GREAT ATHLETES

GREAT ATHLETES

Volume 5

Lindgren–Nicklaus
Indexes

Edited by
The Editors of Salem Press

Special Consultant
Rafer Johnson

SALEM PRESS, INC.
Pasadena, California   Hackensack, New Jersey

Editor in Chief: Dawn P. Dawson

Managing Editor: R. Kent Rasmussen   *Research Supervisor:* Jeffry Jensen
Manuscript Editor: Lauren Mitchell   *Acquisitions Editor:* Mark Rehn
Production Editor: Cynthia Beres   *Page Design and Layout:* James Hutson
Photograph Editor: Philip Bader   *Additional Layout:* William Zimmerman
Assistant Editors: Andrea Miller   Eddie Murillo
Elizabeth Slocum

Cover Design: Moritz Design, Los Angeles, Calif.

© 2002 *Great Athletes, Revised*
© 1994 *The Twentieth Century: Great Athletes, Supplement* (3 volumes)
© 1992 *The Twentieth Century: Great Athletes* (20 volumes)

∞ The paper used in these volumes conforms to the American National Standard for Permanence of Paper for Printed Library Materials, Z39.48-1992 (R1997).

Library of Congress Cataloging-in-Publication Data

Great athletes / edited by the editors of Salem Press ; Rafer Johnson, special consultant.—Rev.
    p. cm.
Includes bibliographical references and index.
    ISBN 1-58765-007-X (set : alk. paper) — ISBN 1-58765-008-8 (v. 1 : alk. paper) —
ISBN 1-58765-009-6 (v. 2 : alk. paper) — ISBN 1-58765-010-X (v. 3 : alk. paper) —
ISBN 1-58765-011-8 (v. 4 : alk. paper) — ISBN 1-58765-012-6 (v. 5 : alk. paper) —
ISBN 1-58765-013-4 (v. 6 : alk. paper) — ISBN 1-58765-014-2 (v. 7 : alk. paper) —
ISBN 1-58765-015-0 (v. 8 : alk. paper)
    1. Athletes—Biography—Dictionaries. I. Johnson, Rafer, 1935-   . II. Salem Press

GV697.A1 G68 2001
796′.092′2—dc21

                                                                                                2001042644

First Printing

Contents

page

Indexes

GREAT ATHLETES

GERRY LINDGREN

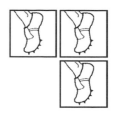

Sport: Track and field (long-distance runs)

Born: March 6, 1946
      Spokane, Washington

Early Life

Gerald (Gerry) Paul Lindgren was born March 6, 1946, in Spokane, Washington. Gerry's parents, Eleanor and Myrl, had two older sons, Lyle and Mickey.

Gerry grew up in Spokane. He was a small, fragile boy who was rejected by his father and fa-vored by his mother. He became a class clown in school to gain acceptance from his peers because he did not get much positive feedback at home.

In junior high school, Gerry began to run long distances while he delivered newspapers. He went out for track, but the longest race was 660 yards. He had only moderate early running success but found that he enjoyed running and that it was about the only sport in which he could physically participate.

Gerry Lindgren leads the field during the U.S. Olympic trials in 1964.

MAJOR CHAMPIONSHIPS

Year	Competition	Event	Place	Time
1960	NCAA Outdoor Championships	3 miles	1st	13:47.2
1964	Olympic Games	10,000 meters	9th	29:20.6
	U.S. v. U.S.S.R. meet	10,000 meters	1st	—
1965	National AAU Championships	3 miles	1st	13:10.6
	National AAU Outdoor Championships	6 miles	1st	27:11.6 WR
1966	NCAA Indoor Championships	3,000 meters	1st	8:41.3
	NCAA Outdoor Championships	3 miles	1st	13:33.7
		6 miles	1st	28:07.0
1967	NCAA Indoor Championships	3,000 meters	1st	8:34.7
	NCAA Outdoor Championships	3 miles	1st	13:33.7
		6 miles	1st	28:44.0
	National AAU Outdoor Championships	3 miles	1st	13:10.6
1968	NCAA Outdoor Championships	6 miles	1st	—

Note: WR = World Record

The Road to Excellence

Gerry attended Rogers High School in Spokane and was coached by Tracey Walters. Walters became the father figure that Gerry had not had, encouraging Gerry to work hard and to develop discipline in his training.

Gerry did not believe he had much talent for distance running, but under the guidance of Coach Walters, he felt that if he worked hard, he would succeed. Gerry trained twice a day, often running hard intervals in the morning and racing long distances in the afternoon. He remained fairly injury-free even though he probably overtrained during his teenage years. He did, however, suffer from stomach ulcers throughout his career.

As a high school sophomore, Gerry finished second at the state cross-country meet. Coach Walters recognized that he had tremendous potential. Gerry, however, did not accept the idea that he might be talented. He felt that he was unworthy to win races or beat more talented runners than himself.

Walters berated Gerry for not pushing himself harder, particularly when he held back in a practice meet and let an upperclassman beat him. Gerry responded by winning the state mile run as a junior.

By the time Gerry graduated from Rogers, he had set national high school records for the mile, two-mile, and three-mile runs, as well as the 5,000-meter distance. He qualified for the national United States track and field team in 1964. He was chosen to race 10,000 meters in the annual United States versus Soviet Union dual meet, a competition that had come to exemplify the Cold War tensions between the two major political powers.

The Emerging Champion

No American had ever won the 10,000-meter race against the Soviets. Gerry was only 5 feet 6 inches tall and was dwarfed by the taller Soviets in the race. Yet, Gerry burst away at about four miles into the race and won handily. The more than fifty thousand fans at the meet cheered him throughout the final mile.

Gerry's victory against the Soviets made him a national hero for the moment. He became known as the small high school boy who beat the older, more mature Soviets. The media noted that Gerry's victory also epitomized the political system of the United States and its citizen's strong sense of nationalism.

Later in 1964, Gerry qualified for the 10,000-meter run in the Tokyo Olympic Games. Unfortunately, he injured an ankle in practice and finished in ninth place, while his teammate, Billy Mills, won in an upset.

Gerry went to Washington State University (WSU) and was coached by Jack Mooberry. While at WSU, Gerry won an unprecedented

RECORDS

Held world 6-mile record (27:11.6)
Held American collegiate records in distance events
Best mark for 1 mile (4:01.5), 2 miles (8:35.4), 3 miles (12:53.0), 5,000 meters (13:33.8), 10,000 meters (28:40.2)

HONORS AND AWARDS

1964	*Track and Field News* High School Runner of the Year

eleven national championships in cross country and indoor and outdoor track.

Continuing the Story

In 1965, Gerry was caught in the middle of a power struggle between the NCAA and the Amateur Athletic Union (AAU), the two major governing bodies for track and field. The NCAA had threatened to terminate the athletic scholarship of any athlete who competed in AAU-sanctioned races. In the summer, Gerry ignored the NCAA boycott and set a shared world record with Billy Mills in the 6-mile run at the National AAU meet. He was not penalized, and he actually became a hero to those in the track and field community who disapproved of the feud between the two governing bodies.

Gerry trained for the Mexico City Olympics of 1968, but an injured Achilles tendon ruined his opportunity. Following his graduation from WSU with a major in political science, Gerry had difficulty finding a job that allowed him to make a decent living while continuing to train. He became a motivational speaker in the early 1970's and gave seminars on how to fulfill one's potential.

In 1971, Gerry resumed heavy training in preparation for the 1972 Munich Olympics. Once again he suffered an injury prior to the Olympic trials and did not qualify. He signed a professional track contract with the International Track Association later in 1972, but the group failed by 1976.

Gerry never made it back to world-class running levels after 1972. He had married in 1970, and he and his wife, Betty, had two sons, Steven and Jeremy.

Strangely, Gerry disappeared in 1980 when he left his family and dropped out of society. His close friend and rival, Kenny Moore, later contacted Gerry and attributed his leaving as primarily the result of personal problems associated with the inability to cope with his early phenomenal running success and later performance failures.

Summary

For many track and field fans, Gerry Lindgren will be remembered as the small, fragile high school boy who beat the mighty Soviet runners in the 1964 10,000-meter race. To others, he will be remembered as an outstanding track athlete who was not afraid to stand up to authority.

Tinker D. Murray

Additional Sources:

Bateman, Hal. *United States Track and Field Olympians, 1896-1980.* Indianapolis, Ind.: The Athletics Congress of the United States, 1984.

Hanley, Reid M. *Who's Who in Track and Field.* New Rochelle, N.Y.: Arlington House, 1971.

Wallechinsky, David. *The Complete Book of the Olympics.* Boston: Little, Brown and Company, 1991.

Watman, Mel. *Encyclopedia of Track and Field Athletics.* New York: St. Martin's Press, 1981.

ERIC LINDROS

Sport: Ice hockey

Born: February 28, 1973
London, Ontario, Canada

Early Life

Eric Lindros was born to Carl and Bonnie Lindros on February 28, 1973, in London, Ontario, Canada. Both parents achieved some success as amateur athletes and would convey their love of sport and competitive spirit to Eric, his younger brother, Brett, and his sister, Robin. Carl and Eric practiced for hours throughout the Canadian winters on backyard ice rinks Carl constructed. When Eric was six, his mother enrolled him in a non-contact hockey league, hoping to drain some of his excess energy. He quickly developed an appreciation for the complexity of the sport.

The Road to Excellence

Blessed with skill, determination, and size, Eric often played in leagues with boys two years older than he was. When he was fourteen, a year he grew 7 inches, he decided that he wanted to become a professional hockey player. By 1989 he was qualified to play in the Ontario Hockey League, a stepping-stone to the National Hockey League (NHL). When the Sault Sainte Marie Greyhounds drafted him, however, Eric refused to report to a team so far from his home. It would have been difficult for him to complete his education there, so during the fall of 1989 he finished high school and played in a less competitive league.

In early 1990 Eric joined the Canadian national junior team, which competed for the junior world championship in Finland. Eric was the youngest player in the tournament, but he scored 4 goals in seven games to help Canada win the world championship. He returned to discover that the Ontario Hockey League had changed its rules to let Eric join the Oshawa Gen-

erals, closer to home. That spring Oshawa captured the Memorial Cup, the championship of the Canadian Hockey League.

During the 1990-1991 season Eric dominated the Ontario Hockey League and won the prestigious Canadian Hockey League Player of the Year award. He was the obvious top choice for the NHL draft in June, 1991. Eric and his parents warned the Quebec Nordiques, who had the first pick, that Eric would not sign with them. He did not speak French, nor would he receive sufficient salary and recognition in Quebec. The Lindroses emphasized that the Nordiques' owner was not committed to winning. Quebec nevertheless drafted Eric, and he refused to sign.

The Emerging Champion

While waiting for the Quebec Nordiques to back down and trade him, Eric completed a remarkable amateur hockey career. In the 1991 world junior championships he dominated the competition, scoring 6 goals and 11 assists in only seven games. It was the first time Canada won back-to-back gold medals in that tournament. Later that year Eric made Team Canada as an eighteen-year-old amateur, the youngest Canadian ever to compete against other nations for the Canada Cup. Playing against NHL stars, Eric scored 3 goals and 2 assists and delivered dozens of devastating body checks. Team Canada was victorious. In the 1992 Olympics Eric tallied 5 goals and 6 assists in eight games for the all-amateur squad, but the Unified Team, of the former Soviet Union, captured the gold. Still, the silver medal was the first Winter Olympic medal for Canada in twenty-four years.

Continuing the Story

On June 30, 1992, the Quebec Nordiques traded Eric to two different teams. An arbitrator finally decided that the Philadelphia Flyers had

STATISTICS

Season	GP	G	Ast.	Pts.	PIM
1992-93	61	41	34	75	147
1993-94	65	44	53	97	103
1994-95	46	29	41	**70**	60
1995-96	73	47	68	115	163
1996-97	52	32	47	79	136
1997-98	63	30	41	71	134
1998-99	71	40	53	93	120
1999-00	55	27	32	59	83
Totals	486	290	369	659	946

Notes: Boldface indicates statistical leader. GP = games played; G = goals; Ast. = assists; Pts. = points; PIM = penalties in minutes

obtained Eric. The Flyers gave Quebec their starting goaltender, five other players, two first-round draft picks, and $15 million. The Flyers' management knew that Eric was the star around whom they could build a championship team.

In his first season Eric missed two months, with knee injuries costing him the Calder Memorial Trophy as the top rookie. He still scored 41 goals and 34 assists, which was remarkable for a center on a next-to-last place team.

The strike-shortened 1994-1995 season did not stop Eric's rise. Only twenty-one, Eric became team captain and led the Flyers to their first playoff appearance in five years. Eric won the Hart Memorial Trophy as the most valuable player. The following year Eric scored 115 points and finished second to Mario Lemieux for the Hart Trophy.

In 1996-1997 the forward line of Eric Lindros, John LeClair, and Mikael Renberg, nicknamed the "Legion of Doom," led the Philadelphia Flyers to the Stanley Cup finals. They supplied a physical presence and scoring punch that few teams could match. Eric led all scorers in the playoffs. In the finals, however, the talented Detroit Red Wings stopped the Legion, and the Flyers lost in four straight games. Late in the next season Eric scored his five

hundredth point; only four players had achieved that goal more quickly. Eric was only twenty-five years old, but he was named captain of the Canadian team for the 1998 Winter Olympics in Nagano, Japan.

On March 7, 1998, Darius Kasparaitis of the Pittsburgh Penguins checked Eric so hard that the latter suffered a serious concussion. A year later, a freak injury during a game in Nashville sent him to the hospital with a collapsed and bleeding lung. The life-threatening condition kept him out of the playoffs and prevented him from achieving another hundred-point season.

Physical problems continued to plague Eric's career. In the last half of the 1999-2000 season he suffered three more concussions. He rejoined the Flyers during the third round of the playoffs, but on May 26, 2000, a vicious hit by an opponent knocked Eric unconscious, leaving Eric's future in doubt. He was ready to play by November,

Eric Lindros of the Philadelphia Flyers in May, 2000.

AP/Wide World Photos

HONORS AND AWARDS

1990	Memorial Cup All-Star Team
1991	Canadian Hockey League Player of the Year
	Canadian Hockey League Plus/Minus Award
	Canadian Hockey League Top Draft Prospect Award
	Red Tilson Trophy
	Eddie Powers Memorial Trophy
	Ontario Hockey League All-Star First Team
1992	Silver Medal with Team Canada at the Olympic Games
1993	NHL All-Rookie Team
1995	*Sporting News* NHL Player of the Year
	Hart Memorial Trophy
	Sporting News All-Star First Team
	Lester B. Pearson Award
1996	Team Canada
1998	Team Canada captain

Eric has a quick and hard wrist shot, and he is a graceful yet powerful skater. At 6 feet 4 inches and 235 pounds, he is difficult for opponents to control. Known as "Captain Crunch" and the "E-Train," Eric delivers checks that leave opponents dazed and intimidated. His skillful passing made the "Legion of Doom" a scoring machine.

His refusal to play for Sault Sainte Marie and Quebec led to accusations that he is arrogant, but this was contradicted by his willingness to represent his country in numerous international events, his teammates' respect, and his work for the Children's Miracle Network to help hospitalized children. Only injuries seemed to limit Eric's achievements in the NHL.

M. Philip Lucas

2000, but was determined to change teams because of strained relations with the coach of the Flyers. He sat out the entire 2000-2001 season, but rumors of his going to another team ended when he was traded to the New York Rangers in August, 2001.

Summary

Hall of Famer Bobby Clarke concluded that at age sixteen Eric Lindros was ready for the NHL.

Additional Sources:

Lindros, Eric. *Pursue Your Goals*. Dallas, Tex.: Taylor Publishing, 1999.

Lindros, Eric, and Randy Starkman. *Fire on Ice*. Toronto: HarperCollins, 1991.

Poulin, Daniel. *Lindros: Doing What's Right for Eric*. Markham, Ont.: Panda Publishing, 1992.

Rappoport, Ken. *Sports Great Eric Lindros*. Springfield, N.J.: Enslow, 1997.

Savage, Jeff. *Eric Lindros: High Flying Center*. Minneapolis, Minn.: Lerner Publishing, 1998.

TED LINDSAY

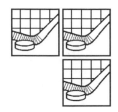

Sport: Ice hockey

Born: July 29, 1925
Renfrew, Ontario, Canada

Early Life

Robert Blake Theodore Lindsay was born on July 29, 1925, in Renfrew, Ontario, Canada. He had a hockey heritage in that his father, Bert Lindsay, had played goal for the Renfrew Million-aires, a team that was famous before the National Hockey League (NHL) existed. Later in his ca-reer, the elder Lindsay played part of a season with the NHL Toronto Arenas, now known as the Toronto Maple Leafs. Young Ted was determined to follow in his father's footsteps and become a pro-fessional hockey player. He got his first set of skates from a neighbor at the age of nine. These did not last very long as Ted wore them out by practicing long hours.

The Road to Excellence

Although small of stature for a hockey player (5 feet 8 inches tall and 155 pounds), Ted had the fierce deter-mination to succeed. Throughout his career, he made a point of never back-ing down from another player. His abil-ity and competitiveness earned him the respect of all his teammates and oppos-ing players. While playing for a junior hockey team in Ontario, Ted attracted the attention of several major league scouts. In 1944, he helped the Oshawa Generals win the Memorial Cup, which was Canada's junior hockey title. That same year, at the age of nineteen, Ted was signed to a professional contract with the Detroit Red Wings. His first year in the professionals was a good one; he scored 17 times in 45 games.

The Emerging Champion

Ted was always known as a tough hockey player and usually was at, or near, the top of the penalties list each year. Along with that, he was a fine playmaker and always a team player. His tal-ents were best displayed when he was teamed with center Sid Abel and left winger Gordie Howe. That trio, known as the "Production Line," helped the Red Wings to win eight league titles and four Stanley Cup championships in the late 1940's and early 1950's. Ted was the heart of

Ted Lindsay of the Detroit Red Wings, in 1956.

STATISTICS

Season	GP	G	Ast.	Pts.	PIM
1944-45	45	17	6	23	43
1945-46	47	7	10	17	14
1946-47	59	27	15	42	57
1947-48	60	**33**	19	52	95
1948-49	50	26	28	54	97
1949-50	69	23	**55**	**78**	141
1950-51	67	24	35	59	110
1951-52	70	30	39	69	123
1952-53	70	32	39	71	111
1953-54	70	26	36	62	110
1954-55	49	19	19	38	85
1955-56	67	27	23	50	**161**
1956-57	70	30	**55**	85	103
1957-58	68	15	24	39	**110**
1958-59	70	22	36	58	184
1959-60	68	7	19	26	91
1964-65	69	14	14	28	173
Totals	1,068	379	472	851	1,808

Notes: Boldface indicates statistical leader. GP = games played; G = goals; Ast. = assists; Pts. = points; PIM = penalties in minutes

that line. He was not the biggest player, but he played tough every game. He was a hard worker along the boards, where few players liked to be.

Ted made the All-Star team nine times and once led the league in scoring. It was an incredible accomplishment for any player during this time. The National Hockey League had only six teams, and each squad was loaded with talent. To stand out from the crowd as a tough player, yet one who could skate, pass, and score, was difficult, but Ted possessed the talent to do just that.

Continuing the Story

Prior to the 1957-1958 season, Ted was traded to the Chicago Black Hawks. In his three seasons there, he was able to help the Black Hawks get out of the cellar and into the playoffs twice. It was well known, however, that he never thought highly of Chicago, and finally, after sixteen years in the big leagues with Detroit and Chicago, Ted retired.

Four years later, however, at age thirty-nine, he returned to the game. His return was not inspired by money, for his business ventures had been successful and Ted was well off. Rather, the thrill of the game and the desire to close off his career in a Detroit uniform brought him back. The Detroit management wanted him back because they knew a team played better when he

was around. Nobody slacked off when Ted was in uniform, and no player melded such ferocity with so much skill.

Almost from the time the game of hockey was invented, good teams had a variety of players. There were the flashy skaters, the goal scorers, the playmakers, and the policemen. In every era of the sport, this latter group, the policemen, helped control the mood and tempo of each game so as to give the scorers an opportunity to perform their magic on the ice. Ted filled this role of "ice cop" throughout his career. In Ted's case, however, he brought considerably more to the game. Not only was his rugged style able to set the tone of the contest, but his natural ability also made him into a scorer and playmaker. This was a rare combination and one that was recognized by fans, teammates, and management. Finally, in the summer of 1965, at age forty, Ted decided it was time to quit for good.

In 1966, Ted was elected into the Hockey Hall of Fame. While honored by the selection, he declined to attend the ceremonies when he learned that members' wives and families would be excluded from some of the events. True to form, Ted scowled, "If my wife and kids can't see the old man honored, what's the point?" Rather than leave the family out, Ted stayed home.

Summary

No man on skates was ever too big or too tough for Ted Lindsay to challenge. His fierce determination, his ability at the game, and the great attitude of a team player gave Ted the edge as a hockey player. At the start of his comeback with

HONORS AND AWARDS

1948, 1950-54, 1956-57	NHL First Team All-Star
1949	NHL Second Team All-Star
1950	Art Ross Trophy
1966	Inducted into Hockey Hall of Fame

Detroit, then League President Clarence Campbell scoffed at the idea, believing it to be a publicity stunt by both the team and the player. After the season was over, he called it one of the most amazing comebacks in professional sports. To Ted, it was just a matter of playing a game he loved. Honored by his peers, his induction into the Hall of Fame proved that Ted was one of the greatest left wingers ever to play the game.

Carmi Brandis

Additional Sources:

Dryden, Steve, and Michael Ulmer, eds. *The Top 100 NHL Hockey Players of All Time.* Toronto: McClelland & Stewart, 1998.

Hickok, Ralph. *A Who's Who of Sports Champions.* Boston: Houghton Mifflin, 1995.

Hollander, Zander, and Hal Bock, eds. *The Complete Encyclopedia of Ice Hockey.* Rev. ed. Englewood Cliffs, N.J.: Prentice-Hall, 1974.

GARY LINEKER

Sport: Soccer

Born: November 30, 1960
Leicester, England

Early Life

Gary Winston Lineker was born on November 30, 1960, in Leicester, England, a city about one hundred miles north of the capital, London. His father, Barry Lineker, was a market trader, running the well-established family fruit and vegetable stall in Leicester.

Gary's father was an average soccer player, but his grandfather had played soccer for a county schoolboy team and for top army teams. When Gary was still a toddler, his father and grandfather would kick a soccer ball to him. It was soon obvious that the grandson had inherited the grandfather's special ability. Gary had the unusual skill of being able to use both feet equally well.

The Road to Excellence

In elementary school, Gary and his brother, Wayne, helped their school win a local trophy. Gary next attended the City of Leicester Boys' Grammar School, a college preparatory school where he especially liked math and sports. He did well there, both academically and athletically. He passed tough examinations in six subjects at the age of sixteen and became the Leicester School's 400-meter sprint champion.

In 1976, Gary left school, and he was good enough in sports to be offered opportunities in both cricket (a game similar to baseball) and soccer. He chose to become an apprentice soccer player with Leicester City, his local club. He was then only 5 feet 6 inches tall and weighed less than 125 pounds. Perhaps because Gary was so small, Leicester was the only soccer club to offer him a chance.

On January 1, 1979, Gary first played for Leicester, and he scored his first goal three months later. He was often mentioned in the

newspapers after that because he was averaging one goal every two games. In 1984, he first played for England's national team, when he came on as a substitute. In 1985, he scored in the first match in which he started for England.

Gary achieved star status when he was transferred to a top club, Everton, in June, 1985, for a fee of £800,000 (approximately $1.6 million). That was the highest fee Everton had ever paid for a player. Everton paid so much for Gary because he was quick, with excellent timing and balance. He also had the reputation of being a likable, levelheaded player, with a great sense of humor.

The Emerging Champion

Gary continued his fantastic scoring rate at Everton, scoring 40 goals in 57 games. He was the top scorer in the entire English League.

The year 1986 was hectic but successful for Gary. He was selected Footballer of the Year by two sports organizations. In June, he was bought by Barcelona, a top team in the Spanish league, for £2.2 million (approximately $4.4 million). Gary wanted to play in international club competition, and English clubs were banned from it at the time because of crowd rowdiness.

Gary played for England in the World Cup in Mexico in 1986 and was the tournament's top scorer, with 6 goals. Just before leaving for Barcelona in July, Gary was married to his girlfriend of seven years.

Gary had acquired two reputations to go with his skill on the field. One was that he was a very sporting competitor who had never even been cautioned by a referee, let alone ejected, in his entire career. Additionally, he was recognized as an excellent thinker and speaker on the game of soccer. He also had one ritual: Because of his poor blood circulation, he liked to have a long, hot bath before a game.

In three other sports, each very different from soccer, Gary was also talented. He played a great game of snooker (similar to pool), he continued to play some cricket, and he had a golf handicap of only 14.

Life in Barcelona had its ups and downs for Gary. First, he had to learn a new language, Spanish, in order to understand what his teammates were saying. Within two years, he was asked to comment about soccer on Spanish television, and did so, in fluent Spanish.

On the field, Gary was told to play a wing position, when he was really a center-forward. He accepted the role without complaint, but he believed that he was not being used to the best of his ability. Nevertheless, in 1989, Gary won a European Cup Winners' Cup Medal with Barcelona and scored the winning goal from his new position.

HONORS AND AWARDS	
1986	World Cup high scorer (6 goals)
	English Footballer of the Year
	English Professional Football Association Player of the Year
1989	European Cup Winners' Cup champion
1991	FA Cup Championship

MILESTONES
80 international appearances for England
48 international goals (through Nov., 1990)

Continuing the Story

Although Gary had adapted well to Spain, he was happy to return to play in England in June, 1989, when he was transferred to Tottenham Hotspur, a top London club, for £1.1 million (approximately $2.2 million). The excitement this caused may be understood from the fact that within two days of Gary's transfer to "Spurs" (Tottenham Hotspur's nickname), more than £100,000 (approximately $200,000) worth of season tickets were sold.

In most of the world, a soccer player receives a percentage of his transfer fee. Gary could have made more money by agreeing to be transferred to a French or Italian club, but he wanted to return to England.

In the 1990 World Cup in Italy, Gary was instrumental in England's unexpectedly getting to the semifinals. He scored a total of 4 goals in the tournament. He also was named the captain of England in 1990. In 1991 Gary joined the Tottenham Hotspur club and won an FA Cup Championship, improving his international goal total to 48, just one behind Bobby Charlton's England record of 49. Gary moved to Japan in 1992 to assist in the launch of the new J-League. While he was playing with Grampus Eight in Japan, a series of foot injuries hampered his debut. Gary announced his retirement in 1994.

Gary was successful in off-the-field business as well. He signed several deals with

Express Newspapers/Archive Photos

equipment manufacturers to endorse their products. Companies were eager to have such a pleasant, articulate person to help sell their merchandise. He also became a successful newspaper columnist and radio announcer.

Summary

Other English players with the same average of a goal in every two games are Bobby Charlton and Geoff Hurst, both players from earlier times. Gary Lineker is the only player to achieve that feat in the 1990's. He brought intense excitement to every game in which he played, and his patience with the press, his modesty, and his clean-cut image on and off the field have made him one of the most remarkable and popular players ever. He credits his parents with giving him the guidance and support necessary to becoming a champion.

Shirley H. M. Reekie

Additional Sources:

Henshaw, Richard. *The Encyclopedia of World Soccer.* Washington, D.C.: New Republic Books, 1979.

Hollander, Zander. *The American Encyclopedia of Soccer.* New York: Everett House, 1980.

Lineker, Gary. *Soccer.* New York: Dorling Kindersley, 2000.

TARA LIPINSKI

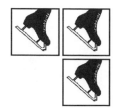

Sport: Figure skating

Born: June 10, 1982
Philadelphia, Pennsylvania

Early Life

Born on June 10, 1982, Tara Lipinski is the only child of Jack Lipinski, an oil refinery executive, and Pat Lipinski, a former Wall Street secretary. Although Tara was born in Philadelphia, the Lipinskis soon moved to Sewell, New Jersey, where they lived until Tara was nine.

Tara was an active toddler, and Pat Lipinski was alert to anything that might help channel the little girl's energy. When Tara was three, Pat signed her up for roller-skating lessons. Tara showed a natural talent for roller skating, and, when the rink gave performances, she loved skating in front of an audience. Soon she was entering and winning roller-skating competitions, including a regional and a national championship.

The Road to Excellence

When Tara was six, her parents took her ice skating at the urging of a family friend. By watching the other skaters she quickly learned to keep her balance on the ice and soon was performing jumps from her roller-skating repertoire. She fell in love with ice skating and immediately started taking lessons.

In 1991 the Lipinskis moved to Sugar Land, Texas, near Houston. Tara tried to continue figure skating in Texas, but she and her mother had to get up at four every morning and drive to the nearest rink so Tara could get enough practice time. In 1993 Tara and her mother moved back to Delaware so she could pursue her skating on a less taxing schedule, while her father remained in Texas. A year later, Tara and Pat moved once again, this time to Bloomfield, Michigan, where she began training with coach Richard Callaghan.

Tara Lipinski won the 1997 world championship at the age of fourteen.

MAJOR CHAMPIONSHIPS

Year	Competition	Place
1994	Midwestern Novice	1st
	Southwestern Novice	1st
	National Novice	2d
	U.S. Olympic Festival	1st
	Blue Swords	1st
1995	Nebelhorn Trophy	4th
	National Juniors	2d
	World Junior Championships	4th
1996	World Junior selections	2d
	Skate Canada	2d
	South Atlantic Juniors	1st
	Nations Cup	2d
	Trophée Lalique	3d
	World Championships	15th
	National Championships	3d
	World Juniors	5th
1997	Trophée Lalique	2d
	World Championships	1st
	Hershey's Challenge (team)	1st
	Champions Series final	1st
	National Championships	1st
	Skate America	2d
1997-98	Champion Series Final	1st
1998	Jefferson Pilot Financial Championships	1st
	National Championships	2d
	Olympic Games	Gold
	Skate TV Championships	1st
	Ice Wars	1st Team USA
	Ice Wars	1st Ladies
	Team Ice Wars	2d Team USA
1998-99	Team Ice Wars	1st Ladies
1999	World Pros	1st
	Team Ice Wars	1st Team USA
	Pro Superteam Challenge	1st

The Emerging Champion

Twelve-year-old Tara gained national attention in 1994 as the youngest athlete ever to win a gold medal at the Olympic Festival. Two years later at the World Championships she placed fifteenth, a respectable accomplishment for a newcomer, and third at the National Championships. She also set a record, becoming the first woman to land a triple loop, triple loop combination jump in competition.

In 1997 Tara unexpectedly swept the World Championships, the National Championships, and Champions Series, placing first in each competition; at fourteen, she had set yet another record as the youngest world champion in the history of the sport. At the 1998 National Championships Tara landed 7 triple jumps in her long program and placed second, qualifying for the American Olympic team.

Tara had been criticized for being a robotic jumper, impressive in her athleticism but unable to interpret music with emotional maturity on the ice. To correct this, she worked with a ballet instructor while polishing her Olympic programs and began to create a more sophisticated image. She used practice sessions to improve her artistic presentation in the days before the Olympic competition. She watched daily videotapes of practice sessions and discussed the balletic elements of her program with her choreographer, Sandra Bezic, via e-mail. Small changes in her movements improved the overall look of her program.

Tara entered the Olympic Village determined to experience everything possible about the event, so that she would have wonderful memories even if she did not win a medal. Her approach was contrasted with that of figure skater Michelle Kwan, who eschewed much of the camaraderie with other athletes and possibilities for entertainment in the Olympic Village. Kwan was expected to win the gold medal, but Tara's wins at the National and World Championships proved that she could also be a serious contender for the gold.

The media focused on a rivalry between the two young women, although Tara and Kwan had been casually friendly. Increasingly distraught by the pressure of competing and the public perception that she was skating to defeat Kwan, Tara briefly considered dropping out of the competition after her short program.

Deciding to go forward, Tara skated a perfect long program. Her 7 triple jumps included her trademark triple-loop combination, a harder element than Kwan's combination jump. Tara won the gold medal, at fifteen the youngest woman to place first in ladies' figure skating at the Olympics.

Continuing the Story

After her gold-medal win in Nagano, Tara immediately wanted to start training for the 2002 Winter Olympics. However, after years of sacrifice and complete dedication to her daughter's skating career, Pat Lipinski wanted to move home to Texas. Tara understood and made the decision to leave amateur competition, officially becoming a professional figure skater in April, 1998.

In the years immediately following her Olympic victory, Tara skated professionally with Scott Hamilton's Stars on Ice tour and made several television specials. She began an acting career as a guest star in prime-time television programs and in a brief role as a college student on the daytime soap opera *The Young and the Restless*. Tara also signed contracts to endorse many products, from Capezio dancewear to Snapple fruit drinks.

Tara taught at skating clinics for young hopeful skaters around the country, visited children in hospitals, and gave lessons to sick children for the Make-A-Wish Foundation. She was also a national spokesperson for Tobacco-Free Kids and for the Boys and Girls Clubs of America. Although she was able to move back to Texas with her parents, her schedule still required many hours of practice and constant travel to make personal appearances.

Summary

Tara Lipinski's Olympic win, her dedication to her sport, and her naturally bubbly personality made her a heroine to many young women and opened up countless opportunities for the young athlete. Her determination was rewarded as she set new records in figure skating and achieved her ultimate dream at the Olympics. She remains one of the most remarkable young women in the history of her sport.

Maureen J. Puffer-Rothenberg

Additional Sources:

Christopher, Matt. *On the Ice with Tara Lipinski.* Boston: Little, Brown, 1999.

Lipinski, Tara, with Simon Bruty and Mark Zeigler. *Totally Tara: An Olympic Journey.* New York: Universe, 1998.

Lipinski, Tara, and Emily Costello. *Tara Lipinski: Triumph on Ice, an Autobiography.* New York: Bantam Books, 1997.

Swift, E. M. "A Holy Tara." *Sports Illustrated* 88, no. 9 (March 2, 1998): 48-53.

FLOYD LITTLE

Sport: Football

Born: July 4, 1942
New Haven, Connecticut

Early Life

Floyd Douglas Little was born on July 4, 1942, in New Haven, Connecticut, the son of Fred and Lula Little. Fred was a factory worker; he died in 1948, when Floyd was six years old. Floyd's mother worked as a clothes presser to support her family of six children. Floyd was shy and not always in good health during his early years. A speech problem made him withdraw even more, and, for a number of years, he refused to talk in class. As he got older, Floyd worked at odd jobs to help support the family. By the time he got to high school, he had proven that his speed could make up for the lack of time he had to devote to practicing football.

The Road to Excellence

At Hillhouse High School in New Haven, Floyd was a prep football All-American in 1962. He felt that he had not received a very good education, so he enrolled in Bordertown Military Academy in New Jersey. He was the first African American student ever accepted at Bordertown. Floyd wanted to go to college, and he wanted to be able to succeed academically as well as play football. When he reached 5 feet 10 inches in height and weighed 196 pounds, and when it was determined that he could handle college scholastically, he was recruited by a number of major colleges. Floyd narrowed down his choices to Notre Dame and Syracuse. Because of a personal appeal by running star Ernie Davis of Syracuse University, who at the time was dying from leukemia, Floyd decided that Syracuse was the college for him. After hearing that Davis had died, he called the Syracuse football coach, Ben Schwartzwalder, and told him that he had chosen Syracuse. Floyd was given the privilege of wearing number 44, which had been worn not only by Ernie Davis but also by another former Syracuse football great, Jim Brown.

Courtesy of the Denver Broncos

STATISTICS

Season	GP	Rushing					Receiving			
		Car.	Yds.	Avg.	TD	Rec.	Yds.	Avg.	TD
1967	13	130	381	2.9	1	7	11	1.6	0
1968	11	158	584	3.7	3	19	331	17.4	1
1969	9	146	729	**5.0**	6	19	218	11.5	1
1970	14	209	**901**	4.3	3	17	161	9.5	0
1971	14	284	**1,133**	4.0	6	26	255	9.8	0
1972	14	216	859	4.0	9	28	367	13.1	4
1973	14	256	979	3.8	**12**	41	423	10.3	1
1974	14	117	312	2.7	1	29	344	11.9	0
AFL Totals	33	434	1,694	3.9	10	45	560	12.4	2
NFL Totals	70	1,082	4,184	3.9	31	141	1,550	11.0	5

Notes: Boldface indicates statistical leader. GP = games played; Car. = carries; Yds. = yards; Avg. = average yards per carry *or* average yards per reception; TD = touchdowns; Rec. = receptions

Floyd decided to major in both history and religion at Syracuse. During his years at Syracuse, Floyd came into his own, his growing self-confidence and his ability making him a popular player and a team leader. As a player, Floyd made an immediate impact by scoring 5 touchdowns in his first college game, against the University of Kansas, the team of the amazing running back, Gale Sayers.

The Emerging Champion

Floyd finished his sophomore year at Syracuse with a total of 12 touchdowns in 10 regular season games. His junior year was to be his most productive scoring season; he scored 19 touchdowns, which led the nation in 1965. For the second year in a row, Floyd was named All-American. His senior year at Syracuse was no less spectacular, as he led the Orangemen to the 1967 Gator Bowl. Floyd also became the first college football player since Doak Walker to be a three-time All-American.

In his career with the Syracuse Orangemen, Floyd scored 46 touchdowns and gained 5,529 total yards. Because of his outstanding college career, he was highly sought after by both the National Football League (NFL) and the American Football League (AFL). Floyd was the number-one draft choice of the Denver Broncos of the AFL in 1967.

Floyd was not sure that he or his wife, Joyce, would enjoy living in Denver, but he accepted the contract offered to him by the Bronco organization. The Littles were pleasantly surprised by the Denver environment, and Floyd looked forward to contributing to his new team. The Broncos also had a new coach, Lou Saban, for Floyd's rookie year. The 1967 season was difficult for Floyd. The Broncos were in a period of development, which meant that it was going to take time before they could be considered a solid team. During his rookie year, Floyd gained only 381 yards rushing. The bright points of the season were that he led the AFL in punt returns and excelled at running back kickoffs.

Continuing the Story

As the Broncos improved over the next few seasons, so did Floyd's individual statistics. During the 1969 season, he gained 729 yards rushing in 9 games and led the league in average yards per carry with 5.0. Floyd was a tough competitor. He was able to make the distinction between what was a real injury and what was merely pain, and he was not about to let pain stop him from doing his best. Floyd wanted to help the team any way he could and, therefore, was willing to work harder and endure more so that his job would get done.

Floyd played for the Denver Broncos for eight seasons and was popular with the fans. In 1971, he led the league in rushing with a total of 1,133 yards, and in 1973, he led the league in touchdowns with 12. During his career, Floyd was selected to *The Sporting News* All-Star team on three occasions, played in the AFL All-Star Game twice, and played in the Pro Bowl (NFL All-Star Game) three times. Starting in 1970, the AFL became part of the NFL and known as the American Football Conference (AFC).

After Floyd retired from professional football in 1975, he earned a master's degree from the University of Denver School of Law and went into the Adolph Coors Company management training program. Floyd had always been active in community service projects, including drug abuse programs and working with disadvantaged children. His wife, Joyce, whom he met at Syracuse, has taught biology. They have two daughters. Floyd has also tried his hand at working for NBC as a sportscaster. After two years with NBC, he went to work for Ford Motor Company, and in 1979, he began to manage Lincoln/ Mercury dealerships in California. Floyd continued to concentrate on business and charitable work, in particular the Special Olympics, Boys and Girls Clubs, and the Leukemia Society.

Summary

Floyd Little succeeded in his chosen sport because of more than mere natural talent. He learned early in life that he would have to work hard to pull himself out of the poverty in which he lived. He knew that he needed an education and he fought to get one, even after being told that he could not handle college classes. Floyd proved to himself and to those around him that he could excel both on the field and off. After his hard work paid off, Floyd accepted the responsibility of giving back something to those who needed encouragement. Floyd is a champion no matter what yardstick is used to measure him.

Michael Jeffrys

HONORS AND AWARDS

1964-66	College All-American
1969	*Sporting News* AFL All-Star Team
1969-70	AFL All-Star Team
1969-71	All-NFL Team
1970-71	*Sporting News* AFC All-Star Team
1971	Football Writers Association of America Outstanding Pro Back
1971-72, 1974	NFL Pro Bowl Team NFL All-Pro Team
1973	Brian Piccolo Award
1980	NFL All-Pro Team of the 1970's
1983	Inducted into College Football Hall of Fame Uniform number 44 retired by Denver Broncos
1984	Made inaugural member of Denver Broncos Ring of Fame

Additional Sources:

College Football Hall of Fame. http://college football.org.

Denver Broncos Ring of Fame. http://www .denverbroncos.com/history/ringoffame .php3.

"Profiles in Connecticut Black History: Floyd Little." http://courant.ctnow.com/projects/ bhistory/little.htm..

LAWSON LITTLE

Sport: Golf

Born: June 23, 1910
    Newport, Rhode Island
Died: February 1, 1968
    Pebble Beach, California

Early Life

William Lawson Little Jr. was the son of Colonel and Mrs. William Lawson Little of the United States Army Medical Corps. Lawson Jr. was born at Fort Adams, the Army base at Newport, Rhode Island, on June 23, 1910. Because of his father's career, the family moved a great deal, as Colonel Little was transferred from post to post. Lawson spent his boyhood and adolescent years at a number of Army posts, including several years in China. One feature found on all these bases was a golf course, and golf became the favorite form of recreation for Lawson.

In the early part of the twentieth century, United States Army bases in countries such as China were rather small, and people from all Western nationalities tended to form friendships across national lines. On this basis Lawson formed many golfing friendships with people in England and Europe.

Courtesy of Amateur Athletic Foundation of Los Angeles

The Road to Excellence

Lawson was rather short, but he developed very powerful arms and shoulders by lifting weights and by gymnastics exercises such as the parallel bars and the rings. His squat, muscular build allowed Lawson to drive the ball unusually long distances on his tee shots. These drives were so fast and so strong that, early in his career, Lawson was nicknamed "Cannonball" Little.

Lawson had fine control over his muscles, however, and once his ball was on the green, the "Cannonball" became a delicate and precise putter. It was as if Lawson had learned the trick of changing from a bull to a dove and back again as he drove or putted. Early in his career, Lawson also learned he could intimidate some of his opponents by adopting a fierce facial expression during the course of the game.

1643

MAJOR CHAMPIONSHIP VICTORIES

1934-35	U.S. Amateur
	British Amateur
1940	U.S. Open

OTHER NOTABLE VICTORIES

1934	Walker Cup Team
1936	Canadian Open
1940	Los Angeles Open
1941	Texas Open
1948	St. Petersburg Open

The Emerging Champion

In 1934, Lawson became an international golfer to be reckoned with. In that year he became the United States Amateur champion by defeating David Goldman; went on to win the British Amateur Championship, defeating James Wallace; and was named a member of America's Walker Cup team. It was quite a year for a young man just out of college.

The next year, 1935, Lawson repeated his feat of winning the amateur titles on both sides of the Atlantic. This alone would have ensured his place in golfing history, because no other player has ever won both the United States and British titles in two consecutive years. In recognition of this unmatched accomplishment, the Amateur Athletic Union named Lawson the 1935 winner of the James E. Sullivan Memorial Award, the highest honor that can come to an amateur athlete.

Continuing the Story

In 1936, Lawson became a professional golfer, playing in tournaments with cash prizes. He immediately made his mark on the professional golf world by winning the Canadian Open and setting a new record for the course on which it was played.

Each year Lawson traveled all over the United States, Canada, and England winning major tournaments. In 1939, World War II broke out in Europe, and Lawson had to restrict his play to North America. Even then his career bloomed. In 1940, 1,100 people played in the qualifying rounds for the United States Open Tournament at Olympia Fields Country Club of Chicago. The lowest score on 36 holes was 134, shot by Lawson Little. In the tournament itself, Lawson played to a tie with Gene Sarazen, 287 strokes each, but Lawson won the tie-breaking round 70 strokes to 73.

Because of shortages of gasoline for travel and to emphasize the seriousness of the war, fewer golf tournaments were held once the United States entered World War II at the end of 1941. Yet, in 1942 and 1944, Lawson was ranked second only to the legendary golfer Ben Hogan. When the war was over, Lawson returned to international golfing and did well in the British Open in 1946 and again in 1947. In 1948, Lawson won his last major tournament, the Saint Petersburg Open held at the Lakewood Country Club, Saint Petersburg, Florida.

The Professional Golfers' Association (PGA) honored Lawson in 1951 and 1952 by naming him co-chair in charge of organizing national tournaments. In 1961, Lawson was inducted into the PGA Hall of Fame at Pinehurst, North Carolina. He died in 1968.

Summary

Although physically quite strong, Lawson Little felt that much of his success was the result of his mental ability. Before addressing the ball on the tee, he always thought out his play and made allowances for unexpected circumstances.

Michael R. Bradley

Additional Sources:

Grimsley, Will. *Golf: Its History, People, and Events.* Englewood Cliffs, N.J.: Prentice-Hall, 1966.

Hickok, Ralph. *A Who's Who of Sports Champions.* Boston: Houghton Mifflin, 1995.

Porter, David L., ed. *Biographical Dictionary of American Sports: Outdoor Sports.* Westport, Conn.: Greenwood Press, 1988.

HONORS AND AWARDS

1934	World Trophy
	Hall of the Athlete Foundation Athlete of the Year
1935	Sullivan Award
1961	Inducted into PGA Hall of Fame
1980	Inducted into PGA/World Golf Hall of Fame

SERGEI LITVINOV

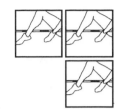

Sport: Track and field (hammer throw)

Born: January 23, 1958
       Krasnodar, U.S.S.R. (now Russia)

Early Life

Sergei Litvinov was born on January 23, 1958, in Krasnodar, near the Black Sea in what was then the Soviet Union. Born at a time of tension between his country and the United States, Sergei was drawn into a life in the Soviet Army as well as into a life in athletics. His military career proved to be a factor in his choice of individual athletic competition as opposed to team competition.

Sergei grew to almost 5 feet 11 inches tall and nearly 240 pounds. His muscular build led to a natural interest in events of strength such as the hammer throw. His competitive spirit resulted in his first official competition in 1972 at the age of fourteen. The first record of his ability in the hammer throw is in 1974, when, at the age of sixteen, he threw the hammer 60.68 meters, or almost 200 feet.

The Road to Excellence

Sergei gained international recognition in 1976, when he set a world junior record with a throw of 72.38 meters (237.5 feet). He raised that record in 1977 and also became a member of the Soviet national track and field team.

Sergei's athletic development was paralleled by his training as a Soviet Army officer. His physical training in the military helped him to develop the arm, shoulder, and back muscles that are vital to success in the hammer throw. Because the hammer is thrown with both hands, tremendous upper-body strength and excellent coordination are required for a championship performance. The hammer is actually a sixteen-pound metal sphere attached to a grip by a steel spring wire, which is almost four feet long. The event, which is believed to have its origin in sledgehammer throwing in England and Scotland during the fifteenth and sixteenth centuries, first appeared in the Olympics in 1900.

I. Timashkov was Sergei's coach in the hammer throw. In 1978, Sergei improved his best to

Sergei Litvinov during the 1988 Olympics in Seoul, South Korea.

STATISTICS

Year	Competition	Place	Distance
1980	Olympic Games	Silver	80.6 meters/264.4 feet
1982	European Championships	3d	78.6 meters/257.9 feet
1983	World Championships	Gold	82.6 meters/271 feet
1986	European Championships	2d	85.7 meters/281.2 feet
1987	World Championships	Gold	83.0 meters/272.3 feet
1988	Olympic Games	Gold	84.8 meters/278.2 feet

76.32 meters (238.5 feet), a mark he raised to 79.82 meters (261.9 feet)in 1979. This performance enabled Sergei to join Yuri Sedykh and Yuri Tamm to form a Soviet trio that would dominate the hammer throw for the next decade.

The Emerging Champion

By 1980, this trio was repeatedly setting and breaking world records. In May, the world record, which was then held by the German Karl-Hans Reihm, was first broken by Sedykh. Tamm followed with a new record, which was erased immediately by Sedykh. Eight days later, Sergei beat both of his countrymen and set his first world record with a mighty throw of 81.66 meters (267.9 feet).

In the 1980 Summer Olympics in Moscow, the Soviet trio had the field to themselves. Because the United States and many Western European nations boycotted the Games in response to the Soviet invasion of Afghanistan, Karl-Hans Reihm, the only threat to the Soviets, could not compete.

Sedykh had won his first gold medal in the 1976 Olympics in Montreal, and he repeated as champion in 1980 with a throw of 81.80 meters (268.4 feet). Sergei's first toss in Moscow was 80.64 meters (264.6 feet), enough for the silver medal. Tamm won the bronze.

Following the 1980 Olympics, the competition between Sergei and Sedykh intensified, inspiring both men to previously unbelievable performances. Because Yuri was three years older and had more experience than Sergei, his advantage held for the next three years; however, Sergei was rapidly narrowing the gap. In 1982, he set his second world record

with a throw of 83.98 meters (275.5 feet). Sergei placed third in the European Championships that year.

The year of 1983 marks a major summit in Sergei's career. Not only did he win the World Championships in Helsinki, Finland, with a throw of 82.68 meters (271.3 feet), but in so doing he defeated Sedykh for the first time in a major competition. It was Sedykh's first such defeat since 1976. Sergei's best effort in 1983 was a tremendous 84.14 meters (276.1 feet) for his third world record.

In 1984, the personal duel again turned in favor of Sedykh. Although Sergei threw for more than 85 meters for the first time at a meet in Cork, Ireland, he placed second to Sedykh, who set a new world record at 86.34 meters (283.3 feet). The Soviet trio missed the 1984 Olympics in Los Angeles as a result of a Soviet boycott of those Games.

In 1986, Sergei reached his personal high point when he threw the hammer 86.04 meters. Sedykh, however, again surpassed him with a new world record of 86.74 meters (282.3 feet). Sedykh did not enter any official competition in 1987 as he trained for the 1988 Olympics. This gave Sergei an easy road to win the European Cup in Prague in June and to successfully defend his World Championship in Rome in September.

The climax of Sergei's career came in the 1988 Summer Olympics in Seoul, Korea. As in 1980, the Soviet trio won all three medals, but this time, the top two positions were reversed. Sergei won the gold medal with a throw of 84.80 meters (278.2 feet). Sedykh followed with 83.76 meters (274.8 feet) for the silver, and Tamm again received the bronze.

RECORDS AND MILESTONES

Set world record in the hammer throw in 1980 (81.66 meters/267.9 feet), 1982 (83.98 meters/275 feet), and 1983 (84.14 meters/276.1 feet)

Set world junior records in the hammer throw in 1976 (72.38 meters/237.5 feet) and 1977 (78.22 meters/256.6 feet)

HONORS AND AWARDS

USSR Merited Master of Sport

Continuing the Story

The friendly rivalry between Sergei and Sedykh left a lasting impact on athletic events with individual competition. With the added incentive of both to stay a throw in front of Tamm, the impact was even greater. As of 1988, Sergei and Sedykh were the only men to ever throw the hammer more than 85 meters (279 feet).

The Soviet Union had many honors for its outstanding athletes. Many were awarded the title of Master of Sport; only the elite, however, were honored as Merited Masters of Sport. Along with Sedykh and Tamm, Sergei was awarded this highest title.

Sergei and his closest rival, Sedykh, retired from active competition after the 1988 Olympics. After the breakup of the Soviet Union in 1991, Tamm competed in the 1992 Barcelona Olympics for his native republic of Estonia.

Sergei retired as a Soviet Army officer about the same time as his retirement from athletics. At the time, he was living in Rostov-on-Don, not far from his place of birth. For several years, Sergei had been a student working on a physical-education diploma, and after his retirement from the army, he began a new career as a physical-education teacher.

Summary

Throughout his many years of training, Sergei Litvinov exhibited tremendous determination to become a champion. His fierce competitive spirit, his consistent improvements, and his many awards all serve as examples of what an athlete can accomplish with hard work and dedication.

Glenn L. Swygart

Additional Sources:

Wallechinsky, David. *The Complete Book of the Olympics.* Boston: Little, Brown and Company, 1991.

Watman, Mel. *Encyclopedia of Track and Field Athletics.* New York: St. Martin's Press, 1981.

REBECCA LOBO

Sport: Basketball

Born: October 6, 1973
Southwick, Massachusetts

Early Life

Rebecca Lobo was born in Southwick, Massachusetts, on October 6, 1973. She grew up with an older brother, Jason, and sister, Rachel. Her parents, RuthAnn and Dennis, were both educators and instilled in their children the importance of schooling. When Rebecca went to high school and college she took this lesson with her and made the dean's list every semester. Rebecca has talked about the need for all student athletes to not neglect their education in favor of the game. For Rebecca the two went hand in hand, and her education made her a better player on the court.

Growing up, Rebecca developed a love for basketball because it gave her an opportunity to daydream and think, a time to be alone. She loved to play the game, whether by herself or with her family and, later, her friends.

The Road to Excellence

While in high school Rebecca did not spend all her time on the basketball court but also played the saxophone in the Southwick Tolland Regional High School band. In addition to starring on the court she also played field hockey and softball and ran track.

By the time her high school days were over, however, Rebecca had become the all-time leading scorer (male or female) in Massachusetts history with 2,710 points. Many of her summers had been spent working at basketball camps preparing for the next season, and all that hard work paid off.

Rebecca Lobo practices during a May, 2000, training session for the New York Liberty.

STATISTICS

Season	GP	FGA	FGM	FG%	FTA	FTM	FT%	Reb.	Ast.	TP	PPG
1997	28	354	133	.376	105	64	.610	203	53	348	12.4
1998	30	281	136	.484	93	66	.710	207	44	350	11.7
1999	1	0	0	—	0	0	—	1	0	0	0.0
Totals	59	635	269	.424	198	130	.657	411	97	698	11.8

Notes: GP = games played; FGA = field goals attempted; FGM = field goals made; FG% = field goal percentage; FTA = free throws attempted; FTM = free throws made; FT% = free throw percentage; Reb. = rebounds; Ast. = assists; TP = total points; PPG = points per game

The Emerging Champion

After high school Rebecca went on to star at the University of Connecticut from 1991 to 1995. During these four years the Lady Huskies had a 106-25 record, including 102 consecutive wins. In 1995, with a 35-0 record, the Huskies won the national championship, and Rebecca was voted the Final Four most valuable player and was named the National Player of the Year. In 1994 and 1995 Rebecca was selected as the Big East Conference Player of the Year and in 1994 was named to the Kodak All-American First Team.

When Rebecca graduated from the University of Connecticut she was the all-time leader in rebounds with 1,286 and in blocked shots with 396. The Lady Huskies had also played in four National Collegiate Athletic Association (NCAA) championships. In addition, she graduated with a degree in political science.

Continuing the Story

In 1996 Rebecca's mother was diagnosed with breast cancer, and the family helped her fight the disease and triumph. Rebecca and her mother wrote a book about the experience, entitled *The Home Team* (1997). As a result of her mother's battle Rebecca made breast cancer research and awareness an important cause. Her work with Yoplait and others resulted in her being named Sportswoman of the Year by the Women's Sports Foundation, and in 1998 she won the Hispanic Heritage Sports Award.

Rebecca's basketball career continued after she played for the Olympic gold-medal-winning team in 1996. Originally drafted to play for the New Jersey Turnpikes in the United States Basketball League (USBL), Rebecca was assigned to the New England Blizzard in the American Basketball League (ABL). Instead, she chose to join the Women's National Basketball Association (WNBA), playing for the New York Liberty in 1997. A torn ligament in her left knee ended her 1999 season only one minute into the first game. After missing the entire 2000 season, she returned to limited action in 2001. Before her knee injury Rebecca had been named to the All-WNBA Second Team in 1997 and to the Eastern Conference All-Star team in 1999.

As a rookie for the New York Liberty, Rebecca played a solid game, averaging just over 12 points a game and a little over 7 rebounds. Rebecca

HONORS AND AWARDS

1991	Junior Select Team U.S. Olympic Festival East Team
1992	Big East Rookie of the Year Junior World Championship Qualifying Team
1993-95	All-Big East First Team
1994	Kodak All-America First Team
1994-95	Big East Conference Player of the Year Big East Tournament Most Outstanding Player Academic All-American Big East Conference Women's Basketball Scholar Athlete of the Year
1995	Final Four most valuable player Consensus National Player of the Year Wade Trophy
1996	Gold Medal with U.S. Women's Olympic Team
1997	All-WNBA Second Team

proved that she was a team player, unselfish and able to work to make her team better through her own play. While injuries have interrupted Rebecca's climb to the top of the charts in the WNBA, the Liberty expected big things from her.

Rebecca is recognized as one of the most popular stars in the WNBA. Although she may not have the top statistics in the league, Rebecca is one of the most popular of all the league's players. Her endorsements for the league range from Mattel to Reebok to General Motors and appearances on ESPN.

Summary

Rebecca Lobo is an inspiration to young female athletes. A role model who took both school and sports seriously, she succeeded in both areas. Court stars Rebecca, Lisa Leslie, and Sheryl Swoopes brought a new image to women's basketball both on and off the court as the threesome have become as well known for their modeling as their for on-court activities.

Leslie Heaphy

Additional Sources:

Duffy, Mary, et al. "Center of Attention." *Women's Sports and Fitness* 18 (March, 1996): 68-71.

Jenkins, Sally. "She's Got Fame." *Women's Sports and Fitness* 2 (July, 1999): 68.

Lobo, RuthAnn, and Rebecca Lobo. *The Home Team: Of Mothers, Daughters and American Champions.* New York: Kodansha International, 1996.

Marks, Robyn. "Supermodels." *Sport* 8 (July, 1997): 46-49.

Savage, Jeff. *Sports Great Rebecca Lobo.* Berkeley Heights, N.J.: Enslow, 2001.

JOHNNY LONGDEN

Sport: Horse racing

Born: February 14, 1907
Wakefield, England

Early Life

John Eric Longden was born in Wakefield, England, on February 14, 1907. His family soon emigrated to Canada. Great athletes generally have arisen in two ways: Some first take up their sport as an avocation, and others seize the chance their ability offers to extricate themselves from poverty. Johnny decidedly belongs to the latter group. He had little formal education and in his teens worked in a coal mine.

Johnny turned what some may view as a handicap into an asset, enabling him to raise his prospects of success. He was very short, standing 4 feet 11 inches and weighing only 110 pounds. Although short people often are at a disadvantage, in one occupation they decidedly have an edge.

Horse racing requires riders of Johnny's dimensions. Thoroughbreds react strongly to weight, and a horse that has to race with a jockey weighing 150 pounds faces an insurmountable obstacle. Johnny saw that a future far superior to that of a coal miner awaited him if he could acquire the skills to become a jockey.

The Road to Excellence

Johnny acquired his earliest experience as a trick rider in Canadian fairs. His riding ability and his talent for handling horses convinced him that he ought to try his hand as a professional jockey, and he began his career in 1927. He immediately started an intensive program of hard work. He arrived at the track each day by 8 A.M. and mingled with the trainers, exercise boys, and walkers. He did not confine himself to learning to ride but endeavored to master every sort of work at the track. To that end, he was willing to perform unpleasant tasks, such as "mucking out" a stable and bandaging a horse's legs.

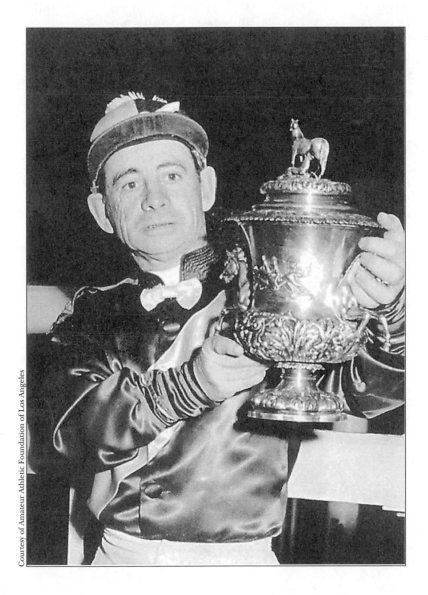

Courtesy of Amateur Athletic Foundation of Los Angeles

1651

MAJOR CHAMPIONSHIP VICTORIES AS A JOCKEY

Year	Race	Horse
1943	Belmont Stakes	Count Fleet
	Kentucky Derby	Count Fleet
	Preakness Stakes	Count Fleet

MAJOR CHAMPIONSHIP VICTORIES AS A TRAINER

Year	Race	Horse
1969	Kentucky Derby	Majestic Prince
	Preakness Stakes	Majestic Prince

By doing so, he acquired a comprehensive knowledge of racing. Joe Hernandez, Johnny's California agent from 1931 to 1966, noted that Johnny excelled not only as a jockey but in every aspect of the sport.

Johnny developed a style of racing that enabled him to realize his riding potential to the fullest. He had an unusual ability to break his horse very fast at the start of a race. Taking advantage of the quick start, he tried to keep his horse ahead for the entire race. Because of his style, he was nicknamed "The Pumper" by fans; he was also called "The Fox." Not all horses like to charge immediately to the front, and if Johnny's mount preferred to keep back of the pack initially, he was perfectly capable of riding in this fashion. A breakneck dash from the starting gate to the finish was, however, his trademark.

The Emerging Champion

Throughout his long career, Johnny rode most of his races from a base in California. His first appearance in the state was in the 1931-1932 season, in which he rode at the Tanforan track near San Francisco. His success was immediate: He rode 54 winners in 51 days.

Southern California became the hub of Johnny's activities from the mid-1930's. He rode at the first meeting of the Santa Anita Race Track in 1936; his first victory there was aboard War Letter on December 26, 1936. For nearly his entire career, Johnny ranked among the best California jockeys.

Two obstacles confronted him in his efforts to reach the top. Because of the speed and power of racehorses, the chance of injury to a jockey is considerable, Johnny suffered breaks in both arms, both legs (one five times), his collarbone, both feet, two vertebrae, and several ribs. Even after reaching an age above that of most jockeys, Johnny never let injuries halt his career. He took them as part of the price he had to pay to remain a leading rider.

Another difficulty stemmed from Johnny's decision to center his career in California. Most of the major racing events in the United States during the 1930's, 1940's, and 1950's took place in the eastern states. A major victory at Santa Anita counted for much less in prestige and financial rewards than a win in an eastern stakes race. Among Johnny's contemporaries was Eddie Arcaro, generally considered the greatest of all jockeys in major stakes races; he was also eclipsed by a younger rival, Willie Shoemaker, in this type of race.

Johnny refused to be discouraged. He did not concentrate on key races but instead aimed to build a consistent run of winners. Because of his extraordinary longevity as a rider—his forty years in the saddle surpassed only by Shoemaker's forty-one—he outranked nearly all other riders in purses and number of wins.

Continuing the Story

Johnny's peak as a jockey was in the early 1940's. He rode one of the twentieth century's greatest horses, Count Fleet, to victory in the Triple Crown in 1943. The Triple Crown consists of the Kentucky Derby, the Preakness Stakes, and the Belmont Stakes, the most important races for three-year-olds. Johnny's wins in 1943 were his only victories in these events as a jockey. He was also the leading money winner in 1943, a feat he repeated in 1945.

RECORDS AND MILESTONES

Only person to ride and train Kentucky Derby winners
Annual money leader (1943, 1945)
Triple Crown winner aboard Count Fleet (1943)
6,032 career victories

HONORS AND AWARDS

1958	Inducted into National Horse Racing Hall of Fame

After his wonderful year, Johnny returned to his usual path of steadiness rather than the spectacular. In 1950, he once again found himself in the limelight. His adept riding of Noor enabled his mount to upset Citation, the 1948 Triple Crown winner, in four successive races.

Johnny closed his career in triumph. His last mount was in the March 13, 1966, San Juan Capistrano Handicap, the eighth race of the day. His horse, George Royal, had not won all year, and Johnny himself, aged fifty-nine, was well past his prime. George Royal was a come-from-behind horse, unamenable to Johnny's front-running style. Johnny responded to the challenge. He won the race, nosing out Bobby Unser, a much younger jockey.

Johnny retired in 1966 with 6,032 wins, at the time the world's record. The total purses won by his horses were more than twenty-four million dollars. After his riding career, he worked for many years as a trainer.

Summary

After a hard youth working as a coal miner in Canada, Johnny Longden decided to become a jockey. Careful study of all aspects of racing enabled him to attain his goal. He was a leading rider for forty years, centering his activities in California. Although he did not specialize in major stakes races, he won the Triple Crown aboard Count Fleet in 1943. He closed his career with a victory in his final race.

Bill Delaney

Additional Sources:

Beckwith, B. K. *The Longden Legend*. South Brunswick, England: A. S. Barnes, 1973.

Davis, Stephanie. "Back on Track." *Sports Illustrated* 81, no. 2 (July 11, 1994): 3-4.

Murray, James. "Johnny Comes Riding Home." *Sports Illustrated* 10, no. 7 (February 16, 1959): 44-45.

JEANNIE LONGO

Sport: Cycling

Born: October 31, 1958
Annecy, France

Early Life

Jeannie Longo was born on October 31, 1958, in Annecy, a city with a population of fifty-three thousand located twenty miles south of Geneva, Switzerland. She was the youngest of three sisters born to athletic parents. Her father was a competitive runner and rugby player; her mother taught sports in school. The family moved to Grenoble, and Jeannie began following her parents down the ski slopes at a young age. She also developed a talent for the piano, which she studied seriously for ten years.

At the age of seventeen, Jeannie enrolled in college and began devoting more time to studying and to skiing. She began cycling during the warmer seasons as a way to stay in shape for skiing. The sports complemented each other, and she became French university champion in skiing. She met her future husband, Patrice Ciprelli, during her competitive skiing career, and he helped coach her in both sports.

The Road to Excellence

Jeannie began to concentrate on cycling, and she won the French national road racing championship in 1979. The next year, she successfully defended that title, picking up the national pursuit championship as well. Both titles were hers for the rest of the decade. She became known for riding at the front of the pack, even though the riders in front work hardest, cutting the wind for the riders behind them.

The 1981 world championships in Prague, Czechoslovakia, marked Jeannie's emergence to world prominence. She missed the gold medal by inches. She claimed that she had promised Ciprelli that she would marry him when she was world champion; she added jokingly that people said she had lost the race to avoid fulfilling her promise. Jeannie also took third place in the individual pursuit competition in 1981. She continued to compete in both skiing and cycling events, earning two more bronze medals in the individual pursuit at the world championships in 1982 and 1983.

Jeannie's breakthrough came in 1984, when she won the Tour of Texas, a series of events that drew riders from all over the world. She took a silver medal in the individual pursuit at the 1984

Jeannie Longo cycles in November, 2000, to a new one-hour women's world record.

MAJOR CHAMPIONSHIP VICTORIES

Year	Competition	Place
1979-89,1992,1995	French National Road Racing Championship	1st
1980-89,1992,1994	French National 3-kilometer Pursuit	1st
1984-85	Tour of Texas	1st
1985-87,1989,1995	World Championships Road Race	1st
1986,1988-89	World Championships 3-kilometer Pursuit	1st
1987	Coors Classic	1st
	Tour of Colombia	1st
	Tour of Norway	1st
1987-89	Tour de France Féminin	1st
1988-89	World Championships 30-kilometer Points Race	1st
1991	Ore-Ida Women's Challenge	1st
1992	Olympic Games Road Race	Silver
	Olympic Games Pursuit	5th
1995	French National Time Trial Championship	1st
1995-97	World Championships Time Trial	1st
1996	Olympic Games Road Race	Gold
	Olympic Games Time Trial	Silver
2000	Olympic Games Time Trial	Bronze

Féminin, a multiday race run in conjunction with the men's Tour de France. In 1985 and 1986, she had finished second to Italy's Maria Canins in the Tour de France Féminin, an event that Jeannie had pushed to get established. The race was first run in 1984.

Training for the 1987 event began in January, with Jeannie riding up mountain roads in the Alps while her husband followed her in a car. She began the year's racing by winning the week-long Tour of Colombia, the week-long Tour of Norway, and the two-week Coors Classic. When the Tour de France Féminin began in July, she was ready for mountain riding. She dueled with Canins for days, then won a decisive stage of the race in the Alps. That stage win effectively clinched the race for her, with Canins coming in second.

world championships, then repeated her win at the Tour of Texas the following year. In 1985, she also chalked up her first world championship, in the road race, along with another second-place finish in the individual pursuit. Soon after, she married Ciprelli as promised. She continued to compete under her maiden name, under which she had become famous.

The Emerging Champion

Jeannie had been a champion almost since her entry into the sport of cycling, but after her first world championship, she dominated the sport. In 1986, she won the world championships in both the road race and the individual pursuit, earning two gold medals in the space of a week and beating Rebecca Twigg of the United States at her home track in Boulder, Colorado.

Jeannie extended her stay in Colorado to take advantage of the thin air at the high altitude. She set a world record for distance traveled in one hour by a female cyclist. Few accomplishments had eluded her, but she still lacked an Olympic medal and a victory in the Tour de France

Jeannie had her eye on further world records, and she returned to Colorado. She set a new world hour record as well as four other records to bring her total to eleven. The records were erased, however, when she tested positive for the drug ephedrine. She had never tested positive before, and she claimed that traces of the drug came from herbal therapy she had undergone in France. Nevertheless, her records were stripped from her, and she faced a one-month suspension from cycling. No major events were held during her suspension, and she returned ready to prove herself.

Major championships continued to be hers. She won the Tour de France Féminin in 1988 and 1989 and also won world championships in the individual pursuit in 1988 and 1989, in the road race in 1989, and in the points race in 1988 and 1989. After her amazing 1989 season, she retired from the sport, as did Canins.

RECORDS

2000	Broke world one-hour women's record (44.767 kilometers)

Continuing the Story

Jeannie's retirement lasted only a year. Many people believed that she missed cycling and the spotlight, particularly after compatriot Catherine Marsal won the 1990 world championship in the road race. Jeannie began her comeback with the 1991 Ore-Ida Women's Challenge road race in Idaho. To maintain a low profile, she entered under the name Jane Ciprelli, using her husband's last name. She won the race.

An Olympic medal was the one major cycling prize that Jeannie had not yet won. A minor accident that broke her bicycle's derailleur had dropped her to sixth place in the 1984 road race, and in 1988 she had tired while chasing the leader, dropping back to finish in twenty-first place. Another chance came in 1992. She finally won her medal, finishing second in the road race to Kathryn Watt. She also placed fifth in the 3,000-meter individual pursuit. She continued to take on challenges, even experimenting with racing mountain bikes in off-road races. She placed second in the 1993 world championship road race. Always a fierce competitor, she was fined for her disregard of the winner's national anthem at the awards ceremony.

In 1994 and 1995, Jeannie put together a string of impressive victories: the French National 3-Kilometer Pursuit, the World Championships Road Race and Time Trial, and the French National Road Racing Championship and Time Trial. Having been denied the gold medal in the 1988 Olympics because of a broken derailleur, Jeannie took the 1996 Olympic Games in Atlanta by storm, winning the gold in the road race competition and the silver in the time trials. She added another World Championship time trial win in 1997 to her considerable list of victories, bringing her total World Championship titles to twelve. At the age of forty-one, Jeannie competed in her fourth Olympic Games in Sydney, taking the bronze medal in the time trial event.

Summary

Jeannie Longo is probably the greatest women's cyclist ever to compete. Her persistent charges to the front and consistent strength made her a formidable competitor.

A. J. Sobczak

Additional Sources:

Chavner, David, and Michael Halstead. *The Tour de France Complete Book of Cycling*. New York: Villard Books, 1990.

Levinson, David, and Karen Christenson, eds. *Encyclopedia of World Sport: From Ancient to Present*. Santa Barbara, Calif.: ABC-CLIO, 1996.

AL LOPEZ

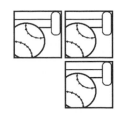

Sport: Baseball

Born: August 20, 1908
Tampa, Florida

Early Life

On August 20, 1908, Alfonso Ramon Lopez was born in the Spanish-speaking section of Tampa, Florida, called Ybor City. His parents had immigrated to the United States from Spain in order to work in the cigar industry. Lopez grew up in a Spanish-speaking neighborhood where the children learned Spanish before English. The youngsters considered Spanish more manly and powerful and refused to speak English to one another. The neighborhood was filled with the unpleasant smells from the cigar factories, which Al detested. As a youngster, he promised himself that he would never work in those factories. His childhood love of baseball allowed him to keep this promise.

The Road to Excellence

In 1924, Al was offered $150 a month to play baseball for the Tampa Smokers. "I took it before they changed their minds," he said. In that first year of his professional career, he played in an exhibition game, catching for Walter Johnson, often considered the finest pitcher of all time. After the game, Johnson praised Al, saying, "Nice game, kid. You're going to make a great catcher someday."

Al spent a year playing for Jacksonville in the Southeastern League. At the end of the season, Jacksonville sold him to the Brooklyn Dodgers for ten thousand dollars after having purchased him for a mere one thousand dollars. He was hitless in the only three games he played, and the next season he was back in the South, playing for Atlanta in the Southern Association. In that sea-

Al Lopez practices catching in 1947.

son, however, he hit .327 in 143 games and was back in Brooklyn in 1930.

The Emerging Champion

Al excelled during his six-year stint with the Dodgers, hitting .309 in 1930 and .301 in 1933 and playing on the All-Star team in 1934. The next four years saw Lopez playing for the financially troubled Boston Bees under Casey Stengel. In order to meet payroll, the team sold him to the Pittsburgh Pirates in 1940, after Stengel's assurance that he could stay. "You and Eddie Miller are the only ones we can get money for," Stengel told him. "So we'll sell Miller." Lopez lost a bet for a one-hundred-dollar suit of clothes to Miller because of that broken promise.

During this period, Lopez married Evelyn M. Kearney, and the couple had a son, Alfonso Ramon, Jr.

Al's stay with Pittsburgh from 1940 to 1946 was highly successful. Again in 1941 he was named to the All-Star team. He was a strong presence on the Pirates, although for the last year and a half, he usually played defensively, coming in at the end of games. His popularity was so great, however, that when the management publicly announced the possibility of firing manager Frankie Frisch, a fan opinion poll conducted by a Pittsburgh newspaper showed that fans overwhelmingly supported Al Lopez as a replacement for Frisch. The next season, 1947, Al was playing for the Cleveland Indians. It was his final season.

Most ballplayers would be content to have completed such a successful seventeen-year career in the majors, but Al's greatest achievements

were still to come. In 1948, he was named manager of Indianapolis in the American Association. After finishes in second place in 1949 and 1950, he was named manager of the Cleveland Indians on November 10, 1950, for a salary of thirty-five thousand dollars a year, replacing Lou Boudreau. In his six-year stay with the Indians, the team never lost more than 66 games of the 154-game season. They won the pennant in 1954, the only team at that point in the decade to break the pennant-winning streak of the New York Yankees in the 1950's. The Indians lost the Series to the New York Giants in a four-game sweep.

Continuing the Story

The greatness of Al's career did not stop in the mid-1950's. In 1956, Al left the Indians and signed with the Chicago White Sox for forty thousand dollars. The next two seasons brought second-place finishes to the Sox. In 1958, Al was named Manager of the Year, and, amid talk that he would retire because of his frustration over the invincible Yankees, he signed on for the next season. "I love baseball and I think we have a good chance of winning the pennant," he said.

Win they did. The 1959 season brought a lifeless Yankee team, leaving the Indians as the strongest competition for the White Sox. After a

STATISTICS

Season	GP	AB	Hits	2B	3B	HR	Runs	RBI	BA	SA
1928	3	12	0	0	0	0	0	0	.000	.000
1930	128	421	130	20	4	6	60	57	.309	.418
1931	111	360	97	13	4	0	38	40	.269	.328
1932	126	404	111	18	6	1	44	43	.275	.356
1933	126	372	112	11	4	3	39	41	.301	.376
1934	140	439	120	23	2	7	58	54	.273	.383
1935	128	379	95	12	4	3	50	39	.251	.327
1936	128	426	103	12	4	8	46	50	.242	.345
1937	105	334	68	11	1	3	31	38	.204	.269
1938	71	236	63	6	1	1	19	14	.267	.314
1939	131	412	104	22	1	8	32	49	.252	.369
1940	95	293	80	9	3	3	35	41	.273	.355
1941	114	317	84	9	1	5	33	43	.265	.347
1942	103	289	74	8	2	1	17	26	.256	.308
1943	118	372	98	9	4	1	40	39	.263	.317
1944	115	331	76	12	1	1	27	34	.230	.281
1945	91	243	53	8	0	0	22	18	.218	.251
1946	56	150	46	2	0	1	13	12	.307	.340
1947	61	126	33	1	0	0	9	14	.262	.270
Totals	1,950	5,916	1,547	206	42	52	613	652	.261	.337

Notes: GP = games played; AB = at bats; 2B = doubles; 3B = triples; HR = home runs; RBI = runs batted in; BA = batting average; SA = slugging average

four-game sweep in August, Chicago won the pennant on September 22, 1959, in a game with the Indians. The Series with the Los Angeles Dodgers did not go as well, with a defeat of 4 games to 2. Al, ever the "nice guy," commented that the Dodgers and manager Walt Alston "played good ball, real good ball."

Mentioned as a successor to Casey Stengel at the helm of the Yankees, Al chose to stay on with the White Sox for sixty thousand dollars in the 1960 season. He remained with the team through 1969, with years off in 1966 and 1967, retiring with the team in fourth place. He was named to the National Baseball Hall of Fame as a manager in 1977.

Summary

One of the few ballplayers whose excellence was seen in both his playing and managing, Al Lopez was a major leaguer who was reliable, smart, and likable. For many years, he held the record for the number of games caught, 1,918, and he was able to steer two very dissimilar teams to the only American League pennants not won by the Yankees in the 1950's. His teams finished second ten times. In a poll taken among retired major leaguers in the mid-1930's, Al was rated seventh best of all time as a defensive catcher and manager. Without the stellar New York Yankees of the 1950's, Al's career would shine even more brightly in the history of baseball.

Vicki K. Robinson

HONORS AND AWARDS	
1934, 1941	National League All-Star Team
1977	Inducted into National Baseball Hall of Fame

Additional Sources:

Hirshberg, Al. *Baseball's Greatest Catchers.* New York: G. P. Putnam's Sons, 1966.

Shatzkin, Mike, et al., eds. *The Ballplayers: Baseball's Ultimate Biographical Reference.* New York: William Morrow, 1990.

Singletary, Wes. *Al Lopez: The Life of Baseball's El Señor.* Jefferson, N.C.: McFarland, 1999.

NANCY LOPEZ

Born: January 6, 1957
Torrance, California

Early Life

Nancy Lopez was born January 6, 1957, in Torrance, California. She grew up in the southern New Mexico city of Roswell. This region of the country, with its abundance of sunshine and mild winters, provides a great environment for year-round outdoor sports activities. As a child, Nancy's small build led her to become involved in gymnastics and swimming. Her father, Domingo, was an avid golfer and took Nancy and her older sister Delma to the golf course with him almost every day. Nancy showed an immediate interest in golf, and her father gave her some clubs when she was only eight years old. She began hitting golf balls daily at the range and, by the time she was nine, she entered her first Pee Wee tournament in Alamogordo, New Mexico, and won.

The Road to Excellence

By the time Nancy was a freshman in high school, she had distinguished herself as a junior golfer and had generated some controversy as well at Goddard High School. She was good enough to play on the boys' golf team, but girls were not permitted to play on boys' teams and there was no girls' team at the high school. Nancy's situation drew national attention, and within a year, girls were allowed to play on boys' teams in noncontact sports (golf, tennis, and track). Nancy not only made the team; she was the best golfer on it and led the team to two state championships. Nancy was a pioneer in the rights of women to participate in school athletics. Because of her great ability, teachers and coaches realized that girls should have teams and opportunities to participate in sports, just like boys.

Nancy's dream in high school was to go to Arizona State University and to play on the Sun Devils golf team. When it came time to pick a college, however, Arizona State did not have full scholarships for women's golf. Dale McNamara, the golf coach at Tulsa University in Oklahoma, had been reading about Nancy in golfing maga-

Nancy Lopez tees off during a 2000 tournament.

AP/Wide World Photos

MAJOR CHAMPIONSHIP VICTORIES	
1978, 1985, 1989	LPGA Championship
1981	Colgate Dinah Shore

OTHER NOTABLE VICTORIES	
1978-79	Colgate European Open
1979	Lady Keystone Open
1980	Rail Charity Classic Women's Kemper Open
1982-83	J & B Scotch Pro-Am
1983	Elizabeth Arden Classic
1984	Chevrolet World Championship of Women's Golf
1989	Atlantic City Classic Nippon Travel-MBS Classic
1990	MBS LPGA Classic
1991	Sara Lee Classic
1992	Rail Charity Golf Classic PING-Cellular LPGA Golf Championship
1993	Youngstown-Warren LPGA Classic
1997	Chick-Fil-A Charity Championship

zines for several years. She convinced the Tulsa Athletic Department to provide a full scholarship for Nancy to play for the Golden Hurricanes.

The Emerging Champion

Nancy was an immediate sensation in college golf. The Tulsa women's team entered nine tournaments in the 1975-1976 season and won six of them. Nancy was the individual winner (medalist) in six of the tournaments and led the team to a second-place national finish. She won the national championship as an individual, was second once in her two years of college golf, and was All-American both years.

With her father's blessing and guidance, Nancy joined the Ladies Professional Golf Association (LPGA) as a touring professional in 1977 and began a career that has made her, perhaps, the greatest woman golfer ever. Nancy's first year on the professional tour was one of the most remarkable years for any athlete in any sport. As a rookie at age twenty-one, she won nine tournaments, including five in a row. She set new records for the amount of prize money won in one

year and had the lowest scoring average (71.76). She was unanimously named Rookie of the Year and Player of the Year, a feat that had never been equaled in professional golf. Her second year on the tour was just as successful. Nancy won eight tournaments that year and again was named Player of the Year. In that two-year period, Nancy elevated her status from golf superstar to sports legend. She took the sporting world by storm and single-handedly brought women's golf to a new level, making it popular as a spectator sport and becoming a celebrity in the process.

Continuing the Story

To be a superstar at age twenty-one can burden one with huge responsibilities, and Nancy found that some of the other golfers on tour resented her great talent and success on the course and her popularity with the media. In addition, playing in a tournament every week and traveling all the time was not as glamorous as Nancy thought it would be. She met sportscaster Tim Melton in Cincinnati, and they were married in 1979. Nancy soon found that being a sports superstar presented special problems in a relationship, and the marriage did not survive them.

Although Nancy continued to win golf tournaments and became a spokesperson for women's golf and a celebrity, she still sought an identity away from golf and the satisfaction and security of a family. In 1982, Nancy married Ray Knight, who at that time was a baseball star for the Houston Astros. Nancy felt it helped to have the support of someone who understood the pressures of being a professional athlete and the emotional aspects of professional golf.

Over the next four years, Nancy took time out from golf to have two daughters, Ashley Marie and Erinn. She and Knight have managed to blend busy, glamorous sports careers with the happiness of a quiet home life. Nancy resumed her winning on the LPGA tour and was inducted into the LPGA Hall of Fame in 1987.

In 1991, Nancy took time off to have her third child, another daughter, but still managed to play in eleven tournaments, with a win at the Sara Lee Classic. The following year, Nancy recorded back-to-back playoff victories in the Rail Charity Golf Classic and the PING-Cellular One LPGA Golf Championship. In 1993, she won her forty-seventh career victory in a sudden-death playoff with Deb Richard in the Youngstown-Warren LPGA Classic.

After two years without a tour victory Nancy won the Chick-Fil-A Charity Championship in 1997, bringing her total LPGA tournament victories to forty-eight. She also finished second in the U.S. Women's Open Championship, an event that she has never won.

Nancy competed in few tournaments in 1999 and 2000 because of knee and gall bladder surgery. During the LPGA's fiftieth anniversary celebration, she was named one of the LPGA's top fifty players.

Summary

Nancy Lopez is perhaps the best woman golfer ever and is the person most responsible for making the Ladies Professional Golf Association a success on television and on tour throughout the United States. Her dazzling smile and warm personality, combined with her tremendous athletic talent, have made her one of the most popular women athletes of all time and an effective role model for millions of young people.

Henry A. Eisenhart

Additional Sources:

Cuniberti, Betty. "Never a Bridesmaid Again." *Golf Digest* 49, no. 6 (1998).

Hahn, James. *Nancy Lopez: Golfing Pioneer.* St. Paul, Minn.: EMC, 1979.

Hasday, Judy L. *Extraordinary Women Athletes.* New York: Children's Press, 2000.

Lopez, Nancy. *The Complete Golfer.* New York: Galahad Books, 2000.

Wilner, Barry. *Superstars of Women's Golf.* Philadelphia, Pa.: Chelsea House, 1997.

RECORDS AND AWARDS

Became the fastest LPGA player ever to reach the $200,000 and $400,000 marks in a single season

Became the second player in 1988 (Amy Alcott was the first) to cross the $2 million mark in career earnings

Youngest player to reach $1 million in earnings at age twenty-six

Holds the record for consecutive LPGA victories (5)

HONORS AND AWARDS

1976	Tulsa University Female Athlete of the Year
1977	Golf Digest Rookie of the Year
1978	Golf Digest Most Improved Golfer LPGA Rookie of the Year Gatorade Rookie of the Year
1978, 1985, 1988	Golf Digest Mickey Wright Award for Tournament Victories
1978-79	GWAA Player of the Year Seagram's Seven Crowns of Sports Award
1978-87	*Golf* magazine Golfer of the Decade
1978-79, 1985	LPGA Vare Trophy
1978-79, 1985, 1988	LPGA Player of the Year Rolex Player of the Year
1987	William and Mousie Powell Award Inducted into LPGA Hall of Fame
1998	Bob Jones Award

STEVEN LOPEZ

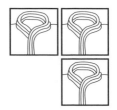

Sport: Martial arts (Tae Kwon Do)

Born: November 9, 1978
New York, New York

Early Life

After having been born in New York in 1978, Steven Lopez moved to Suger Land, Texas, while a child. When he was only five he began training in Tae Kwon Do. He would get up at sunrise to train in the garage with his three siblings. Whatever his older brother did, Steven wanted to try. They shared the two-car garage with tools, junk, and the clothes dryer, which kept the garage warm in the winter while they practiced. He would later say that people thought "the garage" was the nickname of the gym where they practiced.

The Road to Excellence

Although he enjoyed more traditional sports, such as football and basketball, Steven found Tae Kwon Do intriguing. Years later he said that what interested him was that Tae Kwon Do was not a sport that everyone else did. He also liked the fact that winning and losing depended solely on his own performance and abilities.

In addition to rising with the sun to begin training, Steven and his brothers practiced after school and in the evenings. Despite the grueling schedule, he maintained his grades and was an honor student at Kempner High School in Sugar Land. His schedule did, however, force some sacrifices. He was unable to attend either his homecoming or his prom because of upcoming national competitions.

The Emerging Champion

The sacrifices became worth it as he started winning more and more of his matches. In 1994 and 1996 both Steven

and his older brother Jean were a part of the U.S. national team. Jean later left competition in order to become Steven's coach. In 1997 Steven expanded his dominance when he won the World Gold Cup in Cairo, Egypt. From 1996 to 2000 he placed first in international Tae Kwon Do competitions as a featherweight.

In 1998 Sugar Land celebrated its first Olympic star when Tara Lipinski won the gold medal in women's figure skating. Steven hoped that she would not be Sugar Land's only Olympic champion. Before being ready for the Olympics, how-

Steven Lopez won the gold medal in the featherweight Tae Kwon Do competition at the 2000 Olympics.

ever, he had several more years of rigorous training and brutal competition. In 1999 he finished second in the Pan-America regional qualification tournament in his weight class.

The outcome of this match helped propel him to the Olympic trials in May, 2000. Tae Kwon Do was making its debut as an Olympic sport, and Steven hoped to represent the United States in Sydney, Australia. He was just one of three Lopezes competing in those trials. His brother Mark finished third in the men's flyweight division, and his sister, Diana, finished third in the women's welterweight division. Steven made the U.S. team by defeating Glenn Lainfiesta at the trials. He had the possibility of becoming Sugar Land's second Olympic champion.

Continuing the Story

During his first three preliminary rounds at the 2000 Olympics, Steven was an easy winner and had only 1 point scored on him. In his semifinal round he won an easy victory over Germany's Aziz Arhrki; during the Olympic qualifying tournament in Croatia, Aziz had defeated Steven. Steven did, however, dislocate his little finger during the match. The pain was only a momentary distraction to him. The years of training and sacrifice were paying off. He went into the final bout the favorite against South Korean champion Sin Jun-sik.

The final round was Steven's most difficult, however. He fell behind early when Sin, a fast and powerful kicker, scored on him with a head kick. The crowd, composed of several thousand Koreans, erupted in thunderous applause. Steven knew he had to devise a strategy that not only would help him win but also would earn Sin penalty points. At 6 feet 2 inches Steven had an incredible height advantage over his opponent. He

STATISTICS			
Year	Competition	Division	Place
1992	U.S. Open Tae Kwon Do Championships	Junior Finweight	1st
1993	U.S. Open Tae Kwon Do Championships	Junior Finweight	1st
	U.S. Junior Olympic Tae Kwon Do Championships	Flyweight	Silver
1994	U.S. Open Tae Kwon Do Championships	Junior Flyweight	1st
	U.S. National Tae Kwon Do Championships	Finweight	2d
	U.S. National Tae Kwon Do Team Trials	Finweight	1st
	World Cup Tae Kwon Do Championships	Finweight	3d
	Pan American Tae Kwon Do Championships	Finweight	2d
1995	Pan American Games Team Member	Finweight	
	U.S. National Tae Kwon Do Championships	Flyweight	2d
	U.S. National Tae Kwon Do Team Trials	Flyweight	3d
	U.S. Junior Olympic Tae Kwon Do Championships	Featherweight	1st
	U.S. Olympic Festival	Flyweight	1st
1996	U.S. Open Tae Kwon Do Championships	Featherweight	3d
	U.S. National Tae Kwon Do Junior Team Trials	Lightweight	1st
	U.S. National Tae Kwon Do Championships	Featherweight	1st
	U.S. National Tae Kwon Do Team Trials	Featherweight	1st
	World Junior Tae Kwon Do Championships	Lightweight	1st
	Pan American Tae Kwon Do Championships	Featherweight	1st
1997	U.S. Open Tae Kwon Do Championships	Featherweight	1st
	World Cup Tae Kwon Do Championships	Featherweight	1st
	U.S. National Tae Kwon Do Team Trials	Featherweight	1st
1998	U.S. Open Tae Kwon Do Championships	Lightweight	1st
	Spain Open Tae Kwon Do Championships	Lightweight	1st
	World Cup Tae Kwon Do Championships	Featherweight	3d
	U.S. National Tae Kwon Do Team Trials	Featherweight	1st
	U.S. Olympic Weight Division Tournament	Featherweight	Gold
	National Collegiate Tae Kwon Do Championships	Featherweight	1st
	Choson International Tae Kwon Do Cup	Featherweight	1st
	Pan American Tae Kwon Do Championships	Featherweight	1st
1999	U.S. Olympic Weight/Pan Am Games Team Trials	Featherweight	1st
	U.S. National Tae Kwon Do Team Trials	Lightweight	1st
	Pan American Games	Featherweight	1st
	Pan Am Olympic Qualification Tournament	Featherweight	2d
2000	U.S. Olympic Tae Kwon Do Team Trials	Featherweight	1st
	U.S. National Tae Kwon Do Team Trials	Lightweight	1st
	Olympic Games	Featherweight	Gold

knew that he would have to use his long reach to keep the Korean away from him. Sin was unable to score and was given a penalty point for a lack of aggression. Shortly after the penalty Steven landed a foot kick, but the crowd was so loud that the judges were unable to hear it.

With only one minute remaining in the match Steven knew he had to pull out all the stops. He remembered that he had not thrown a back kick the entire day and so devised a new strategy. He left his chest open. Sin took the bait, and Steven was ready for him. His back kick was perfect, and he scored. Although the match ended in a 1-1 tie, Steven won the gold medal because of

Sin's penalties. Steven became the first Latino and the first American to win a gold medal in the sport's debut.

Summary

Steven Lopez discovered his talent and his love early when he began practicing Tae Kwon Do with his brothers and sister. Although it meant years of sacrifice, he wanted to have his chance to compete. He moved steadily up the ranks of his weight class and established himself as a champion. When Tae Kwon Do debuted as an Olympic sport in 2000, Steven was ready to compete. When he won the gold he credited his family for giving him the drive to win.

Deborah Service

Additional Sources:

Baranger, Walter R. "Lopez Takes Gold." *The New York Times*, September 29, 2000, p. 5.

Bleiker, Cecil. "Steven Lopez Wins the First Official Olympic Gold Medal in Taekwondo." *U.S. Taekwondo Union.* http://www.ustu.org/pubs/lopezgold.html.

"Lopez Seizes Gold Medal." *MSNBC News Services.* http://www.msnbc.com/news/4687554.asp.

"Lopez, U.S. Win Inaugural Gold." *The Washington Post*, September 29, 2000, p. D12.

Waddell, Robert. "Steven Lopez Makes History Winning First Olympic Gold for Taekwondo." *Latino.com.* http://www.latino.com/article.phtml/000929lope.

RONNIE LOTT

Sport: Football

Born: May 8, 1959
Albuquerque, New Mexico

Early Life

Ronald Mandel Lott was born in Albuquerque, New Mexico, on May 8, 1959, the oldest of three children of Mary and Roy Lott. At the age of five, Ronnie and his family moved to Washington, D.C., when his father accepted an assignment in the United States Air Force. During his early years, Ronnie loved all sports and enjoyed watching all kinds of sports on television, but his favorite was basketball. His childhood in the inner city toughened him. At the age of nine, his family moved to San Bernardino, California, and a year later to Rialto, California.

The Road to Excellence

Ronnie attended Eisenhower High School in Rialto. While there, he made All-Conference in baseball and basketball and in football for three consecutive years. Upon graduating from high school in 1977, he enrolled at the University of Southern California (USC) on a football scholarship as a free safety. During his sophomore year USC won the Rose Bowl over Michigan and shared the number-one ranking in football with the University of Alabama.

Ronnie was ranked second in the nation, with 8 interceptions. He was also elected to the All-American team two years in a row, and he won recognition as the USC Trojans' most valuable and inspirational player. While at USC Ronnie also played as a reserve guard on the basketball team. In 1981 he was the eighth pick of the first round of the National Football League (NFL) draft to be chosen to play cornerback and safety for the San Francisco 49ers team.

The Emerging Champion

As a 6-foot, 203-pound defensive back, Ronnie made an immediate impression. On his first day of training camp, he became the starting left cornerback for the 49ers. During his first season with the NFL, Ronnie helped the 49ers win the Super Bowl in 1982. Ronnie became the second rookie in the history of the NFL to return 3 interceptions for touchdowns. Along with Lawrence Taylor of the New York Giants, he received Rookie of the Year honors.

Ronnie Lott in a 1990 game.

STATISTICS

Season	Int.	Yds.	TD	Sac.
1981	7	117	3	0.0
1982	2	95	1	0.0
1983	4	22	0	1.0
1984	4	26	0	1.0
1985	6	68	0	1.5
1986	**10**	134	1	2.0
1987	5	62	0	0.0
1988	5	59	0	0.0
1989	5	34	0	0.0
1990	3	26	0	0.0
1991	**8**	52	0	1.0
1992	1	0	0	0.0
1993	3	35	0	1.0
1994	0	0	0	1.0
Totals	63	730	5	8.5

Notes: Boldface indicates statistical leader. Int. = interceptions; Yds. = yards; TD = touchdowns; Sac. = sacks

During his fourteen-year career in the NFL, Ronnie became known for his hard-hitting style. As a versatile defensive back he earned ten Pro Bowl invitations and played three different defensive positions: free safety, strong safety, and cornerback. By 1986, he was playing the position of free safety, a position that enabled him to cover the entire field.

Continuing the Story

Ronnie played his final season with the 49ers in 1990, and on March 25, 1991, he signed a two-year contract to play the position of strong safety with the Los Angeles Raiders. In 1992 Ronnie led the team in tackles and was second in passes defended, with only 1 interception. The Raiders lost nine games and did not make the playoffs. In March, 1993, Ronnie signed a $3.1 million contract with the New York Jets. During his first year with the Jets, he was second on the team, with 3 interceptions. In his final year with the Jets, he took a $325,000 pay cut, which enabled the Jets to have more money under the salary cap. He retired from the Jets and from the NFL at the end of his 1994 season.

On July 29, 2000, Ronnie was formally inducted into the Pro Football Hall of Fame in Canton, Ohio. This is the highest honor awarded to veterans of the NFL and recognizes the achieve-

ments Ronnie made during his fourteen years with the league. During his career with the 49ers (1981-1990), Los Angeles Raiders (1991-1992), and the New York Jets (1993-1994) Ronnie made 63 career interceptions and twice led the league. He surpassed the 1,000-tackle mark in 1993 and had five seasons of at least 100 tackles. In his ten seasons with the 49ers, that team won eight NFC Western Division titles and four Super Bowls. In 20 playoff contests, Ronnie recorded 9 interceptions, 89 tackles, 1 forced fumble, 1 fumble recovery, and 2 touchdowns.

Respected coach George Seifert called him as football's greatest safety and the most committed football player he had ever known. Once, while playing in a NFL game, Ronnie smashed the tip of his little finger and chose to have it amputated because it would heal more quickly than it would if he waited for a bone graft. Although he lost part of his little finger, he did not spend much time on the sidelines.

Ronnie owns his own sports marketing company, the Hitters Club. He also serves as a Fox Sports Net analyst and is the co-owner of a Toyota dealership. He settled in Cupertino, California, with his wife and their three children. Close friends of Joe Montana, the Lotts have worked with him to launch a television program for children, *Adventures with Kanga and Roddy.*

Summary

Ronnie Lott is one of the best defensive players to play in the NFL. He played in four Super Bowl games with the San Francisco 49ers and ten Pro Bowl games. He was named All-Pro eight times, All-NFC six times, and All-AFC once and was enshrined into the Pro Football Hall of Fame in 2000.

Lloyd Johnson

Additional Sources:

Cooney, Frank. "'Couch Potato' is Number 1 Motivator." *The Sporting News,* January 23, 1989, 14.

Lott, Ronnie, and Jill Lieber. *Total Impact Straight Talk from Football's Hardest Hitter.* New York: Doubleday, 1991.

Silver, Michael. "Together Forever." *Sports Illustrated,* July 24, 2000, 56.

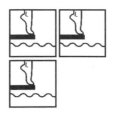

GREG LOUGANIS

Sport: Diving

Born: January 29, 1960
El Cajon, California

Early Life

Gregory Efthimios Louganis is of Samoan and Northern European background. He was adopted by Frances and Peter Louganis nine months after his birth on January 29, 1960.

Greg has an older sister, Despina, who is also adopted. They grew up in El Cajon, a working-class suburb of San Diego, California. Both children began taking dancing lessons when they were very small.

Greg's early school experiences were difficult. The other children called him a sissy because of his dancing. They called him stupid because he stammered and had a severe reading problem. He was even a physical misfit, with dark hair and skin in a school of mostly blond, blue-eyed children. Greg also had problems with his father, a hard-living tuna fisherman who could not understand his more sensitive son.

The Road to Excellence

Greg learned gymnastics as a child. When he began tumbling off the diving board in the family's backyard pool, Peter Louganis decided to enroll his son in local diving classes.

To make up for his difficulties at school, Greg concentrated on his only success: diving. At age eleven, just two years after starting lessons, Greg scored a perfect 10 in diving at the 1971 Amateur Athletic Union (AAU) Junior Olympics in Colorado Springs, Colorado.

Greg impressed the spectators at this competition. One of the them was Dr. Sammy Lee, gold medalist in both the 1948 and 1952 Olympics. Four years later, when Peter Louganis asked Dr. Lee to coach Greg for the upcoming 1976 Olympics, Lee quickly agreed.

Life at home was growing increasingly difficult for Greg, so he moved in with his coach's family. Lee was a strict disciplinarian. He set up a rigorous training schedule and helped Greg to build self-confidence. Under Lee's coaching, Greg qualified to enter both the springboard and platform events for the 1976 Olympics. He finished

MAJOR CHAMPIONSHIPS

Year	Competition	Event	Place	Points
1976	Olympic Games	3-meter springboard	6th	528.96
		10-meter platform	Silver	576.99
1978	World Championships	10-meter platform	1st	844.11
1979	World Cup	10-meter platform	1st	588.90
	Pan-American Games	3-meter springboard	1st	627.84
		10-meter platform	1st	592.71
1981	World Cup	3-meter springboard	1st	643.20
1982	World Championships	3-meter springboard	1st	752.67
		10-meter platform		643.26
1983	World Cup	3-meter springboard	1st	717.03
		10-meter platform	1st	687.90
	Pan-American Games	3-meter springboard	1st	724.02 PAR
		10-meter platform	1st	677.58 PAR
	World University Games	3-meter springboard	1st	—
		10-meter platform	1st	—
1984	Olympic Games	3-meter springboard	Gold	754.41
		10-meter platform	Gold	710.91
1986	World Championships	3-meter springboard	1st	750.06
		10-meter platform	1st	668.58
1987	World Cup	3-meter springboard	1st	707.46
	Pan-American Games	3-meter springboard	1st	754.14
		10-meter platform	1st	694.68
1988	Olympic Games	3-meter springboard	Gold	730.80
		10-meter platform	Gold	638.61

Note: PAR = Pan-American Record

lem was caused by a learning disorder—dyslexia. He finally believed that he was not really intellectually limited.

Greg continued to dive fearlessly. Experts expected him to win two gold medals at the 1980 Olympics. Unfortunately, the United States boycotted the 1980 games to protest the Soviet Union's invasion of Afghanistan, and Greg was unable to compete.

In January, 1981, he transferred to the University of California at Irvine so he could train with Ron O'Brien, head coach at the famous Mission Viejo Swim Club. Greg received his B.A. degree from Irvine in 1983, with a theater major and dance minor.

During these years, Greg was virtually unchallenged. In the 1982 World Aquatic Championship, he became the first diver ever to earn a perfect score from all seven judges in international competition. In 1982, he won the 1-meter and 3-meter springboard and the 10-meter platform diving events at the national indoor and outdoor diving championships. This winning streak was not broken until 1987.

Greg developed new, difficult dives and introduced them into his sport. He was classically proportioned for a diver. He had great flexibility and balance because of early dance and gymnastic training. Because his legs were strong, he was able to jump high off the board and have more time for twists and turns in his dives. By raising his own standards of excellence, Greg also raised the standards of world diving competition.

sixth in springboard diving. He did even better in platform diving, finishing second behind the favorite, two-time gold medal winner Klaus Dibiasi.

Greg returned home feeling that he had failed. Back in his high school, he was now a hero, but he was still withdrawn and without real friends. Greg experienced a long period of illness and injuries. As he became more and more unhappy, he started to smoke and drink.

For a while, Greg did not train much or compete. By spring, 1978, however, he was again winning titles at competitions such as the National AAU Indoor and Outdoor Diving Championships, the Hall of Fame International Diving Meet, and the World Aquatic Championship.

The Emerging Champion

In the fall of 1978, Greg accepted a scholarship at the University of Miami, mostly because it was far away from his life in California. There he learned for the first time that his reading prob-

HONORS AND AWARDS

1984	Sullivan Award
1985	Inducted into U.S. Olympic Hall of Fame
1986	Jesse Owens International Trophy
1988	Olympic Spirit Award
1993	Inducted into the International Swimming Hall of Fame

Despite his diving success, he still had personal problems. In 1983, an incident gave Greg the strength to change his life. During a break in a swim meet, he saw a young diver smoking. When questioned, the boy said he wanted to be just like Greg Louganis, and Greg Louganis smoked.

That made Greg take a long, hard look at himself. He stopped smoking and drinking and started to accept himself for what he was. He began to take himself less seriously and decided that it was acceptable to be shy.

When the time came for the 1984 Olympic competition, Greg was prepared both physically and mentally. He won gold medals in both the springboard and platform diving competitions, becoming the first man in fifty-six years to do so. He also became the first diver ever to earn more than 700 points in a single Olympic event.

Continuing the Story

After facing his own fears, Greg felt that he had something to offer others. He began telling his story to thousands of teenagers at school assemblies. He began doing television commercials and public-service spots, moving toward his long-time goal of an acting career. In 1984, Greg won the prestigious James E. Sullivan Memorial Award as the Outstanding Amateur Athelete of the Year. In 1985, he was inducted into the United States Olympic Hall of Fame. In 1986, he was awarded the Jesse Owens International Trophy for excellence in athletics and international relations.

In the 1988 Olympics, Greg again won both the springboard and platform competitions, as he had done in 1984. This time, though, he did so after hitting his head on the springboard in a preliminary dive. With stitches in his scalp and his confidence shaken, Greg immediately went back up to dive again and did so almost perfectly.

The coach of the Chinese team later said: "We must all learn from Louganis's grit and determination. In adversity, he was able to rise up and win the championship."

Unlike many world-class athletes, Greg is motivated by an inner search for artistic perfection rather than an outer desire to excel. In this, he has been encouraged by his mother, who told him to do his best and that she would love him no matter what.

In 1988, Greg retired from competitive diving. He spent time speaking to dyslexia organizations, youth clubs, drug and alcohol rehabilitation groups, and diving clinics about the challenges in his life. He made his professional dance debut with the Indiana Repertory Theatre and continued to pursue a serious acting career.

In 1995 Greg published his autobiography, *Breaking the Surface*, in which he discussed openly for the first time his struggle for acceptance as a gay man and the turmoil of living with AIDS. In the years following his historic diving career, he became an inspiration to athletes and fans alike.

In addition to a growing list of film and theater credits, Greg has also received recognition as an advocate for those living with AIDS. Greg was inducted into the International Swimming Hall of Fame in 1993.

Summary

Greg Louganis is considered to be the world's greatest diver. An equally important achievement may be his personal victory over self-doubt. By recognizing his fears and rising above them, Greg grew from an introverted, troubled child into a relaxed, confident adult who is comfortable with himself and others.

Greg is a diver of unequaled grace and power. His goal has always been not only to win but also to raise his own level of performance and the standards of his sport. Greg says, "I don't want to be remembered as the greatest diver who ever lived. I want to be able to see the greatest diver. I hope I live to see the day when my records are broken."

Jean C. Fulton

Additional Sources:

Edelson, Paula. *Superstars of Men's Swimming and Diving*. Philadelphia, Pa.: Chelsea House, 1999.

Hickok, Ralph. *A Who's Who of Sports Champions*. Boston: Houghton Mifflin, 1995.

Knapp, Ron. *Top Ten American Men's Olympic Gold Medalists*. Springfield, N.J.: Enslow, 2000.

Louganis, Greg, with Eric Marcus. *Breaking the Surface*. New York: Plume, 1996.

Milton, Joyce. *Greg Louganis: Diving for Gold*. New York: Random House, 1989.

JOE LOUIS

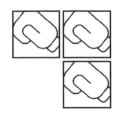

Sport: Boxing

Born: May 13, 1914
   Lafayette, Alabama
Died: April 12, 1981
   Las Vegas, Nevada

Early Life

Joseph Louis Barrow was born on May 13, 1914, about six miles outside the small village of Lafayette, Alabama. The town is located in the Buckalew Mountains, a hilly area of red clay soil that was difficult to work for the farmers who lived there.

Joe was the seventh of eight children born to Lillie and Munroe Barrow. His family, like most farm families in the Buckalew Mountains, was poor. They lived in an unpainted, windowless shack that had no electricity. Shoes were seldom worn by the Barrow children, and kerosene lamps lit the small home.

Joe worked hard for his family, especially his mother, by washing floors and doing other chores around the house and in the fields. Although he got into several rock fights as a child, there were few indications of the boxer Joe would become.

The Road to Excellence

Like thousands of other Southern African American families who went north in search of a better life during the 1920's, Joe's family moved to Detroit in 1926. In Detroit, Joe gradually took an interest in boxing when he began taking part in friendly fights among the boys who lived on Catherine Street, quickly earning recognition as the best fighter in the neighborhood.

It was at the Brewster Recreation Center, a local athletic club, that Joe, now sixteen, gained serious training in the sport of boxing. Fearing his mother would not approve of his interest in boxing, Joe dropped his last name and came to be known as Joe Louis.

At about the same time, Joe quit school and began to work full-time

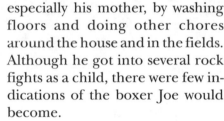

RECOGNIZED WORLD HEAVYWEIGHT CHAMPIONSHIPS

Date	Location	Loser	Result
June 22, 1937	Chicago, Ill.	James J. Braddock	8th-round knockout
Aug. 30, 1937	New York City, N.Y.	Tommy Farr	15th-round unanimous decision
Feb. 23, 1938	New York City, N.Y.	Nathan Mann	3d-round knockout
Apr. 1, 1938	Chicago, Ill.	Harry Thomas	5th-round knockout
June 22, 1938	New York City, N.Y.	Max Schmeling	1st-round knockout
Jan. 25, 1939	New York City, N.Y.	John Henry Lewis	1st-round knockout
Apr. 17, 1939	Los Angeles, Calif.	Jack Roper	1st-round knockout
June 28, 1939	New York City, N.Y.	Tony Galento	4th-round technical knockout
Sept. 20, 1939	Detroit, Mich.	Bob Pastor	11th-round knockout
Feb. 9, 1940	New York City, N.Y.	Arturo Godoy	15th-round split decision
Mar. 29, 1940	New York City, N.Y.	Johnny Paychek	2d-round knockout
June 20, 1940	New York City, N.Y.	Arturo Godoy	8th-round technical knockout
Dec. 16, 1940	Boston, Mass.	Al McCoy	6th-round technical knockout
Jan. 31, 1941	New York City, N.Y.	Red Burman	5th-round knockout
Feb. 17, 1941	Philadelphia, Pa.	Gus Dorazio	2d-round knockout
Mar. 21, 1941	Detroit, Mich.	Abe Simon	13th-round technical knockout
Apr. 8, 1941	St. Louis, Mo.	Tony Musto	9th-round technical knockout
May 23, 1941	Washington, D.C.	Buddy Baer	7th-round disqualification
June 18, 1941	New York City, N.Y.	Billy Conn	13th-round knockout
Sept. 29, 1941	New York City, N.Y.	Lou Nova	6th-round technical knockout
Jan. 9, 1942	New York City, N.Y.	Buddy Baer	1st-round knockout
Mar. 27, 1942	New York City, N.Y.	Abe Simon	6th-round knockout
June 9, 1946	New York City, N.Y.	Billy Conn	8th-round knockout
Sept. 18, 1946	New York City, N.Y.	Tami Mauriello	1st-round knockout
Dec. 5, 1947	New York City, N.Y.	Jersey Joe Walcott	15th-round split decision
June 25, 1948	New York City, N.Y.	Jersey Joe Walcott	11th-round knockout
Sept. 27, 1950	New York City, N.Y.	Joe Louis (Ezzard Charles, winner)	15th-round unanimous decision

at a nearby factory while continuing to box on the weekends. In 1932, he fought his first amateur bout against former Olympian Johnny Miler. The more experienced Miler quickly defeated Joe, knocking him down seven times in two rounds.

Joe's mother encouraged him to continue while his stepfather urged him to get a job at the Ford Motor Company. Joe took his stepfather's advice and stayed away from the ring for seven months. In mid-1933, Joe went back to boxing and later reached the light heavyweight finals of the National Amateur Athletic Union championships, where he lost in three rounds.

His third and final amateur defeat (out of fifty-four fights) marked a turning point in Joe's boxing career. John Roxborough, a leading businessman in Detroit's African American community, was impressed enough with Joe's skill to lend his financial support to the promising boxer.

Roxborough also hired Jack Blackburn, a former professional boxer, to train Joe. Blackburn taught Joe balance in the ring, showed him how to throw punches with both hands, and discussed strategy and conditioning with the young fighter.

The Emerging Champion

Blackburn's coaching paid off, as Joe won his first twenty-two fights in the heavyweight division upon turning professional in 1934. Eighteen of these victories came when Joe knocked his opponent out with powerful punches from both hands, and it was this strength that captured the imagination of fight fans around the country. In 1935, he won the Associated Press Male Athlete of the Year award.

Joe's first professional defeat came in 1936 at the hands of a German fighter named Max Schmeling. Although some began to doubt Joe's ability after this bout, he dedicated himself to training and studying under the direction of Blackburn. His hard work earned him the heavyweight championship in 1937 and another fight with Schmeling in 1938. Joe defeated Schmeling this time, and people began to speak of him as one of the best boxers ever.

Joe defended his title twenty-five times without a loss between 1937 and 1948, more than any other champion. Joe's willingness to defend his title so many times, his skill inside the ring, and his respectable conduct outside the arena

STATISTICS

Bouts, 66
Knockouts, 49
Bouts won by decision, 13
Bouts won by fouls, 1
Knockouts by opponents, 2
Bouts lost by decision, 1

RECORDS

Successfully defended his world boxing title for almost twelve years—the longest of any world heavyweight champion

HONORS AND AWARDS

1934	National Amateur Athletic Union light heavyweight champion
1935	Associated Press Male Athlete of the Year
1936, 1938-39, 1941	*Ring* magazine Merit Award
1940	Schomberg Collection of the New York Public Library and the Association for the Study of Negro Life and History Award for Improving Race Relations
1941	Neil Trophy
1944	Legion of Merit Award
1954	Inducted into *Ring* magazine Boxing Hall of Fame
1967	Walker Memorial Award
1990	Inducted into International Boxing Hall of Fame

brought to boxing a dignity that the sport had been missing since the 1920's.

As an African American, Joe's ability gave other African American men and women a sense of pride and dignity in a nation that treated African Americans unfairly, if not harshly. Despite his great success, Joe never lost contact with the ordinary man and woman in the neighborhood, so that his success was in some ways shared by African Americans of lesser fame. They saw their struggles in everyday life as similar to those that Joe faced in the ring against an opponent.

Continuing the Story

Joe's popularity with white America came mainly from his service in the Army during World War II. Joe continued to defend his title while carrying out his military duties, and he won praise for donating much of his prize money to the Navy Relief Society to help the war effort. His actions won the respect of people the world over. Many Americans saw Joe as demonstrating the love of country that every citizen should possess, and as time passed, Joe came to be a national hero. His strength in the ring was seen as an example of America's strength as a nation, and songs and posters celebrated his patriotism.

Joe continued to box after the war was over, but, as with any athlete, age had begun to erode his skills. Joe had been a great boxer because his hands were quicker and stronger than those of his opponents. Although he was still powerful, Joe's quickness had diminished. In 1950 he lost his heavyweight crown to Ezzard Charles in a unanimous decision. His last (non-title) fight, which ended in only his third loss as a professional, was against Rocky Marciano on October 26, 1951.

Despite the money he had earned in the ring, Joe spent much of his life after boxing with little or no money because most of his business plans failed. He had also been generous with friends and charities throughout his life, donating heavily to educational causes. Joe spent most of his retired life golfing and working at Caesar's Palace in Las Vegas, where he died on April 12, 1981, among friends.

Summary

Joe Louis's brilliance in the ring, and his generosity outside it, gave to African Americans, white Americans, and the sport of boxing a sense of dignity during a difficult time in American history. Joe is still regarded as one of the best boxers, and one of the most popular athletes, in the nation's history.

Jill Dupont

Additional Sources:

Bak, Richard. *Joe Louis: The Great Black Hope*. Dallas: Taylor, 1996.

Barrow, Joe Louis, and Barbara Munder. *Joe Louis: Fifty Years an American Hero*. New York: McGraw-Hill, 1988.

Jakoubek, Robert E. *Joe Louis: Heavyweight Champion.* New York: Chelsea House, 1990.

Libby, Bill. *Joe Louis: The Brown Bomber.* New York: Lothrop, Lee & Shepard Books, 1980.

Louis, Joe, Edna Rust, and Art Rust. *Joe Louis: My Life.* New York: Harcourt Brace Jovanovich, 1978.

Mead, Chris. *Champion: Joe Louis: Black Hero in White America.* New York: Charles Scribner's Sons, 1985.

CLYDE LOVELLETTE

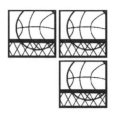

Sport: Basketball

Born: September 7, 1929
Terre Haute, Indiana

Early Life

Clyde Edward Lovellette was born on September 7, 1929, in Terre Haute, Indiana. He was the son of John and Myrtle Lovellette. His father was a railroad engineer. Clyde attended Terre Haute Garfield High School and was a two-time All-State basketball player for Garfield. He led his team to the 1947 Indiana state tournament championship game, which Garfield lost to Shelbyville High School 68-58. Clyde was known for his pleasant disposition and sharp elbows, a combination that served him well in college and professional basketball. He was recruited by the colorful Coach Forrest C. "Phog" Allen to play at the University of Kansas from 1949 to 1952. Allen was a master of the game who taught Clyde all the inner workings of the sport, including the psychological aspects of getting motivated for games.

The Road to Excellence

As a sophomore in 1949, Clyde made his University of Kansas debut against Rockhurst College at Mason-Halpin Fieldhouse in Kansas City, Missouri. Kansas won 55-34 and Clyde scored 21 points, thus beginning his sensational collegiate basketball career. He went on to become the only player in college basketball history to lead the nation in scoring in the same year that his team won the National Collegiate Athletic Association (NCAA) championship. He played at 6 feet 9 inches, 235 pounds, and became one of the first great scoring centers. He led the Big Eight Conference in scoring as a sophomore, averaging 21.8 points per game. As a junior averaging 22.8 points per game, Clyde again won the scoring title. In his final season, he averaged 28.4 points per game and led the Jayhawks to an 80-60 victory over St. John's in Seattle for the NCAA championship. He was the most valuable player in the title game and averaged 35 points per game in the tournament, including 44 points against St. Louis University. His performance capped a season that few players ever ex-

Courtesy of Amateur Athletic Foundation of Los Angeles

STATISTICS

Season	GP	FGM	FG%	FTM	FT%	Reb.	Ast.	TP	PPG
1953-54	72	237	.423	114	.695	419	51	588	8.2
1954-55	70	519	.435	273	.686	802	100	1,311	18.7
1955-56	71	594	.434	338	.721	992	164	1,526	21.5
1956-57	69	574	.426	286	.717	932	139	1,434	20.8
1957-58	71	679	.441	301	.743	862	134	1,659	23.4
1958-59	70	402	.454	205	.820	605	91	1,009	14.4
1959-60	68	550	.468	316	.821	721	127	1,416	20.8
1960-61	67	599	.453	273	.856	687	172	1,471	22.0
1961-62	40	341	.471	155	.829	350	68	837	20.9
1962-63	61	161	.440	73	.745	177	29	395	6.5
1963-64	45	128	.420	45	.789	126	24	301	6.7
Totals	704	4,784	.444	2,379	.760	6,673	1,099	11,947	17.0

Notes: GP = games played; FGM = field goals made; FG% = field goal percentage; FTM = free throws made; FT% = free throw percentage; Reb. = rebounds; Ast. = assists; TP = total points; PPG = points per game.

perience. He was a two-time All-American, and he scored what was then a collegiate record of 1,888 points in his career with an average of 24.5 points per game. Sportswriters dubbed him "The Great White Whale" and "Colossal Clyde."

The Emerging Champion

Along with six of his Kansas teammates and Coach Allen, Clyde was a part of the 1952 Olympic team that won a gold medal in Helsinki, Finland, defeating the Soviet Union 36-25 in the final game. He spent a year playing Amateur Athletic Union (AAU) basketball and then went on to the National Basketball Association (NBA), playing eleven years with the Minneapolis Lakers, Cincinnati Royals, St. Louis Hawks, and Boston Celtics.

He was part of the Lakers team that won the NBA championship in 1954 and of the Celtics teams that won titles in 1963 and 1964. He be-

came the first player to play on an NCAA, Olympic, and NBA championship team.

Continuing the Story

When he entered the Naismith Memorial Basketball Hall of Fame in 1988, Clyde recalled that basketball had given him an identity and a purpose in life. After his remarkable career in the sport, he spent a number of years trying to refocus that life. He retired from the NBA after the 1964 season at the age of thirty-five. Over the next sixteen years, he sought his niche by serving as a sheriff in Indiana, television sportscaster, advertising salesman, auto salesman, cattleman, operator of an ice cream parlor, and antique store owner in Cape Cod, among other pursuits. His first marriage ended in divorce during this period. After all the accolades he had received during his basketball playing days, he felt unfulfilled.

In 1980, Clyde was lifted from depression by a religious experience. At about that time, he received an offer to become a basketball coach and teacher at White's Institute in Treaty, Indiana. White's is the largest residential child-care facility in the state. Clyde became the director of the Vocational Education program.

HONORS AND AWARDS

1951-52	Consensus All-American
1952	U.S. Olympic gold medalist Helms Division I Player of the Year Citizens Savings College Basketball Player of the Year NCAA Tournament Most Outstanding Player NCAA All-Tournament Team
1956, 1960-61	NBA All-Star Team
1956	All-NBA Team
1988	Inducted into Naismith Memorial Basketball Hall of Fame

Summary

When Clyde Lovellette was inducted into the Naismith Memorial Basketball Hall of Fame in 1988, he noted that he was proud of what he had accomplished and what he was part of: "The days I spent in Lawrence were just super. I will love

Kansas and Lawrence for the rest of my life. But I've had my time in the limelight. It was a long, long time ago. There are more important things now." He remarked that his work with troubled teenagers gave him the chance to "give these kids as much love and direction as I can. They've helped me find myself." These are youngsters who need more help than others, and Clyde's life work is elevated to that calling. At White's, Clyde has said, "I feel nine feet tall."

Arthur F. McClure

Additional Sources:

Brown, Gene, ed. *The New York Times Encyclopedia of Sports.* 15 vols. New York: Arno Press, 1979-1980.

Groliers Educational Corporation. *Pro Sports Halls of Fame.* 8 vols. Danbury, Conn.: Groliers Educational Corporation, 1996.

Porter, David L., ed. *Biographical Dictionary of American Sports: Basketball and Other Indoor Sports.* Westport, Conn.: Greenwood Press, 1989.

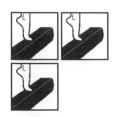

LU LI

Sport: Gymnastics

Born: August 30, 1976
Hunan Province, China

Early Life

Lu Li was born August 30, 1976, in Hunan Province in southern China. Because of her government's one-child-per-family policy, Li was an only child. Chinese parents have a custom of naming a child for a quality they hope he or she will grow to embody. Li's name means "earth flower." (Lu is her family name, Li her given name.)

Li began gymnastics when her mother, thinking the slim five-year-old should do something to build her physique, took her to the gym. Sports training is provided free by the Chinese government with an eye toward Olympic success.

Li's short, strong, yet flexible body proved to be well suited for the sport. So was her mentality: quick, tough, and obedient. She would need these qualities for the hard work ahead. Young gymnasts in China follow a strict regimen of stretching and strengthening exercises that will allow them to perform the spectacular moves modern gymnastics requires. China, with its long acrobatic tradition, is also known for the innovative and artistic gymnastics made possible by this disciplined foundation.

Li rose through the ranks of youth competitions and eventually was selected to train at the national training center in Beijing. There, gymnasts live together and train with the national coaches (at the time Gao Jian and Luo Xe Lian), who keep close watch on their prodigies. Meals, schooling, and housing are furnished by the state. National team members see their parents just once or twice a year, but their families know that their children are enjoying a better standard of living than they could have at home. In addition, top athletes are able to travel abroad, an opportunity denied the average Chinese citizen.

Simon Bruty/Allsport

Lu Li in 1992.

MAJOR CHAMPIONSHIPS

Year	Competition	Event	Place	Event	Place
1992	Olympic Games	Balance beam	Silver	Uneven parallel bars	Gold
	Pacific Alliance Championship	All-Around uneven bars	1st	Floor exercise	1st
		Uneven bars	2d		
	World Championships	Uneven parallel bars	4th		
1993	Chunichi Cup	All-Around	7th	Balance beam	3d
		Uneven bars	1st		
	Tokyo Cup	Balance beam	1st	Uneven bars	1st

The Road to Excellence

In the spring of 1991, fourteen-year-old Lu Li attended Moscow's prestigious Stars of the World competition. The meet often functions as a coming-out party for young gymnasts of the former Eastern Bloc countries, but Li failed to make a big impression. The winner that year, Tatiana Gutsu of the then-Soviet Union, would become the 1992 Olympic all-around champion.

Li's world debut came at the World Championships in Paris a year later. The competition boasted a new, individual-events-only format, which should have worked to the advantage of the Chinese gymnasts. Though they are often weak on vaulting and floor exercise, the Chinese women are acknowledged as the best in the world on the bars and beam. Finally, they would be able to focus on their strong points and with luck, bring home medals.

In Paris, Li dazzled the knowledgeable crowd with her unique bars work, swinging with superb technique and amplitude. The 4-foot 6-inch 66-pounder set a new standard for the event, using complicated elements her coaches had adapted from the men's horizontal bar. Her routine included inverted giant swings (swinging around the bar with the shoulders literally inside out), which require a high degree of both flexibility and strength—if the shoulders are too tight, inverted giants are impossible, but without sufficient strength, injury would result. Thanks to her early training, Li was able to walk that fine line with consummate ease.

Li had the lead after preliminary competition, and it looked as if she would become the first Chinese woman to win a world title in three years. After cruising through a perfect set in the finals, however, Li made a classic mistake. She jumped forward on her difficult double layout dismount, and the resulting deduction kept her out of the medals. She—and her many new fans—would have to wait for the Olympic Games.

Ironically, the Chinese are known for such errors as much as for their beam and bars work. The subjective world of gymnastics judging compounds the problem, as dismount errors tend to be overemphasized.

The Emerging Champion

Her disappointing finish in Paris lit a fire under Li, and she arrived in Barcelona for the 1992 Summer Olympics well prepared. She worked well through the early stages of competition, qualifying for the finals of the all-around, the balance beam, and her specialty, the uneven bars.

During the all-around finals, though, Li fell from the beam, not once but twice. Her resulting drop in place (to thirty-fourth out of thirty-six competitors) was less devastating than the psychological impact of such a disaster in the Olympic Games. Fortunately, she had two days to collect herself for the finals.

The uneven bars final was one of the toughest of the Games. Two world champions and several medalists packed the field. Li, with her novel combinations, precision, and technical superiority, was the favorite, but she would have to "stick" her dismount to win.

As she had in Paris, Li reeled off a superb set, with not so much as a hair out of place. This time, she erased her memories of Paris with a perfect landing. The judges were unanimous, giving Li her first 10.0, one of just two perfect scores in the 1992 Games. Li was the Olympic champion.

Immediately after receiving her gold medal, Li almost won another on the very apparatus that

1679

had foiled her two days before, the beam. The delighted sixteen-year-old happily claimed a silver medal, but some observers felt she deserved gold.

In October, Li took her act to the previous Olympic city, Seoul, South Korea, where she won the all-around and floor exercise at the Pacific Alliance Championships, featuring the best from Asia, Australia, and the Americas. Ironically, the Olympic champion was just second on the bars. Afterward, she dropped out of sight. Some future Chinese stars graced the World Championships in April, 1993, but Lu Li was missing.

Continuing the Story

Finally, in late fall, a familiar name appeared at Japan's prestigious internationals, the Chunichi and Tokyo Cups. Li was back, taller, leggier, and better than ever. Her Olympic bars set was already well ahead of its time, but she added even more difficulty, winning easily in both meets. Additionally, Li pranced through a new beam routine as if she had never been away.

Instead of pursuing coaching or exhibitions at the end of her competitive career, like most gymnasts, Li went on to college. There she studied English and international cultures. In 1999, she moved to the United States and began coaching gymnastics in Southern California.

Summary

The Chinese gymnasts have never failed to impress both gymnastics fans and the general public, but they often fail to deliver the goods with world and Olympic medals at stake. As only the second gymnast to earn perfect scores at the Games, Lu Li turned the "curse" on its ear. She aced two of the best routines of the 1992 Olympics while the world watched, awestruck.

Nancy Raymond

Additional Sources:

Drozdiak, William. "10s Perfect for Lu, Milosovici; 5 Medals Great for Miller." *The Washington Post*, August 2, 1992, p. D11.

Normile, Dwight. "Two 10.0s for Women, Four More Golds for Scherbo." In *International Gymnast*, October, 1992, p. L48.

"Where Are They Now: Lu Li." *International Gymnast* Online. http://www.intlgymnast.com/paststars/psmay99.html. August, 2000.

JERRY LUCAS

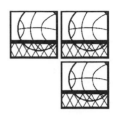

Sport: Basketball

Born: March 30, 1940
Middletown, Ohio

Early Life

Jerry Ray Lucas was born on March 30, 1940, in Middletown, Ohio, a steel and paper mill city located in the southwestern corner of the state. Jerry's parents worked in the local factories. Middletown considered itself the basketball capital of Ohio. The city's parks contained many basketball courts, and its high school won state basketball championships regularly.

The Road to Excellence

Jerry began playing competitive basketball in the fourth grade, and he was already being recruited by colleges when he was in the eighth grade. Playing with a star of Jerry's caliber was difficult for his teammates, however. In his sophomore year, other team members, resentful that a first-year player should dominate, refused to pass the ball to Jerry and set him up for shots. The team's coach was sensitive to this and in one game benched Jerry so that he would not break a scoring record as a sophomore.

Instead of complaining, Jerry waited to rebound and tap in shots. He also developed the passing skills that would be a trademark throughout his career. In his senior year, he was elected team captain. During his three years as a high school player, Jerry made 2,460 points and beat the record held by Wilt Chamberlain. Recruiters from more than 150 colleges scouted his games.

Jerry had to cope with recruiters at all hours of the day. Many illegal offers were made, including homes, jobs for his parents, unlimited spending money, and cars. Jerry was aware of the recruiting regulations of the National Collegiate Athletic Association (NCAA). He also sensed that any school he attended would be closely investigated. He declined all such offers.

Never a hero worshiper, Jerry was not awed by the famous coaches and other personalities who contacted him. Adolph Rupp, renowned coach

1681

STATISTICS

Season	GP	FGM	FG%	FTM	FT%	Reb.	Ast.	TP	PPG
1963-64	79	545	**.527**	310	.779	1,375	204	1,400	17.7
1964-65	66	558	.498	298	.814	1,321	157	1,414	21.4
1965-66	79	690	.453	317	.787	1,668	213	1,697	21.5
1966-67	81	577	.459	284	.791	1,547	268	1,438	17.8
1967-68	82	707	.519	346	.778	1,560	251	1,760	21.5
1968-69	74	555	.551	247	.755	1,360	306	1,357	18.3
1969-70	67	405	.507	200	.784	951	173	1,010	15.1
1970-71	80	623	.498	289	.787	1,265	293	1,535	19.2
1971-72	77	543	.512	197	.791	1,011	318	1,283	16.7
1972-73	71	312	.513	80	.800	510	317	704	9.9
1973-74	73	194	.462	67	.698	374	230	455	6.2
Totals	829	5,709	.499	2,635	.783	12,942	2,730	14,053	17.0

Notes: Boldface indicates statistical leader. GP = games played; FGM = field goals made; FG% = field goal percentage; FTM = free throws made; FT% = free throw percentage; Reb. = rebounds; Ast. = assists; TP = total points; PPG = points per game

from the University of Kentucky, was given ten seconds with Jerry between classes. Jerry's family turned down an invitation to a luncheon at the Galbreath Mansion because they knew it would make no difference to Jerry when he made his choice.

Amid some controversy over the appointment of a new coach from a field of candidates that included Jerry's coach from Middletown, Jerry chose to attend Ohio State University (OSU). Jerry, a high school honors student, stated that his studies came first and basketball second, and he accepted a full academic scholarship.

The Emerging Champion

At the time, NCAA regulations did not permit freshmen to play on varsity teams. In two scrimmage games with the varsity squad, Jerry scored an unbelievable 92 points. The coach developed an offense around "Big Luke," his star of the future.

Always poised and showing little emotion on or off the court, Jerry admitted that he was scared before his first game. Although the team won, he did nothing in the first half and had a mediocre performance in the second half. Observers wondered if the former high school center had what it took to make it in college basketball. Jerry himself was convinced that he "was going to be the biggest disappointment in the history of college basketball."

In the second game, however, he scored 34 points and proved to himself and everyone else

that he could meet their expectations. OSU went on to win the NCAA Championship and lead the nation in scoring, and Jerry had a phenomenal .637 shooting percentage. Using the ball-handling skills he had developed in high school, he would often pass off to a teammate rather than take a shot. No one was surprised when he was named All-American.

Jerry married after his sophomore year and continued to maintain high scholastic standards. He was a consistently strong player with a large repertoire of shots. His sense of timing when rebounding, his genius for getting the ball on defense, and his passing skills assured him of a position on the 1960 United States Olympic team that went on to win the gold medal.

In his junior year, Jerry averaged 25 points and 17 rebounds per game. The team won 17 straight games and was called the best college team in history.

Jerry had always maintained that he did not want to play professional basketball. He had aspirations to go to graduate school or into business. In his senior year, he earned a Phi Beta Kappa key for his academic performance and was drafted by both Cleveland in the American Basketball League (ABL) and Cincinnati in the National Basketball Association (NBA).

When Cleveland offered him a contract that considered some of his concerns about season length, contract length, and investments, he signed. Jerry believed that he could have more influence as a role model if he continued in basketball and in the limelight. The ABL folded in the middle of the 1962-1963 season, though, and Jerry began his pro career with the NBA's Cincinnati Royals in 1963.

Continuing the Story

Considered one of the all-time great college players, the rookie Jerry Lucas was a boost to the NBA. He played in Cincinnati for six years, averaging 20 points a game in his new position as forward. He also developed a chain of restaurants and established himself in business.

In 1969, Jerry asked to be traded to San Francisco. He received a rousing welcome and played with the Warriors until he was traded to the New York Knicks in 1971. Here he was given back his position as center. Because of his size, however, Jerry lost his starting position and became the league's best backup center. He was a success in his new role, and he helped the Knicks to the 1973 NBA title before his retirement from basketball in 1974.

Jerry had always possessed a remarkable memory, and after his retirement he began to use his extraordinary talent of memorizing and manipulating letters, words, and numbers as the basis of a new career. He gave lectures at colleges and to businesses and co-wrote *The Memory Book* (1974), which sold over two million copies. He developed his hobby of performing magic and used his basketball fame to break into entertainment. Performing as "Luke the Magician," Jerry created and hosted the television special *The Jerry Lucas Super Kids Day Magic Jamboree*, which featured educational word games, number puzzles, and magic tricks. Later, a newfound relationship with God led him to write *Remember the Word* (1975) and to form Memory Ministries, Inc., to help others memorize the Bible.

During the late 1980's, Jerry established Lucas Learning, an educational company that pub-

lished learning and memory materials for children. It later became Lucas Educational Systems. Jerry has authored more than sixty books in the field of memory training and learning systems. His ideas for fun and easy memory retention have resulted in the "The Lucas Learning System" and have earned him the title of "Doctor Memory."

Being inducted into the Basketball Hall of Fame in 1980 was Jerry's crowning athletic honor. He was likewise honored when he named to the NBA's 50 Greatest Players of All Time Team during the 1996-1997 season. Jerry was an NBA All-Star seven times and a member of the All-NBA First Team three times. In 1999, he was chosen by *Sports Illustrated* as one of the five most outstanding college basketball players of the twentieth century.

Summary

Jerry Lucas grew up as one of the most sought-after basketball players of his time. A talented

MILESTONES
One of only seven NCAA players to average more than 20 points and 20 rebounds

HONORS AND AWARDS	
1960	U.S. Olympic gold medalist Inducted into U.S. Olympic Hall of Fame
1960-61	NCAA Tournament Most Outstanding Player
1960-62	NCAA All-Tournament Team Consensus All-American
1961	Citizens Savings College Basketball Player of the Year *Sports Illustrated* Sportsman of the Year
1961-62	Rupp Trophy United Press International Division I Player of the Year U.S. Basketball Writers Association Division I Player of the Year *Sporting News* College Player of the Year
1964	NBA Rookie of the Year NBA All-Rookie Team
1964-68	All-NBA Team
1964-69, 1971	NBA All-Star Team
1965	NBA All-Star Game most valuable player
1980	Inducted into Naismith Memorial Basketball Hall of Fame
1996	NBA 50 Greatest Players of All Time Team
1999	One of *Sports Illustrated*'s five most outstanding basketball players of the 20th century

1683

athlete as well as a scholar, he was idolized by children and took his position as a role model seriously. As a player, he avoided the theatrics of many of his colleagues. It seems ironic, therefore, that he became a showman once he left basketball.

Cathy M. Buell

Additional Sources:
Bjarkman, Peter C. *The Biographical History of Basketball.* Chicago: Masters Press, 1998.

Lucas, Jerry, and Harry Lorayne. *The Memory Book.* Rev. ed. New York: Ballantine Books, 1996.

Mallozzi, Vincent M. *Basketball: The Legends and the Game.* Willowdale, Ont.: Firefly Books, 1998.

Sachre, Alex. *One Hundred Greatest Basketball Players of All Time.* New York: Simon and Schuster, 1997.

Shouler, Kenneth A. *The Experts Pick Basketball's Best Fifty Players in the Last Fifty Years.* Lenexa, Kans.: Addax, 1998.

SID LUCKMAN

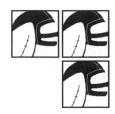

Sport: Football

Born: November 21, 1916
     Brooklyn, New York
Died: July 5, 1998
     Aventura, Florida

Early Life

The most famous Jewish football player in American sports history was born on November 21, 1916, in Brooklyn, New York. Sidney Luckman was the son of Meyer Luckman, a Jewish immigrant. Growing up on the streets of New York, the short and stocky Sid liked playing football with his friends. No one had a ball, so they made one out of rags. He enjoyed the game, so when he was eight his father bought him a football. Sid played football with the boys in his neighborhood, who talked constantly about their idol, Red Grange, the great Illinois halfback. Young Sid's idol, however, was Benny Friedman, the Michigan quarterback.

Quarterback for the Chicago Bears Sid Luckman in 1943.

STATISTICS

Season	GP	PA	PC	Pct.	Yds.	Avg.	TD	Int.
1939	11	51	23	.451	636	**12.5**	5	4
1940	11	105	48	.457	941	8.9	4	9
1941	11	119	68	.571	1,181	9.9	9	6
1942	11	105	57	.543	1,024	9.8	10	13
1943	10	202	110	.545	**2,194**	10.9	**28**	12
1944	7	143	71	.497	1,018	7.1	11	12
1945	10	217	117	.539	1,727	8.0	**14**	10
1946	11	229	110	.480	**1,826**	8.0	**17**	16
1947	12	323	176	.545	2,712	8.4	24	31
1948	12	163	89	.546	1,047	6.4	13	14
1949	8	50	22	.440	200	4.0	1	3
1950	7	37	13	.351	180	4.9	1	2
Totals	121	1,744	904	.518	14,686	8.4	137	132

Notes: Boldface indicates statistical leader. GP = games played; PA = passes attempted; PC = passes completed; Pct. = percent completed; Yds. = yards; Avg. = average yards per attempt; TD = touchdowns; Int. = interceptions

The Road to Excellence

Sid attended Erasmus High School and there developed his great skills as a passer and all-around player. He became the most publicized high school player in New York City.

Sid's talent caught the eye of Lou Little, the head football coach of Columbia University. Coach Little persuaded Sid to attend Columbia even though he was offered scholarships from many other colleges. Sid worked his way through college washing dishes, running errands, and baby-sitting.

At Columbia, Sid's star shone even brighter. Under Coach Little's guidance, he developed into one of the greatest quarterbacks in college football history. From 1936 through 1938, Sid started at tailback and was a true triple-threat player: a great passer, runner, and kicker (he once punted a ball 72 yards).

Although the Columbia team never had a winning season during these years, it did have some great moments. In his senior year, Sid led Columbia to a 20-18 victory over a powerful Army team. He completed 18 passes for 2 touchdowns and ran back a kickoff 85 yards for a third. He also kicked 2 extra points. Despite Columbia's losing record, Sid earned All-American honors in his senior year.

Again Sid's playing caught the attention of a great coach. This time, George Halas, coach of the Chicago Bears, wanted Sid to lead his Bears. Coach Halas traded for the first choice in the 1939 college draft and chose Sid. Sid was reluctant to play professional football after breaking his nose three times in college, but Coach Halas's offer of ten thousand dollars persuaded him.

The Emerging Champion

Coach Halas needed a smart athlete for the key position of quarterback in his new T-formation, and he knew that Sid was the man for the job. Sid quickly learned four hundred plays as well as all the quarterback strategies. He studied and mastered the T-formation. Coach Halas later said that Sid never called a wrong play. By 1939, Sid became the first quarterback of the modern

HONORS, AWARDS, AND RECORDS

1938	College All-American
1940, 1942	NFL Pro Bowl Team
1941-44, 1947	NFL All-Pro Team
1943	Carr Trophy NFL record for the most touchdown passes in a game (7) (record shared)
1960	Inducted into College Football Hall of Fame
1963	NFL All-Pro Team of the 1940's
1965	Inducted into Pro Football Hall of Fame Uniform number 42 retired by Chicago Bears

T-formation, a strategy that forever changed the game of football.

Prior to 1939, before Sid took over as quarterback, the Bears had not won a championship since 1933. With Sid at the helm, the Bears achieved their glory years and won four championships in the next six years. The most memorable of these occurred in 1940, when the Bears crushed the powerful Washington Redskins 73-0. Led by Sid, the Bears achieved the most devastating victory of all time and scored the most points ever in a professional football game, a record that still stands.

Sid rivaled the Redskins' Sammy Baugh as the greatest quarterback of the 1940's. He was selected as an All-Pro five times. Perhaps his greatest game was in 1943 against the New York Giants. The day of that game, Sid's friends had given him a two-thousand-dollar war bond in honor of "Sid Luckman Day." Sid responded by throwing a league-record 7 touchdown passes to lead the Bears to a 56-7 pounding of the Giants. During his twelve-year career, Sid threw 1,744 passes and completed 904, for 14,686 yards gained and 137 touchdowns.

Sid also served his country during World War II. He enlisted in the United States Merchant Marine in 1943 and played football during shore leave.

Continuing the Story

When the All-American Football Conference was formed in 1946, the Chicago Rockets offered Sid a job as player-coach for twenty-five thousand dollars a year. Sid turned it down out of loyalty to the Bears.

In 1950, Sid was replaced at quarterback, but Coach Halas let him have one last chance to play.

Sid managed to lead the team to a touchdown in a game against the Detroit Lions and left the field to a standing ovation. During that year, however, Sid suffered a shoulder injury that ended his career. He retired at the end of the 1950 season.

Following his retirement, Sid served as an assistant coach for the Bears, working closely with the quarterbacks. Coach Halas always sent him a check at the end of the season for his work, but Sid would send it back. He felt he owed to the Bears the success he had achieved and was glad to help them in return. Sid later achieved success in the business world as an executive in a Chicago cellophane company.

Sid's great career in college and professional football was capped with his selection to the National Football Foundation College Football Hall of Fame, and the Pro Football Hall of Fame.

Summary

Sid Luckman's combination of athletic skill and football talent helped lead the Chicago Bears to their greatest years. He will be remembered not only as one of the greatest quarterbacks ever to play football but also as the first quarterback of the modern era. Sid played a key role in changing football to the game it is today.

Nan White

Additional Sources:

Luckman, Sid. *Luckman at Quarterback.* New York: Ziff-Davis, 1949.

_____. *Passing for Touchdowns.* New York: Ziff-Davis, 1948.

Whittingham, Richard. *What a Game They Played: An Historical Narrative of Early Twentieth Century Pro Football.* New York: Harper & Row, 1984.

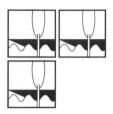

JON LUGBILL

Sport: Canoeing/Kayaking

Born: May 27, 1961
       Wauseon, Ohio

Early Life

Jon Lugbill was born on May 27, 1961, in the northwestern Ohio farming community of Wauseon, some thirty miles west of Toledo. One of four children of Ralph and Viva Lugbill, Jon's midwestern ties were short. When he was three, his family moved to Fairfax, a Virginia suburb of Washington, D.C. Life in the middle-class neighborhood was good. Jon's younger years produced a strong interest in sports, particularly football and basketball.

At the age of ten, a family outing planted a seed that would change Jon's life. Along with his father and older brother, Jon went on a white-water raft trip in West Virginia. There the youngster saw his first canoe and kayak race. Upon the family's return home, they purchased a canoe and launched a career.

A year later, Jon was back in West Virginia to enter the Petersburg downriver race. How did he do? "Bad," says Jon. "I swam twice."

Jon Lugbill in 1988.

The Road to Excellence

Jon and his older brother, Ron, began paddling in slalom races. In slalom, a series of "gates" are hung over a whitewater course. Racers are scored on the basis of elapsed time with penalty points added for hitting or missing gates. If Jon found downriver racing a challenge, slalom was more so.

It was early in his high school career that Jon made a major decision. Naturally athletic, he was also short. At 5 feet 9 inches, his height was a major disadvantage in basketball and football. In canoeing, he found it to be an advantage. It meant a lower center of gravity and greater boat stability. He would concentrate his efforts on canoeing.

Jon took full advantage of both the number of competitions and the quality of the athletes to be found in the Washington, D.C., area and along the Eastern seaboard. Quick to learn and with a natural love of whitewater, he progressed quickly and rose through the ranks. In 1975, the year he graduated from Oakton High School, he made the United States national canoe team.

The Emerging Champion

A month after graduation, Jon was in Yugoslavia competing in his first World Slalom Championships. That first taste of championship competition led to a commitment: Jon would explore the possibilities of hard training, of pushing himself to the limits. He would, he promised himself, become as good as he possibly could.

In 1977, Jon found a mentor in Bill Endicott, a former world-class paddler who had moved to Bethesda, Maryland. Endicott assumed coaching duties for the United States team.

Under the watchful eye of his coach and with a practice schedule that demanded twenty hours a week on the water and additional time for endurance and weight training, Jon began a program that would mold him into a world-class athlete.

"I liked the day-to-day training, being finetuned," says Jon. "I also liked competition and doing well, and I really enjoyed paddling on whitewater." With that combination of desire and an unswerving dedication to excellence, Jon was able to advance his canoeing skills steadily and, at the same time, continue his education. (He holds a B.A. degree in environmental science from the University of Virginia.)

MAJOR CHAMPIONSHIPS

Year	Competition	Event	Place
1978	Pan-American Championships	One-person canoe	1st
1979	World Championships	One-person canoe	1st
		Team canoe	1st
1981	World Championships	One-person canoe	1st
		Team canoe	1st
1983	World Championships	One-person canoe	1st
		Team canoe	1st
1984	Europa Cup	One-person canoe	1st
	Pan-American Championships	One-person canoe	1st
1985	World Championships	Team canoe	1st
1987	World Championships	One-person canoe	1st
		Team canoe	1st
1988	Europa Cup	One-person canoe	1st
1988-90	World Cup	One-person canoe	1st
1989	World Championships	One-person canoe	1st
		Team canoe	1st
1991	World Championships	Team canoe	1st

His first World Championship wins came in 1979 at Jonquière, Quebec, Canada. There he took both the individual gold medal and the team gold (three boats race together) in C-1 (one-person canoe). It was the beginning of a remarkable string.

Continuing the Story

Between 1979 and 1990, Jon won a total of eleven gold medals in the biennial World Championship competitions. Five golds were in individual events, six in team. Only in 1985, when he placed second a fraction of a second behind teammate Davy Hearn in the one-person event, did he fall short in a World Championship effort. In that same time span, Jon won the World Cup championship each of the three years it was held, the Pan-American Games Championship once, and the Europa Cup twice.

Perhaps Jon's greatest accomplishment, the one that gave him the most satisfaction, came at the 1989 World Championships on Western Maryland's Savage River. Jon's second run (each contestant is given two runs and the best time is counted) is ranked by many as the best effort in the history of whitewater slalom.

In a sport where world championships are

1689

usually decided by tenths or even hundredths of a second, Jon blazed through the twenty-five gates hung along 600 meters of thrashing Savage whitewater in 205 seconds. He beat the second-place boat by an unheard of margin of nearly 12 seconds.

"In spite of winning, one seldom paddles to his full potential," says Jon. "This is one time I could say 'I did the best I could,' and that is really rare." To do it under the pressure of the World Championships and the difficult course made it all the more spectacular. The fact that it was in the United States simply added to the thrill.

Jon continued his reign as one of the world's best in whitewater slalom by winning the gold medal at the 1991 World Championships and was the heavy favorite to win the gold in Barcelona in 1992. In fact, he did win the race by a narrow margin of .007 seconds. However, the judges determined that his life-vest had brushed one of the gates, incurring a 5-second penalty that removed him from medal contention altogether.

After retiring from competition, Jon became a commentator for NBC-TV.

Summary

Many things have contributed to Jon Lugbill's outstanding career. There is, of course, his natural athletic ability. There is also his ability to manage priorities, to complete an education and raise a family while maintaining a commitment to excellence in his sport.

There is also his quiet inner strength. It can best be summed up by recounting an incident at the World Championships on the Savage. Between runs, Jon retired to the privacy of his car. There, away from the crowds and his fellow competitors, he spent time by himself. He looked within and found the strength and determination to return to the course for that remarkable second run to the gold.

Chuck Weis

Additional Sources:

Levinson, David, and Karen Christenson. *Encyclopedia of World Sport: From Ancient Times to Present.* Santa Barbara, Calif.: ABC-CLIO, 1996.

Mallon, Bill, and Ian Buchanan. *Quest for Gold: The Encyclopedia of American Olympians.* New York: Leisure Press, 1984.

Richards, Gordon, and Paul Wade. *The Complete Book of Canoeing and Kayaking.* London: Batsford, 1981.

Wallechinsky, David. *The Complete Book of the Olympics.* Boston: Little, Brown and Company, 1991.

HANK LUISETTI

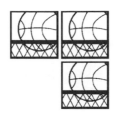

Sport: Basketball

Born: June 16, 1916
San Francisco, California

Early Life

Angelo Joseph Luisetti was born June 16, 1916, in an Italian neighborhood in San Francisco, California. His father, Steven, worked as a chef at a local restaurant. His mother, Amalia, took care of the family.

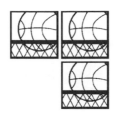

Hank Luisetti revolutionized the game of basketball with his one-handed jump shot.

As a child, Angelo suffered from severe bowed legs and wore braces until age ten. The braces limited his activity, but Angelo developed an interest in basketball and began playing the game at a playground near his home.

Angelo frequently played with older and taller youngsters. Because of his small size, he was forced to shoot the ball a distance from the basket. Consequently, Angelo developed a one-handed shooting style quite different from the traditional two-handed set-shot style of that era. Other youth criticized and laughed at Angelo's shooting technique, but, with continued practice, Angelo became an accurate shooter.

The Road to Excellence

Angelo, called "Hank" by his friends, played on his first organized team as a freshman at Galileo High School in San Francisco. Despite his shooting ability, Hank's playing time was limited because of his small size.

Not to be discouraged, he developed a running one-handed shot and began to experiment with dribbling and passing behind his back. Hank also began to grow, reaching a height of 6 feet, 2½ inches and 165 pounds by his senior year.

During his junior and senior years, Hank made his team's starting lineup, but again, his size hindered his game. He was one of the tallest players on the team, so his coach moved him under the basket to rebound, thus reducing his scoring effectiveness.

Hank was a competitive player and soon became an effective rebounder. College coaches, however, felt he was not big enough to play center in college. Only John Bunn, Stanford University basket-

1691

ball coach, recognized Hank's offensive potential and offered him a scholarship.

The Emerging Champion

Hank entered Stanford University in the fall of 1934. Concerned about his unusual shooting style, he asked Coach Bunn if he could continue his one-handed technique. Following Hank's impressive shooting demonstration, Coach Bunn grinned and said, "Stick with it boy."

Hank took Coach Bunn's advice. He continued to develop physically, improving his coordination, jumping ability, speed, and quick reactions. These attributes, along with his offensive skills and fierce competitiveness, helped Hank lead the Stanford freshman team to an undefeated 18-0 season.

In his sophomore season, 1935-1936, Hank led Stanford to the first of three consecutive Pacific Coast Conference championships. He scored a total of 416 points for an 18-point-per-game average and received All-American honors. Following the 1935-36 season, Hank joined the Stanford University track and field team as a high jumper.

As a junior, Hank added a running one-handed jump shot to his offensive arsenal and was moved to the forward position. With his new shot and a new playing position, Hank led Stanford to a 25-2 record and the school's second conference championship in two years.

On December 30, 1936, at Madison Square Garden in New York, Hank played one of the best games of his career. Although he scored only 15 points, he rebounded, shot, dribbled, and passed Stanford to a 45-31 win over Long Island University, ending the Blackbirds' 43-game winning streak. As Hank left the court, the crowd gave him a standing ovation. Long Island University coach Clair Bee praised Hank: "I can't remember anybody who could do more things."

Hank completed the 1936-1937 season with 410 points for a 15.2-points-per-game average. He received All-American honors for the second time and was named College Player of the Year.

By his senior year, 1937-1938, Hank's weight increased to 184 pounds, but it did not slow him down. His teammates elected him team captain, and Hank responded by leading Stanford to a 21-3 record and the school's third straight conference title. Hank's outstanding game as a senior

HONORS AND AWARDS	
1936-38	College All-American
1937	Helms Foundation Outstanding College Player
1937-38	College Player of the Year
1938	Citizens Savings World Trophy Citizens Savings Northern California Co-Athlete of the Year
1957	Inducted into Stanford University Sports Hall of Fame
1959	Inducted into Naismith Memorial Basketball Hall of Fame

was a 50-point performance on January 1, 1938, as Stanford defeated Duquesne University 92-27. It was the first time a collegiate player had scored that many points in one game. For the second time, Hank was named College Player of the Year, and his 1,596 career point total set a new four-year college scoring record.

Continuing the Story

After completing his college career and graduating with a business degree in 1938, Hank opted to play Amateur Athletic Union (AAU) basketball with Stewart Chevrolet Company in San Francisco. Before the season began, however, Hank accepted ten thousand dollars to play the role of a basketball player in the film *Campus Confessions* (1938) with Betty Grable. The AAU suspended Hank for one year because his basketball playing performance in the film made him a professional player.

After his suspension, Hank returned to AAU competition for the 1939-1940 season. He averaged 19 points per game and led his Stewart Chevrolet team to the AAU national tournament, where he set a tournament record with 72 points in four games and was named the tournament's outstanding player.

Hank joined the AAU Phillips 66 Oilers for the 1940-1941 season, but he played sparingly after sustaining a knee injury early in the season. On April 18, 1941, Hank married Jane Rossiter, with whom he had two children, a daughter, Nancy, and a son, Steven.

Hank enlisted in the United States Navy during World War II, and averaged 30 points per game while playing basketball for the St. Mary's Preflight School. In 1944, Hank was hospitalized with spinal meningitis and lost forty pounds. He recovered, but doctors advised him that playing basketball would endanger his health.

Following his discharge from the Navy, Hank returned to Stewart Chevrolet Company and coached its team for five seasons, guiding it to the AAU Championship in 1950-1951. Hank left coaching after his title season and served as sales manager for Stewart Chevrolet Company and conducted basketball clinics in the San Francisco area. In 1958, Hank joined E. F. McDonald Travel Company as president of its West Coast region until retiring in 1984.

Summary

Hank Luisetti never played in a postseason college basketball tournament, but because his playing style was showcased during one game at Madison Square Garden, he became the most heralded player of his era. His one-handed, jump-shooting style revolutionized basketball and helped to make the game as it is played today.

Jerry Jaye Wright

Additional Sources:

Fimrite, Ron. "A Call to Arms." *Sports Illustrated* 75, no. 18 (Fall, 1991): 98-108.

Herzog, Brad. *The Sports One Hundred: The One Hundred Most Important People in American Sports History.* New York: Macmillan, 1995.

Hickok, Ralph. *A Who's Who of Sports Champions.* Boston: Houghton Mifflin, 1995.

JOHNNY LUJACK

Sport: Football

Born: January 4, 1925
Connellsville, Pennsylvania

Early Life

The youngest of four sons in a family of six children, John C. Lujack, Jr., was born on January 4, 1925, in Connellsville, Pennsylvania. Johnny's father worked as a boilermaker for the railroad in Connellsville and was extremely supportive of his son's athletic pursuits.

Johnny grew up in a town where the name "Lujack" was synonymous with athletic ability. With the exception of two years, there was at least one Lujack brother on the high school sports teams from 1928 to 1941.

Johnny was only fourteen when he was assigned the position of running back on the Connellsville high school football team. He was a multisport talent and went on to letter in baseball, basketball, and track and field.

The Road to Excellence

By the time Johnny was a high school senior, he was offered a contract by the Pittsburgh Pirates major league baseball team. Johnny declined that offer, as well as numerous college scholarships, and enrolled at the University of Notre Dame.

Johnny's rookie season with the Fighting Irish (1943) fulfilled coach Frank Leahy's fondest expectations. In Johnny's first start against undefeated Army, he completed 8 of 15 passes for 237 yards and 2 touchdowns. Johnny plunged for a third touchdown to give Notre Dame an astounding 26-0 upset victory. The Irish were named national champions that year.

In 1944, Johnny joined the United States Navy and served on a submarine chaser in the Atlantic Ocean during World War II. Upon his honorable discharge from the Navy in 1946, Johnny returned to Notre Dame to guide its football team to further victories.

In 1946, and again in 1947, the Irish were named national champions. Johnny was dubbed "coach on the field" by Frank Leahy because of the leadership, poise, and daring he displayed. In

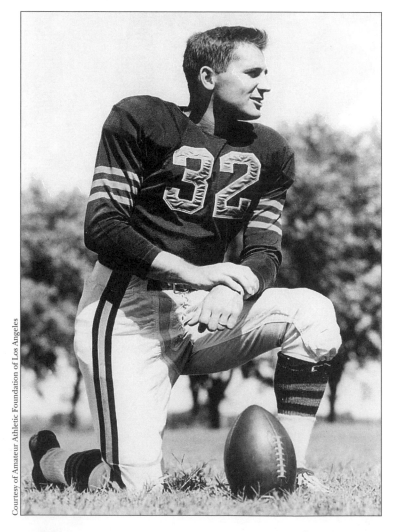

HONORS AND AWARDS

1946-47	Consensus All-American
1947	Heisman Trophy Camp Award Associated Press Male Athlete of the Year
1948, 1950	NFL All-Pro Team
1951-52	NFL Pro Bowl Team
1960	Inducted into College Football Hall of Fame

the three seasons Johnny played for the Irish (all three national championship seasons) he completed 144 passes in 280 attempts for 2,080 yards. Among the honors given to Johnny during his college career were the Heisman Trophy (1947) and membership on the consensus All-American team in 1946 and 1947.

The Emerging Champion

Johnny was already a legend in the minds of many people when he signed an $18,750 four-year contract with the National Football League's Chicago Bears. Fresh in people's memories were amazing athletic feats, both offensive and defensive, such as his jarring open-field tackles in the historic scoreless tie with Army in 1946. It was on defense that Johnny first played for the Bears.

As a defensive back, Johnny's performances were stellar. He stalked the defensive backfield, frustrating the offensive effort of some of the best quarterbacks and running backs in the league. For his dominance, Johnny was named All-Pro defensive back in 1948.

In 1949, however, Johnny was to resume his role as quarterback. In a game against the Chicago Cardinals, the Bears' legendary quarterback, Sid Luckman, was injured. Johnny was called on as replacement.

In that game, Johnny broke Sammy Baugh's single-game record by passing for 468 yards and also threw 6 touchdown passes. The next year, he became the Bears' starting quarterback and was named All-Pro at the season's end. By 1951, however, Johnny's arm had lost its accuracy and power, and he decided to retire. Johnny's career with the Chicago Bears had been remarkable. In four years, he completed 404 of 808 passes for 6,295 yards and 41 touchdowns.

Continuing the Story

After Johnny retired as a professional player at the age of twenty-six, he served as an assistant coach under Frank Leahy at Notre Dame. As a coach, Johnny was highly regarded by Leahy, who once said of Johnny, "He has everything it takes for success—brains, character, and personality. He can make a million dollars if he wants to."

Johnny never went on to become a head coach, but he did make a million dollars. He opened a successful automobile dealership in 1954 in Davenport, Iowa, and also served as a television color announcer for college and professional football games.

Johnny married Patricia Ann Schierbrock in 1948, and they have three children, Mary Jane, John Frances, and Carolyn Elizabeth. He plays golf to relax.

Johnny never regretted turning down a career as a professional baseball player to become one of the all-time great players on the University of Notre Dame's football team and an All-Pro for the Chicago Bears. Asked what game he preferred, college or professional, Johnny said, "I would rather see one pro game than six played by top-ranking collegiate teams. The pros offer far more variety."

Nevertheless, Johnny is remembered most for his performances as a college player. Notre Dame historian Jim Beach said, "Johnny was the kind of quarterback who called runs when passes were expected, and passed on fourth down. He kept the defense in a state of confusion and his teammates on their toes. He knew the job of every man on every play." For his achievements as a Notre Dame quarterback, Johnny was elected to the National Football Foundation College Football Hall of Fame in 1960.

Summary

As a college athlete, Johnny Lujack quarterbacked the University of Notre Dame to three national championships: 1943, 1946, and 1947. He was a consensus All-American in 1946 and 1947 and was awarded the Heisman Trophy as a senior. Picked first in the draft by the Chicago Bears in 1948, Johnny played four years, earning the distinction as an All-Pro on both defense and offense. He won the acclaim of sportswriters and fans throughout the United States.

Rustin Larson

Additional Sources:
Hickok, Ralph. *A Who's Who of Sports Champions.* Boston: Houghton Mifflin, 1995.

LaBlanc, Michael L., and Mary K. Ruby, eds. *Professional Sports Team Histories: Football.* Detroit: Gale, 1994.

Porter, David L., ed. *Biographical Dictionary of American Sports: Football.* Westport, Conn.: Greenwood Press, 1987.

STEVE LUNDQUIST

Sport: Swimming

Born: February 20, 1961
    Atlanta, Georgia

Early Life

Born on February 20, 1961, in Atlanta, Georgia, Stephen Kent Lundquist grew up in the small town of Jonesboro, Georgia, on the shores of Jonesboro's Lake Spivey. Living so close to the water had a strong impact on the young Steve, who was waterskiing and swimming as soon as he learned how to walk.

Eventually, as his affinity for swimming grew and he began to train in the lake, it became clear that he would need better facilities in order to improve. Unfortunately, there was no indoor pool in Jonesboro or the surrounding towns. His father, understanding the importance of adequate facilities for Steve's development, undertook to build a pool for his son on land donated by a man named Al Tallman. This was the beginning of the Tallman swim team, for which Steve swam during high school.

The Road to Excellence

During his early years of age-group swimming in Jonesboro, Steve, nicknamed "Lunk" by his friends, worked on developing a new style of racing start that would come to be known as the "pike" start. Rather than leaving the starting blocks with his back straight and parallel to the water, as in the traditional racing start, Steve would jump in an arc with his body jackknifed. This motion would take him both higher in the air and farther out over the water than other swimmers, giving him an initial head start in the race.

Steve's early swimming success culminated in his first world record, set in 1978 at the age of seventeen. At the 1978 Amateur Athletic Union (AAU) Long Course (50-meter pool) Championships, Steve broke the world record in the 200-meter individual medley (50 meters of each stroke). A year later, at the AAU Short Course (25-meter pool) Championships, he followed up with a world record in the 200-meter breaststroke, becoming the first to break the two-minute mark.

His early success in swimming led to what some might consider cockiness; during his se-

nior year at Jonesboro High School, Steve decided to play football rather than swim. His lack of training led him to miss the finals of the 100-meter breaststroke at the Long Course Championships just before his freshman year of college. His attitude improved in college, however, through his association (as a roommate) with J. D. Browder, who was 4 feet 7 inches tall. Browder's positive outlook and buoyant spirit in the face of physical difficulties inspired Steve by giving him a different perspective on his own success.

The Emerging Champion

Steve was prohibited from participating in the 1980 Olympics as a result of the United States' refusal to participate in the games. Nevertheless, he regained his winning edge, grabbing five National Collegiate Athletic Association (NCAA) championships during his first three years of college at Southern Methodist University, while working toward a degree in business.

The year 1982 was a big one for Steve; he broke the world record in the 100-meter breaststroke twice and won gold medals in the 100-meter breaststroke and the 4×100 medley relay (an event in which each of four team members swims 100 meters in one of the four strokes). In recognition of his superior performance that year, Steve was named the United States Swimmer of the Year by the national governing body of swimming. The next year brought continued success, this time at the Pan-American Games in Caracas, Venezuela. There he won gold in the 100- and 200-meter breaststroke and the 4×100 medley, as well as a bronze in the 200-meter individual medley.

Riding this wave of success, Steve seemed primed for success at the 1984 Olympics in Los Angeles. Unfortunately, the September before the games, he suffered a severe shoulder separation while waterskiing. His injury caused him to finish very poorly at the 1984 United States Swimming Indoor Championships (he placed 26th in the 100-meter breaststroke). The outlook seemed bleak for the upcoming Olympics.

Continuing the Story

The same enthusiasm and energy that had perhaps contributed to past excesses (like overconfidence or aggressive waterskiing) were now needed in order for Steve to regain his winning form. He fought back, with the help of his team trainer, Dr. Ted Becker, and the inspiration of teammate John Moffet. As a result of Becker's therapy and Moffet's competition and encouragement, Steve was stunningly successful in Los Angeles. He won gold in the 100-meter breaststroke, breaking the world record for the fifth time in two years. He was also a member of the United States' gold medal medley relay team, which also set a new world record.

Steve's success at the Olympics marked the end of his career in

MAJOR CHAMPIONSHIPS

Year	Competition	Event	Place	Time
1978	World Championships	100-meter breaststroke	7th	—
		200-meter individual medley	4th	—
1979	Pan-American Games	100-meter breaststroke	1st	1:03.82
		200-meter breaststroke	1st	2:21.97
		4×100-meter medley relay	1st	3:47.20
1980	NCAA Championships	100-yard breaststroke	1st	53.59
		200-yard breaststroke	2d	—
		200-yard individual medley	2d	—
1981	NCAA Championships	100-yard breaststroke	1st	52.93
		200-yard breaststroke	1st	1:55.01
1982	World Championships	100-meter breaststroke	1st	1:02.75
		200-meter individual medley	7th	2:06.22
		4×100-meter medley relay	1st	3:40.84
	NCAA Championships	100-yard breaststroke	1st	53.09
		200-yard breaststroke	1st	1:56.84
		200-yard individual medley	2d	—
1983	Pan-American Games	100-meter breaststroke	1st	1:02.28 WR, PAR
		200-meter breaststroke	1st	2:19.31 PAR
		200-meter individual medley	3d	2:06.36
		4×100-meter medley relay	1st	3:40.42
	NCAA Championships	100-yard breaststroke	1st	52.48
		200-yard individual medley	1st	1:45.54
1984	Olympic Games	100-meter breaststroke	Gold	1:01.65 WR, NR, OR
		4×100-meter medley relay	Gold	3:39.30 WR, OR

Notes: OR = Olympic Record; WR = World Record; NR = National Record; PAR = Pan-American Record

competitive swimming. Indeed, prior to the 1984 Olympics, he had said that he felt old for the sport (at twenty-three years). He claimed that he would have retired in 1980 if not for the United States' boycott of the 1980 games.

Steve has managed to remain in the limelight. His athletic, all-American good looks brought him modeling contracts for *Vanity Fair, L'Uomo Vogue,* and *Interview* magazines in 1983-1984. He then moved on to film work, getting parts in *Return of the Killer Tomatoes* (1988) and *Earth Girls Are Easy* (1989). He has managed to combine his college training in business, his brief flash of Olympic stardom, and his looks and acting talent into a promising new profession.

RECORDS
Broke world and American records on 15 occasions
Set world records in the 100-meter breaststroke and 200-meter individual medley
Set American records in the 100 and 200 yard and meter breaststrokes

HONORS AND AWARDS	
1980	Men's U.S. Olympic Swimming Team
1982	U.S. Swimming Swimmer of the Year
1990	Inducted into International Swimming Hall of Fame

Summary

Over the course of his career, Steve Lundquist managed to combine his exceptional natural ability with a strong sense of determination and commitment, as well as a good dose of all-around intensity. His intensity has in fact created some problems for him, but he has been able to learn from his mistakes and from the experiences of others. As a result, he has persevered over a relatively long and successful reign as swimming's premier breaststroker and has made the difficult transition to a second career in show business.

Mark Rogers

Additional Sources:

Johnson, Steven. "Steve Lundquist." *Swimming World and Junior Swimmer* 39, no. 9 (1998).

Levinson, David, and Karen Christenson, eds. *Encyclopedia of World Sport: From Ancient Times to Present.* Santa Barbara, Calif.: ABC-CLIO, 1996.

Mallon, Bill, and Ian Buchanan. *Quest for Gold: The Encyclopedia of American Olympians.* New York: Leisure Press, 1984.

Wallechinsky, David. *The Complete Book of the Olympics.* Boston: Little, Brown and Company, 1991.

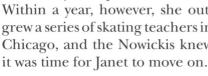

JANET LYNN

Sport: Figure skating

Born: April 6, 1953
Chicago, Illinois

Early Life

Janet Lynn was born Janet Lynn Nowicki, the daughter of Florian Walter Nowicki, a druggist, and Ethleyne Gehrke Nowicki, in Chicago, Illinois, on April 6, 1953.

Janet's parents first put her on skates at age two and a half at a Cub Scout skating outing. She fell often, but she laughed rather than cried and refused to let anyone help her up. Before long, she had taught herself to skate backward, and her parents had enrolled her in a skating class. By age three, she had moved from the children's to the teenagers' class, and by three and a half, was outskating the teenagers. By age four, she had gone beyond anything a class could teach her and was ready for private lessons. Within a year, however, she outgrew a series of skating teachers in Chicago, and the Nowickis knew it was time for Janet to move on.

The Road to Excellence

During a summer visit to the Wagon Wheel Resort near Rockford, Illinois, in 1958, Janet performed for renowned skating coach Slavka Kahout, who accepted her as a student. Kahout was thrilled about coaching the talented child, and the two began an extremely successful collaboration that eventually led Janet to the heights of the figure skating world. In 1961, the entire Nowicki family—including four children and a grandfather—moved to Rockford so Janet would be closer to the Wagon Wheel and her coach.

Janet worked hard, practicing six to eight hours every day. She was coached in her school figures, always the weakest aspect of her skating, by Pierre Brunet, the brilliant coach of the 1960 Olympic

MAJOR CHAMPIONSHIPS

Year	Competition	Place
1966	U.S. National Junior Ladies Championship	1st
1967	U.S. National Senior Ladies Championship	4th
1968	U.S. National Senior Ladies Championship	3d
	Olympic Games	9th
	World Championship	9th
1969	U.S. National Senior Ladies Championship	1st
	World Championship	5th
1970	U.S. National Senior Ladies Championship	1st
	World Championship	6th
1971	U.S. National Senior Ladies Championship	1st
	World Championship	4th
1972	U.S. National Senior Ladies Championship	1st
	Olympic Games	Bronze
	World Championship	3d
1973	U.S. National Senior Ladies Championship	1st
	World Championship	2d

champion Carol Heiss and himself an Olympic gold medalist. According to Kahout, Janet had the two qualities a skater has to be born with: excellent balance and a strong character. She also had great drive and, in Kahout's opinion, was an instinctive winner.

The Emerging Champion

At seven, Janet began her career in earnest. She dropped her last name for professional purposes (Lynn was simply easier for the rink announcers and the media to pronounce and spell than Nowicki) and entered her first competition, placing thirteenth in the Midwestern Juvenile Ladies' Competition. The following year, she won the Upper Great Lakes Novice Ladies' title. An unbroken string of successes followed, beginning at age twelve with the National Junior Ladies' title and, at thirteen, fourth place in the National Senior Ladies' competition.

At fourteen, Janet became the youngest person ever to make the United States figure skating team for the world championships, where she placed ninth. The same year, she took third in the National Senior Ladies' competition and ninth in the 1968 Winter Olympics, showing great promise for the future.

Janet won her first national title in 1969 at the age of fifteen and continued to reign as National Senior Ladies' champion for five consecutive years, from 1969 to 1973. That level of success continued to elude her in world competition, however. She placed fifth in the world in 1969, sixth in 1970, and fourth in 1971, never taking home the gold in either world or Olympic competition.

Janet's second chance at an Olympic medal came in 1972 at Sapporo, Japan. She was eighteen, at the top of her skating form, and was a favorite for medal contention. After the compulsory school figures, usually the weakest portion of her performance, she was ranked fourth, which put her in good position to take a gold medal on the strength of her free-skating program. Unfortunately, Janet fell during a comparatively easy sit spin in her free-skating exhibition and finished third with a bronze medal.

Despite not winning the gold medal, Janet's gamin good looks and radiant smile made her, as always, a crowd pleaser, and the Japanese were particularly taken with her during the Olympics. For months after the Games, Japanese journalists trekked to her home in Illinois, hoping for an interview or picture.

In 1973, a new compulsory short program was added to the figure skating competition. Janet had trouble with this portion of the competition from the beginning. At the 1973 national championships, she was beaten in the short program by the up-and-coming Dorothy Hamill, although she won the overall competition. In the 1973 world championships, her compulsory school figures were good and her freestyle program was, as usual, excellent, but she fell twice during the short program and took the silver medal rather than the gold.

Some of her critics charged she did not practice the short program seriously enough, but perhaps, after eighteen years of skating, Janet Lynn was ready to retire.

Continuing the Story

Janet retired from amateur skating in 1973 and signed a lucrative contract with the Ice Follies, becoming the highest paid female athlete in the world in 1974.

Throughout both her amateur and professional careers, Janet suffered from what had been diagnosed as asthma. She often collapsed after an exhausting competition or performance and was finally forced to retire from the Ice Follies because of this condition.

She married Richard Marc Salomon on October 18, 1975, and taught skating for a year. After the birth of her first son and during her pregnancy with twins, Janet's health began to worsen. Doctors finally correctly diagnosed her problems as allergies, and she soon recovered. She reentered professional skating and won the first professional figure skating competition in 1983.

Summary

As a very young child, Janet Lynn constantly told her mother that she wanted to skate, and skate she did, six to eight hours every day for more than twenty years. Although she never won Olympic gold or became a world champion, she skated brilliantly, winning a place as one of America's most popular figure skaters. Whatever disappointments she may have encountered in the rink, Janet, a devout Christian, has had a very strong faith to sustain her.

Mary Virginia Davis

Additional Sources:

Altman, Linda Jacobs. *Janet Lynn: Sunshine on Ice.* St. Paul, Minn.: EMC, 1974.

Lynn, Janet, with Dean Merrill. *Peace and Love.* Carol Stream, Ill.: Creation House, 1973.

Markel, Robert, Susan Waggoner, and Marcella Smith, eds. "Janet Lynn Nowicki." In *The Women's Sports Encyclopedia.* New York: Henry Holt, 1997.

May, Julian. *Janet Lynn: Figure Skating Star.* Mankato, Minn.: Crestwood House, 1975.

Morse, Ann. *Janet Lynn.* Chicago: Children's Press, 1975.

BOB McADOO

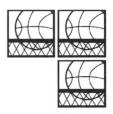

Sport: Basketball

Born: September 25, 1951
Greensboro, North Carolina

Early Life

Robert Allen McAdoo, Jr., was born September 25, 1951, in Greensboro, North Carolina, the son of Vandalia and Robert McAdoo, Sr. He had a younger sister, Pamela. Bob's mother was a schoolteacher, his father a painter and carpenter. A gifted musician, Bob began with the piano and had progressed to the saxophone by the time he joined the school band.

When his family lived in an apartment building, Bob began playing basketball on the apartment's playground. After buying a house of their own, the McAdoos installed a basket in their driveway at which Bob could practice. His mother, who had played basketball in college, jokingly took credit for his interest and ability in the sport.

The Road to Excellence

As an eighth-grader in 1964, Bob tried out for the school basketball team. He stood 6 feet 4 inches, and there was not a uniform that would fit him. Bob did not make the team that time. He did, however, in the next season.

Bob decided to attend Ben L. Smith High School in Greensboro, a predominantly white school. Bob believed his basketball career would receive more publicity at the white school. During the summer, Bob would play

on the playground until well past dark. The practice paid off; by the time he was a senior, Bob, by then 6 feet 8 inches tall, was considered one of the top high school players in North Carolina. When Bob was graduated, Smith retired his number, 24—quite an honor for a high school player.

In 1969, Bob went to Vincennes Junior College in Vincennes, Indiana. In his freshman year

Bob McAdoo of the Los Angeles Lakers making a jump shot.

he averaged 19.3 points per game, and Vincennes won the National Junior College Championship. Bob starred in the semifinal game, despite having the flu. In the next season Bob was named a junior-college All-American. The summer before transferring to the University of North Carolina, Bob played for the United States team in the Pan-American Games and made the winning shot against Brazil in the semifinals.

Bob had a successful season at North Carolina in 1972. He led coach Dean Smith's team in scoring and rebounding and was named the Atlantic Coast Conference (ACC) Tournament's most valuable player. The team also fared well, as the Tar Heels reached the Final Four in the National Collegiate Athletic Association (NCAA) Championship Tournament.

Never doubting his own abilities, Bob made himself eligible for the National Basketball Association (NBA) draft that spring and was selected in the first round by the Buffalo Braves.

The Emerging Champion

Adjusting to life in the NBA is tough for first-year players, and Bob, only twenty-one, had some difficulties early in his rookie season. Although he had played at the center position all his life, Buffalo made Bob a forward, and he had trouble guarding smaller, faster players. He also shot poorly, a problem he had never had before, and was relegated to the bench.

Midway through the season, however, Bob began to play more. His shooting improved, and he averaged 18 points per game. After the season was over, Bob was named 1973 NBA Rookie of the Year, an award that he knew he deserved to win.

The next season, Bob was moved to his natural center position. Said Bob of the position change: "I was convinced last year I could play center in this league. It's where I've always played and I feel more at home there."

The move helped the Braves, who won nearly twice as many games as they had the season before. Bob, with his knack for scoring and his natural shooting touch, became the youngest player ever to win an NBA scoring title. He continued to improve, leading the league in scoring and rebounding in 1975 and being named the NBA's most valuable player.

The Braves were improving also, and reached the second round of the playoffs. Bob's shooting prowess continued in the 1975-1976 season, and he won his third straight scoring title with 31.1 points per game. He had trouble renegotiating his contract with Buffalo, however, and was traded to the New York Knicks.

A once-proud franchise, the Knicks then were a shell of the team that had won two NBA championships in the early 1970's. In his new environment, Bob was never able to perform up to his capabilities. He was still a star, however, and finished as the league's fourth-leading scorer in 1978.

STATISTICS

Season	GP	FGM	FG%	FTM	FT%	Reb.	Ast.	TP	PPG
1972-73	80	585	.452	271	.774	728	139	1,441	18.0
1973-74	74	901	**.547**	459	.793	1,117	170	2,261	**30.6**
1974-75	82	1,095	.512	641	.805	1,155	179	2,831	**34.5**
1975-76	78	934	.487	559	.762	965	315	2,427	**31.1**
1976-77	72	740	.512	381	.738	926	205	1,861	25.8
1977-78	79	814	.520	469	.727	1,010	298	2,097	26.5
1978-79	60	596	.529	295	.656	520	168	1,487	24.8
1979-80	58	492	.480	235	.730	467	200	1,222	21.1
1980-81	16	68	.433	29	.707	67	30	165	10.3
1981-82	41	151	.458	90	.714	159	32	392	9.6
1982-83	47	292	.520	119	.730	247	39	703	15.0
1983-84	70	352	.471	212	.803	289	74	916	13.1
1984-85	66	284	.520	122	.753	295	67	690	10.5
1985-86	29	116	.462	62	.765	103	35	294	10.1
Totals	852	7,420	.503	3,944	.754	8,048	1,951	18,787	22.1

Notes: Boldface indicates statistical leader. GP = games played; FGM = field goals made; FG% = field goal percentage; FTM = free throws made; FT% = free throw percentage; Reb. = rebounds; Ast. = assists; TP = total points; PPG = points per game

HONORS AND AWARDS

1971	Consensus All-American
1972	ACC Tournament most valuable player NCAA All-Tournament Team *Sporting News* All-American
1973	NBA Rookie of the Year NBA All-Rookie Team
1974-78	NBA All-Star Team
1974-75	All-NBA Team
1975	NBA most valuable player Seagram's Seven Crowns of Sports Award
2000	Inducted into Naismith Memorial Basketball Hall of Fame

Because of his sensitivity to criticism about his possible lack of defensive skills and his withdrawn manner, Bob had a rather difficult time adjusting to life in the NBA. Because of his perception that the teams he played for wanted him to be their leading scorer and rebounder, he was never really happy playing for Buffalo, the Knicks, the Boston Celtics, the Detroit Pistons, or the New Jersey Nets. Midway through the 1981-1982 season, Bob was acquired from the Nets by the Los Angeles Lakers. In the role of coming off of the bench for the Lakers, Bob felt less pressure and discovered that he could perform optimally.

Continuing the Story

The Lakers needed to add a veteran scorer to their frontcourt, and Bob certainly fit that bill. Finally, he was a member of a team that had a chance to win the NBA championship, the one thing that had eluded him throughout his professional career. In 1982, Los Angeles won the NBA crown, fulfilling Bob's dream of playing for a championship team.

In Bob's four seasons with the Lakers, they made it to the NBA finals four times, winning the championship twice. As the Lakers added younger players to their bench, Bob did not resign in 1985. He played the 1985-1986 season with the Philadelphia 76ers.

After the 1985-1986 season, Bob left the NBA for the Italian League, where he was annually among the top scorers. Bob led Milan to the Ital-

ian and European Championship in 1987. During his seven seasons in the Italian League, Bob averaged 26.6 points and 8.7 rebounds per game. Although the competition was not NBA-caliber, the fact that Bob excelled against players ten and fifteen years younger than himself is certainly a testament to his physical conditioning and his dedication to the game.

Bob was the first big man in NBA history to shoot regularly from the outside. He was a phenomenal jump shooter who could get his shot off with great accuracy with only a minimal amount of daylight. As part of the celebration of the golden anniversary of the NBA in 1996, Bob received strong consideration to be included as a member of the NBA's 50 Greatest Players of All Time Team. In 2000, he received the ultimate honor for a basketball player when he was inducted into the Naismith Memorial Basketball Hall of Fame.

Summary

Most great basketball players can point to one aspect of their game that separates them from the other players. Bob McAdoo's was his scoring ability, a talent that made him one of the top NBA players of the 1970's. When his teammates got the ball to the supremely confident Bob, they knew that they were never out of the game.

Stephen T. Bell

Additional Sources:

Bjarkman, Peter C. *The Biographical History of Basketball.* Chicago: Masters Press, 1998.

Dolin, Nick, Chris Dolin, and David Check. *Basketball Stars: The Greatest Players in the History of the Game.* New York: Black Dog and Leventhal, 1997.

Haskins, James. *Bob McAdoo, Superstar.* New York: Lothrop, Lee, & Shepard Company, 1978.

Sachre, Alex. *One Hundred Greatest Basketball Players of All Time.* New York: Simon and Schuster, 1997.

Shouler, Kenneth A. *The Experts Pick Basketball's Best Fifty Players in the Last Fifty Years.* Lenexa, Kans.: Addax, 1998.

CHRIS McCARRON

Sport: Horse racing

Born: March 27, 1955
Dorchester, Massachusetts

Early Life

Christopher McCarron was born on March 27, 1955, in Dorchester, Massachusetts, a Boston suburb; Chris was one of nine children of Herbert and Helen (Maguire) McCarron. His father worked as secretary for the Massachusetts Knights of Columbus. Chris grew up in Dorchester and graduated in 1972 from Christopher Columbus High School, where he played varsity ice hockey. He dreamed of playing professional hockey for the Boston Bruins and idolized their star defenseman, Bobby Orr.

His 5-foot 2-inch, 95-pound frame and the success of his older brother, Gregg, as a jockey shifted his sights toward thoroughbred racing. He never saw a racetrack until he was fifteen years old, but soon began watching Gregg ride thoroughbreds. In 1972, Gregg landed Chris a job with leading trainer Odie Clelland.

MAJOR CHAMPIONSHIP VICTORIES

Year	Race	Horse
1974	Kentucky Derby	Go for Gin
1985	Breeders' Cup Sprint	Precisionist
1986	Belmont Stakes	Danzig Connection
1987	Kentucky Derby	Alysheba
	Preakness Stakes	Alysheba
1988	Breeders' Cup Classic	Alysheba
1989	Breeders' Cup Classic	Sunday Silence
1992	Preakness Stakes	Pine Bluff
1994	Kentucky Derby	Go for Gin
1996	Breeders' Cup Classic	Alphabet Soup
1997	Belmont Stakes	Touch Gold
2000	Breeders' Cup Classic	Tiznow

The Road to Excellence

Odie patiently taught Chris thoroughbred racing at his St. Matthews, South Carolina, farm in 1973. Chris learned the qualities that separate a genuine horseman from mere riders while earning $90 a week for grooming and walking horses, filling food tubs, and washing saddle clothes and bandages. Chris was terrified the first time he ever mounted a horse, staying on it for only 4 seconds. On January 24, 1974, Chris entered his first race as an apprentice jockey. His filly finished last at Bowie Race Track in Bowie, Maryland. He rode in unusual fashion, tucking his right leg higher up in the irons than his left leg.

The Emerging Champion

In 1974, Chris tirelessly accepted a record 2,199 mounts and earned about $250,000. His first victory came on February 4 aboard his eleventh mount, but it took several more weeks for the eighteen-year-old to make much impact on the Maryland racing circuit. On March 21, Chris triumphed on four of six mounts. He consistently rode at least three daily winners and even recorded six victories one day at Pimlico Race Track in Baltimore, Maryland. The fall season saw Chris racing six days a week in Maryland and competing Saturday nights and Sunday afternoons at Penn National Race Track in Harrisburg, Pennsylvania.

The competition facing Chris, however, did not rival that of the California or New York State racetracks. On December 17, 1974, he broke Canadian Sandy Hawley's record for most victories by a jockey in one year. Sandy in 1973 had become the first jockey to attain five hundred victories in one year. Chris set the record with his 516th triumph of 1974 aboard Ohmylove at Laurel Race Track in Maryland. He ended 1974 with 546 winners, earning his first Eclipse Award as the nation's top apprentice jockey. His record lasted until jockey Kent Desormeaux incredibly rode 597 winners in 1989.

Continuing the Story

In 1975, Chris repeated as the nation's most winning jockey with 468 triumphs. Two years later, he moved to California and faced stiffer competition at Hollywood Park in Inglewood. Racing style adjustments brought him immediate success. In 1980, Chris led the nation's jockeys for the first time in money earned ($7,663,300), paced them in victories (405), and won his second Eclipse Award. His busy fall 1980 schedule of eight daily races at Aqueduct Race Track in Ozone Park, New York, and nightly races at the Meadowlands in New Jersey helped him become only the fourth rider to lead the nation's jockeys in both wins and earnings and to amass more than four hundred victories in the same year. Chris also paced all jockeys in money earned in 1981 ($8,397,604) and 1984 ($12,045,813). Seagram's, using computerized analysis of performances, rated Chris as the best jockey in 1982, 1983, and 1984. In 1983, Chris became the youngest jockey to reach $50 million in purses and to ride 3,000 career winners. He rode John Henry during the last four years of that great gelding's career and guided Precisionist to the Breeders' Cup Sprint title in 1985.

No victory in a Triple Crown race came for Chris until 1986. At the Preakness Stakes, his Desert Wine finished second in 1983 and his Eternal Prince placed third in 1985. In 1986, he guided Bold Arrangement to second place in the

Jockey Chris McCarron after winning the Pacific Classic in August, 1998.

AP/Wide World Photos

Kentucky Derby, Broad Brush to third in the Preakness, and Danzig Connection to first on a sloppy track in the Belmont Stakes.

Chris was sidelined by a terrible accident in October, 1986, at Santa Anita Race Track in Arcadia, California. Three thoroughbreds suddenly fell about six lengths in front of Chris, causing him to be thrown from his horse. Jockey Laffit Pincay, Jr., fell on Chris, breaking the latter's leg in four places. During surgery, a twelve-inch stainless steel rod was attached to the thigh bone of his left leg. Chris courageously resumed racing two months later.

Alysheba was the best horse Chris ever rode. Chris won his first Kentucky Derby in 1987 when

---

MILESTONES

Annual money leader (1980-81, 1984, 1991)
6,846 victories—through 1999, the tenth-highest all-time record

HONORS AND AWARDS

1974	Eclipse Award, Outstanding Apprentice Jockey
1980	Eclipse Award, Outstanding Jockey
1989	Inducted into National Horse Racing Hall of Fame

Alysheba defeated Bet Twice by three-fourths of a length. Alysheba was clipped by Bet Twice and nearly fell but won the race with a brilliant final stretch. Chris earned his third Triple Crown race when Alysheba edged Bet Twice by one-half length in the Preakness. After finishing a disappointing fourth in the Belmont Stakes, Alysheba won the $1 million Super Derby at Louisiana Downs in September, 1987. Chris steered Alysheba to victory in the 1988 Breeder's Cup Classic at Churchill Downs in November. Alysheba, the richest racehorse of all time, earned Eclipse Awards in 1987 as best three-year-old colt and in 1988 as Horse of the Year.

In November, 1989, Chris replaced suspended jockey Pat Valenzuela aboard Sunday Silence in the Breeder's Cup Classic at Gulfstream Park in Florida. Sunday Silence, 1989 Horse of the Year as Kentucky Derby and Preakness winner, edged arch-rival Easy Goer by a neck. The following month, Chris rode Frankly Perfect to victory in the Hollywood Turf Cup. In June, 1990, Chris took a spill at Hollywood Park that resulted in a broken right arm and two fractured legs, requiring surgery, but in less than three months, he was riding and winning again.

Chris won his second Preakness Stakes in 1992, aboard Pine Bluff, and his second Kentucky Derby in 1994, on Go for Gin. In 1997 he foiled Silver Charm's bid for the Triple Crown by riding Touch Gold to victory at the Belmont Stakes. At the age of forty-five, Chris won the 2000 Breeder's Cup Classic aboard Tiznow—his fourth Breeder's Cup win.

Summary

Chris McCarron is among the best jockeys in racing history, ranking sixth in career victories and first in purses won, reaching the $230 million mark in 2000. The National Horse Racing Hall of Fame inducted him in August, 1989. He has won all the most important races and remains devoted to racing with no plans to retire, as of early 2001.

David L. Porter

Additional Sources:

Nack, William. "Silence Roars Once More." *Sports Illustrated* 71 (November 13, 1989): 28.

Pierce, Charles P. "Psycho." *Gentlemen's Quarterly* 63, no. 5 (1993).

Williams, Gene. "Chris' Craft." *Louisville Magazine* 47, no. 5 (1996).

Reed, William F. "Rolling in Clover." *Sports Illustrated* 76 (May 25, 1992): 66.

PAT McCORMICK

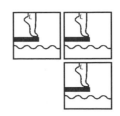

Sport: Diving

Born: May 12, 1930
      Seal Beach, California

Early Life

Patricia Joan Keller was born on May 12, 1930, in Seal Beach, California, one of three children of Robert and Harriet Shipman Keller. Her father, an oilman and World War I veteran, was seldom home. She was reared mostly by her mother, who worked as a nurse. Living near the ocean, Pat began riding waves while still a toddler and soon became a good swimmer.

She and her brother Bob often played at Muscle Beach. There they worked out with the strongmen, who tossed Pat into the air and taught her various stunts. That was the way she learned many acrobatic tricks that she later used in diving and developed the strength that was important for her sport.

Even though she had no coaches, Pat learned to dive quite well. By the time she was fourteen, she was the Long Beach diving champion. That attracted the attention of diving coach Aileen Allen. She invited Pat to join the famous Los Angeles Athletic Club (LAAC), as her pupil.

The Road to Excellence

At first, Pat went to the LAAC only twice a week, but as she improved, she began to work out daily. She was allowed to leave high school at two o'clock for the long trolley ride to Los Angeles

and did not return home until nine o'clock at night.

In 1948, she graduated from Long Beach High School and got a new coach, Russell Smith. That summer, Pat missed making the U.S. Olympic diving team by less than one point. Even though it was a big disappointment, she did not

U.S. Olympic diver Pat McCormick, center, wins gold in the 1956 Olympic Games in Australia.

give up on her Olympic dreams. She was determined to try even harder. She moved to Los Angeles and lived with her aunt so that she would have more time to practice.

It was not easy to be a woman athlete in the 1940's. Girls were often told that if they were very good in sports, boys would not want to date or marry them. Some people even believed that girls who competed seriously in sports like diving or track could never have children. Pat proved them all wrong. On June 1, 1949, she married a diving coach named Glenn McCormick. It was a very successful partnership. Pat soon became a world champion diver and the mother of two children.

She won her first national championship in 1949, the Amateur Athletic Union (AAU) outdoor platform diving title. The next year, she also won both the AAU outdoor platform and the 3-meter springboard championships.

The Emerging Champion

Pat worked hard and made many sacrifices to become a champion. She practiced six days a week, doing between eighty-five and one hundred dives every day. She also suffered many accidents and injuries, including chipped teeth, broken ribs, and a six-inch scalp wound. Her first try at college also failed, as she found out in a few months that being a wife and champion diver took all of her time.

The work really started to pay off in 1951. That year, Pat won one gold and one silver medal at the Pan-American Games. She also became the first person ever to win all five AAU national diving titles in one year. In 1952, she made the U.S. Olympic team.

By then she was famous for being a daring and courageous athlete. She did dives so difficult that few men would try them. Some were so hard that the International Olympic Committee (IOC) would not allow them in women's competition.

Even though some of her best dives had been banned by the IOC, Pat won gold medals in both springboard and platform diving at the Olympics in Helsinki, Finland. She was the first woman to win both events at the same Olympics. The reason is that very few athletes are world class in both diving events. Fewer than half of all Olympic champions compete in both springboard and platform diving like Pat McCormick.

Continuing the Story

By 1956, Pat had won fifteen more AAU championships and the springboard and platform gold medals at the 1955 Pan-American Games. Eight months before the 1956 Olympics, Pat gave birth to her first child, a son. She had trained throughout her pregnancy and easily made the Olympic team. Soon after, her husband Glenn was named the Olympic diving coach.

During the Olympics at Melbourne, Australia, in December, Pat got an early Christmas present. She again won both of the diving gold medals. She was the first athlete ever to win back-to-back golds in both Olympic diving events. This achievement won her many honors and fame as the greatest woman diver of all time.

After the 1956 Olympics, Pat retired from diving to spend more time with her family. She also graduated from Long Beach State College in 1968. For many years she owned and managed a diving camp before becoming president of her own company, Pat McCormick Enterprises. She also became a popular speaker and a college teacher.

In 1984, she was one of the former Olympic champions selected to carry the American flag in the opening ceremonies at the Los Angeles Olympic Games. There Pat also watched as her daughter Kelly won the silver

---

HONORS, AWARDS, AND RECORDS

1949-55	Won twenty-seven national AAU diving titles
1952	First woman diver to win both the springboard and platform diving gold medals at the Olympic Games
1952, 1956	First diver to score a double-double in springboard and platform diving at two consecutive Olympic Games
1956	Sullivan Award Associated Press Female Athlete of the Year Babe Zaharias Woman Athlete of the Year
1965	Inducted into International Swimming Hall of Fame
1984	Inducted into Sudafed International Women's Sports Hall of Fame
1985	Inducted into U.S. Olympic Hall of Fame

1710

medal in springboard diving. After that happy event, mother and daughter gave their first-ever interview together for national television.

Summary

Pat McCormick was fortunate to grow up in California, where she learned to swim and to dive around some excellent coaches and outstanding athletes. She was creative and tried many dangerous stunts, but she also practiced hard for thousands of hours to become one of the greatest divers, male or female, ever to compete in the sport.

Pat also proved that world champion women athletes can marry and have children and still compete. The mother of two, she won four Olympic gold medals, four Pan-American Games medals, and twenty-seven national AAU diving titles. More important, she won at a time when women athletes did not get much support. Because of champions like Pat McCormick, girls are no longer discouraged from becoming world-class ath-

letes. Many, including her own daughter, have followed her example.

Mary Lou LeCompte

Additional Sources:

Hickok, Ralph. *A Who's Who of Sports Champions.* Boston: Houghton Mifflin, 1995.

Levinson, David, and Karen Christenson, eds. *Encyclopedia of World Sport: From Ancient to Present.* Santa Barbara, Calif.: ABC-CLIO, 1996.

Schapp, Dick. *An Illustrated History of the Olympics.* New York: Alfred A. Knopf, 1975.

MAJOR CHAMPIONSHIPS

Year	Competition	Event	Place	Points
1951	Pan-American Games	3-meter springboard	Gold	128.083
		10-meter platform	Silver	65.716
1952	Olympic Games	3-meter springboard	Gold	147.30
		10-meter platform	Gold	79.37
1955	Pan-American Games	3-meter springboard	Gold	142.42
		10-meter platform	Gold	92.05
1956	Olympic Games	3-meter springboard	Gold	142.36
		10-meter platform	Gold	84.85

WILLIE McCOVEY

Sport: Baseball

Born: January 10, 1938
Mobile, Alabama

Early Life

Willie Lee McCovey, the seventh of ten children of Frank and Esther McCovey, was born on January 10, 1938, in Mobile, Alabama. Willie's father, Frank, worked for a railway company, and, although the McCoveys were poor, they always managed to scrape by. Frank McCovey was a quiet man who seldom spoke, but when he did, the entire family paid attention to what he said.

It was difficult growing up in Mobile in the

1940's; poor African American children had few options. Some joined neighborhood gangs; others hung around street corners or played sports. Willie and a group of his friends preferred to play baseball, football, and basketball. In baseball, Willie always played first base. As a youngster, Willie also tried to help his family by working, first as a newspaper boy and later in a factory.

The Road to Excellence

When Willie reached the age of sixteen, he quit school, left Mobile, and moved to Los Angeles to join his older brother, Wyat. Alex Pompez, a New York Giants scout, heard from a friend that the young first baseman had potential. When Willie had just turned seventeen, the Giants sent him a bus ticket and asked him to report to a tryout camp in Melbourne, Florida. At the tryout, the team management recognized his talent and signed him to a professional contract to play with their farm team in Sandersville, Georgia.

Willie climbed up the minor league ladder, playing for four years for different Giant farm teams across the country. In his last year in the minors in 1958, playing for Phoenix at the Triple-A level, the toughest competition in the minors, he hit an astounding .372 with 29 home runs.

The Emerging Champion

Despite that terrific season, the Giants did not call Willie up to the majors right away. The Giants, who had just moved to San Francisco, had an enviable dilemma. They had another young star, Orlando Cepeda, who had won the Rookie of the Year award in 1958 and played the same position that Willie did, first base.

Finally, on July 30, 1959, Willie got the call to the big leagues. He reported to old Seals Stadium in San Francisco and responded in his first game against the Philadelphia Phillies star pitcher (and a future Hall of Famer) Robin Rob-

STATISTICS

Season	GP	AB	Hits	2B	3B	HR	Runs	RBI	BA	SA
1959	52	192	68	9	5	13	32	38	.354	.656
1960	101	260	62	15	3	13	37	51	.238	.469
1961	106	328	89	12	3	18	59	50	.271	.491
1962	91	229	67	6	1	20	41	54	.293	.590
1963	152	564	158	19	5	**44**	103	102	.280	.566
1964	130	364	80	14	1	18	55	54	.220	.412
1965	160	540	149	17	4	39	93	92	.276	.539
1966	150	502	148	26	6	36	85	96	.295	.586
1967	135	456	126	17	4	31	73	91	.276	.535
1968	148	523	153	16	4	**36**	81	**105**	.293	**.545**
1969	149	491	157	26	2	**45**	101	**126**	.320	**.656**
1970	152	495	143	39	2	39	98	126	.289	**.612**
1971	105	329	91	13	0	18	45	70	.277	.480
1972	81	263	56	8	0	14	30	35	.213	.403
1973	130	383	102	14	3	29	52	75	.266	.546
1974	128	344	87	19	1	22	53	63	.253	.506
1975	122	413	104	17	0	23	43	68	.252	.460
1976	82	226	46	9	0	7	20	36	.204	.336
1977	141	478	134	21	0	28	54	86	.280	.500
1978	108	351	80	19	2	12	32	64	.228	.396
1979	117	353	88	9	0	15	34	57	.249	.402
1980	48	113	23	8	0	1	8	16	.204	.301
Totals	2,588	8,197	2,211	353	46	521	1,229	1,555	.270	.515

Notes: Boldface indicates statistical leader. GP = games played; AB = at bats; 2B = doubles; 3B = triples; HR = home runs; RBI = runs batted in; BA = batting average; SA = slugging average

erts by rapping 4 consecutive hits in four at bats. In the remaining fifty-two games of the season, Willie batted .354 and hit 13 home runs, earning the Rookie of the Year award in the National League (NL).

After that great start, things did not go smoothly for Willie during the next few seasons. At the plate, the pitchers found that they could get him out by throwing him pitches high and inside. In the field, he was called on to play the outfield and first base, shuttling back and forth. Another problem was that Willie did not play in the starting lineup every day.

Willie came of age in the 1962 World Series against the New York Yankees. Willie hit a home run to win a game, but, ironically, it was an out that gained him greater recognition. In the seventh and deciding game, with two men on base, Willie hit a blistering line drive toward right field that would have won the Series for the Giants if the Yankees' second baseman Bobby Richardson had not snared it for the final out.

Finally, Willie became a fixture in the Giants' lineup. With the exception of an off-year in 1964, when he was saddled with injuries and saddened by the death of his father, Willie's slugging made him a feared hitter in the National League. After 1965, "Stretch," as he was affectionately nicknamed (no doubt for his lanky, 6-foot 4-inch, 198-pound frame), stopped shuffling between the outfield and the infield and found a regular niche at first base. Batting cleanup behind the legendary Willie Mays and just ahead of the Giants' hard-hitting third baseman, Jim Ray Hart, Willie was an integral part of the Giants' potent offense. Unfortunately, the Giants never had the pitching staff to go along with their offense, so the 1962 Series was Willie's only World Series opportunity throughout his twenty-two-year career.

MAJOR LEAGUE RECORDS

Most intentional walks in a season, 45 (1969)
Most pinch-hit grand slam home runs, 3 (record shared)

NATIONAL LEAGUE RECORDS

First to hit 18 grand slam home runs
Most home runs by a first baseman, 439

Continuing the Story

In many ways, Willie McCovey was overshadowed during the early part of his big-league career by Willie Mays, the Giants' center fielder. Mays could do it all—run, throw, and hit—and with his lively personality had captured the imagination of the entire nation, and especially the Giants fans. Not surprisingly, there was always a bit of rivalry between the two superstars, and they never really got along well. It was not until the late 1960's that the younger and quieter Willie McCovey emerged from Mays's shadow and put together two phenomenal seasons. In 1968 and 1969, Stretch led the National League in home runs, runs batted in, and slugging percentage, becoming the first player in National League history to finish first in all three categories in consecutive years. In the 1969 All-Star game, Willie hit 2 home runs to help the National League beat the American League.

In recognition of his accomplishments, Willie was an obvious choice for the National League most valuable player in 1969. What is amazing is that he put together such an awesome campaign despite painful calcium deposits that caused bleeding in his right hip when he swung hard or when he extended himself in the field. An indication of the respect that pitchers accorded Willie was his walk total—in 1969, he received 121 walks, and in 1970, a league-leading 137, including a National League record of 45 intentional walks—demonstrating that hurlers preferred to pitch around him rather than take any chances. He hit 3 homers in a game twice in his career and hit 2 home runs in the same inning twice.

Injuries continued to plague Willie, and he was traded in 1974 to the San Diego Padres. The Giants, who had traded Willie Mays to the New York Mets a year before, was trying to rebuild its fortunes, but the moves to trade the two Willies were very unpopular with the Giants' fans. After a few seasons in San Diego, the Giants' management, in an effort to bolster its sagging attendance, brought the popular Stretch home to finish his playing career in San Francisco. Willie retired in 1980 after twenty-two seasons in the big leagues.

After he retired, the Giants gave him a seven-year contract and a front-office position working

HONORS AND AWARDS	
1959	National League Rookie of the Year
1963, 1966, 1968-71	National League All-Star Team
1969	National League most valuable player
	Sporting News Major League Player of the Year
	All-Star Game most valuable player
1986	Inducted into National Baseball Hall of Fame
2000	Pacific Bell Park opened; an area of China Basin Channel is dubbed "McCovey Cove." Uniform number 44 retired by San Francisco Giants

in community relations in the Bay Area. After ballplayers finish their playing careers, they are still popular with fans, especially youngsters, and public appearances by Willie or Mays often helped with ticket sales and promotions. In April, 2000, the San Francisco Giants played their first game in Pac Bell Park, their new $319 million ballpark on San Francisco Bay. A small channel of water beyond the right-field wall was named McCovey Cove to honor the Giants Hall of Famer.

Summary

Willie McCovey in his prime was an imposing sight. His muscular build and powerful swing struck fear in opposing pitchers. His accomplishments, including 521 home runs and more than 2,200 hits, meant that he was assured a spot in the National Baseball Hall of Fame. Stretch became only the sixteenth player in history to be voted into baseball immortality in his first year of eligibility.

Allen Wells

Additional Sources:

Asnen, Alan R. "McCovey, Willie Lee 'Stretch,' 'Big Mac.'" In *Biographical Dictionary of American Sports: Baseball*, edited by David L. Porter. Westport, Conn.: Greenwood Press, 1987.

The Hall of Fame Giants: In Commemoration of Willie McCovey's Induction, Summer 1986. San Francisco: Woodford, 1986.

"McCovey, Willie." In *The Lincoln Library of Sports Champions.* Vol. 8. Columbus, Ohio: Frontier Press, 1993.

FLORETTA DOTY McCUTCHEON

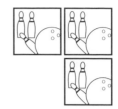

Sport: Bowling

Born: July 22, 1888
    Ottumwa, Iowa
Died: February 2, 1967
    Pasadena, California

Early Life

Floretta Doty McCutcheon was born in Ottumwa, Iowa, on July 22, 1888. She lived there until 1901, when her family moved to Denver, Colorado. In 1921, they moved again to Pueblo, Colorado, where Floretta lived for many years. In Pueblo, she met and later married Robert McCutcheon, a clerk for Colorado Fuel and Iron Corporation. They soon had their only child, Barbara.

For many years, Floretta was a housewife who enjoyed quilting and an occasional round of golf. Unlike so many sports champions, she did not enter her sport until late in life. She began to bowl in Pueblo as a hobby, and on November 23, 1923, at the age of thirty-five, Floretta rolled a 69 in her first game.

The Road to Excellence

Floretta continued to bowl in Pueblo, participating in two leagues, but then stopped bowling until 1926, when she joined league play again. Her career as a bowler was enhanced when an accomplished and well-known bowler, Jimmy Smith, gave an exhibition in Pueblo. Soon thereafter, Floretta adopted a style similar to Smith's, and a year later, she defeated the Hall of Famer in a three-game exhibition, 704 to 687.

With this victory, "Mrs. Mac," as she became affectionately known, began a tour of exhibition matches, traveling through New York, Ohio, Missouri, Minnesota, Michigan, California, Oregon, and Colorado. In 1930, at the age of forty-two, Mrs. Mac began the Mrs. McCutcheon School of Bowling with her partner, C. J. Cain, who had been Jimmy Smith's manager. She continued to travel to major cities throughout the United States, giving exhibition matches and conducting teaching clinics for women. Mrs. Mac was far superior to other women bowlers, as bowling had not been widely popular with women in the United States. Her competitors were men, many of whom she defeated.

The Emerging Champion

Mrs. Mac weighed 185 pounds when she began bowling. A year after her tour began, she had lost 42 pounds. In 1935, she traveled eighteen thousand miles, giving exhibitions, running bowling "schools," and competing in tournaments.

HONORS AND AWARDS

1956	Inducted into WIBC Hall of Fame

Mrs. Mac continued her tours and exhibitions and compiled an impressive list of records. She bowled ten 300-pin games, eleven 800-pin three-game series, and more than one hundred series above 700 pins. In Morris, Minnesota, on January 20, 1931, she rolled her highest three-game total of 832 pins. Once, she hit 248 in twelve-game blocks. She averaged 201 for 8,076 games on strange alleys over a ten-year period. No woman had ever scored better than her 248 twelve consecutive games.

Mrs. Mac also placed first among the women in the 1932 Olympic Games, and, during the 1938-1939 season, she averaged 206 pins in New York, a record that stood until the 1963-1964 season. None of Mrs. Mac's records is included in Women's International Bowling Congress (WIBC) records because she scored in instructional exhibitions or unsanctioned match play.

In spite of the many records she set, Mrs. Mac's greatest contribution to bowling was her school. She traveled extensively throughout the United States and is credited with instructing as many as 300,000 women in the game of bowling. She maintained that women would eventually bowl as well as men because bowling required rhythm, control, timing, and coordination rather than strength and speed. Although bowling had been popular with women, its popularity increased dramatically among women thirty-five and older because of Mrs. Mac's tours, exhibitions, and instruction. Her contributions made bowling the most popular amateur sport in the United States during the Depression.

Continuing the Story

Mrs. Mac continued to travel, compete, and instruct during the decade of the 1930's. She was a spot bowler who used the four-step delivery and was highly regarded because of her consistent accuracy. She made further contributions to the game by writing bowling booklets, organizing leagues, and creating an instructional series for female bowlers.

In 1939, she became an instructor at the Capital Health Center in New York City. In 1944, she moved to Chicago, Illinois, where she continued her instruction at the Bowlium.

In 1954, she announced her retirement and moved to San Gabriel, California, to help care for her two grandchildren. She left the game after dominating bowling for fifteen years and molding champions for fifteen more years. Although she held all of the bowling records for women, she never won a tournament. Yet, for her many contributions as teacher and athlete, she was inducted into the WIBC Hall of Fame in 1956 as a Star of Yesteryear and was later named as an honorary member of WIBC. She died in 1967.

Summary

Floretta "Mrs. Mac" Doty McCutcheon was known as both a teacher and an athlete. She began her career late in life, at the age of thirty-five. After defeating Jimmy Smith, a well-known champion, she established herself as the dominant woman bowler of the 1930's. For many years, she toured the United States from coast to coast, giving exhibitions and conducting clinics for more than 300,000 women. She also wrote booklets advocating the four-step delivery and spot bowling. During this time, she bowled more than eight thousand matches, averaging over 200 per game. The most notable of her achievements include eleven 800 series, more than one hundred 700 series, nine 299 games, and ten perfect games. In the 1938-1939 season, she set a WIBC league average of 206, a record that stood for twenty-five years. For these achievements and her many contributions to bowling, Mrs. Mac was inducted into the WIBC Hall of Fame in 1956 and later named as an honorary member of the organization.

Susan J. Bandy

Additional Sources:

Jacobs, Helen H. *Famous American Women Athletes.* New York: Dodd, Mead, 1964.

Layden, Joe. *Women in Sports.* Santa Monica, Calif.: General Publishing, 1997.

Woolum, Janet. *Outstanding Women Athletes: Who They Are and How They Influenced Sports in America.* Phoenix, Ariz.: Oryx Press, 1998.

HUGH McELHENNY

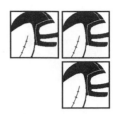

Sport: Football

Born: December 31, 1928
      Los Angeles, California

Early Life

The boy who would someday become one of football's best broken-field runners of all time was born on December 31, 1928, in Los Angeles, California, to a petite mother and a wiry, 130-pound, 5-foot 4-inch father. Hugh Edward McElhenny, Jr., was born to defy the odds against him.

When he was eleven years old, Hugh stepped on a broken milk bottle and severed all the ten-dons in one foot. Not only was he bedridden for five months and on crutches for seven, but doctors proclaimed he would never walk again.

Hugh began a series of exercises that gradually strengthened his foot. Instead of facing a life of dragging himself around with a cane, he was eventually able to join the George Washington High School football team. He still had to take painkiller shots before each game, and he wore a steel plate in the sole of his shoe.

One other incident had actually served to further Hugh's future career. When he was six, a

San Francisco 49er Hugh McElhenny (left) in 1955.

man with a shotgun chased Hugh and his friends off a vacant lot. Hugh was shot in the back. From then on, he ran scared. Whenever he played football, he ran as fast as he could, imagining that man with the gun chasing him. At a high school track meet, he was clocked at 9.7 seconds for the 100-yard dash and he set the world's interscholastic 120-yard hurdles record of 14 seconds.

The Road to Excellence

Hugh's father, a prosperous coin machine operator, disliked football and refused to sign Hugh's permission slip to play the game in high school. His mother signed it, and Hugh made her proud by playing brilliantly. Consequently, forty colleges wooed him with scholarships. Hugh wanted to be near his childhood sweetheart, Peggy Ogston (whom he later married), so he chose Compton Junior College.

Standing 6 feet 1 inch and weighing 205 pounds, Hugh scored 23 touchdowns at Compton and led the school to the national junior college championship. Meanwhile, another sixtythree colleges courted Hugh, hoping to recruit him. Rumors went around that he chose the University of Washington because the road there was "paved with twenty-dollar bills." Hugh's may have been the first celebrated recruiting case to come to public attention. While at the University of Washington, Hugh openly admitted to having

three cars, $30,000 in the bank, two professional teams paying his way through school, and the promise of a lifetime job from four companies.

In his junior year, Hugh made 5 touchdowns and gained 296 yards in a single game; he also set a Pacific Coast Conference single-season rushing record. The following year, he made All-American after scoring 17 touchdowns and 125 total points.

The Emerging Champion

Hugh signed on with the San Francisco 49ers after confidently asking them for $30,000. He soon agreed to a compromise—only $7,000—and became known as the first college star to take a cut in salary in order to play professionally.

As a rookie in 1952, Hugh led the league in rushing average with 7 yards per carry. He scored 60 points. He was named All-Pro and Rookie of the Year. Few NFL players have had a finer first season. That year and from then on, Hugh ran with the ball the way boys do in their happiest dreams: with speed, power, instinct, and a complete mastery of moves such as faking, sudden bursts, spinning, pivoting, and sidestepping. He also made full use of his keen intuition and wideangle vision that told him where his opponents lurked. Sometimes he made instinctive plays like criss-crossing a field 40 yards in order to gain 5 yards.

STATISTICS

| Season | GP | Rushing | | | | | Receiving | | | |
		Car.	Yds.	Avg.	TD	Rec.	Yds.	Avg.	TD
1952	12	98	684	**7.0**	6	26	367	14.1	3
1953	12	112	503	4.5	3	30	474	15.8	2
1954	6	64	515	**8.0**	6	8	162	20.3	0
1955	12	90	327	3.6	4	11	203	18.5	2
1956	12	185	916	5.0	8	16	193	12.1	0
1957	12	102	478	4.7	1	37	458	12.4	2
1958	12	113	451	4.0	6	31	366	11.8	2
1959	10	18	67	3.7	1	22	329	15.0	3
1960	9	95	347	3.7	0	14	114	8.1	1
1961	13	120	570	4.8	3	37	283	7.6	3
1962	11	50	200	4.0	0	16	191	11.9	0
1963	14	55	175	3.2	0	11	91	8.3	2
1964	8	22	48	2.2	0	5	16	3.2	0
Totals	143	1,124	5,281	4.7	38	264	3,247	12.3	20

Notes: Boldface indicates statistical leader. GP = games played; Car. = carries; Yds. = yards; Avg. = average yards per carry *or* average yards per reception; TD = touchdowns; Rec. = receptions

HONORS AND AWARDS

1951	College All-American
1952-53	NFL All-Pro Team
1953-54, 1957-59, 1962	NFL Pro Bowl Team
1958	NFL Pro Bowl Co-Player of the Game
1963	NFL All-Pro Team of the 1950's
1970	Inducted into Pro Football Hall of Fame
1981	Inducted into College Football Hall of Fame
	Uniform number 39 retired by San Francisco 49ers

Because he was a superb pass receiver and an outstanding running back, Hugh McElhenny was soon nicknamed the "King" by his teammates. At times, owing to his body rhythm and balance, the 49ers also referred to him as "Slider" because of his skill at sliding away from or eluding tacklers.

Hugh's best playing years were from 1952 to 1958, when he wore out six pairs of shoes a season. He played in six Pro Bowl games. His team never won a title during his years with it, however. In his short career with San Francisco, Hugh amassed 4,288 yards in rushing for second place in the league's lifetime standings. He also made 264 pass receptions and 360 points.

Continuing the Story

In 1955, Hugh injured the same foot he had maimed as a child. Still, he managed to average 3.6 yards per carry. His playing began to go into a slump, however. After quarreling with his new coach, the tough taskmaster Red Hickey, Hugh asked to be traded.

He went on to play for the Minnesota Vikings, where he was team captain and most valuable player in 1961. Soon, however, the years of twisting and turning the cartilage in his knees caught up with him. When he was traded to the New York Giants in 1963, he knew he had to prove he was not washed up. In striving to do his best,

Hugh pulled a muscle in his thigh. Soon after helping the Giants win the Eastern Conference championship, he tired of the pain and retired to San Francisco.

There, Hugh worked for Allen and Darwood, an advertising agency, where he handled the NFL's merchandising account. He was inducted into the Pro Football Hall of Fame in 1970.

As the preeminent ball carrier of the 1950's, the King had what it took to be the best: dedication, speed, and size.

Another reason the King was so successful was that he was the first of football's running specialists. He was the first running back able to concentrate exclusively on his forte, which was running with the ball. Before his time, backfield men had had to play on both defense as well as offense. The era of the specialist began with Hugh McElhenny, among others. By the time he retired in 1964, all players were able to specialize in what they did best.

Summary

Hugh McElhenny earned his nickname "the King" for his many gridiron-royal qualities that enabled him to rank among the world's top running backs. His statistics show he was more than just a runner, for he caught 264 passes in his career. He retired with one of the best averages in yards per carry in pro football history.

Nicholas White

Additional Sources:

Hickok, Ralph. *A Who's Who of Sports Champions.* Boston: Houghton Mifflin, 1995.

LaBlanc, Michael L., and Mary K. Ruby, eds. *Professional Sports Team Histories: Football.* Detroit: Gale, 1994.

Porter, David L., ed. *Biographical Dictionary of American Sports: Football.* Westport, Conn.: Greenwood Press, 1987.

JOHN McENROE

Sport: Tennis

Born: February 16, 1959
Wiesbaden, West Germany

Early Life

John Patrick McEnroe, Jr., was born on February 16, 1959, in Wiesbaden, West Germany, where his father served in the United States Air Force. He was the first of John Patrick and Kay McEnroe's three sons. John was nine months old when the family relocated in Flushing in the Borough of Queens. When John was four, the family moved to Douglastown, where John grew up.

John discovered tennis when he was eight. His family joined the Douglastown Club, which had five tennis courts. When John showed an interest in tennis, his father began to play with him and regularly defeated his son, a model child who was chiefly concerned with doing well in school and sports.

John attended Buckley Country Day School near his home until he was thirteen. Then he went to Trinity School, the oldest continuously operated school in Manhattan, from which he was graduated in 1977. He played tennis, football, and soccer at Trinity. Although he was already playing in significant tournaments, John never missed school and never fell behind in his academic work.

After Trinity, John attended Stanford University, where he was on the tennis team. He won the National Collegiate Amateur Athletic (NCAA) Championship as a freshman. By 1978, however, tennis came to assume so important a role in

John McEnroe won his fourth U.S. Open in 1984, beating Czech Ivan Lendl.

John's life that he left Stanford to join the professionals.

The Road to Excellence

While he was still at Trinity School, John won several U.S. junior singles and doubles matches. Eliot Teltscher remembers playing John in a competition in Dallas when both were fourteen. By 1977, he had won the junior titles in the French Open mixed doubles and singles. The next year, having become a professional, he won the Italian Indoor Doubles Championship. He defeated Tim Gullikson in both the Stockholm Open and the Benson and Hedges Championships at Wembley in the same year. He also beat Dick Stockton in the TransAmerica Open, going on in 1979 to beat Vitas Gerulaitis, 7-5, 6-4, 6-3, in the U.S. Open and Arthur Ashe, 6-7, 6-3, 7-5, in the Masters.

John, shorter than most of his peers and pudgy in his early teens, had an intensity that became legendary among tennis fans. His furrowed brow bespoke a seriousness and competi-tiveness seldom seen even in championship tennis circles. His jutting lip and chin suggested unbending determination.

The Emerging Champion

Björn Borg was in many ways John's most formidable opponent. Therefore, beating him 7-5, 4-6, 6-2, 7-6 in the World Championship Tennis (WCT) finals of 1979 was particularly sweet. The victory marked an important prelude to other impressive victories that would place John first among U.S. tennis players and eventually first among all tennis players.

He defeated Borg, 7-6, 6-1, 6-7, 5-7, 6-4, in the men's singles of the U.S. Open the following year and again, 4-6, 6-2, 6-4, 6-3, in 1981. He also prevailed in the U.S. Open in 1984. In 1981, John claimed his most important victory over Borg at Wimbledon, where he and Peter Fleming had already taken the men's doubles titles in 1979 and 1981. He trounced Borg 4-6, 7-6, 7-6, 6-4 in the men's singles and won again in 1983 and 1984.

These victories over Borg were more important to John than his conquest of Jimmy Connors in the U.S. Indoor Championship men's singles in Memphis in 1980 or of Vitas Gerulaitis in the Custom Credit Australian Indoor Championship men's singles in Sydney, Australia, the same year, impressive as these victories were.

Having won the U.S. Pro Indoor Championship men's singles from 1982 to 1985 and the U.S. Indoor Championship in both 1980 and 1983, John slackened his pace during his courtship of actress Tatum O'Neal, which resulted in their marriage in 1986. The couple and their children settled in Malibu.

He prevailed, nevertheless, in the men's singles competitions of the AT&T Challenge of 1987, in the Japan Open the following year, and in the U.S. Hardcourt

---

MAJOR CHAMPIONSHIP VICTORIES AND FINALS

1977	French Open mixed doubles (with Mary Carillo)
1978, 1982	Wimbledon doubles finalist (with Peter Fleming)
1979-81, 1984	U.S. Open
1979, 1981, 1983, 1989	U.S. Open doubles (with Fleming; with Mark Woodforde)
1979, 1981, 1983-84, 1992	Wimbledon doubles (with Fleming; with Michael Stich)
1980	U.S. Open doubles finalist (with Fleming)
1980, 1982	Wimbledon finalist
1981, 1983-84	Wimbledon
1984	U.S. Open finalist

OTHER NOTABLE VICTORIES

1978	NCAA Championship
1978-79	Italian Indoor Championship doubles (with Fleming)
1978-80	The Masters doubles (with Fleming)
1979	WCT World doubles (with Fleming)
1979, 1981-82	On winning U.S. Davis Cup team
1979, 1981, 1983-85	WCT Finals
1979, 1984	Canadian Open doubles (with Fleming)
1979, 1984-85	The Masters
1980-81	WCT Tournament of Champions doubles (with Fleming)
1980	U.S. Indoor Championship doubles (with Brian Gottfried) U.S. Clay Court Championship doubles (with Gene Mayer)
1980, 1982, 1984	U.S. Pro Indoor doubles (with Fleming)
1980, 1983	U.S. Indoor Championship
1981	ATP Championship
1981, 1982	ATP Championship doubles (with Ferdi Taygan; with Fleming)
1982-85	U.S. Pro Indoor
1984-85	Canadian Open
1989	U.S. Hardcourt Championship

Championship singles of 1989. Fatherhood made John more attentive to his behavior on court. He began to try to create a more favorable image. Although his marriage ended in 1994, John has said that rearing children has helped him to become a more real person.

HONORS AND AWARDS

1978	All-American
1978-84, 1987-91	Davis Cup team
1979-81, 1983-85	Ranked number one by the ATP
1981	Associated Press Male Athlete of the Year
1983-84	International Tennis Federation Player of the Year
1999	Inducted into International Tennis Hall of Fame

Continuing the Story

When John played at Wimbledon in 1988 after a two-year absence, he was in excellent form. He was, however, eliminated early in the competition and left England bemoaning the kind of tennis that was now being played and muttering darkly about the future of the sport. The game of power and pace at which players like Boris Becker, Stefan Edberg, and Ivan Lendl excel was a new brand of championship tennis that clearly delineated a new generation of tennis champions.

John may have mellowed through the years but did not lose his ardor. In 1992 John teamed up with German Michael Stich to win the doubles title at Wimbledon in dramatic fashion with a 19-17 fifth set. He retired from the men's tour in 1993 and became a tennis sportscaster for the USA Network. In 1994, John began playing on the Worldwide Senior Tennis Circuit. He was in-ducted into the International Tennis Hall of Fame in 1999. He was also named captain of the U.S. Davis Cup team in that same year, but he resigned from the position in 2000. A man of many interests, John is also the owner of an art gallery in New York City and is involved with many charities through his own foundation.

Summary

Recognized as an unusually complex individual, John McEnroe was a fierce competitor who expected perfection from himself on the court. Considered by many authorities to be one of the true geniuses of tennis, John left an indelible mark on the game that he loved. He will be remembered as one of the best doubles players to ever play the game. His impact on tennis goes beyond just the court. Always forthright and articulate, John injected fresh and sometimes controversial ideas into tennis as well. He was a unique kind of champion who asked for better from himself and from those who dared to stand in his way.

R. Baird Shuman

Additional Sources:

Drucker, Joel. "Mac the Nice." *Tennis* 35 (June, 1999): S8-11.

Esterow, Milton. "John McEnroe: From Center Court to Soho." *ARTnews* 95 (April, 1996): 114-117.

Evans, Richard. *McEnroe, Taming the Talent.* Lexington, Mass.: S. Greene, 1990.

Leand, Andrea. "Watch Your Back Mac." *Tennis* 36 (February, 2000): 8-10.

Lidz, Franz. "An Invasion of Privacy." *Sports Illustrated* 85 (September 9, 1996): 66-73.

MARK McGWIRE

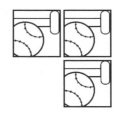

Sport: Baseball

Born: October 1, 1963
Pomona, California

Early Life

Mark David McGwire was born to Ginger and John McGwire, a dentist, in 1963 in Pomona, California. He attended Damien High School in Claremont, California, where he played basketball, golf, and baseball. Mark's younger brother, Dan, would later play as a quarterback for the Seattle Seahawks of the National Football League from 1991 to 1994 and with the Miami Dolphins in 1995.

Graduating from high school in 1981, Mark declined an offer to sign with the Montreal Expos as a pitcher and opted to attend the University of Southern California (USC) in 1982. Although a promising young pitcher at USC, he was switched to third base in his sophomore year because of his hitting ability.

The Road to Excellence

At USC in 1984, Mark hit .387 and established a Pacific-10 Conference season record of 32 home runs. He was named the 1984 College Player of the Year and was selected to the College All-American team. He played on the 1984 United States Olympic team, winning a silver medal.

Drafted by the Oakland Athletics, Mark chose to forego his senior year at USC. He played two full seasons in the minor leagues, spending 1985 with Modesto, California, and 1986 with Huntsville, Alabama, and Tacoma, Washington. At the end of the 1986 season, he was called up to the major leagues and played in eighteen games for the Athletics.

After making numerous errors at third base, Mark was switched to first base by the

Athletics in 1987. His 49 home runs in 1987 established a major league record for the most home runs ever hit by a rookie. His .618 slugging percentage also set the American League record for a rookie. Mark tied the major league record for most home runs in two consecutive games

Mark McGwire in May, 2000. This home run tied him with Mickey Mantle for the eighth-highest number of career homers, 536.

STATISTICS

Season	GP	AB	Hits	2B	3B	HR	Runs	RBI	BA	SA
1986	18	53	10	1	0	3	10	9	.189	.377
1987	151	557	161	28	4	**49**	97	118	.289	**.618**
1988	155	550	143	22	1	32	87	99	.260	.478
1989	143	490	113	17	0	33	74	95	.231	.467
1990	156	523	123	16	0	39	87	108	.235	.489
1991	154	483	97	22	0	22	62	75	.201	.383
1992	139	467	125	22	0	42	87	104	.268	**.585**
1993	27	84	28	6	0	9	16	24	.333	.726
1994	47	135	34	3	0	9	26	25	.252	.474
1995	104	317	87	13	0	39	75	90	.274	.685
1996	130	423	132	21	0	**52**	104	113	.312	**.731**
1997	156	540	148	27	0	58	86	123	.274	.646
1998	155	509	152	21	0	**70**	130	147	.299	**.752**
1999	153	521	145	21	1	**65**	118	**147**	.278	.697
2000	89	236	72	8	0	32	60	73	.305	.746
Totals	1,777	5,888	1,570	248	6	554	1,119	1,350	.267	.593

Notes: Boldface indicates statistical leader. GP = games played; AB = at bats; 2B = doubles; 3B = triples; HR = home runs; RBI = runs batted in; BA = batting average; SA = slugging average

when he hit 3 on June 27, 1987, and 2 the following night. He was named the 1987 American League Rookie of the Year by the Baseball Writers' Association of America.

The Emerging Champion

With more experience, Mark became a very selective hitter at the plate. He learned to drive the ball in clutch situations and take equal satisfaction in reaching base on a walk. Mark was selected to the American League All-Star Team eight times between 1987 and 1997. Although he helped lead the Athletics to a number of postseason appearances, he never performed very well in the playoffs or the World Series. In four American League Championship Series (1988, 1989, 1990, 1992), he hit .258 with 3 home runs and 11 runs batted in (RBIs). During three World Series (1988, 1989, and 1990), he managed only a meager .188 average with 1 home run.

Mark worked hard to improve his fielding and won the Gold Glove for American League first basemen in 1990 and 1992. He was named the first baseman on the *Sporting News* American League Silver Slugger Team in 1992, 1996, and 1998. During much of the 1993 and 1994 seasons, Mark was sidelined with injuries. In 1995, he made a resounding comeback, hitting 39 home runs with 90 RBIs in only 104 games.

Mark's home-run production between 1996 and 1999 was truly amazing. In 1996, he clubbed 52 home runs, batted .312, had a .730 slugging percentage, and drove in 113 runs. He became the first major league player to hit 50 home runs in fewer than 140 games. Playing in 105 games with the Athletics in 1997, he hit 34 home runs with 81 RBIs.

In July, 1997, he was traded to the St. Louis Cardinals. Mark then clouted 24 home runs in 59 games, bringing his home-run total in 1997 to 58—the most home runs hit in the major leagues in a season since Roger Maris hit 61 in 1961. Ironically, although he led the major leagues in home runs for the season, he was not listed

RECORDS AND MILESTONES

1987	Set record for home runs hit by a rookie (49)
	Set American League rookie record for slugging average (.618)
	Tied major league record for most home runs in two consecutive games (3 and 2)
1998	400th major league home run; reached the mark in fewer games than any player before him
	Most home runs in a single season (70)
	Set National League record for walks in a season (162)
1999	500th major league home run; fastest player to reach the mark
1997-99	Averaged 64.3 home runs per season

among the home run leaders in either league. Mark was selected as the 1997 Sportsman of the Year by *The Sporting News*.

Continuing the Story

Early in the 1998 season, Mark hit his four hundredth career major league home run, reaching that plateau faster than any other player in history. He went on to shatter the major league record for home runs in a season by hitting 70. He hit number 62 on September 8 to surpass the record of Roger Maris. Throughout the record-setting period, Mark showed his humility, as he paid his respect to the Maris family and to Sammy Sosa of the Chicago Cubs, who challenged Mark by hitting 66 home runs during the same season.

The home-run chase between Mark and Sosa captivated people throughout the world and re-invigorated the game of baseball, which had been slumping since the player strike in 1994. Mark's 1998 statistics also included a .299 batting average, 147 RBIs, and a .752 slugging percentage. He homered every 7.3 at bats and set the National League record of 162 walks in a season. With such a super season, Mark was selected as the Major League Player of the Year in 1998. He finished second to Sosa in the balloting for the National League most valuable player award.

In 1999, Mark reached the 500 home-run mark. Again, it was faster than anyone else in major league history. The achievement also made him the first player to reach multi-hundred homer totals in consecutive seasons. He went on to hit 65 home runs, bat .278, and drive in 147 runs. He played for the National League in the 1998 and 1999 All-Star games. Mark was named to the United States Baseball All-Time Team in 1999. In 2000, he was plagued with tendinitis in his knee and back pain and played in only eighty-nine games, hitting 32 home runs and batting .305. He started the 2001 season but went back on the disabled list after only a few games. When he returned to the lineup two months later, he hit a home run in his first game. He then re-

HONORS AND AWARDS	
1984	College Player of the Year College All-American Silver Medal with U.S. Olympic baseball team
1987	American League Rookie of the Year
1987-1992, 1995-1997	American League All-Star Team
1990, 1992	American League Gold Glove, first base
1992, 1996, 1998	*Sporting News* American League Silver Slugger Team
1997	*Sporting News* Sportsman of the Year
1998	Major League Player of the Year
1998-2000	National League All-Star Team
1999	U.S. Baseball All-Time Team
2000	Major League Baseball All-Century Team

sumed his climb up the list of all-time leaders in career home runs.

Summary

Mark McGwire is one of the greatest pure-power hitters to play in the major leagues, being the all-time leader in home runs hit per time at bat. He is the only player to hit 50 or more home runs in four consecutive seasons and set the single-season mark of 70. Mark was selected as a member of Major League Baseball's All-Century Team.

Alvin K. Benson

Additional Sources:

Allen, Bob, and Bill Gilbert. *The Five Hundred Home Run Club: Baseball's Sixteen Greatest Home Run Hitters from Babe Ruth to Mark McGwire.* Champaign, Ill.: Sports Publishing, 2000.

Gallagher, Jim. *Mark McGwire.* Bear, Del.: Mitchell Lane, 2000.

Noden, Merrell, ed. *Home Run Heroes: Mark McGwire and Sammy Sosa and a Season for the Ages.* New York: Simon & Schuster, 1998.

Stewart, Mark. *Mark McGwire: Home-Run King.* Chicago: Children's Press, 1999.

Stewart, Mark, and Mike Kennedy. *Home Run Heroes: Mark McGwire and Sammy Sosa.* Brookfield, Conn.: Millbrook Press, 1999.

KEVIN McHALE

Sport: Basketball

Born: December 19, 1957
      Hibbing, Minnesota

Early Life

Kevin Edward McHale was born in Hibbing, Minnesota, on December 19, 1957, to Paul Mc-

Courtesy NBA

Hale, an "iron ranger" who loaded ore from Minnesota's Mesabi Iron Range for the U.S. Steel Corporation, and his wife, Josephine.

Kevin grew up playing hockey, yet once he got to Hibbing High School—which also had produced National Basketball Association (NBA) star Dick Garmaker and pop-music icon Bob Dylan—he gravitated to basketball, as he shot upward to 6 feet 10 inches. In his senior year, the Hibbing High Bluejackets, led by Kevin's superior play at the high post, reached the state finals. Although courted by a number of collegiate basketball powers, Kevin opted to stay in state to attend the University of Minnesota.

The Road to Excellence

From 1976 to 1980, Kevin helped to make Minnesota a force in college basketball. Playing as a power forward, Kevin led Minnesota into the National Invitational Tournament (NIT) finals in his senior year. In 1979 and 1980, Kevin was named Minnesota's most valuable player; he was also elected to the All-Big Ten Conference team.

In 1980, the Boston Celtics of the National Basketball Association (NBA) made the highly touted Minnesotan the third choice overall in the NBA draft. When queried about Boston's decision, he replied with typical drollery, "Where else would a six-ten, white, Irish Catholic kid want to play?"

The Emerging Champion

Kevin had an immediate impact on the Celtics. Boston head coach Bill Fitch made the freshman the team's "sixth man." In Boston, the sixth man had become a venerated position previously filled by such stalwarts as Frank Ramsey, John Havlicek, and Paul Silas. Kevin's main job was to enter each game, usually late in the first quarter, to spell a starter who was in foul trouble or in need of a breather.

Opponents soon found him a worthy adversary. Kevin's virtually unstoppable fade-away jumper, effective shot-blocking, and aggressive rebounding at both ends of the court made him equally effective on defense and offense. In 1980-81, his first year, Kevin played in all eighty-two regular-season contests and averaged 10.0 points a game, a performance that earned him selection to the NBA's All-Rookie team. Kevin also played a key role in Boston's six-game defeat of the Houston Rockets for the 1981 NBA championship.

During the early and mid-1980's, Boston— bolstered by superstar forward Larry Bird and such solid performers as center Robert Parish, power forward Cedric Maxwell, and guard Dennis Johnson—was one of the NBA's dominant franchises. Kevin became an increasingly vital part of the Celtics' success story. During his first four years, Kevin appeared in all eighty-two games of each regular season. During the same span, his scoring average rose from 10.0 points per game in 1980-81 to 13.6 in 1981-82, 14.1 in 1982-83, and 18.4 in 1984-85. Kevin's status as one of the NBA's elite players was confirmed after the 1983-84 and 1984-85 seasons, when he was selected as the NBA's best sixth man.

Kevin also enjoyed successful stints as a starter during periods when Larry Bird or Robert Parish were sidelined with injuries. In 1985-86, finally a regular starter, he broke the 20-points-per-game barrier with a 21.3 scoring average. His career personal best came during the 1986-87 season, when his per-game scoring average zoomed to 26.1 while he scored 2,008 points.

Continuing the Story

Under coach K. C. Jones, who had replaced Bill Fitch at the onset of the 1983-84 season, the Celtics continued to thrill their fans, who thronged to the Boston Garden to witness the heroics of Bird, Parish, McHale, and company. In 1984, the Celtics topped their West Coast rivals, the Los Angeles Lakers, to take another NBA championship. Though the Lakers returned the favor by besting Boston for the 1985 NBA crown, the Celtics again ascended to the top spot by defeating the Houston Rockets in 1986. Once more in 1986-87, Jones swept his troops to the NBA's Eastern Conference summit, qualifying them for another joust for the championship, and again the Celtics were up against the Lakers. In an-

STATISTICS

Season	GP	FGM	FG%	FTM	FT%	Reb.	Ast.	TP	PPG
1980-81	82	335	.533	108	.679	359	55	818	10.0
1981-82	82	465	.531	187	.754	556	91	1,117	13.6
1982-83	82	483	.541	193	.717	553	104	1,159	14.1
1983-84	82	587	.556	336	.765	610	104	1,511	18.4
1984-85	79	605	.570	355	.760	712	141	1,565	19.8
1985-86	68	561	.574	326	.776	551	181	1,448	21.3
1986-87	77	790	**.604**	428	.836	763	198	2,008	26.1
1987-88	64	550	**.604**	346	.797	536	171	1,446	22.6
1988-89	78	661	.546	436	.818	637	172	1,758	22.5
1989-90	82	648	.549	393	.893	677	172	1,712	20.9
1990-91	68	504	.553	228	.829	480	126	1,251	18.4
1991-92	56	323	.509	134	.822	330	82	780	13.9
1992-93	71	298	.459	164	.841	358	73	762	10.7
Totals	971	6,810	.554	3,634	.798	7,122	1,670	17,335	17.0

Notes: Boldface indicates statistical leader. GP = games played; FGM = field goals made; FG% = field goal percentage; FTM = free throws made; FT% = free throw percentage; Reb. = rebounds; Ast. = assists; TP = total points; PPG = points per game

other hard-fought campaign, Los Angeles beat Boston in six games to take the 1987 NBA title.

During the Celtics' glory days of the 1980's, Kevin continued to amass impressive numbers and honors. A respected shot-blocker and re-bounder, Kevin was tapped for the NBA's All-De-fensive First Team in 1986-87, 1987-88, and 1988-89. In 1987-88, his .604 field goal percentage led the NBA. One of pro basketball's most accurate shooters, Kevin in 1986-87 became the first NBA player to shoot over 60 percent from the field and 80 percent from the foul line. In 1989-1990, Kevin, Larry Bird, and Magic Johnson were the only NBA players to shoot over 50 percent from the floor and 90 percent from the free-throw line. Kevin also was chosen to play in seven NBA All-Star games.

Playing thirteen seasons for the Celtics, Kevin scored 17,335 points, collected 7,122 rebounds, blocked 1,690 shots, and had a .554 completion percentage from the field. Players and coaches agree that he was probably the most difficult low-post player to defend in the history of the NBA. His variety of drop steps, head fakes, pump fakes, hook shots, shovel shots, and fadeaway jumpers always kept the best defenders guessing what was coming next.

After retiring as a player, Kevin joined the Minnesota Timberwolves as a television analyst and special assistant during the 1993-1994 sea-son. He became assistant general manager of the Timberwolves in August, 1994, and continued as one of their broadcasters. In May, 1995, he was promoted to vice president of basketball opera-tions for the organization and was instrumental in adding young stars, such as Kevin Garnett, to the roster. It quickly paid dividends as the Wolves reached the NBA playoffs for the first time in their history in 1997.

As part of the celebration of the golden anni-versary of the NBA in 1996, Kevin was selected as a member of the NBA's 50 Greatest Players of All Time Team. As further recognition of his achieve-ments in basketball, Kevin was inducted into the Naismith Memorial Basketball Hall of Fame in 1999.

Summary

Kevin McHale finished his thirteen-year ca-reer with Boston at the end of the 1992-1993 sea-son. He had become the fourth-leading scorer in Boston's distinguished history, behind only Havlicek, Bird, and Parish. His now-retired num-ber 32 hangs from the rafters of Boston's Fleet Center, a tribute to his unique abilities as a low-post scoring machine and to his exuberant per-sonality.

Chuck Berg

Additional Sources:

Bjarkman, Peter C. *The Biographical History of Bas-ketball.* Chicago: Masters Press, 1998.

_____. *The Boston Celtics Encyclopedia.* Cham-paign-Urbana, Ill.: Sports Publishing, 1999.

Doling, Nick, Chris Doling, and David Check. *Basketball Stars: The Greatest Players in the History of the Game.* New York: Black Dog and Leventhal, 1997.

Ryan, Bob. *The Boston Celtics: The History, Legends, and Images of America's Most Celebrated Team.* New York: Gallery Books, 1989.

Shouler, Kenneth A. *The Experts Pick Basketball's Best Fifty Players in the Last Fifty Years.* Lenexa, Kans.: Addax, 1998.

HONORS AND AWARDS

1979	Gold Medal, Pan-American Games Gold Medal, World University Games
1981	NBA All-Rookie Team
1983, 1989-90	NBA All-Defensive Second Team
1984, 1986-91	NBA All-Star Team
1984-85	NBA Sixth Man Award
1986-88	NBA All-Defensive First Team
1987	All-NBA First Team
1996	NBA 50 Greatest Players of All Time Team
1999	Inducted into Naismith Memorial Basketball Hall of Fame Uniform number 32 retired by Boston Celtics

REGGIE McKENZIE

Sport: Football

Born: July 27, 1950
Detroit, Michigan

Early Life

Reginald McKenzie was born on July 27, 1950, in Detroit, Michigan. His family's home, however, was just outside the city in Highland Park. Reggie was one of eight children of Nettie and Henry McKenzie. Like many in Highland Park, Reggie's family was poor, but Reggie's parents worked hard to see that their children made the most of their opportunities. They encouraged Reggie to be a positive part of his community by participating in such organized recreation as Little League and Boy Scout Troop 1286.

Scouting was an important part of Reggie's early life. Scout Master Sam Smith taught Reggie about leadership and stressed the importance of caring for others and believing in oneself. Reggie remained an active member of the Boy Scouts right through his years at Highland Park High School.

The Road to Excellence

At Highland Park High School, Reggie excelled as a two-way football star, playing both offensive and defensive tackle. He credits his line coach Jim Bobbitt with encouraging the kind of positive thinking and self-confidence that gave him the goal of becoming a professional football star. It was that kind of attitude that helped Reggie deal with the disappointment he felt when a recruiter from Michigan State Uni-

versity told him that he did not have what it took to be a major college football player. The University of Michigan disagreed, however, and soon afterward offered Reggie an athletic scholarship.

As an offensive guard on a Michigan Wolverines team that ran the ball often and with great success, Reggie gained considerable national attention. During his four years at Michigan, Reggie played on two Rose Bowl teams and was selected to play in the Hula Bowl and College All-

Reggie McKenzie of the Buffalo Bills, in 1977.

Star games. In 1972, after earning All-Big Ten honors as a junior and senior, Reggie was named a consensus All-American. Just as there were those who questioned his ability to play college football, there were a few professional scouts who wondered if Reggie's lack of pass-blocking experience at Michigan would limit him as a professional. The Buffalo Bills, however, never doubted his ability and were surprised and pleased when they were able to draft him in the second round of the 1972 National Football League (NFL) draft.

The Emerging Champion

When Reggie joined the Bills in 1972, the team was in desperate need of offensive line help. Even though "the Juice," O. J. Simpson, one of the greatest running backs ever, was a member of the Bills backfield the previous three seasons, the team compiled disappointing 4-10, 3-10-1, and 1-13 records. That began to change when Reggie joined the team.

It was after his first professional game, a pre-season match in Chicago against the Bears, that Reggie realized his new team also needed a team leader. In that game, the Bills held a commanding 24-0 half-time lead, but the Bears rallied and ended up tying the game 24-24. In the locker room afterward, a disgusted Reggie announced that he would not be a part of a team that just quits. In his rookie season, Reggie not only became a starter but, by most accounts, the most solid performer on the offensive line. Although their 4-9-1 record in 1972 was not much to speak of, it was the best the team had done since 1966.

That season, behind Reggie's lead blocks, O. J. led the NFL in rushing with 1,251 yards.

During the off-season, Reggie suggested to O. J. that, because the offensive line blocked well enough in 1972 for him to gain 1,251 yards, they should be able to get him 2,000 yards in 1973. When training camp opened, Reggie told the rest of his teammates his new goal. Most, including O. J., thought Reggie's dream was farfetched.

By the seventh game of the 1973 season, however, O. J. had already rushed for more than 1,000 yards. Suddenly, the Bills' players began to believe in Reggie's prediction. In the final game of the season, O. J. needed 197 yards to hit the 2,000-yard mark. Behind the blocking of Reggie and the rest of the offensive line, O. J. gained 200 yards and became the first running back to rush for more than 2,000 yards in a season. For his efforts, Reggie, in just his second professional season, was named All-NFL by the Associated Press (AP), Professional Football Writers of America (PFWA), and *Football News*.

Continuing the Story

A fixture in the Bills starting lineup from his first game of his rookie season, Reggie played in 142 consecutive games, tying a team record. His streak came to an end in 1981 only after a serious knee injury sidelined him for the season's final ten games.

In 1983, after eleven seasons in a Buffalo Bills uniform, Reggie was traded to the Seattle Seahawks. There he rejoined former Bills head coach Chuck Knox. Knox, who had coached the Bills from 1978 until 1982, was known for his successful run-oriented offenses. When he traded for Reggie, he knew he got a player who not only could demonstrate his "run-offense" first-hand but was a proven team leader as well.

Although new and nagging old injuries began to take their toll, Reggie managed to play twenty-four of a possible thirty-two games with the Seahawks. His inspirational play earned him respect and admiration from fans and players alike.

Summary

Although Reggie McKenzie retired as an active player after the 1984 season, he was quickly moved into a management position with the Seahawks as director of marketing and sales.

HONORS AND AWARDS

1971-72	All-Big Ten Conference Team
1972	Chicago College All-Star Team Hula Bowl All-Star Team Consensus All-American
1973	Wisconsin Pro Football Writers NFL Top Blocking Lineman Associated Press All-NFL Team *Sporting News* All-AFC Team Professional Football Writers of America All-NFL Team *Football News* All-NFL Team
1973, 1980	United Press International All-AFC Team
1983	University of Michigan Second-Fifty-Year All-Time Team

Knowing the importance of positive role models and opportunities in education, Reggie founded and would continue to run the Reggie McKenzie Foundation, which tutors needy Detroit-area youngsters in reading and life skills so they too might someday realize their potential. The foundation has been very successful and has received a number of awards for its work.

Joseph Horrigan

Additional Sources:

Maiorana, Salvatore. *Relentless: The Hard-Hitting History of Buffalo Bills Football.* Lenexa, Kans.: Quality Sports, 1994.

"Reggie McKenzie." http://www.geocities.com/bflobuzrd_2000/reggie.html.

Rothaus, James R. *The Buffalo Bills.* Mankato, Minn.: Creative Education, 1981.

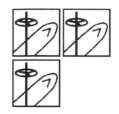

TAMARA McKINNEY

Sport: Skiing

Born: October 16, 1962
Lexington, Kentucky

Early Life

Tamara McKinney was born in Lexington, Kentucky, on October 16, 1962. She was the youngest in a family of seven children. Her father, Rigan, had been an outstanding steeplechase jockey, and Tamara was reared on a horse farm. She became an accomplished horseback rider.

Tamara's mother, Frances, took her children to rented winter homes in the Lake Tahoe area. There Tamara learned to ski, as did her brothers and sisters, four of whom would also make the United States ski team.

Frances and her children often lived in cabins without heat or running water during these winters near Lake Tahoe, and Tamara's education suffered, as she often took only correspondence courses.

The Road to Excellence

As Tamara's talent for skiing emerged, her sister, Sheila, sustained a serious accident. While racing in a downhill, she crashed and slammed into a post. She was left partially paralyzed, was unconcious for a month, and when she came to was unable to walk or speak. She recovered slowly, although she gave up competitive skiing.

Tamara pressed on with her skiing, though, and a year later she made the U.S. ski team at the age of fifteen.

She raced in her first World Cup race during the 1977-1978 season, although her performance did not stand out. The following season, however, she finished third in her first big European race. Publicity roared around Tamara, and she was proclaimed an up-and-coming star in World Cup skiing. She was only seventeen.

Tamara McKinney during the World Ski Championships in 1989.

Tamara slumped, though, and she failed to finish in her next nine races. More disappointments waited ahead for Tamara. She was a highly touted prospect for the U.S. team at the Lake Placid Winter Olympics the following season. Tamara fell, however, in both the slalom and giant slalom events during the games in Lake Placid, ending her hopes for a medal.

Still, Tamara pressed on, and in the 1980-1981 season, she charged back onto the World Cup circuit. Tamara won three World Cup giant slalom races that year, and she captured the World Cup giant slalom championship.

The Emerging Champion

Finally, Tamara had established herself as a world-class skier. Yet, the ups and downs continued, in her personal life as well as in her skiing career. In 1981, her father suffered a stroke. Soon after, Tamara broke her right hand, and she had to ski during much of the 1981-1982 season with her hand in a cast. She taped her ski pole to the cast and was able to continue skiing, but the season was essentially lost. She won nothing that year.

When Tamara recovered from her hand injury, her career went on the rise again. She skied superbly during the 1982-1983 season and won the overall World Cup title. She was the first American woman ever to win the World Cup.

Tamara's skiing style was light-footed, quick, and fast. She was a small woman at 5 feet 4 inches tall and about 117 pounds. After the World Cup victory she began to train to develop more strength in order to gain better control. She began karate workouts to increase what she called her body awareness. In addition, she began lifting weights, borrowing a training program from the Dallas Cowboys football team.

As times were good in 1983, so they went bad again in 1984, as Tamara's life continued its series of ups and downs. Favored to win the giant slalom at the Winter Olympics in Sarejevo, Yugoslavia, she finished fourth. In the slalom at Sarejevo she fell when she hooked a gate with a ski.

She did, however, win the World Cup standings that season. Tamara has said she continued skiing and continued competing because it made her happy. She said she just wanted to have fun and do her best.

MAJOR CHAMPIONSHIPS

Year	Competition	Event	Place
1979	World Cup	Overall	25th
		Giant slalom	13th
		Slalom	23d
1980	World Cup	Overall	14th
		Giant slalom	14th
		Slalom	10th
1981	World Cup	Overall	6th
		Giant slalom	1st
		Slalom	7th
1982	World Championships	Giant slalom	6th
	World Cup	Overall	9th
		Giant slalom	4th
		Slalom	12th
1983	World Cup	Overall	1st
		Giant slalom	1st
		Slalom	2d
1984	Olympic Games	Giant slalom	4th
	World Cup	Overall	3d
		Giant slalom	3d
		Slalom	1st
		Combined	9th
1985	World Championships	Slalom	3d
		Downhill	22d
		Combined	3d
	World Cup	Overall	8th
		Giant slalom	11th
		Slalom	2d
		Combined	17th
1986	World Cup	Overall	24th
		Giant slalom	20th
		Slalom	14th
		Super-giant slalom	22d
		Combined	28th
1987	World Championships	Giant slalom	18th
		Combined	3d
	World Cup	Overall	6th
		Giant slalom	10th
		Slalom	2d
		Super-giant slalom	22d
1989	World Championships	Combined	1st
		Downhill	3d

She continued to ski well over the next several seasons, but it was the European women who began to dominate the World Cup. Although Tamara earned bronze medals in the overall at both the 1985 and 1987 World Alpine Ski Championships, she could not catch the best Europeans.

In 1985, tragedy struck when Tamara's father died. He had been sick since his stroke four years earlier. Still Tamara persevered.

HONORS, AWARDS, AND RECORDS	
1980, 1984, 1989	Women's U.S. Olympic ski team
1983	First American woman to win the World Cup (two gold medals in the overall and giant slalom, and a silver medal in the slalom)
1989	First American woman to win the World Championships (a gold medal in the combined, and a bronze medal in the downhill)

Continuing the Story

The 1988 Winter Olympics in Calgary approached. They would be Tamara's third Olympics. The year got worse and worse for her, though. Tamara broke her left ankle early in the season. Although she would be able to ski at Calgary, she was not fully recovered when the Olympics arrived.

Her Olympic performance was again disappointing. She did not finish in either the slalom or the giant slalom. Then later in the year her mother died of cancer, and a brother, McLean, committed suicide. Another brother was injured in a helicopter accident. Tamara's up-and-down life had hit perhaps its lowest point.

She came back to ski again in the 1988-1989 season, however. At the 1989 World Alpine Ski Championships, she came from behind to capture the gold medal in the women's overall. Chasing Swiss star Vremi Schneider, who had won ten consecutive slalom and giant slalom races that season, Tamara clinched the victory in the downhill event—even though she seldom raced the downhill.

Schneider had started the downhill eighth, and her time, though not exceptional, kept her in first place in the overall standings, since she had skied so strongly in the slalom and giant slalom. Few thought Tamara could catch Schneider, especially in the downhill. Tamara started sixteenth, but halfway down the course she had the second-best time in the event. The crowd began to roar. She said later that she could hear the crowd, a rarity in the downhill, in which racers travel at 50 or 60 miles per hour. Tamara finished in third place in the race, but nearly 2 seconds ahead of Schneider, a big enough margin to earn her the first-place overall title. Tamara's gold medal was the first by an American skier in the World Alpine Ski Championships since 1985.

After more injuries, including a broken leg in 1989, Tamara decided to retire in 1991, making her home in Squaw Valley, California. She continued to participate in various skiing events, including the MCI Relays in 1999, where she and U.S. teammates Phil Mahre and Doug Lewis competed against ski legends Franz Klammer and Franz Weber.

Summary

During her eleven-year career, Tamara McKinney won eighteen World Cup races, more than any other American, male or female, and she was the first American woman to win the World Cup combined title. Her career—indeed, her life—was a series of ups and downs, of triumphs and disappointments, but she continued through the bad times as well as the good. Most of all, she skied for fun and to enjoy herself, and to do her best.

Robert Passaro

Additional Sources:

Campbell, Stu, and Dave Merriam. "Something in the Way She Moves." *Ski* 59, no. 4 (1994).

Hickok, Ralph. *A Who's Who of Sports Champions: Their Stories and Records.* Boston: Houghton Mifflin, 1995.

Levinson, David, and Karen Christenson, eds. *Encyclopedia of World Sport: From Ancient to Present.* Santa Barbara, Calif.: ABC-CLIO, 1996.

Wallechinsky, David. *The Complete Book of the Olympics.* Boston: Little, Brown and Company, 1991.

1734

JIM McMAHON

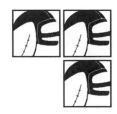

Sport: Football

Born: August 21, 1959
Jersey City, New Jersey

Early Life

James Robert McMahon was born on August 21, 1959, to Roberta (Williams) McMahon and James Francis McMahon in Jersey City, New Jersey. Jim was the second child in a family that would grow to six children. Jim's mother Roberta, a Mormon, and father James Francis, a Catholic, moved the family to San Jose, California, when Jim was three years old.

When Jim was halfway through high school, the McMahons moved again. Jim started his junior year of high school in Roy, Utah, and he quickly made a name for himself in his new town. Jim lettered in three sports, baseball, basketball, and football. He was named All-State most valuable player in football in 1977; as a Catholic, Jim would have attended the University of Notre Dame if he had been recruited by the school. He was not, however, and, noticing the pass-oriented offense at Brigham Young University, Jim found himself playing college football as a quarterback in the Western Athletic Conference (WAC).

The Road to Excellence

Jim was obviously a talented young athlete, and his performance with the Cougars at Brigham Young was awesome. In 1978, his sophomore year, he shared the quarterback position, yet he still won All-WAC honors. In 1979, Jim shattered college football records. In one season, Jim passed for more than 4,000 yards and tied two National Collegiate Athletic Association (NCAA) records. He also set thirty-two NCAA total-offense and season-passing records.

In 1980, Jim threw for 47 touchdowns, gaining a total of 4,627 yards with 4,571 yards passing. He gained an average of 385.6 total yards per game

Chicago Bears

and threw for an average of 380.9 yards per game. In the 1980 season alone, Jim passed for more than 300 yards in eleven consecutive games, averaging 10.7 yards per pass attempt. He was chosen All-WAC for the second consecutive year, and his passing totals were the best in the country. He played most of the season with a hyperextended knee that caused him to miss two games, but he played in the July and Senior Bowls and was selected a consensus All-American. At the end of the season, Jim was honored as the country's best signal-caller with the first annual Davey O'Brien National Quarterback Award. As the Cougars' full-time quarterback for two years, Jim threw 81 touchdowns, passing for 8,126 yards. Not surprisingly, the Cougars won WAC titles and Holiday Bowl championships both years.

The Emerging Champion

In Jim's years at Brigham Young, he set fifty-six separate NCAA records; this in itself was a record, as the previous highest total was only eighteen. He threw for 84 touchdowns with 9,723 total yards and 9,536 yards passing. His completion rate at Brigham Young surpassed 64 percent, while his interception rate stayed at less than 3 percent.

In the first round of the 1982 National Football League (NFL) draft, Jim was picked fifth, the first choice of the Chicago Bears. His ability to throw repeatedly and accurately carried him through seven years with the Bears in which he threw for 67 touchdowns, completing 874 passes for 11,203 yards. In 1984, Jim received a high 97.8 rating as quarterback, but after nine games he was knocked out for the season with a lacerated kidney.

Jim was back in great form in 1985. The Bears compiled a 15-1 regular season record, and Jim threw for 15 touchdowns and 2,392 total yards, completing 56.9 percent of his 313 passes. In postseason play, both the New York Giants and the Los Angeles Rams lost to the unstoppable Bears, who dominated the New England Patriots in Super Bowl XX, winning 46-10. In the Super Bowl, Jim threw 2 touchdown passes, completing 12 of 20 passes for 256 yards. He became a national celebrity, as much for his trademark headbands and outrageous behavior as for his football talent. The Bears were compared to the greatest NFL teams ever, and it seemed that Jim and his teammates were on top of the world.

Continuing the Story

Jim's body, however, was not going to be able to take much more. In 1986, he was out frequently with injuries, although he threw 5 touchdown passes in six games. The Bears, with their awesome Buddy Ryan-coached defense, hardly missed a beat in the regular season, going 14-2

STATISTICS

Season	GP	PA	PC	Pct.	Yds.	Avg.	TD	Int.
1982	8	210	120	57.1	1,501	7.15	9	7
1983	14	295	175	59.3	2,184	7.40	12	13
1984	9	143	85	59.4	1,146	8.01	8	2
1985	13	313	178	56.9	2,392	7.64	15	11
1986	6	150	77	51.3	995	6.63	5	8
1987	7	210	125	59.5	1,639	7.81	12	8
1988	9	192	114	59.4	1,346	7.01	6	7
1989	12	318	176	55.3	2,132	6.70	10	10
1990	5	9	6	66.7	63	7.00	0	0
1991	12	311	187	60.1	2,239	7.20	12	11
1992	4	43	22	51.2	279	6.49	1	2
1993	12	331	200	60.4	1,967	5.94	9	8
1994	3	43	23	53.5	219	5.09	1	3
1995	1	1	1	100.0	6	6.00	0	0
1996	5	4	3	75.0	39	9.75	0	0
Totals	120	2,573	1,492	58.0	18,147	7.05	100	90

Notes: GP = games played; PA = passes attempted; PC = passes completed; Pct. = percent completed; Yds. = yards; Avg. = average yards per attempt; TD = touchdowns; Int. = interceptions

and again winning the Central Division title.

Jim, however, could not play in the post-season. After a December game against the Bears' old rivals, the Green Bay Packers, Jim's shoulder required surgery. The Bears were not the same without him and failed to repeat as Super Bowl champions.

In the next two seasons, Jim struggled to stay in the lineup. He showed flashes of brilliance, but his best days were clearly behind him. Moreover, he quarreled publicly with Bears coach Mike Ditka, and after the 1988 season he was traded to the San Diego Chargers.

After only one season as a starter at San Diego, he moved on to Philadelphia and, after three seasons there, to the Minnesota Vikings. He had become primarily a backup quarterback; as his career wound down, he devoted more time to his family. He had married Nancy Daines in 1982, and they had two children, Ashley and Sean. He then spent one season with Arizona and two more with Green Bay and retired from pro football at the end of the 1996 season. In the next few years Jim appeared in Sherwin Williams commercials presented during Super Bowls XXXIII and XXXIV and the Nike "Fun Police" commercials with Gary Payton. He also participated in several charitable events, including the Charity

---

HONORS AND AWARDS
1981 O'Brien National Quarterback Award
1982 United Press International NFC Rookie of the Year
1985 NFL Pro Bowl
1991 *Pro Football Weekly* Comeback Player of the Year

Golf Tournament in Arizona and the Children's Miracle Network activities.

Summary

Jim McMahon's determined career in football was perhaps best characterized by his tremendous spirit and athleticism. His natural athletic talent combined with his leadership skills, intelligence, and determination helped make him one of the great players of his era.

Alicia Neumann

Additional Sources:

Dufresne, Jim. *Quarterbacks: McMahon, Eason, Elway, Fouts*. Worthington, Ohio: Willowisp, 1986.

Hewitt, Brian. *Jim McMahon, The Zany Quarterback*. Chicago: Children's Press, 1986.

McMahon, Jim, and Bob Verdi. *McMahon!* New York: Warner Books, 1986.

STEVE McNAIR

Sport: Football

Born: February 14, 1973
Mount Olive, Mississippi

Early Life

Steve LaTreal McNair was born in Mount Olive, Mississippi, in 1973. His mother, Lucille, gave him the nickname "Monk" (short for "monkey") as a child because of his ability to climb trees near his home. His older brother, Fred, played quarterback for the Arena Football League Florida Bobcats.

Steve attended Mount Olive High School, where he excelled at football and participated in basketball and baseball. He played quarterback and defensive end, tying a state career record with 30 interceptions (15 in his senior year alone). In his last year he was named a high school All-American selection by *Prep Magazine* and made the All-State team. Following graduation, he was recruited primarily as a defensive back and chose to attend Alcorn State University, where he went on to become one of the top quarterbacks in the National Collegiate Amateur Athletic (NCAA) history.

The Road to Excellence

As a freshman at Alcorn State in 1991, Steve rushed for 242 yards, passed for 2,895 yards, and had 30 touchdowns (6 rushing, 24 passing). *Sports Illustrated* named him their Offensive Player of the Year in 1991 for all NCAA divisions. He was also named to

the All-Southwestern Athletic Conference First Team.

By the time Steve was a senior he had become the only player in NCAA history to gain over 16,000 yards (16,823) in total offense during his career. He had earned the nickname "Air McNair" for his passing skills. He also set a colle-

Steve McNair looks to pass to a fellow Tennessee Titan during a wild card playoff game in January, 2000.

giate record by averaging 400.5 yards in total offense per game, and he threw for a total of 119 career touchdowns. He broke every Alcorn State game, season, and career passing and total offense record.

In 1994, Steve made his fourth consecutive All-Southwestern Athletic Conference Team and was a unanimous Associated Press All-American choice. He won the Walter Payton Award for the top NCAA Division I-AA player, was awarded the Eddie Robinson Trophy for the top player in the black college ranks, and finished third in the Heisman Trophy balloting. He was the first quarterback and third overall player selected in the 1995 National Football League (NFL) draft, by the Houston Oilers.

The Emerging Champion

As a rookie Steve was placed on the inactive list as the Oilers' third-string quarterback for most of the season. The management's goal was to bring Steve along slowly as a promising future NFL starting quarterback. He did play in four games (two as a starter) and passed for 569 total yards, with 3 touchdowns and 1 interception. He also rushed for 38 yards on 11 carries.

In 1996, Steve played in nine games and started four times. He completed 61.5 percent of his passes (88 of 143) for 1,197 yards and 4 touchdowns. He rushed for an additional 169 yards on 31 carries with 2 touchdowns.

The owner of the Houston Oilers, Bud Adams, moved the team from Houston, Texas, to Nashville, Tennessee, in 1997 and changed its name to the Tennessee Titans. Steve was the Titans' starting quarterback in sixteen games. He

helped set a team record for the fewest interceptions (13) in a single season. He also led the team in rushing touchdowns (8) and ranked second in team rushing with 674 yards, the third most in NFL history by a quarterback.

Continuing the Story

Steve set career highs in 1998 in passes attempted (492), completions (289), yards (3,228), and passing touchdowns (15). He led all NFL quarterbacks in rushing (599 yards) for the second consecutive season and helped set a new team record for fewest interceptions (10). Steve also gained a reputation as a "comeback player" as he led the team to several last-minute scores during the year.

In 1999, he missed five games because of back surgery, and his backup, Neil O'Donnell, led the Titans so well in his absence that some fans did not want Steve to return immediately as the starter. However, coach Jeff Fisher did name Steve as the starter following his recovery, and he went on to win nine of his eleven starts. In fact, he led the team into the NFL playoffs and the NFL championship game, where the Titans beat the Jacksonville Jaguars 33-14 to advance to the Super Bowl against the St. Louis Rams.

In the 2000 Super Bowl, Steve led his team to a remarkable comeback after trailing the Rams at halftime 16-0. Although he only threw for 214 yards, compared to Rams quarterback Kurt Warner's 414 yards, his performance on critical drives kept the Titans in the game until the last play. He set a Super Bowl record for quarterbacks when he rushed for 64 yards. Unfortunately, Steve and the Titans were stopped one yard short of send-

STATISTICS

Season	GP	PA	PC	Pct.	Yds.	Avg.	TD	Int.
1995	6	80	41	.512	569	7.11	3	1
1996	10	143	88	.615	1,197	8.37	6	4
1997	16	415	216	.520	2,665	6.42	14	13
1998	16	492	289	.587	3,228	6.56	15	10
1999	11	331	187	.565	2,179	6.58	12	8
2000	16	396	248	.626	2,847	7.19	15	13
Totals	75	1,857	1,069	.576	12,685	6.83	65	49

Notes: GP = games played; PA = passes attempted; PC = passes completed; Pct. = percent completed; Yds. = yards; Avg. = average yards per attempt; TD = touchdowns; Int. = interceptions

ing the game into overtime when Kevin Dyson was tackled by Rams linebacker Mike Jones to end the game.

Summary

Steve McNair became one of the best quarterbacks in the NFL after his rookie season in 1995. He is a double threat to defenses because he has a strong arm and is an explosive runner. His athletic skills and competitive nature helped him carry his team and challenge the Rams in one of the most exciting Super Bowls of all time. The Titans looked forward to greater successes for him in the future.

Tinker D. Murray

Additional Sources:

Pompei, Dan. "More Air for McNair." *The Sporting News,* August 7, 2000, 39.

Stewart, Mark. *Steve McNair: Running and Gunning.* Brookfield, Conn.: Millbrook Press, 2001.

JULIANNE McNAMARA

Sport: Gymnastics

Born: October 11, 1965
Flushing, New York

Early Life

Julianne (Juli) Lynn McNamara was born in Flushing, New York, on October 11, 1965. While Juli was in elementary school, her family moved to California and settled near San Francisco. She enrolled in her first gymnastics classes at the

Burlingame (California) Sports Center and was classified as a Class II (Intermediate) gymnast. By 1977, she was competing in the Class I Division and qualified for the state championships, as she had while in Class II.

In 1978, her family moved across San Francisco Bay to Danville. There she met Mas Watanabe, the first of five outstanding coaches who had much to do with Julianne's rapid rise in artistic gymnastics. Unfortunately, the American Gymnastics Center where Mas was coaching fell upon hard times and closed. Juli had no place to practice for some months.

The Road to Excellence

After Juli had resumed practice at a local gymnasium, her first real opportunity came in 1979, when her family decided to send her to the National Academy of Gymnastics in Eugene, Oregon. There she came under the guidance of Linda and Dick Mulvihill, both of whom were later elected to the Gymnastics Hall of Fame. Dick was also the first person elected to the Hall of Fame established by the United States Association of Independent Gymnastics Clubs (USAIGC). Linda was a gymnast who had represented the United States in three Olympiads (1964, 1968, 1972).

Juli had found a level of training that was exactly suited to her ambition to be a top gymnast. Almost immediately, she became a member of the Academy's elite

MAJOR CHAMPIONSHIPS

Year	Competition	Event	Place	Event	Place
1981	U.S. National Championships	All-Around	4th		
	American Cup	All-Around	1st		
	World Championships	All-Around	7th	Balance beam	5th
		Uneven parallel bars	3d	Team	6th
1982	U.S. National Championships	All-Around	2d	Balance beam	1st
		Floor exercise	3d	Vault	4th
	American Cup	All-Around	1st		
	World Championships	All-Around	8th	Vault	3d
		Balance beam	7th		
1983	U.S. National Championships	All-Around	2d	Vault	4th
		Uneven parallel bars	1st		
	American Cup	All-Around	2d		
	World Championships	Uneven parallel bars	7th	Team	7th
		Vault	6th		
1984	U.S. National Championships	All-Around	2d	Balance beam	3d
		Floor exercise	2d	Vault	5th
		Uneven parallel bars	1st		
	Olympic Games	All-Around	4th	Uneven parallel bars	Gold
		Floor exercise	Silver	Team	Silver

team, and in 1980 she won the all-around title at the U.S. Championships, beating her teammate, Tracee Talavera. She had also become a member of the 1980 Olympic team, overcoming an ankle sprain and placing sixth. Unfortunately, 1980 was the year of the U.S. Olympic boycott proclaimed by President Jimmy Carter. None of the U.S. Olympians was able to compete in Moscow. Julianne would have to wait for an Olympic medal, but she was determined to win one.

In five short years, Juli had progressed from a Class II gymnast to an Olympian. She continued to work very hard to maintain her skill level. The World Gymnastics Championships were coming and would also be held in Moscow. This competition was not the target of a boycott, since gymnastics had less press coverage than other sports and was less likely to be used for political purposes than the Olympics.

The Emerging Champion

Juli made the U.S. World Championship team in 1981 and traveled to Moscow. She had concentrated very well upon her specialty, the uneven bars, and tied for the bronze medal competing against strong teams from the Soviet Union, East Germany, and China. Her medal was earned despite her feeling ill and missing one of her most difficult tricks. The fact that she was the first gymnast to compete in the uneven bars finals was also a negative factor. Very often, the judges are particularly strict when awarding scores to the first gymnast in an event. Julianne was one of the few American women to win a medal in international competition when all of the strong Eastern European teams have been present.

In 1982, Juli returned to California to train with the Southern California Acro Teams, better known as the SCATS. The SCATS had previously produced the first U.S. gymnast to win a medal in World Championship competition, Cathy Rigby.

Cathy had been coached by an American pioneer in women's gymnastics, Bud Marquette, who organized the SCATS in Long Beach. Bud had retired, and Juli's new mentor was Don Peters, who had been appointed coach of the 1984 women's Olympic gymnastics team. One of the problems encountered by top gymnasts in the United States has been its failure to fund national teams. Many foreign gymnastics teams receive state funding and provide food, housing, and other benefits for their national sports teams. American athletes, particularly promising women, have moved frequently with little guidance from the national governing body. This pattern was beginning to emerge in the life of the young champion.

1742

Juli progressed with the SCATS and her new coach, learning a number of new elements that would improve her world-class uneven bars routine. Then she heard about Bela Karolyi's new club in Texas. She knew that he was a controversial individual and tough to work with, but he had developed Nadia Comaneci, the Romanian gymnast. She decided at last to go to Karolyi's club early in 1984. She had a new teammate, Mary Lou Retton. She would train harder than ever to achieve her goal—winning an Olympic medal.

Continuing the Story

Julianne had to prepare for two competitions prior to the Olympics in late summer. First was the Championships of the USA in Illinois and then the Olympic trials in Florida. She finished a very close second to Mary Lou Retton in both meets, with as many as four of her former SCATS teammates challenging her all the way. Juli was the best on uneven bars in both of the meets, however.

Her training had resulted in an athletic "peak" by the end of the summer. She was ready for the Olympic Games. Once again, a boycott was established. This time the Soviet Union stayed away, and a number of gymnastically powerful Eastern European countries participated. Many experts are fairly certain that of the fourteen medals won by Americans, the tie for the gold medal on the uneven bars won by Julianne McNamara was one of few that would have stood, even with the boycotting teams present.

Although doing a little acting, television commentary, and touring after retiring from competition in 1986, Julianne settled into a life of wife and mother. She married professional baseball star Todd Zeile in 1989 and had two children, Garrett and Hannah.

Summary

By 1984 Julianne McNamara had become one of only three American women to have won a gold medal in world-class gymnastics competition. The first was Marcia Frederick, who also won a gold for uneven bars against the world's best. Juli's career was highlighted by her tremendous talent and rapid rise to the top.

A. Bruce Frederick

Additional Sources:

Crumlish, John. "Julianne McNamara: In Full Bloom." *International Gymnast*, November, 1999, 24-25.

Normile, Dwight. "10 Years After." *International Gymnast*, December, 1994, 8.

"Where Are They Now: Julianne McNamara." *International Gymnast* Online. http://www.intl gymnast.com/paststars/psdec99/psdec99 .html. December, 1999.

HONORS AND AWARDS

1980	Women's U.S. Olympic gymnastics team
1981-82	U.S. Gymnastics Federation Gymnast of the Year

GREG MADDUX

Sport: Baseball

Born: April 14, 1966
San Angelo, Texas

Early Life

Gregory Alan Maddux was born in San Angelo, Texas, in 1966. Because his father was a career military man, the Maddux family lived in many different places. Greg's father began teaching him how to play baseball at the age of five. He played Little League baseball in Madrid, Spain.

In 1984 Greg graduated from Valley High School in Las Vegas, Nevada. During his junior and senior seasons, he was an All-State baseball player. Even then, the key to his pitching was amazing control. Opting not to attend college, Greg was selected in the second round of the 1984 major league baseball draft by the Chicago Cubs.

The Road to Excellence

Greg spent three seasons in the minor leagues prior to joining the Cubs in September, 1986. One of the first games that he pitched was against his older brother Mike, who was a rookie pitcher for the Philadelphia Phillies. It marked the first time that rookie brothers had ever pitched against each other in the major leagues. To his great delight, Greg defeated his older brother.

The 1987 campaign was very disappointing for Greg, as he compiled a 6-14 record and a hefty 5.61 earned run average (ERA) for the Cubs. Following the advice of Cubs pitching coach Dick Pole to concentrate on making good pitches instead of trying to retire every bat-

Greg Maddux of the Atlanta Braves pitching in September, 2000.

ter, Greg had an excellent year in 1988. He was selected as a member of the National League All-Star Team and finished the season with an 18-8 mark and a 3.18 ERA. Four more excellent seasons ensued with the Cubs, culminating in 1992

STATISTICS

Season	GP	GS	CG	IP	HA	BB	SO	W	L	S	ShO	ERA
1986	6	5	1	31.0	44	11	20	2	4	0	0	5.52
1987	30	27	1	155.2	181	74	101	6	14	0	0	5.61
1988	34	34	9	249.0	230	81	140	18	8	0	3	3.18
1989	35	35	7	238.1	222	82	135	19	12	0	1	2.95
1990	35	35	8	237.0	242	71	144	15	15	0	2	3.46
1991	37	37	7	263.0	232	66	198	15	11	0	2	3.35
1992	35	35	9	268.0	201	70	199	20	11	0	4	2.18
1993	36	36	8	267.0	228	52	197	20	10	0	1	2.36
1994	25	25	10	202.0	150	31	156	16	6	0	3	1.56
1995	28	28	10	209.2	147	23	181	19	2	0	3	1.63
1996	35	35	5	245.0	225	28	172	15	11	0	1	2.72
1997	33	33	5	232.2	200	20	177	19	4	0	2	2.20
1998	34	34	9	251.0	201	45	204	18	9	0	5	2.22
1999	33	33	4	219.1	258	37	136	19	9	0	0	3.57
2000	35	35	6	249.1	225	42	190	19	9	0	3	3.00
Totals	471	467	99	3,315.9	2,986	733	2,350	240	135	0	30	2.83

Notes: Boldface indicates statistical leader. GP = games played; GS = games started; CG = complete games; IP = innings pitched; HA = hits allowed; BB = bases on balls (walks); SO = strikeouts; W = wins; L = losses; S = saves; ShO = shutouts; ERA = earned run average

when Greg won twenty games and the Cy Young Award.

The Emerging Champion

Greg became a member of the Atlanta Braves after signing as a free agent after the 1992 season. Joining a pitching rotation that already included Tom Glavine, John Smoltz, and Steve Avery, Greg soon emerged as the ace of the staff. Greg pitched against the Cubs in Wrigley Field on opening day of 1993 and won the game. In his first season with the Braves, he won twenty games, posted a 2.36 ERA, and won the Cy Young Award for the second straight year.

In the strike-shortened season of 1994, Greg won sixteen games, pitched ten complete games, and claimed the Cy Young Award for the third year in a row. No one had previously won that award more than two consecutive years. His 1.56 ERA set a record for the Braves and was the third best in major league baseball since 1919.

Greg had another remarkable year in 1995, compiling a 19-2 record and a 1.63 ERA. He became the first player since Walter Johnson (1918-1919) to pitch back-to-back seasons with an ERA below 1.70. For an amazing fourth consecutive year, Greg won the Cy Young Award. According to Greg, his greatest moment in sports came when the Braves won the 1995 World Series. As the Braves defeated the Cleveland Indians for the world championship, Greg pitched a brilliant two-hitter against the potent Indians' attack in game 1. Although the Indians defeated Greg in game 5, the Braves won the series in six games.

In 1996 Greg slipped to a 15-11 record but still had a 2.72 ERA. The Braves lost the World Series to the New York Yankees. Greg returned to his old form in 1997, compiling a 19-4 record and a 2.20 ERA. It was the tenth consecutive season in which he had won at least fifteen games. In 232 innings pitched, he gave up only 20 walks, 6 of which were intentional.

Continuing the Story

Greg won his fourth National League ERA title in 1998 with a 2.22 mark and struck out a career-high 204 batters. Pitching nine complete games, Greg hurled a career-high five shutouts. He was the National League starting pitcher in the All-Star game, which marked the seventh time he had played in the midsummer classic. Although Greg won nineteen games in 1999, he had his highest ERA (3.57) since 1987. Once again, the Braves lost the World Series to the New York Yankees. In 2000 Greg had another stellar year, going 19-9 with a 3.00 ERA.

Although his hardest fastball only approaches about 87 miles per hour, Greg has great movement on the ball, running it in and out on the opposing hitter. He also throws a curve, a sharp slider, a circle changeup, and numerous other breaking pitches that fall somewhere in between. He constantly keeps batters off stride by changing the speed on his pitches. Greg concluded the 1990's with a 2.54 ERA, the third-lowest ERA in any decade since the early 1900's, behind only Hoyt Wilhelm's 2.16 and Sandy Koufax's 2.36.

Greg is an excellent fielding pitcher. He won the National League Gold Glove for pitchers ten straight seasons (1990-1999). On seven occasions, Greg has led the major leagues in putouts by a pitcher, which is a major league record. Greg is also a good hitting pitcher, possessing a career .179 average with 4 home runs. One of his goals each season is to have a higher batting average than his ERA (when both statistics are expressed as whole numbers).

Greg became actively involved in community affairs in Las Vegas. He and his wife, Amanda, established the Greg Foundation, which is involved in several charitable activities, including the donation of tickets to Braves games for nonprofit organizations.

Summary

Greg Maddux is one of the most durable and one of the best control pitchers in major league baseball history. With the exceptional movement he puts on a baseball and his pinpoint control, Greg was the most dominant pitcher in the major leagues during the 1990's. An emblem of consistency, he won the Cy Young Award an unprecedented four consecutive years (1992-1995).

Alvin K. Benson

Additional Sources:

Brenner, Richard J. *Baseball Superstars Album.* New York: Beech Tree Books, 1999.

Christopher, Matt. *On the Mound with Greg Maddux.* Boston: Little, Brown, 1997.

Macht, Norman. *Greg Maddux.* New York: Chelsea House, 1997.

Saccoman, John. *The Most Dominating Starting Pitcher of All Time?* Cleveland, Ohio: Society for American Baseball Research, 1998.

Torres, John A. *Greg Maddux: Ace.* Minneapolis, Minn.: Lerner Publishing, 1997.

BILL MADLOCK

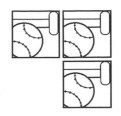

Sport: Baseball

Born: January 12, 1951
Memphis, Tennessee

Early Life

William Madlock, Jr., was born on January 12, 1951, in Memphis, Tennessee. Almost from the beginning of his life, Bill was an outstanding athlete.

He excelled at many sports, most notably baseball and football. He hit over .700 as a Little Leaguer and over .500 during his high school baseball career.

By the time Bill reached high school, his family had moved to Illinois. As good as he was in baseball, football was his best sport at Eisenhower High School in Decatur, Illinois. After his senior year, he received more than one hundred scholarship offers because of his ability as a running back.

The Road to Excellence

Bill thought about college, and even went to junior college for a year in Iowa to improve his grades for a four-year school, but he was hitting the ball so well that the old Washington Senators (now the Texas Rangers) picked him in baseball's collegiate draft in 1970.

Bill showed promise as a hitter in the minors, batting .338 with 90 runs batted in in Class AAA. The Rangers were so impressed that they invited him up to the majors to finish out the season. He batted .351 in twenty-one games with the Rangers in 1973.

Even though he was powerfully built, Bill was not the typical slug-

ging third baseman. Instead, he was a more consistent line-drive hitter. Whereas other players might swing as hard as they could for home runs, Bill preferred to swing more carefully, placing the ball as best he could. It was that ability that first drew the attention of baseball scouts and made him into a batting champion.

Just when everything seemed to be going perfectly, Bill was traded. That winter, he was dealt to the Chicago Cubs with another player for veteran pitcher Ferguson Jenkins. Cubs fans missed

Pittsburgh Baseball Club

1747

Jenkins and had no idea who this untested young player at third base was.

The Emerging Champion

Bill quickly became a fan favorite. He was a hard-nosed, fiery competitor, just the kind of player the long-losing Cubs needed. He batted .313 as a rookie, the fifth-best mark in the National League. Baseball fans everywhere got their first taste of what Bill could do in the All-Star game the next season. Bill, then still largely unknown outside of Chicago, won the game for the National League with a 2-run single in the ninth.

By the end of 1975, Bill's second full season in the major leagues, he had won the league batting title, hitting a whopping .354. He went on to win the batting crown in 1976 as well, and finished with four titles in all during his fifteen-year major league career.

His reputation as a great hitter and a fiery competitor continued to grow. His teammates nicknamed him "Mad Dog" because of his single-mindedness when it came to hitting and winning.

Bill was traded to the San Francisco Giants in 1977 and to the Pittsburgh Pirates two years later. This was not a happy time for Bill. Critics pointed out that he never had played on a championship team and that he did not hit home runs or field particularly well at third base.

In 1979, Bill set out to change their minds. He went to the Pirates in the early part of the 1979 season and was the missing piece in the puzzle for that team. Pittsburgh went on to win the World Series that year, playing their best baseball after Bill joined the team in June.

Bill decided that he was not the kind of hitter who could swing for the fences, so he kept hitting singles and doubles. He worked diligently on his fielding and in time became solid defensively.

In the World Series that season, Bill batted .375 in the seven games against Baltimore and participated in 4 double plays at third base, tying a World Series record.

Continuing the Story

Bill also played for the Los Angeles Dodgers and the Detroit Tigers during his career. He helped both of those teams win divisional titles. In 1985, he hit .275 during the regular season for the Dodgers and .333 with 3 homers in the playoffs. He played primarily as a designated hitter for the Tigers in 1987 but helped them win the American League East that season.

Once his career was complete, Bill could be satisfied that he had left his mark on the game—despite the criticism he endured at times during his career. He became the first man to win four National League batting titles since Hall of Famer Stan Musial.

STATISTICS

Season	GP	AB	Hits	2B	3B	HR	Runs	RBI	BA	SA
1973	21	77	27	5	3	1	16	5	.351	.532
1974	128	453	142	21	5	9	65	54	.313	.442
1975	130	514	182	29	7	7	77	64	**.354**	.479
1976	142	514	174	36	1	15	68	84	**.339**	.500
1977	140	533	161	28	1	12	70	46	.302	.426
1978	122	447	138	26	3	15	76	44	.309	.481
1979	154	560	167	26	5	14	85	85	.298	.438
1980	137	494	137	22	4	10	62	53	.277	.399
1981	82	279	95	23	1	6	35	45	**.341**	.495
1982	154	568	181	33	3	19	92	95	.319	.488
1983	130	473	153	21	0	12	68	68	**.323**	.444
1984	103	403	102	16	0	4	38	44	.253	.323
1985	144	513	141	27	1	12	69	56	.275	.402
1986	111	379	106	17	0	10	38	60	.280	.404
1987	108	387	102	18	0	17	61	57	.264	.442
Totals	1,806	6,594	2,008	348	34	163	920	860	.305	.442

Notes: Boldface indicates statistical leader. GP = games played; AB = at bats; 2B = doubles; 3B = triples; HR = home runs; RBI = runs batted in; BA = batting average; SA = slugging average

HONORS AND AWARDS

1975	All-Star Game most valuable player
1975, 1981, 1983	National League All-Star Team

In addition, he finished as one of only about 150 players in the history of the game with a lifetime batting average that surpassed .300, finishing at .305, the same mark Hank Aaron had achieved. Also, Bill was one of only 175 players at the time of his retirement who had recorded more than 2,000 lifetime base hits.

Summary

Bill Madlock was, in many ways, an unusual third baseman. Usually, baseball fans like a hard-hitting player who can hit homers at that position. Bill realized early that he was not that kind of ballplayer so, ignoring his critics, he stuck to what he felt he could do best, worked on his weaknesses defensively, and became a solid all-around performer.

John McNamara

Additional Sources:

Feehny, Charley. "Sweet-Swinger Madlock Made It the Hard Way." *The Sporting News* 192, no. 4 (1981).

McDonnell, Joe. "A Batting Leader Who Merits More Recognition." *Baseball Digest* 42, no. 3 (1983).

Sahadi, Lou. *The Pirates.* New York: Times Books, 1980.

LARRY MAHAN

Sport: Rodeo

Born: November 21, 1943
Salem, Oregon

Early Life

Larry Mahan was born on a farm near Salem, Oregon, on November 21, 1943. Larry's love for riding horses was evident early in his life. By the time he was ten years old, he was spending most of his time at the Oregon State Fairgrounds, breaking every colt he could find. At the age of twelve, he entered his first junior rodeo, roping and riding calves, where he won six dollars and a belt buckle. By the time he graduated from high school, he was ready to trade his job sacking groceries for a chance to make it big in rodeo.

The Road to Excellence

Even though Larry was a good rider, his days did not go by without injury. After graduating from high school, he entered a rodeo in Stockton, California, where he rode a bull named Rattler. A few seconds out of the chute, Larry flew off and learned why they called the bull Rattler. Once he was off the bull, it came after him and stepped on his jaw, breaking it in five places. This injury kept Larry from riding for several months while he was recuperating. During this time, he married Darlene, and they moved to Arizona, where they would attend Arizona State University. Like most newlyweds, they had little money, so Larry went to what he knew best—the rodeo—to earn money for tuition.

The Emerging Champion

Larry Mahan broke into the professional rodeo circuit in 1965. As a new face in rodeo, he attracted attention quickly when, during his rookie year, he took first place in the Professional Rodeo

Cowboys Association (PRCA) bull riding category and seventh in the All-Around Cowboy championship. Larry soon became widely recognized because of his frequent exposure at rodeos. To participate in as many rodeos as he could, he would fly his own plane to rodeos across the country, often competing in two a day.

Larry's success involved some serious injuries. For example, he was kicked by a bull in the back of his neck, breaking three vertebrae. When he was X-rayed at the hospital, the doctor did not see the broken bones and told Larry it was all right to ride. A month and about twelve bull rides later, the doctor discovered that he had missed

1750

the broken vertebrae. Larry's neck had healed on its own; he simply complained of a stiff neck.

Larry competed in professional rodeo for about thirteen years. The late 1960's were his glory years. He held the record for the most consecutive PRCA World Champion All-Around Cowboy titles from 1966 to 1970. He emerged at the top again in 1973, taking a record six All-Around Cowboy championships. He consistently won first to fourth place in bull riding, bareback riding, and saddle bronc riding.

Continuing the Story

Larry Mahan differed from other rodeo athletes in that he was also a successful businessman and public relations manager. He was called "Goldfinger" because, unlike other cowboys who spent what money they earned, Larry invested in different businesses. He had a talent for making money out of almost anything. Jim Shoulders, another well-known cowboy, once suggested that Larry had been important in promoting rodeo by using the media and promoting himself in business.

After his rodeo career, Larry Mahan became involved in a wide range of activities. For a while, he broke into television to assist with rodeo commentary, and he even formed his own group as a singer, touring the country and playing during rodeos. His business ventures kept him busy as well; he established the "Larry Mahan Collection" of boots and western clothing. He was also involved in the longhorn cattle business, and in the early 1980's, he bought a cattle ranch in Colorado. He became interested in horse cutting (training horses to "cut" or separate cattle from a herd) and bought another ranch in Bandera, Texas.

Larry had learned an important lesson when he was competing on the rodeo circuit: To get to the top, he had had to put aside many other things in his life. His dedication to rodeo cost him a marriage, and his two children grew up without seeing much of their father. He remarried after retiring from rodeo, and his goals centered more on spending time with his wife, Robin.

Summary

Larry Mahan was different from other cowboys. While in the arena, he became one of the most successful rodeo athletes, with six All-Around Cowboy titles plus numerous other individual event titles. Outside the arena, he was able to promote himself and rodeo while investing his money in business. By the end of his rodeo career, he had learned that fame, money, and success were not everything. The more important things in his life became his family and ranching.

Rodney D. Keller

Additional Sources:

"The Legendary Larry Mahan." The About Network. http://rodeo.about.com/sports/rodeo/library/weekly/aa082597.htm.

Thorson, Juli S., and Jim Bortvedt. "Urbane Cowboy." *Horse and Rider* 32, no. 5 (1993).

MILESTONES

1965, 1967	PRCA Bull Riding Champion
1966	Inducted into Rodeo Hall of Fame, the National Cowboy Hall of Fame
1966-70, 1973	PRCA World Champion All-Around Cowboy
1967	NFR Saddle Bronc Riding Average Winner
1979	Inducted into Pro Rodeo Hall of Fame

RECORDS

Most PRCA World Championship All-Around Cowboy titles, 6 (record shared with Tom Ferguson)

Qualified in twenty-six events in the National Finals Rodeo (NFR)—the most in NFR history (record shared with Olin Young)

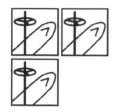

PHIL MAHRE

Sport: Skiing

Born: May 10, 1957
Yakima, Washington

Early Life

Phillip Mahre was born on May 10, 1957, in Yakima, Washington. His twin brother, Steven, was born four minutes later. The twins were the fifth and sixth of nine children in the Mahre family.

Phil's father, David Mahre, reluctantly gave up apple farming when he found it would not support his growing family. He was offered a job managing a ski area at White Pass, Washington, in the Cascade Mountains, and when Phil was four, the family moved into a house located about thirty yards from the ski lift. Phil started skiing when he was six.

Living in the mountains, the Mahre twins rode a bus an hour and a half each way to the nearest school in Naches, Washington. They did their homework on the bus ride home and were off skiing as soon as they got back to White Pass.

The Road to Excellence

Phil began winning junior ski races at White Pass in the mid-1960's and, with Steve, soon came to dominate the Buddy Werner League races held there. Eventually, Phil and Steve were essentially competing only with each other. They took first and second places consistently, one winning some days, the other winning on the other days.

Phil and Steve were close, even for twin brothers. They competed with each other, but they helped each other and pushed each other to work harder. This relationship would continue throughout their careers.

When Phil was eleven, he was selected as one of a dozen boys to attend the national training camp of the U.S. ski team. Then, just after graduating from high school, when Phil was seventeen, he made the U.S. ski team and began competing internationally on the World Cup circuit.

Phil raced at Innsbruck, Austria, in the 1976 Olympic Games and finished fifth in the giant slalom. It was the best finish by an American alpine skier that year, but Phil had not yet reached his prime.

The Emerging Champion

Phil began to excel on the World Cup circuit, the highest level of international skiing. Phil

American Phil Mahre skis a giant slalom race in 1976.

STATISTICS

Year	Competition	Event	Place
1976	Olympic Games	Giant slalom	5th
		Slalom	18th
	World Cup	Overall	14th
		Giant slalom	10th
		Slalom	7th
1977	World Cup	Overall	9th
		Giant slalom	4th
		Slalom	12th
1978	World Championships	Giant slalom	5th
	World Cup	Overall	2d
		Giant slalom	3d
		Slalom	3d
1979	World Cup	Overall	3d
		Giant slalom	19th
		Slalom	2d
1980	Olympic Games	Giant slalom	10th
		Slalom	Silver
		Downhill	14th
1980	World Cup	Overall	3d
		Giant slalom	9th
		Slalom	12th
1981	World Cup	Overall	1st
		Giant slalom	3d
		Slalom	2d
		Downhill	32d
1982	World Cup	Overall	1st
		Giant slalom	1st
		Slalom	1st
		Downhill	25th
1983	World Cup	Overall	1st
		Giant slalom	1st
		Slalom	6th
		Downhill	18th
1984	Olympic Games	Giant slalom	Silver
		Slalom	Gold

won five World Cup races in 1977 and 1978, equaling a record set by Billy Kidd for the most World Cup races won by an American. Phil finished ninth in the overall standings (combined results from slalom, giant slalom, and downhill) in 1977, and he finished second to Ingemar Stenmark in 1978. He had another excellent year in 1979, finishing third in the overall standings.

Then in 1979, at pre-Olympic races, Phil shattered his ankle in a fall. Phil had suffered injuries before, breaking his leg in an avalanche in 1973 and tearing liga-

ments in his ankle in 1974, causing him to miss much of that season, but the broken ankle was severe and required surgery. Doctors installed screws and a metal plate to hold the bones together, and Phil's chances for success in the 1980 Lake Placid Olympics looked bleak.

On the World Cup circuit that year, his performance suffered. He roared back at the Olympics, though, and won the silver medal in the slalom, second only to Stenmark.

The following season Phil was back on top of his form, and he won the overall title in the World Cup, finally beating Stenmark. He was the first American to win the title in the fifteen-year history of the World Cup. He won the overall title again in 1982 and then for a third consecutive year in 1983.

Phil's career culminated at the Olympics in Sarajevo, Yugoslavia, in 1984. Having already planned to retire at the end of the year, Phil made public statements that a gold medal was not that important to him. He felt there was too much emphasis on winning medals. He said the important thing was that he enjoy himself and the competition and that he was satisfied with his career so far. The press criticized him for his remarks and what appeared to be a lackadaisical attitude. Phil, however, was far from lackadaisical.

He attacked a very difficult slalom course and ended up narrowly defeating his brother Steve to win the gold medal in the slalom. He was the first American ever to win an Olympic gold medal in skiing.

Continuing the Story

After Sarajevo, both Phil and Steve retired from amateur ski racing. Phil planned to spend more time with his family.

For Phil, skiing was simply sport; it was meant to be fun. He avoided the limelight and once said

HONORS, AWARDS, AND RECORDS

1976-80	U.S. Male Alpine Racer of the Year
1981	First U.S. skier to win the World Cup (a gold medal in the overall, a silver medal in the slalom, and a bronze medal in the giant slalom)
1984	First American man to win the Olympic gold medal in skiing (slalom)
1992	Inducted into U.S. Olympic Hall of Fame

he would probably be just as happy if he were flat broke.

Phil and Steve competed together on the U.S. ski team for years, and they pushed each other to higher and higher levels. While the twins competed against each other, each admitted that he enjoyed the other's success almost as much as his own. Yet one would not slack off to help the other win. Steve once took points from his brother in a crucial World Cup race. If he had purposely skied more slowly, he would have allowed Phil to clinch the overall title. Eventually, Phil did clinch the title, but Steve made him work for it. They helped each other too, but by offering advice and encouragement. When it came time to ski, they always went all-out.

Although the twins did not train during the off-season—they spent summers in other pursuits, like building a house for Phil near Yakima, Washington—they dedicated themselves in the winter.

Often the twins would get up while it was still dark. They would hike the slopes and ski several runs before the sun came up, well before other skiers reached the mountain.

In 1989, after four years in retirement, the Mahre brothers returned to competitive skiing, this time on the professional tour. Phil started placing in races right away, although pro skiing is not as competitive as the amateur World Cup. Moreover, both Phil and Steve brought more popularity to pro skiing, especially among American spectators, who came to watch perhaps the best male skier the United States has ever produced.

Phil has remained active in skiing as a teacher with his brother Steve at the Mahre Training Center in Keystone, Colorado, and a competitor in numerous professional ski events with other legendary skiers like Franz Klammer. He has also become interested in professional auto racing. He was inducted into the U.S. Olympic Hall of Fame in 1992.

Summary

Phil Mahre has been hailed many times as the greatest U.S. skier ever, and his accomplishments attest to that. Still, he has said that gold medals and fame and glory are not that important to him. He skis because he loves the sport, but he competes aggressively, skiing a wild, all-out style even when he can afford to ski a conservative race. To him skiing is just fun, and he has said he will stop racing when he stops having fun.

Robert Passaro

Additional Sources:

Hickok, Ralph. *A Who's Who of Sports Champions: Their Stories and Records.* Boston: Houghton Mifflin, 1995.

Levinson, David, and Karen Christenson, eds. *Encyclopedia of World Sport: From Ancient to Present.* Santa Barbara, Calif.: ABC-CLIO, 1996.

Mahre, Phil, Steve Mahre, and John Fry. *No Hill Too Fast.* New York: Simon & Schuster, 1985.

Wallechinsky, David. *The Complete Book of the Olympics.* Boston: Little, Brown and Company, 1991.

HERMANN MAIER

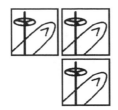

Sport: Skiing

Born: December 7, 1972
Flachau, Austria

Early Life

Hermann Maier's parents ran a ski school in their hometown of Flachau, Austria. Hermann began skiing at the age of three. By the time he was six, he was racing against other children. Because he had the potential for being a fine ski racer, he was enrolled in a special high school for promising skiers. At age fifteen, he won the title of the Austrian junior national champion. He was called an aggressive skier, but because of his

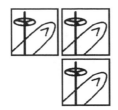

Hermann Maier captured two gold medals in the 1999 World Alpine Ski Championships.

small size—he only weighed 110 pounds—and his bad knees and shin splints, he was asked to leave the school.

From the ski school, Hermann went to a trade school to become a bricklayer. He continued to ski; he trained in the mornings and taught at the ski school on weekends. He also continued to enter regional races.

The Road to Excellence

In 1996, Hermann was asked to be a forerunner for the World Cup super-giant slalom (Super-G) in Flachau. A forerunner is a skiier who is not part of the race but who goes down the course before the racers to set a time for the course. The course of the Super-G is quite steep and has many gates the racers must go through. Although the gates are far apart, the racers must make tight turns on a straight run to finish in a faster time. Hermann's time as a forerunner in the World Cup event was the fourth fastest of the day. Because of his performance in Flachau, he was invited to participate on the Europa Cup travel squad.

The Emerging Champion

In 1997, in the first three races of the ski season, Hermann finished in the top three. He was invited to participate on the World Cup Austrian team. His skiing was described as relaxed, but he was known to always take risks and often had a "wild-eyed" look.

Hermann went to the 1998 Winter Olympic Games in Nagano, Japan, with the World Cup Austrian alpine ski team. He was set to participate in three alpine skiing events— the downhill, the Super-G, and the giant slalom. The first was the downhill. During the race, Hermann had a huge crash: He flew off the course, went through the air, and

1755

HONORS, AWARDS, AND RECORDS

1988	Austrian Junior National Champion
1996	Europa Cup Travel Squad
1997	World Cup Austrian Alpine Ski Team
1998	Gold Medal, Olympic skiing: Super-G Gold Medal, Olympic skiing: Giant slalom
2000	Crystal Globes: Overall title, Downhill title, Super-G title, Giant slalom title Set World Cup record for reaching 2,000 in overall points standings

landed on his head. He continued to crash through two safety mesh fences and was finally stopped by a third safety fence. Amazingly, he walked away complaining only of a headache, a painful shoulder, and a sore knee.

Three days later, Hermann won the gold medal in the men's Super-G. Three days after that, the giant slalom event took place. The giant slalom is one of two technical events in ski racing. Racers take two runs in one day down a course that is shorter than the speed event courses. Gates are set fairly close together, and racers must make wide turns to make it through these gates. Hermann earned his second gold medal, finishing a full eight-tenths of a second before the silver medalist.

The media has nicknamed Hermann "The Herminator," "Das Monster," and "Racin' Mason" (after his days as a bricklayer). His fearless, go-for-it style and spectacular crash in the downhill race helped to earn him these nicknames.

Continuing the Story

Hermann continued to ski on the Austrian team, winning races and earning praise. He skied his best Super-G race ever in Bormio, Italy, in March, 2000. In this race, the final World Cup Super-G of the 2000 race season, Hermann finished almost 2 seconds ahead of the second-place finisher. The 1.91-second margin was the greatest ever in a World Cup Super-G event. Hermann took the Super-G title and the overall title during this season. Points are given to racers in every event in which they compete. The points are assigned according to the field of racers and the racer's finish. Hermann reached the 2,000-point plateau in overall point standings—the highest ever for a ski racer.

After only three years on the World Cup circuit as a ski racer, Hermann had won 15 races in the Super-G, as well as Olympic and World Championships titles. At the completion of the 2000 race season, he had his twenty-eighth win. In March, 2001, Hermann won another World Cup Super-G title at Kvitjell, Norway. He is the third ski racer ever, and the first since 1987, to take home four crystal globes in one season, winning the titles in the overall, the downhill, the Super-G, and the giant slalom.

Summary

Born and raised in Austria to parents who ran a ski school, Hermann Maier seemed to have an ideal environment in which to become a ski racer. In fact, he has become one of the greatest ski racers in the history of the sport. Though he showed early promise, he was forced to take time off to grow to a more mature height and weight. Continuing to train and race, Hermann eventually was recognized as an exceptional ski racer. After racing on the World Cup circuit for only three years, Hermann Maier had earned more titles and points than anyone in the sport. His daredevil attitude on the racecourse and his charming personality make him a favorite of fans and the media.

Betsy L. Nichols

Additional Sources:

Bechtel, Mike. "High and Tight." In *Sports Illustrated 2000 Sports Almanac*. New York: Time, 1999.

Fisher, David, and Reginald Bragonier, Jr., eds. *What's What in Sports: The Visual Glossary of the Sports World*. Maplewood, N.J.: Hammond, 1984.

Levinson, David, and Karen Christensen, eds. *Encyclopedia of World Sport III: From Ancient Times to the Present*. Santa Barbara, Calif.: ABC-CLIO, 1996.

KARL MALONE

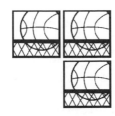

Sport: Basketball

Born: July 24, 1963
　　　　Summerfield, Louisiana

Early Life

Karl Malone, one of eight children of J. B. and Shirley Malone, was born on July 24, 1963, in Summerfield, a small Louisiana farming community. When Karl was five years old, his father abandoned the family, and his mother went to work in sawmills and poultry houses to support her children. Karl learned to play basketball on a makeshift clay court behind the family home, where his older brother Danny would test him with rough play to toughen him up. Karl soon became a star player at Summerfield High School, setting scoring records and leading the team to three state championships.

The Road to Excellence

Karl's impressive high-school performance drew the attention of college recruiters, and he accepted a scholarship to Louisiana Tech University in nearby Ruston in 1981. Buoyed by his success, however, he became arrogant and overconfident, and he neglected his schoolwork. His grades plummeted, and his scholarship was suspended; he had to take out a student loan to finish his freshman year.

Chastened, Karl applied himself both on the court and in the classroom, and the effort was rewarded. In three years at Louisiana Tech, the powerfully built 6-foot 9-inch forward averaged 18.7 points and 9.3 rebounds per game and twice led the school's team into the National Collegiate Athletic Association (NCAA) tournament. Fans of the school nicknamed Karl "The Mailman"—because, they

Karl Malone makes a slam dunk in a Utah Jazz-Boston Celtics game in February, 1998.

said, he always delivered. After his junior season, Karl decided to turn professional, and he was selected by the Utah Jazz of the National Basketball Association (NBA) with the thirteenth pick of the 1985 NBA draft.

The Emerging Champion

Karl had expected to be chosen much higher, and he soon made teams that had passed him over in the draft regret their decisions. In his first season with the Jazz, Karl averaged 14.9 points and 8.9 rebounds a game, earned selection to the NBA's All-Rookie team, and finished third in the league's Rookie of the Year voting. Yet he drew occasional criticism for a lack of intensity and for a reluctance to play near the basket. Though he was tall and powerful, he was also somewhat soft.

Utah's coach, Frank Layden, prodded Karl to take his play more seriously, and he began an intensive regimen of weightlifting. The formerly soft Malone bulked up to more than 250 pounds, and he acquired the physique of a bodybuilder. His hard work paid off, and he raised his averages to 21.7 points and 10.4 rebounds per game in his second NBA season. The next year, averaging 27.7 points and 12.0 rebounds per game, he was chosen to play in his first NBA All-Star game.

Continuing the Story

At Utah, Karl teamed with star point guard John Stockton to give the Jazz one of the most effective player combinations in basketball. NBA fans soon grew accustomed to the sight of Stockton, a brilliant passer, feeding the ball to Karl, whose enormous strength made him al-most unstoppable near the basket. In the 1988-89 season, Karl finished second in the NBA in scoring with a 29.1 points-per-game average, behind only perennial scoring champion Michael Jordan. Karl also used his size and strength to make himself one of the league's premier rebounders.

In the 1989 NBA All-Star game, Karl outperformed the game's brightest stars to earn most valuable player honors. The following year, he raised his scoring average still further, to 31.0 points per game, but again finished second to Jordan in the race for the league scoring title. In 1992, Karl's status as one of the world's best players was confirmed by his selection to the U.S. "Dream Team," which romped to the gold medal in basketball at the Barcelona Olympics.

Karl is arguably the best power forward to ever play in the NBA. Karl can run the floor, rebound, hit the medium range jumper, defend, and make a variety of powerful moves to score on the inside. He is extremely durable, having missed only four games in his NBA career. By late November, 2000, Karl had scored 31,323 points, the third best in the history of the game. He credits much of his scoring success to the numerous assists he has received from Jazz point guard John Stockton. Karl and Stockton led the Jazz to the NBA finals in 1997 and again in 1998.

STATISTICS

Season	GP	FGM	FG%	FTM	FT%	Reb.	Ast.	TP	PPG
1985-86	81	504	.496	195	.481	718	236	1,203	14.9
1986-87	82	728	.512	323	.598	855	158	1,779	21.7
1987-88	82	858	.520	552	.700	986	199	2,268	27.7
1988-89	80	809	.519	703	.766	853	219	2,326	29.1
1989-90	82	914	.562	696	.762	911	226	2,540	31.0
1990-91	82	847	.527	684	.770	967	270	2,382	29.0
1991-92	81	798	.526	673	.778	909	241	2,272	28.0
1992-93	82	797	.552	519	.740	919	308	2,217	27.0
1993-94	82	772	.497	611	.694	940	328	2,063	25.2
1994-95	82	830	.536	516	.742	871	285	2,187	26.7
1995-96	82	789	.519	512	.723	804	345	2,106	25.7
1996-97	82	864	.550	521	.755	809	368	2,249	27.4
1997-98	81	780	.530	628	.761	834	316	2,190	27.0
1998-99	49	393	.493	378	.788	463	201	1,164	23.8
1999-00	82	752	.509	589	.797	779	304	2,095	25.5
2000-01	81	670	.498	536	.793	669	361	1,878	23.2
Totals	1,273	12,105	.524	8,636	.738	13,287	4,365	32,919	25.0

Notes: GP = games played; FGM = field goals made; FG% = field goal percentage; FTM = free throws made; FT% = free throw percentage; Reb. = rebounds; Ast. = assists; TP = total points; PPG = points per game

HONORS AND AWARDS

1986	NBA All-Rookie Team
1988	All-NBA Second Team
	NBA All-Defensive Second Team
1988-98, 2000	NBA All-Star Team
1989-99	All-NBA First Team
1989, 1993	NBA All-Star Game most valuable player
1992, 1996	Gold Medal, Olympic basketball
1996	NBA 50 Greatest Players of All Time Team
1997, 1999	NBA most valuable player
1997-99	NBA All-Defensive First Team
1999	Named one of twenty best NBA players of all time

After winning a gold medal as a member of Dream Team I in 1992, Karl won another gold medal in 1996 as a member of Dream Team III. In 1996 he was named to the NBA's 50 Greatest Players of All Time Team. In 1999 he was selected as one of the twenty best NBA players of all time. Karl has been named to the All-NBA First Team eleven times, which is an NBA record. He has played in eleven All-Star games, being named the most valuable player (MVP) twice. The second time was as the co-MVP with Stockton. Karl has been selected to the NBA All-Defensive First Team twice. Karl was the NBA most valuable player for the 1996-1997 season and again for the 1999-2000 campaign. On December 5, 2000, Karl passed Wilt Chamberlain to become the second-highest scorer in NBA history, with 31,443 points. Only Kareem Abdul-Jabbar has scored more points.

Karl purchased car dealerships in Utah and New Mexico, a bed and breakfast in Salt Lake City, and Malone Enterprises, a trucking company. He appeared in the motion picture *Rockwell* and became an honorary member of the Avikan Witanuche Ute Indian Tribe in 1997. In 2000 he made an exercise video that demonstrates his approach to maintaining physical fitness.

Summary

Karl Malone augmented his enormous natural ability with a training regimen that made him one of the most imposing athletes in any sport. His success is a striking example of the results that can be achieved when talent is supplemented by hard work.

Robert McClenaghan

Additional Sources:

Bjarkman, Peter C. *The Biographical History of Basketball.* Chicago: Masters Press, 1998.

Deseret News Firm. *The Jazz: Utah's Dream Team.* Salt Lake City, Utah: Deseret News, 1997.

Doling, Nick, Chris Doling, and David Check. *Basketball Stars: The Greatest Players in the History of the Game.* New York: Black Dog and Leventhal Publishers, 1997.

Lewis, Michael C. *To the Brink: Stockton, Malone, and the Utah Jazz's Climb to the Edge of Glory.* New York: Simon & Schuster, 1998.

Shouler, Kenneth A. *The Experts Pick Basketball's Best Fifty Players in the Last Fifty Years.* Lenexa, Kans.: Addax, 1998.

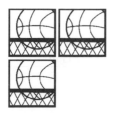

MOSES MALONE

Sport: Basketball

Born: March 23, 1955
Petersburg, Virginia

Early Life

Moses Eugene Malone was born on March 23, 1955, in Petersburg, Virginia. Petersburg, a city of about forty thousand people in southeastern Virginia, was the site of important military conflicts during the American Civil War.

Life was not easy for Moses growing up as a young boy in the late 1950's and the 1960's. For as long as he can remember, Moses was bigger than the other boys and girls in the neighborhood. At times, they would choose him first to be on their team because they knew he could help them win. On other occasions, however, they would make fun of him because of his size.

Moses did not have any brothers or sisters, so when neighborhood playmates were not around, he would play games by himself, usually basketball. His mother, Mary, was a nurse's aide who did not make enough money to be able to provide Moses with everything he wanted, but she was always there to provide him with the encouragement he needed.

The Road to Excellence

Like many young boys and girls who enjoy sports today, Moses began his life in sports during his grade school years. Moses was always taller than the rest of the boys on his team, and, even in those early years when he was learning to play basketball, people could notice that Moses was a special player.

During grade school and on through high school, Moses continued to improve as a basketball player. He spent many hours on the playground by himself practicing his shooting skills. It was during team practice sessions and in games against other schools, however, that his trademark as a player began to appear—his rebounding.

While playing on the varsity basketball team at Petersburg High School for four years, he set

Moses Malone in 1978.

nine school records. During his senior year, he scored 52 points in one game and 895 points for the entire season. For his four-year varsity career, he scored 2,124 points. His other records include the most field goals and free throws in one game, during one season, and for a high school career at Petersburg.

By his senior year, he had grown to 6 feet 11 inches tall and had become known as the best high school basketball player in the United States. More than three hundred colleges offered him scholarships. Which one to accept was a difficult decision for this nineteen-year-old who signed his autograph "Sweet Moses."

The Emerging Champion

The determination that made Moses a champion basketball player in high school caught the attention not only of college coaches but also of the professionals. After sorting through all the offers from the many colleges that wanted him to play for them, he decided to accept the scholarship from the University of Maryland, where Lefty Driesell was the coach. About the same time he chose Maryland, the Utah Stars of the American Basketball Association (ABA) drafted him and offered him a large sum of money to play professional basketball.

No player had ever gone directly from high school to professional basketball. Moses's mother, who was his constant encouragement and the most important person in his life, allowed him to make this very difficult decision. Much to the disappointment of Coach Driesell and to the surprise of the sports world, Moses chose to sign the contract with the Utah Stars. It made him the highest salaried teenage athlete in the United States. He was also offered a large scholarship by the Utah Stars to attend any college of his choice in the off-season.

Many people believed the Stars had selected Moses as a publicity stunt because no high school player had ever made the move directly to the professional ranks. Many others did not believe Moses could be successful as a professional at only nineteen years of age. The same determination that made him a champion in high school, however, would now make him a champion as a professional. When most people said he could not, Moses said he would.

Continuing the Story

In his two years with the Utah Stars of the ABA, Moses gained the praise of his coach for how quickly he learned the professional game of basketball. His shooting was consistent and his rebounding continued to amaze both teammates and opposing players.

STATISTICS

Season	GP	FG	FG%	FTM	FT%	Reb.	Ast.	TP	PPG
1974-75	83	591	.571	375	.635	1,209	82	1,557	18.8
1975-76	43	251	.512	112	.612	413	58	614	14.3
1976-77	82	389	.480	305	.693	1,072	89	1,083	13.2
1977-78	59	413	.499	318	.718	886	31	1,144	19.4
1978-79	82	716	.540	599	.739	1,444	147	2,031	24.8
1979-80	82	778	.502	563	.719	1,190	147	2,119	25.8
1980-81	80	806	.522	609	.757	1,180	141	2,222	27.8
1981-82	81	945	.519	630	.762	1,188	142	2,520	31.1
1982-83	78	654	.501	600	.761	1,194	101	1,908	24.5
1983-84	71	532	.483	545	.750	950	96	1,609	22.7
1984-85	79	602	.469	737	.815	1,031	130	1,941	24.6
1985-86	74	571	.458	617	.787	872	90	1,759	23.8
1986-87	73	595	.454	570	.824	824	120	1,760	24.1
1987-88	79	531	.487	543	.788	884	112	1,607	20.3
1988-89	81	538	.491	561	.789	956	112	1,637	20.2
1989-90	81	517	.480	493	.781	812	130	1,528	18.9
1990-91	82	280	.468	309	.831	667	68	869	10.6
Totals	1,290	9,709	.493	8,486	.769	16,772	1,796	27,908	21.6

Notes: GP = games played; FGM = field goals made; FG% = field goal percentage; FTM = free throws made; FT% = free throw percentage; Reb. = rebounds; Ast. = assists; TP = total points; PPG = points per game

When the ABA merged with the National Basketball Association (NBA) in 1976, Moses was challenged again to raise the quality of his play to another level. In his first five seasons in the NBA, while playing for the Houston Rockets, he won the NBA rebounding title twice, finished second twice, and third, once. His scoring average rose steadily with each season, reaching a personal high of 31.1 points per game in the 1981-1982 season. That season, as well as the 1978-1979 season, when he led the league with 17.6 rebounds per game, he was named the most valuable player of the NBA while playing for the Houston Rockets. During his first year of play for the Philadelphia 76ers in 1982-1983, he gained his third most valuable player award.

During his career in the NBA, Moses has done for the offensive rebound what Boston Celtic Bill Russell did for the blocked shot: He made it into an art that other players can only envy. His selection to the NBA All-Star Team twelve times speaks to the high standard set by the man who is the leading rebounder among active NBA players. Moses signed a two-year contract to play for the Milwaukee Bucks in July, 1991, after being released by the Atlanta Hawks.

Moses will be remembered not only for his greatness as an all-around player, but also for his longevity. He played for twenty-two years and was a member of two ABA teams and eight NBA teams. Ferocious on the boards, he was the first player in NBA history to lead the league in rebounding for five consecutive seasons. Moses finished his long career with the San Antonio Spurs in 1995. His combined totals for ABA and NBA play were 29,580 points and 17,834 rebounds. Former NBA player and coach John Lucas noted that Moses was the greatest "blue-collar worker" in the history of basketball.

As part of the celebration of the golden anniversary of the NBA in 1996, Moses was selected as a member of the NBA's 50 Greatest Players of All Time Team. In 2001, he was elected to the Naismith Memorial Basketball Hall of Fame. After retiring from basketball, Moses took some college courses but had no regrets about bypassing college for his pro basketball career. He became involved in providing counsel and guidance for young players who are considering an NBA career.

Summary

Determination and hard work have made Moses Malone one of the best NBA players ever. In overcoming the limitations of his boyhood and the doubts of many who said he would never become a successful professional player, Moses has made himself a place in NBA history and a place among sports champions.

Robert R. Mathisen

Additional Sources:

Aaseng, Nathan. *Basketball's Power Players*. Minneapolis, Minn.: Lerner Publishing, 1985.

Bjarkman, Peter C. *The Biographical History of Basketball*. Chicago: Masters Press, 1998.

Doling, Nick, Chris Doling, and David Check. *Basketball Stars: The Greatest Players in the History of the Game*. New York: Black Dog and Leventhal, 1997.

Lundgren, Hal. *Moses Malone: Philadelphia's Peerless Center*. Chicago: Children's Press, 1983.

Shouler, Kenneth A. *The Experts Pick Basketball's Best Fifty Players in the Last Fifty Years*. Lenexa, Kans.: Addax, 1998.

NBA RECORDS

Most free throws made in career, 7,999

HONORS AND AWARDS

1975	ABA All-Star Team ABA All-Rookie Team
1978-89	NBA All-Star Team
1979, 1982-83	NBA most valuable player
1979-85, 1987	All-NBA Team
1979, 1983	NBA All-Defensive Team
1983	NBA Finals most valuable player
1987	All-NBA Second Team
1996	NBA 50 Greatest Players of All Time Team Uniform number 24 retired by Houston Rockets
2001	Elected to Naismith Memorial Basketball Hall of Fame

MILESTONES

Most honored NBA player to play professional basketball right out of high school

LLOYD MANGRUM

Sport: Golf

Born: August 1, 1914
Trenton, Texas
Died: November 17, 1973
Apple Valley, California

Early Life

Lloyd Eugene Mangrum was born on August 1, 1914, in Trenton, Texas. He grew up on a dirt farm just outside the city, the youngest of three brothers. His older brother, Ray, eventually became a golf professional and won several Professional Golfers' Association (PGA) events, until a leg ailment forced him to quit.

The Mangrum family was very poor. Lloyd did not grow up with any of the toys that many American children around him had. He mostly played outdoors on the family farm.

When he was older, his impoverished father decided things might get better if the family moved to Dallas. There Lloyd dropped out of school before he was legally old enough to do so. The young boy began playing golf, not only for fun but also for money.

The Road to Excellence

At age fifteen, Lloyd turned professional. Playing golf actually earned him enough money to live on. The next year, at age sixteen, he paid his own way to Los Angeles, where he played against amateurs for five and ten dollars. A child of the Depression, Lloyd had to play golf to win money because it was the only way he could afford to play the game, and he did so at a time when golf was still considered a game primarily for aristocrats. Lloyd was anything but that.

In fact, he was an ornery, tough player—a maverick at the game. He had to be, because the

Courtesy of Amateur Athletic Foundation of Los Angeles

men he played against were a rough bunch. One of his opponents, it turned out, was wanted for bank robberies. Another stuffed Lloyd's partner into a locker after losing to him. Once Lloyd gambled with a professional who lost by three putts. The man was so angry that he took his putter into the creek and jammed it knee-deep into the mud.

Because of the world he lived in, Lloyd grew up fast. At age nineteen, he married Eleta, the

MAJOR CHAMPIONSHIP VICTORIES

1946	U.S. Open

OTHER NOTABLE VICTORIES

1947, 1949, 1951, 1953	Ryder Cup team
1948	Greater Greensboro Open
1948, 1953	Bing Crosby National Pro-Am
1949, 1951, 1953, 1956	Los Angeles Open
1950	Eastern Open
1952, 1953	Phoenix Open
1952, 1954	Western Open
1953	Ryder Cup team captain

operator of a beauty salon, who was eleven years older than Lloyd. She brought to the marriage her three children, the eldest child only eight years younger than her new stepfather. Lloyd addressed Eleta as "Mother" and let her handle the handsome income his golf playing soon began to generate. In spite of the age difference, Lloyd's and Eleta's marriage turned out to be a very successful one.

The Emerging Champion

In order to secure backing for some of his tournaments, Lloyd went to his brother Ray, who was then a successful golfer himself. Ray is said to have pulled out a wad of bills and peeled off two one-dollar bills, telling his younger brother to get a job because he was not good enough at golf.

By 1943, Lloyd Mangrum had become a golfer to contend with. That year, he won four PGA events, the first four out of a total of thirty-four that he would win over the course of his lifetime.

He was drafted and served in the armed forces as an infantry sergeant on the front lines. Later, he was a member of a reconnaissance team that headed the 90th Division of General Patton's Third Army on D day at Omaha Beach. After the ensuing battles, Lloyd was one of only two surviving members of his original platoon. For this and his multiple injuries, he was awarded two Purple Hearts.

After the war, the heroic Mangrum returned to golf on the PGA tour. It took him a while to get back into the game and to win

enough to make a living. In 1946, he won the United States Open, and, by 1951, he led all the professionals, winning four tournaments for a grand total of $26,088. He was then able to buy his own airplane.

Although his career was interrupted by the war, Lloyd Mangrum still made it to the top. In addition to winning many PGA events, he won the Vardon Trophy twice. He won the Los Angeles Open four times and was on four Ryder Cup teams, serving as captain once.

Continuing the Story

Golf professionals and teachers were amazed by Lloyd Mangrum's success. To them, his game was nothing exceptional. Many of them could outdrive him and hit straighter. Somehow, the game just came naturally to him, according to Lloyd. The "how" was not important to him; the "how many" was.

However it may have happened, Lloyd's putts, chips, pitches, and bunker shots were nearly matchless, and he was considered one of the least nervous of putters in golf history. In fact, he was known for his calmness on the fairways. A thin, leathery-looking fellow, he always managed to appear constantly bored, as if there were nothing better for him to do. He would even putt with a cigarette hanging out of his mouth.

Violence continued to be a part of Lloyd's life, on and off the fairways. During one tournament, he received a telephone call threatening his life if he won the game. He refused to withdraw and went on to win, surrounded by uniformed police.

Eventually, by 1953, Lloyd became only an occasional winner. In 1949, his first book was published, *Golf, A New Approach.* In this book, Lloyd

MILESTONES

The Masters runner-up (1940)
Among the top ten money leaders between 1946 and 1954
Won four times in 1949; four times in 1950; five times in 1951; five times in 1952
Won a career total of thirty-four PGA tournaments

HONORS AND AWARDS

1951, 1953	PGA Vardon Trophy
1964	Inducted into PGA Hall of Fame

revealed that he deliberately tried to copy the short game of Johnny Revolta, the swing of Sam Snead, and the putting style of Horton Smith. On November 17, 1973, when he was fifty-nine years old, Lloyd Mangrum died at home in Apple Valley, California, of his twelfth heart attack. He was survived by his wife, Eleta, his son, Robert, and his two daughters, Reina and Shirley. Lloyd was a member of both the California Golf Hall of Fame and the PGA Hall of Fame.

Summary

Lloyd Mangrum's golf successes were remarkable for a man whose career was interrupted by the war and by injuries sustained in battle. In addition to winning thirty-four PGA events, Lloyd won the 1946 United States Open, won the Vardon Trophy twice, and played on four Ryder Cup teams.

Nan White

Additional Sources:

Brown, Gene, ed. *The New York Times Encyclopedia of Sports.* 15 vols. New York: Arno Press, 1979-1980.

Grimsley, Will. *Golf: Its History, People, and Events.* Englewood Cliffs, N.J.: Prentice-Hall, 1966.

Porter, David L., ed. *Biographical Dictionary of American Sports: Outdoor Sports.* Westport, Conn.: Greenwood Press, 1988.

VALENTIN MANKIN

Sport: Yachting

Born: August 19, 1938
Kiev, U.S.S.R. (now Ukraine)

Early Life

Valentin Mankin, one of the finest sailors in the world, was born on August 19, 1938, in the ancient city of Kiev. Kiev, a port city on the Dnieper River, is the capital of the Ukraine and one of the largest cities in the former Soviet Union.

Not all of the citizens of Kiev are of Ukrainian heritage; such is the case of Valentin, who is of Russian descent. This city, which recovered well from immense damage sustained during World War II, is considered one of the most beautiful in Europe. Along with its parks and gardens, it is well known for its wealth of medieval art and architecture. It was in this atmosphere that Valentin was raised as an only child. He attended school in Kiev and planned to become a building engineer.

Legend has it that, as a young man, Valentin was concerned that certain activities, such as running, would cause blood to be concentrated in his feet, thereby limiting the flow to his brain. The resultant lack of oxygen to his brain, he reasoned, could lead to diminished intelligence. He therefore looked to activities that might stimulate a stronger blood flow to his head.

One sport that Valentin felt might accomplish this was water polo, and as a young teenager he looked forward to the challenge of playing on the water polo team. Unfortunately, he was not selected for the team, because his hands were considered too small for him to handle the ball effectively. Little did Valentin realize what a blessing those small hands would be in shaping the course of his brilliant future.

The Road to Excellence

As Valentin walked dejectedly along the banks of the Dnieper pondering his failure to make the water polo team, he saw young rowers practicing on the river. Spotting a man whom he thought was the rowing coach, the ambitious youngster asked what it would take to be a rower. The man responded that he did not know, because he was the sailing coach, whereupon the undaunted Valentin asked what he needed to do to be on the sailing team. The coach, no doubt taken with the enthusiasm and hopefulness of the boy, directed him to the sailing team.

MAJOR CHAMPIONSHIPS

1968	Olympic gold medalist (winning score of 11.7) (Finn class)
1972	Olympic gold medalist (winning score of 28.1) (Tempest class)
1973	World Championship (Finn class)
1976	Olympic silver medalist (score of 30.40) (Tempest class)
1980	Olympic gold medalist (winning score of 24.7) (Star class)

While the young mariner enjoyed the mere act of sailing, he set himself apart from other young sailers because he was mature enough to learn everything he could about the principles underlying the practice of sailing. His complete dedication to the sport was rewarded when he won his first race within a year of his talk with the coach along the banks of the Dnieper. Three years later, at the age of nineteen, he qualified for the Soviet national team. He won his first national championship when he was twenty-one.

Valentin was racing Finn-class boats. These boats are 14 feet 9 inches long and weigh 314 pounds. Having only one sail and a center board (a structure that hangs down into the water from the bottom center of the boat for stability in currents), the Finn is a very small craft that requires only one person to sail it in competitive events.

The Emerging Champion

In 1964, at the age of twenty-six, Valentin was selected as an alternate to the Tokyo Olympics. Four years later, in 1968, he represented the Soviet Union at the Mexico Olympics, thus beginning one of the most brilliant records in Olympic sailing history. In Mexico, he won the gold medal in the Finn class.

During the ensuing four years, Valentin switched to a Tempest-class boat. The Tempest, at 977 pounds and almost 22 feet in length, with a jib (the small forward sail on sloop-styled boats), a mainsail, and a spinnaker (a large balloon-like sail used in racing), requires a racing crew of two people. In the 1972 Munich Olympics, Valentin won his second gold medal with his crewman, Vitalii Drydyra.

In the 1976 Olympics at Montreal, Valentin and his new crewman, Vladislav Akimenko, were beaten in the Tempest competition by a team from Sweden and finished with a silver medal. In preparation for the 1980 Olympics in Moscow,

Valentin moved up to a Star-class boat. The Star is about nine inches longer and five hundred pounds heavier than the Tempest and has a jib and mainsail. Valentin took the gold medal in the Star class at Moscow, and in so doing, he became the first Olympic sailor in history to win a gold medal in his home waters.

Valentin, who retired from competitive sailing in 1980, has other championships to his credit, including the 1973 World Championship in the Finn class.

Continuing the Story

By the time he retired from the Soviet national team, Valentin was regarded by his peers as a sailor of legendary strength and intelligence who had elevated competitive sailing to a sport requiring elegant precision and technical and strategical superiority, as well as courage, stamina, and physical strength. He continued his valuable contributions to Soviet sailing by setting up an Olympic training camp on the Black Sea. After being named head coach of the Soviet national team in 1988, he moved to Moscow. In 1990, he moved to Alassio, Italy, a coastal village near the port city of Genoa, home of the Italian Sailing Federation. Here the delightful Valentin has been warmly welcomed, as much for his wit and gracious enthusiasm as for his immense, well-earned sailing wisdom.

Summary

As a fifteen-year-old Russian boy, rejected from a Kiev water polo team he had earnestly hoped to join, Valentin Mankin showed the maturity and cheerful fortitude that destined him for one of the finest sailing records in Olympic history. He stopped brooding and sought another activity in which he could excel. The activity was sailing. His complete devotion to this sport for over thirty-five years has earned him the genuine respect of his peers, as well as a permanent place among the world's finest competitive sailors.

Rebecca J. Sankner

Additional Sources:

Levinson, David, and Karen Christenson, eds. *Encyclopedia of World Sport: From Ancient Times to Present.* Santa Barbara, Calif.: ABC-CLIO, 1996.

PEYTON MANNING

Sport: Football

Born: March 24, 1976
New Orleans, Louisiana

Early Life

Peyton Williams Manning, born March 24, 1976, in New Orleans, is the second of three sons born to Archie and Olivia Manning. He was welcomed into a family with a strong background in football. His father, Archie Manning, had been a renowned quarterback at the University of Mississippi and was enjoying a successful career with the New Orleans Saints.

Young Peyton played basketball and baseball for recreation, but football was his passion. He grew up watching his father play quarterback for the Saints and looked up to his father as a role model and ideal.

The Road to Excellence

At Isidore Newman High School, Peyton and older brother Cooper were teammates on the football team. As a freshman at the University of Mississippi, Cooper was diagnosed with spinal stenosis, a narrowing of the spinal canal, and was forced to end his athletic career. In his honor, Peyton took his brother's jersey, number 18, which was also the number their father had worn at the University of Mississippi.

Although Peyton excelled in baseball, amassing a .440 batting average in his junior year and a berth on the Louisiana All-State Second Team as a shortstop, he focused ever more intensely on football. By the end of his high school career, Peyton was rated as one of the top three high school quarterbacks in the nation. In three years as a starter, he helped the team to a 34-5 record and was responsible for 92 touchdowns.

The Indianapolis Colts' Peyton Manning in November, 2000.

The Emerging Champion

Peyton was heavily recruited by college athletic programs during his high school career, and many expected him to follow the lead of his father and older brother into the ranks of the Rebels of the University of Mississippi. However, a desire to be his own person took Peyton to the University of Tennessee at Knoxville. The Tennesee tradition of outstanding quarterbacks and excellent facilities also figured in his decision.

Peyton was not slated to be a starter his freshman year, but when injuries sidelined senior Jerry Colquitt in the season opener and junior Todd Helton in the fourth game, Peyton found himself as Tennessee's primary quarterback. Gradually, through hard work and increasing experience, Peyton began setting records at Tennessee, leading the Volunteers to a 7-1 record as a starter his freshman year and earning the title of Southeastern Conference (SEC) Freshman of the Year for 1994.

The next two years were golden for Peyton. In the 1995 season he set Tennessee single-season records for pass completions (244), yards gained (2,954), consecutive passes without an interception (132), and lowest interception percentage (1.05 percent). During the 1996 season he became Tennessee's first quarterback to throw for more than 3,000 yards in a single season. He was twice honored as SEC Offensive Player of the Week and was named the Citrus Bowl most valuable player.

Peyton worked as hard in the classroom as on the field. He was selected for Phi Beta Kappa in 1997 and graduated cum laude after only three years, earning a bachelor's degree in speech communication with a minor in business. His 3.6 grade point average brought him numerous student athlete honors.

After his early graduation, Peyton faced a major decision. He could elect to turn pro, with offers of up to $30 million, or he could return to Tennessee to use his final year of eligibility. Suspense mounted in the press and among Volunteer fans until Peyton declared he would return to the campus to work toward a master's degree in sports management.

Peyton generated great attention in the media and among fans while at Tennessee. His father took out a $7 million insurance policy on his son through Lloyds of London—the largest policy ever written for a college athlete—which only added to Peyton's larger-than-life image. Fan mail for the much-loved quarterback included requests to autograph three hundred to five hundred items per week. A football office coordinator was assigned to handle the great volume of Peyton-related mail.

During Peyton's final collegiate season, he amassed 3,000 yards passing for the second consecutive year and earned another SEC Player of the Week title, and he was named SEC Player of the Year. He finished as Tennessee's all-time leader in touchdown passes (89).

Peyton's college career included a National College Athletic Association record for the lowest interception percentage (2.39 percent). He was also the all-time leading passer (11,201 yards) and all-time offense leader (11,020 yards). Peyton was named Player of the Year for 1997 by many organizations, including the Associated Press, Walter Camp Football Foundation, and *Football News*. One final honor eluded Peyton, however. In a hotly contended Heisman Trophy contest, Peyton was named runner-up in his third year as a top candidate.

Continuing the Story

Peyton Manning was the number one National Football League (NFL) draft choice in 1998, going to the Indianapolis Colts. His initiation into professional football was rough, however, with 11 interceptions in his first four games. By midseason, however, Peyton regained his composure. During his rookie season, he set five

STATISTICS

Season	GP	PA	PC	Pct.	Yds.	Avg.	TD	Int.
1998	16	575	326	.567	3,739	6.50	26	28
1999	16	533	331	.621	4,135	7.76	26	15
2000	16	571	357	.625	**4,413**	7.73	33	15
Totals	48	1,679	1,014	.604	12,287	7.32	85	58

Notes: Boldface indicates statistical leader. GP = games played; PA = passes attempted; PC = passes completed; Pct. = percent completed; Yds. = yards; Avg. = average yards per attempt; TD = touchdowns; Int. = interceptions

NFL passing records: most passing yards (3,739), touchdown passes (26), attempts (575), completions (326), and consecutive games with at least 1 touchdown pass (13). He also became the first quarterback in Colts history to take every snap of the season.

The 1999 season saw Peyton duplicate his 26 touchdown passes and raise his percentage of pass completions from 56 to 62. Off the field, Peyton turned his energy from the classroom to the community, devoting time to assisting youth-oriented organizations such as Boys Town and Special Olympics.

In 2000, he threw 33 touchdown passes and led the league in passing yardage, with 4,413 yards—a figure that raised his average for his first three pro seasons above 4,000 yards.

Summary

Peyton Manning exemplifies the ideal athlete. Self-effacing and hardworking, he credits his family with his success, although his coaches attribute his achievements to relentless study and a constant quest for improvement. He combines a desire to be the best with a genuine love of the game and strives to return to fans and to the community the support they have long offered him.

Carol G. Fox

Additional Sources:

Frisaro, Joe. *Peyton Manning: Passing Legacy.* Champaign, Ill.: Sports Publishing, 1999.

Manning, Archie, et al. *Manning: A Father, His Sons, and Football Legacy.* New York: Harper, 1999.

Stewart, Mark. *Peyton Manning: Rising Son.* Champaign, Ill.: Sports Publishing, 2000.

NIGEL MANSELL

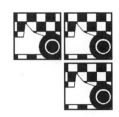

Sport: Auto racing

Born: August 8, 1953
Upton-on-Severn, England

Early Life

Nigel Mansell was born on August 8, 1953, in Upton-on-Severn, England, a village ninety miles northwest of London. Nigel became involved with motor-cart racing through his father, Eric, an engineer with some small-time racing experience. When Nigel was thirteen, he sailed through a fence at a track while going one hundred miles per hour in a cart. Upon arriving at the hospital, Nigel's condition was so severe that a priest administered last rites. Nigel gave an indication of his toughness when he regained consciousness and told the priest to leave.

The Road to Excellence

Nigel was no stranger to adversity. In a Formula Ford race in 1979, he broke his neck in two places when his car left a racecourse going backward at 120 miles per hour. Unfortunately for Nigel, he had just resigned from an engineering job at an aerospace company to pursue racing full-time. He found himself with no job and no money, and for a period of time he had no movement in his arms and legs. Nigel, though, was not one to quit.

Nigel was told that he had to remain flat on his back or risk permanent paralysis. Ignoring his doctor's advice, Nigel discharged himself from the hospital and was back racing in less than two months. Wearing a neck brace, he won the Formula Ford driving championship by winning thirty-two of forty-two starts, despite driving at times in great pain.

Nigel's family was not wealthy enough to sponsor his jump to the next level of competition, so he wrote four hundred letters pleading for finan-

Racer Nigel Mansell with his French Grand Prix trophy in 1987.

cial backing from potential sponsors. Unable to secure a sponsor, he sold his house and many of his belongings in 1978 to buy a race car. After four races, Nigel was out of money.

Nigel, a fully qualified engineer, took a job as a window washer in the middle of winter so he could keep racing. Finally, in 1979, he signed on with an established racing team. The move provided him with cash and some valuable exposure.

The Emerging Champion

In 1980, Nigel made the jump to Formula One, the top level of racing. He quickly established himself as one of the finest drivers in British racing history. He was admired by many for his determination and never-say-die attitude, as demonstrated in a race in Dallas, Texas, in 1984. In that race, he pushed his car across the finish line to wind up in sixth place, then collapsed from heat exhaustion.

Nigel was at or near the top of Formula One racing during the 1980's and early 1990's. During 1985 and 1986, he won a total of thirteen races and narrowly missed the world driving champi-

onship. In 1987, Nigel won six races and broke a thirty-four-year-old record by qualifying on the front row for fifteen consecutive races. A late-season crash relegated him to another second-place finish in the world driving championship.

In 1992, it all came together for Nigel. He set several records, including most wins (nine), most pole position starts (fourteen), and most consecutive wins at the start of a season (five). This tremendous string of success helped Nigel to clinch the Formula One championship in August, the earliest the crown had been won since 1971.

In 1993, Nigel did something that no other reigning Formula One champion had ever done: He switched to Indy car racing. In his first Indy car race, in Australia, Nigel won both the pole position and the race, both at record average speeds. His first full year of Indy car racing was an unbelievable success. Nigel won the championship by posting five wins in fifteen starts. He also won seven pole positions, captured nine top-five finishes, and eleven top-ten finishes, and led an incredible 603 out of a possible 2,112 laps.

Continuing the Story

Nigel's accomplishments in the 1993 Indy car series are even more impressive when considering that, prior to the 1993 Indianapolis 500, Nigel had never raced on an oval track. Furthermore, Nigel had to overcome serious back injuries incurred in a crash during his attempt to qualify for a race in Phoenix, Arizona. Doctors had to clean out his lower back with hypodermic needles and vacuum tubes, then surgically repair damaged muscle. One hundred sutures were left deep inside his lower back to reduce swelling. During the week of practice and qualifying before a race in Long Beach, California, a doctor drained one hundred cubic centimeters of blood from his back almost every morning to reduce the swelling. Nigel finished his career following the 1993 season with thirty-one Grand Prix victories, third all-time behind only Alain Prost and Ayrton Senna.

GRAND PRIX AND OTHER VICTORIES

1985	European Grand Prix
1985, 1992	South African Grand Prix
1986	Belgian Grand Prix Canadian Grand Prix
1986-87, 1991-92	French Grand Prix British Grand Prix
1986, 1990, 1992	Portuguese Grand Prix
1987	Austrian Grand Prix
1987, 1992	San Marino Grand Prix
1987, 1991-92	Spanish Grand Prix
1987, 1992	Mexican Grand Prix
1989	Hungarian Grand Prix
1989, 1992	Brazilian Grand Prix
1991	Italian Grand Prix
1991-92	German Grand Prix
1993	Australian Grand Prix Miller 200 Marlboro 500 New England 200 Bosch Grand Prix

HONORS AND AWARDS

1992	World Championship of Drivers
1993	CART/PPG Indy Car Championship

Summary

Nigel Mansell will be remembered as one of history's greatest racing drivers. His perseverance culminated in his being knighted by the Queen of England; on the Isle of Man, his name is on the currency, and his face appears on postage stamps.

Bill Swanson

Additional Sources:

Hilton, Christopher. *Nigel Mansell: The Lion Returns.* Newbury Park, Calif.: Haynes, 1995.

Levinson, David, and Karen Christenson, eds. *Encyclopedia of World Sport: From Ancient Times to Present.* Santa Barbara, Calif.: ABC-CLIO, 1996.

Mansell, Nigel, and Jeremy Shaw. *Nigel Mansell's Indy-Car Racing.* Osceola, Wis.: Motorbooks International, 1993.

MICKEY MANTLE

Sport: Baseball

Born: October 20, 1931
Spavinaw, Oklahoma
Died: August 13, 1995
Dallas, Texas

Early Life

Mickey Charles Mantle was born on October 20, 1931, in Spavinaw, Oklahoma. His parents, Elvin Clark Mantle and Lovell Richardson Mantle, were both natives of Oklahoma. Life was hard during the Great Depression. After working for a time as a tenant farmer, Elvin Mantle moved his family to Commerce, a small, dreary town in northeastern Oklahoma, about twenty miles from Joplin, Missouri, to take a job as a shoveler in the zinc mines.

It was in Commerce that Mickey attended school. Aside from his family, Elvin Mantle's great love was baseball; despite his many hours of toil in the mines, he still made time to practice with his son Mickey, the oldest of five children, teaching him to be a switch-hitter.

The Road to Excellence

By the time Mickey was twelve, he often walked two or three miles with his best friends to play for a sandlot team in Dauthat, Oklahoma. A serious infection of a bone in his leg, osteomyelitis, threatened Mickey's hopes for a career in sports when he was only fifteen. Although the infection was cleared up by use of the then-new miracle drug, penicillin, Mickey would always have to worry about the chance of the infection return-

ing. For that reason, his draft board later ruled him ineligible for military service during the Korean War.

In 1947, a New York Yankees' scout, Tom Greenwade, spotted Mickey playing on an amateur team, the Whiz Kids, in Baxter Springs, Kansas, and was impressed with his ability with the bat and with his blazing speed. On the very day he graduated from high school in 1949, Mickey accepted Greenwade's offer of $400 in salary to

STATISTICS

Season	GP	AB	Hits	2B	3B	HR	Runs	RBI	BA	SA
1951	96	341	91	11	5	13	61	65	.267	.443
1952	142	549	171	37	7	23	94	87	.311	.530
1953	127	461	136	24	3	21	105	92	.295	.497
1954	146	543	163	17	12	27	**129**	102	.300	.525
1955	147	517	158	25	**11**	**37**	121	99	.306	.611
1956	150	533	188	22	5	**52**	**132**	**130**	**.353**	**.705**
1957	144	474	173	28	6	34	**121**	94	.365	.665
1958	150	519	158	21	1	**42**	127	97	.304	.592
1959	144	541	154	23	4	31	104	75	.285	.514
1960	153	527	145	17	6	**40**	**119**	94	.275	.558
1961	153	514	163	16	6	54	**132**	128	.317	**.687**
1962	123	377	121	15	1	30	96	89	.321	.605
1963	65	172	54	8	0	15	40	35	.314	.622
1964	143	465	141	25	2	35	92	111	.303	.591
1965	122	361	92	12	1	19	44	46	.255	.452
1966	108	333	96	12	1	23	40	56	.288	.538
1967	144	440	108	17	0	22	63	55	.245	.434
1968	144	435	103	14	1	18	57	54	.237	.398
Totals	**2,401**	**8,102**	**2,415**	**344**	**72**	**536**	**1,677**	**1,509**	**.298**	**.557**

Notes: Boldface indicates statistical leader. GP = games played; AB = at bats; 2B = doubles; 3B = triples; HR = home runs; RBI = runs batted in; BA = batting average; SA = slugging average

play a season of Class D baseball for the Yankees' Independence, Kansas, farm team.

The next year, Mickey moved up one notch to the Yankees' Joplin, Missouri, farm team in Class C. There Mickey became a sensation. Now nearly 5 feet 11 inches and 170 pounds, Mickey hit .383 and showed tremendous power, which he attributcd to strong shoulders and wrists; he believed his strength had come from milking cows during the two years his family had lived on a farm while he was in his early teens. His one weakness seemed to be in fielding; he played shortstop, but his Joplin manager believed his future would be as an outfielder.

The Emerging Champion

Mickey worked in the mines during the off-season and then went to spring training with the Yankees in 1951, skipping over several levels of minor league baseball. Hitting above .400 in spring training games, Mickey opened the season in right field. Despite belting one of the tape-measure home runs of about 500 feet for which he became famous, Mickey struck out so often that his playing time was reduced.

In July, he was sent to the Kansas City Blues in Class AAA ball. He thought of quitting baseball. Chastised by his father for being a crybaby,

Mickey quickly broke out of his slump and rejoined the Yankees in time to open the 1951 World Series in right field.

During the off-season, Mickey married his high school sweetheart, Merlyn. They had four sons: Mickey, Jr., David, Billy, and Danny.

Continuing the Story

In 1952, Mickey replaced the great Joe Di-Maggio in center field. Replacing a legend was not easy. The media added to the pressure by describing Mickey as the fastest player and the hardest hitter in baseball, creating enormous expectations of him. Mickey, his character shaped in a town where struggle and hard work were normal, came through brilliantly. During his first fourteen years with the Yankees, Mickey helped get the team into twelve World Series and set an all-time record by hitting 18 home runs in Series competition. In the regular season, he hit more than 50 home runs twice and 40 or more two other times, and batted .300 or more ten times. In 1956, he won the American League's Triple Crown.

During his first few seasons with the Yankees, Mickey developed bad habits off the ballfield, especially in his heavy drinking. He could have ruined his life and career, but fortunately, he real-

MAJOR LEAGUE RECORDS

Most consecutive home runs, 4 (1964)
Most World Series home runs, 18
Most World Series runs batted in, 40
Most World Series runs, 42
Most World Series walks, 43
Most World Series total bases, 123

HONORS AND AWARDS

1952-65, 1967-68	American League All-Star Team
1952, 1956-57	*Sporting News* Major League All-Star Team
1956	*Sporting News* Major League Player of the Year Associated Press Male Athlete of the Year Hickok Belt
1956-57, 1962	American League most valuable player
1956-62	*Sporting News* Outstanding American League Player
1961-62, 1964	*Sporting News* American League All-Star Team
1962	American League Gold Glove Award
1974	Inducted into National Baseball Hall of Fame
1999	MLB All-Century Team Uniform number 7 retired by New York Yankees

ized the harm drink could bring to himself and others after being involved in a driving accident in which his wife narrowly escaped a serious injury.

In 1963, he signed his first $100,000 contract, a huge salary then, but his peak years were coming to an end. The leg injuries that had always troubled him became more frequent, and by 1965 his career began going downhill; he shifted to first base in 1967. Mickey played his final game in September, 1968, worked out briefly just before spring training in 1969, and retired. In 1974, he was inducted into the National Baseball Hall of Fame.

Mickey and his family made their permanent home in Dallas, Texas. After retiring, he briefly tried broadcasting but found that he was most successful in public relations. He represented the companies that employed him at such events as charitable dinners and celebrity golf tournaments. Mickey continued to struggle with alcohol, and in 1994 he checked in to the Betty Ford Clinic. The following year, he underwent a liver transplant operation, but his health did not last. Mickey died of cancer on August 13, 1995, in Dallas. He was sixty-three. In 1999, Mickey was selected for major league baseball's All-Century team.

Summary

Enduring the pain that two bad knees caused him throughout his major league career, Mickey Mantle was a marvelous all-around ball player. Although the playing style of the 1950's did not emphasize base-stealing, he ran the bases well, ranged all over Yankee Stadium's large center field, hit for average, and batted with more power than any other switch-hitter in the history of baseball. At a time when such other outfield immortals as Willie Mays, Duke Snider, Hank Aaron, Al Kaline, and Roberto Clemente were having their peak seasons, Mickey ranked second to none.

Lloyd J. Graybar

Additional Sources:

Berger, Phil. *Mickey Mantle*. New York: Park Lane Press, 1998.

Faulkner, David. *The Last Hero: The Life of Mickey Mantle*. New York: Simon & Schuster, 1995.

Mantle, Mickey, with Herb Gluck. *The Mick*. Garden City, N.Y.: Doubleday, 1985.

Mantle, Mickey, and Phil Pepe. *My Favorite Summer, 1956*. New York: Doubleday, 1991.

DIEGO MARADONA

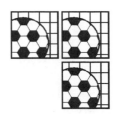

Sport: Soccer

Born: October 30, 1960
Buenos Aires, Argentina

Early Life

Diego Armando Maradona was born on October 30, 1960, to a poor family in a suburb of Buenos Aires, Argentina. At his birth, the midwife said to his mother that there was no need to worry—her son was all muscles.

He had eight brothers and sisters. Like many other poor kids in South America, the children spent much of their time playing soccer with a makeshift ball in the back streets. Diego's remarkable talent marked him from an early age.

In later years he said he had two reasons to make money in soccer: The first was to earn enough so that his father would not have to work hard; the second was to buy a pair of trousers of his own.

The Road to Excellence

With the exception of Pelé, perhaps no soccer player ever showed as much natural talent as Diego. By the time Diego was fifteen, the Argentine national team coach, Cesar Menotti, said, he already had first-class technique. Diego was already an excellent soccer player before he started serious training. Still, several years were to pass before he reached true greatness.

The coach of Argentine Juniors, a local team, first spotted Diego's talents when Diego was thirteen. Diego's ball control amazed everyone who saw him.

Though Diego was short (he grew to only 5 feet 6 inches as an adult), he was stocky and immensely fast. By the age of sixteen he was playing professionally. At seventeen he made his international debut for Argentina. To Diego's annoyance, however, Menotti left him off the Argentina squad for the 1978 World Cup, which Argentina won.

Over the next few years, Diego's honors mounted. In 1979 and 1980, he was the top marksman in the Argentine league. In 1979 and 1980, he was named South American Player of the Year. In 1981, his new team, Boca Juniors,

Diego Maradona celebrates a goal in a 1997 soccer match.

won the Argentine League Championship. Still, experts believed that Diego was not achieving his true potential. They complained that in a team game he played as an individualist.

The 1982 World Cup confirmed their suspicions. A poor Argentine team was defeated early by Brazil, and Diego was ejected for kicking an opposing player. The same year he transferred to the Barcelona team in Spain for a fee of $10 million. His two years there before a transfer to the Napoli club in Italy proved unhappy ones. Injury and illness prevented him from showing his best form.

The Emerging Champion

Not until the World Cup finals in 1986 did Diego finally emerge as the truly great player people had always said he could become. He had gradually matured as a person and a player, and he had learned to handle the adulation that had been heaped on him since his mid-teens. On the soccer field he still showed fantastic individual touches, but now he played as one player in a team.

Argentina appointed a new national coach in 1983, Carlos Bilardo. Bilardo immediately flew to Europe to meet with Diego. Bilardo told Diego that he would have to follow his orders at all times. Eventually Bilardo grew to have such confidence in Diego that he made him captain of the Argentina team.

Before the 1986 World Cup finals, two players were most often mentioned as contenders for the title of the greatest soccer player in the world: Diego and Michel Platini of France. Many, including Pelé, believed that Platini, with his accurate passing and great team play, had the edge. In addition, the teams on which Platini played usually won.

By the competition's end, Diego was undisputedly number one. Reporters said that some of his 5 goals would be talked about for fifty years. To score his second goal against England in the World Cup quarterfinal, he collected the ball on the halfway line and beat three opponents and the goalkeeper before placing the ball in the back of the net. Two more goals followed in the semifinal versus Belgium. In the final, Diego set up all 3 Argentine goals as his team beat West Germany and became the world champion.

Continuing the Story

Diego's success continued with the Napoli club, which won the Italian League championship in 1986-1987 and again in 1989-1990. In between, they collected the Union of European Football Associations (UEFA) Cup, winning a competition held among some of the greatest teams in Europe.

No longer could anyone say that Diego did not play with successful teams or that he could not blend his talent with a team's overall strategy. Moreover, he still had uncanny ball control with his left foot. It seemed as though no space was too small for him to beat an opponent. Rival teams assigned two players to mark Diego, and he still won games by setting up goals for his teammates. Though Diego disliked training, he was always fit for important matches. Sometimes, as in 1989, he gained weight, but when he needed to lose it, he did. Though he was officially a striker, he roamed over soccer fields, always in the thick of the action. People talked about his goals as miracles, goals only he could have scored.

By the late 1980's, Diego was probably the most famous sportsman in the world outside the United States. Wherever soccer was played, Diego was recognized as its most talented exponent. By the time of the 1990 World Cup, Argentina had lost many of its best players. Sometimes three opponents would mark Diego, and when he would beat them he would be fouled. Troubled by a foot injury, Diego failed to score in any match. Nevertheless, his team reached the final game before losing to West Germany. Such was Diego's popularity with Neapolitan fans that when Argentina played Italy in Naples some cheered for Argentina against their own country.

Diego's career was interrupted in 1991, how-

HONORS AND AWARDS

1979, 1980	South American Player of the Year
1981	Argentine League champion
1986	World Cup champion World Cup most valuable player (Golden Ball)
1987	Italian League Cup champion
1987, 1990	Italian League champion
1989	UEFA Cup champion

ever, when he was arrested by police in Buenos Aires for drug possession. The result was a fifteen-month suspension from Italian and world competition, effectively marking the beginning of the end of his career. Following his reinstatement, he tried to revive his career in Seville and later with Argentina. He returned to World Cup competition in 1994 but was banished when he tested positive for cocaine use. Diego finished his career with the Boca Juniors and formally retired in 1997.

Summary

In the history of soccer, Diego Maradona's achievements rank him with the greatest players of all time: Pelé, Alfredo di Stefano, Franz Beck-enbauer, Johan Cruyff. The ball control of his left foot, his explosive speed, his passing ability, and his team leadership made him a unique player with an instantly recognizable style. His amazing skills brought him fame and wealth; sadly, they brought him troubles as well.

Philip Magnier

Additional Sources:

"Argentines Ponder Maradona's Fall." *Economist* 354, no. 8153 (2000).

Burns, Jimmy. *Hand of God: The Life of Diego Maradona.* New York: Lyons & Burford, 1996.

McCallum, Jack, and Richard O'Brien. "Cornered Kicker." *Sports Illustrated* 81, no. 2 (1994).

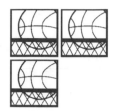

PETE MARAVICH

Sport: Basketball

Born: June 22, 1947
Aliquippa, Pennsylvania
Died: January 5, 1988
Pasadena, California

Early Life

Peter Press (Pistol Pete) Maravich was born June 22, 1947, in Aliquippa, Pennsylvania. Pete was the first of two children born to Peter "Press" and Helen Maravich.

Pete's father was a basketball coach, so Pete's involvement in the game was almost a requirement. Press developed his son's interest for the game, and did a masterful job of "creating" a youngster hungry for the game of basketball. With his father a coach, the opportunities were present for Pete to become one of the top scorers in basketball history.

The Road to Excellence

Young Pete was developed by his father from a very early age for a life in the game of basketball. When he was too young to play the game, his father would shoot baskets in the back yard, and Pete would itch to try it himself. His father would not allow it, trying to instill a desire for the sport that would be unparalleled.

Pete received a basketball as a Christmas present one year, and the time had arrived for him to learn of his father's extensive plan for his future. Pete's basketball debut took place at Daniel High School in Clemson, North Carolina, where his father was the coach of the Clemson Tigers of the Atlantic Coast Conference.

Pete was a 90-pound eighth-grader and took constant jeers and teasing from other children, as he was considerably smaller than his teammates. Although at first he was ignored on the basketball court because of his size, when Pete was given the opportunity to contribute he did so with great success.

In 1963, the Maravich family moved to Raleigh, North Carolina, where Pete's father would be the assistant coach at North Carolina State University. Pete attended Needham-Broughton High School and at this point had grown to almost 6 feet in height. Still very skinny, young Pete was anxious to display his rapidly developing talents to his new coach.

When Pete was graduated from high school and still rather slight in build, he and his father decided that another year would be helpful before Pete tried college basketball. Pete left Needham-Broughton with a 32-points-per-game

New Orleans Jazz guard Pete Maravich in 1979.

1780

average to attend Edwards Military Academy in Salemburg, North Carolina.

"Pistol Pete" was now 6 feet 4 inches tall and preparing for his college career. When his father accepted the head coaching position at Louisiana State University (LSU), Pete signed to play under his father, although he was not happy with the move because LSU was primarily a football school at the time.

The Emerging Champion

Averaging 43 points per game on the freshman team his first year at LSU, Pete was anxious to begin his varsity experience. He did so with a bang, averaging 43.8 points per game and setting a collegiate record.

Pete's junior year at LSU was another success. His two-year total of 2,097 points broke both Bob Pettit's LSU career scoring record and the National Collegiate Athletic Association (NCAA) record for the most points in two seasons. His total of 1,148 points that season was the second-highest in NCAA history up to that time.

In his final season at LSU, he set still more records. Pete broke Oscar Robertson's NCAA career scoring record, Elvin Hayes's NCAA single-season scoring record, and Calvin Murphy's NCAA single-game record all in the same year. He finished his college career with 3,667 points and a 44.2-points-per-game average, both records.

Pete signed a million-dollar contract with the Atlanta Hawks of the National Basketball Association (NBA), which, at the time, was the largest contract in professional sports. Although all seemed to be going well, the anger of some veteran players over Pete's large salary made his acceptance into the NBA difficult.

After four years with the Hawks and no positive changes regarding his acceptance on the team, Pete was traded to the New Orleans Jazz for the 1974-1975 season. Pete's dreams of being on a championship team now seemed less likely, but his free-flowing, aggressive, and creative style of play fit in much better with the young team. Pete played with New Orleans through the middle of the 1979-1980 season, when he was traded to the Boston Celtics.

Continuing the Story

Pete found it difficult to find a place on the team with stars such as Larry Bird, Robert Parish, Dave Cowens, and Nate Archibald. During the remainder of the 1979-80 season with Boston, his ailing knees bothering him, Pete was used primarily as a substitute. The Celtics were defeated by the Philadelphia 76ers in the playoffs.

At the beginning of the 1980-1981 season, Pete lost his desire to play the game and decided to retire. He worked hard at maintaining his interests with business ventures and his family: his wife Jackie, and their two boys, Jaeson and Joshua.

The final years of Pete's life were made difficult by the death of his father, Press, in 1987, and the memories of his life's incomplete goals and dreams. Pete found peace and happiness as a

STATISTICS

Season	GP	FGM	FG%	FTM	FT%	Reb.	Ast.	TP	PPG
1970-71	81	738	.458	404	.800	298	355	1,880	23.2
1971-72	66	460	.427	355	.811	256	393	1,275	19.3
1972-73	79	789	.441	485	.800	346	546	2,063	26.1
1973-74	76	819	.457	469	.826	374	396	2,107	27.7
1974-75	79	655	.419	390	.811	422	488	1,700	21.5
1975-76	62	604	.459	396	.811	300	332	1,604	25.9
1976-77	73	886	.433	501	.835	374	392	2,273	31.1
1977-78	50	556	.444	240	.870	178	335	1,352	27.0
1978-79	49	436	.421	233	.841	121	243	1,105	22.6
1979-80	43	244	.449	91	.867	78	83	589	13.7
Totals	658	6,187	.441	3,564	.820	2,747	3,563	15,948	24.2

Notes: GP = games played; FGM = field goals made; FG% = field goal percentage; FTM = free throws made; FT% = free throw percentage; Reb. = rebounds; Ast. = assists; TP = total points; PPG = points per game

born-again Christian and in travel, speaking engagements, clinics, and television commentary.

On January 5, 1988, Pistol Pete died of a heart attack shortly after a pick-up basketball game.

Summary

Pete Maravich became a crusader for youngsters in his attempts to enrich their lives and give back some of what he believed he had been blessed with in his life. His accomplishments during that last phase of his life will not soon be forgotten.

Meanwhile, the memories of the court magician—his baggy socks, long hair, fancy dribbling, pinpoint passes through his legs and behind his back, and his numerous records—will survive and will always be associated with the name "Pistol Pete." His induction into the Naismith Memorial Basketball Hall of Fame in 1987 marked his farewell to the basketball world. "The Pistol," however, will never be forgotten.

Hal J. Walker

Additional Sources:

Berger, Phil. *Forever Showtime: The Checkered Life of Pistol Pete Maravich.* Dallas: Taylor, 1999.

Finney, Peter. *Pistol Pete: The Story of College Basketball's Greatest Star.* Baton Rouge, La.: Levee Press, 1969.

Gutman, Bill. *Pistol Pete Maravich: The Making of a Basketball Superstar.* New York: Grosset & Dunlap, 1972.

Maravich, Pete, and Darrel Campbell. *Heir to a Dream.* Nashville, Tenn.: Thomas Nelson, 1987.

NCAA DIVISION I RECORDS

Most points, 3,667
Highest scoring average, 44.2
Most games with at least 50 points, 28
Most points in a season, 1,381 (1969-70)
Highest scoring average in a season, 44.5 (1969-70)
Most games with at least 50 points, one season, 10 (1969-70)
Most free throws made in a game, 30 (1969)

HONORS AND AWARDS

1968-70	Consensus All-American
1970	Rupp Trophy
	United Press International Division I Player of the Year
	U.S. Basketball Writers Association Division I Player of the Year
	Naismith Award
	Sporting News College Player of the Year
	Helms Athletic Foundation Division I Player of the Year
	Citizens Savings College Basketball Co-Player of the Year
1971	NBA All-Rookie Team
1973-74, 1977-79	NBA All-Star Team
1973, 1976-78	All-NBA Team
1987	Inducted into Naismith Memorial Basketball Hall of Fame
	Uniform number 7 retired by Utah Jazz

ALICE MARBLE

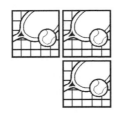

Sport: Tennis

Born: September 28, 1913
        Beckwourth, California
Died: December 13, 1990
        Palm Springs, California

Early Life

Alice Marble was born on September 28, 1913, in Beckwourth, California, the fourth child in a family of five. Life was hard in the early years as her father, a farmer, died when she was only six. By this time, the family had moved to San Francisco, and Alice's eldest brother, Dan, and her mother, Jessie, worked to support the family. Dan was seven years older than Alice and was an enormous influence in guiding her toward a career in tennis.

Her first love, though, was baseball, which Alice spent her spare time playing. At this time, however, it was rather unusual for girls to play baseball, and her brother was concerned that she might be thought "unfeminine." It was Dan, then, who gave Alice her first tennis racket and paid for her to join a tennis club. By now, Alice was sixteen years old.

The Road to Excellence

Alice began to practice regularly, curtailing the usual social engagements of a teenager in favor of the disciplined life of a serious athlete. She quickly became good enough to start playing junior tournaments, and she won the State Junior tournament in 1931, at age seventeen.

Her next step was to seek out the woman who was to be her coach, Eleanor Tennant. "Teach" Tennant was the leading coach of her day. She had several movie stars as her pupils, including Carole Lombard and Errol Flynn.

Teach immediately recruited Alice as her pupil, and in return, Alice performed secretarial duties for her coach. The system paid dividends because a year later, Alice rose to number seven in the national rankings and won her first significant tournament—the State Women's Championship.

Later in 1932, Alice took lessons from another coach, Harwood White, who helped her learn some new stroke techniques that greatly improved her game.

Alice continued to advance, and in 1933 she was chosen to play for the U.S. Wightman Cup team in the annual challenge match against Great Britain. She had now risen to number three in the United States, behind the great contemporaries Helen Wills Moody and Helen Jacobs. It was in this year that Alice first contracted the illness that dogged her for most of the next two years. Playing in Easthampton, Long Island, Alice collapsed due to sunstroke after play-

ing 108 games in 104 degrees Fahrenheit. Although she quickly recovered, more serious illness was around the corner.

The Emerging Champion

Following this incident, Alice fell prey to anemia, a condition resulting from a deficiency of iron in the body. Alice felt tired most of the time and was not able to play her best tennis.

In 1934, however, the Wightman Cup team made a trip to France. That was exceptional, since the team usually played only against Great Britain and had not traveled to the continent of Europe before. The trip by ocean liner took six days, and the excitement of a new language and the strange red clay court surface took their toll on Alice.

Alice was playing in the Stade Roland Garros in Paris when once again she collapsed on the court. It was first thought that she had tuberculosis, a lung disease that was often fatal in those days. A later diagnosis, however, revealed pleurisy, less dangerous but still a serious and painful illness. She was told by two doctors that she would never play tennis again.

Alice was hospitalized, first in Paris and then in Los Angeles, where she spent several months recovering in a sanatorium. As she convalesced, Alice started to do secretarial work once more for Teach Tennant. She gradually got stronger and never let go of her dream to play tennis again.

It was almost a year later before Alice was back on court—as her coach's assistant—helping to give lessons to movie-star pupils such as Marlene Dietrich.

Continuing the Story

Despite the reservations of officials of the United States Lawn Tennis Association, Alice resumed her career in 1935. She and her coach Teach were now inseparable, and their hard work was rewarded with a win for Alice in the California State Championships of that year.

This win was a turning point for Alice. Her repertoire of shots widened as she capitalized on the developments made with her other coach, Harwood White, three years earlier. Unlike other women players of her day, she possessed a hard American twist serve that she would often follow with secure volleys. Her ground strokes were not always as powerful as those of her backcourt rivals, but her agility and determination in the attack made up for anything she lacked.

Few women had attempted to play this type of game before, and Alice seemed to draw inspiration from the male players of her day, such as Fred Perry and Don Budge, as she leapt for overheads and constantly hit the ball on the rise.

Her first taste of major success came in 1936, when she won the U.S. National Championship, beating Helen Jacobs in the final. Three more U.S. National Championship victories came in 1938, 1939, and 1940.

Wimbledon, the British national championship, was another conquest in 1939, where she won not only the singles but also the doubles and the mixed

---

MAJOR CHAMPIONSHIP VICTORIES AND FINALS

1936, 1938-40	U.S. National Championship U.S. National Championship mixed doubles (with Gene Mako; with Donald Budge; with Harry Hopman; with Bobby Riggs)
1937-38, 1939	Wimbledon mixed doubles (with Budge; with Riggs)
1937-40	U.S. National Championship doubles (with Sarah Palfrey Fabyan)
1938-39	Wimbledon doubles (with Helen Jacobs)
1939	Wimbledon

OTHER NOTABLE VICTORIES

1933, 1937-39	On winning U.S. Wightman Cup team
1940	U.S. Clay Court Championship U.S. Clay Court Championship doubles (with Mary Arnold)

HONORS, AWARDS, AND MILESTONES

1933, 1937-39	U.S. Wightman Cup team
1936-40	Nationally ranked number one
1939-40	Associated Press Female Athlete of the Year
1964	Inducted into National Lawn Tennis Hall of Fame
1984	Service Bowl Award

doubles. In 1939 and 1940, Alice Marble was totally dominant and received the Associated Press Female Athlete of the Year award in both years.

In 1940, Alice turned professional and toured with Mary Hardwick, Donald Budge, and Bill Tilden. She also made her debut as a singer, performing at the Waldorf Astoria Hotel in New York City. She died on December 13, 1990, in Palm Springs, California.

Summary

Alice Marble's dominance was based on her strong serve and incisive volleys. Her style paved the way for postwar women champions such as Margaret Osborne and Louise Brough.

If the war years had not intervened, it is certain that Alice would have won even more major titles. She overcame not only some illustrious rivals but also severe ill health. Alice was a pivotal figure in women's tennis in the twentieth century.

Elizabeth C. E. Morrish

Additional Sources:

Davidson, Sue. *Changing the Game: The Stories of Tennis Champions Alice Marble and Althea Gibson.* Seattle, Wash.: Seal Press, 1997.

Marble, Alice. *The Road to Wimbledon.* New York: Charles Scribner's Sons, 1946.

Marble, Alice, and Dale Leatherman. *Courting Danger.* New York: St. Martin's Press, 1991.

HORTENCIA MARCARI

Sport: Basketball

Born: September 23, 1959
São Paulo, Brazil

Early Life

Hortencia de Fa'tima Marcari was born in 1959 to a poor family in São Paulo, a sprawling metropolis in southeastern Brazil that is one of the world's largest cities. Although soccer is South America's most popular sport, Hortencia became fascinated with basketball after she first learned the game as a thirteen-year-old schoolgirl. Within two years of taking up the game, the lanky teenager had become good enough to compete for a spot on Brazil's national women's team.

The Road to Excellence

Hortencia became a member of the Brazilian national team in 1979, and she soon became a star both in international competition and on the club level in Brazil, where professional women's basketball is popular. A slender 5-foot 8-inch shooting guard, she earned respect for her accurate outside shooting, her quick, acrobatic drives to the basket, and her fiery competitive nature. By 1983, Hortencia was known to fans around the world by her first name alone. American colleges, including the powerful University of Tennessee, tried to lure her to the United States to play basketball, but all of them were unsuccessful. "I always wanted to come to the United States—not to earn money but because they have the best basketball," she told a reporter. "Tennessee offered me an education, but I needed money to support my family. I couldn't leave Brazil." By the mid-1980's, she was earning the equivalent of $5,000 per month playing Brazilian club basketball.

The Emerging Champion

By then, Hortencia had established herself as perhaps the biggest female star in the sport. In a game for the São Paulo city championship, she scored 120 points to lead her team to a landslide victory. She was also a major celebrity in South America; at one point, she drew considerable publicity for her decision to pose for the Brazilian edition of *Playboy* magazine. Yet she remained almost unknown to North American fans. In part, this was because the Brazilian women's team had never qualified to play in the Olympics, the showcase of international women's basketball. Moreover, the Brazilian women had not managed to defeat the perennially powerful United States team since the 1971 Pan-American Games.

At the first Goodwill Games, held in Moscow in July of 1986, Hortencia and backcourt partner Maria Da Silva united to propel the Brazilian team in an impressive run-and-gun attack pattern against their opponents. (In Brazil, the two guards had become so dominant that they were not allowed to play on the same club team; in one eleven-year span, their teams met for the league championship ten times.) Yet even the duo's combined performance was not good enough to stop the U.S. team, which won the gold medal.

The following year, Hortencia and her teammates got a measure of revenge by routing Tennessee, the National Collegiate Athletic Association (NCAA) champions, by the score of 105-68. Hortencia scored 34 points on 10 of 14 shooting opportunities and dominated the court, causing Tennessee coach Pat Summitt to compare her play to that of National Basketball Association (NBA) great Larry Bird.

Continuing the Story

The 1987 Pan-American Games at Indianapolis, Indiana, were thus eagerly anticipated by fans in both Brazil and the United States. During an early-round game, the U.S. team narrowly beat Brazil 84-81, as Hortencia struggled with fouls,

AAF/Janus Jeszensky

feature the inside play of center Marta Souza and forward Janeth Dos Santos. In the critical semifinal game, the Brazilian and U.S. squads squared off again. With seconds remaining and the pro-Brazil Cuban crowd cheering wildly, Hortencia drove around U.S. defender Teresa Edwards and scored on a baseline jump shot to put the game away. Brazil held on to win 87-84, ending the U.S. team's nine-year, forty-two-game winning streak in international competition; after the buzzer, Da Silva did cartwheels across the court. In the finals, Brazil downed Cuba to take the gold medal, putting an end to years of national frustration.

By then, Hortencia had begun playing for teams in Europe at salaries that approached $200,000 a year. She had also married José Victor Oliva, a wealthy Brazilian nightclub owner, and the couple had become renowned for their jet-set lifestyle.

In 1994, Hortencia's career reached its apex. In the semifinals of the World Championships, she scored 32 points as the Brazilian team again upset the U.S. team by a score of 110-107. In the finals against China, she scored 27 points to lead the Brazilians to their first world title. Having reached the summit of women's basketball at last, after the game she retired from international competition.

shots that missed the mark, and frustrating offensive plays. In a final-round rematch between the U.S. and Brazilian teams, Hortencia had control of the court at the beginning of the game. She scored many three-point shots and banked in underhand shots off the glass. At one point, she even slapped her hand on the press table as she ran down the court. Yet her energetic play was again not enough; despite her 30 points, the U.S. team prevailed 111-87. In the late 1980's, Hortencia appeared in a ten-page layout in the Brazilian *Playboy* magazine, with the front cover reading "Our Queen, Hortencia," which referred to her status as possibly the best woman basketball player in the world.

In the 1991 Pan-American Games in Havana, Cuba, Brazil fielded a more balanced team. Rather than relying entirely on Hortencia and Da Silva, the Brazilians diversified their attack to

Because of her exploits on the basketball floor, Hortencia was regarded in Brazil as the female equivalent of Pelé. The heart and soul of Brazilian basketball, she was known by only her first name and was often referred to as the queen of sports in Brazil. With the advent of the 1996 Olympic Games in Atlanta, Georgia, Hortencia came out of retirement to participate at the age of thirty-six. In Brazil's win over Ukraine in a semifinal game, Hortencia scored 20 points on 8 out of 13 shooting opportunities from the field. Although she slipped to 11 points in the gold-medal game against the United States, the play of Hortencia and Paula da Silva garnered the silver medal for the Brazilian team.

Hortencia played in five Olympics, leading the run-and-gun Brazilian team. Most of the people of Brazil still regard her as the biggest star to ever play women's basketball. Hortencia became the general manager and director of the Paran basketball team in the Confederation of Brazilian Basketball, which represents the national and international basketball organization in Brazil. She and her husband have one boy, Joao Victor Oliva, who was born in February, 1996.

Summary

Hortencia Marcari enjoyed unprecedented success on both the national and international levels of women's basketball. Her outstanding performances on the court and her colorful life-

HONORS AND AWARDS	
1991	Gold Medal, Pan-American Games
1994	Gold Medal, World Basketball Championships
1996	Silver Medal, Olympic basketball

style off it made her one of the few celebrities known around the world by first name alone.

Marcia J. Mackey

Additional Sources:

Brill, Marlene Targ. *Winning Women in Basketball.* Haupauge, N.Y.: Barrons Educational Series, 2000.

Corbett, Sara. *Venus to the Hoop.* New York: Doubleday, 1997.

Sandelson, Robert. *Ball Sports.* New York: Crestwood House, 1991.

GINO MARCHETTI

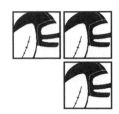

Sport: Football

Born: January 2, 1927
Antioch, California

Early Life

Gino John Marchetti was born on January 2, 1927, in Antioch, California, to Italian American parents. Gino's father, Ernest, was an immigrant who owned a bar and grill called The Nevada Club.

Gino had an unusually difficult childhood. When he was fourteen years old, the Americans entered World War II against Fascist Italy, Japan, and Germany. In the name of national security, all Japanese and Italian immigrants in the United States were sent to detention camps. This was especially hard on Gino because he considered himself a patriotic American.

After four years behind barbed wire, Gino decided to prove his feelings for his adopted nation. He petitioned his draft board to induct him into the United States armed forces. After initially refusing, the board eventually signed him up. Gino soon found himself fighting with the 69th Infantry on the Siegfried Line in Nazi Germany.

Gino served during the difficult time of the Battle of the Bulge. Somehow, the worst circumstances brought out the best in him, and soon Gino was winning medals. When news of his valiant performance reached his hometown papers, Gino's parents were finally released from detention camp.

The Road to Excellence

After the war, Gino finished high school in Antioch, where he had already demonstrated talent as a football player and was named team most valuable player. He also tended bar and became a motorcycle stunt rider. Upon graduation, Gino attended Modesto Junior College for a year, until assistant coach Brad Lynn of the University of San Francisco recruited him.

Gino Marchetti, defensive end for the Baltimore Colts, in 1959.

AP/Wide World Photos

In 1948, Gino enrolled at the University of San Francisco, where he played with some fine teammates, eleven of whom (including quarterback Ed Brown, offensive tackle Bob St. Clair, and All-American Ollie Matson) eventually went on to the National Football League (NFL).

Gino became known for being an extremely rough player who rarely missed a chance to get in some cheap shots. The war had left its imprint on his playing style—he had become a hatchet man. Fortunately, one of his opponents, Doak Walker, gave him a look that helped Gino see what unsportsmanlike tricks he had been resorting to. The experience caused him to clean up his style. From then on, he was on the lookout for others who played dirty and gave them his own version of justice. At San Francisco, Gino was named All-Pacific Coast and All-Catholic tackle in 1951.

The Emerging Champion

The next year, Gino was picked by the Dallas Texans in the second round of the NFL draft. Although he played well as an offensive tackle, the team did so poorly that it was re-formed and moved to Baltimore. The resulting new team was called the Baltimore Colts. As offensive tackle, Gino played well but not exceptionally. Then, Weeb Ewbank became head coach in 1954, and he switched Gino back to defensive end. Gino began to shine in the role, having gained a valuable education from his various positions. He had learned a number of deceptive moves from his opponents and incorporated them into his own play.

With time, the Colts became champions, and Gino turned out to be one of the finest defensive ends ever. He won all-league honors from 1955 through 1965, playing in ten Pro Bowl games and being named All-Pro eight times. In 1970, he was selected the best defensive end in the NFL's first fifty years. Eventually, the Pro Football Hall of Fame named him to its AFL-NFL 1960-1984 All-Star Team.

Continuing the Story

Gino's strongest asset was his skill at viciously rushing the passer. At 6 feet 4 inches and 245 pounds, he had what it took to impress his opponents. He was able to knock down any interfer-

ence, and it was nearly impossible to keep him away from the opposing passer and ball carrier. More than any player before him, Gino proved that it was possible to be quick as a defensive end, in spite of his height and heavy weight.

Although he had a vicious streak on the field, off the field Gino was another kind of person. A modest man who never complained or talked about himself, he simply loved life. Each January, he happily returned to his wife and three children in Antioch, California, and worked in a cocktail lounge. Then one winter, the Colts' owner, Carroll Rosenbloom, offered Gino the capital for his own restaurant if he would move his family to Baltimore. The resulting Gino's Restaurant grew into a chain of Gino's along the East Coast, all featuring the Ginoburger.

In 1958, Gino broke his leg in two places during the NFL championship game. When he announced his decision to retire in 1963, he was given an enormous farewell party by the Colts. Twice he was persuaded to return and play, in 1965 and 1966. He led the Colts to their first conference title since 1959 and to their tenth straight victory. When he retired again, after thirteen years with the Colts, Gino was given another fabulous retirement party.

Summary

Gino Marchetti was one of the finest defensive ends ever. His strongest asset was his skill at viciously rushing the passer. It was nearly impossible for opponents to keep him away from their passer and the ballcarrier. More than any player

HONORS AND AWARDS

1951	All-Pacific Coast Conference Team All-Catholic Team
1955-58, 1960-65	NFL Pro Bowl Team
1957-64	NFL All-Pro Team
1958	Associated Press NFL Player of the Year
1963	NFL All-Pro Team of the 1950's
1964	NFL Pro Bowl Co-Player of the Game
1970	All-First-Fifty-Year NFL Team
1972	Inducted into Pro Football Hall of Fame
1985	AFL-NFL 1960-1984 All-Star Team Uniform number 89 retired by Indianapolis Colts

before him, Gino proved it was possible to be quick as a defensive end in spite of size. He competed in ten Pro Bowl games, was named All-Pro eight times, and was selected best defensive end in the NFL's first fifty years.

Nicholas White

Additional Sources:

Anderson, Dave. *Great Defensive Players of the NFL.* New York: Random House, 1967.

Hickok, Ralph. *A Who's Who of Sports Champions.* Boston: Houghton Mifflin, 1995.

LaBlanc, Michael L., and Mary K. Ruby, eds. *Professional Sports Team Histories: Football.* Detroit: Gale, 1994.

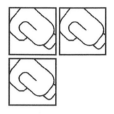

ROCKY MARCIANO
Rocco Francis Marchegiano

Sport: Boxing

Born: September 1, 1923
   Brockton, Massachusetts
Died: August 31, 1969
   near Newton, Iowa

Early Life

Rocky Marciano (born Rocco Francis Marchegiano on September 1, 1923, in Brockton, Massachusetts) was the oldest of six children born to Pierino and Pasqualena Marchegiano. His parents, both Italian immigrants, lived with his maternal grandfather in Brockton, Massachusetts, throughout most of Rocky's adolescence.

Rocky's father, a World War I veteran who had been seriously wounded at the battle of Château Thierry, worked in a shoe factory in Brockton most of his adult life. The shoe factory job paid only a modest wage. The poverty in which the Marchegiano family lived was deepened by the Great Depression, but Rocky's father always managed to keep food on the table. Rocky's fear of spending his life in a job similar to his father's made him determined to excel at sports in order to escape the Italian-Jewish-Irish ghetto in which he grew up.

The Road to Excellence

Rocky and his small circle of friends all dreamed of becoming major league baseball players. The boys spent most of their spare time playing sandlot games in a park near Rocky's home. Rocky himself was a good hitter but was painfully slow and had only an average throwing arm. None of the group was interested in schoolwork, and most dropped out before finishing high school. Rocky left school at age sixteen and took a series of jobs doing manual labor in order to help his father support his family. He continued to spend many hours every week during seasons of good weather playing baseball with his friends. Although never a bully, Rocky established himself as the best street fighter in the neighborhood, but he never considered a career in boxing.

In March, 1943, Rocky was drafted by the United States Army. Assigned to a supply unit in England, he did not see combat action during World War II. After the surrender of Germany in May, 1945, Rocky was sent back to the United States and stationed at Fort Lewis, Washington. He quickly learned that successful participation in sports would exempt him from routine duties. In addition to playing baseball, he began to box for the Fort Lewis team.

In the spring of 1946, an overweight Rocky Marciano arrived at his parents' home in Brockton on leave. Needing money, Rocky convinced his maternal uncle to arrange with a fight

RECOGNIZED WORLD HEAVYWEIGHT CHAMPIONSHIPS

Date	Location	Loser	Result
Sept. 23, 1952	Philadelphia, Pa.	Jersey Joe Walcott	13th-round knockout
May 15, 1953	Chicago, Ill.	Jersey Joe Walcott	1st-round knockout
Sept. 24, 1953	New York City, N.Y.	Roland LaStarza	11th-round technical knockout
June 17, 1954	New York City, N.Y.	Ezzard Charles	15th-round unanimous decision
Sept. 17, 1954	New York City, N.Y.	Ezzard Charles	8th-round knockout
May 16, 1955	San Francisco, Calif.	Don Cockell	9th-round technical knockout
Sept. 21, 1955	New York City, N.Y.	Archie Moore	9th-round knockout

promoter for him to compete in local prizefighting. Rocky was inexperienced and not in peak physical condition; he consequently lost the fight, for which he received thirty dollars. In later years, he related that he learned a valuable lesson from this first fight: Before all his fights for the rest of his career, he trained his body mercilessly. However inauspiciously, Rocky had launched his career in professional boxing.

The Emerging Champion

After his discharge from the army, Rocky embarked on a career as a boxer, despite his mother's almost hysterical objections. He entered a local Amateur Athletic Union tournament, for which he trained hard. Although he scored two first-round knockouts, he lost in the final bout primarily because he had dislocated one of his knuckles during the second knockout.

Rocky entered several more amateur tournaments, during which he demonstrated devastating punching power, clumsiness, and inexperience. He ended his amateur career the next year with an unimpressive 8-4 record. During the spring of 1948, he secured a manager, changed his name to Marciano, and began to train hard and to fight regularly. In 1948, Rocky had eleven fights, winning all of them by knockout within the first three rounds. In 1949, he added thirteen more victories, eleven by knockout, and had achieved the status of featured fighter at Madison Square Garden in New York.

By 1950, Rocky was receiving large purses for his fights and was rated by many as a top contender for the heavyweight championship. During that year, he married Barbara Cousins, with whom he had one daughter, Mary Anne. Over the next two and one-half years, he scored seventeen more victories, including a knockout over the legendary Joe Louis. On September 23, 1952, he finally got his chance at the world champion-

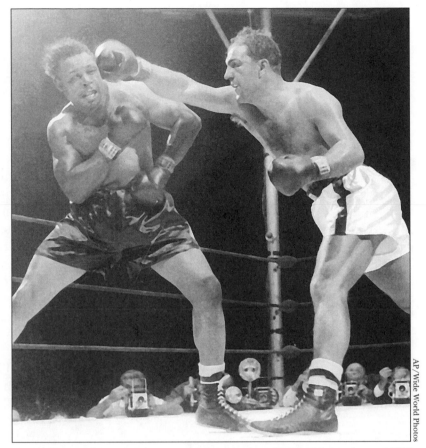

Rocky Marciano (right) pummels opponent Archie Moore in a 1955 bout.

ship and responded by knocking out Jersey Joe Walcott in the thirteenth round of a brutal fight. The poor Italian kid from a Brockton slum was heavyweight champion of the world.

Continuing the Story

During the next three years, Rocky defended his championship six times. He won five of those fights by knockout and won the other in a fifteen-round decision over Ezzard Charles. In April, 1956, he retired with a record of 49-0 as the only undefeated heavyweight champion in the history of boxing. Rocky intended, according to his friends, to spend his time in retirement with his family, making up to them for the neglect of his boxing days, when he had subordinated everything to pursuing the championship and the financial security it represented. Instead, Rocky spent most of his time after retirement traveling.

Always fearful of descending again into the poverty in which he grew up, Rocky spent most of

1793

his time from 1956 to 1969 as a professional celebrity. He was in great demand for personal appearances at clubs and on television. He often made three or four of those appearances a week, in widely separate parts of the world. He also made movies and pursued many business ventures. Rocky never trusted banks and hid most of the money he made from these endeavors in various places around the country. Very little

of the money he hid was found after his death. On August 31, 1969, the plane carrying Rocky Marciano to a personal appearance in Des Moines crashed near Newton, Iowa, killing everyone aboard.

Summary

Rocky Marciano achieved the pinnacle of boxing success despite his relatively small size for a heavyweight (5 feet 10 inches, 185 pounds) because of the same attributes that mark most sports champions. He had an indomitable will to win and utter confidence in himself, and trained perhaps harder than any other fighter in the history of the sport, subordinating everything to his goal. In a computer simulation in 1971 of a boxing tournament involving all the heavyweight champions, Rocky was the projected winner.

Paul Madden

Additional Sources:

Cutter, Robert A. *The Rocky Marciano Story.* New York: William Allen, 1954.

Mayes, Harold. *Rocky Marciano.* London: Hamilton, 1956.

Mee, Bob. *Boxing: Heroes and Champions.* Edison, N.J.: Chartwell Books, 1997.

Skehan, Everett M. *Rocky Marciano: Biography of a First Son.* Boston: Houghton Mifflin, 1977.

STATISTICS

Bouts, 49
Knockouts, 43
Bouts won by decision, 6
Losses, 0

RECORDS

First undefeated world heavyweight champion in professional boxing history

HONORS AND AWARDS

1952	Neil Trophy
	Hickok Belt
1952, 1954-55	*Ring* magazine Merit Award
1959	Inducted into *Ring* magazine Boxing Hall of Fame
1990	Inducted into International Boxing Hall of Fame

JUAN MARICHAL

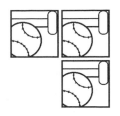

Sport: Baseball

Born: October 20, 1937
      Laguna Verde, Dominican Republic

Early Life

Juan Antonio Sanchez Marichal was born on October 20, 1937, at Laguna Verde, Dominican Republic. His family was very poor, farming a small patch of ground and living in a palm bark shack. When Juan was only three years old, his father died, and he was raised by his mother and older brother Gonzalo.

Gonzalo loved baseball and fostered a similar interest in Juan. They could not afford store-bought equipment, but Gonzalo taught his brother how to fashion a baseball out of a piece of rubber, threads unwound from an old silk stocking, and adhesive tape. The ball was lop-sided and hard to throw accurately, but that actually helped young Juan develop the control that would become one of his hallmarks as a major league pitcher.

Juan quit school after eleventh grade to pitch and play shortstop for several Dominican amateur teams. In 1958, a scout from the San Francisco Giants signed him to a contract for a $500 bonus.

The Road to Excellence

Juan's progress through the minor leagues was rapid. In 1958, he led the Midwest League in victories, innings pitched, and earned run average. The next year, he led the Eastern League in the same categories and added the leadership in strikeouts. He began 1960 with Tacoma of the Pacific Coast League, only a step away from the major leagues. When he had eleven wins by mid-July, the Giants decided to bring him up.

On July 19, the "Dominican Dandy," as he was already being called, made his first major league start against the Philadelphia Phillies. For 7 innings, he held them hitless. A Philadelphia batter finally broke the spell with a single in the eighth, but that was the only hit Marichal allowed in pitching a 2-0 shutout. He won five more games before the season ended, losing only two.

Besides marvelous control, Juan possessed an excellent fastball and curve. Throwing out of a high-kicking motion, he delivered either pitch overhand, three-quarters sidearm, sidearm, or even underhand. Batters were mystified, never knowing which pitch would come from what angle. Equally frustrating to hitters was that he threw with such ease, almost effortlessly, and all the while with a big grin on his face. They called him "Laughing Boy."

The Emerging Champion

Juan was ready for his first big season in 1962. By early September, he had won eighteen games. Then, after a foot injury sidelined him for several starts, he lost three games. The Giants tied the Los Angeles Dodgers for the pennant and then won a three-game playoff, but Juan reinjured his foot while pitching the deciding game. The 1962 World Series would be the only one in which he would ever appear, and it was not a happy experience. He started game 3 but had to leave after 4 shutout innings when he was hit on the hand by a pitch while batting.

Although the Giants won no more pennants while Juan pitched for them, he kept them in the pennant races throughout the 1960's. From 1963 through 1969, he won twenty or more games six times. In 1963, he led the National League in victories with twenty-five, including a no-hitter against Houston. He had twenty-five wins again in 1966 and again led the league with twenty-six in 1968. In only one of those golden years did his earned run average rise above 2.50, and his sparkling 2.10 topped the league in 1969.

Surprisingly, although he won more games than any other pitcher in the decade, he never received the Cy Young Award, emblematic of the season's best pitcher. Each year, it seemed, another hurler—Sandy Koufax, Dean Chance, Bob Gibson, or Tom Seaver—would have an even more spectacular season to win the honor. When Juan had an off-year in 1967 and slipped to fourteen wins, his teammate Mike McCormick had the only twenty-win season of his career to earn the Cy Young.

Continuing the Story

Juan was at his best when the competition was the strongest. One example is his outstanding record in the All-Star game. Facing the best players in the American League, he was the winning pitcher in 1962 and 1964 and was chosen the game's most valuable player in 1965. In 18 All-Star innings, he allowed only 2 runs.

Los Angeles was San Francisco's arch-rival.

STATISTICS

Season	GP	GS	CG	IP	HA	BB	SO	W	L	S	ShO	ERA
1960	11	11	6	81.1	59	28	58	6	2	0	1	2.66
1961	29	27	9	185.0	183	48	124	13	10	0	3	3.89
1962	37	36	18	262.2	233	90	153	18	11	1	3	3.36
1963	41	40	18	321.1	259	61	248	**25**	8	0	5	2.41
1964	33	33	22	269.0	241	52	206	21	8	0	4	2.48
1965	39	37	24	295.1	224	46	240	22	13	1	**10**	2.13
1966	37	36	25	307.1	228	36	222	25	6	0	4	2.23
1967	26	26	18	202.1	195	42	166	14	10	0	2	2.76
1968	38	38	30	325.2	295	46	218	**26**	9	0	5	2.43
1969	37	36	27	300.0	244	54	205	21	11	0	**8**	**2.10**
1970	34	33	14	243.0	269	48	123	12	10	0	1	4.11
1971	37	37	18	279.0	244	56	159	18	11	0	4	2.94
1972	25	24	6	165.0	176	46	72	6	16	0	0	3.71
1973	34	32	9	209.0	231	37	87	11	15	0	2	3.79
1974	11	9	0	57.1	61	14	21	5	1	0	0	4.87
1975	2	2	0	6.0	11	5	1	0	1	0	0	13.50
Totals	471	457	244	3,507.0	3,153	709	2,303	243	142	2	52	2.89

Notes: Boldface indicates statistical leader. GP = games played; GS = games started; CG = complete games; IP = innings pitched; HA = hits allowed; BB = bases on balls (walks); SO = strikeouts; W = wins; L = losses; S = saves; ShO = shutouts; ERA = earned run average

HONORS AND AWARDS

1962-69, 1971	National League All-Star Team
1963	Citizens Savings Northern California Athlete of the Year
1963, 1965-66, 1968	*Sporting News* National League All-Star Team
1965	All-Star Game most valuable player
1983	Inducted into National Baseball Hall of Fame Uniform number 27 retired by San Francisco Giants

Juan was 37-18 in games against the Dodgers. When facing Los Angeles before a home crowd at Candlestick Park, he was nearly unbeatable: 24-1.

The rivalry between the Giants and Dodgers spawned the most controversial incident of Juan's career in 1965. During a hard-fought series in August, charges flew that pitchers on both sides intentionally threw at batters. Juan was batting in the third inning of a game when a return throw from Dodger catcher John Roseboro whizzed past his ear. He warned Roseboro not to throw so close, and when the next return throw narrowly missed him, he turned on the catcher. Roseboro started toward him, and Juan swung his bat, hitting the catcher in the head. A bench-clearing brawl ensued.

Juan received a nine-day suspension and a $1,750 fine, the largest ever levied to that time. The incident was completely out of character for the easygoing Juan, but many fans who knew only his pitching record assumed that he was a thug. That Roseboro later became one of Juan's staunchest supporters for election to the Baseball Hall of Fame shows what kind of person the "Dominican Dandy" really was.

In 1970, a bad reaction to penicillin led to chronic arthritis and ended Juan's days as a great pitcher. In 1975, he retired with his family to a one-thousand-acre, mechanized farm in Santo Domingo.

Following his retirement at age 37, Juan divided his time between his family farm in the Dominican Republic and San Francisco. He was hired by the Oakland A's as the director for Latin American scouting, a post that he held for twelve years. In 1996, Juan was asked by Dominican president Leonel Fernandez to serve on his cabinet as minister of sports, physical education, and recreation. In that role, he often developed relationships between young Dominican players and major league scouts.

Summary

Juan finished his sixteen-year career with a 243-142 record, a 2.89 lifetime ERA, 2,303 strikeouts, and nine All-Star Team selections. In six out of seven years during the 1960's, he won more than twenty games, including three seasons of over twenty-five wins. Despite these formidable statistics, Juan was never given the Cy Young Award. In 1983, however, he became the first Latin American player to be elected to the Hall of Fame through the regular selection process.

Bob Carroll

Additional Sources:

Devaney, John. *Juan Marichal, Mister Strike.* New York, Putnam, 1970.

Gutierrez, Paul. "Catching up with Juan Marichal." *Sports Illustrated* 87, no. 11 (1997).

Libby, Bill. *Star Pitchers of the Major Leagues.* New York: Random House, 1971.

Marichal, Juan, with Charles Einstein. *A Pitcher's Story.* Garden City, N.Y.: Random House, 1967.

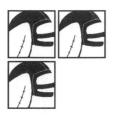

DAN MARINO

Sport: Football

Born: September 15, 1961
Pittsburgh, Pennsylvania

Early Life

Daniel Constantine Marino, Jr., was born on September 15, 1961, in Pittsburgh, Pennsylvania, the son of *Pittsburgh Post-Gazette* truck driver Daniel Constantine Marino and his wife, Veronica Marino. Dan started his quarterbacking career as a fourth grader at St. Regis Elementary School. A gifted, all-around athlete, Dan lettered in football and baseball at Central Catholic High School in Oakland, a working-class neighborhood in Pittsburgh. Though he was chosen by the Kansas City Royals in the fourth round of the 1979 amateur baseball draft, the heavily recruited 6-foot 4-inch, 200-pound signal-caller opted to pursue a football career at the University of Pittsburgh.

The Road to Excellence

Dan proved himself almost immediately. In the middle of his freshman year, he was installed by Pitt coach Jackie Sherrill as the Panthers' starting quarterback, and he responded by leading the team to an 11-1 record and a Fiesta Bowl win over Arizona State. Blessed with a strong arm and the capacity to throw long passes with pinpoint precision, Dan also guided the Panthers to 11-1 seasons and bowl victories in his sophomore and junior years. In his senior year, with expectations of a national championship and a Heisman Trophy, the Panthers "slumped" to 9-3. In spite of the disappointment, Dan was graduated as a communications major and set records as Pitt's all-time total of-

fensive leader in passing yards, passes attempted, and touchdown passes.

Dan was the number-one choice of the Los Angeles Express in the inaugural draft of the United States Football League, but he chose to sign with the National Football League (NFL) Miami Dolphins, who had made him their number-one choice in the quarterback-rich draft of 1983—a draft that also included future stars John Elway, Jim Kelly, and Ken O'Brien.

Courtesy Miami Dolphins

The Emerging Champion

In Dan's first appearance with the Dolphins, a relief stint against the Los Angeles Raiders, he engineered touchdown drives on his first two possessions. It was an auspicious beginning. As the Dolphins' new signal-caller, Dan took the Miami team to the playoffs, in the process earning the NFL's Rookie of the Year Award. He also became the first rookie quarterback named to start in the Pro Bowl.

In his sophomore season of 1984-85, with further mentoring from Miami head coach Don Shula, Dan turned in one of the finest campaigns ever by an NFL quarterback. Most impressive were Dan's three NFL records: 48 passing touchdowns, 5,084 total passing yards, and 362 completions. Dan also led Miami to an appearance in Super Bowl XIX, where he completed 29 of 50 passes for 318 yards and a touchdown in a hard-fought loss to the San Francisco 49ers. In just two seasons, Dan had established himself as one of the game's premier passers, a member of an elite cadre that included Super Bowl adversary Joe Montana.

Working with an offense that Shula had designed to capitalize on Dan's rifle arm and quick release, the Dolphins continued to be one of the powerhouses of the NFL's Eastern Division. In 1985, Dan again topped the NFL in total passing yards (4,137), completions (336), and touchdowns (30) and again took Miami to the playoffs. In 1986, he once more set the pace for the NFL in total passing yardage (4,746), completions (378), and passing touchdowns (44). In a September game that season, Dan established a personal best with 6 touchdown passes against the New York Jets.

During 1987, 1988, and 1989, Dan continued his assaults on the Miami and NFL record books. Though his 1989 total of 3,997 passing yards just missed giving him a fifth 4,000-yard season, Dan continued to demolish team benchmarks set by Bob Griese, Miami's outstanding quarterback of the 1970's.

Continuing the Story

In 1990, Dan put the Dolphins back into the playoffs. Although Miami lost to the Buffalo Bills in the American Football Conference (AFC) championship game, Dan's 3,363 passing yards made him only the eleventh quarterback in NFL history to have thrown for more than 30,000 yards, a plateau he reached faster than any previous quarterback. In 1991, Dan threw for 3,000 yards for the eighth time, establishing a new NFL record for 3,000-yard seasons.

In 1992, Dan had another banner year, throwing for more than 4,000 yards and again leading

STATISTICS

Season	GP	PA	PC	Pct.	Yds.	Avg.	TD	Int.
1983	11	296	173	58.4	2,210	7.47	20	6
1984	16	**564**	**362**	64.2	**5,084**	**9.01**	**48**	17
1985	16	567	**336**	59.3	4,137	7.30	**30**	21
1986	16	**623**	**378**	60.7	**4,746**	7.62	**44**	23
1987	12	444	263	59.2	3,245	7.31	26	13
1988	16	**606**	**354**	58.4	4,434	7.32	28	23
1989	16	550	308	56.0	3,997	7.27	24	22
1990	16	531	306	57.6	3,563	6.71	21	11
1991	16	549	318	57.9	3,970	7.23	25	13
1992	16	**554**	**330**	59.6	**4,116**	7.43	24	16
1993	5	150	91	60.7	1,218	8.12	8	3
1994	16	615	385	62.6	4,453	7.24	30	17
1995	14	482	309	64.1	3,668	7.61	24	15
1996	13	373	221	59.2	2,795	7.49	17	9
1997	16	548	319	58.2	3,780	6.90	16	11
1998	16	537	310	57.7	3,497	6.51	23	15
1999	11	369	204	55.3	2,448	6.63	12	17
Totals	242	8,358	4,967	59.4	61,361	7.20	420	252

Notes: Boldface indicates statistical leader. GP = games played; PA = passes attempted; PC = passes completed; Pct. = percent completed; Yds. = yards; Avg. = average yards per attempt; TD = touchdowns; Int. = interceptions

NFL RECORDS

Most yards passing, 61,361
Most touchdown passes, 420
Most pass attempts, 8,538
Most pass completions, 4,967

HONORS AND AWARDS

1981	College All-American
1983-87, 1991-95	NFL Pro Bowl Team
1983	*Sporting News* NFL Rookie of the Year
1984	Associated Press NFL Player of the Year
	Bert Bell Trophy
	Professional Football Writers Association Player of the Year
	Sporting News NFL Player of the Year
	United Press International AFC Offensive Player of the Year

the Dolphins into the AFC title game. As in 1990, however, the Dolphins fell to quarterback Jim Kelly and the Buffalo Bills. Still, Dan won the Dolphins' most valuable player award for the tenth consecutive year. With 330 completions, he joined Dan Fouts and Fran Tarkenton as the only quarterbacks in NFL history to have completed 3,000 passes. Dan was also named the starting quarterback for the 1992 AFC Pro Bowl team. It was his seventh career Pro Bowl selection overall and his fifth as a starter.

After only ten NFL seasons, the gifted Miami quarterback had amassed 39,502 total yards passing. As the 1993 season unfolded, he moved past the 40,000-yard mark and, shortly thereafter, Johnny Unitas' career record of 40,239 yards. Now, only Fouts at 43,040 and Tarkenton at 47,003 stood between Dan and yet another NFL record.

In 1993, Dan might have passed Fouts's mark had it not been for a midseason injury to his Achilles tendon that kept him on the bench for the duration of the season. Though he had bounced back from five previous surgeries on his left knee, this was the first long-term, injury-caused absence for the durable quarterback. Dan's durability at the hazardous quarterback position was a tribute both to Miami's staunch offensive line and to Dan's own rugged constitution, athleticism, and confidence.

Dan retired from pro football at the end of the 1999 season. In his last six seasons with the Dol-

phins he continued to set records and be honored accordingly. He was selected two more times to the Pro Bowl, in 1994 and 1995. He held the league's records in touchdown passes (420), yards passing (61,361), pass attempts (8,358), and completions (4,967). During the halftime of a Miami-Baltimore game on September 17, 2000, Dan's number 13 jersey was retired.

One of the brightest stars of the sports world, Dan has balanced the trials of being a celebrity with the joy of his wife, Claire, his three sons, and his two daughters. His ongoing work for the community is centered on the Dan Marino Foundation for children's charities of South Florida. In 1997 Dan embarked on a new major league sports venture, making his debut as a NASCAR Winston Cup team co-owner with race legend Bill Elliot. The Elliot-Marino Motorsports team began full-time competition in 1997. In 2000 Dan joined the executive management team of Dreams, Incorporated, as director of business development. He also became a host on HBO's weekly football program *Inside the NFL*.

Summary

Dan Marino is one of the most recognizable and popular sports figures in the entire world. After seventeen consecutive seasons with the Miami Dolphins, Dan managed to rewrite the NFL record book by establishing twenty records, including being the all-time leading passer in NFL history. A symbol of competitiveness and efficiency, Dan has ensured himself a place in American sports and entertainment culture.

Chuck Berg

Additional Sources:

Beckett Publications editors. *Dan Marino: The Making of a Legend.* Dallas: Beckett, 1999.

Holmstrom, John. *Dan Marino, Joe Montana.* New York: Avon Books, 1985.

Marino, Dan, and Steve Delsohn. *Marino!* Chicago: Contemporary Books, 1986.

Rubin, Bob. *Dan Marino: Wonder Boy Quarterback.* Chicago: Children's Press, 1985.

Wilner, Barry. *Dan Marino.* New York: Chelsea House, 1996.

ROGER MARIS

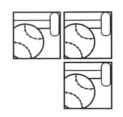

Sport: Baseball

Born: September 10, 1934
   Hibbing, Minnesota
Died: December 14, 1985
   Houston, Texas

Early Life

Roger Eugene Maris was born in Hibbing, Minnesota, a northern Iron Range town, on September 10, 1934. His parents, Rudy, a railroad worker, and Connie, were of Austrian, German,

Courtesy of Amateur Athletic Foundation of Los Angeles

and Polish ancestry. The original family name Maras was changed to Maris in 1955. Roger's older brother, Rudy Jr., was born in 1933. When the children were infants, the family moved to Grand Forks, North Dakota, and finally settled in Fargo when Roger was twelve. Roger's home town of Fargo is a small city in the fertile Red River Valley of eastern North Dakota, which produces sugar beets, wheat, and barley.

School was difficult for Roger, who preferred outdoor activities and lacked patience for academic work. From an early age, Roger stood out as a gifted athlete in a variety of sports including hockey, a favorite pastime of his father.

The Road to Excellence

Urged to play baseball by his brother, who was also a fine athlete, Roger soon looked to Ted Williams as his idol. Shanley Catholic High School, which Roger attended, did not have a baseball team, but the youngster excelled there in track, basketball, and football while continuing to play baseball in the City League and American Legion programs. During his senior year in 1953, Roger, an All-State halfback, received football scholarship offers from a dozen universities. Although he considered attending Oklahoma, Roger's dislike for books and classes and a timely offer from a Cleveland Indians scout persuaded him to choose baseball.

From the Class C Fargo-Morehead club, where he hit

.325, the left-handed right fielder moved up through the Indians' farm system to Keokuk, Tulsa, Reading, and finally the Indianapolis Triple-A team in 1956. In the minors, Roger had his ups and downs, experiencing injuries and problems with some managers, as he would in his later career. In Keokuk and Reading, Roger's manager was Jo Jo White, an easygoing person with the patience to handle a tense young ballplayer. White, who was the most significant influence on Roger's baseball career, advised him to worry less about hitting singles and concentrate on power hitting by pulling the ball to right field. The result was very promising. In 1957, at age twenty-three, the future star was ready for his major league debut.

The Emerging Champion

Roger's first three major league seasons were not especially notable. On June 15, 1958, Cleveland traded Roger to the Kansas City Athletics. Roger was content in this familiar midwestern setting. In 1956, he had married his high school sweetheart, Patricia Carvell. The couple bought a home in suburban Raytown and started to rear the first of their six children.

The farsighted New York club management recognized Roger's possibilities as a natural home-run hitter in Yankee Stadium, with its short distance to the right field fence. Through a trade on December 11, 1959, Roger joined baseball's tradition-rich team and reluctantly stepped into the

spotlight of national scrutiny in the "house that Ruth built."

In his first Yankee season, Roger received the League's most valuable player award with a .283 average, 39 home runs, and a league-leading 112 runs batted in (RBIs). This valuable new Yankee was a compact 6-foot, 195-pound athlete with powerful shoulders. Baseball experts praised Roger's picture-perfect, lashing home-run stroke. Furthermore, Roger was a complete ballplayer who had good speed on the bases, made spectacular outfield plays, and won respect from base runners for his strong, accurate throwing arm. On the field, Roger was an unselfish, loyal team player and a serious competitor.

Roger made the 1961 season an unforgettable year in baseball when he and teammate Mickey Mantle chased Babe Ruth's mammoth record of 60 homers in one season. Mickey finished with 54, and Roger broke the record with 61 on the last day of the season, while driving in 142 runs. The huge Yankee Stadium crowd that came to witness this historic baseball moment gave Roger the unrestrained, joyous ovation he deserved.

Continuing the Story

Roger paid a high price for glory. Boos, hate mail, and disparaging comparisons issued from Ruth loyalists, who felt that Roger was an unworthy twenty-six-year-old upstart. Baseball Commissioner Ford Frick announced that, because Ruth had played the old 154-game schedule instead of

STATISTICS

Season	GP	AB	Hits	2B	3B	HR	Runs	RBI	BA	SA
1957	116	358	84	9	5	14	61	51	.235	.405
1958	150	583	140	19	4	28	87	80	.240	.431
1959	122	433	118	21	7	16	69	72	.273	.464
1960	136	499	141	18	7	39	98	**112**	.283	**.581**
1961	161	590	159	16	4	**61**	**132**	**142**	.269	.620
1962	157	590	151	34	1	33	92	100	.256	.485
1963	90	312	84	14	1	23	53	53	.269	.542
1964	141	513	144	12	2	26	86	71	.281	.464
1965	46	155	37	7	0	8	22	27	.239	.439
1966	119	348	81	9	2	13	37	43	.233	.382
1967	125	410	107	18	7	9	64	55	.261	.405
1968	100	310	79	18	2	5	25	45	.255	.374
Totals	1,463	5,101	1,325	195	42	275	826	851	.260	.476

Notes: Boldface indicates statistical leader. GP = games played; AB = at bats; 2B = doubles; 3B = triples; HR = home runs; RBI = runs batted in; BA = batting average; SA = slugging average

HONORS AND AWARDS

1959-62	American League All-Star Team
1960	American League Gold Glove Award
1960-61	American League most valuable player
1961	*Sporting News* Major League Player of the Year Associated Press Male Athlete of the Year Hickok Belt Major league record for the most home runs in a season (61)
1962	Major league record for the most intentional walks in a game (4) Uniform number 9 retired by New York Yankees

the current 161 games, an asterisk explaining this would go into the record book if Babe's total was surpassed in more than 154. Roger also suffered from poor relations with the press; he was a shy, blunt man of few words who preferred the privacy of family life. Before the 1961 season ended, Roger was losing his hair as a result of stress.

In 1962, Roger hit 33 homers with 100 RBIs, but the boos and bad press persisted because he did not duplicate the previous year's achievement. Roger would never regain the form of the 1961 season, which had taken its toll on him. The Yankees traded Roger to the St. Louis Cardinals in December, 1966. Pleased with the move, Roger played enthusiastically before appreciative fans; he had an excellent 1967 World Series and retired at the end of the next season.

Roger moved to Gainesville, Florida, where the Cardinals' owner had given him a beer distributorship. In his remaining years, he avoided returning to Yankee Stadium for Old Timers' Day and turned down proposals to make a movie of his life. On December 14, 1985, Maris died at age fifty-one, following a two-year struggle against lymphatic cancer. Roger's body was laid to rest on the northern plains where his roots were, among his people. The large funeral in Fargo was attended by many former Yankee teammates who came to pay him tribute.

Summary

Roger Maris's achievement should not be diminished by the infamous asterisk. The great Babe Ruth hit 60 home runs under less hectic circumstances without the media pressures and hostile critics. Under similar conditions, Roger may have topped Ruth's mark in less than 154 games. Roger deserves credit for persevering and hitting 61 home runs against these formidable obstacles. Mickey Mantle called Roger's achievement the greatest single feat he ever saw in baseball.

When Mark McGwire finally broke Roger's record in 1998, it had stood for thirty-seven years—longer than Ruth's record had stood. The attention attracted by McGwire's pursuit of the record focused new interest in Roger himself. In 2001 Billy Crystal produced and directed a film for HBO about Roger's great season titled *61*.

David A. Crain

Additional Sources:

Allen, Maury. *Roger Maris: A Man For All Seasons.* New York: Donald L. Fine, 1986.

Maris, Roger, and Jim Ogle. *Roger Maris at Bat.* New York: Duell, Sloan and Pearce, 1962.

_____. *Slugger in Right.* New York: Argonaut Books, 1963.

McNeil, William. *Ruth, Maris, McGwire and Sosa: Baseball's Single Season Home Run Champions.* Jefferson, N.C.: McFarland, 1999.

Rosenfeld, Harvey. *Roger Maris: A Title to Fame.* Fargo, N.D.: Prairie House, 1991.

RUBE MARQUARD

Sport: Baseball

Born: October 9, 1889
Cleveland, Ohio
Died: June 1, 1980
Baltimore, Maryland

National Baseball Library, Cooperstown, New York

Early Life

Richard William Marquard was born on October 9, 1889, in Cleveland, Ohio. Ever since he was a child, all that he would think about was baseball. He loved the game and, as he was always tall for his age, he generally played ball with a group of older boys. The shortest of Richard's four siblings was his sister. She grew to be 6 feet 2 inches tall. Richard finally stopped growing at 6 feet 3 inches.

In his early teens, Richard was a batboy for Cleveland of the American League. At the time, Cleveland was known as the Blues or Bronchos, and later as the Naps; the team later became the Indians. Working beside heroes such as Nap Lajoie, Elmer Flick, and Addie Joss, Richard decided that he was going to be a professional baseball player.

The Road to Excellence

Richard's father, chief engineer of Cleveland, was against his son's becoming a ballplayer. He felt that the only way Richard could get a good job was to finish high school and then go to college. Richard argued that he wanted to be a ballplayer and that he could get good pay doing so, but his father did not believe him.

In the summer of 1906, Richard gained a tryout with the minor league baseball club in Waterloo, Iowa. The club was in desperate need of a left-handed pitcher, so Waterloo's catcher, Howard Wakefield, suggested that his friend

Richard Marquard be given a try. Richard, knowing that his father would never loan him money for the long trip, hitchhiked his way from Cleveland to Waterloo. Although he pitched well for Waterloo and even won a game, Richard was not offered a contract. Disappointed, he returned to Cleveland.

The next summer, Richard got a job with a local ice-cream company. On Sundays, he was the star pitcher for the company's semiprofessional baseball team. The Cleveland Naps were impressed with Richard's pitching and offered him $100 a month to sign with their organization, but Richard turned them down. He was already making that much money with the ice-cream company and wanted more. Eventually, he got more when he signed for $200 a month with the Indianapolis Indians of the minor league American Association.

Richard told his father about his new job as a professional baseball player. His father told Richard not to come back home; he never wanted to see his son again. Richard vowed to make his father proud of him.

The Emerging Champion

Indianapolis optioned Richard to Canton, Ohio, of the Central League. His 1907 season with Canton was excellent. He led the league with twenty-three wins and held opposing batters to a cumulative batting average of .119.

The next year, Richard played for Indianapolis and led the Indians to the AA pennant. An Indianapolis newspaper noted that his pitching resembled that of star major leaguer Rube Waddell. From then on, Richard was known as "Rube."

In 1908, Rube led the AA with 28 wins and 250 strikeouts. That July, it was announced that the National League New York Giants had purchased Rube from Indianapolis for $11,000. At the time, that was the greatest amont of money ever paid for a minor league baseball player.

Rube finished out the AA season with the Indians and then went to New York. The Giants were in the middle of one of the tightest pennant races of all time. Every game was important and manager John McGraw was wary to start the rookie pitcher. McGraw felt that if Rube lost his first game, he might easily lose his confidence and not be effective for a long time afterward. Never-

HONORS AND AWARDS
1912 Major league record for the most consecutive victories in a season (19)
1971 Inducted into National Baseball Hall of Fame

theless, pressured by Giants owner John Brush, McGraw started the highly touted Rube against Cincinnati on September 25. Rube was hit hard and lasted only 5 innings, giving up 5 runs and earning the loss. He did not pitch again that season.

Over the next two years, Rube fulfilled Mc-Graw's prophecy by struggling to a 9-17 record with the Giants. With the aid of pitching coach Wilbert Robinson, Rube regained his confidence and bounced back in 1911 with a record of 24-7 and a league-leading 237 strikeouts.

The following year, Rube won his first nineteen decisions, tying the record for most consecutive games won in a season set by Tim Keefe in 1888. Under today's scoring rules, Rube actually would be credited with twenty consecutive wins. Rube finished the 1912 season leading the league in victories with twenty-six.

His final twenty-win season came in 1913, when he finished at 23-10. Over the previous three years, he had a cumulative record of 73-28 and

STATISTICS

Season	GP	GS	CG	IP	HA	BB	SO	W	L	S	ShO	ERA
1908	1	1	0	5.0	6	2	2	0	1	0	0	3.60
1909	29	21	8	173.0	155	73	109	5	13	0	0	2.60
1910	13	8	2	70.2	65	40	52	4	4	0	0	4.46
1911	45	33	22	277.2	221	106	**237**	24	7	2	5	2.50
1912	43	38	22	294.2	286	80	175	**26**	11	0	1	2.57
1913	42	33	20	288.0	248	49	151	23	10	2	4	2.50
1914	39	33	15	268.0	261	47	92	12	22	2	4	3.06
1915	33	23	10	193.2	207	38	92	11	10	2	2	4.04
1916	36	20	15	205.0	169	38	107	13	6	5	2	1.58
1917	37	29	14	232.2	200	60	117	19	12	0	2	2.55
1918	34	29	19	239.0	231	59	89	9	**18**	0	4	2.64
1919	8	7	3	59.0	54	10	29	3	3	0	0	2.29
1920	28	26	10	189.2	181	35	89	10	7	0	1	3.23
1921	39	35	18	265.2	291	50	88	17	14	0	2	3.39
1922	39	24	7	198.0	255	66	57	11	15	1	0	5.09
1923	38	29	11	239.0	265	65	78	11	14	0	3	3.73
1924	6	6	1	36.0	33	13	10	1	2	0	0	3.00
1925	26	8	0	72.0	105	27	19	2	8	0	0	5.75
Totals	536	403	197	3,303.4	3,233	858	1,593	201	177	14	30	3.08

Notes: Boldface indicates statistical leader. GP = games played; GS = games started; CG = complete games; IP = innings pitched; HA = hits allowed; BB = bases on balls (walks); SO = strikeouts; W = wins; L = losses; S = saves; ShO = shutouts; ERA = earned run average

his earned run average was consistently around 2.50.

It was during these years that Rube starred in vaudeville during the off-seasons. He married actress Blossom Seeley in 1913, although their conflicting careers eventually brought about a divorce in 1920. Rube remarried twice.

Continuing the Story

Rube had an off-year in 1914. Struggling again the following year, he was sold to the National League Brooklyn Dodgers, managed by Rube's former pitching coach, Wilbert Robinson. Ironically, Rube's best game that year was against the Dodgers on April 15, when he pitched a no-hitter.

In 1916, Rube helped the Dodgers to their first pennant since 1890. Four years later, coming back from a broken leg the previous season, Rube again pitched on a pennant winner in Brooklyn. Although Rube pitched for five National League champion teams, he was never on a World Series winner.

Rube was traded to the National League Cincinnati Reds for 1921 and won seventeen games. He was traded again the following winter, and pitched four years with the Boston Braves.

Rube followed his major league career with ten years of playing, managing, coaching, and even umpiring in the minor leagues. At forty-three years of age, Rube retired from baseball for good. He settled in Baltimore and worked at mutuel windows at nearby racetracks. On June 1, 1980, Rube died of cancer.

Summary

The popular Rube Marquard never drank alcohol or smoked. Although he often experienced times when his performance was mediocre, he always seemed to bounce back with periods of exceptional pitching.

Once, after pitching a game for Brooklyn, Rube was told that his father had come from Cleveland to see him. Rube was sure that there was some mistake. "My father wouldn't go across the street to see me," he said. Yet it was his father, and he was very proud of his son after all.

Tom Shieber

Additional Sources:

Hynd, Noel. *Marquard and Seeley.* Hyannis, Mass.: Parnassus Imprints, 1996.

Mansch, Larry D. *Rube Marquard: The Life and Times of a Baseball Hall of Famer.* Jefferson, N.C.: McFarland, 1998.

Shatzkin, Mike, et al., eds. *The Ballplayers: Baseball's Ultimate Biographical Reference.* New York: William Morrow, 1990.

JIM MARSHALL

Sport: Football

Born: December 30, 1937
Danville, Kentucky

Early Life

James Laurence Marshall was born on December 30, 1937, in Danville, Kentucky. His family later moved to Columbus, Ohio. Jim was a good student and a fine athlete in high school. He attended East High School where his art teacher, Mrs. Barlow, was one of his favorites. Jim was a two-time All-League selection in football while helping East High School to city championships in 1954 and 1955. His coach was Ralph Webster, who Jim credits, along with his coach at Ohio State University, Woody Hayes, with instilling in him the importance of making the most out of life. He always did. Besides being a great football player, Jim participated in track. He even lettered twice in track at Ohio State while earning All-Big Ten and All-American honors in football. Jim majored in psychology and biology at Ohio State.

Jim Marshall of the Minnesota Vikings, in 1963.

The Road to Excellence

Woody Hayes was intent on recruiting Jim to stay in his hometown and play college football at Ohio State. He sent one of his top former athletes, Jim Parker, over to East High School to be a coach and a friend. In the process of coaching and helping Jim, Parker convinced him to go to Ohio State.

Now Jim met the real Woody Hayes. Woody had been nice to Jim and Jim had gotten to know Mrs. Hayes, who Jim thought was a wonderful person. Woody, however, was a tough coach. It was that toughness that Jim later said was the most important thing he learned from Woody.

Jim disappointed Woody when he left school early to pursue professional football, but Jim made the most of the opportunity.

After being named to the 1958 All-American team at the tackle position, Jim began his professional career with Saskatchewan in the Canadian Football League. After one successful season in Canada, Jim was drafted by the Cleveland Browns of the National Football League (NFL) in 1960. He was the Browns' number-four draft choice.

Jim was impressive during his rookie season,

NFL RECORDS

Most opposition fumbles recovered, 29
Most consecutive games played, 282

HONORS AND AWARDS

1958	College All-American
	All-Big Ten Conference Team
1969-70	NFL Pro Bowl Team

playing all twelve games for the Browns. During training camp the following year, Jim became ill. He had contracted encephalitis, which is often called "sleeping sickness." Jim eventually won a life-threatening battle with the illness. Even though Coach Paul Brown thought Jim was going to be a star in the NFL, the Browns needed a healthy defensive tackle right away as they set their sights on the championship. The Browns reluctantly traded Jim to the Minnesota Vikings.

The Emerging Champion

The Vikings were about to play their first season in the NFL. Coach Norm Van Brocklin was happy to have a player of Jim's potential on his new team. Jim stood out among the other players because of his quickness and tenacity. Jim immediately became a star for the Vikings, but the team was not very good because of problems on offense and with coach Van Brocklin. While other players were bitter toward the coach, Jim tried to achieve harmony with everyone. Jim told a sportswriter: "Understanding is what the world needs. . . . I don't like bad vibes. I hate being phoney. We are all as one. Thinking otherwise is phoney." Needless to say, Jim had strong leadership abilities and he was soon named captain of the defensive unit.

In 1967, Bud Grant became the Vikings head coach and the Minnesota team improved greatly. Coach Grant added Alan Page and eventually, Carl Eller and Gary Larsen, to join Jim on the defensive line. They became known as the "Purple People Eaters" for the ferocious way they attacked NFL quarterbacks. Jim was selected to the NFL Pro Bowl team in 1969 and 1970.

Although much of the attention from sportswriters was focused on Alan Page and Carl Eller,

this did not bother Jim. To him, it was the team and improving his skills as a player that mattered the most. It was that kind of attitude and leadership that enabled the Vikings to play in four Super Bowls during Jim's career. Coach Grant was always quick to point out the influence Jim had on the entire team. He said that Jim loved the game more than any player he had ever seen and that he thrived on an atmosphere of teamwork. Jim brought energy, enthusiasm, and joy to everything he did. He was considered the heart and soul of the Vikings.

Continuing the Story

What Jim Marshall is most remembered for in sports is his longevity. Although he was the first of the "Purple People Eaters," he was still playing after the others had retired. Jim's professional football career spanned two full decades. He holds NFL records for the most consecutive games played in a lifetime (282) and most consecutive starts with one team (269). Some observers, including Jim's defensive line coach, Jack Patera, say that Jim had his best season at age thirty-six, an age when most careers are over. Jim continued to play well for the Vikings beyond the age of forty.

Considered too small for his position, his speed and technical skills enabled him to persevere. Jim's record for durability and longevity may never be equaled. Coach Grant said Jim's body was a physical impossibility because it did not "rip, bust, or tear." Jim said the secret of his longevity was that he had mental control over his physical being. "There are things we are physically capable of doing but push away from because our minds tell us to," he said. Jim was determined to keep his streak of consecutive starts alive, even coming out of the hospital on a couple of occasions to play. At the end of his career, he was still called on to make big plays in critical situations.

"I'm a doer," Jim once said. "I want to know what life is about and what I'm about." As a result of his adventurous and joyful approach, Jim became accomplished in a number of hobbies. He read poetry, became a skydiver, a skier, a scuba diver, a mountain climber, a rifleman, and a chess player and even managed a rock group. It was not that he needed anything special to be happy, he simply had a zest for life. Jim has spent many of his post-football days helping inner-city youth and working for charities, including Life's Missing Link, a nonprofit fund-raising support group for troubled youth. In August, 2000, Jim was diagnosed with prostate cancer.

Summary

Jim Marshall was a unique athlete and a multi-faceted person. He played football with an enthusiasm that inspired his teammates. His determination to improve himself constantly enabled him to have one of the longest professional football careers ever. His commitment to the team rather than personal glory set the standard for the success of the Minnesota Vikings.

Kevin R. Lasley

Additional Sources:

"Ex-Viking Marshall Has Cancer." *The Washington Post*, August 16, 2000, p. D2.

"Vikings Great Jim Marshall Has Cancer." *Minneapolis Star Tribune*, August 16, 2000, p. 4C.

Zimmerman, Paul. "Gangs of Four, the Four-Man Defensive Lines Born in the 50's, Ruled the NFL Until Changes in the Game Spelled Their Doom." *Sports Illustrated* 83, no. 14 (October 6, 1995): 66-73

SLATER MARTIN

Sport: Basketball

Born: October 22, 1925
El Mina, Texas

Early Life

Slater Martin was born on October 22, 1925, in the rural community of El Mina, Texas, outside the city of Houston. A descendant of a Scots-Irish father and a Native American mother, Slater was small in physical stature as a child, but he quickly developed fiery competitive instincts because he always played with much bigger children.

Slater played unorganized football and baseball at an early age in the dusty, grassless fields near his home. It was in football that Slater developed exceptional speed and quickness, a necessity to escape injury.

At age eleven, Slater and his family moved to Houston, Texas. Here, Slater's new neighbor and close friend, Jamie Owens, introduced him to basketball.

On the playground near their home, the two boys shot baskets for hours each day. Slater loved his new-found game. In addition to his speed and quickness, Slater soon became an excellent set shooter and a pesky defensive player.

The Road to Excellence

The first team on which Slater played was in junior high school, but during those two years he played very little.

At Jefferson Davis High School in Houston, Slater failed to make the freshman team. Somewhat discouraged, he turned to baseball, a sport in

which he was highly skilled. He soon returned to basketball, however, and worked even harder on his skills. As a sophomore, Slater made the varsity team and became a starter in the last twelve games of the 1941-42 season.

By his junior year, Slater had grown to 5 feet 8½ inches and 140 pounds, small for a basketball

STATISTICS

Season	GP	FGM	FG%	FTM	FT%	Reb.	Ast.	TP	PPG
1949-50	67	106	.351	59	.634	—	148	271	4.0
1950-51	68	227	.362	121	.684	246	235	575	8.5
1951-52	66	237	.375	142	.747	228	249	616	9.3
1952-53	70	260	.410	224	.780	186	250	744	10.6
1953-54	69	254	.388	176	.724	166	253	684	9.9
1954-55	72	350	.381	276	.769	260	427	976	13.6
1955-56	72	309	.358	329	.833	260	445	947	13.2
1956-57	66	244	.332	230	.790	288	269	718	10.9
1957-58	60	258	.336	206	.746	228	218	722	12.0
1958-59	71	245	.347	197	.776	253	336	687	9.4
1959-60	64	142	.371	113	.729	187	330	397	6.2
Totals	745	2,632	.364	2,073	.762	—	3,160	7,337	9.8

Notes: GP = games played; FGM = field goals made; FG% = field goal percentage; FTM = free throws made; FT% = free throw percentage; Reb. = rebounds; Ast. = assists; TP = total points; PPG = points per game

player of that era. Nevertheless, Slater was emerging into a fine ball handler and excellent passer. Also, he could score whenever the situation required. With these skills, Slater led his high school team to two Texas State Basketball titles, as a junior in 1942 and as a senior in 1943.

Following high school graduation, in the midst of World War II, Slater joined the United States Navy. During his thirty-three months of service, Slater had limited opportunity to play basketball. He grew to a height of 5 feet 10 inches and weighed 155 pounds.

Having completed his military service in 1945, Slater enrolled at the University of Texas, where he quickly rejuvenated his dormant basketball skills. Under the tutelage of Texas head coach Jack Gray, Slater became a stellar all-around player at the guard position. Along with his playmaking talent, Slater was called upon to be more of a scorer. He responded by averaging 10 and 12 points per game as a sophomore and junior, respectively. As a senior, Slater averaged 16 points per game and led the Longhorns in scoring.

In his sophomore and junior years, 1946-1947 and 1947-1948, Slater led the University of Texas into the National Collegiate Athletic Association (NCAA) Tournament, but lost in the first round each time. Slater's senior season, 1948-1949, was his most outstanding. Although the Longhorns did not make the NCAA Tournament, Slater's 16-points-per-game scoring average included a 49-point performance against Texas Christian University; he was also named Southwest Conference (SWC) most valuable player. Slater graduated from the University of Texas in 1949 with a bachelor's degree in physical education and married his college sweetheart, Faye.

The Emerging Champion

In the spring of 1949, the Minneapolis Lakers of the National Basketball Association (NBA) were building a dynasty. The Lakers had legendary players George Mikan and Jim Pollard, but the team needed a playmaking guard. Slater joined the Lakers for the 1949-1950 season and directed the team from the guard position.

In his rookie season, Slater scored 271 points in sixty-seven games for a 4-points-per-game average and led the Lakers to the NBA championship. It was the first of four NBA titles for Slater and the Lakers. He set up many baskets for George Mikan and Jim Pollard during the Lakers' championship years. In 1955, Slater led the league with 427 for an average of nearly 6 assists per game.

During his career with the Lakers, Slater earned the reputation as the best small defensive player in the league and the nickname "Dugie" for his persistence and drive. These attributes contributed to Slater's being selected to the All-NBA Second Team from 1954-1955 through 1958-1959.

Following a contract dispute with the Lakers, Slater was traded to the New York Knickerbockers for the 1956-1957 season. He played only thir-

HONORS AND AWARDS

1949	SWC most valuable player *Sporting News* All-American
1953-59	NBA All-Star Team
1955-59	All-NBA Second Team
1966	Inducted into Texas Sports Hall of Fame
1981	Inducted into Naismith Memorial Basketball Hall of Fame

teen games before being traded to the St. Louis Hawks.

Slater played with St. Louis from 1956 to 1960, during which time he won his fifth NBA title as he led the Hawks to the championship in the 1957-1958 campaign. He was named to the All-NBA Second Team for the fifth time in his career.

During eleven regular NBA seasons, Slater played in 745 games, scored 2,632 field goals and 2,073 free throws for 7,337 points and a 9.8-points-per-game average.

Continuing the Story

During his early years in the NBA, Slater played semiprofessional baseball in Texas during the summer months. He also took up golf, which he would continue to play to nearly a scratch handicap. Upon retirement from professional basketball, Slater worked in the building construction business in Houston, Texas. He would also own and operate a restaurant, but he spent much of his time on the golf course.

Summary

Slater Martin's physical size was never a deterrent to his athletic success. He was a gifted athlete whose drive, determination, and enthusiasm for a physical challenge made basketball fun. An outstanding playmaker, Slater was the original mold from which the modern-day basketball point guard is cast.

Jerry Jaye Wright

Additional Sources:

Heuman, William. *Famous Pro Basketball Stars.* New York: Dodd, Mead, 1970.

Hickok, Ralph. *A Who's Who of Sports Champions.* Boston: Houghton Mifflin, 1995.

LaBlanc, Michael L., and Mary K. Ruby, eds. *Professional Sports Team Histories: Basketball.* Detroit: Gale, 1994.

Porter, David L., ed. *Biographical Dictionary of American Sports: Basketball and Other Indoor Sports.* Westport, Conn.: Greenwood Press, 1989.

EDGAR MARTINEZ

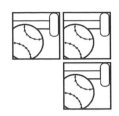

Sport: Baseball

Born: January 2, 1963
New York, New York

Early Life

Although born in New York, Edgar Martinez knew nothing of this city until many years later, for when he was two years old his parents moved to Dorado, in their native Puerto Rico. He was raised by his grandparents there, to whom he gave much credit for teaching him the value of hard work and living an upright life. He started to play baseball in his back yard in Dorado with his brother and a few friends. The next year he joined the local Little League and fell in love with

the game. He also played at Dorado High School, from which he graduated in 1979, and at American College in Puerto Rico.

The Road to Excellence

Major league scouts, aware of the tradition of baseball in Puerto Rico, often established try-out camps there. In 1982, when he was nineteen, Edgar decided to attend one of these camps. He impressed two scouts for the Seattle Mariners of the American League, Marty Martinez and Coco LaBoy, who signed him to a contract. The next year he found himself far from Puerto Rico, in Bellingham, Washington, playing in the Northwest League. Everything seemed different: the language, the weather, and especially the caliber of the players. It turned out to be a difficult season for Edgar. He got into only thirty-two games at third base and batted a woeful .173.

Edgar's grandparents had taught him to persevere, though, and at Wausau of the Midwest League in 1984, he put together a solid season, batting .303 with 15 home runs. He continued to advance, splitting the following season between Class AA Chattanooga of the Southern League and Calgary, Alberta, of the Class AAA Pacific Coast League. Although he batted .353 in twenty games with the latter team, the Mariners decided that Edgar needed another year at the AA level, so back he went to Chattanooga in 1986, where he was used at both second and third base. He played well and in 1987, his fifth season of professional baseball,

Seattle Mariner Edgar Martinez led the league in RBIs in 2000.

AP/Wide World Photos

1813

he got his first look at the major leagues when the Mariners called him up in September from Calgary, where he had enjoyed his best year to date with a .329 batting average and league-leading totals in putouts and assists among Pacific Coast League third basemen. Performing in thirteen games as a third baseman and designated hitter for Seattle, he hit a resounding .372.

The Emerging Champion

In the spring of 1988 Edgar got off to a slow start and was dispatched to Calgary for the third time. The Mariners liked his hitting but had reservations about using him as an everyday player. He was slow afoot and did not seem strong enough defensively to play regularly at either second or third base. Edgar had such an outstanding year at Calgary, however, leading the league with a .363 average, that he was again called up near the end of the season.

Aware of his slowness, Edgar had been working hard on his base running. He also studied opposing defensive players and was quick to take advantage of any defensive lapses. He began the 1989 season as the Mariners' third baseman but hit only .240 in sixty-five games and again was sent back to Calgary. Now in his seventh professional season, he still had not made the grade as a major league player, but he went to work, batted .345 for the remainder of the season, and earned yet another shot at a place on the Seattle roster in

1990. This time he was there to stay. He added muscle to his 5-foot 11-inch frame and began to hit for power while remaining a good contact hitter. He became one of the few major league hitters with more walks than strikeouts.

Continuing the Story

In the 1990's Edgar established himself as one of the premier major league hitters. Despite nagging injuries in 1993 and 1994, he began to pile up impressive career totals of extra-base hits. He played at third and at first base but most often was a designated hitter. In 1992 he led the American League in doubles with 46 and repeated in 1995 with 52, when his .356 batting average led the league—a remarkable figure for a man who got few "leg hits." He also led the league in runs scored with 121.

In the five-game Division Series that fall against the New York Yankees, Edgar hit an amazing .571 but cooled off in the Championship Series as the Mariners fell to Cleveland. In the seasons that followed, he continued to demonstrate consistency in both batting average and extra-base power. For the six-season period ending in 2000 he never hit less than .322 or fewer than 24 home runs. At the age of thirty-seven in 2000, taking up the slack created by the move of his longtime teammate Ken Griffey, Jr., to Cincinnati, Edgar drove in a remarkable 145 runs to lead the American League. The boy who grew up in

STATISTICS

Season	GP	AB	Hits	2B	3B	HR	Runs	RBI	BA	SA
1987	13	43	16	5	2	0	6	5	.372	.581
1988	14	32	9	4	0	0	0	5	.281	.406
1989	65	171	41	5	0	2	20	20	.240	.304
1990	144	487	147	27	2	11	71	49	.302	.433
1991	150	544	167	35	1	14	98	52	.307	.452
1992	135	528	181	**46**	3	18	100	73	**.343**	.544
1993	42	135	32	7	0	4	20	13	.237	.378
1994	89	326	93	23	1	13	47	51	.285	.482
1995	**145**	511	182	**52**	0	29	**121**	113	**.356**	.628
1996	139	499	163	52	2	26	121	103	.327	.595
1997	155	542	179	35	1	28	104	108	.330	.554
1998	154	556	179	47	1	29	86	102	.322	.567
1999	142	502	169	35	1	24	86	86	.337	.554
2000	153	556	180	31	0	37	100	**145**	.324	.579
Totals	1,540	5,432	1,738	404	14	235	980	925	.320	.529

Notes: Boldface indicates statistical leader. GP = games played; AB = at bats; 2B = doubles; 3B = triples; HR = home runs; RBI = runs batted in; BA = batting average; SA = slugging average

Puerto Rico also became an entrepreneur, establishing the Caribbean Embroidery Company in his adopted home state of Washington.

Summary

Edgar Martinez, despite an early start in professional baseball, did not establish himself as a major leaguer until he was twenty-seven. After that time, however, he became one of the rare hitters who combined power and a consistently high batting average to rack up the hits despite lack of running speed. By the end of the 2000 season he had amassed more than 400 doubles and over 750 extra-base hits. His lifetime average stood at .320 and his slugging average at .529. A few players have exceeded each of these marks, but none matched him in both aspects of batting excellence.

Robert P. Ellis

Additional Sources:

Martinez, Edgar, with Greg Brown. *Patience Pays.* Bothell, Wash.: Positively for Kids, 1992.

Shatzkin, Mike, et al., eds. *The Ballplayers: Baseball's Ultimate Biographical Reference.* New York: William Morrow, 1999.

Edgar Martinez Zone. http://www.edgarzone.com.

PEDRO MARTINEZ

Sport: Baseball

Born: October 25, 1971
Manoguayabo, Dominican Republic

Early Life

Pedro Jaime Martinez was born in a small town in the Dominican Republic to parents who were civil servants. Pedro's parents divorced when he was eight years old. Being the fifth of six children, he was reared by his mother. Like Pedro, an older brother, Ramon, also made it to the major leagues as a pitcher, while another brother, Jesus, pitched in the minor leagues.

While Pedro was growing up, conditions were extremely poor for the Martinez family. Pedro hustled the streets selling orange juice and shining shoes for pennies in order to help his family survive. Being too poor to buy a baseball, Pedro and his brothers would play ball with rolled-up socks, fruit, or even their sister's doll heads. The brothers would often get into trouble when their sister came home from school and found her doll with no head.

The Road to Excellence

Pedro was signed to a professional baseball contract by the Los Angeles Dodgers in June, 1988. He pitched in the minor leagues for five seasons, with Santo Domingo, Dominican Republic, in 1988 and 1989; Great Falls, Montana, in 1990; Bakersfield, California, and San Antonio, Texas, in 1991; and Albuquerque, New Mexico, for parts of the 1991-1993 seasons. He was named the Minor League Player of the Year in 1991 after compiling an 8-0 record and a 2.05 earned run average (ERA) with Bakersfield, a 7-5 record with a 1.76 ERA for San Antonio, and a 3-3 record with a 3.66 ERA for Albuquerque.

After a brief stint in the major leagues in 1992, Pedro compiled a 10-5 record, 2.61 ERA, and 119 strikeouts

Pedro Martinez pitching in 2000, the year he won his second consecutive Cy Young Award and the third of his career.

in 107 innings of relief work for the Dodgers in 1993. In November, 1993, he was traded to the Montreal Expos and placed into the starting rotation in the strike-shortened 1994 season. He compiled an 11-5 record, 3.42 ERA, and 142 strikeouts in 144.2 innings. In 1995, he slipped a little, compiling a 14-10 record with a 3.51 ERA. The 1996 season featured 222 strikeouts in 216.2 innings of work, but his record fell slightly to 13-10 with a 3.70 ERA.

The Emerging Champion

On June 3, 1995, it finally became apparent what would eventually lie ahead for Pedro in the big leagues. He pitched nine perfect innings against the San Diego Padres. Unfortunately, the Expos also failed to score, and Pedro was relieved after yielding a leadoff double in the tenth inning.

Besides compiling a 17-8 record in 1997, Pedro led the major leagues with an amazing 1.90 ERA and became the first ERA leader to also garner 300 strikeouts in the same season since the feat was accomplished by left-hander Steve Carlton in 1972. No right-handed pitcher had done so since Walter Johnson in 1912. Against Pedro, National League opponents only managed to bat a major league low of .184. Pedro pitched in the 1997 All-Star game and earned the National League Cy Young Award. To show his respect to fellow Dominican Juan Marichal, a standout pitcher for the San Francisco Giants in the 1960's, Pedro offered him his Cy Young Award; Marichal gracefully declined.

HONORS AND AWARDS	
1991	Minor League Player of the Year
1996, 1997	National League All-Star Team
1997	National League Cy Young Award
1998, 1999	American League All-Star Team
1999	American League Triple Crown
1999, 2000	American League Cy Young Award, unanimous choice

Facing a large arbitration salary to retain Pedro for the 1998 season, Montreal opted to let him go. In December, 1997, he signed a six-year, $75 million deal with the Boston Red Sox, becoming the highest paid player in major league history. He did not disappoint, registering a 19-7 record and a 2.89 ERA, helping the Red Sox into the American League Division Series. Pedro finished second in the balloting for the American League Cy Young Award.

Continuing the Story

Pedro won the 1999 All-Star game, striking out five batters in 2 innings of work. After going 23-4 with a 2.07 ERA and 313 strikeouts in 213.1 innings, Pedro won the 1999 American League Cy Young Award with a unanimous vote. Opposing batters hit a meager .205 against him. He was also a close second in the voting for the American League's most valuable player. His best pitching performance of the season came against the New York Yankees in Yankee Stadium on September 10, when he struck out seventeen batters and yielded only 1 hit. Thereafter, some of the Yankee players, including Derek Jeter and

STATISTICS

Season	GP	GS	CG	IP	HA	BB	SO	W	L	S	ShO	ERA
1992	2	1	0	8.0	6	1	8	0	1	0	0	2.25
1993	65	2	0	107.0	76	57	119	10	5	2	0	2.61
1994	24	23	1	144.2	115	45	142	11	5	1	1	3.42
1995	30	30	2	194.2	158	66	174	14	10	0	2	3.51
1996	33	33	4	216.2	189	70	222	13	10	0	1	3.70
1997	31	31	**13**	241.1	158	67	305	17	8	0	4	**1.90**
1998	33	33	3	233.2	188	67	251	19	7	0	2	2.89
1999	31	29	5	213.1	160	37	**313**	**23**	4	0	1	**2.07**
2000	29	29	7	217.0	128	32	**284**	18	6	0	**4**	**1.74**
Totals	278	211	35	1,574.0	1,178	442	1,818	125	56	3	15	2.68

Notes: Boldface indicates statistical leader. GP = games played; GS = games started; CG = complete games; IP = innings pitched; HA = hits allowed; BB = bases on balls (walks); SO = strikeouts; W = wins; L = losses; S = saves; ShO = shutouts; ERA = earned run average

Paul O'Neill, labeled Pedro as the best pitcher in the major leagues.

Once again he pitched the Red Sox into the American League Division Series as the wild card team and then on to the American League Championship Series, where the Yankees triumphed. Although his back was hurt, Pedro started throwing fastballs from all sorts of arm angles to pitch 13 scoreless innings against the Cleveland Indians and the Yankees in the postseason games. Pedro won the Cy Young Award again in 2000, becoming the first pitcher to win the award unanimously in consecutive years.

Many experts say that Pedro is one of the best pitchers in baseball. Although small in size, Pedro is known for an excellent fastball (92 to 98 miles per hour), great curveball, and superb change-up. He has mastered his change-up in order to throw it three different ways with three different actions, so batters never know when it is coming. In addition to his pitching expertise, Pedro has a warm personality, brings great enthusiasm to major league ball parks, and devotes hours of his time to off-the-field charity projects.

Summary

Pedro Martinez is only the third pitcher in the history of major league baseball to win the Cy Young Award in both the National and the American Leagues. He can be so dominating and is the master of so many different kinds of pitches that most major league players have ranked him as the best pitcher in the big leagues. During an era of high baseball offense, Pedro completely dominated the opposition.

Alvin K. Benson

Additional Sources:

Gallagher, Jim. *Pedro Martinez*. Bear, Del.: Mitchell Lane, 1999.

Gillette, Gary, Matt Silverman, and Stuart Shea, eds. *Total Red Sox 2000*. Kingston, N.Y.: Total Sports, 2000.

Prime, Jim, and Bill Nowlin. *Tales from the Red Sox Dugout*. Champaign, Ill.: Sports Publishing, 2000.

Shalin, Mike, and Rob Rains. *Pedro Martinez: Throwing Strikes*. Champaign, Ill.: Sports Publishing, 1999.

Stewart, Mark. *Pedro Martinez: Pitcher Perfect*. Chicago: Children's Press, 2000.

EDDIE MATHEWS

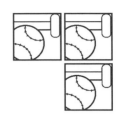

Sport: Baseball

Born: October 13, 1931
        Texarkana, Texas
Died: February 18, 2001
        La Jolla, California

Early Life

Edwin Lee Mathews was born in Texarkana, Texas, on October 13, 1931. Encouraged by his father, Eddie was an athlete throughout his boyhood and was heavily scouted in high school. He and his father carefully scouted also. They determined that, of all major league teams, the Boston Braves would need a replacement most quickly for their veteran third baseman, Bob Elliott. Eddie signed with the team on the night of his high school graduation in 1949.

The Road to Excellence

From 1949 to 1952, Eddie played in the minors in High Point, North Carolina, Atlanta, and Milwaukee, with a two-month stay in the Navy, ended by his father's hospitalization for tubercular pneumonia.

Within three years of his high school graduation, Eddie was the starting third baseman for the Boston Braves. Only twenty years old and quite shy, Eddie, along with pitcher Lew Burdette and shortshop Johnny Logan, gave hope to the seventh-place team. Eddie's fielding and long-ball hitting were impressive. In the 1952 season, he had 25 home runs, with over-the-wall blasts in Philadelphia, St. Louis, and Cincinnati, and 3 in one day on September 26 in Ebbets Field off Joe

Black and Ben Wade. Eddie was a strong fielder also; Baseball Commissioner Ford Frick was astounded at one of his foul-ball saves in spring training.

The Emerging Champion

Braves Field drew small crowds, and in the spring of 1953, the Braves franchise was moved to Milwaukee. They seemed like a changed team after the move. The fans doted on them and they acquired excellent new talent in Hank Aaron, Bob Buhl, and Wes Covington, and saw improvement in veterans Joe Adcock and others. Eddie

STATISTICS

Season	GP	AB	Hits	2B	3B	HR	Runs	RBI	BA	SA
1952	145	528	128	23	5	25	80	58	.242	.447
1953	154	579	175	31	8	**47**	110	135	.302	.627
1954	138	476	138	21	4	40	96	103	.290	.603
1955	141	499	144	23	5	41	108	101	.289	.601
1956	151	552	150	21	2	37	103	95	.272	.518
1957	148	572	167	28	9	32	109	94	.292	.540
1958	149	546	137	18	1	31	97	77	.251	.458
1959	148	594	182	16	8	**46**	118	114	.306	.593
1960	153	548	152	19	7	39	108	124	.277	.551
1961	152	572	175	23	6	32	103	91	.306	.535
1962	152	536	142	25	6	29	106	90	.265	.496
1963	158	547	144	27	4	23	82	84	.263	.453
1964	141	502	117	19	1	23	83	74	.233	.412
1965	156	546	137	23	0	32	77	95	.251	.469
1966	134	452	113	21	4	16	72	53	.250	.420
1967	137	436	103	16	2	16	53	57	.236	.392
1968	31	52	11	0	0	3	4	8	.212	.385
Totals	2,388	8,537	2,315	354	72	512	1,509	1,453	.271	.509

Notes: Boldface indicates statistical leader. GP = games played; AB = at bats; 2B = doubles; 3B = triples; HR = home runs; RBI = runs batted in; BA = batting average; SA = slugging average

followed suit. From his 1952 Boston season of .242 with 25 home runs and 58 runs batted in (RBIs), he gained adulation in 1953 with a .302 batting average, 47 home runs, and 135 RBIs. Suddenly the Braves were in second place in the National League and remained strong throughout the 1950's.

With what Ty Cobb called one of the "three or four perfect swings," Eddie had unprecedented success in his early years. In five years, before he reached the age of twenty-five, he hit 190 home runs, more than Babe Ruth, even while his batting average remained below .300 in all but the 1953 season. His performances in the World Series and All-Star games were less impressive: .080 in All-Star games with 3 hits and 6 errors, and .200 in Series play.

The remainder of Eddie's career was up and down. Always a long-ball hitter, he made important contributions to the Braves' 1957 World Series win. He and Hank Aaron added a one-two punch to the team, producing 76 home runs and 226 RBIs. His own home-run season total of 32 was capped in the seven-game World Series with a game-winning home run in the tenth inning of the fourth game off Yankee Bob Grim. In addition, his fielding of Bill Skowron's hit down the third-base line killed the Yankees expected seventh-game win.

Unfortunately, Eddie's best years did not coincide with those of his team. His weak .251 average in 1958 did not contribute much to the team's pennant win. Conversely, his strong 1959 season with a career-high batting average of .306 and 46 home runs did not help the team to avoid defeat in the pennant race at the hands of a suddenly strong Los Angeles Dodger team in a three-game playoff.

Continuing the Story

Although Eddie's skill declined after 1959, except in the 1965 season (32 home runs), he remained on the team through 1966, the first year the franchise played for Atlanta. Eddie became the only player to belong to one franchise that had played in three cities.

Eddie completed his career with a year divided between Houston and Detroit, a few years coaching for the Braves in the early 1970's, and

HONORS AND AWARDS

1953, 1955-62	National League All-Star Team
1955, 1957, 1959-60	Sporting World Outstanding Third Baseman
1978	Inducted into National Baseball Hall of Fame
	Uniform number 41 retired by Atlanta Braves

three years managing the team, from 1972 to 1974. In those years, the team only attained fourth and fifth place in the division, but in 1974, the batting order contained the first three-man set of 40-home-run hitters: Hank Aaron, Davey Johnson, and Darrell Evans. Eddie Mathews was inducted into the National Baseball Hall of Fame in 1978 in a ceremony attended by his wife Verjean and children Eddie Jr., John, and Stephanie.

In early 2001, Eddie died in his sleep in a Southern California hospital after suffering a respiratory problem aggravated by pneumonia. He was sixty-nine years old.

Summary

Eddie Mathews achieved unprecedented early career success and excellence in both fielding and hitting. Blessed with an ideal athlete's body of strength and quickness, Eddie was a major contributor to the success of the Milwaukee Braves in the 1950's.

Vicki R. Robinson

Additional Sources:

Hirshberg, Al. *The Eddie Mathews Story.* New York: J. Messner, 1960.

King, Kelley. "Eddie Mathews, Braves Hall of Famer." *Sports Illustrated* 91, no. 25 (1999).

Mathews, Eddie, and Bob Buege. *Eddie Mathews and the National Pastime.* Milwaukee, Wis.: Douglas American Sports Publications, 1994.

Schulian, John. "National Pastime." *Sports Illustrated* 88, no. 22 (1998).

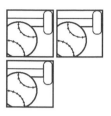

CHRISTY MATHEWSON

Sport: Baseball

Born: August 12, 1880
Factoryville, Pennsylvania
Died: October 7, 1925
Saranac Lake, New York

Early Life

Christopher Mathewson was born in the small northeastern Pennsylvania town of Factoryville on August 12, 1880. Factoryville was a calm and quiet town, and many of its people were deeply religious.

Christy's mother wanted him to be a preacher, but from an early age, he aspired to become a professional baseball player.

Christy's talents became evident early, as he first played for pay at the age of fourteen. He developed as a pitcher while attending a local school, the Keystone Academy. His Protestant, middle-class upbringing influenced Christy to attend college, which was uncommon for the majority of ballplayers of his time.

The Road to Excellence

From the Keystone Academy, Christy went to Bucknell College, where he would dominate the athletic scene as both a football and baseball star. The collegiate rules of that time allowed him to play semiprofessional baseball in the summers.

Christy also became a prominent personality on campus through his involvement in several literary societies, glee club, the Phi Gamma Delta fraternity, his ability as a checker player, and as class president.

At almost 6 feet 2 inches tall and 200 pounds, the blond and blue-eyed Christy Mathewson was a handsome and commanding figure. One sportswriter would describe him as a good-looking boy with sparkling eyes and a low, melodious voice. Christy would later become one of the first professional athletes to function as a role model for America's young.

Christy began his professional baseball career with the Taunton, Massachusetts, club of the New England League in 1899. He posted a pitching record of five wins and two losses while earning a salary of $90 a month. It was at Taunton where Christy began developing his famous "fadeaway" pitch, which modern pitchers call the screwball. The Taunton club eventually went broke.

Still pursuing his dream of becoming a professional baseball player, nineteen-year-old Christy joined the Norfolk, Virginia, club of the Virginia

STATISTICS

Season	GP	GS	CG	IP	HA	BB	SO	W	L	S	ShO	ERA
1900	5	1	1	33.2	35	14	15	0	3	0	0	4.76
1901	40	38	36	336.0	288	97	221	20	17	0	5	2.41
1902	34	32	29	276.2	241	73	159	14	17	0	8	2.11
1903	45	42	37	366.1	321	100	**267**	30	13	2	3	2.26
1904	48	46	33	367.2	306	78	**212**	33	12	0	4	2.03
1905	43	37	33	338.2	252	64	**206**	**31**	8	2	8	1.27
1906	38	35	22	266.2	262	77	128	22	12	1	6	2.97
1907	41	36	31	315.0	250	53	**178**	**24**	13	2	**8**	1.99
1908	56	44	34	390.2	285	42	**259**	**37**	11	**5**	**12**	**1.43**
1909	37	33	26	275.1	192	36	149	25	6	2	8	**1.14**
1910	38	35	27	318.1	292	60	184	27	9	0	2	1.90
1911	45	37	29	307.0	303	38	141	26	13	3	5	**1.99**
1912	43	34	27	310.0	311	34	134	23	12	4	0	2.12
1913	40	35	25	306.0	291	21	93	25	11	2	4	**2.06**
1914	41	35	29	312.0	314	23	80	24	13	2	5	3.00
1915	27	24	11	186.0	199	20	57	8	14	0	1	3.58
1916	13	7	5	74.2	74	8	19	4	4	2	1	3.01
Totals	634	551	435	4,779.2	4,216	838	2,502	373	188	27	80	2.13

Notes: Boldface indicates statistical leader. GP = games played; GS = games started; CG = complete games; IP = innings pitched; HA = hits allowed; BB = bases on balls (walks); SO = strikeouts; W = wins; L = losses; S = saves; ShO = shutouts; ERA = earned run average

League for the 1900 season. It was there that the young pitcher first hinted at his eventual greatness, winning twenty games while losing only two.

The Emerging Champion

Christy's major league debut was not promising. Having been called up to the National League's New York Giants in July of 1900, Christy appeared in five games. With a record of no wins and three losses, the Giants sent him back to Norfolk.

The Cincinnati club then drafted him, after which he was traded back to the Giants, who must have had second thoughts about the young right-hander. "Matty," as Christy would be called by baseball fans, justified his return to the Giants by winning twenty games in his first full major league season.

During the 1902 season, the Giants fell to last place and Christy experienced a record of fourteen wins and seventeen losses. In July of that season, however, a new manager had come to the Giants whose name would forever be linked with Christy's—John McGraw.

McGraw realized that his team's fortunes depended greatly upon the right arm of Christy Mathewson. So, in the spring of 1903, he worked

hard to earn the pitcher's friendship and trust. Spring training served as a honeymoon for Christy and his new wife, Jane, whom he had met while in college. When the Giants returned to New York to begin the season, the McGraws and Mathewsons agreed to share an apartment in the city.

The bond that grew between Christy Mathewson and John McGraw has been called unlikely. It was improbable that the tall, gentlemanly, and soft-spoken pitcher would get along with his short, often crude, and critical manager. Both men were intent on winning, however, and the combination of Mathewson and McGraw would work to transform the Giants.

Continuing the Story

Christy became a star in 1903 with a record of thirty wins and thirteen losses, and the Giants jumped to second place. That marked the beginning of twelve straight seasons of more than twenty wins for Christy, including four of 30 or more. In 1908, he set the record for wins in the National League with thirty-seven. Christy also shares the record for the third-highest number of wins in major league history, with 373.

Perhaps Christy's greatest season was 1905, when he led the league in victories (31), winning

MAJOR LEAGUE RECORDS

Most wins in one World Series, 3 (1905) (record shared)
Most shutouts in one World Series, 3 (1905) (record shared)
Most World Series complete games, 10
Most World Series shutouts, 4

HONORS AND AWARDS

1936	Inducted into National Baseball Hall of Fame
	Honorary number retired by San Francisco Giants

percentage (.775), earned run average (1.27), strikeouts (206), and shutouts (8), capturing the first of two Triple Crowns for pitching (he won the second in 1908). In the World Series against the Philadelphia Athletics that fall, he pitched 3 shutouts in six days while allowing 14 hits and one base on balls in 27 innings.

A master of control and an easy worker, Christy could go many innings without issuing a base on balls. During the 1913 season, he pitched 68 consecutive innings without walking a batter, still a league record. Christy delivered his fade-away, fastball, curve, and floater with a smooth overhand motion.

The last big season for Christy was 1914, when he won twenty-four and lost thirteen. The thirty-five-year-old pitcher struggled to only eight wins and fourteen losses in 1915. The Giants traded Christy to Cincinnati in July of 1916 so he could become a playing manager. He pitched only one game for the Reds and was victorious.

Christy left the Reds in August, 1918, to join the military and severely damaged his lungs when he accidentally inhaled poison gas. He recovered enough to return to the Giants in 1919 as a coach for John McGraw. He was soon diagnosed as having tuberculosis, however. Christy died in October of 1925 at the age of forty-five.

Summary

Giants manager John McGraw called Christy Mathewson "the greatest pitcher that ever lived." Pittsburgh Pirate star Honus Wagner said, "Mathewson knew more in five minutes about batters than the modern pitcher does in a whole season." Various sources rank Christy with other great right-handed pitchers such as Cy Young, Walter Johnson, Bob Feller, Tom Seaver, and Nolan Ryan.

Yet, perhaps Christy's noblest attribute was that he was the first American sports hero whose personal appeal crossed all social, economic, and cultural boundaries. He proved that a professional athlete could remain a gentleman.

Ronald L. Ammons

Additional Sources:

Macht, Norman L. *Christy Mathewson.* New York: Chelsea House, 1991.

Mayer, Ronald. *Christy Mathewson: A Game-by-Game Profile of a Legendary Pitcher.* Jefferson, N.C.: McFarland, 1993.

Robinson, Ray. *Matty: An American Hero, Christy Mathewson of the New York Giants.* New York: Oxford University Press, 1993.

Will, George F. "The First Michael Jordan: And Before DiMaggio, There Was Christy Mathewson." *Newsweek* 133, no. 12 (March 22, 1999): 61.

BOB MATHIAS

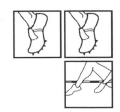

Sport: Track and field (decathlon)

Born: November 17, 1930
Tulare, California

Early Life

On November 17, 1930, Robert Bruce Mathias was born in the small agricultural town of Tulare in central California. His father, Dr. Charles Mathias, was a physician and surgeon of Scots-Irish ancestry. Bob's father met his future wife, Lillian Harris, when they were students at the University of Oklahoma, where Charlie Mathias was an All-State football player.

Bob was the second-born in the family of three boys and one girl. Even as a youngster, Bob became known for his remarkable gift of all-around athletic coordination. In spite of suffering from childhood anemia, Bob played whatever sport was in season.

While in grade school, he built a small track in his backyard. There he practiced jumping, running, and throwing. Even though Bob was frail from his blood disorder, the gangling twelve-year-old still managed to high-jump 5 feet 6 inches.

The Road to Excellence

By the time Bob entered high school, his parents' long-term efforts to combat their son's anemia with a proper diet and iron supplements began to pay off. The handsome, blue-eyed high school student was to grow to a strapping 6 feet tall and 190 pounds before graduation.

Bob earned a reputation for being one of California's outstanding high school athletes in basketball, football, and track. By the time he was a senior, his track and field versatility had won him forty first-place finishes and twenty-one high school records. He was also the California Interscholastic Federation discus and shot-put champion in 1947.

Tulare High School's track coach, Virgil Jack-

son, had a hunch that Bob might be a potential Olympic athlete. Shortly before Bob was to graduate, the coach suggested that he enter the decathlon event at the annual Pacific Coast games in Pasadena, California.

With his coach's help, Bob quickly trained for the grueling ten-event competition. The kid from Tulare then amazed everyone in California by not only competing well but also winning his first-ever decathlon.

Shortly afterward, Coach Jackson and Bob were on their way to the National Decathlon and Olympics tryouts in New Jersey, thanks to financial contributions from Bob's hometown.

There Bob won again, stunning the nation by landing a berth on the Olympic team. In the space of a few months, this seventeen-year-old had gone from being a regional prep star to be-

ing the youngest member ever on the American Olympic track team.

The Emerging Champion

In August, 1948, at Wembley Stadium in London, England, Bob lined up with thirty-four other decathletes from nineteen nations to compete in the Olympic decathlon. The two-day competition was held in spite of terrible weather conditions. Between his events, Bob spent most of the time huddled under a blanket as he tried to protect himself from the cold and heavy rain. Because of the large number of competitors, the last three events lasted well into the night.

When the 1,500-meter run finally concluded, Bob Mathias had done the incredible. He not only had won the gold medal but also had become the youngest men's track and field gold medal winner in the history of the modern Olympic Games.

After his triumphant return home, the Olympic hero began to concentrate on his academic studies. Although still a dedicated decathlete while he was a student at Stanford University, Bob also played football. As a fullback, he once ran 96 yards for a touchdown against Southern California and was a member of Stanford's Rose Bowl team on January 1, 1952.

By the summer of 1952, for the fourth time in his career, Bob was the National Decathlon champion. Now 6 feet 3 inches tall and weighing 205 pounds, he led the American decathletes in Helsinki, Finland, the site of the fifteenth mod-

MAJOR DECATHLON CHAMPIONSHIPS			
Year	Competition	Place	Points
1948	Olympic Games	Gold	7,139
	National AAU Championships	1st	7,224
	Southern Pacific AAU	1st	7,094
1949	National AAU Championships	1st	7,556
1950	National AAU Championships	1st	8,042
	Swiss Championships	1st	7,312
1952	Olympic Games	Gold	7,887 WR, OR
	National AAU Championships	1st	7,825 WR

Notes: OR = Olympic Record; WR = World Record

ern Olympic Games. Given his international reputation as the reigning world-record holder, Bob was the man to beat in 1952.

No one, however, could match his remarkable performance. Overcoming a leg injury suffered during the competition, Bob still won the decathlon gold medal by the largest margin in Olympic history. In the process, he broke his own world record and achieved the then-unprecedented feat of winning the Olympic decathlon for the second time.

Continuing the Story

To the ancient Greeks, the way to find the best athlete of the times was to hold an all-around competition. The modern decathlon, a track meet within a track meet, is just such a competition because it tests skill, stamina, speed, strength, and even character.

Until Bob Mathias won back-to-back decathlons, most observers of the sporting world had agreed that Jim Thorpe, winner of the 1912 Olympic decathlon and pentathlon, was the greatest all-around athlete. Bob's eight-year dominance of the modern decathlon caused the sporting press to speculate that Bob may have been even better than Thorpe.

The two athletes shared a common character trait. They both could relax anywhere, anytime. One competitor said of Bob Mathias that he seemed to relax so completely between his events that one thought he had actually gone to sleep.

Bob's later life career opportunities have called for as much versatility as the decathlon de-

RECORDS
Set a world record in the decathlon in 1952 (7,690 points)
Youngest Olympic gold medalist in men's track and field

HONORS AND AWARDS	
1948	Sullivan Award
	World Trophy
1949	Honorary Degree, Chevalier, Order of DeMolay
	American Legion Good Citizenship Citation
1952	Associated Press Male Athlete of the Year
	Hall of the Athlete Foundation Athlete of the Year
1974	Inducted into National Track and Field Hall of Fame
1975	Pierre de Coubertin International Fair Play Trophy
1980	Inducted into U.S. Olympic Hall of Fame

manded of him. He served as an officer in the Marine Corps, a Hollywood actor, and a director of his own boys' camp. Bob's reputation eventually took him to Washington, D.C., where he served four terms as a representative to the United States Congress.

After Congress, his leadership skills carried him to the directorship of the Olympic Training Center and, later, of the National Fitness Foundation. Continuing his interest in helping the youth of America by promoting healthy sporting activities, he later served as the president of the American Kids Sports Association.

Summary

After overcoming childhood illness, schoolboy Bob Mathias came out of nowhere to win the decathlon gold medal in the 1948 Olympic Games. As a young man, four years later, he became the first athlete ever to repeat the feat with his victory at the Helsinki Games.

Bob's athletic accomplishments helped glamorize the decathlon. He was a role model for countless youngsters who were inspired by his good character habits, his belief in fair play, and his old-fashioned determination and hard work. Bob was a champion in every sense of the word.

William Harper

Additional Sources:

Hickok, Ralph. *A Who's Who of Sports Champions.* Boston: Houghton Mifflin, 1995.

The Lincoln Library of Sports Champions. 16 vols. Columbus, Ohio: Frontier Press, 1993.

Mathias, Bob, and Bob Mendes. *A Twentieth-Century Odyssey: The Bob Mathias Story.* Champaign, Ill.: Sports Publishing, 2000.

Wallechinsky, David. *The Complete Book of the Olympics.* Boston: Little, Brown and Company, 1991.

Watman, Mel. *Encyclopedia of Track and Field Athletics.* New York: St. Martin's Press, 1981.

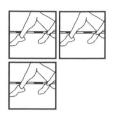

RANDY MATSON

Sport: Track and field (shot put)

Born: March 5, 1945
Kilgore, Texas

Early Life

James Randel Matson was born on March 5, 1945, in Kilgore, Texas. He was the second of three children and was educated in the public schools of Pampa, Texas. In elementary school, he stood out not only because of his height and size but also because of his skill and poise. The young giant, far from being clumsy, moved fluently in a variety of athletic activities.

As with so many young athletes, early training was critical in providing the platform for eventual success. In the eighth grade, Randy was spotted by Pampa High School track coach Dwayne Lyons. Coach Lyons saw, in Randy, an exciting future prospect in the "heavy" section of field events.

The Road to Excellence

Coach Lyons found Randy to be a willing learner who trained enthusiastically for the special demands of the shot put and discus throw. In both events, enormous force is applied over a wide range of movement to launch the object (shot or discus) as if it were a missile.

Randy, early on, set age-group records at the state and national levels. In the shot, Randy had to master the complex mechanics of putting a 12-pound metal shot from the confines of a circle 7 feet in diameter. Records tum-

bled and his performances in track and field would have been even better if he had been able to devote the time to additional strength-training programs. As it was, he complemented his shot/discus prowess with excellence in high school basketball, baseball, and football.

Upon graduating from Pampa High School in 1963, Randy faced a dilemma in choosing a college. From an avalanche of offers, he had to decide which was the best option. A major reason

1828

for his selection of Texas Agricultural and Mechanical University (Texas A&M) was the renowned strength- and weight-training program offered there by Emil Mamaligia. Randy knew full well that if he wanted to become a world-ranked field event athlete, skill and technique would be only part of his strategy. If he could make himself into a herculean figure, then success would be much more likely.

The Emerging Champion

Built more like a powerful basketball player than a squat, heavy thrower, Randy worked on his strength and technique. If both areas were developed, then he would acquire the consistency that frequently escapes throwers, not only in the shot, but also in discus, javelin, and hammer throwing.

In 1964, he putted the now 16-pound (senior) shot 64 feet 11 inches for an Amateur Athletic Union (AAU) record. Later that year at the Tokyo Olympics, he won a silver medal with a throw of 66 feet 3¾ inches.

In Japan, it was very much the battle of the young American giants. Randy, at 6 feet 6½ inches and 265 pounds, faced Dallas Long, 6 feet 4 inches and 260 pounds. Randy was all of nineteen and Long, a year older.

In mid-competition, Randy was leading. In the final stages, however, Long unleashed a toss of 66 feet 8½ inches to win by less than 5 inches.

Early in 1965, Randy set a world indoor record of 65 feet 8¼ inches. In meet following meet, he surpassed his own top performance and eventually Dallas Long's world record of 67 feet 10 inches. Another American, Parry O'Brien, had broken the 60-foot barrier in the shot with a throw of 60 feet 5¼ inches on May 10, 1954. On May 8, 1965 (exactly eleven years to the day since England's Roger Bannister beat the 4-minute mark for the mile) Randy, throwing on his home campus at College Station, Texas, reached a distance of 70 feet 7¼ inches.

In the 1965-1966 indoor track season, Randy retired tempo-

rarily from track and field competition. He concentrated on playing basketball for Texas A&M and ended the season as the Southwest Conference Sophomore of the Year.

Despite losing weight during the basketball season, he returned a year later to continue his successes in the track and field arena. For example, in June, 1966, he won the shot/discus double at the National Collegiate Athletic Association (NCAA) Outdoor Championships.

Randy won the shot-put gold medal at the 1967 Pan-American Games with a distance of 65 feet 4¾ inches. Another great honor for Randy in 1967 was being awarded the James E. Sullivan Memorial Award, the highest honor of the Amateur Athletic Union.

Athletic setbacks toughen the mental resolve of returning Olympians, and Randy was eager to follow his 1964 silver medal with a 1968 gold. The early jitters of Olympic qualifying (he only placed third at the Olympic trials) had evaporated by 1968 in Mexico City. In the finals, his first throw of 67 feet 4¾ inches demolished the rest of the field, and his winning margin was about 16 inches.

An Associated Press story carried by *The New York Times* on May 9, 1965, quoted Baylor track coach Clyde Hart as having said: "We'll see Matson standing on the middle platform at the Olympics, getting his gold medal. He'll pull off

MAJOR CHAMPIONSHIPS

Year	Competition	Event	Place	Distance
1964	Olympic Games	Shot put	Silver	66′ 3¼″
	National AAU Outdoor Championships	Shot put	1st	64′ 11″
1965	NCAA Indoor Championships	Shot put	1st	63′ 2¼″
1966	NCAA Outdoor Championships	Shot put	1st	67′ ½″ WR
		Discus	1st	197′ 0″
	National AAU Championships	Shot put	1st	64′ 2½″
1967	Pan-American Games	Shot put	1st	65′ 4¾″
	NCAA Outdoor Championships	Shot put	1st	67′ 9½″
		Discus	1st	190′ 4″
	National AAU Championships	Shot put	1st	66′ 11″
1968	Olympic Games	Shot put	Gold	67′ 4¾″ OR
	National AAU Championships	Shot put	1st	67′ 5″
1970	National AAU Championships	Shot put	1st	67′ 10¼″
1972	National AAU Championships	Shot put	1st	69′ 6½″

Notes: OR = Olympic Record; WR = World Record

his A. and M. warm-up suit, and underneath he'll have on a cape and a big S on his chest. Then he'll fly away and we'll all wonder whether we really saw him."

Continuing the Story

Following his 1968 Olympic success, Randy returned to Texas A&M. There he successfully completed a graduate degree in business administration on an academic scholarship awarded by the NCAA.

In the Olympic trials four years later, Randy attempted a comeback but only managed to place fourth with a throw of 67 feet 5¾ inches, and, thus, he failed to attend a third consecutive Olympics.

Randy's greatest contribution was to redefine excellence as it applied to the shot put. Although Parry O'Brien of the United States had revolutionized the throwing technique in the 1950's by introducing a snapped-down glide from the back of the throwing circle, it was Randy who took it to

another level. One coach described him as a marvelous collection of muscular levers linking together like a firecracker. The overall picture was of a giant with an explosive throwing arm.

Summary

As an eighteen-year-old, Randy Matson was a sensation when he broke the 60-foot barrier. Only five years later, he added another 10 feet to this distance and was the Olympic champion.

A much-beloved son of Texas, he was roundly cheered by his fellow students. At College Station, when he competed, whole sections of the crowd urged him to greater efforts.

Randy was much more than a big strongman who heaved the 16-pound shot. He had sufficient skill and quickness to sling the discus more than 200 feet. In every sense, he was a versatile athlete. He was drafted by the Atlanta Falcons in the National Football League, by Seattle in the National Basketball Association, and by Dallas in the American Baseball Association. For a time, he was executive director of the booster club at West Texas State.

Scott A. G. M. Crawford

Additional Sources:

Bateman, Hal. *United States Track and Field Olympians, 1896-1980.* Indianapolis, Ind.: The Athletics Congress of the United States, 1984.

Hickok, Ralph. *A Who's Who of Sports Champions.* Boston: Houghton Mifflin, 1995.

Wallechinsky, David. *The Complete Book of the Olympics.* Boston: Little, Brown and Company, 1991.

Watman, Mel. *Encyclopedia of Track and Field Athletics.* New York: St. Martin's Press, 1981.

RECORDS

Two world records in shot put: 1965 (70′ 7¼″), 1967 (71′ 5½″)
World indoor record in shot put in 1965 (65′ 8¼″)
Won 47 shot-put competitions after the 1964 Olympic Games

HONORS AND AWARDS

1965	DiBeneditto Award
1967	World Trophy
	Sullivan Award
1970	*Track and Field News* World Athlete of the Year
1984	Inducted into National Track and Field Hall of Fame

ROLAND MATTHES

Sport: Swimming

Born: November 17, 1950
Erfurt, East Germany

Early Life

Roland Matthes, whom many consider the greatest backstroke swimmer who ever lived, was born on November 17, 1950, in Erfurt, in what was then East Germany. Roland was definitely different. Although the East Germans had thousands of children training in swimming, the leaders of the pack of potential champions were all girls except for Roland.

Roland went on winning throughout his youth and somehow stayed popular with the other boys, whom he always defeated in practice and meets. He grew to become the German Democratic Republic's first swimming prodigy, followed in a few years by dozens of great women performers.

The Road to Excellence

Roland began to swim seriously at age ten with coach Hans Schneemann. He swam with Hans for three years and learned the basics. Roland had talent in the freestyle and butterfly, but his strongest stroke was the backstroke. He moved from the basics to fine-tuning his strokes with Marlies Grohe, who coached Roland from 1963 through the Montreal 1976 Olympics. At age seventeen, Roland was a champion backstroker, winning against all of his contemporaries. Roland's selection to the national swimming team of East Germany made his family as well as his country very proud.

The magic behind Roland Matthes's success is difficult to pinpoint, because at that time in history, the East Germans did not publicly discuss their research or the training regimens of their most successful sports champions. Roland's success probably came from a combination of his excellent coaching and his own natural talent and

MAJOR CHAMPIONSHIPS

Year	Competition	Event	Place	Time
1968	Olympic Games	100-meter backstroke	Gold	58.7 OR
		200-meter backstroke	Gold	2:09.6 OR
		4×100-meter medley relay	Silver	—
1970	European Championships	100-meter freestyle	2d	—
		100-meter backstroke	1st	56.9 WR, ER
		200-meter backstroke	1st	2:06.1 WR, ER
		4×100-meter medley relay	1st	3:54.4
1972	Olympic Games	100-meter backstroke	Gold	56.58 OR
		200-meter backstroke	Gold	2:02.82 WR, OR
		Relay	Silver	—
		Relay	Bronze	—
1973	World Championships	100-meter backstroke	1st	57.47
		200-meter backstroke	1st	2:01.87
		4×100-meter freestyle relay	3d	3:33.33
		4×100-meter medley relay	2d	3:53.24
1974	European Championships	100-meter backstroke	1st	58.21
		200-meter backstroke	1st	2:04.64
		100-meter butterfly	2d	56.68
1975	World Championships	100-meter backstroke	1st	58.15
1976	Olympic Games	100-meter backstroke	Bronze	57.22

Notes: OR = Olympic Record; WR = World Record; ER = European Record

deep determination to win and represent his country. Whatever his particular combination, it worked, and Roland was unbeaten from 1967 to 1974.

The Emerging Champion

During this seven-year period, he broke the 100-meter backstroke record seven consecutive times and the 200-meter backstroke record nine times. Altogether, he set nineteen world records. He won the gold medal in both the 100- and the 200-meter backstroke in two back-to-back Olympics, in 1968 in Mexico City and in 1972 in Munich, West Germany. In 1968, Roland beat United States swimmer Charlie Hickcox, who had temporarily taken the East German's world record and held all the yard records for the backstroke before the 1968 Olympics.

Roland also won a silver medal in the 400-meter medley relay, in which he swam the backstroke leg even though he was the fastest East German swimmer in the butterfly and freestyle strokes as well. At the 1972 Games, Roland beat Mike Stamm to take the double gold in the 100- and 200-meter

backstroke events, and went on to help his teammates win a silver and a bronze in the medley and sprint freestyle relay competitions as well. The United States, with more good swimmers, won both.

Continuing the Story

Although the backstroke was Roland's best event, he also was a world-class butterflyer and freestyler, winning silver medals in the 1970 European Championships in the 100-meter freestyle and in 1974 in the 100-meter butterfly. In the 1976 Olympic Games, Roland, competing against the United States' John Naber, took the bronze in the 100-meter backstroke event and did not place in the 200-meter event. He retired after the 1976 Games, considered by many as the world's greatest backstroker of all time. Only Adolph Kiefer over the same long period of time and John Naber at his peak could contest the point.

Two years later, Roland married swimming superstar Kornelia Ender in May, 1978. The marriage did not last, but it produced a daughter, Francesca.

Summary

Roland Matthes from East Germany won medals in three Olympics and set nineteen world records in the 100- and 200-meter backstroke events. He is remembered for these wins and his

RECORDS

Set 19 world records

Won 22 East German championships

Unbeaten in world competition for 7 years (1967-74)

During the period from 1967 to 1974, broke the 100-meter backstroke record 7 consecutive times and the 200-meter backstroke record 9 times

HONORS AND AWARDS

1981	Inducted into International Swimming Hall of Fame

seven-year reign over world competition in the backstroke events. He won five European Championships and twenty-two East German Championships. Roland was one of the few male swimmers to stand out in the record book in East Germany, as East German women largely dominated the sport in the 1970's. Roland was elected to the International Swimming Hall of Fame in 1981.

Buck Dawson

Additional Sources:

Besford, Pat. *Encyclopedia of Swimming.* New York: St. Martin's Press, 1976.

Levinson, David, and Karen Christenson, eds. *Encyclopedia of World Sport: From Ancient Times to Present.* Santa Barbara, Calif.: ABC-CLIO, 1996.

Schapp, Dick. *An Illustrated History of the Olympics.* New York: Alfred A. Knopf, 1975.

Wallechinsky, David. *The Complete Book of the Olympics.* Boston: Little, Brown and Company, 1991.

SIR STANLEY MATTHEWS

Sport: Soccer

Born: February 1, 1915
Hanley, England

Early Life

Stanley Matthews was born in Hanley, in the English Midlands, on February 1, 1915. His father, Jack Matthews, a barber and a professional boxer, was known as "The Fighting Barber of Hanley." Jack Matthews instilled in his son a habit of rigorous self-discipline. He trained Stanley as a sprinter, and at the age of six Stanley competed in a 100-yard race at nearby Stoke-on-Trent. Every morning Stanley was expected to rise at six o'clock and exercise with his father and two brothers.

Stanley always wanted to be a professional soccer player. He practiced endlessly, either dribbling a rubber ball on his own or joining in games with his school friends wherever they could find a suitable place—in streets or on strips of wasteland. Stanley's father, on the other hand, wanted him to become a boxer. Nevertheless, he agreed to support his son's soccer ambitions if Stanley was selected for the England schoolboy side before he left school.

The Road to Excellence

Stanley met the condition. When he was thirteen he was selected to play for England against Wales in a schoolboy international game. He played well in what was for him the unusual position of outside right. To his bitter disappointment, however, he was not selected for the following international game against Scotland. Stanley remembered the advice of his father, who had told him never to take anything for granted in life, and this helped him to recover his spirits.

Stanley later attributed much of his success to the training and upbringing he had received from his father. It was Jack Matthews who warned his son not to get a swollen head over some early praise he had received in the newspapers. It was also Jack Matthews who watched all Stanley's early matches, offering constructive advice and criticism after each game. The levelheaded, self-disciplined attitude that Stanley's father instilled in his son helped Stanley cope with the adulation he was later to receive.

In 1930, at the age of fifteen, Stanley began work as an office boy with the Stoke City Football Club. He also played more than twenty games for the Stoke City reserve team before signing as a professional when he was seventeen. By 1933, he was playing regularly on the Stoke first team. The following year, Stanley played his first match for England's national team, against Wales at Cardiff, and scored a goal in England's victory.

The Emerging Champion

During the 1930's, Stanley established himself as a favorite of the Stoke City and England fans. They realized that he was destined to become one of the greatest soccer players of all time.

Playing at outside right, Stanley was a superb dribbler of the ball. His balance was perfect, and no one could match his speed over the first ten yards. Time after time, Stanley would dribble the ball, at a leisurely pace, up to the opposing fullback. Then he would sway in one direction, get-

1834

ting the fullback off balance, and then sway back in the other direction, eluding the despairing lunge of his opponent. At that point Stanley would take off at top speed down the wing leaving the unfortunate defender either flat on his back or trailing hopelessly behind. Stanley would often beat two or three defenders in this way before crossing the ball into the goal area. His crosses were so accurate that they would always land within a yard of a teammate.

One sign of Stanley's extraordinary reputation came in 1938, when he requested a transfer from Stoke City. Three thousand people attended a public meeting to protest. Leaflets circulated throughout the town saying "Stanley Matthews Must Not Go." Stanley agreed to stay on, and he remained with Stoke for another eight years before he was transferred to Blackpool in 1946.

Continuing the Story

By the 1940's, Stanley Matthews had become a soccer legend. In those days, before matches were televised, people would travel hundreds of miles just to see him play. His presence on the field seemed to lend a kind of magic to the atmosphere. He seemed like a miracle worker, and opposing defenses were often driven to panic as soon as he got the ball. The wizard of English soccer was held in awe by fans the world over.

Perhaps Stanley's finest match came in 1953, when he played for Blackpool in the Football Association Cup final against the Bolton Wanderers. With twenty minutes of the game remain-

Sir Stanley Matthews (on shoulders at right) with his teammates after winning the Football Association Cup final in 1953, dubbed the "Matthews Final."

ing, Bolton had a 3-1 lead. Then Stanley turned on his deadly skill. After one long run down the wing that left several defenders beaten, Stanley crossed the ball and Mortensen scored for Blackpool. With Stanley creating havoc every time he got the ball, Bolton struggled to hold on to its lead. A goal from a free kick tied the score, and 30 seconds from the end Stanley set off on another incredible run. Two defenders were left sprawling before Stanley made a perfect pass to his colleague Perry, who scored the winning goal. The match became known as the "Matthews Final."

Stanley's sportsmanship was also legendary. He was a modest man, and he always remained calm and dignified on the field. He would never retaliate, even when he was badly fouled by his opponents.

Stanley's remarkable physical fitness enabled him to continue playing long after other players of his age had retired. He was past the age of forty when he played for England for the fifty-fourth time in 1957, and in 1965 he became the oldest player ever to appear in a Football League match.

After Stanley's retirement, he became the first soccer player to be knighted, by Queen Eliza-beth II, for his services to professional soccer. For a brief period he became manager of Port Vale. Some years later, he and his family emigrated to Canada.

Summary

Many soccer experts regard Sir Stanley Matthews as the greatest soccer player of all time. His astonishing ball control and body swerve seemed to mesmerize defenders, and his speed left them floundering. In a playing career that spanned thirty-five years, he consistently brought to English soccer a level of artistry that it has rarely seen, before or since.

Bryan Aubrey

Additional Sources:

Henshaw, Richard. *The Encyclopedia of World Soccer.* Washington, D.C.: New Republic Books, 1979.

LaBlanc, Michael L., and Richard Henshaw. *The World Encyclopedia of Soccer.* Detroit: Gale, 1994.

Matthews, Stanley. *The Stanley Matthews Story.* London: Oldbourne, 1960.

Miller, David. *Stanley Matthews: The Authorized Biography.* London: Pavilion, 1989.

DON MATTINGLY

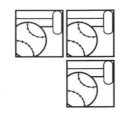

Sport: Baseball

Born: April 20, 1961
         Evansville, Indiana

Early Life

Donald Arthur Mattingly was born on April 20, 1961, in Evansville, Indiana, youngest of the five children of Bill and Mary Mattingly. His father's 12-hour shifts at the post office gave him three or four days off a week, which he used to play sports with his sons.

Don and his brothers all had athletic ability. His brother Randy played professional football in Canada. His brother Mike was a star pitcher in high school and played basketball at the University of Evansville. His oldest brother, Jerry, who died tragically in a construction accident at the age of twenty-three, also played basketball at the University of Evansville.

The Road to Excellence

Don showed promise as a ballplayer at an early age. At nine years old he won the most valuable player award for children nine to twelve years old in Little League, although the award was taken away from him because it was decided to give it to an older child. Don was an all-around athlete in high school. He was a quarterback on the football team, a point guard in basketball, and a pitcher and first baseman on the baseball team.

In high school, Don developed a highly disciplined approach to baseball. He credits his high school baseball coach, Quentin Merkle, with instilling in him the motivation to attain the goals he established for himself. Don also learned to accept his athletic success without becoming conceited. He never wore a letter sweater because he did not want to show off.

Don began playing professional baseball for the New York Yankees organization in the minor leagues the summer after he graduated from high school. Don was the most valuable player of the South Atlantic League in 1980. He was named Yankee Minor League Player of the Year in 1981. Although he earned a batting average of .332 in his four years with the minor leagues, he never hit more than 10 home runs in a season.

Don Mattingly of the New York Yankees in 1995.

STATISTICS

Season	GP	AB	Hits	2B	3B	HR	Runs	RBI	BA	SA
1982	7	12	2	0	0	0	0	1	.167	.167
1983	91	279	79	15	4	4	34	32	.283	.409
1984	153	603	**207**	**44**	2	23	91	110	**.343**	.537
1985	159	652	211	**48**	3	35	107	**145**	.324	.567
1986	162	677	**238**	**53**	2	31	117	113	.352	.573
1987	141	569	186	38	2	30	93	115	.327	.559
1988	144	599	186	37	0	18	94	88	.311	.462
1989	158	631	191	37	2	23	79	113	.303	.477
1990	102	394	101	16	0	5	40	42	.256	.335
1991	152	587	169	35	0	9	64	68	.288	.396
1992	157	640	184	40	0	14	89	86	.287	.416
1993	134	530	154	27	2	17	78	86	.291	.445
1994	97	372	113	20	1	6	62	51	.304	.411
1995	128	458	132	32	2	7	59	49	.288	.413
Totals	1,785	7,003	2,153	442	20	222	1,007	1,099	.307	.471

Notes: Boldface indicates statistical leader. GP = games played; AB = at bats; 2B = doubles; 3B = triples; HR = home runs; RBI = runs batted in; BA = batting average; SA = slugging average

When he moved up to the major leagues in 1983, Don still needed to become powerful enough to hit home runs frequently.

The Emerging Champion

Don did not make the first string immediately when he went up to the major leagues to play for the Yankees. In 1984, he was assigned to fill in as needed at first base and in left and right field. Instead of becoming discouraged, Don resolved to improve his batting. He devoted time to extra batting practice so that he would improve enough to be a regular player. Not only did he meet his goal, but his batting was outstanding enough to earn him the American League batting title in 1984 with a batting average of .343. He also proved to be an excellent defensive player, making only 5 errors the entire season. *The Sporting News* declared Don to be the American League Player of the Year in 1984.

In the 1985 season, Don established one of the greatest records of any ballplayer in the history of the Yankees. He led the American League with 145 runs batted in, the highest total in the American League in thirty-two years. No other Yankee player had equaled his 211 hits in the previous forty-six years.

He was the first Yankee to collect 200 hits two years in a row since Joe DiMaggio did it in 1936-1937. He was presented with his first Gold Glove Award for his performance at first base. He was named American League most valuable player and *The Sporting News* Major League Player of the Year.

Even though Don did not make many hits in the beginning of the 1986 season, he still finished it with a .352 batting average. He established Yankee records by earning 238 hits and 53 doubles. His 1987 season also started off with few hits. After recuperating from a back injury, however, he broke the American League record and tied the National League record by hitting at least one home run in eight consecutive games.

HONORS, AWARDS, AND RECORDS

1984	*Sporting News* American League Player of the Year
1984-89	American League All-Star Team
1985	American League most valuable player *Sporting News* Major League Player of the Year
1985-89	American League Gold Glove Award
1987	Major league record for the most grand slams in a season (6) Major league record for the most consecutive games hitting a home run (8) (record shared)
1993	Lou Gehrig Memorial Award
1997	Uniform number 23 retired by New York Yankees

He established a single-season record of 6 grand slams and finished the 1987 season with a .327 batting average.

Continuing the Story

After the 1988 season, Don was plagued by a long-standing back problem. He managed to bat over .300 in 1988 and 1989 in spite of it. The Yankees awarded him a five-year contract worth $19 million at the beginning of the 1990 season, the highest contract any Yankee had received up to that time. His back problem kept him from playing almost two months that year, and his batting average fell below .300 for the first time since his first season in the major leagues. Don not only continued to fight his back problem but also kept working to make the Yankees become a championship team again.

While Don's batting suffered because of his back problems, his fielding remained strong. He led the American League three straight years in fielding percentage (1992-1994), and his lifetime fielding percentage of .996 at first base tied him for the all-time lead.

Don was replaced at first base by the young Tino Martinez in 1995 and slipped into an unofficial retirement. He made an official announcement of retirement in 1997 when he decided that his back problems would prevent a successful comeback. His number, 23, was retired by the Yankees that same year.

Don was not a big man, his shoulders were not broad, and he did not move fast, yet he was an outstanding ballplayer. His success came from his determination to improve his skills, no matter how superior his performance in comparison to that of other players. He maintained a low profile because he considered himself an ordinary, hardworking player. He did not seek the praise of others but concentrated on his job and his family.

Don has supported the activities of many charitable organizations, including Easter Seals and the Special Olympics. In the 1988 season, he donated $1,000 for every home run he hit to a health project for homeless children in New York City.

Summary

Don Mattingly became an outstanding ballplayer through hard work and dedication. He learned motivation and discipline as a teenager. If he had not been willing to devote extra time to improve his batting at the beginning of his major league career, many of the batting records he broke would still be standing.

Evelyn Toft

Additional Sources:

Gutman, Bill. *Baseball's Hot New Stars.* New York: Pocket Books, 1988.

Honig, Donald. *The Greatest First Basemen of All Time.* Chicago: Follett, 1988.

Rushin, Steve. "First-Rate." *Sports Illustrated* 79, no. 9 (1993).

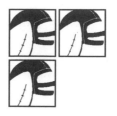

DON MAYNARD

Sport: Football

Born: January 25, 1935
Crosbyton, Texas

Early Life

Donald Rogers Maynard was the son of Ernest Thomas Maynard and Marian Arletta Sharpe Maynard. He was born in Crosbyton, in the Texas Panhandle, east of Lubbock, on January 25, 1935.

His father was in the cotton and construction businesses, and the family moved often. Don went to many public schools in both New Mexico and Texas, including five different high schools.

Even with all of the changing of schools, Don still found time to play sports. He competed in junior high baseball and track and American Legion baseball. As a high school freshman, Don attended a school so tiny that they competed in six-man football instead of the regular eleven-man game. Through all of the moving around, Don ran track and played baseball, basketball, and football. He rarely had the same coach two years in a row and seldom moved beyond the "B" team. Yet sports did help Don to make friends at each new school.

The Road to Excellence

When he finally stayed in one place long enough, Don became a star. He spent his junior and senior years at Colorado City High School, Texas. There he lettered in football, baseball, basketball, and track and was the state champion in both the high and low hurdles. In both his junior and senior years, he was named the high school's best all-around athlete. He graduated in 1953.

Even though he was an outstanding high school athlete, Don received only a few college offers. He decided to take a combination track and football scholarship at Rice University in Houston, Texas. Houston was a big city far from the small west Texas towns

New York Jet Don Maynard in 1968.

where he had usually lived, and Don was not very happy there.

After one semester, he transferred to Texas Western University (now the University of Texas at El Paso). He liked it much better, and would live in El Paso for many years. At Texas Western, he lettered in both track and football, was the Border Conference champion in the low and high hurdles, and played offensive halfback and defensive safety on the Miners' football team.

The Miners won the Border Conference football championship in 1956, and Don was named to the All-Conference team in 1956 and 1957. They also played in the 1957 Sun Bowl. As a senior, Don led the team in scoring with 52 points. He graduated in 1958. By that time, Don had married Marilyn Francis Weaver. They had two children but were divorced in 1978.

The Emerging Champion

In 1957, Don was drafted ninth as a future choice of the New York Giants of the National Football League (NFL). Don played on special teams with the division-winning Giants in 1958 but was cut the next year. That was a big disappointment, but he went on to play the 1959 season with the Hamilton Tiger-Cats, division winners in the Canadian Football League.

It was not a very good start on a professional

STATISTICS					
Season	GP	Rec.	Yds.	Avg.	TD
1958	12	5	84	16.8	0
1960	14	72	1,265	17.6	6
1961	14	43	629	14.6	8
1962	14	56	1,041	18.6	8
1963	12	38	780	20.5	9
1964	14	46	847	18.4	8
1965	14	68	1,218	17.9	**14**
1966	14	48	840	17.5	5
1967	14	71	**1,434**	**20.2**	10
1968	13	57	1,297	**22.8**	10
1969	10	47	938	20.0	6
1970	10	31	525	16.9	0
1971	14	21	408	19.4	2
1972	14	29	510	17.6	2
1973	3	1	18	18.0	0
AFL Totals	133	546	10,289	18.8	84
NFL Totals	53	87	1,545	17.8	4

Notes: Boldface indicates statistical leader. GP = games played; Rec. = receptions; Yds. = yards; Avg. = average yards per reception; TD = touchdowns

career, but Don's luck was about to change. In 1960, the American Football League (AFL) was formed. The New York Titans of the AFL hired Texan Sammy Baugh as their first head coach. Having recently coached college football in Texas, Baugh remembered Don Maynard as an outstanding athlete.

Because of Sammy Baugh, Don became the first player signed by the Titans. In his first season in the AFL, the 6-foot 1-inch, 175-pound wide receiver caught 72 passes for 1,265 yards and 6 touchdowns.

In 1964, the Titans were renamed the Jets. With a new coach and quarterback Joe Namath, they soon reached the top. Don was Namath's favorite target. Don's biggest game was the 1968 AFL Championship, in which he caught 6 passes for 118 yards and 2 touchdowns to help the Jets beat the Oakland Raiders 27-23 and win the title.

That victory meant the Jets would meet the heavily favored Baltimore Colts (now the Indianapolis Colts) in the 1969 Super Bowl. To the surprise of almost everyone, the Jets won that Super Bowl, one of the most famous upsets in pro football history.

Continuing the Story

During his twelve years with the Jets, Don also won a place in football history. By his 1972 retire-

HONORS AND AWARDS

1956-57	All-Border Conference Team
1958	Blue-Gray College All-Star Team
1965-68	AFL All-Star Team
1968	AFL All-Star Game Co-Outstanding Offensive Player
1969	All-AFL Team All-Time AFL Team
1985	Texas Sports Hall of Fame All-Time AFL Team
1987	Inducted into Pro Football Hall of Fame Uniform number 13 retired by New York Jets

ment, he held every team record for pass receptions. He had been named to various all-star teams and set many NFL records as well.

He was the first player ever to gain 10,000 yards in pass receptions, and also the first to gain 11,000. He played in the first overtime game, in the first Monday Night Football game, and was the first NFL player shown on instant replay.

He played his final professional season with the St. Louis Cardinals and Los Angeles Rams in 1973. For the next two years, he was a player-coach in the World Football League (WFL). When the WFL folded, Don returned home to El Paso, where he owns a business.

Although his playing days were over, Don Maynard's achievements were not forgotten. He was elected to the Texas Sports Hall of Fame in 1985 and the Pro Football Hall of Fame in 1987. Almost twenty years after he retired, Don was still listed in the record books and still held several NFL records. In 2001 he still had the fifth-highest single-season receiving yardage in NFL history. He and other former Jets teammates have been engaged in work for charitable organizations, such as the Larry Grantham Freedom House, a rehabilitation center for alcoholics. Don and the other Jets support and take part in the Larry Grantham Save A Life Golf Classic.

Summary

Don Maynard grew up in west Texas and moved around so much that he rarely had a chance to know his coaches or his teammates. In spite of this, he worked hard and became an outstanding four-sport athlete in high school and a football and track star in college.

His professional career got off to a slow start until Don joined the New York Jets and played in one of the most famous Super Bowls in history. Although small in stature, he was an outstanding receiver, All-Star performer, and Hall of Fame Honoree.

Mary Lou LeCompte

Additional Sources:

Devaney, John. *Star Pass Receivers of the NFL.* New York: Random House, 1972.

Eskenazi, Gerald. *Gang Green.* New York: Simon and Schuster, 1998.

Pro Football Hall of Fame. http://www.pro footballhof.com.

WILLIE MAYS

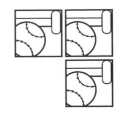

Sport: Baseball

Born: May 6, 1931
Westfield, Alabama

Early Life

Willie Howard Mays, Jr., was born on May 6, 1931, in the small town of Westfield, Alabama, just outside the major city of Birmingham.

Willie started his sports career at a very early age. It helped that his family was athletically gifted. One of his grandfathers pitched for a black baseball team. His mother, Ann Mays, was a track star in high school. His father, William Howard Mays, was an outfielder with the Birmingham Black Barons. Later, at the steel mill where he worked, his father played on the semiprofessional company team.

When he was only three, Willie was already practicing on the steel mill's baseball field with his father. Because his high school had no baseball team, Willie played basketball and football at school, but he continued to practice baseball on his own. At fourteen, he became a pitcher for his father's steel mill team.

His parents were divorced while Willie was still in school. His mother and her second husband, Frank McMorris, had ten children, making Willie part of a large family of half-brothers and half-sisters.

The Road to Excellence

Willie's father did not want his son to be a mill worker, so he actively helped him to develop his baseball potential. He took him to the manager of the Birmingham Black Barons, Lorenzo "Piper" Davis. Willie, only seventeen at the time, so impressed the manager with his workout that he was given a contract as an outfielder for the season.

Willie played home games with the team on Sundays during the school year and went on the road during summer vacations. That gave scouts from major teams an opportunity to watch him play. Bill Harris and Ed Montague, two scouts from the New York Giants, recommended him to their team. So it was that on the day Willie graduated from high school—June 20, 1950—he signed a contract with the major league New York team.

At first, Willie played with their Class B Interstate League farm team in Trenton, New Jersey.

1843

STATISTICS

Season	GP	AB	Hits	2B	3B	HR	Runs	RBI	BA	SA
1951	121	464	127	22	5	20	59	68	.274	.472
1952	34	127	30	2	4	4	17	23	.236	.409
1954	151	565	195	33	**13**	41	119	110	**.345**	**.667**
1955	152	580	185	18	**13**	**51**	123	127	.319	**.659**
1956	152	578	171	27	8	36	101	84	.296	.557
1957	152	585	195	26	**20**	35	112	97	.333	**.626**
1958	152	600	208	33	11	29	**121**	96	.347	.583
1959	151	575	180	43	5	34	125	104	.313	.583
1960	153	595	**190**	29	12	29	107	103	.319	.555
1961	154	572	176	32	3	40	**129**	123	.308	.584
1962	162	621	189	36	5	**49**	130	141	.304	.615
1963	157	596	187	32	7	38	115	103	.314	.582
1964	157	578	171	21	9	**47**	121	111	.296	**.607**
1965	157	558	177	21	3	**52**	118	112	.317	**.645**
1966	152	552	159	29	4	37	99	103	.288	.556
1967	141	486	128	22	2	22	83	70	.263	.453
1968	148	498	144	20	5	23	84	79	.289	.488
1969	117	403	114	17	3	13	64	58	.283	.437
1970	139	478	139	15	2	28	94	83	.291	.506
1971	136	417	113	24	5	18	82	61	.271	.482
1972	88	244	61	11	1	8	35	22	.250	.402
1973	66	209	44	10	0	6	24	25	.211	.344
Totals	2,992	10,881	3,283	523	140	660	2,062	1,903	.302	.557

Notes: Boldface indicates statistical leader. GP = games played; AB = at bats; 2B = doubles; 3B = triples; HR = home runs; RBI = runs batted in; BA = batting average; SA = slugging average

In 1951, he was sent to their Class AAA American Association team in Minneapolis, where he hit 8 home runs in thirty-five games. Meanwhile, the major team was not doing well. They sent their scout to Minnesota to see if Willie was ready for the major leagues. He was very impressed and referred to Willie as the "outstanding player on the Minnesota team."

Willie, however, apparently did not believe that he was ready for the big leagues. In fact, his first few games in the major leagues in 1951 were not impressive. He wanted to be sent back to the minor leagues, but the New York manager, Leo Durocher, refused to let him go. It was this manager who turned out to be Willie's favorite manager as well as the most influential person in his career.

The Emerging Champion

With the faith of the Giants' manager to keep him in New York, Willie soon proved himself to be the fresh young talent the team needed. The Giants ended the 1951 season by beating the Brooklyn Dodgers and winning the National League pennant. Leo Durocher credited Willie as the "spark" that won the victory. In his 1988 autobiography, *Say Hey,* Willie credited Leo with inspiring him to believe in himself.

Although Willie's career was interrupted in 1952 when he was drafted into the United States Army, he continued to play baseball all through his military service. In 1954, discharged from the Army, he returned to the Giants.

His team had not won the pennant while Willie was gone, but with him, the Giants won the pennant and then the World Series against the Cleveland Indians. In one of the four games against the Indians, Willie made such a superb catch that it was widely talked about in public and was even considered the greatest ever made on a baseball field. Willie was an impressive defensive player because of his famous catches and his perfect throws at home plate that caught runners out.

With his batting average of .345 and his 41 home runs, Willie led the league in 1954. Awards and honors were showered upon him. He was voted the National League most valuable player in 1954, named Player of the Year by *The Sporting News,* and voted Male Athlete of the Year by the

Associated Press poll. He also received the Hickok Belt, studded with diamonds worth $10,000, as the professional athlete of the year.

In 1956, Willie married a divorced woman two years older than he was. He and Marghuerite Wendell Kennedy Chapman adopted a three-year-old boy, Michael, in 1959. Although the couple divorced in 1961, Willie and his son remained close.

Continuing the Story

For the next few years, Willie had an outstanding career. When the Giants left New York City to move to San Francisco in 1958, Willie temporarily felt insecure. In his 1966 autobiography, *Willie Mays: My Life In and Out of Baseball,* he wrote that San Francisco fans did not like him the way New York fans did. San Francisco already had its own baseball hero, Joe DiMaggio. Also, Willie felt that being black and from New York did not help him on the West Coast.

In 1962, when the Giants won the pennant again, Willie felt more comfortable in San Francisco. He was appointed team captain in 1964 and went on to hit 52 home runs in 1965, in what was perhaps his best season. Again, he was named the National League most valuable player.

As a professional athlete, Willie drove himself hard. Sometimes he had fainting spells from nervous exhaustion, although he tried to take good care of himself. He did not drink or smoke and he slept regularly. Moreover, he was admired for his ability to keep the peace among the players when bitter fights seemed to threaten. He remarried, in 1971, to social worker Mae Allen.

Willie was traded to the New York Mets in 1972, and in 1973, he retired from baseball. The Mets, however, gave him a ten-year pact to keep him as a part-time coach and goodwill ambassador. In 1979, he was inducted into the National Baseball Hall of Fame. In 1999, Willie was honored again by being selected for the starting lineup of major league baseball's thirty-man All-Century team.

Summary

With his 660 home runs in twenty-two years of playing ball, Willie Mays ranks third, behind Hank Aaron and Babe Ruth, on the all-time list. Willie seemed destined to play baseball from the age of six months, when his father tried to get him to walk by getting him to chase a ball. His record-breaking achievements as well as his entertaining autobiographies show how well he used his talents to raise the status of the game he loved.

Shakuntala Jayaswal

Additional Sources:

Grabowski, John F. *Willie Mays.* New York: Chelsea House, 1990.

Hano, Arnold. *Willie Mays.* New York: Grosett & Dunlap, 1970.

Mays, Willie, and Jeff Harris. *Danger in Center Field.* Larchmont, N.Y.: Argonaut Books, 1963.

Mays, Willie, with Lou Sahadi. *Say Hey: The Autobiography of Willie Mays.* New York: Simon and Schuster, 1988.

HONORS AND AWARDS	
1951	National League Rookie of the Year
1954	*Sporting News* Major League Player of the Year Associated Press Male Athlete of the Year Hickok Belt
1954, 1965	National League most valuable player
1954-73	National League All-Star Team
1957-68	National League Gold Glove Award
1963, 1968	All-Star Game most valuable player
1970	*Sporting News* Baseball Player of the Decade First Commissioner's Award
1973	Inducted into California Sports Hall of Fame
1975	Inducted into Black Athletes Hall of Fame
1979	Inducted into National Baseball Hall of Fame Inducted into Alabama Sports Hall of Fame
1999	MLB All-Century Team Uniform number 24 retired by San Francisco Giants

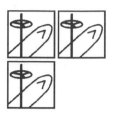

ANDREA MEAD LAWRENCE

Sport: Skiing

Born: April 19, 1932
Rutland, Vermont

Early Life

Born into a family who skied, Andrea Mead Lawrence and her brother could ski almost before they could walk. Their parents, Bradford and Janet Mead of Rutland, Vermont, skied at the Pico Peak Ski Resort. It was there that their two children learned to ski with the help of their parents and the instructional ski program at Pico.

Although Andrea had no formal training in ski racing, she began training for races when she was six. By the age of eight, she began to compete in local races. She was eleven when she skied in her first major event against adults; she took second place in the Eastern Slalom Championship Race. At age fourteen, she qualified for the U.S. Olympic ski team by winning the slalom and coming in second in the downhill events at the Olympic trials.

The Road to Excellence

There are two types of events in alpine ski racing. The technical events are the slalom and the giant slalom, and the speed events are the super-giant slalom (Super-G) and the downhill. Before the 1950's, the combined event existed as one of the technical events. In this event, racers were given two runs, and the racer with the fastest combined time won. The giant slalom replaced the combined event in the 1950's. In the giant slalom, skiers make turns, but the gates are placed farther apart than in the slalom, in which the skier must make short turns through tightly placed gates on a relatively short, steep course.

In 1948, Andrea was the youngest member of the U.S. Women's Olympic alpine ski team. She took eighth place in the slalom (the bronze medal winner skied a mere one-tenth of a second faster), twenty-first in the combined event, and thirty-fifth in the downhill.

The next ski season, 1949, Andrea won all the events at the Fédération International de Ski try-outs in Whitefish, Montana. With her wins in the slalom, combined event, and downhill, Andrea earned the right to represent the U.S. on the international ski team.

Andrea Mead Lawrence after winning the slalom and giant slalom in the 1955 International Downhill Championship.

MAJOR CHAMPIONSHIPS

Year	Competition	Event	Place
1944	Eastern Slalom Championship	Slalom	2d
1947	Olympic Trials	Slalom	1st
		Downhill	2d
1948	Olympic Games	Slalom	8th
		Combined	21st
		Downhill	35th
1952	Olympic Games	Giant slalom	Gold
		Slalom	Gold
1956	Olympic Games	Slalom	4th

Although Andrea skied poorly during the ski season of 1950, she worked hard to regain her championship style for the next season. Of the sixteen races in which she competed during the 1951 season, Andrea won ten and placed second in four. This was the first time in history that American skiers were performing at a top level.

The Emerging Champion

The 1952 Winter Olympics were held in Oslo, Norway, the first time the Winter Olympics had been held in a Scandinavian country. From February 14 to 25, 500,000 fans watched athletes from thirty countries compete in the Games. A new women's ski event was introduced to replace the combined event: the giant slalom. Andrea, at age nineteen, won the giant slalom by more than 2 seconds, becoming the youngest athlete at Oslo to win a gold medal.

In the downhill event, Andrea fell and was disqualified. During the first run of the slalom event, Andrea's ski caught a gate, and she missed the turn; she had to backtrack up the course to go through the gate. Despite the delay, Andrea finished fourth in that run. Andrea's second, and final, run of the slalom was near-flawless. She won the event with eight-tenths of a second to spare. She became the first American to earn two gold medals in a Winter Olympics.

Continuing the Story

Andrea continued to compete in national and international ski events. She married skier Dave Lawrence and had three of their five children before the 1956 Olympics. During this Olympics, Andrea finished fourth in the giant slalom (one-tenth of a second behind the bronze-medal winner).

Because of her outstanding finishes in national and international ski racing events, Andrea was honored with many awards. In 1958, she was inducted into the U.S. National Ski Hall of Fame. She was invited to ski the torch into the stadium for the opening of the 1960 Winter Olympics in Squaw Valley, California. In 1983, she was named to the International Women's Sports Hall of Fame.

Summary

Being surrounded by snow and mountains from the very beginning, Andrea Mead Lawrence learned to ski at an early age. Even when she was a young girl she showed amazing promise as a ski racer. She kept up her training, and with her strength and determination she earned places on U.S. ski teams. Her exemplary ski racing career, which included two Olympic gold medals, is an example for all young skiers. Although her career ended in the 1950's, Andrea still shines as a model of excellence for ski racers.

Betsy L. Nichols

Additional Sources:

Drummond, Siobhan, and Elizabeth Rathburn, eds. *Grace and Glory: A Century of Women in the Olympics.* Chicago: Multi-Media Partners and Triumph Books, 1996.

Greenberg, Stan. *Olympic Games Records: 776 BC to AD 1988.* Enfield, Middlesex, England: Guinness Superlatives, 1987.

Woolum, Janet. *Outstanding Women Athletes: Who They Are and How They Influenced Sports in America.* Phoeniz, Ariz.: Oryx Press, 1992.

HONORS AND AWARDS

1949	White Stag Trophy (Best Ladies Combined Downhill)
1952	Beck International Trophy (Outstanding U.S. Skier in International Competition)
1958	Inducted into National Ski Hall of Fame
1960	Skied Olympic torch into stadium to open Winter Olympic Games at Squaw Valley, California
1983	Inducted into International Women's Sports Hall of Fame

MARY T. MEAGHER

Sport: Swimming

Born: October 27, 1964
Louisville, Kentucky

Early Life

Mary Terstegge Meagher was born on October 27, 1964, the tenth of eleven children in an Irish Catholic family from Louisville, Kentucky. A swimmer from a very early age, she got her start in swimming by following her brother and sisters down to the pool.

She won her first meet at the age of six. A couple of years later, she decided to specialize in the butterfly, considered to be the most challenging stroke in swimming. Even at such a young age, she says that the stroke came to her "naturally."

In a sport known for the youthfulness of its participants, Mary T.—or, as she is called by her friends, simply T—was even younger than most. Yet her exceptional drive and determination to win pushed her to overcome her lack of a "normal" childhood through success in the pool.

The Road to Excellence

For Mary, the road to excellence was a short one. Less than ten years passed between the time that she won her first meet and the time that she set her first world record at the age of fourteen. At the 1979 Pan-American Games in San Juan, Puerto Rico, she swam the 200-meter butterfly in 2 minutes 9.77 seconds.

She was in the eighth grade and swimming for the Lakeside Swimming Club in Louisville when she set that record. At that point, she was still wearing braces on her teeth and traveling with a stuffed frog named Bubbles. Denny Pursley, her coach at the time, had to suggest to her the idea of training for the upcoming 1980 Olympics because she had not thought of it.

She went on to qualify for the United States Olympic team, but, like the other United States athletes, was unable to compete because the United States chose not to participate in the games to protest the invasion of Afghanistan by the Soviet Union. Even without Olympic competition, however, she set another record time (this time in the 100-meter butterfly) of 59.26 seconds that year. Bill Peak, an age-group coach for the Lakeside Swimming Club at the time that Mary T. set her first world record, became her coach after the 1980 Olympics. He helped her to focus her desire not only to win but also to improve on her own world record.

The Emerging Champion

It took Mary only a year to surpass her previous best in the 100-meter butterfly in a remarkable meet: the United States Long Course Championships in Brown Deer, Wisconsin, in August of 1981. On August 13, at the age of sixteen, she swam the 200-meter butterfly in a world-record 2 minutes, 5.96 seconds.

Three days later, Mary also beat the world-record 100-meter butterfly mark she had set a year earlier. Finishing in 57.93 seconds, she took a full 1.33 seconds off her previous record. This was a remarkable accomplishment in swimming, where races are won by hundredths of a second.

The two world records she set that week in Wisconsin are the oldest in amateur swimming, and nobody, not even Mary T. herself, has come close to beating them. It was around this time that people began to refer to her as "Madame Butterfly." This name acknowledged her absolute supremacy in her sport.

Those records also created a lot of pressure for Mary, because she knew that everyone expected her to top them, especially in the 1984 Los Angeles Olympics. After training with Mark Schubert in Mission Viejo, California, in preparation for the Olympics, she went on to win three gold medals in the Los Angeles games. She won one each in the 100- and 200-meter butterfly, as well as one in the 4×100-meter medley relay.

Continuing the Story

After the 1984 Olympics, Mary attended the University of California at Berkeley and swam with coach Karen Moe Thornton. During her time there, she continued to dominate the butterfly events, winning fourteen consecutive races in 1985 and six of eight in 1986.

MAJOR CHAMPIONSHIPS

Year	Competition	Event	Place	Time
1979	Pan-American Games	200-meter butterfly	Gold	2:09.77 WR, PAR
	U.S. Nationals	100-meter butterfly	1st	—
		200-meter butterfly	1st	—
1981	U.S. Nationals	200-meter freestyle	2d	—
		100-meter butterfly	1st	57.93 WR
		200-meter butterfly	1st	2:5.96 WR
1982	World Championships	100-meter butterfly	1st	59.41
		200-meter butterfly	2d	2:09.76
		4×100-meter medley relay	2d	4:08.12
	U.S. Nationals	100-meter butterfly	1st	—
		200-meter butterfly	1st	—
1983	Pan-American Games	200-meter butterfly	1st	2:10.06
	NCAA Championships	100-yard butterfly	2d	—
		200-yard butterfly	1st	1:56.71
	U.S. Nationals	200-meter butterfly	1st	—
1984	Olympic Games	100-meter butterfly	Gold	59.26
		200-meter butterfly	Gold	2:06.90 OR
		4×100-meter medley relay	Gold	4:08.34
1985	World University Games	100-meter butterfly	1st	59.81 UR
		200-meter butterfly	1st	2:07.32 UR
		4×200-meter medley relay	—	4:11.24
	NCAA Championships	100-yard butterfly	1st	53.50
		200-yard butterfly	1st	1:55.13
	U.S. Nationals	100-meter butterfly	1st	—
		200-meter butterfly	1st	—
1986	World Championships	200-meter freestyle	3d	2:00.14
		100-meter butterfly	3d	59.98
		200-meter butterfly	1st	2:08.41
		4×100-meter freestyle relay	2d	3:44.04
		4×200-meter freestyle relay	—	8:02.12
		4×100-meter medley relay	2d	4:07.75
	NCAA Championships	200-yard butterfly	1st	1:54.52
		100-yard butterfly	2d	—
1987	NCAA Championships	100-yard butterfly	1st	52.42
		200-yard butterfly	1st	1:55.54
1988	Olympic Games	200-meter butterfly	Bronze	—
		4×100-meter relay	Silver	—

Notes: OR = Olympic Record; WR = World Record; PAR = Pan-American Record; UR = University Record

After winning both the 100- and 200-yard butterfly events at that National Collegiate Athletic Association Championships in 1987, she decided to take a break from the sport that had consumed her life for the past ten years. Nearing the point of graduation from Berkeley, she quit swimming. The pressure to beat marks she had posted years earlier, combined with a desire to see something of life outside the pool, led her to take some time off to live a "normal" life.

Five months later, she was back in the swimming pool, but she had lost some of her momen-

RECORDS AND MILESTONES

Held 7 world records and 8 national records
Won 21 national titles
Won 6 NCAA individual awards

HONORS AND AWARDS

1980	Women's U.S. Olympic swimming team
1981	U.S. Swimming Swimmer of the Year
1984	Olympia Award
1986-87	Honda Broderick Cup
1987	NCAA Today's Top Six Award
1993	Inducted into International Swimming Hall of Fame

tum because she had not been training. After some poor meets in late 1987 and early 1988, she made a tearful phone call to Bill Peak, her coach in the early 1980's. He said that he would help her, under one condition: She had to make a commitment to train for a world record and not only to make the Olympic team.

She went on to become only the fourth woman in history to qualify for three Olympics (1980, 1984, and 1988), but was not as successful as she might have hoped in the 1988 competition. Although she received a bronze medal for the 200-meter butterfly and a silver for her part in the 4×100-meter relay, she finished a disappointing seventh in the 100-meter butterfly and did not succeed in breaking her earlier records.

Yet the longevity of her records and the length and successfulness of her swimming career testify to Mary's unique combination of natural ability and exceptional drive.

In 1993, Mary was inducted into the International Swimming Hall of Fame.

Summary

Odd as it may sound, Mary T. Meagher's success was perhaps also her greatest obstacle. At a very early age, she established a standard of excellence that no one, not even she, could surpass. Yet she did not rest on that success. Instead, she strove to go beyond it, and in the process fashioned one of the most impressive careers in swimming history.

Mark Rogers

Additional Sources:

Hickok, Ralph. *A Who's Who of Sports Champions.* Boston: Houghton Mifflin, 1995.

Levinson, David, and Karen Christenson, eds. *Encyclopedia of World Sport: From Ancient Times to Present.* Santa Barbara, Calif.: ABC-CLIO, 1996.

Mallon, Bill, and Ian Buchanan. *Quest for Gold: The Encyclopedia of American Olympians.* New York: Leisure Press, 1984.

Wallechinsky, David. *The Complete Book of the Olympics.* Boston: Little, Brown and Company, 1991.

RICK MEARS

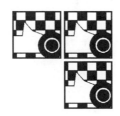

Sport: Auto racing

Born: December 3, 1951
　　　　Wichita, Kansas

Early Life

Rick Ravon Mears was born on December 3, 1951, in Wichita, Kansas, to Bill Ravon Mears and Mae Louise (Simpson) Mears. As a boy, Rick was quiet and shy, so shy that in school he would take an "F" rather than speak in front of a group. Yet Rick was very competitive.

He entered the world of racing in 1968, when he started racing motorcycles in the California desert. He was very successful, winning more than sixty trophies before switching to racing sprint buggies in the Mojave Desert. Rick soon was graduated to off-road races and even competed in the famous Pikes Peak Hill Climb. In 1973, Rick captured seven off-road victories and started racing sportsman stock cars at local California speedways.

The Road to Excellence

In 1976, Rick jumped into the world of big-time racing, making his Indy car debut with an eighth-place finish in the California 500. He finished ninth in each of the final two events of the 1976 season and was named Rookie of the Year by the United States Auto Club.

In 1977, Rick attempted to qualify for the Indianapolis 500 for the first time, sacrificing his job and home in California. He did not qualify for the race; however, he picked up four top-ten finishes in the eight Indy car races in which he competed that year.

Rick's fortunes as a professional racer took off through a chance occurrence. While participating in a motorcycle expedition in the Colorado Rockies, he met Roger Penske, a highly successful race-car owner who offered him an opportunity to drive for his team during the 1978 racing season. Rick jumped at the chance.

The Emerging Champion

The 1978 racing season saw the beginning of one of the most successful owner-driver teams in automobile racing history. Rick's driving talent and the near-military ambitiousness of the Penske program proved to be a formidable combination for the next fourteen years.

Rick qualified on the outside of the front row, in third position, for the 1978 Indianapolis 500.

Rick Mears celebrates his victory in the 1991 Indy 500.

1851

He was the first rookie to break 200 miles per hour in qualifying and was named the Indianapolis 500 Rookie of the Year. Rick won his first Indy car race in Milwaukee, Wisconsin, that year, then went on to capture two more wins and three second-place finishes.

In 1979, Rick captured the pole position for the Indianapolis 500 and recorded the first of his four Indianapolis 500 victories. Rick won two other races that year and finished in the top ten in all fourteen races in which he competed.

Continuing the Story

During the remainder of Rick's racing career, which ended with his retirement after the 1992 racing season, he was a model of consistency. Perhaps no other driver in racing devoted as much time to understanding his car's handling. During testing sessions, Rick would closely examine the computer data between runs, working with engineers to perfect a car's handling. On the road, Rick would sit in his hotel room with a computer, playing with the numbers, trying to make connections between the computer read-outs and what he felt on the track. He constantly strove for perfection.

Rick also had to overcome some serious accidents during his career. While competing in the 1981 Indianapolis 500, Rick narrowly escaped a potentially fatal burning. During 1985, the condition of his feet limited his racing to oval tracks, as road racing requires more footwork for braking and shifting.

Competition, not a love of speed, was the motivating factor for Rick's success. He was not a gambler on the track but would take calculated risks when the situation called for it. With Indy cars typically traveling more than the length of a

CART AND OTHER VICTORIES	
1978-79,1981-82	Atlanta
1978	Brands Hatch
1978,1988-91	Milwaukee
1979,1984,1988,1991	Indianapolis 500
1979	Trenton
1980-81	Mexico City
1981,1983	Michigan
1981-82	Riverside
1981	Watkins Glen
1982,1989-90	Phoenix
1982,1985	Pocono 500
1989	Laguna Seca

football field each second, a driver must understand when a risk can be taken. Rick's judgment rarely was wrong.

Rick's success won the respect of his fellow drivers as well as the media. Indy car driver Danny Sullivan stated, "Rick is the best guy I've ever seen on an oval . . . he's the yardstick for all of us." In 1989, Rick was named the Driver of the Decade by the Associated Press. In 1992, he was the youngest of ten drivers named "Champions for Life" at the Driver of the Year awards ceremony.

Summary

Rick always maintained that he was not motivated by records. He was true to his words when he announced his retirement in 1992. In retiring at the relatively young age of forty-one, he passed up the chance to establish some new racing records, perhaps the most important being a chance to become the first driver to win the Indianapolis 500 five times.

Bill Swanson

Additional Sources:

Hickok, Ralph. *A Who's Who of Sports Champions: Their Stories and Records.* Boston: Houghton Mifflin, 1995.

Levinson, David, and Karen Christenson, eds. *Encyclopedia of World Sport: From Ancient Times to Present.* Santa Barbara, Calif.: ABC-CLIO, 1996.

McKenna, A. T. *Indy Racing.* Edina, Minn.: Adbo & Daughters, 1998.

Sakkis, Tony. *Indy Racing Legends.* Osceola, Wis.: Motorbooks International, 1996.

Sowers, Richard. *Stock Car Racing Lives.* Phoenix, Ariz.: David Bull, 2000.

MILESTONE
Only driver to win six Indy 500 poles

HONORS AND AWARDS	
1976	USAC Rookie of the Year
1978	Indianapolis 500 Rookie of the Year
1979	Jerry Titus Memorial Award
1979,1981-82	CART National Champion
1989	Associated Press Driver of the Decade

ALEXANDER MEDVED

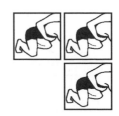

Sport: Wrestling

Born: September 16, 1937
Near Belaya Tserkov, Ukraine, U.S.S.R.
(now Ukraine)

Early Life

Alexander Vasilyevich Medved was born September 16, 1937, near the town of Belaya Tserkov, which is near Kiev, in the Ukraine. His father, Vasily Zenkovich Medved, was a forest ranger. His father believed children should work hard, and Alexander learned the lesson well. The years following World War II, which ended in 1945 when Alexander was eight years old, were difficult for everyone living in the war-ravaged Ukraine. Each family struggled to obtain even the bare necessities of life. When Alexander was fifteen years old, his father became an invalid and could no longer work. Alexander, as the old-est child, went to work in a factory to help support the family.

Alexander entered a school for young persons who worked during the day to continue his high school education. While at this school, he first took an interest in wrestling at age seventeen.

The Road to Excellence

Following high school, Alexander entered his country's army and was stationed in Byelorussia. Military service was required of all young men by the government. His army commander was a wrestler and selected Alexander, who had grown into a big, strong young man, as a training partner. Alexander improved his wrestling skills greatly during his army years. In his last year of military service, he finished third in the Soviet National Championships.

Following his service in the army, Alexander decided to attend a college for teachers located in Minsk, Byelorussia. Here Alexander began serious wrestling, training under the coaching of Pavel V. Grigoryev and Bogeslav M. Ribalko in 1959. In the short span of two years, his hard work helped him become his country's representative at the World Championships held in Yokohama, Japan.

The Emerging Champion

Alexander Medved competed in fifteen international championships between 1961 and 1972. During this period, he won seventy-three matches and lost only two. He lost to the West German Wilfried Dietrich at his first World Championships in 1961, finish-

Olympic wrestling champion Alexander Medved at the 1964 Games.

MAJOR CHAMPIONSHIPS

Year	Competition	Weight Class	Place
1961	World Championships	+87 kilograms	3d
1962	World Championships	97 kilograms	1st
1963	World Championships	97 kilograms	1st
1964	Olympic Games	97 kilograms	Gold
1965	World Championships	97 kilograms	2d
1966	European Championships	+97 kilograms	1st
	World Championships	97 kilograms	1st
1967	World Championships	+97 kilograms	1st
1968	European Championships	+97 kilograms	1st
	Olympic Games	+97 kilograms	Gold
1969	World Championships	+100 kilograms	1st
1970	World Championships	+100 kilograms	1st
1971	World Championships	+100 kilograms	1st
1972	European Championships	+100 kilograms	1st
	Olympic Games	+100 kilograms	Gold

ing third. In 1965, he lost to the Turk Ahmet Ayuk and finished second at the World Championships. Both losses were on points. He was not pinned in any of his seventy-five matches in international championship competition.

Alexander won thirteen international championships (the most by any wrestler in history). Included in these were three Olympic gold medals (1964, 1968, and 1972).

Alexander became a great wrestling champion because of his many outstanding qualities. His technical skill was outstanding, he was always in excellent physical condition (6 feet 6 inches tall and as much as 220 pounds), and he possessed enormous willpower and an ability to give 100 percent concentration during a match. For Alexander to win on points was hardly a victory. He wanted to dominate his opponent and pin him.

During his matches, Alexander overwhelmed his opponents with his unbelievable attacking style. His great number of wrestling moves, along with his relentless pursuit, caused most opponents to fear him. Generally, when his opponents avoided a pin and lost on points, they were proud to say they had lost to a great champion. Alexander's favorite hold was the half nelson. He became the greatest wrestler in the world in spite of

the fact that he started wrestling at the rather advanced age of seventeen.

The Soviet freestyle wrestling system is well known throughout the world because of the many Olympic champions it has produced. The first Soviet wrestling championships were held in 1945. The first Soviet Olympic champions were David Tsimakuridze and Arsen Mekokishvili in 1952. There were more than 715,000 wrestlers in the Soviet Union in the late 1980's. Every year, the Soviet national team was replenished by dedicated, talented, and eager young wrestlers. Each newcomer had survived intense competition at home and at the many youth world championships. Those who rose to the top possessed excellent technique, great endurance, and lightning-fast reflexes.

Continuing the Story

Alexander gained revenge against the West German Wilfried Dietrich during the 1968 Olympic Games in Mexico City. The high altitude placed great stress on all the athletes. Alexander valiantly battled fatigue and a dislocated thumb in the final against Dietrich to finish first. He ended his career on a high note in the 1972 Olympic finals in Munich, Germany. Alexander, now thirty-five years old, won the gold medal against the Bulgarian Osman Duraliv who was also competing in the Olympics for the last time.

Alexander Medved is the most meritorious wrestler in wrestling history. In addition to receiving numerous international and Soviet awards, he was recognized by UNESCO for his "nobility in sport." In his honor, a major international wrestling tournament, "Tournei Medved," is held in Minsk.

Following his retirement as a wrestler, Alexander dedicated his efforts to becoming an outstanding international wrestling referee. In a few short years, he achieved his goal. In keeping with the Soviet tradition of past champions aiding youthful wrestlers, Alexander became the director of a wrestling club in Minsk to train future Olympic champions. He was elected president of the Wrestling Federation of Byelorussia. Alexander also became a radio engineer in Minsk. His son, Alexei, won the 1986 Junior World Cup Championship and in 1988 became a member of the Soviet national team at age twenty-one.

Summary

Alexander Medved won more international wrestling championships (thirteen) than any other wrestler in history. He was known for overwhelming his opponents through superior conditioning, technical skill, determination, and concentration. Following his retirement, he became an internationally ranked wrestling referee and director of a wrestling club to train future Olympic champions.

Walter R. Schneider

Additional Sources:

Levinson, David, and Karen Christenson, eds. *Encyclopedia of World Sport: From Ancient Times to Present.* Santa Barbara, Calif.: ABC-CLIO, 1996.

Schapp, Dick. *An Illustrated History of the Olympics.* New York: Alfred A. Knopf, 1975.

Wallechinsky, David. *The Complete Book of the Olympics.* Boston: Little, Brown and Company, 1991.

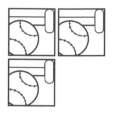

JOE MEDWICK

Sport: Baseball

Born: November 24, 1911
Carteret, New Jersey
Died: March 21, 1975
St. Petersburg, Florida

Early Life

Joseph Michael (Ducky) Medwick was born on November 24, 1911, in Carteret, New Jersey, a small town that is part of the New York metropolitan area. His parents were immigrants from Hungary. Although not a large boy, Joe grew muscu-

Joe Medwick in 1934.

AP/Wide World Photos

lar and strong. Very aggressive, he loved action and starred in four sports—track, football, basketball, and baseball—in high school. His dream in those days was to go to the University of Notre Dame and play football.

The Road to Excellence

In 1930, the year of his graduation, the St. Louis Cardinals organization convinced Joe to forgo college in favor of a career as an outfielder in professional baseball. Sent to a minor league team for the balance of that season, Joe demonstrated power, speed, and instinctive ability in the field. He completely overmatched the Middle Atlantic League pitchers, in only seventy-five games batting .419 with 100 runs batted in.

Promoted to Houston the next year, he tore into Texas League pitchers also. In 1931, he led the league in runs batted in, and in 1932, he batted .354 and led the league's outfielders in fielding percentage.

At Houston, he acquired his nickname. There are two or three versions of the story. According to the most likely one, a young woman in the stands decided that he walked like a duck and called him her "Ducky Wucky." The nickname, usually abbreviated Ducky, stuck, although Joe himself preferred to be called Mickey, and, later, Muscles.

Joe's great strength and aggressiveness, advantageous to him as a hitter, also proved to be a weakness, for his combative nature and chip-on-the-shoulder attitude often got him into trouble. No one doubted, however, that Ducky Medwick was ready to play major league baseball, and late in the 1932 season, the twenty-year-old outfielder was promoted to the Cardinals.

The Emerging Champion

From the start, Joe hit major league pitching as solidly as he had always hit every previous vari-

STATISTICS

Season	GP	AB	Hits	2B	3B	HR	Runs	RBI	BA	SA
1932	26	106	37	12	1	2	13	12	.349	.538
1933	148	595	182	40	10	18	92	98	.306	.497
1934	149	620	198	40	**18**	18	110	106	.319	.529
1935	154	634	224	46	13	23	132	126	.353	.576
1936	155	636	**223**	**64**	13	18	115	**138**	.351	.577
1937	156	633	**237**	56	10	**31**	111	**154**	**.374**	**.641**
1938	146	590	190	**47**	8	21	100	**122**	.322	.536
1939	150	606	201	48	8	14	98	117	.332	.507
1940	143	581	175	30	12	17	83	86	.301	.482
1941	133	538	171	33	10	18	100	88	.318	.517
1942	142	553	166	37	4	4	69	96	.300	.403
1943	126	497	138	30	3	5	54	70	.278	.380
1944	128	490	165	24	3	7	64	85	.337	.441
1945	92	310	90	17	0	3	31	37	.290	.374
1946	41	77	24	4	0	2	7	18	.312	.442
1947	75	150	46	12	0	4	19	28	.307	.467
1948	20	19	4	0	0	0	0	2	.211	.211
Totals	1,984	7,635	2,471	540	113	205	1,198	1,383	.324	.505

Notes: Boldface indicates statistical leader. GP = games played; AB = at bats; 2B = doubles; 3B = triples; HR = home runs; RBI = runs batted in; BA = batting average; SA = slugging average

ety. He batted .349 in twenty-six games in 1932 and became a fixture in left field for the Cardinals. Joe had amazingly keen eyes. Whereas most batters simply follow the path of a pitched ball, he could see the rotation and gauge instantly what sort of pitch it was. Then his powerful arm muscles whipped the bat around in a split second.

In his first full season, he batted .306 and knocked in 98 runs. Like his teammate Pepper Martin, Joe slid into every base and went after every ball in the field as though his life depended on it. It became clear that the Cardinals, winners of four pennants from 1926 to 1931, were assembling another championship team.

Everything came together in 1934, when the Cardinal pitching ace Dizzy Dean won thirty games, Martin led the league in stolen bases, and Joe Medwick crashed 76 extra-base hits, including a league-leading 18 triples. Frank Frisch's Cardinals had won the right to meet the Detroit Tigers in the World Series.

Joe lashed out 11 hits in the seven-game Series, but in the seventh inning of the final game in Detroit, he caused one of the most unusual incidents in Series history. It started when he slid hard, spikes flying, into third baseman Marv Owen in the seventh inning.

The Cardinals were now leading 9-0 behind Dean, and the Tiger fans were frustrated. As Joe took his position in left field in the bottom of the seventh inning, the fans in the seats behind him began to hurl fruit, bottles, and other debris at him.

When the groundskeepers could not clear the field, Baseball Commissioner Kenesaw Mountain Landis, from his box seat, decided to restore order by removing Joe Medwick from the game. Had the score been close, Joe and the Cardinals would no doubt have protested vigorously, but as things stood, they complied, the game resumed, and the Cardinals reigned as world champions.

Continuing the Story

Over the next few seasons, Joe continued his heavy hitting for the Gashouse Gang, as the Cardinals of that era were called. From 1935 through 1939, he batted .353, .351, .374, .322, and .332, with at least 117 runs batted in each year. For three consecutive years, he led the league in doubles, with his 64 in 1936 setting a league record that remained unbroken more than a half century later.

In 1936, he amassed a stupendous 95 extra-base hits, only to top that total with 97 the following year. In 1937, he won the Triple Crown and was chosen the National League most valuable player. He never curbed his fighting instincts entirely, but he learned to be agreeable to the

MAJOR LEAGUE RECORDS

Three consecutive seasons as RBI leader (record shared)

NATIONAL LEAGUE RECORDS

Ten consecutive hits (1936) (record shared)

HONORS AND AWARDS

1934-40, 1942, 1944	National League All-Star Team
1937	National League most valuable player
1968	Inducted into National Baseball Hall of Fame

young fans who clamored for his autograph as one of the game's great players.

Between 1935 and 1940, the Cardinals won no pennants, and in June of the latter year, they traded Joe and pitcher Curt Davis to the Brooklyn Dodgers for four players and $125,000. A few days later, a pitch from one of his old Cardinal teammates struck Joe in the head.

Although he continued to be a feared hitter for several more years, Joe never reached the batting heights again after that beaning. He played with two other league teams, in 1947 returning to St. Louis as a part-time player. The following year he was back in the Texas League with Houston again.

Joe loved baseball too much to quit, so he became a playing manager for several minor league teams from 1949 to 1952. Later, he served as a batting instructor in the Cardinals' farm system and did some coaching at St. Louis University.

The National Baseball Hall of Fame received Joe Medwick in 1958. Joe was at work at the Cardinals' St. Petersburg, Florida, training camp when he died on March 21, 1975, at the age of sixty-three.

Summary

Joe Medwick's competitive spirit made him a key ingredient of the Gashouse Gang in the 1930's. He was an individual star who always recognized the importance of team success. No one ever played a more all-out brand of baseball.

Had he not been hit in the head at the age of twenty-eight, he undoubtedly would have posted some amazing career batting marks. Despite the decline in the second half of his career, he finished with a .324 average and 540 doubles for seventeen seasons. For a half dozen seasons, he was one of the game's greatest right-handed hitters.

Robert P. Ellis

Additional Sources:

Appel, Martin, and Burt Goldblatt. *Baseball's Best: The Hall of Fame Gallery.* New York: McGraw-Hill, 1977.

Liss, Howard. *Triple-Crown Winners.* New York: Julian Messner, 1969.

Shatzkin, Mike, et al., eds. *The Ballplayers: Baseball's Ultimate Biographical Reference.* New York: William Morrow, 1990.

EDDY MERCKX

Sport: Cycling

Born: June 17, 1945
　　　　Meensel-Kiezegem, Belgium

Early Life

Eddy Merckx (pronounced "merks") was born in the small Belgian village of Meensel-Kiezegem, some twenty-five miles from the French border, on June 17, 1945. His father worked as a grocer. Eddy decided at a young age that cycling was going to be his great love. He found it hard to con-centrate on his schooling and preferred to be out working on his cycling. Eddy finally convinced his mother that he should try his hand at professional cycling. At the age of sixteen, Eddy dropped out of school to devote himself full-time to being the best cyclist he could be.

The Road to Excellence

Eddy did not waste any time in his pursuit. In between races, he learned quickly the value of

Eddy Merckx in 1977.

hard work. Conditioning was important to him. Throughout his career as a cyclist, he always kept himself in great shape. Conditioning, combined with desire, made Eddy a powerful rider. Eddy also had developed an amazing amount of stamina. In 1962, he won his first title, the Junior Championship of Belgium. Two years later he won the amateur World Road Championship. At this point, Eddy knew that he was ready to turn professional.

In 1965, he began competing as a professional cyclist. In that first year Eddy proved that he was on the verge of greatness. He won a number of races, including ones at Vilvoorde, Torhout, Visé, and Saint Jansteen. Eddy also finished second in the Belgian Pro National Championship. For his next challenge, he decided to compete in events known as classics. In 1966, Eddy won the 180-mile Milan-San Remo race that has been dubbed the King of the Classics.

Eddy won the Milan-San Remo race again the next year. He was truly beginning to look like the great rider that his coach of 1962, Felicien Vervaecke, had predicted. In 1967, Eddy won his first professional World Road Championship at Heerlen, Netherlands. He had not won the Tour de France yet, but he was about to break through to the top of the cycling elite. Eddy amazed a number of critics with his win in the 1968 Tour of Italy. The race is 2,400 miles long and lasts twenty-three days. Eddy proved that he definitely had the physical stamina for such a grueling race.

The Emerging Champion

In 1969, Eddy became the world's premiere cyclist by winning three classic events and also his first Tour de France. He was the first cyclist to be so successful in the classic races and win the 2,600-mile Tour de France in the same year. The Tour de France is considered the leading road race in the world. It is an event of just longer than twenty days that takes the rider through the European countryside and ends in Paris. Eddy not only won the race but also finished first in six stages of the race. Because of his success during the year, Eddy won the top cycling award: the Super Prestige Pernod Trophy. He had compiled a total of 412 points, which was almost 130 points higher than the previous record.

Eddy, because of his stamina, was at his best in the long-distance road races. He won the Tour de France again in 1970, as well as his second Tour of Italy. Eddy was in top form and, seemingly, no other cyclist was in his class. From 1969 to 1975, he won the Super Prestige Pernod Trophy. In 1971, Eddy amassed a point total of 570 to win the trophy. Even though he was the premiere cyclist, winning the tough Tour de France did not come easily. In the 1971 race, Eddy was several minutes behind Luis Ocana in total time, but the Spaniard crashed while descending the Pyrenees Mountains, causing Eddy and another cyclist to crash into Ocana. Ocana was unable to resume the race because of his injuries, but Eddy was able to recover from his fall and pedal to his third victory at the Tour de France. He won his fourth Tour de France in a row in 1972.

Continuing the Story

Eddy decided to go to Mexico City to attempt to set a world's record for one-hour unpaced cycling. At Mexico City's Velodrome, he was able to cover thirty miles and 1,231 yards on the wood track in the one-hour time limit. In this particular event Eddy's only opponent was the clock—a new type of challenge for him.

During his career, Eddy won most of the classic events in which he raced. The classics were the

---

RECORDS

One of only three cyclists to win the Tour de France five times—the current world record
One of only two cyclists to capture competitive cycling's unofficial version of the Triple Crown, winning the Tour de France, the Tour of Italy, and the World Road Championships Professional Road Race in 1974
Set world record for the most first-place finishes in a classic, with seven victories in the 180-mile-long Milan-San Remo

HONORS AND AWARDS

1969-75	Super Prestige Pernod Trophy

MAJOR CHAMPIONSHIPS

Year	Competition	Place
1962	Belgian Junior Championships	1st
1964	World Road Championships, Amateur Road Race	Gold
1965	Belgian Pro National Championship	2d
1966-67, 1969, 1971-72, 1975-76	Milan-San Remo	1st
1967, 1971, 1974	World Road Championships, Professional Road Race	Gold
1968, 1970, 1972-74	Tour of Italy	1st
1969-71	Paris-Nice	1st
1969-72, 1974	Tour de France	1st
1973	Tour of Spain	1st

important short races of the season. He was at his best, however, in the multi-stage long races that are known as tours. The tours were the most demanding, since they covered more than 2,000 miles.

In 1973, Eddy won his fourth Tour of Italy. He also won the Tour of Spain that year, which put him in line to become the first cyclist ever to win the three most prestigious tours in the same year. The season took too much out of Eddy, however, and he decided not to compete in the Tour de France. This broke his string of Tour de France victories at four. Eddy knew that he could not extend himself anymore for the season. In 1974, though, he came back to win both the Tour de France and the Tour of Italy. Eddy also won his third professional World Road Championship race that year. He had proven himself to be one of cycling's greatest road race champions. There are few athletes whose careers can compare with Eddy's accomplishments. What he did as a cyclist must be considered phenomenal. Eddy retired from racing in 1978 and became a respected bicycle designer and businessman.

Summary

Eddy Merckx won the Tour de France five times, the Tour of Italy five times, the professional World Road Championships race three times, and the Milan-San Remo Classic seven times. He won countless other races and is in a class by himself. Eddy always believed in being the best-conditioned athlete around, and some highly regarded medical experts have said that no one else has ever been in better condition than Eddy. Any cycling champion who comes after him will have Eddy's legacy with which to compete.

Michael Jeffrys

Additional Sources:

Chavner, David, and Michael Halstead. *The Tour de France Complete Book of Cycling.* New York: Villard Books, 1990.

Henderson, N. G. *Yellow Jersey, from Eugene Christophe to Eddy Merckx.* Silsden, England: Kennedy Bros., 1970.

Levinson, David, and Karen Christenson, eds. *Encyclopedia of World Sport: From Ancient to Present.* Santa Barbara, Calif.: ABC-CLIO, 1996.

Vanwalleghem, Rik. *Eddy Merckx: The Greatest Cyclist of the 20th Century,* translated by Steve Hawkins. Boulder, Colo.: Velo Press, 1996.

Wadley, J. B. *Eddy Merckx and the 1970 Tour de France.* Silsden, England: Kennedy Bros., 1970.

MARK MESSIER

Sport: Ice hockey

Born: January 18, 1961
Edmonton, Alberta, Canada

Early Life

Mark Douglas Messier was born on January 18, 1961, in Edmonton, Alberta, Canada, to Douglas and Mary Jean Messier. His father, who had a long career as a minor-league hockey player, often took Mark and his older brother Paul to practice with him. As a result, both boys developed a keen appreciation for the game at an early age.

Mark was fifteen when he attended his first junior hockey training camp. His father was the coach, and Paul, two years older than Mark, was the team's star player. Because he had not physically matured yet, Mark was somewhat intimidated by his brother's superior play. Concerned that he might not make the team, Mark began to concentrate on his physical conditioning as well as on honing his hockey skills.

The Road to Excellence

In 1978, after two seasons of junior hockey, Mark turned professional at the age of seventeen, signing a five-game tryout contract with the Indianapolis Racers of the World Hockey Association. Ironically, he was signed to replace future teammate and hockey superstar Wayne Gretzky, who was sold to the Edmonton Oilers. After five games with the Racers, Mark joined the Cincinnati Stingers, with whom he spent the rest of the 1978-79 season. Mark scored just one goal in forty-seven games with the Stingers. Still, his talents were evident enough to Glen Sather, general manager of the Oilers, to make Mark Edmonton's second choice in the 1979 National Hockey League (NHL) draft.

Mark played his first NFL game on October 10, 1979, against the Chicago Black Hawks and scored his first goal three days later in a game against the Detroit Red Wings. Even though he

Mark Messier practices in November, 2000, shortly after returning to the New York Rangers.

demonstrated tremendous potential, Sather felt that Mark was undisciplined, so he sent him down to the minors for four games. The demotion had a sobering effect on Mark, causing him to rededicate himself to the game he loved. It was the last time he would be sent to the minors.

The Emerging Champion

Traditionally, left wings are better known for their bone-rattling checks than for their shooting skills. As Oilers' opponents quickly began to realize, however, in Mark, Edmonton had the complete package. At 6 feet and 207 pounds, he was not only big—his nickname was "Moose"—he was also fast.

Mark, like the Oilers of the early 1980's, improved with each new season. He scored 12 goals his first season, 23 the next, and 50 in 1981-82, a feat that earned him NHL All-Star team selection. Even with his personal successes, however, Mark was ultimately disappointed, as the Oilers were swept out of the 1981-1982 playoffs by the Los Angeles Kings, a team that many in hockey believed that Edmonton should have beaten.

Mark and the Oilers came roaring back the next season as the team skated to the Stanley Cup Finals for the first time in franchise history. Despite a sore shoulder throughout the playoffs, Mark led the Oilers with 15 goals in fifteen games, including a 4-goal outing against Calgary. His season mark of 106 points (48 goals and 58 assists) was second only to that of teammate Wayne Gretzky.

Mark had clearly emerged as one of the best left wings in the NHL. The trouble was, not many outside Edmonton were aware of just how dominating a player he had become. The reason was simple: Wayne Gretzky. Mark was, as one teammate put it, "the crash that followed the flash." Playing on the same team as "Number 99" was the surest way for a player to remain anonymous. Yet Mark was never bothered by his own lack of notoriety; he believed that there were enough pressures in the game without worrying about who got the most attention. For Mark, having Gretzky as a teammate meant having a winner in his corner and a friend both on and off the ice.

In the 1983-1984 season, Mark again scored more than 100 points. Midway through the season, however, the raw-boned wing man was shifted to center ice. Without skipping a beat, he continued his on-ice assault of NHL opponents, leading the Oilers to a 57-18-5 record and the team's first Stanley Cup championship.

Mark, who tallied 8 goals and 18 assists for 24 points in the playoffs, captured the Conn Smythe Trophy as the most valuable player of the playoffs.

Just before the start of the 1988-1989 season, a shock wave was sent through the hockey world when the Oilers traded superstar and team captain Wayne Gretzky to the Los Angeles Kings. The trade left Edmonton in transition and struggling; Mark dropped below the 100-point mark for the first time in three years. The Oilers' team leader was gone.

The 1989-1990 campaign, however, was different. Mark, who replaced Gretzky as team captain, knew that the Oilers needed a leader to step forward. With a sense of determination and a contagious level of enthusiasm, Mark carried his leadership duties onto the ice, registering a career year in nearly every department and leading the Oilers to their fifth Stanley Cup championship in eight years. Once again, it was Mark who led the way in the postseason, providing 9 goals and a league-leading 22 assists. Although he received numerous awards and All-Star recognition, none of it equaled the satisfaction he received when, as the Oilers' new leader and team captain, he ac-

STATISTICS

Season	GP	G	Ast.	Pts.	PIM
1979-80	75	12	21	33	120
1980-81	72	23	40	63	102
1981-82	78	50	38	88	119
1982-83	77	48	58	106	72
1983-84	73	37	64	101	165
1984-85	55	23	31	54	57
1985-86	63	35	49	84	68
1986-87	77	37	70	107	73
1987-88	77	37	74	111	103
1988-89	72	33	61	94	130
1989-90	79	45	84	129	79
1990-91	53	12	52	64	34
1991-92	79	35	72	107	76
1992-93	75	25	66	91	72
1993-94	76	26	58	84	76
1994-95	46	14	39	53	40
1995-96	74	47	52	99	122
1996-97	71	36	48	84	88
1997-98	82	22	38	60	58
1998-99	59	13	35	48	33
1999-00	66	17	37	54	30
2000-01	82	24	43	67	89
Totals	1,561	651	1,130	1,781	1,806

Notes: GP = games played; G = goals; Ast. = assists; Pts. = points; PIM = penalties in minutes

cepted the Stanley Cup trophy from NHL President John A. Ziegler, Jr.

Continuing the Story

Following an injury-plagued 1990-1991 season and stalemated contract negotiations with the Oilers' management, Mark surprised Oilers fans by asking to be traded. On October 4, 1991, in one of the biggest trades in club history, Mark was acquired by the New York Rangers. The Rangers, confident that they were getting a team leader as well as a great player, named Mark team captain just three days later.

Mark wasted no time showing New York fans why he was considered one of the most dominant players in the game. In his first season with the Rangers, he led the team in scoring with 107 points, and his 72 assists were the most ever by a Ranger center. His play earned him the Hart Memorial Trophy as the NHL's most valuable player, the Lester B. Pearson Award as the NHL's top player as selected by all NHL players, and his fourth NHL All-Star First Team selection.

After a disappointing season in 1992-1993, and with Mike Keenan as the new head coach, Mark helped the Rangers earn the league's best record, finishing the season with 26 goals and 58 assists. Facing elimination in the semifinals of the Stanley Cup championship, Mark scored a hat trick in game 6 against New Jersey, and the Rangers went on to defeat Vancouver in seven games to win their first Stanley Cup since 1953.

With a shortened season in 1994-1995 due to a labor dispute, and with the loss of head coach Mike Keenan to St. Louis, Mark and the Rangers barely made the playoffs. They were eliminated in the second round by Philadelphia.

Mark recorded 47 goals and 52 assists during the 1995-1996 season and passed Hall of Famer Stan Mikita to become the fifth leading scorer in NHL history. Mark was also nominated for the Hart Trophy as the league's most valuable player, although the award was given to Mario Lemieux. Once again, the Rangers were defeated in the second round of playoffs, this time by Lemieux and the Penguins.

In 1996 Mark was reunited with former teammate Wayne Gretzky, and the Rangers were poised to make another run for the Stanley Cup. Mark had a solid season, scoring 36 goals and 48 assists, including his 1,500th career point. In the Eastern Conference finals, however, the Rangers lost in five games to the Flyers, led by Eric Lindros.

Mark left the Rangers as a free agent in 1997 and signed with the Vancouver Canucks. Hampered by elbow and wrist injuries, Mark averaged just under 18 goals per year in his three years with Vancouver. In July, 2000, Mark returned to New York, signing a two-year, $11 million deal with the Rangers. General manager Glen Sathers and new head coach Ron Low hoped that Mark, at the age of thirty-nine, could help his younger teammates with his considerable experience and leadership skills.

Summary

With his blend of talent and toughness, Mark Messier has earned the respect and admiration of his teammates, opponents, fans, and critics alike. Although he played in Gretzky's shadow for much of his career, "Moose" eventually proved that he too was among the best players of his era.

Joe Horrigan

Additional Sources:

Carpiniello, Rick. *Messier: Hockey's Dragonslayer.* Tampa, Fla.: McGregor, 1999.

_____. *Messier: Steel on Ice.* Toronto: Stoddard, 1999.

Duhatschek, Eric. "Medicine Man." *Sports Illustrated* 93, no. 3 (2000).

Hollander, Zander, ed. *The Complete Encyclopedia of Hockey.* 4th ed. Detroit: Visible Ink Press, 1993.

NHL RECORDS
First to score 11 career playoff shorthanded goals First to score 12 career All-Star Game assists

HONORS AND AWARDS	
1982-83, 1990, 1992	NHL All-Star First Team
1982-86, 1988-92	NHL All-Star Game
1984	Conn Smythe Trophy NHL All-Star Second Team
1990, 1992	Hart Memorial Trophy Lester B. Pearson Award *Sporting News* NHL Player of the Year

LINDA METHENY

Sport: Gymnastics

Born: August 12, 1947
Olney, Illinois

Early Life

Linda Jo Metheny, a three-time United States gymnastics Olympian, was born in Olney, Illinois, on August 12, 1947. At an age when Nadia Comăneci was already on the verge of a World Championship, Linda was introduced to gymnastics at a local dancing school in Tuscola, Illinois, her hometown.

Gymnastics for girls and women was rare outside cities like Chicago and Philadelphia during the 1950's. Girls could learn some very elementary gymnastics and acrobatics at dancing schools and, infrequently, instruction was offered in elementary school. At the beginning, Linda's backyard was her only gym.

It was not until she was fourteen that Linda was able to receive instruction at Pond's Palaestrum, a kind of camp that had been opened by the very innovative Charles (Charlie) Pond, the coach at the University of Illinois. Luckily, some of the best gymnasts in the United States visited the Palaestrum regularly, including Muriel Grossfeld, who had been on the 1956 and 1960 Olympic teams, and JoAnne Matthews, one of the best tumblers in the country.

The Road to Excellence

Traveling the thirty miles to the Palaestrum on a regular basis, Linda soon fell in love with the balance beam. It was on the beam that she achieved her greatest fame. Like other children who have been exposed to champions, she worked hard to mimic some of the "tricks" she had ob-

Linda Metheny competes in the balance beam exercise during the Pan-American Games in 1971.

served. She was naturally gifted and, being small, well suited to gymnastics. She claims that she did not stop growing until she was a senior in college. Smallness has some advantages in gymnastics. For example, lighter gymnasts are easier to catch when they fall and usually do not suffer as many injuries as larger gymnasts. In her first competition, Linda represented McKinley YMCA (Champaign, Illinois) at a meet in Louisville, Kentucky. She won the balance beam event and placed second in all-around. She was off to a good start.

Her coach was Dick Mulvihill. He would become her husband after she retired from gymnastics in 1973. Mulvihill had been hired to direct Pond's Palaestrum from 1961 to 1964. Later, he was named Olympic coach. Under his tutelage, Linda placed seventh at the National Amateur Athletic Union (AAU) Championships and won a place on the U.S. Olympic team in 1964. She had moved up three places by the time of the Olympic trials.

The Emerging Champion

In 1964, Coach Mulvihill left the Palaestrum to coach exclusively at the McKinley YMCA in Champaign. Linda followed him there a year later. These were difficult years for gymnastics. The federation movement was developing, and there was an ongoing struggle with the AAU to gain control of the sport nationally. Many athletes such as Linda were caught in the cross fire. Coach Mulvihill favored the AAU's position and entered Linda in AAU-sanctioned meets. Her name is not found among those who competed in early championships sponsored by the United States Gymnastic Federation (USGF), despite the fact that she undoubtedly would have placed well in such meets.

At the McKinley YMCA, Linda developed into the nation's most prominent female gymnast, making both the 1968 and 1972 Olympic teams.

Dominating American gymnastics for six years, Linda won the outstanding performer's trophy in the first U.S. North/South meet for women. It was one of the few times she had an opportunity to compete against Cathy Rigby at a national meet. Rigby was then thirteen and was coached by "Bud" Marquette. Coach Marquette was dedicated to the emerging federation and helped to organize the first Women's Committee.

Linda first entered the North American Gymnastics Championships in 1966 and placed fourth. Between 1967 and 1970, however, she was the all-around champion. She accumulated six gold medals in Pan-American Games competition: five in 1967 and one in 1971. She won the AAU National all-around title in 1966, 1968, and 1970.

Linda was also one of those gymnasts who were able to compete at the very beginning of intercollegiate gymnastics for women in the United States. In 1966, she contemplated attending Springfield College, but she decided to enter the University of Illinois at Champaign, where

STATISTICS

Year	Competition	Event	Place	Event	Place
1964	Olympic Games	All-Around	36th	Team	9th
1966	U.S. National Championships	All-Around	1st	Balance beam	1st
		Floor exercise	4th	Vault	5th
		Uneven parallel bars	6th		
1967	NCAA Championships	All-Around	1st		
	Pan-American Games	All-Around	1st	Balance beam	1st
		Floor exercise	1st	Vault	1st
		Uneven parallel bars	1st		
1968	U.S. National Championships	All-Around	1st	Balance beam	2d
		Floor exercise	2d	Vault	4th
		Uneven parallel bars	3d		
	Olympic Games	Balance beam	4th	Team	6th
1970	U.S. National Championships	All-Around	1st	Balance beam	1st
		Floor exercise	1st	Vault	7th
		Uneven parallel bars	1st		
1971	U.S. National Championships	All-Around	2d	Balance beam	3d
		Floor exercise	1st	Vault	6th
		Uneven parallel bars	2d		
	Pan-American Games	All-Around	2d	Balance beam	2d
		Floor exercise	1st	Vault	6th
		Uneven parallel bars	3d		
1972	U.S. National Championships	All-Around	1st	Balance beam	1st
		Floor exercise	1st	Vault	3d
		Uneven parallel bars	2d		
	Olympic Games	Team	4th		

she could continue to train at the McKinley YMCA. At Illinois, she became a one-woman team and continued to work with Dick Mulvihill, who coached her throughout her eleven years in gymnastics.

In 1967, she placed third all-around in the National Collegiate Championships and won the U.S. Nationals all-around again in 1968. At last, the Division of Girls and Women's Sports of the American Association for Health, Physical Education, and Recreation sponsored the first nationally recognized Collegiate Gymnastics Championships for Women in 1969. Linda, not surprisingly, was the all-around champion. She was an honors student at the University of Illinois both as an undergraduate and as a graduate. She earned a master's degree in dance in 1971.

Continuing the Story

Linda had become a world-class competitor by 1968. That year, the year of the Mexican Olympiad, proved to be the most meaningful of her international career. Cathy Rigby was getting most of the publicity and finished sixteenth in the all-around ahead of Linda, but it was Linda who became the first American woman to compete well enough to advance to the final individual competition—on the balance beam. No American woman had advanced that far in the past. In order to go on to the finals, she had to perform a compulsory routine, one performed by every gymnast, and an optional routine of her own design. She finished second in the compulsory beam and third with her optional. In the finals, however, Linda placed fourth, narrowly missing third place by only .025 of a point. Larissa Petrik of the Soviet Union won the bronze.

Linda had a serious back injury in 1970, but after several months without training, she showed the American gymnastic community that she could indeed win a USGF Championship. She was also the USGF all-around champion in 1971 and 1972. She

made the Olympic team for the third time in 1972 but was injured on the last day of the Olympic Training Camp. Despite the injury, Linda finished in the top thirty-six. She retired from gymnastics after the Olympic Games and went on to become a very successful coach.

Summary

Linda Metheny will be remembered primarily as an outstanding gymnast and coach. Her eleven-year gymnastic career and her scholarly preparation in dance and physical education qualified her as one of the first truly professional women coaches in the United States. With her husband, Dick Mulvihill, she established one of the first live-in gymnastics academies in the United States. She coached a number of Olympians, the most famous of whom was Julianne McNamara. She has served the United States as a coach on a number of occasions and was assistant coach of the 1976 Olympic team. In honor of her outstanding career as a gymnast and coach, she was elected to the Gymnastics Hall of Fame in 1985.

A. Bruce Frederick

Additional Sources:

Hickok, Ralph. "Metheny, Linda J." *A Who's Who of Sports Champions: Their Stories and Records.* New York: Houghton Mifflin, 1995.

Simons, Minot. *Women's Gymnastics, a History: Volume 1, 1966-1974.* Carmel, Calif.: Welwyn Publishing Company, 1995.

HONORS AND AWARDS

1964, 1968, 1972	Women's U.S. Olympic Gymnastics Team
1966	Women's U.S. World Championships Gymnastics Team
1967-70	North American All-Around Champion
1969	First DGWS National Intercollegiate Gymnastics Champion
1968	First U.S. gymnast to reach the finals in an event in the Olympic Games
1981	USGF Artistic Gymnastics Choreographer of the Year
1985	Inducted into Gymnastics Hall of Fame

RECORDS AND MILESTONES

Premier U.S. gymnast on the balance beam and in the floor exercises for eight years
Member of the U.S. Olympic Committee, Athlete's Advisory Council, for six years
Gymnastics advisor and clinician, the President's Council on Physical Fitness

DEBBIE MEYER

Sport: Swimming

Born: August 14, 1952
Haddonfield, New Jersey

Early Life

Deborah Elizabeth Meyer was born in Haddonfield, New Jersey, on August 14, 1952. Her father was with the Campbell Soup Company. Debbie was four years old when Murray Rose (considered by many to be the all-time world's greatest swimmer) set world records in the 400-meter and 1,500-meter freestyle. Twelve years later, Debbie Meyer broke these world records herself. She began modestly, swimming as a youngster at the Camden YMCA. Her swimming there and at the famed Vesper Boat Club in Philadelphia was undistinguished, but she quickly found herself when her family was transferred to the Campbell's soup operation in Sacramento, California.

The Road to Excellence

Swimming with Mike Burton at coach Sherm Chavoor's Arden Hills Swimming and Tennis Club, Debbie at thirteen was already becoming the world's best woman swimmer. Good-looking, fun-loving, smart, and willing to work hard, Debbie swam thirty thousand miles in the next seven years, setting hitherto undreamed of training standards in the pool. Debbie was not only the world's fastest female swimmer from age fourteen to seventeen but also the world's best trainer and hardest worker.

The Emerging Champion

In 1967, after her double gold medal performance at the Winnipeg, Canada, Pan-American Games, the Soviet News Agency, Tass, picked Debbie as Woman Athlete of the Year. The following year, she won the James E. Sullivan Memorial Award as the top amateur athlete in the United States. She was named World Swimmer of the Year three successive years (1967, 1968, and 1969).

At the 1968 Olympics in Mexico City, despite being ill, Debbie became the first woman to win three Olympic gold medals in individual events. She set Olympic records in the 200-meter and 800-meter freestyle events and a world record in the 400-meter freestyle, all grueling distance races. During her career, Debbie was the first woman in the world to swim the 1,500 meters in less than 18 minutes, the first to swim the 400 meters in less than 4 minutes 30 seconds, and the first to swim the 500-yard short course (25-yard pool) in less than 5 minutes. In the 1,650 yards, she was the first woman to finish in less than 17 minutes, a standard that, not too many years before, had belonged to Hall of Famer George Breen, a male swimmer.

Continuing the Story

Altogether, Debbie won nineteen United States national championships at almost every freestyle distance and in the four-stroke 400-meter individual medley. She set twenty-four American short course records and fifteen world long course records—all before she was nineteen. In two years and five weeks (from July 9, 1967, to August 17, 1969), she set fifteen world marks.

STATISTICS

Year	Competition	Event	Place	Time
1967	Pan-American Games	400-meter freestyle	1st	4:32.64
		800-meter freestyle	1st	9:22.86
	AAU Outdoor Championships	440-yard freestyle	1st	4:29.0 WR
		1,500-meter freestyle	1st	17:50.2
	AAU Indoor Championships	1,650-yard freestyle	1st	17:38.1
1968	Olympic Games	200-meter freestyle	Gold	2:10.05 OR
		400-meter freestyle	Gold	4:31.8 WR, OR
		800-meter freestyle	Gold	9:24.0 OR
	AAU Outdoor Championships	440-yard freestyle	1st	4:26.7
		1,500-meter freestyle	1st	17:38.5
	AAU Indoor Championships	500-yard freestyle	1st	4:54.1
		1,650-yard freestyle	1st	17:04.4
1969	AAU Outdoor Championships	440-yard freestyle	1st	4:26.4
		1,500-meter freestyle	1st	17:19.19
	AAU Indoor Championships	1,650-yard freestyle	1st	17:04.4
	AAU Outdoor Championships	400-meter individual medley	1st	5:08.6
1970	AAU Outdoor Championships	440-yard freestyle	1st	4:24.3
		1,500-meter freestyle	1st	17:28.4
	AAU Indoor Championships	500-yard freestyle	1st	5:00.7
		1,650-yard freestyle	1st	16:54.6
		400-yard individual medley	1st	4:34.2
1971	AAU Indoor Championships	500-yard freestyle	1st	5:03.8
		1,650-yard freestyle	1st	17:11.8

Notes: OR = Olympic Record; WR = World Record

RECORDS

Set 15 world records and 24 American records
Won 19 national AAU championships

HONORS AND AWARDS

1967	Tass News Agency Woman Athlete of the Year
1967-69	World Swimmer of the Year
1968	Sullivan Award
	Robert J. H. Kiphuth Award, Short Course
1969	Associated Press Female Athlete of the Year
1977	Inducted into International Swimming Hall of Fame
1986	Inducted into U.S. Olympic Hall of Fame
1987	Inducted into Sudafed International Women's Sports Hall of Fame

In her favorite event, the 1,500, her ultimate women's world record was 39 seconds faster than Murray Rose's time in winning the same event for men in the 1956 Olympics in Melbourne and only .3 seconds slower than John Konrads's winning time in Rome in 1960.

After the 1968 Olympics, Debbie went on swimming with enthusiasm, even setting more world records through the 1970 outdoor nationals. Then, suddenly, as seems to happen to many athletes, it was not fun anymore. "It was still fun to race," she said, "but it's no longer fun to train." Debbie was smart enough to know that she could not swim fast in races unless she swam fast in practice. She quit, gained weight, and, after a year in which she was not happy with herself or her life in general, she made herself get trim again. She went on to do commercials for television, got married, and coached the women's varsity swim team at her alma mater, Stanford University.

Summary

Debbie Meyer came the closest of any modern female swimmer to breaking the men's world records. She was enshrined in the International Swimming Hall of Fame in Fort Lauderdale, Florida, in 1977, and in the United States Olympic Hall of Fame in 1986.

Buck Dawson

Additional Sources:

Besford, Pat. *Encyclopedia of Swimming.* New York: St. Martin's Press, 1976.

Hickok, Ralph. *A Who's Who of Sports Champions.* Boston: Houghton Mifflin, 1995.

Mallon, Bill, and Ian Buchanan. *Quest for Gold: The Encyclopedia of American Olympians.* New York: Leisure Press, 1984.

Schapp, Dick. *An Illustrated History of the Olympics.* New York: Alfred A. Knopf, 1975.

Wallechinsky, David. *The Complete Book of the Olympics.* Boston: Little, Brown and Company, 1991.

ANN MEYERS

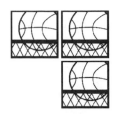

Sport: Basketball

Born: March 26, 1955
San Diego, California

Early Life

Ann Elizabeth Meyers was born on March 26, 1955, in San Diego, California. Ann came from a family of eleven children, and she was very shy and insecure. As in many large families, there was a lot of sibling rivalry and hand-me-downs.

Basketball was the main sport in the Meyers family, but Ann also lettered in track, volleyball, badminton, tennis, field hockey, and softball before her graduation from Sonora High School in La Habra, California, in 1975. Because of her success in track, Ann had aspirations of participating in the Olympics and competing in the high jump.

Basketball, however, became a real love for Ann. She found that basketball was a sport she could play by herself. Despite lettering in seven sports in high school, Ann had the same dream as her older brother David. Her dream was to be able to play basketball for a living. Ann spent many hours on the courts dribbling and shooting to work toward that dream. Basketball became her release.

The Road to Excellence

While still a senior in high school, Ann became the first female athlete to play for a United States national basketball team. Because of her great success in basketball, the University of California at Los Angeles (UCLA) offered her its first women's athletic scholarship. UCLA seemed to be a natural choice for Ann, because it was close to home and her brother Dave was playing basketball there, too. Friends and family could travel to UCLA and watch Ann reach for her dream and also see her brother Dave play. The full athletic scholarship also assisted the Meyers family, and the fact that big brother Dave was on campus provided a sense of security.

During her senior year in high school, Ann participated in the 1975 Pan-American Games and World Championships. Ann's senior year was filled with travel and excitement. From 1975 to 1977, Ann had the opportunity to participate in the World University Games. Adding still another feather to her cap in 1976, Ann guided the United States women's basketball team to a silver medal in the Montreal Olympics.

Ann became the first four-time women's All-American basketball guard during her career at UCLA (1975-1978). In 1978, Ann's play led the UCLA Bruins to the Association of Intercolle-

Courtesy of Amateur Athletic Foundation of Los Angeles

1871

giate Athletics for Women (AIAW) National Collegiate Women's Basketball Championship, defeating the University of Maryland 90-74 before a crowd of 9,351. During that game Ann scored 20 points, grabbed 10 rebounds, handed out 9 assists, and made 8 steals.

Ann completed her four-year career with 1,685 points, averaging 17.4 points per game and 8.4 rebounds. In 1978, she was named the AIAW Basketball Player of the Year and was the recipient of the Honda Broderick Cup as the outstanding female collegiate athlete of the year.

During the time Ann played for the Bruins, women's sports were not supported well. While the men's basketball team traveled to away games by bus or plane, the women's team would travel by vans or station wagons. Practicing in the women's gym was quite different from practicing in the men's gym. Still, many times the men's basketball coaches assisted Ann in getting the classes she wanted, and despite the lack of program equality, Ann made a name for herself at UCLA. Even with her astonishing four-year basketball career, Ann found time to run track, play volleyball, and try out for the tennis team.

The Emerging Champion

Ann finished her four-year basketball career with All-American distinction. The future for Ann was not as clear as it was for her brother Dave, who became a professional basketball player for the Milwaukee Bucks. Ann was glad she had pursued a college degree; because there was not a major professional women's league for basketball, she could not use her four years of college as a stepping-stone for a professional basketball career as many males had done. Ann was grateful just to be given the opportunity to play a sport she loved and to obtain a degree.

On September 6, 1979, though, Ann became the first women to be signed by a National Basketball Association (NBA) team. The Indiana Pacers signed Ann to a one-year, $50,000, no-cut contract. The contract guaranteed her a paid salary but not a spot on the team. The Pacers would promote Ann as a three-point threat. Many people felt the Pacers used the contract as a publicity stunt to attract more spectators. Earlier in the year, Ann had had the opportunity to sign with a women's professional league, but she decided to wait in order to participate in the 1980 Olympics. By turning pro and signing with the Pacers, Ann turned down the opportunity to play in the 1980 Olympics in Moscow, but Ann felt that the Pacers' offer was a chance of a lifetime.

Many people worried about Ann's signing with the Pacers. Even her brother Dave showed concern because of the talent his sister had and the possibility of her getting hurt physically and emotionally. Dave knew how brutal the media could be and was worried about situations where Ann could be made fun of or mocked.

On September 12, 1979, two days after tryouts began for the Pacers, Ann was cut from the team. Ann knew the game and had the fundamentals, but her 5-foot 9-inch frame was too small for the NBA. She was retained as a radio color commentator for the Pacers' games. Ann was also the color commentator for the 1979 UCLA men's basketball team.

Continuing the Story

After Ann was cut, two professional women's basketball teams, the New Jersey Gems and the Houston Angels, sought her talent. At that time the Women's Professional Basketball League

STATISTICS

Season	GP	FGM	FG%	FTM	FT%	Reb.	Ast.	TP	PPG
1974-75	23	183	.528	56	.767	191	125	422	18.3
1975-76	23	129	.426	65	.730	189	128	323	14.0
1976-77	22	160	.505	82	.828	161	109	402	18.3
1977-78	29	221	.526	96	.800	278	182	538	18.6
Totals	97	693	.500	299	.785	819	544	1,685	17.4

Notes: GP = games played; FGM = field goals made; FG% = field goal percentage; FTM = free throws made; FT% = free throw percentage; Reb. = rebounds; Ast. = assists; TP = total points; PPG = points per game

(WPBL) could pay its players only $7,000 to $20,000 a season. The salary that was being offered to play on the women's professional team was much lower than the $50,000 Ann was receiving as color commentator for the Indiana Pacers. On November 15, 1979, after a series of salary negotiations, Ann signed a three-year contract with the New Jersey Gems for $130,000. Ann competed as a New Jersey Gem for two years, sitting out in protest part of the last year as a result of contract disagreements. Meyers won both most valuable player trophies of the short-lived WPBL.

In 1986, Ann married retired Los Angeles Dodgers pitcher Don Drysdale and had one child. She also worked as a sports broadcaster. Ann was among the first UCLA basketball players to officially have her UCLA Bruins jersey, number 15, retired, on February 3, 1990, along with Bill Walton's and Kareem Abdul-Jabbar's.

Ann has served as a color analyst on broadcasts of many different Olympic events, including softball, tennis, volleyball, soccer, and women's basketball. She covered several Women's National Collegiate Athletic Association (NCAA) basketball tournaments during the 1990's. In 2000, Ann was a broadcaster for the NCAA Women's Final Four and for the Summer Olympics in Sydney, Australia. She worked for the National Broadcasting Corporation (NBC) as a commentator for the NBA and for the Women's National Basketball Association (WNBA).

Ann was the first inductee into the Women's Sports Hall of Fame. In 1993, she was inducted into the Naismith Memorial Basketball Hall of Fame in Springfield, Massachusetts. She said that

HONORS, AWARDS, AND MILESTONES	
1975	Women's U.S. Pan-American Games Gold Medalist
1975-77	World University Games, Women's U.S. Team
1975-78	Kodak All-American
1975, 1979	World Championships, Women's U.S. Team
1976	Gold medal, Jones Cup U.S. Olympic Silver Medalist
1978	AIAW Basketball Player of the Year Honda Broderick Cup AIAW Championship Team UCLA Athlete of the Year All-Western Collegiate Athletic Association Team All-Region 8 Team
1980	WPBL co-most valuable player
1981	WPBL most valuable player
1985	Inducted into Sudafed International Women's Sports Hall of Fame
1990	Uniform number 15 retired by UCLA Athletic Department
1993	Inducted into Naismith Memorial Basketball Hall of Fame

her greatest mentor was her late husband, Don Drysdale. They were the first married couple ever to be inducted into the halls of fame in their respective sports.

Summary

Ann Meyers was truly a pioneer of women's basketball. Her participation and fortitude also paved the way for women in their quest for a dream.

Carol L. Higy

Additional Sources:

Bjarkman, Peter C. *The Biographical History of Basketball.* Lincolnwood, Ill.: Masters Press, 1998.

Gutman, Bill. *Shooting Stars: The Women of Pro Basketball.* New York: Random House, 1998.

Hult, Joan S., and Marianna Trekell, eds. *A Century of Women's Basketball: From Frailty to Final Four.* Reston, Va.: National Association for Girls and Women in Sport, 1991.

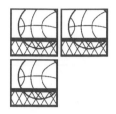

GEORGE MIKAN

Sport: Basketball

Born: June 18, 1924
Joliet, Illinois

Early Life

George Lawrence Mikan was born on June 18, 1924, in Joliet, Illinois. The first child of Joseph, a Croatian, and Minnie Mikan, a Lithuanian, he grew to a height of 6 feet 10 inches and a weight of 245 pounds. George and his brothers, Joe and Ed, worked in the family restaurant after school. George aspired to be a concert pianist; he would enjoy the musical skills he developed as a youngster throughout his life.

George had few basketball skills as a boy. At age thirteen, he broke his leg in a game. He left Joliet Catholic High School to pursue the Catholic priesthood at Quigley Seminary in downtown Chicago. The Joliet coach had already discouraged him from basketball because of George's poor eyesight. Quigley, a thirty-five-mile commute from home, left no time for basketball. His height had done little but make George awkward, shy, and self-conscious.

The Road to Excellence

George tried out for basketball at Notre Dame University. Coach George Keogan said he would never succeed with his quarter-inch-thick glasses. Notre Dame assistant coach Ray Meyer had just become head coach at Chicago's DePaul University and decided to work with George.

Skipping rope, shadowboxing, and scrimmaging one-on-one with more agile teammates improved George's timing. George played four years of varsity basketball for DePaul.

In 1942-1943, George's first season, DePaul won nineteen games and lost five. George's ability to block shots on their way downward into the basket contributed to a new National Collegiate

George Mikan in 1948.

Athletic Association (NCAA) rule against goal-tending. DePaul lost in the finals of the National Invitational Tournament (NIT) in 1944 but won the next year. George scored 120 points in the final three games, with a high of 53. He was a three-time All-American, from 1944 to 1946. In all, George scored 1,870 points, a collegiate record to that time, and DePaul's record was 83-18.

In the off-season, George was a baseball pitcher, attracting offers from major league scouts. At 6 feet 10 inches tall, it was inevitable that George would choose basketball.

The Emerging Champion

The National Basketball League (NBL) had begun in 1937, but with teams in Anderson, Indiana, and Sheboygan, Wisconsin, it was a small-time operation until World War II. George's team, the Chicago American Gears, was sponsored by a business, as bowling teams still are. George earned $12,000 per season. The year George became a professional, 1946, he married Patricia Lu Deveny. They had four sons and two daughters.

When the Gears disbanded after twenty-five games, George joined the Minneapolis Lakers. In 1947-1948, he scored an average of 21.3 points per game and was chosen unanimously as most valuable player in the NBL. That year was the start of a dynasty as the Lakers won their first title.

In 1948-1949, the Lakers were one of four NBL teams to join a new league, the National Basketball Association (NBA). Commissioner Maurice Podoloff added eleven teams from his

Basketball Association of America (BAA). George, wearing his familiar number 99, was the drawing card that professional basketball needed. Everywhere crowds came to see him.

In the NBA's first year, the Lakers won another title. The league's leading scorer was George Mikan, averaging 28.3 points. A dramatic moment in that season came when George's wrist was broken in the playoffs. George played the last two games with one hand dangling in a cast and averaged 30 points.

George, Vern Mikkelson, Jim Pollard, Arnie Ferrin, and Slater Martin, on one of the greatest teams ever assembled, won a third consecutive championship in 1949-1950. Again the league's leading scorer, George averaged 27.4 points per game.

In 1950-1951, George again led the NBA in scoring with 28.4 points per game. With George out because of a broken ankle, the Lakers lost in the semifinals to the Rochester Royals. November 22, 1950, witnessed one of the strangest games ever played in professional basketball. Fort Wayne defeated the Lakers 19-18 despite George's 15 points. Games like this led to the 24-second rule in 1954-1955, which forced a team to shoot within 24 seconds. No longer could professional teams use a stall to keep the ball from superstars like George.

The next season, 1951-1952, the 3-second lane (the corridor from the free throw line to the basket) was enlarged from six to twelve feet across. Great centers like George had to get out from under the basket sooner. George's comment: "They

STATISTICS

Season	GP	FG	FG%	FTM	FT%	Reb.	Ast.	TP	PPG
1946-47	25	147	—	119	.726	—	—	413	16.5
1947-48	56	406	—	383	.752	—	—	1,195	21.3
1948-49	60	583	.416	532	.772	—	218	**1,698**	28.3
1949-50	68	649	.407	567	.779	—	197	**1,865**	27.4
1950-51	68	678	.428	576	.803	958	208	**1,932**	28.4
1951-52	64	545	.385	433	.780	866	194	1,523	23.8
1952-53	70	500	.399	442	.780	**1,007**	201	1,442	20.6
1953-54	72	441	.380	424	.777	1,028	174	1,306	18.1
1955-56	37	148	.395	94	.770	308	53	390	10.5
Totals	520	4,097	—	3,570	.778	—	—	11,764	22.6

Notes: Boldface indicates statistical leader. GP = games played; FGM = field goals made; FG% = field goal percentage; FTM = free throws made; FT% = free throw percentage; Reb. = rebounds; Ast. = assists; TP = total points; PPG = points per game

made the game better . . . more wide-open play and outside shooting." It did not slow him down; in an early-season game he scored 61 points. The Lakers won their fourth title.

Continuing the Story

After the 1953-1954 season and the Lakers' fifth title in seven years, George shocked coach Larry Kundla by announcing his retirement. He was thirty years old. Nicknamed "Mr. Basketball," George had dominated the game from 1946 to 1954. In New York City, the Madison Square Garden marquee always read: "Tonite George Mikan vs. Knicks."

George then became Laker general manager. Without him on the team, the Lakers slumped. Absent a year and a half, George returned to the lineup, but weighing 265 pounds and out of shape, he averaged only 10.5 points. George retired for good in 1956. With attendance down, the team later moved to Los Angeles.

George had become a lawyer in 1949 through

off-season study, and his business career proved quite successful. He was the first commissioner of the new American Basketball Association (ABA) in 1967. The red, white, and blue ball, the ABA trademark, was George's conception. He resigned in 1969 to continue his law practice in Minneapolis.

Summary

Without the 24-second rule, basketball was a game of low scores. George Mikan's 28-point average (in 1951) under these conditions was incredible. Although slow getting downcourt, George was a deadly shooter and a fine playmaker, great on defense, and rugged. Much injured, he gave as well as he got. He made weapons out of his elbows to survive. Usually double- or triple-teamed, he often fouled but seldom fouled out.

In six professional seasons, George led the league in scoring three times, was second twice, and was fourth once. He made the All-NBA First Team six consecutive years. In 1950, he was named the Associated Press Player of the Half Century. George revolutionized basketball, making it more offense-oriented. Professional basketball's first superstar was inducted into the Naismith Memorial Basketball Hall of Fame in 1959.

Daniel C. Scavone

Additional Sources:

Fimrite, Ron. "Big George." *Sports Illustrated* 71, no. 19 (November 6, 1989): 128-139.

Mikan, George, and Bill Carlson. *Mr. Basketball: George Mikan's Own Story.* New York: Greenburg, 1951.

Mikan, George L., and Joseph Oberle. *Unstoppable: The Story of George Mikan, the First NBA Superstar.* Indianapolis, Ind.: Masters Press, 1997.

HONORS AND AWARDS	
1944-45	Helms Athletic Foundation Division I Player of the Year Citizens Savings College Basketball Player of the Year
1944-46	Consensus All-American
1948	NBL most valuable player
1949-54	All-NBA Team
1950	Associated Press Player of the Half Century
1951-54	NBA All-Star Team
1953	NBA All-Star Game most valuable player
1959	Inducted into Naismith Memorial Basketball Hall of Fame
1970	NBA 25th Anniversary All Time Team
1980	NBA 35th Anniversary All Time Team

STAN MIKITA
Stanislaus Gvoth

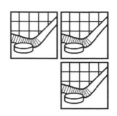

Sport: Ice hockey

Born: May 20, 1940
Sokolce, Czechoslovakia (now
Slovakia)

Early Life

On May 20, 1940, Stan Mikita was born Stanislaus Gvoth in the Slovakian village of Sokolce, near the Tatra mountains of eastern Czechoslovakia. The villagers were mostly impoverished small farmers and laborers. Stanislaus was the second of Juraj and Emelia Gvoth's three children. Stan's home was an apartment with one all-purpose room and a small kitchen in a building without indoor plumbing.

In 1948, Stan's aunt and uncle, Joe and Anna Mikita, who lived in Canada, arrived for a six-month visit. Before returning home, the Mikitas persuaded their relatives to allow Stan to come and live with them in a country where he would have more opportunities.

In St. Catharines, Ontario (an industrial city near Niagara Falls), where Uncle Joe was a building contractor, Stan entered the third grade and began the difficult task of learning English.

The Road to Excellence

Stan's initial adjustment was tough. Other children taunted him because he was a foreigner. He frequently got into fights and developed a feisty personality. His outstanding skill on the soccer field soon made him a school hero, however. Stan also had

great ability in many other sports such as lacrosse, basketball, football, and baseball. Later, he turned down offers from major league baseball scouts because of his love for hockey.

The young immigrant was introduced to hockey shortly after he arrived in Canada. "Puck" and "stick" were among the first English words Stan learned from neighborhood boys playing street hockey. Many of Stan's hockey skills were

STATISTICS

Season	GP	G	Ast.	Pts.	PIM
1958-59	3	0	1	1	4
1959-60	67	8	18	26	119
1960-61	66	19	34	53	100
1961-62	70	25	52	77	97
1962-63	65	31	45	76	69
1963-64	70	39	50	**89**	149
1964-65	70	28	59	**87**	154
1965-66	68	30	48	78	58
1966-67	70	35	62	**97**	12
1967-68	72	40	47	**87**	14
1968-69	74	30	67	97	52
1969-70	76	39	47	86	50
1970-71	74	24	48	72	85
1971-72	74	26	39	65	46
1972-73	57	27	56	83	32
1973-74	76	30	50	80	46
1974-75	79	36	50	86	48
1975-76	48	16	41	57	37
1976-77	57	19	30	49	20
1977-78	76	18	41	59	35
1978-79	65	19	36	55	34
1979-80	17	2	5	7	12
Totals	1,394	541	926	1,467	1,273

Notes: Boldface indicates statistical leader. GP = games played; G = goals; Ast. = assists; Pts. = points; PIM = penalties in minutes

learned from Vic Teal, his Bantam and Midget coach, who stressed defense and fundamentals.

When Stan was thirteen, the Chicago Black Hawks of the National Hockey League (NHL) acquired first rights to sign him in the future and agreed to finance his education. Stan played several high school sports and also ran with a tough neighborhood street gang. He quit the gang around age sixteen to dedicate himself to hockey as a member of the prestigious St. Catharines Junior A TeePees in the Black Hawks farm system. By his third amateur season, 1958-1959, sportswriters were calling him Canada's best junior player. During that same season, the Black Hawks called up Stan for three games to fill in for an injured forward. After tryouts at the Black Hawks' training camp in the summer of 1959, Stan signed a professional contract.

The Emerging Champion

Stan's rookie year at center position was not very impressive (8 goals, 18 assists, 119 penalty minutes). Despite his small size—5 feet 9 inches and only 165 pounds—Stan was determined not to be intimidated by big players who targeted him because of his reputation as a scoring threat. As experience complemented his natural aggressiveness and skill, Stan's scoring output increased yearly. In 1961, when Chicago won the Stanley Cup, his 6 playoff goals led the league. The next season, Stan's third full year, he joined the ranks of the NHL's leading scorers with 77 points. Moreover, his 15 assists and 21 total points in postseason action were new league records. Stan went on to win successive league scoring titles in 1963-1964 and 1964-1965.

On the ice, Stan skillfully used every trick to win. He was the little guy who made the big plays in crucial situations to beat other teams. Chicago's other superstar, Bobby Hull, called his teammate the NHL's smartest player. Stan had tremendous reflexes and anticipation. He could change his mind in mid-stride while shooting or skating. He constantly analyzed opposing teams and players to find exploitable weaknesses. Stan also worked creatively on equipment. He introduced the now-popular curved "banana blade" stick, which permits a greater variety of shots to confound goalies, and had a lightweight helmet with webbed suspension designed for him after a head injury.

Stan scored with a hard wrist shot. He was an elusive, swift skater and a superb playmaker. He was unsurpassed at stick-handling and winning face-offs. Passing, defense, checking, and penalty killing were also strong points of this versatile star.

Continuing the Story

If Stan had a fault, it was his hot temper and "chippy" style of play. Stan's frequent resort to using stick, elbows, fists, and verbal provocation during his first six NHL seasons prompted French-Canadian fans to name him "Le Petit Diable" (The Little Devil).

While sitting out a penalty in November, 1966, Stan finally decided he was more valuable to his team on the ice than in the box. Thereafter, Stan avoided unnecessary penalties and took a "later and legal" approach to retaliating against fouls. The Little Devil's transformation stunned hockey observers. In 1967, he won not only the Hart and Ross trophies as hockey's most valuable player (MVP) and top scorer, but also the Lady Byng Trophy for gentlemanly and sportsmanlike conduct. Stan's sweep of the NHL's top awards was a historic first. The next season he repeated this feat.

In 1963, Stan married Jill Cerny, who many credit with exercising a calming influence on this fiery superstar. Stan is the father of four children. He also maintained ties with his family in Czechoslovakia, exchanging visits. In 1969, he became vice president of Christian Brothers, Incorporated, a Minnesota firm that makes hockey sticks.

Overcoming terrific pain from old and new injuries, Stan continued to have superstar seasons. In 1972-1973, he tallied 83 points, although missing twenty-one games with a broken heel, and scored 20 postseason playoff points skating with a bad back and tender foot. When an old back injury forced his retirement after twenty-two seasons in 1980, he was third among NHL career scoring leaders. Career highlights included four scoring titles, two MVP awards, and eight All-Star team selections. He is also Chicago's all-time point and assist leader. The Black Hawks retired his jersey number (21), and in 1983, he was elected to the Hockey Hall of Fame.

In 1974, Stan was inspired by a friend's deaf son to open the Stan Mikita Hockey School for the Hearing Impaired. From this weeklong training camp came the formation of the U.S. National Deaf Hockey Team, which in 1995 won the gold medal in the World Winter Games for the Deaf. Stan made a cameo appearance as the surly owner of an Aurora, Illinois, doughnut shop in the popular 1997 film *Wayne's World*.

Summary

Stan Mikita's story is inspirational. Rescued from poverty during childhood, he took advantage of new opportunities and battled his way to enduring sports fame. Stan was a fearless competitor who always strove to do better. Although the little athlete's fighting spirit became a problem at times, he demonstrated that he was a big enough man to change and mature by making the right personal choices in life.

David A. Crain

Additional Sources:

Mikita, Stan. *I Play to Win.* New York: Morrow, 1969.

Mikita, Stan, with George Vass. *Inside Hockey.* Chicago: Regnery, 1971.

Wahl, Grant. "Blackhawks Center Stan Mikita." *Sports Illustrated* 86, no. 21 (1997).

HONORS AND AWARDS

1962-65, 1967-68	NHL First Team All-Star
1964-65, 1967-68	Art Ross Trophy
1966, 1970	NHL Second Team All-Star
1967-68	Lady Byng Memorial Trophy Hart Memorial Trophy
1972	Team Canada Member
1976	Lester Patrick Trophy
1983	Inducted into Hockey Hall of Fame Uniform number 21 retired by Chicago Black Hawks

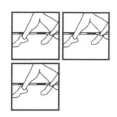

ROD MILBURN

Sport: Track and field (hurdles)

Born: May 18, 1950
    Opelousas, Louisiana
Died: November 11, 1997
    Port Hudson, near Baton Rouge,
    Louisiana

Early Life

Rodney Milburn, Jr., was born on May 18, 1950, in Opelousas, Louisiana, a farming town situated in the south central part of the "Bayou State." Life was not easy for the Milburn family.

When Rod was a young boy, his father died, and consequently the family faced difficult financial circumstances.

Rod, like many African Americans in Louisiana, also faced racial segregation. Because the segregation laws were strictly enforced in Louisiana in the early 1960's, Rod attended J. S. Clark High, an all-black high school in Opelousas. It was there that Rod began to run track.

One day at practice, assistant track coach Eddie Gilbeau saw Rod hurdling over some old

Rod Milburn in his gold medal winning hurdles race at the 1972 Olympics.

STATISTICS

Year	Competition	Event	Place	Time
1970	NAIA Indoor Championships	60-yard hurdles	1st	7.1
1971	Pan-American Games	110-meter high hurdles	1st	13.4
	NCAA Outdoor Championships	120-yard high hurdles	1st	13.6
	National AAU Outdoor Championships	110-meter high hurdles	1st	13.1
1972	Olympic Games	110-meter high hurdles	Gold	13.24 WR
	National AAU Outdoor Championships	110-meter high hurdles	1st	13.4
	National AAU Indoor Championships	60-yard high hurdles	1st	7.1
	NAIA Indoor Championships	60-yard hurdles	1st	7.0
1973	NCAA Outdoor Championships	120-yard high hurdles	1st	13.1
	NCAA Indoor Championships	55-meter high hurdles	1st	6.9
	National AAU Indoor Championships	60-yard high hurdles	1st	7.0
	NAIA Indoor Championships	60-yard hurdles	1st	7.0

Note: WR = World Record

Rod would have the opportunity to train with a person considered the fastest in the world.

Rod proved he was ready for college competition. Although he was considered short for a high hurdler at 6 feet tall, Rod used his great technique and blazing speed to outrun his taller opponents. In 1970, his freshman year, Rod began to gain national attention. He twice ran the high hurdles in 13.5 seconds and once in a wind-aided 13.3 seconds, which tied Davenport's Olympic record. His freshman year culminated with a fourth place finish at the Amateur Athletic Union (AAU) Championships. That was to be Rod's last defeat for more than a year. Davenport, who won the AAU Championship and had defeated Rod, proclaimed that one day Rod would be the best.

The Emerging Champion

In 1971, Rod was the best hurdler in the world. As a sophomore at Southern, Rod astonished the track world with a season that ranks among the greatest of any athlete. Undefeated in twenty-eight starts, Rod became the first track man in history to win the National Association of Intercollegiate Athletes, the National Collegiate Athletic Association (NCAA) College Division, and the NCAA University Division all in one year. Rod also won the AAU, the meets against the Soviet Union and Africa, and the gold medal at the Pan-American Games.

Of his twenty-eight first-place finishes, two races were sensational. On June 4, Rod was timed in the high hurdles at 13.0 seconds, but the world record was disallowed because the race was wind-aided. Three weeks later, however, Rod broke the world record when he ran a nonwind-aided 13.0 seconds for 120 yards. For his exceptional season, Rod was named the 1971 World Track Athlete of the Year by *Track and Field News*. Rod also won the James J. Corbett Award as Louisiana's best amateur athlete.

The only track championship left for Rod to win was the Olympic gold. Rod said that as long

wooden hurdles and recommended him to head coach Claude Paxton. Coach Paxton quickly recognized Rod's hurdling talent and convinced Rod that track could provide an excellent avenue beyond Opelousas and could be used as a vehicle to improve his life. With Paxton's instruction and guidance, Rod was able to win the Louisiana state championships in the high hurdles in his junior year. In his senior year, Rod repeated as champion and ran the hurdles in 13.7 seconds, the fastest time for a high school athlete. Before leaving J. S. Clark High, Rod realized that he could become the greatest hurdler in the world.

The Road to Excellence

Rod's hurdling accomplishments aroused interest from dozens of colleges around the United States. Rod decided to run at Southern University, a predominantly African American university in Baton Rouge, less than one hundred miles from his hometown.

His decision was based on several reasons. Coach Paxton, his high school coach and good friend, had decided to take a position as an assistant coach at Southern. Southern also had an excellent track program and had already produced one of the best hurdlers in U.S. history, Willie Davenport, who won the gold medal in the 1968 Olympics and set an Olympic record at 13.3 seconds. Because Davenport was still at Southern,

RECORDS
World record at 110-meter high hurdles in 1971 (13.0)
Four world records at 110-meter high hurdles
Two world records at 120-yard high hurdles

HONORS AND AWARDS	
1971	Corbett Award
	Track and Field News World Track Athlete of the Year
	Dieges Award, Outdoor
1972-73	DiBeneditto Award
1992	Inducted into Southwestern Athletic Conference Hall of Fame
1993	Inducted into Track and Field Hall of Fame

as he remained physically and mentally fit, there was no one who could beat him. He vowed to win every meet in 1972, including the Olympic Games.

In the summer of 1972, Rod attempted to qualify for the Olympic team. He was considered the favorite but hit two hurdles in the finals and barely qualified in third place. Nevertheless, he had made the Olympic team.

Continuing the Story

In its Olympic preview, *Sports Illustrated* wrote that, before Rod's mishap at the Olympic trials, he was considered the favorite to win the gold at Munich. After barely qualifying, however, the sports magazine predicted that either Davenport or Thomas Hill, the two hurdlers who beat Rod at the trials, would finish ahead of him.

At Munich, however, the twenty-two-year-old regained his form. Rod was the first man over the first hurdle and had a two-meter lead at the sixth hurdle. He hit the finish line at 13.24 seconds, equaling the world record.

After winning the gold medal, Rod continued to run for Southern University. In 1973, he ran another 13.0 seconds in the 120-yard hurdles and improved his 110-meter hurdle time to 13.1.

After graduation from Southern in 1973, Rod turned to professional track the following year and joined the International Track Association (ITA) circuit. He established another winning streak of thirty-one races.

When the ITA folded in 1976, Rod applied for reinstatement as an amateur. He was finally allowed to run as an amateur four years later, in 1980. At thirty years old, Rod made a brilliant comeback and was ranked sixth in the world with a time of 13.4 seconds in the 110-meter high hurdles. Rod, however, failed in his attempt to make the United States Olympic team in 1980, the trials being held before the United States decided to boycott the Moscow Games.

After this disappointment, Rod Milburn continued to race in the 110-meter high hurdles. He ran 13.59 seconds in 1981, 13.46 seconds in 1982, and 13.6 seconds in 1983 as a thirty-three-year-old hurdler. Following his retirement from competition in 1983, Rod served as the head track and field coach at his alma mater, Southern University, in 1987.

In 1997 Rod's body was discovered in a freight car at the Georgia Pacific paper plant, where he had worked since 1988. It is believed that he was overcome by fumes from the freight car's contents, liquid sodium chlorate, which he had been assigned to unload.

Summary

During the 1970's Rod Milburn dominated the 110-meter hurdles event, winning twenty-eight consecutive races and setting or matching the world record five times. He was inducted as an inaugural member into the Southwestern Conference Hall of Fame in 1992, and a year later he was inducted into the National Track and Field Hall of Fame.

William G. Durick

Additional Sources:

Bateman, Hal. *United States Track and Field Olympians, 1896-1980*. Indianapolis, Ind.: The Athletics Congress of the United States, 1984.

Hickok, Ralph. *A Who's Who of Sports Champions*. Boston: Houghton Mifflin, 1995.

Wallechinsky, David. *The Complete Book of the Olympics*. Boston: Little, Brown and Company, 1991.

Watman, Mel. *Encyclopedia of Track and Field Athletics*. New York: St. Martin's Press, 1981.

CHERYL MILLER

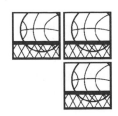

Sport: Basketball

Born: January 3, 1964
Riverside, California

Early Life

Cheryl DeAnne Miller was born on January 3, 1964, in Riverside, California, a city located east of the metropolitan Los Angeles area. Cheryl's father, a career Air Force man and professional musician, had been a prep All-American basketball player and college All-Conference player. A registered nurse, Cheryl's mother considered her first daughter her "little nurse."

Cheryl was the middle of five children. Her oldest brother, a talented athlete with little patience, became a musician. The other children all became athletes. The second brother was a professional baseball player, a younger brother was a highly recruited college basketball player, and the youngest daughter chose volleyball as her sport.

The Road to Excellence

At age five, Cheryl began playing basketball with her older brothers. Throughout elementary school, she played with boys. She learned to be aggressive and hold her own against players who were bigger and stronger. In her first game, when she was only in third grade, she scored 40 points.

Her father schooled Cheryl and her younger brother Reggie in the basics of the game. He built a basketball practice court in their yard and coached and practiced with his children daily.

Throughout her career, Cheryl continued to call her father her coach, her trainer, and her best friend.

The brother and sister were more like twins, as well as each other's greatest fan. During their early teen years, Reggie would challenge other players to a game with him and his sister while Cheryl hid. Then Cheryl would come out from hiding and surprise their prey.

During her four years as a high school basket-

The U.S. basketball team, led by Cheryl Miller (left) won the gold at the 1984 Olympics.

ball star, Riverside Poly won eighty-nine straight games. Cheryl scored 3,026 total points. On January 27, 1982, Cheryl scored a record 105 points and made history by becoming the first girl to stuff the ball in a high school game.

The first (male or female) four-time prep All-American and four-time member of the All-American junior national team, Cheryl received playing offers from more than two hundred colleges and universities. The B-average student, who enjoyed drawing and often read before a game to calm herself, looked for a school with a strong communications program. She chose to attend the University of Southern California (USC) and to play basketball for the Trojans.

The Emerging Champion

In 1983, as a 6-foot 3-inch first-year student at USC, Cheryl distinguished herself with an aggressive style of play formerly attributed to male basketball stars. She demonstrated high-flying tip-ins, full-court passes, and jumping ability unusual for a woman. Setting freshman records in scoring average, rebounds, free throws, steals, blocked shots, and points per game, Cheryl led the already strong Trojan team to its first national championship. For Cheryl, this was the biggest thrill of her life.

The team won a second championship in 1984. With her intense, high-caliber play, Cheryl continued to demonstrate that women's basketball had begun a new era. Her exuberant antics, such as her Hotdog Wrist (a showy modification of a follow-through training technique used by Cheryl's father) and cartwheels on the court, raised the eyebrows of conservative coaches and fans. Although Cheryl was called a "hotdog," she argued that her conduct was not an act but a spontaneous reaction to the emotion and stress of the game.

Cheryl credited her talent to God. Some people, including several well-known former women basketball players, said that she was a star only because women's sports were finally being acknowledged and supported. Others, however, recognized her hard work to excel in all phases of the sport and the 100 percent effort she gave in every game.

Training for the 1984 Olympics was mentally and physically the most challenging time in Cheryl's career, but the work paid off as she led the team to a gold medal. This team was called the greatest ever to play women's basketball. Cheryl was flattered by the comparisons to the Soviet star Ulyana Semenova and to male players like Magic Johnson, but she resented the expectation that she improve each time she stepped onto the court. Cheryl played basketball because she loved basketball.

During her last two years as a player at USC, Cheryl was sometimes discouraged by seasons that did not result in national championships. Even though her game continued to improve, she was getting burned out and even considered retiring after her junior year. She did not quit, but her impulsive style of play was somewhat tempered by the circumstances.

Continuing the Story

A four-time All-American, three-time winner of the coveted Naismith Trophy, winner of the Wade Trophy, and Player of the Decade for the 1980's, Cheryl's legacy to basketball did not end with her final USC game in 1986. She was drafted by the United States Basketball League, a men's league, as well some other professional leagues.

STATISTICS

Season	GP	FG	FG%	FTM	FT%	Reb.	Ast.	TP	PPG
1983	33	268	.551	137	.737	320	115	673	20.4
1984	33	281	.570	164	.752	350	120	726	22.0
1985	30	302	.528	201	.696	474	86	805	26.8
1986	32	308	.609	198	.753	390	93	814	25.4
Totals	128	1,159	.563	700	.734	1,534	414	3,018	23.6

Notes: GP = games played; FGM = field goals made; FG% = field goal percentage; FTM = free throws made; FT% = free throw percentage; Reb. = rebounds; Ast. = assists; TP = total points; PPG = points per game

USC RECORDS
Most points, 3,018
Highest scoring average, 23.6
Most field goals, 1,159
Most free throws made, 700
Most rebounds, 1,534
Highest average in rebounds per game, 12.0
Most blocked shots, 320
Most steals, 462
Most games played, 128

HONORS AND AWARDS	
1983	Gold Medal, Pan-American Games, Women's U.S. Team
1983-84	NCAA Tournament Most Outstanding Player
1983-86	College All-American All-Conference Team
1984	Collegiate Woman Athlete of the Year U.S. Olympic Gold Medalist
1984-85	Broderick Cup
1984-86	Naismith Trophy
1985	Wade Trophy
1985-86	Women's Basketball Coaches Association Player of the Year
1986	Gold Medal, Goodwill Games, Women's U.S. Team NCAA Today's Top Six Award
1991	Women's Basketball Coaches Association Player of the Decade
1995	Inducted into Naismith Memorial Basketball Hall of Fame

Though injuries kept her from playing pro ball or being on the 1988 Olympic team, she continued to be involved with basketball as a Trojans assistant coach from 1986 to 1991. In addition, Cheryl pursued a career in telecommunications by working as a color commentator for ABC Sports college basketball telecasts.

In 1993 Cheryl was appointed the head coach of the women's basketball team at USC. During her two seasons there, Cheryl coached the team to a 44-14 record. In 1994 her team won the Pac-10 Conference title. Cheryl was the first basketball player to have her uniform number retired by USC.

Cheryl gave up her coaching position at USC so she could resume her broadcasting career. Initially she worked for the American Broadcasting Corporation (ABC), handling a variety of assignments for *Wide World of Sports*. She joined Turner Sports in 1995 as an analyst and an NBA reporter on Turner Network Television (TNT). The ultimate honor in basketball was bestowed upon her in 1995, when she was inducted into the Naismith Memorial Basketball Hall of Fame.

Off of the court, Cheryl served as the commissioner of the 1985 Los Angeles Olympic Committee Summer Youth Games. She has also been a spokesperson for the Los Angeles Literacy Campaign; the Muscular Dystrophy Association; and the American Lung, Diabetes, and Cancer Associations. In 1997 Cheryl became the head coach and general manager of the Phoenix Mercury in the Women's National Basketball Association (WNBA). During four seasons at Phoenix, Cheryl led the team to the playoffs three times. At the end of 2000, she resigned and turned her attention to full-time broadcasting work.

Summary

Cheryl Miller finished her college career with virtually every USC record as well as with a National Collegiate Athletic Association academic award. Cheryl's influence extended beyond the boundaries of the basketball court. She revolutionized the game of basketball by demonstrating that it was possible and acceptable for girls and women to play hard, be physical, be competitive, and still have fun. Little girls sported the Cheryl haircut, and no longer were playground hoops only for their brothers.

Cathy M. Buell

Additional Sources:

Bjarkman, Peter C. *The Biographical History of Basketball.* Lincolnwood, Ill.: Masters Press, 1998.

Dollar, Sam. *The History of the Phoenix Mercury.* New York: Creative Education, 2000.

Gutman, Bill. *Shooting Stars: The Women of Pro Basketball.* New York: Random House, 1998.

Hult, Joan S., and Marianna Trekell, eds. *A Century of Women's Basketball: From Frailty to Final Four.* Reston, Va.: National Association for Girls and Women in Sport, 1991.

Owens, Tom, and Diana Star Helmer. *Teamwork: The Phoenix Mercury in Action.* Logan, Iowa: Powerkids Press, 1999.

REGGIE MILLER

Sport: Basketball

Born: August 24, 1965
Riverside, California

Early Life

Born into a large middle-class family of ambitious achievers, Reggie Miller was the fourth of five children of Saul and Carrie Miller. From the time of his birth, August 24, 1965, in Riverside, California, his family was concerned about his health. The immediate problem was his legs and pelvis, which were severely twisted and contorted, leaving doctors to believe he might not ever be able to walk. The medical team decided braces were required to straighten and strengthen Reggie's legs. Accordingly, while still a baby, he was fitted with the heavy braces he would have to wear for the first four years of his life.

Three decades later, Reggie could clearly remember the sadness and frustration he felt about being forced into nearly total immobility. He also suffered from an inability to gain or maintain adequate weight, causing him to appear practically gaunt. These health concerns did not signal a promising beginning for a future professional athlete.

Indiana Pacer Reggie Miller makes a shot in a 1996 game.

The Road to Excellence

Reggie's father, a chief master sergeant in the Air Force, and his mother, a nurse, were loving parents and strict disciplinarians, and they never allowed their son a moment of self-pity. Fortunately, the braces worked, and Reggie's legs developed normally. His parents built a basketball court, and all the Miller children, especially Reggie and his sister Cheryl, played and practiced as often as possible. Reggie liked other sports too, such as baseball, but only basketball offered the nonstop action he craved.

With the help of his father and Cheryl, Reggie developed a skilled jump shot and perfected it by taking approximately 700 shots daily. Playing for Riverside Polytechnic High School, he became a starter during his sophomore year and scored 35 and 45 points in his first two games, respectively.

Not wanting to leave his family, Reggie wanted to attend the University of California, Los Angeles (UCLA). The Bruins, however, had questions about his endurance, and the school did not offer him a scholarship until three other players had turned it down. At UCLA, Reggie became an outstanding player. Despite having a sometimes strained relationship with coach Walt Hazzard and having to work himself into a starting position, Reggie averaged over 17 points a game over the course of his college career and ended his college years as the second leading scorer in UCLA history, trailing only Kareem Abdul-Jabbar (Lew Alcindor at UCLA).

Reggie's dream to play in the National Basketball Association (NBA) was about to come true. He had long known, played with, and socialized with several Los Angeles Lakers, such as Michael Cooper and Byron Scott, and they had no doubts about Reggie's ability to excel at the highest level. He was ready to show the world he belonged with the best.

The Emerging Champion

The Indiana Pacers made Reggie their 1987 first-round draft pick, the eleventh choice overall. Being selected by the Pacers was not a total surprise, as Donnie Walsh, the Pacers' general manager, had often spoken admiringly of Reggie, but the selection was controversial. Many Indiana fans were outraged that the Pacers had not selected Steve Alford, the All-American guard who had just led Indiana University to the national championship. Walsh believed Reggie was a more complete player, and Reggie promptly proved him right. As an NBA rookie in 1987, he averaged more than 10 points a game despite starting only a handful of contests. In that first year, Reggie proved he had not only the ability but also the mental toughness to star in the league.

Continuing the Story

Reggie soon developed a reputation for two things: his lethal outside shooting and his trash talking. He loved verbally abusing his opponents, believing it gave him a competitive advantage. This practice, not surprisingly, made him controversial, and he was disliked by many. He was selected to the All-Star team four times, he made more than 100 three-point goals for ten successive years, and he was a member of the victorious United States Olympic team in both 1992 and 1996. Reggie played even better during the

STATISTICS

Season	GP	FGA	FGM	FG%	FTA	FTM	FT%	Reb.	Ast.	TP	PPG
1987-88	82	627	306	.488	186	149	.801	190	132	822	10.0
1988-89	74	831	398	.479	340	287	.844	292	227	1,181	16.0
1989-90	82	1,287	661	.514	627	544	.868	295	311	2,016	24.6
1990-91	82	1,164	596	.512	600	551	**.918**	281	331	1,855	22.6
1991-92	82	1,121	562	.501	515	442	.858	318	314	1,695	20.7
1992-93	82	1,193	571	.479	485	427	.880	258	262	1,736	21.2
1993-94	79	1,042	524	.503	444	403	.908	212	248	1,574	19.9
1994-95	81	1,092	505	.462	427	383	.897	210	242	1,588	19.6
1995-96	76	1,066	504	.473	498	430	.863	214	253	1,606	21.1
1996-97	81	1,244	552	.444	475	418	.880	286	273	1,751	21.6
1997-98	81	1,081	516	.477	440	382	.868	232	171	1,578	19.5
1998-99	50	671	294	.438	247	226	**.915**	135	112	920	18.4
1999-00	81	1,041	466	.448	406	373	**.919**	239	187	1,470	18.1
2000-01	81	1,176	517	.440	348	323	**.928**	285	260	1,527	18.9
Totals	1,094	14,636	6,972	.476	6,038	5,338	.884	3,447	3,323	21,319	19.5

Notes: Boldface indicates statistical leader. GP = games played; FGA = field goals attempted; FGM = field goals made; FG% = field goal percentage; FTA = free throws attempted; FTM = free throws made; FT% = free throw percentage; Reb. = rebounds; Ast. = assists; TP = total points; PPG = points per game

playoffs and seemed to take particular delight in harassing the New York Knicks and one of their celebrity fans, filmmaker Spike Lee.

In the 1994 Eastern Conference finals against the Knicks, the Pacers trailed by 12 points entering the fourth quarter of game 5. Inspired by the hostile New York crowd and Lee's off-court antics, Reggie proceeded to score 25 points, including 5 three-point baskets, and lead the Pacers to an amazing victory.

In the 1995 Eastern Conference semifinals, the Pacers trailed the Knicks 105-99 in game 1, with only twenty seconds left. Reggie proceeded to score 8 points in only 8.9 seconds, leading the Pacers to another victory. In game 3 of the 1998 Eastern Conference finals against the Chicago Bulls, Reggie scored 13 of his 28 points in the last four and a half minutes to seal another come-from-behind victory. Clearly, Reggie was a player who could break the spirit of his opponents by burying them under a barrage of long-distance shots or sarcastic barbs. Reggie finally led the Pacers to the finals in the 1999-2000 season, but they lost to the Los Angeles Lakers.

HONORS AND AWARDS

1987-1988	NBA All-Rookie Second Team
1994-95, 1995-96, 1997-98	All-NBA Third Team
1992, 1996	U.S. Olympic Gold Medalist
1997-98	NBA All-Interview Second Team
2000	NBA All-Star Team

Summary

Reggie Miller won many individual awards and accomplishments. After twelve years his team made it to the finals. Reggie is one of the most exciting players in NBA history.

Thomas W. Buchanan

Additional Sources:

Bjorkman, Peter C. *Reggie Miller: Star Guard*. New York: Enslow, 1999.

Frisaro, Joe. *Reggie Miller from Downtown*. Champaign, Ill.: Sports Publishing, 2000.

Miller, Reggie, and Gene Wojciechowski. *I Love Being the Enemy*. New York: Simon and Shuster, 1995.

Wilner, Barry. *Reggie Miller*. Philadelphia: Chelsea House, 1997.

MILESTONES

1994	Set an NBA Playoff record for the most three-point field goals made in one quarter (5)
1994, 1995	Tied the NBA Playoff record for most three-point field goals made in one half (6)
1995	Became the first Pacer to start in an NBA All-Star Game
1998	Scored 1,500th career three-pointer Closed the season as the NBA's all-time career leader in three-pointers made (1,596) and attempted (3,950) Became the first player in NBA history to hit 100 three-pointers in nine consecutive seasons (1988-89 to 1997-98)
1999	Scored 18,000th career point Closed the season as the NBA's all-time career leader in three-pointers made (1,702) and attempted (4,225)
2000	Held Pacers' franchise records for most points (17,402), field-goals made (5,695) and attempted (11,748), free throws made (4,416) and attempted (5,037), and three-pointers made and attempted

SHANNON MILLER

Sport: Gymnastics

Born: March 10, 1977
  Rolla, Missouri

Early Life

Shannon Lee Miller was born on March 10, 1977, in Rolla, Missouri. She grew up in Edmond, Oklahoma, where her father, Ronald, was a college physics professor and her mother, Claudia, was a bank vice president and gymnastics judge. Shannon started practicing gymnastics at home but soon enrolled in a local club and dedicated herself to developing her talent. She continued to maintain a straight A average in school and became a member of the National Honor Society.

The Road to Excellence

In 1985, Shannon's parents sent their eight-year-old daughter to the Soviet Union for a two-week training program. The Soviets, whose athletes dominated gymnastics, paid special attention to the young American and encouraged her to develop her talent. Steve Nunno, who attended the camp and later became her coach, recognized her determination and skill. He refined her style and helped her to overcome her shyness and learn to play to an audience.

Under his direction, Shannon trained six days a week. She spent hours each day practicing basic gymnastics skills as well as studying ballet, running, and stretching. She went to the gym early in the morning, then to school, and returned to gymnastic practice until 9 P.M. She ate a late dinner, did homework, and saved time for her family and pets before bed. Her rigorous schedule required strict self-discipline seldom demanded of children so young.

Her work paid off. Shannon had all the qualities required of a good gymnast: strength, agility, discipline, determination, and the ability to project her charming personality to the audience. She dominated local gymnastic meets, then won

national recognition, and finally emerged as one of the top international competitors. Shannon placed second in the 1988 Junior Pan-American Games in Puerto Rico and ranked first that year in her age category in the United States Championships.

The Emerging Champion

In the 1970's and 1980's, women's gymnastics had become one of the world's most popular sports. Television made international stars of Olga Korbut, Nadia Comǎneci, and Mary Lou Retton. At age twelve, Shannon began to stand out in the crowded field of talented young women vying for recognition. In 1989 she placed third in the Olympic Festival and sixth in a strong field of gymnasts at the Japanese Junior International. In 1990 Shannon ranked second at the American Classic and led the field as the top all-around gymnast at the prestigious Catania Cup competition in Italy.

In 1991 she continued her drive to the top. In June, Shannon competed in the U.S. Championships against thirty other athletes. She performed beautifully in most events but faltered on one routine and ranked seventh. Kim Zmeskal, her major future rival, won the event. At the 1991 World Championships, Shannon placed sixth in the all-around competition. She made a near-perfect score in the compulsory vault, which had been regarded as her weakest event. She also became the first American gymnast ever to qualify for all four individual event finals. She stood out in other international meets, and in December, she and her partner, Scott Keswick, won first all-around in the mixed competition at the Swiss Cup.

As 1992 opened, attention focused on the upcoming Summer Olympics. Shannon missed the U.S. Championships because she had had surgery on her right elbow, but she was ready in

MAJOR CHAMPIONSHIPS					
Year	Competition	Event	Place	Event	Place
1991	U.S. National Championships	All-Around	7th	Balance beam	1st
				Vault	3d
	World Championships	All-Around	6th	Balance beam	6th
		Floor exercise	4th	Vault	6th
		Uneven bars	2d	Team	2d
1992	Olympic Games	All-Around	Silver	Balance beam	Silver
		Floor exercise	Bronze	Vault	6th
		Uneven parallel bars	Bronze	Team	Bronze
	American Cup	All-Around	3d		
1993	U.S. National Championships	All-Around	1st	Floor exercise	1st
		Uneven parallel bars	1st		
	World Championships	All-Around	1st	Floor exercise	1st
		Uneven parallel bars	1st		
	American Cup	All-Around	1st	Vault	1st
		Uneven parallel bars	1st	Floor exercise	1st
1994	Goodwill Games	All-Around	2d	Balance beam	1st
		Floor exercise	1st	Vault	2d
		Uneven bars	2d	Team	4th
	World Gymnastics Championships	All-Around	1st	Balance beam	1st
		Floor exercise	4th	Vault	7th
	U.S. National Championships	All-Around	2d	Vault	2d
1994	U.S. National Championships	Uneven parallel bars	2d	Balance beam	2d
		Floor exercise	2d		
1995	World Championships	All-Around	12th	Team	3d
		Uneven parallel bars	7th	Balance beam	4th
	U.S. National Championships	All-Around	2d	Vault	1st
		Floor exercise	3d		
1996	Olympic Games	Team	Gold	Balance beam	Gold
		All-Around	8th	Vault	8th
	U.S. National Championships	All-Around	1st		
1997	World University Games	All-Around	1st	Team	2d
2000	U.S. Gymnastics Championships	Balance beam	2d		

June, 1992, for the Olympic trials in Baltimore. The nation's best gymnasts competed for the six spots on the U.S. team that would go to the Olympics in Barcelona, Spain. Shannon faltered on the vault but then settled down to perform brilliantly. She came in first and startled the experts by upsetting Kim Zmeskal.

At Barcelona, Shannon and Kim competed against athletes from 172 nations. Media attention centered on Kim, the first American ever to win the all-around title in the World Championships. She was known for her dynamic, explosive style, while Shannon combined grace with technical brilliance. Kim thrived on audience adulation and usually blossomed under pressure; Shannon displayed composure, consistency, and concentration.

Shannon and Kim faced intense competition from other young women. The Soviet Union had ceased to exist as a nation, but its athletes still competed together as the Unified Team. Despite the political turmoil in their homeland, they retained their superior techniques. Kim faltered under the intense pressure, and the contest for the all-around gold medal narrowed to Shannon Miller and Tatiana Gutsu from the Ukraine. Shannon led in the compulsory competition but lost to Tatiana in the finals. It was the closest loss in Olympic history. Shannon won the silver medal in the all-around competition, a silver medal on the balance beam, and three bronze medals.

Shannon entered the Olympics overshadowed by her better-known rivals but emerged as the leading medalist among women. She was the star of the U.S. team, and her coach, Steve Nunno, told the press, "Everyone has to finally realize the greatness of Shannon Miller."

Shannon did not let celebrity affect her. She was still shy and unconceited and became uncomfortable when people mentioned her medals. She seemed more excited at meeting other famous athletes than at her own success. Her quiet and modest personality wore well with her fans. She did not let media acclaim and endorsement money destroy her perspective; the money she received went into her college savings account.

She continued to win honors; in early 1993, she was named one of the Sportswomen of the Year by the U.S. Olympic Commission. More important, she showed that her performance at the Olympics was not a fluke. In April, 1993, she won first in the all-around, uneven bars, and floor exercise at the World Championships in Birmingham, England. She continued to dominate women's gymnastics as the year went on, winning the all-around medals at the Olympic Festival and the U.S. Championships.

Shannon dominated world women's gymnastics from 1992 to 1994. She gathered awards and honors from around the country for her mastery of the sport. Although she came in second to Dominique Dawes at the 1994 nationals, she became only the fourth woman in history, from any country, to repeat as the world all-around champion. Careers in the top levels of gymnastics are usually short because the "ideal" body type is tiny, extremely strong, and exceedingly flexible, which usually means young. The rigors of the sport cause many, often career-ending, injuries. By the end of 1994 Shannon was, by gymnastics standards, old—at seventeen—and tall, at 5 feet 1 inch. She was also plagued by injuries.

Shannon's hallmark determination, however, led her to train and redesign her routines to accommodate her height, accentuating the beauty of long lines and graceful, controlled flow of movement. She was going to compete in her second Olympics. A mature, seasoned veteran, Shannon won the all-around title at the U.S. National Championships in 1996, and she went to the 1996 Olympic Games in Atlanta, Georgia, as leader of the "Magnificent Seven," the name bestowed on the American women's gymnastics team.

The depth and strength of this American team, as defined by Shannon, was reflected in their winning the team gold medal, the first time the team gold went to a Western country since Germany won the title in 1936, at the second Olympics in which the event existed. A step out of bounds on during her floor exercise routine took a very disappointed Shannon out of the all-around competition. Shannon, however, won

Shannon Miller performs her gold medal winning routine on balance beam in the 1996 Olympics.

AP/Wide World Photos

the gold medal on the balance beam by perfectly executing her signature move—the "Miller," created by and named for her—and her dismount.

Continuing the Story

Shannon toured with the very popular "Magnificent Seven" after the Olympics, was co-Grand Marshal in the 1997 Tournament of Roses Parade, in Pasadena, California, and continued to compete. She placed first in the all-around competition of the 1997 World University Games. She moved away from top-level competitive gymnastics in 1998 and 1999. During this time, she continued her studies at the University of Oklahoma; wrote a book, *Winning Every Day* (1998); and stayed involved with her aggressive charity work, especially as national spokesperson for the Children's Miracle Network. On June 12, 1999, she married Dr. Chris B. Phillips in Edmond, Oklahoma. Her guest list of nine hundred included the most notable names in American gymnastics, including the entire "Magnificent Seven" team, Kim Zmeskal, Bart Conner, and Nadia Comăneci.

Shannon attempted a comeback to gain a spot on the 2000 Olympic team. Injuries, however, kept her from competing to her full potential and, ultimately, kept her off the team.

Summary

Gymnastics requires hard work and discipline from young women barely in their teens. Fortunately for Shannon Miller, coach Steve Nunno encouraged her to balance gymnastics with her family and educational future. Gymnastic officials cited her as an example of all that was best in young people. She maintained her perspective while, barely out of middle school, she emerged as one of the best athletes in the world.

Shannon was America's first true international gymnastics superstar. She had a career enviable even to Russians and Romanians, the sport's traditional powerhouses. Shannon brought steely nerves, consistency on all events, innovative moves, and gorgeous artistry to a very unforgiving sport that demands perfection. Shannon did all this for more than a decade while also staying close to her family, maintaining high academic standards, attending college, and giving back generously to the community. She is an outstanding individual in all life's events.

Martha E. Pemberton

Additional Sources:

Green, Septima. *Going for the Gold: Shannon Miller.* New York: Avon Books, 1996.

Kleinbaum, Nancy. *Magnificent Seven: The Authorized Story of American Gold.* New York: Bantam Books, 1996.

Miller, Claudia Ann, with Gayle White. *Shannon: My Child, My Hero.* Norman: University of Oklahoma Press, 1999.

Miller, Shannon, with Nancy Ann Richardson. *Winning Every Day: Gold Medal Advice for a Happy, Healthy, Life!* New York: Bantam Books, 1998.

Quiner, Krista, and Steve Lange. *Shannon Miller, America's Most Decorated Gymnast: A Biography.* 2d ed. East Hanover, N.J.: Bradford, 1997.

BILLY MILLS

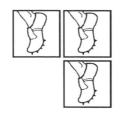

Sport: Track and field (long-distance runs)

Born: June 30, 1938
　　　Pine Ridge, South Dakota

Early Life

William Mervin (Billy) Mills brought about one of the most spectacular upsets in Olympic history when he, an unknown in the sports world, beat record holder Ron Clarke in the 10,000 me-ters at the 1964 Tokyo Games and set an Olympic record. Billy was born on June 30, 1938, in Pine Ridge, South Dakota. A seven-sixteenths Sioux Indian, he grew up on the Sioux Reservation at Pine Ridge. He was orphaned when he was twelve and was raised by his sister. He attended Haskell Indian Institute (Jim Thorpe was an alumnus) in Lawrence, Kansas, where he took up boxing. He ran as a part of his training and, after getting battered in a few matches, he decided to devote himself entirely to running.

The Road to Excellence

In Kansas, Billy broke the high school record for cross-country. He was twice state champion in the mile, and he broke the high school mile record when he was a senior. Billy went on to the University of Kansas, where he ran cross-country and was captain of the team. There was nothing distinguished about his performance there, although no one thought he lacked potential.

After his university experience, Billy joined the Marines and became a motor-pool lieutenant at Camp Pendleton in California. There he competed on the Marine Corps team. After two decades of running, he quit in 1962. Billy probably never would have thought about competing in the Tokyo Olympics if his wife, Pat, had not encouraged him to come out of retirement. Billy had become difficult to live with, and Pat, a track fan herself, knew that he missed the competition. She

At the 1964 Olympics, Billy Mills won the 10,000 meters, the first Ameri-can ever to win the event.

1893

STATISTICS

Year	Competition	Event	Place	Time
1964	Olympic Games	10,000 meters	Gold	28:24.4 OR
		Marathon	14th	—
1965	National AAU Outdoor Championships	6-mile run	Gold	27:11.6

kept insisting that they go to track meets, hoping that he would overcome his feelings of failure and be inspired to run again. She knew her husband well, and her efforts finally succeeded.

The Emerging Champion

Billy set for himself the goal of making the United States Olympic team and running the 10,000 meters at the Tokyo Games. The 10,000 meters was hardly a glamour event and attracted little interest in the United States. The closest an American had ever come to winning an Olympic gold medal in the event was when Louis Tewanima, another athlete of American Indian descent, won the silver in the 1912 Stockholm Games. His faith in his abilities renewed, Billy set out, in obscurity, on a rigorous training schedule. He sprinted at distant trees, imagining them to be the finish for the 10,000 meters. He kept a workout book to note his progress and wrote inspirational messages to himself to develop his winning mentality.

At the Olympic trials, Billy took second in the 10,000 meters and also qualified for the marathon. His performance was completely overshadowed by his fellow teammate Gerry Lindgren, who was expected to be a top competitor in the event. The 5-foot 11-inch, 160-pound Mills was hardly noticed, and most thought his finest moment had already passed. His best time was almost a full minute slower than Ron Clarke's world record of 28 minutes 15.6 seconds, and Clarke himself, when asked what he thought about Billy Mills, said he had never heard of him. American reporters did not even interview Billy during the two weeks the team was in Tokyo before the games. When he went to the Olympic Village store, where shoe manufacturers were distributing track shoes free to recognized distance runners, Mills had to purchase his. All of that would change the next day.

Continuing the Story

On October 14, 1964, the track world "discovered" Billy Mills. It had rained that morning and the track was still wet as the contestants gathered for the 10,000 meters. The race was predicted to be a tough battle among Clarke, the world record holder; Murray Halberg of New Zealand, the defending 5,000 meters Olympic champion; and the Soviet Pyotr Bolotnikov, the defending Olympic champion in the distance. Clarke started fast and by the halfway mark had outdistanced all but four runners. Billy, to everyone's surprise, was one of them. With two and one-half laps to go, Clarke seemed assured of victory because Billy and Mohamed Gammoudi of Tunisia, the only two still in contention, had never broken 29 minutes.

On the final lap, the three were jockeying with one another for the lead, and stragglers, whom they were lapping, cluttered the track. Caught between a straggler and Billy, Clarke tapped the American to pass, but when Billy would not move, Clarke shoved him aside. Billy was momentarily put off stride, and Gammoudi pushed his way between the two and took a quick ten-yard lead. Clarke caught up with Gammoudi and passed him on the homestretch, but Gammoudi recovered. The crowd cheered them on and Billy appeared to be out of the race. What happened next electrified the sports world.

Billy always knew that his strength was his finishing kick. If he was anywhere near his competition at the finish, he could outsprint them. He shot by Clarke and Gammoudi in the final stretch and won by three yards. The crowd went

RECORDS

First American to win a gold medal in the 10,000 meters
Held world 6-mile run record

HONORS AND AWARDS

1964	DiBeneditto Award
1965	Dieges Award
1972	Named One of America's Ten Outstanding Young Men
1976	Inducted into National Track and Field Hall of Fame
1984	Inducted into U.S. Olympic Hall of Fame

wild even though most of them, and at least one Japanese official, did not even know who he was. His time of 28 minutes 24.4 seconds bettered his previous best by 46 seconds and set a new Olympic record. Later, he would also finish fourteenth (Clarke finished ninth) in the marathon.

Billy returned home a hero, the first American ever to win the gold in the 10,000 meters. When he went back to his hometown in South Dakota, the Oglala Sioux tribal elders presented him with a gold ring and made him a warrior. They gave him a Sioux name that meant "He Thinks Very Good of His Country," and a building was dedicated in his name. Billy proved that his performance at Tokyo was no accident when he shattered Ron Clarke's 6-mile world record in 1965.

Summary

In 2000, Billy remained the only American ever to win the 10,000-meter race in the Olympics. He overcame a disadvantaged childhood, obscurity, and a lack of confidence to stun the world with his victory in the 10,000 meters at the 1964 Tokyo Olympics. Seldom has an athlete had such an uphill battle, and his triumph will always be a contender for the top Olympic Cinderella story. He is the perfect example of what one can accomplish with hard work, family support, and belief in oneself.

Robert B. Kebric

Additional Sources:

Bateman, Hal. *United States Track and Field Olympians, 1896-1980.* Indianapolis, Ind.: The Athletics Congress of the United States, 1984.

Hickok, Ralph. *A Who's Who of Sports Champions.* Boston: Houghton Mifflin, 1995.

Wallechinsky, David. *The Complete Book of the Olympics.* Boston: Little, Brown and Company, 1991.

Watman, Mel. *Encyclopedia of Track and Field Athletics.* New York: St. Martin's Press, 1981.

LAVINIA MILOSOVICI

Sport: Gymnastics

Born: October 21, 1976
Logoj, Romania

Early Life

Lavinia Corina Milosovici was born on October 21, 1976, in Logoj, Romania, close to the Yugoslavian border. She was the second of two children born to athletic parents, a former wrestler and a volleyball player.

Lavinia began gymnastics when she was selected from her kindergarten class at age six. In Romania, sports coaches go to the schools and observe the youngsters, inviting the talented children to come try their sport. Gymnastics holds a high place in the hearts of Romanians, so it is an honor to be chosen. Little Romanian girls want to be like Nadia Comăneci, the star of the 1976 Olympics, and Lavinia was no different.

Lavinia was stronger than the other girls her age, and her desire to succeed was deep. She joined the Cetate Deva club in Deva, some miles away, where she was coached by Leo Cosma and assistants Mirela Sucala and Petre Sebu. Though initially regarded as one of the most promising young athletes in her club, Lavinia was constantly injured, losing precious training time. Her gymnastics future was in doubt.

The Road to Excellence

A lesser gymnast might have given up, but Lavinia and Coach Cosma pressed on, spending extra hours in the gym to catch up with her teammates. The work paid off when she qualified for the junior national team in 1989. She was now a 1992 Olympic hopeful, and she would be just the right age for the Barcelona Games.

The Romanian revolution of 1989 raised a serious question about the future of its gymnasts: Would government support continue? Cosma left to pursue a life in Germany, and the national team members were sent from the training facility at

Deva back to their own clubs for a short time. By early 1990, the team had returned to Deva. That spring, Lavinia placed third at both the national championships and the Balkan Championships.

The Western world caught its first glimpse of the spunky thirteen-year-old when Great Britain hosted the Romanians in the spring of 1990. There, Lavinia electrified the crowd with her uneven bars routine, which included four release elements. Most gymnasts at the time were capable of just two releases. Her feat was all the more spectacular in light of the fact that Romanian gymnasts were traditionally weak at bars routines.

By 1991, Lavinia was ready to take on the world. Though the prestigious European Junior Championships ended in disappointment for her, she did win two events and set the tone for her career: all-around defeats followed by single-event victories. Later that year, she became Romania's national champion.

The Emerging Champion

The most important meet of 1991 was the World Championships, held in Indianapolis. Before an overpoweringly pro-American crowd and some stiff judging, the Romanians lost to the host in the team competition, and Lavinia managed just seventh in the all-around.

In the event finals, she gave a taste of things to come. Her excellent amplitude on vault won Lavinia her first world title, and she followed it with a bronze-medal performance on the beam. Though she came away from the floor exercises without a medal, Lavinia premiered an amazing combination tumbling pass never done before, showing incredible air sense, timing, and strength.

The major pre-Olympic meet for Lavinia was the individual-event World Championships in Paris. There, she won her second world title, this time for her unique bars work. Still, with an ankle

AP/Wide World Photos

Romanian Lavinia Milosovici performs on the floor in a 1996 meet. She won the bronze in the all-around at the Olympics later that year.

injury, she could not yet show her full potential.

In Barcelona, a new, improved Lavinia and her teammates took revenge on the Americans with a late charge to beat out the U.S. team for the silver medal; both countries were bested by the Unified Team from the former Soviet republics. Lavinia was fourth after the prelims, with her best routines to come. Unfortunately, small errors in the all-around once again left Lavinia to watch the battle for the gold medal, but the bronze was hers. Once again, she would save her revenge for the event finals.

In her first event, the vault, Lavinia "stuck" both attempts, sharing her first gold medal with Hungary's Henrietta Onodi, who had succeeded

her as world champion in Paris. Her performance on the bars produced only a fourth-place finish, as she was upstaged by the astounding work of China's Lu Li. Lavinia finished eighth in the beam competition after a fall, but the beam had never been her event. While Romanians are known for superb beam work, Lavinia was an accomplished all-arounder.

Finally, she shone during the floor exercise. With a spirited interpretation of boogie-woogie music and an outrageous new middle series in which she worked the floor as if it were a trampoline, the title was hers as soon as she finished. The magic 10.0 went up, and Romanian coach Octavian Belu hoisted her on his shoulders to acknowledge the cheering crowd.

Lavinia was the only female gymnast at the Barcelona Games to win two gold medals. She was also one of only two competitors to qualify for the finals for every event, an accomplishment in itself.

After the Olympics, Lavinia went home a heroine. The Romanian government rewarded her with the equivalent of $18,000. In early December of 1992, she won Germany's prestigious DTB Cup and more cash. A new world of professionalism was emerging for the gymnasts, one which might keep them in the sport longer—all to the advantage of an athlete such as Lavinia.

After the Games, the code of points for judging were revised, Lavinia "suffered" a growing spurt (a phenomenon that usually ends gymnastics careers), and the public demands of being a national hero affected her. She was not her best at the 1993 World Championships. She did, however, win the gold medal on balance beam, the only individual apparatus event for which she did not already hold an Olympic or world championship gold medal. Regaining her confidence and focus, Lavinia continued to compete at the top world levels. At the 1994 World Championships,

MAJOR CHAMPIONSHIPS

Year	Competition	Event	Place	Event	Place
1991	World Championships	All-Around	7th	Balance beam	3d
		Floor exercise	4th	Team	3d
		Vault	1st		
1992	Olympic Games	All-Around	Bronze	Balance beam	8th
		Floor exercise	Gold	Team	Silver
		Uneven parallel bars	4th	Vault	Gold
	World Championships	Floor exercise	8th	Vault	4th
		Uneven parallel bars	1st		
	Chunichi Cup	All-Around	1st	Vault	1st
		Uneven parallel bars	3d	Floor exercise	3d
1993	European Cup	All-Around	3d	Floor exercise	2d
		Uneven parallel bars	1st	Vault	1st
	World Championships	All-Around	8th	Balance beam	1st
		Uneven parallel bars	5th	Floor exercise	5th
		Vault	2d		
	Chunichi Cup	All-Around	1st	Vault	1st
		Uneven parallel bars	3d	Balance beam	2d
		Floor exercise	5th		
1994	World Championships	All-Around	2d	Team	1st
		Vault	3d	Floor exercise	2d
		Uneven parallel bars	6th	Balance beam	5th
1994	European Championships	All-Around	6th	Team	1st
		Vault	1st	Floor exercise	2d
		Uneven parallel bars	7th	Balance beam	3d
	Chunichi Cup	All-Around	2d	Vault	1st
		Floor exercise	1st	Balance beam	2d
		Uneven parallel bars	5th		
1995	World Championships	All-Around	3d	Team	1st
		Uneven parallel bars	5th		
	Chunichi Cup	All-Around	1st	Floor exercise	1st
		Vault	2d	Balance beam	2d
		Uneven parallel bars	4th		
1996	Olympic Games	All-Around	Bronze	Team	Bronze
		Uneven parallel bars	8th		
	European Championships	All-Around	3d	Team	1st
		Uneven parallel bars	4th	Floor exercise	1st

she barely lost the all-around title to American gymnast Shannon Miller, and she placed in the floor exercise and vault events.

Lavinia continued to gather world, European, and other championship titles from 1994 through early 1996, making her a veteran team leader going into the 1996 Olympic Games in Atlanta, Georgia. Lavinia's performances were steady and composed, giving her the bronze medal in the all-around and team competitions. She retired from competition shortly after the Games.

Continuing the Story

For the next year and a half Lavinia participated in the Gold World Tour, giving exhibitions around the world. She then returned to Roma-nia to relax, build a home, and go to school to qualify as a coach. Later, Lavinia and her Olympic teammate Gina Gogean were named to the coaching staff of the Romanian junior national team. She married her longtime boyfriend at the end of 1999.

Summary

No female gymnast since Czechoslovakia's Vera Časlavská in the 1960's has owned Olympic and world titles on all the apparatus. Lavinia Milosovici may be the best gymnast, even the best all-around gymnast, never to have won an Olympic or world all-around gold medal. She earned medals in every World Championship and Olympic Games from 1991 to 1996, a remarkable achievement in a sport that regularly sees top athletes rise and fall within a year or two. Lavinia will be remembered as one of the best of a rapidly changing generation of gymnastics "machines" whose innovation, personality, and lasting power set her apart from the crowd.

Nancy Raymond

Additional Sources:

Citroen, Nicole. "Lavinia Milosovici." *International Gymnast*, April, 1992, 14.

Normile, Dwight. "Lavinia's Legacy: Milosovici Represents the Latest Chapter in Romania's Rich History of Women's Gymnastics." *International Gymnast*, January, 1997, 28-32.

Perlez, Jane. "Romanian Coach Keeps up the Fight." *The New York Times*, July 13, 1995, p. B19.

"Where Are They Now: Lavinia Milosovici." *International Gymnast* Online. http://www.intl gymnast.com/paststars/psdec98.html. October, 1999.

ROSI MITTERMAIER

Sport: Skiing

Born: August 5, 1950
Reit-im-Winkl, West Germany

Early Life

Rosi Mittermaier grew up in a skiing family. She was born in West Germany on August 5, 1950. Her twin sister died at birth. Rosi's father, Heinrich, operated a ski school. He had been a good Nordic skier and a member of the German national team. Unfortunately, he reached his athletic peak during World War II. He never had the opportunity to experience top international competition. All of his children learned to ski at an early age. Rosi began at two.

The Road to Excellence

Rosi; her younger sister, Evi; and her older sister, Heidi, all were talented skiers. Each of them went on to become a member of the German national ski team.

In 1967, the International Ski Federation developed a series of races called the World Cup. The World Cup was designed to test the skills of a racer over an entire season. World Cup competition at that time included three events: the slalom, the giant slalom, and the downhill. Rosi competed in all three. As a teenager, Rosi skied on the World Cup circuit in its first year, finishing twenty-seventh in the world.

The Emerging Champion

Rosi skied in the World Cup series for ten years. During the first nine years, she never finished the season ranked higher than third. She competed in the Winter Olympic Games for the first time in 1968, in Grenoble, France. Her results were not good. She finished twentieth in the giant slalom and twenty-fifth in the downhill, and was disqualified in the slalom.

Four years later, Rosi skied in her second Olympic Games at Sapporo, Japan. Once again, she failed to win a medal, but her performance was better than

Rosi Mittermaier skiing the slalom course en route to winning the women's European Cup in 1973.

the one at Grenoble. Her best result was a sixth in the downhill. She finished twelfth in the giant slalom and seventeenth in the slalom.

Injuries were a problem for Rosi at key points in her career. She suffered two serious injuries that delayed her emergence as a major star. In 1973, she was a contender for the World Cup slalom title, but she was struck by a surfboard in Hawaii and could not complete the season. Two years later, she was in second place in the World Cup standings. Late in the season, a recreational skier ran into her during one of her training runs. Once again, she was unable to compete in important races at the end of the season. She was forced to miss races in Japan and North America and finished the year in third place.

Although Rosi did not emerge as a superstar during the first nine years of her World Cup career, she was always a consistent performer. Following her rookie season on the World Cup tour, she finished the season in the top fifteen every year between 1968 and 1975, and usually was in the top ten.

Also, during this period of her career, Rosi developed her abilities in all three Alpine skiing events. Whereas many skiers specialize in one or two events, Rosi was capable of doing well in slalom, giant slalom, and downhill.

Continuing the Story

Throughout her career, Rosi was recognized as a well-rounded person. She warned against taking ski racing too seriously. Unlike many elite skiers, who seemed to be interested only in skiing, Rosi had outside interests. She enjoyed deep sea diving and spent her summers working on pottery and ceramics.

By the time of the 1976 Winter Olympic Games at Innsbruck, Austria, Rosi had been on the international ski scene for ten years. Although she was only twenty-five, her teammates called her "Omi," German for "Granny." The nickname referred to her long experience as a leading racer.

She was considered to be an excellent racer but not a top star. Prior to the 1976 Olympic Games, most experts believed that she might win one medal. One American sports magazine predicted that she would finish third in the slalom. Another magazine stated that she might "sneak in" for a medal in the downhill.

MAJOR CHAMPIONSHIPS

Year	Competition	Event	Place
1967	World Cup	Overall	27th
1968	Olympic Games	Downhill	25th
		Giant slalom	20th
	World Cup	Overall	15th
1969	World Cup	Overall	7th
1970	World Championships	Downhill	20th
		Slalom	14th
		Combined	5th
	World Cup	Overall	12th
1971	World Cup	Overall	14th
1972	Olympic Games	Downhill	6th
		Slalom	17th
		Giant slalom	12th
	World Cup	Overall	6th
1973	World Cup	Overall	4th
1974	World Championships	Slalom	6th
	World Cup	Overall	7th
1975	World Cup	Overall	3d
1976	Olympic Games	Slalom	Gold
		Giant slalom	Silver
		Downhill	Gold
	World Cup	Overall	1st

No one expected what was to happen. The night before the downhill, Rosi dreamed that she would win the race. The next day, to the surprise of almost everyone, including Rosi, that is exactly what she did. The next race was the slalom. Her main rival was the Swiss skier Lise-Marie Morerod. Morerod had defeated Rosi six times in slalom races during the 1976 season. In the Olympic race, however, Morerod missed a slalom gate and was disqualified. Rosi completed two strong runs down the course and had her second gold medal.

The final race of the Olympic competition was the giant slalom. With more than thirty-five thousand fans lining the course, Rosi had another excellent race. She finished .12 of a second behind the winner, Kathy Kreiner of Canada.

Suddenly Rosi became a major sports star. In just a few days, she had won two Olympic gold medals and one silver. Following the Olympic Games, Rosi was a hero in Germany. When she returned to her small hometown of Reit-Im-Winkl, more than twenty-five thousand people lined the road to greet her.

1901

HONORS AND AWARDS

| 1976 | World Cup Competitor of the Year |
| | *Ski Racing* magazine Competitor of the Year |

At the end of the 1976 season, Rosi retired from ski racing. Her success in 1976 caused many companies to seek her services as a spokesperson. She married German Olympic teammate Christian Neureuther, and they settled in Garmisch, Germany, where they would pursue several business interests.

Summary

Rosi Mittermaier's triumph at Innsbruck was the culmination of a long and successful career. At the 1976 Olympic Games, she was the only woman competing who had also skied the World Cup circuit during its first year. Sometimes in sports, an athlete will somehow perform at a higher level than she has ever done before and will be able to stay at that level for several days or weeks. Rosi's three-medal Olympic performance was one of those special moments.

Wayne Wilson

Additional Sources:

Levinson, David, and Karen Christenson, eds. *Encyclopedia of World Sport: From Ancient to Present.* Santa Barbara, Calif.: ABC-CLIO, 1996.

Schapp, Dick. *An Illustrated History of the Olympics.* New York: Alfred A. Knopf, 1975.

Scharff, Robert, ed. *Ski Magazine's Encyclopedia of Skiing.* New York: Harper and Row, 1970.

Wallechinsky, David. *The Complete Book of the Olympics.* Boston: Little, Brown and Company, 1991.

RON MIX

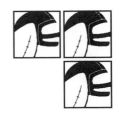

Sport: Football

Born: March 10, 1938
Los Angeles, California

Early Life

Ronald Jack Mix was born on March 10, 1938, in Los Angeles, California. Ron and his younger brother, Alan, were raised by their mother, Daisey Mix, after their parents divorced when Ron was four years old. The two boys grew up in the aircraft industry town of Hawthorne, just a few miles southwest of Los Angeles.

As a youngster, Ron had aspirations of being a baseball player. Unfortunately, in his sophomore year at Hawthorne High School, the baseball coach advised the 5-foot 5-inch Ron that scorekeeping might be his only baseball skill.

Although Ron was fairly successful in track, he shifted his interest to football. By his senior year, Ron had grown to 6 feet tall and weighed 155 pounds. As an end on the Hawthorne High School football team, he played well enough to earn a scholarship to the University of Southern California (USC).

The Road to Excellence

It was at USC that Ron first began an intensive weightlifting and bodybuilding program that would eventually develop him into one of football's strongest linemen. By the time he was a senior at USC, he had grown to 6 feet 4 inches and increased his weight to 255 pounds. Because of his size and strength, and partially because of a vision problem, Ron was moved by USC coach Don Clark from the end position to a tackle spot. Ron's vision was so bad, Coach Clark claimed, that, on more than one occasion, Ron had tackled the blocker instead of the ball carrier. While weightlifting developed his body, Coach Clark ordered contact lenses to correct Ron's vision.

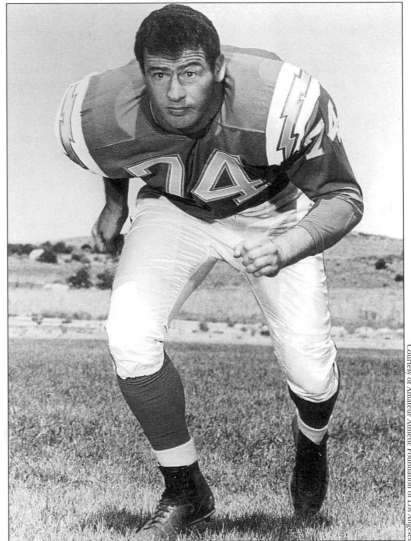

Although Ron was not eager to change positions, he excelled as a tackle and earned All-Coast and All-American honors and was voted team co-captain his senior year (1959) as well as Most Valuable Lineman. Undersized for a lineman, Ron made up for that with his tremendous strength and mobility. Coach Clark described his toughness and intensity as "incredible." Still, he missed playing "a fun position."

In 1960, the Baltimore Colts of the National Football League (NFL) picked Ron in the first round of the annual college football draft. At the same time, the Boston (now the New England) Patriots of the rival American Football League (AFL) obtained negotiation rights to Ron but quickly traded them to the Los Angeles Chargers. Because they offered more money and Los Angeles was home, Ron signed with the Chargers.

The Emerging Champion

A big part of Ron's decision to play in Los Angeles was based on his plan to continue his education at USC. Ron planned to play professional football for only a year or two and then to go into teaching. He loved his English and physical education courses at USC and originally wanted to teach both.

As his on-the-field successes continued, however, Ron's plans began to change. For the first time since he had changed from the "fun" end position to a tackle, Ron was again beginning to enjoy football. He combined his intensity and toughness with his articulate off-the-field manners to rise above the "unknown" status of an offensive lineman to that of a star. He often found himself receiving attention from the media generally reserved for "skilled players" such as quarterbacks and running backs.

With the Chargers, who in 1961 relocated to San Diego, Ron was an All-AFL selection his first nine seasons. Eight times he was the AFL's All-League tackle and once, in 1961, earned the honor as a guard. He played in seven AFL All-Star games and in five of the league's first six championship games. When the Pro Football Hall of Fame Board of Selectors picked an All-Time AFL team in 1969, Ron was a unanimous choice for one of the offensive tackle positions.

During Ron's tenure, the Chargers were con-

sidered one of the most offensively potent teams in professional football. Ron provided unparalleled blocking for running backs Keith Lincoln and Paul Lowe while giving in-the-pocket protection to All-League quarterback John Hadl.

Early in his professional career, Ron relied upon his speed and strength to become the AFL's best offensive tackle. As time went on and AFL defenses improved, Ron determined that speed and strength alone were no longer enough. Just as he had used the weight room to build his strength, Ron focused his attention on creating new moves and techniques to help him remain the best tackle in the league. While Ron continued to excel on the field, he also continued to prepare for his life after football.

Continuing the Story

Throughout the off-seasons of his professional football career, Ron continued to pursue his dream of teaching. Nicknamed the "Intellectual Assassin," Ron became a published writer in 1963 when he wrote a training camp story for a national sports magazine.

Following the 1969 season, Ron retired from professional football and enrolled at the University of San Diego, where he completed his law degree. His one-year retirement, however, came to an abrupt end in 1971 when he joined the Oakland Raiders for one final playing season. When Ron finally ended his professional pro football career following the 1971 season, he returned to San Diego, where he began his successful law practice.

Ron continued to work as a personal injury

HONORS AND AWARDS	
1959	College All-American All-Coast Conference Team
1960-63	All-AFL Team
1962-64, 1968	Sporting News AFL All-Star Team
1962-65, 1967-69	AFL All-Star Team
1962-69	NFL Pro Bowl Team
1964-68	Associated Press All-AFL Team United Press International All-AFL Team
1969	All-Time AFL Team
1979	Inducted into Pro Football Hall of Fame

lawyer in the San Diego area with the firm of Klodny and Pressman. Ron has worked with many social causes, such as Project Hope, and has worked on a project selling a special limited edition set of football trading cards featuring the living members of the Pro Football Hall of Fame. The funds raised from this project would be used to assist former football greats and Hall of Fame members on limited incomes.

Summary

Ron Mix always worked hard for what he wanted to achieve. He overcame physique and vision problems as well as personal hardships to become one of professional football's premier players. Consistent with his will to succeed, Ron never quit working to improve himself and can reflect with great pride on his success on and off the field.

Of all the praise and awards Ron received as a player, he once said that the most flattering came when Chargers head coach Sid Gillman said that he wanted his own son to be like Ron Mix.

In 1979, Ron was accorded professional football's highest honor, election to the Pro Football Hall of Fame.

Joseph Horrigan

Additional Sources:

Holden, Anthony. "Player Profile: Ron Mix, San Diego Chargers." CBS Online. http://cbs .sportsline.com/u/football/nfl/legends/ player991231.htm.
Pro Football Hall of Fame. http://www.pro footballhof.com.

JOHNNY MIZE

Sport: Baseball

Born: January 7, 1913
　　　　Demorest, Georgia
Died: June 2, 1993
　　　　Demorest, Georgia

Early Life

John Robert Mize was born on January 7, 1913, in Demorest, Georgia. As a youngster, he had little interest in baseball. His first love was tennis, and in high school varsity sports he preferred basketball, at which he excelled. In 1929, while John was still in school, the coach of the Piedmont College baseball team asked him to join the team. He had seen John play in some sandlot games and knew that the big, moon-faced kid could whack the ball a country mile. Thus it was that Johnny Mize became one of the youngest college players ever. He would later note that he used up his college eligibility before earning his first college credit.

The Road to Excellence

At Piedmont, Johnny earned the nickname "The Big Cat" because, despite his large frame, he could move gracefully. He soon attracted the attention of major league scouts, including Frank Rickey, chief recruiter for the St. Louis Cardinals and brother of the "Mahatma," Branch Rickey, that team's general manager. The Cardinals signed Johnny and started him in their farm system, although Rickey was dubious about his prospects. Rickey thought that Johnny might be injury prone, and Johnny seemed to confirm it when he developed a trick knee and began to pull muscles.

Rickey sold Johnny to the Cincinnati Reds, whose hopes for him ran high during a sensational spring training camp, but Johnny went lame again, and the Reds canceled the sale. Playing for Rochester, Johnny continued to be plagued by knee and leg injuries.

Johnny Mize in 1943.

AP/Wide World Photos

He finally consulted Dr. Robert Hyland, who discovered that a growth on the player's pelvic bone was causing most of his problems. Despite the fact that the delicate operation to correct the condition could have left him lame for life, Johnny chose to go through with it.

The Emerging Champion

The next spring, in 1936, Johnny reported to the Cardinals' training camp with little hope of making the team. St. Louis still had one of the famous Gashouse Gang, Rip Collins, holding down first base. Manager Frank Frisch was impressed with John's smooth, effortless swing, and he soon put him in the regular lineup. Johnny quickly justified the move, finishing with a .329 batting average and 19 homers.

The next year, he beat the sophomore jinx with 25 homers and a sizzling .364 batting average, second in the league behind teammate Joe Medwick's .374. Two years later, in 1939, he won the batting crown with a .349 average but also began his verbal battles with Branch Rickey.

Despite Johnny's achievements, Rickey seemed bent on justifying his first appraisals of him. Their worst falling out came after the 1940 season. That year, Johnny led the league with 43 homers and 137 runs batted in, and he had every reason to expect a raise, but Rickey told him his salary was cut because his average had dropped to .314.

In September of 1941, Johnny sustained a serious shoulder injury, and Rickey made up his mind to sell him to the Giants, whose new manager, Mel Ott, was looking to build a team centered on power hitters.

When Johnny first reported to the Giants, it appeared that the Mahatma had pulled off a very clever deal; Johnny could not throw a ball ten feet. Then an osteopath, "Doc" Ferguson, discovered that Johnny had a misplaced ligament and eventually corrected the problem.

In 1942, his first season with the Giants, Johnny hit 26 homers and drove in 110 runs. He might have done even better, but it took time for him to adjust to the Polo Grounds, where balls lined deep to center usually turned into long outs. Johnny, a straightaway hitter, had to learn to pull the ball to take advantage of the short right field line, and in time he did.

Continuing the Story

At the close of his first year with the Giants, Johnny was inducted into the Navy. By that time, his weight had climbed toward 250 pounds, and it was assumed that his baseball career was over. Johnny fooled the experts, however. He went on a diet and conditioning regimen, and when he returned to the Giants, trimmed down to 205, he began setting some new career records. In 1947, he hit 51 homers, winning the league's home-run crown, and the next year, with 40 homers, he won it again.

In mid-season of 1948, Leo Durocher replaced Ott as the Giants' manager, and Johnny had trouble adjusting to the change. The two men never got along. Durocher, always energetic and aggressive, could not understand Johnny's mildness and deceptive calm and placidity, and in August of 1949, he traded Johnny to the Yankees.

Events first made it seem that Durocher had made a very timely deal. Johnny reinjured his shoulder in a defensive play and could not take the field again until the World Series, when he

STATISTICS

Season	GP	AB	Hits	2B	3B	HR	Runs	RBI	BA	SA
1936	126	414	136	30	8	19	76	93	.329	.577
1937	145	560	204	40	7	25	103	113	.364	.595
1938	149	531	179	34	**16**	27	85	102	.337	.614
1939	153	564	197	44	14	**28**	104	108	**.349**	**.626**
1940	155	579	182	31	13	**43**	111	**137**	.314	**.636**
1941	126	473	150	**39**	8	16	67	100	.317	.535
1942	142	541	165	25	7	26	97	**110**	.305	**.521**
1946	101	377	127	18	3	22	70	70	.337	.576
1947	154	586	177	26	2	**51**	**137**	**138**	.302	.614
1948	152	560	162	26	4	**40**	110	125	.289	.564
1949	119	411	108	16	0	19	63	64	.263	.440
1950	90	274	76	12	0	25	43	72	.277	.595
1951	113	332	86	14	1	10	37	49	.259	.398
1952	78	137	36	9	0	4	9	29	.263	.416
1953	81	104	26	3	0	4	6	27	.250	.394
Totals	1,884	6,443	2,011	367	83	359	1,118	1,337	.312	.562

Notes: Boldface indicates statistical leader. GP = games played; AB = at bats; 2B = doubles; 3B = triples; HR = home runs; RBI = runs batted in; BA = batting average; SA = slugging average

HONORS AND AWARDS

1937, 1939-42, 1946-49	National League All-Star Team
1953	American League All-Star Team
1981	Inducted into National Baseball Hall of Fame

promptly proved his worth. He won the third and crucial game as a pinch hitter, a role he filled well during his last playing years. The Yankee manager, Casey Stengel, knew that Johnny was excellent in clutch situations and used him brilliantly. It was Johnny who devastated the Dodgers in the 1952 World Series, batting .400 and hitting 3 homers. Clearly, to the very end of his playing days, the Big Cat remained a potent weapon with a bat in his hands.

After his retirement in 1953, Johnny spent some time as both scout and coach, then settled in Deland, Florida, where he would maintain a citrus grove and manage other business interests.

Summary

The reason selectors failed to elect Johnny Mize to the Baseball Hall of Fame long before 1981 remains a mystery. The genial Johnny was one of the league's great power hitters, but he was also a steady player who, when injury-free, was extremely dependable. His career batting average of .312 and his high slugging average should have guaranteed him early selection, but for some reason he was repeatedly overlooked. It is typical of Johnny that he never made any great fuss about the oversight, although he was well aware that he deserved the honors.

John W. Fiero

Additional Sources:

Porter, David L., ed. *Biographical Dictionary of American Sports: Baseball.* Westport, Conn.: Greenwood Press, 1987.

Rizzuto, Phil, and Tom Horton. *The October Twelve: Five Years of New York Yankee Glory, 1949-1953.* New York: Forge, 1994.

Shatzkin, Mike, et al., eds. *The Ballplayers: Baseball's Ultimate Biographical Reference.* New York: William Morrow, 1990.

EARL MONROE

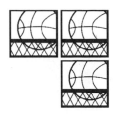

Sport: Basketball

Born: November 21, 1944
       Philadelphia, Pennsylvania

Early Life

Vernon Earl Monroe was born on November 21, 1944, in Philadelphia, Pennsylvania, to Vernon and Rose Monroe. His father worked as a night watchman and his mother managed a grocery store. Earl, their only son, has an older sister, Anna, and a younger sister, Theresa. When Earl was five years old, his parents divorced. He grew up on the south side of Philadelphia, a rough part of the city. His mother's influence helped Earl stay out of trouble.

He also fell in love with athletics at an early age. Earl was a good soccer player, but after breaking his leg, he decided to concentrate on basketball, practicing many hours a day. Earl attended John Bartram High School in south Philadelphia. It was not until his junior year that Earl began to excel, when he had grown to 6 feet 2 inches and was moved to the center position. He became adept at a number of trick shots so as to score against the bigger centers on the other high school teams.

The Road to Excellence

In his senior year at John Bartram, Earl averaged more than 21 points per game and was named All-City. Because he did not possess a strong scholastic re-

cord, Temple University of Philadelphia decided against offering Earl a scholarship. He went to work in a factory and learned what life would be like if he did not get a college education. After a year of factory work, Earl was recruited by Winston-Salem State College, a small, predomi-

nantly African American college located in North Carolina. At Winston-Salem, he majored in elementary education. On the basketball court, Earl was moved to the guard position. As a freshman, he averaged only 7 points per game, but as a sophomore, Earl raised his average to 23 points. The more he played, the better he got. Earl was on the verge of becoming a star in the college ranks.

Earl put everything he had into being the best that he could be on the basketball court. He was spectacular to watch. He looked flashy, but it was merely his natural style. Whereas some critics believed that Earl was showing off, his coach, Clarence Gaines, knew that he was working harder than anyone to help the team win. During his junior year, Earl raised his average to 30 points per game, but his greatest college season was still ahead of him. In 1966-1967, he scored a total of 1,329 points, a small-college record for total points. Earl again raised his average, this time to 41.5 points per game. Because of all his efforts, the Winston-Salem Rams won the National Collegiate Athletic Association (NCAA) College Division Championship, and Earl was named NCAA College Division Player of the Year.

The Emerging Champion

Earl was chosen by the Baltimore Bullets in the 1967 National Basketball Association (NBA) draft. The Bullets had been a last-place team in the Eastern Division, but they hoped, with the addition of Earl, that their luck would change. He turned out to be the missing ingredient that they needed. During the 1967-1968 season, Earl was an instant success. He averaged 24.3 points per game and was voted NBA Rookie of the Year. The Bullets also made it to the playoffs. In addition to Earl, the Bullets were blessed with Wes Unseld and Gus Johnson. These three players helped spark one of the most potent fast breaks in the NBA. Earl ran the offense and brought excitement to Baltimore. He stayed with the Bullets for four years before he asked to be traded. During those four seasons, Baltimore made it into the playoffs each year and Earl averaged 23.7 points per game. He was not happy in Baltimore, however, finding the city to be "dull."

In 1971, Earl was traded to the New York Knicks for Dave Stallworth, Mike Riordan, and some cash. Earl had been allowed to run the offense as he saw fit in Baltimore, but in New York, the situation was completely different. The New York coach, Red Holzman, believed in a more disciplined, team-oriented style of play. The Knicks were also endowed with a number of extremely talented players, including Walt Frazier, Willis Reed, Bill Bradley, Dave DeBusschere, Dick Barnett, and Jerry Lucas. It took some time, but Earl eventually learned the Knicks' team concept and was able to contribute to the their success. During his first season with the Knicks, Earl

STATISTICS

Season	GP	FG	FG%	FTM	FT%	Reb.	Ast.	TP	PPG
1967-68	82	742	.453	507	.781	465	349	1,991	24.3
1968-69	80	809	.440	447	.768	280	392	2,065	25.8
1969-70	82	695	.446	532	.830	257	402	1,922	23.4
1970-71	81	663	.442	406	.802	213	354	1,732	21.4
1971-72	63	287	.434	175	.781	100	142	749	11.9
1972-73	75	496	.488	171	.822	245	288	1,163	15.5
1973-74	41	240	.468	93	.823	121	110	573	14.0
1974-75	78	668	.457	297	.827	327	270	1,633	20.9
1975-76	76	647	.478	280	.787	273	304	1,574	20.7
1976-77	77	613	.517	307	.839	223	366	1,533	19.9
1977-78	76	556	.495	242	.832	182	361	1,354	17.8
1978-79	64	329	.471	129	.838	74	189	787	12.3
1979-80	51	161	.457	56	.875	36	67	378	7.4
Totals	926	6,906	.464	3,642	.807	2,796	3,594	17,454	18.8

Notes: GP = games played; FGM = field goals made; FG% = field goal percentage; FTM = free throws made; FT% = free throw percentage; Reb. = rebounds; Ast. = assists; TP = total points; PPG = points per game

averaged 11.9 points per game but became an important component of the team.

Continuing the Story

The Knicks won the 1973 NBA Championship with the help of Earl the "Pearl," as he was known. He was a crowd pleaser and a fierce competitor. Walt Frazier was always cool and steady, whereas Earl was dramatic. He and Frazier had to contribute even more to the offense in the mid-1970's with the retirement of Willis Reed and Dave DeBusschere. Earl himself retired after the 1979-1980 season because his knees were giving him problems. The years of twisting and slashing had taken their toll. Earl finished with a total of 17,454 points for his career and an 18.8 points-per-game average.

After his retirement from basketball, Earl became involved in the management of his Tiffany Entertainment Corporation and Pretty Pearl Records. He managed several notable singing groups. For the most part, he put basketball behind him and his energies into entertainment.

On March 6, 1985, Earl was named the commissioner of the United States Basketball League. During the late 1980's and the 1990's, Earl worked as a television commentator on NBA games. In 1990, he was elected to the Naismith Memorial Basketball Hall of Fame. The National Association of Intercollegiate Athletics (NAIA) had recognized his college career earlier by inducting him into its Hall of Fame in 1975.

As part of the celebration of the golden anniversary of the NBA in 1996, Earl was honored for his contributions to basketball by being selected as a member of the NBA's 50 Greatest Players of All Time Team. During his playing days, Earl "the Pearl" had helped usher in a new era in basketball by displaying amazing individual skills within the team concept. He uncovered and perfected the "shake-and-bake" style of one-on-one basketball. Some basketball experts think that Earl may

HONORS AND AWARDS		
1966	*Sporting News* All-American	
1967	NCAA College Division Player of the Year NCAA College Division Tournament Outstanding Player	
1968	NBA Rookie of the Year NBA All-Rookie Team	
1969	All-NBA Team	
1969, 1971, 1975, 1977	NBA All-Star Team	
1975	Inducted into NAIA Basketball Hall of Fame	
1990	Inducted into Naismith Memorial Basketball Hall of Fame	
1996	NBA 50 Greatest Players of All Time Team Uniform number 15 retired by New York Knicks	

have been the most exciting player to ever play in the NBA.

Summary

Earl Monroe will be remembered for his flamboyant style on the court. He had an amazing way of spinning around larger defenders and driving toward the basket for the score. The New York crowd came alive when Earl put on a move. The 1973 NBA Championship team must be considered one of the greatest teams ever assembled, and Earl was an essential component of the Knicks' success.

Michael Jeffrys

Additional Sources:

Bjarkman, Peter C. *The Biographical History of Basketball.* Chicago: Masters Press, 1998.

Dolin, Nick, Chris Dolin, and David Check. *Basketball Stars: The Greatest Players in the History of the Game.* New York: Black Dog and Leventhal, 1997.

Kalinsky, George, and Phil Berger. *The New York Knicks: The Official Fiftieth Anniversary Celebration.* New York: Macmillan, 1996.

Mallozzi, Vincent M. *Basketball: The Legends and the Game.* Willowdale, Ont.: Firefly Books, 1998.

Shouler, Kenneth A. *The Experts Pick Basketball's Best Fifty Players in the Last Fifty Years.* Lenexa, Kans.: Addax, 1998.

JOE MONTANA

Sport: Football

Born: June 11, 1956
Monongahela, Pennsylvania

Early Life

Joseph C. Montana, Jr., was born on June 11, 1956, in the town of Monongahela, Pennsylvania, which is situated to the south of Pittsburgh. The town gets its name from the Monongahela River, which runs through it.

Joe was the only child of Joseph, Sr., and Teresa Montana. Before he was even a year old, Joe was given his first bat and ball by his father. Later, his father installed a hoop for him to shoot baskets and a tire through which he was to throw footballs. Joe Namath, the great quarterback of the New York Jets—and a native of Pennsylvania—was Joe's childhood hero.

The Road to Excellence

Although a thin child, Joe excelled in many sports. He batted .500 and pitched three perfect games in Little League. At Ringgold High School in Monongahela, Joe continued his development as an all-around athlete. He was an excellent baseball player and was All-State in basketball and All-American in football. Joe also could high jump 6 feet 9 inches. North Carolina State University offered him a scholarship in basketball, but he turned it down when the University of Notre Dame offered him a football scholarship. The coach at Notre Dame was Dan Devine. Devine was not impressed by how Joe performed in practice, so he was not the starting quarterback for Notre Dame for most of his career there.

Joe had his greatest impact at Notre Dame by coming off the bench to lead the Fighting

Joe Montana, quarterback for the 49ers, looks for an opening in a 1989 game.

AP/Wide World Photos

Irish from behind to comeback victories. He was known as "the Comeback Kid" for his heroics in a number of memorable games. His first year did not include any extraordinary efforts, but during his second season, in 1975, the legendary comebacks began. Joe was sent into the game against the University of North Carolina with Notre Dame trailing 14-6 in the fourth quarter. He brought the Fighting Irish back, and they won the game by the score of 21-14. In even more dramatic fashion, Joe brought his team back from a 30-10 deficit with 3 touchdown passes against the Air Force Academy after entering the game in the second half. These two remarkable efforts highlighted his sophomore year.

In 1976, Joe was forced to sit out because of a shoulder separation. The next year, though, he took up where he had left off in 1975. At the start of the year, he was the third-string quarterback behind Rusty Lisch and Gary Forystek, but, after bringing the Fighting Irish back from a loss in the third game of the year against Purdue University, he became the starting quarterback. Notre Dame went to the Cotton Bowl that season and played an undefeated University of Texas that was favored. Notre Dame won the game 38-10 and was voted the number-one team by the Associated Press and the United Press International polls. Joe's last year at Notre Dame was no less dramatic, with a crowning Cotton Bowl victory in January, 1979, against the University of Houston. Joe left Notre Dame with a degree in marketing and the status of a hero in the hearts of Fighting Irish fans.

The Emerging Champion

Even with his reputation for being the Comeback Kid and also being the subject of a student song, "The Ballad of Joe Montana," at Notre Dame, the professional scouts were not convinced that he had a place in professional football. Joe was passed over in the first two rounds of the 1979 professional draft. Bill Walsh, the coach and general manager of the San Francisco 49ers, was convinced that Joe deserved a chance, so he drafted him in the third round.

His first year in professional football was a learning year for Joe. Walsh and the 49er quarterback coach, Sam Wyche, had Joe and rookie receiver Dwight Clark work on the fundamentals together. San Francisco had a record of 2-14 in 1979 and Joe only threw 23 passes the entire season. He was not to edge out starting quarterback Steven DeBerg until about midway through the next season.

Joe was still learning and remained cautious as he began mastering the Walsh way of football. Clark became his principal target for his passes and, by the end of the season, Joe had completed 176 passes for a total of 1,795 yards. His pass-

STATISTICS

Season	GP	PA	PC	Pct.	Yds.	Avg.	TD	Int.
1979	16	23	13	.565	96	4.2	1	0
1980	15	273	176	**.645**	1,795	6.6	15	9
1981	16	488	311	.637	3,565	7.3	19	12
1982	9	346	213	.616	2,613	7.6	**17**	11
1983	16	515	332	.645	3,910	7.6	26	12
1984	16	432	279	.646	3,630	8.4	28	10
1985	15	494	303	.613	3,653	7.4	27	13
1986	8	307	191	.622	2,236	7.3	8	9
1987	13	398	266	.668	3,054	7.7	**31**	13
1988	14	397	238	.599	2,981	7.5	18	10
1989	13	386	271	**.702**	3,521	**9.1**	26	8
1990	15	520	321	.617	3,944	7.6	26	16
1992	1	21	15	.714	126	6.0	2	0
1993	11	298	181	.607	2,144	7.2	13	7
1994	14	493	299	.606	3,283	8.3	16	9
Totals	192	5,292	3,409	.632	40,551	7.5	273	139

Notes: Boldface indicates statistical leader. GP = games played; PA = passes attempted; PC = passes completed; Pct. = percent completed; Yds. = yards; Avg. = average yards per attempt; TD = touchdowns; Int. = interceptions

completion percentage led the league at .645. The 49ers had improved as a team and finished 1980 with a 6-10 record.

The 49ers traded Steven De-Berg in the summer of 1981. Joe realized at this point that the 49er organization had put their faith in him. By the time the season started, he was more relaxed and less insecure than he had been at any point in his professional career. He was to have his first great season and also help lead San Francisco to the National Football Conference (NFC) West Division title and eventually Super Bowl XVI on January 24, 1982, against the Cincinnati Bengals. The 49ers won the game 26-21 after building a first half lead of 20-0, and Joe was named the most valuable player of the game.

Joe was proving himself as a quarterback who knew how to win the big games in the National Football League (NFL). Other players commented on how calm he appeared to be, no matter the situation in which he found himself. An NFL players' strike shortened the 1982 season and the San Francisco 49ers finished with a 3-6 record.

Because of his statistics as a quarterback, as well as the intangibles that were making him a winner, Joe was becoming a legitimate sports hero. This new celebrity status not only led to increased monies for playing football, but also to contracts to endorse products. Joe did not become caught up in this newfound celebrity status. His cool detachment served him well both on and off the field.

Continuing the Story

San Francisco went as far as the NFC Championship Game in 1983, but the team's bid to reach the Super Bowl once again was not to be. Joe had an excellent season, though, and was named to the NFL Pro Bowl team for that season. The 49ers bounced back the next year and reached Super Bowl XIX. Joe set a Super Bowl record for

NFL RECORDS
Most seasons with at least 3,000 yards passing, 7
Highest passing efficiency rating in a season, 112.4 (1989)
Highest completion percentage in a postseason game, .867 (1989)
Most touchdown passes in a Super Bowl game, 5 (1990)
Most yards passing in a Super Bowl game, 357 (1989)

HONORS AND AWARDS	
1982, 1985, 1990	NFL Super Bowl most valuable player
1982, 1984-86, 1989-90, 1993-94	NFL Pro Bowl Team
1989	Associated Press NFL Player of the Year
	Associated Press NFL Offensive Player of the Year
	United Press International NFC Offensive Player of the Year
	Professional Football Writers of American NFL Player of the Year
	Sporting News NFL Player of the Year
	Bell Trophy
	Football News NFC Player of the Year
	Pro Football Weekly NFL Offensive Player of the Year
	Football Digest NFL Player of the Year
	Sporting News NFL All-Star Team
	All-NFL Team
	Associated Press NFL All-Pro Team
	United Press International All-NFC Team
	Professional Football Writers of America NFL All-Pro Team
	Associated Press Male Athlete of the Year
	Sporting News Sportsman of the Year
1990	*Sports Illustrated* Sportsman of the Year
2000	Inducted into Pro Football Hall of Fame

passing with a total of 331 yards in San Francisco's 38-16 victory over the Miami Dolphins. Once again, Joe was named most valuable player.

The 49ers did not make it back to the Super Bowl until 1988. Joe suffered a serious injury in 1986, when he ruptured a disk and had to undergo spinal surgery. This could have been a career-ending injury for many players, but Joe decided not to give up and endured an extensive rehabilitation program. Against his physician's recommendation, he rejoined the team after only fifty-five days from the date of the injury.

Joe was never considered big for a quarterback at 6 feet 2 inches and 195 pounds, but he proved himself tougher than anyone could have imagined. The 49ers won the 1988 Super Bowl under Joe's leadership, even though during the season he had to have cortisone treatment for swelling in his right elbow. Always at his best under pressure, Joe proved himself a remarkable player and an inspiration to his teammates. The 49ers won the Super Bowl again in 1989 and

1990. The latter was a 55-10 victory over the Denver Broncos.

Joe was forced to miss the 1991 season after undergoing elbow surgery on October 9, 1991, to replace a torn tendon in his right elbow. He was traded to the Kansas City Chiefs and was with them for the last three seasons of his career, 1992-1994. Joe was again selected to the Pro Bowl for the 1993 and 1994 seasons. He was voted to the Pro Bowl eight times, which was a league record for a quarterback at the time. In 1994 Joe became only the fifth quarterback to pass for more than 40,000 yards in a career. He retired at the end of the 1994 season and was inducted into the Pro Football Hall of Fame in 2000. At the time of his retirement, Joe ranked fourth in career passing yardage (40,551 yards), attempts (5,391), and passing touchdowns (273). His 3,409 completions ranked third highest of all time, and his career passing rating of 92.3 ranked second highest of all time.

Summary

Joe Montana demonstrated throughout his professional career a unique drive that did not allow him or his team to fail. He overcame more than most players would have been willing to endure, and he did it with a special poise. Joe was a superstar who truly earned that accolade. He can rightfully be considered one of the great quarterbacks of all time.

Michael Jeffrys

Additional Sources:

Appleman, Marc. *Joe Montana.* Boston: Little, Brown, 1991.

Kavanaugh, Jack. *Sports Great Joe Montana.* Hillside, N.J.: Enslow, 1992.

Montana, Joe. "Joe Cool: My Four NFL Titles." *Sports Illustrated* 84, no. 3 (January 22, 1996): 14-18.

Reilly, Rick. "Back in the Groove." *Sports Illustrated* 70, no. 1 (January 9, 1989): 37-39.

Wiener, Paul. *Joe Montana.* New York: Chelsea House, 1995.

HELEN WILLS MOODY

Sport: Tennis

Born: October 6, 1905
    Centerville, California
Died: January 1, 1998
    Carmel, California

Early Life

Helen Newington Wills was born on October 6, 1905, in Centerville, California. Her parents were Dr. and Mrs. Clarence Wills. When she was very young, the family moved to Berkeley, California, where Helen was raised in a privileged social environment.

She learned tennis as a small child from her father, and as a present for her fourteenth birthday, she was given a membership in the Berkeley Tennis Club. Soon, she was playing every day, receiving help from the volunteer coach at the Club, William Fuller, who also arranged matches for her. Next, she started entering local tournaments and was soon winning them all.

The Road to Excellence

In 1921, when Helen was fifteen, she was sent East to play in the National Junior Tournament for girls 18 and under and to play on the women's circuit. She won the National Junior Championship and did extremely well in the other tournaments. Her career as an outstanding tennis player had begun.

The next year, 1922, Helen again won the National Junior Singles title and also won the National Junior Doubles with Helen Hooker. In the United States National Championship singles she reached the finals, where she was beaten by the defending champion, Molla B. Mallory. The defeat bothered Helen and motivated her to practice even harder when she returned to California. However, she did win the United States National Championship doubles title paired with Marion Z. Jessup. At the end of the year, when the United States Lawn Tennis Association (USLTA) released the rankings of the top ten women, seventeen-year-old Helen was rated third.

In 1923, Helen won the U.S. National

Helen Wills Moody, who won eight Wimbledon titles, in 1938.

Championship singles title, beating Mallory in the finals, and earned the number-one ranking. She was also selected as a member of the inaugural U.S. Wightman Cup team to play in an annual match between the top women players of the United States and England.

By this time the press had given Helen Wills the nickname "Miss Poker Face" for her incredible concentration on the court coupled with her expressionless behavior. They soon had to call her "Queen Helen," because for the next fifteen years she was the outstanding figure in women's tennis.

The Emerging Champion

In 1924, Helen for the first time traveled overseas and played at Wimbledon. She reached the finals, where she lost in three sets to the best British player, Kitty McCane, but she won the doubles title playing with Hazel Wightman, donor of the Wightman Cup. Then she and Wightman went to Paris for the 1924 Olympic Games, where Helen won two gold medals, one in singles and one in doubles paired with Wightman.

Returning home to America, Helen accomplished a "hat trick" by winning all three titles at the United States National Championships: the singles, the doubles with Wightman, and the mixed doubles with Vincent Richards. When the rankings came out for 1924, Helen was number one again.

Continuing the Story

From then on Helen's record was amazing. She won the United States National Championship singles five more times—in 1925, 1927, 1928, 1929, and 1931; she did not enter the 1926, 1930, and 1932 tournaments. In her last year in the U.S. Championship singles, 1933, she played in her most controversial match. Losing in the finals to her perennial rival, Helen Jacobs, she claimed she was ill and defaulted. Critics still wonder if she pretended to be sick to avoid outright defeat.

MAJOR CHAMPIONSHIP VICTORIES AND FINALS	
1922, 1924, 1926, 1928	U.S. National Championship doubles (with Marion Zinderstein Jessup; with Hazel Wightman; with Mary K. Browne)
1922, 1933	U.S. National Championship finalist
1923-25, 1927-29, 1931	U.S. National Championship
1924	Wimbledon finalist
1924, 1927, 1930	Wimbledon doubles (with Wightman; with Elizabeth Ryan)
1924, 1928	U.S. National Championship mixed doubles (with Vincent Richards; with John B. Hawkes)
1927-30, 1932-33, 1935, 1938	Wimbledon
1929	Wimbledon mixed doubles (with Francis T. Hunter)
1928-30, 1932	French Championship
1930, 1932	French Championship doubles (with Ryan)

OTHER NOTABLE VICTORIES	
1923, 1927, 1929, 1931-32, 1938	On winning U.S. Wightman Cup team
1924	Olympic Gold Medal Olympic Gold Medal doubles (with Wightman)

Helen won the U.S. National Championship doubles title two more times, once with Wightman as partner again and another time with Mary K. Browne. In 1928, she won another mixed doubles title with John B. Hawkes.

At Wimbledon, Helen Wills won the singles championship eight times. Her record of eight wins, which she had held since 1938, was not broken until 1990, when Martina Navratilova won her ninth Wimbledon singles title. After a two-year layoff between 1935 and 1937, Helen Wills competed at Wimbledon for the last time in 1938, and she defeated her rival, Helen Jacobs, in the final. Helen's victory after her long layoff earned her the Comeback Player of the Year Award.

In the French Championships, she won the singles three times and the doubles twice, both times with Elizabeth Ryan as a partner, and she played on the Wightman Cup teams ten times, serving as captain in 1930 and 1932.

Helen Wills married Fred Moody, a California stock broker, in 1929. In 1937, they were divorced, and she married Aidan Roark, a writer and polo player. When she retired from tennis in 1938, she participated in very few events connected with the game. She was an accomplished artist whose works were exhibited in galleries all over the world. She also wrote several books, the most well-known being her autobiography, *Fifteen-thirty: The Story of a Tennis Player* (1937). Later, she retired to live a quiet, private life in California.

HONORS AND AWARDS

1923-31	Nationally ranked number one
1927-33, 1935, 1938	Ranked number one in the world
1935	Associated Press Female Athlete of the Year
1938	Comeback Player of the Year
1959	Inducted into National Lawn Tennis Hall of Fame
1981	Inducted into Bay Area [California] Sports Hall of Fame

MILESTONES

U.S. Wightman Cup team (1923-25, 1927-32, 1938)
U.S. Wightman Cup team captain (1930, 1932)
30 Grand Slam titles

Summary

Helen Wills Moody competed for eighteen years, and for most of those years she dominated women's tennis, winning thirty national and international championships. Between 1927 and 1933 she did not lose a set in singles; she won 180 matches in a row until the default to Helen Jacobs at the U.S. Championships. The USTA listed her in its Top Ten rankings nine times, seven of those years at number one. In world rankings she was number one for nine years. Some tennis experts rate her as the most controlled champion the game has ever seen. In 1959, the National Lawn Tennis Hall of Fame inducted Helen, calling her "the greatest woman player in the annals of lawn tennis."

Joanna Davenport

Additional Sources:

Engelmann, Larry. *The Goddess and the American Girl: The Story of Suzanne Lenglen and Helen Wills.* New York: Oxford University Press, 1988.

Jacobs, Helen H. *Gallery of Champions.* New York: A. S. Barnes, 1949.

Wills, Helen. *Fifteen-thirty: The Story of a Tennis Player.* New York: Charles Scribner's Sons, 1937.

WARREN MOON

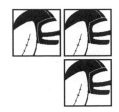

Sport: Football

Born: November 18, 1956
 Los Angeles, California

Early Life

Harold Warren Moon was born on November 18, 1956, in a rough, racially mixed neighborhood in Los Angeles, California. When Warren was seven, his father died, leaving Warren the only male in a household that included his mother, Pat, and six sisters. Warren quickly learned about responsibility. His mother and sisters taught him to cook, sew, and iron his own clothes. Outside the house, he contributed to the family's finances by working as a paper boy and, later, in a restaurant.

The Road to Excellence

As a youngster, Warren demonstrated a talent for throwing a football. His first involvement in organized football was in the Pop Warner League. Although he also enjoyed other sports, when it came time to enter Hamilton High School, he decided that he would play only football. Warren was a three-year letterman at Hamilton and was the team's starting quarterback in both his junior and senior years. Following his senior season, he was selected All-City most valuable player and named a high-school All-American.

Although Warren was recruited by several major colleges, none recruited him as a quarterback. This disturbed him. He could not help but wonder if it was because he was an African American. Although he was disappointed, he was also determined to destroy the myth that African Americans could not play quarterback. Eventually, Warren enrolled at West Los Angeles Junior College. There, he believed, he would have a chance to prove the major colleges wrong.

After just one year of junior college, Warren was offered a football scholarship to the University of Washington. Head coach Don James was so impressed by Warren's ability that after only a few weeks of practice, he named Warren the starting quarterback, ahead of the incumbent senior.

With Warren at quarterback, the Huskies changed from perennial losers to conference contenders. As a senior, he led the Huskies to a 27-20 upset victory over the University of Michigan in the 1978 Rose Bowl. For his part, he was named the game's most valuable player and Pacific Eight Conference Player of the Year.

The Emerging Champion

Even after Warren's outstanding senior year at Washington, no National Football League (NFL) team showed serious interest in drafting him. Again, he wondered if he was being judged as a quarterback or as an African American quarterback. He decided not to wait for the NFL draft, instead opting to sign a professional contract with the Edmonton Eskimos of the Canadian Football League (CFL).

In the CFL, where the playing field is longer and wider than in U.S. football, the game favors mobile, strong-armed quarterbacks. In this setting, Warren was nothing short of sensational. During his six seasons with the Eskimos, he passed for more than 20,000 yards and led his team to five consecutive Grey Cup championships. In doing so, Warren finally began to gain the recognition he deserved. By 1983, teams from both the NFL and the new United States Football League were trying to woo Warren back to the States. Finally, on February 3, 1984, he accepted a five-year, $6 million contract from the Oilers that made him the highest-paid player in professional football.

Oilers fans, however, were a little slow to accept the new quarterback. After all, he was succeeding Dan Pastorini and Ken Stabler, two popular players. In his first season in a Houston uniform, Warren started all sixteen games and completed 259 of 450 passes for a then-club record of 3,338 yards and 12 touchdowns. His accomplishments earned him All-NFL Rookie team honors.

Success with the Oilers, however, was not to come easily. Midway through the 1986 season, after two years of turmoil and a constant on-the-field pounding, Warren openly questioned the Oilers' conservative offensive game plan. Head coach Jerry Glanville listened to Warren's concerns and, surprisingly, agreed. Glanville totally revamped the offense for the final seven games of the 1986 season, emphasizing the pass. The team, which had won just one game in its first eight, went on to win four of its final seven. Warren finished the season with a streak of 66 completions without an interception.

The Oilers continued to build their offense around Warren's passing and advanced to the playoffs the next three seasons. Warren's consistently great play earned him a spot in the Pro Bowl every year from 1988 to 1995.

In 1990, under the direction of new head coach Jack Pardee, the Oilers introduced a new scheme called the run-and-shoot offense. The run-and-shoot, which employs four wide receivers and a single running back, was tailor-made for a passing quarterback like Warren. He responded by leading the league in pass attempts (584), completions (362), and yards gained (4,689).

The following season, Warren set an NFL single-season record for completions (404) and attempts (655). He again ranked first in total passing yards (4,690) and became only the third NFL quarterback to record back-to-back 4,000-yard seasons. Although he was injured and missed five games during the 1992 season, Warren still earned Pro Bowl selection for the fifth consecutive time.

Continuing the Story

On December 16, 1990, after watching Warren tear apart the Kansas City Chiefs' defense for 527 passing yards, Hall of Fame coach Sid Gillman said that he felt Warren was possibly "the best ever." This was high praise from a coach who had seen many outstanding performers.

Warren's career has always reflected a balanced commitment to football excellence and community service. In 1989, he founded the Crescent Moon Foundation to assist disadvantaged youngsters and the homeless in Houston. When an area church needed more than $200,000 to complete a new community center, Warren donated the entire amount. A tireless worker for charity, he was recognized in 1989 as

STATISTICS

Season	GP	PA	PC	Pct.	Yds.	Avg.	TD	Int.
1984	16	450	259	57.6	3,338	7.42	12	14
1985	14	377	200	53.1	2,709	7.19	15	19
1986	15	488	256	52.5	3,489	7.15	13	**26**
1987	12	368	184	50.0	2,806	7.63	21	18
1988	11	294	160	54.4	2,327	7.91	17	8
1989	16	464	280	60.3	3,631	7.83	23	14
1990	15	**584**	**362**	62.0	**4,689**	8.03	**33**	13
1991	16	**655**	**404**	61.7	**4,690**	7.16	23	**21**
1992	11	346	224	64.7	2,521	7.29	18	12
1993	15	520	303	58.3	3,485	6.70	21	21
1994	15	601	371	61.7	4,264	7.09	18	19
1995	16	606	377	62.2	4,228	6.98	33	14
1996	8	247	134	54.3	1,610	6.52	7	9
1997	15	528	313	59.3	3,678	6.97	25	16
1998	10	258	145	56.2	1,632	6.33	11	8
1999	1	3	1	33.3	20	6.67	0	0
2000	2	34	15	44.1	208	6.12	1	1
Totals	208	6,823	3,988	58.4	49,325	7.23	291	233

Notes: Boldface indicates statistical leader. GP = games played; PA = passes attempted; PC = passes completed; Pct. = percent completed; Yds. = yards; Avg. = average yards per attempt; TD = touchdowns; Int. = interceptions

NFL RECORDS

First to attempt 655 passes, single season
First to complete 404 passes, single season

HONORS AND AWARDS

1977	Pacific Eight Conference Player of the Year
1978	Rose Bowl most valuable player
1983	CFL Most Outstanding Player
1988-95	NFL Pro Bowl Team
1990	United Press International AFC Offensive Player of the Year

1998 while with the Seahawks, he passed for a total of 5,310 yards and 36 touchdowns. Warren spent the 1999 and 2000 seasons with the Kansas City Chiefs and entered his twenty-second professional football year and sixteenth in the NFL in 2000. He retired at the end of the 2000 season.

Summary

Warren Moon had to prove himself in Canadian football before he got the chance to lead an NFL team. When he returned to the United

the outstanding "citizen athlete" and was named the NFL's Man of the Year.

By the 1993 season, though, Houston management had come to believe that Warren was slowing down. When the season opened, he found himself relegated to the bench. The Oilers got off to a slow start behind young Cody Carlson, however, and Warren soon returned to the starting lineup. The move seemed to revitalize the team, which finished the season with a long winning streak and advanced to the playoffs. Warren was clearly not yet over the hill, and he was named to his sixth consecutive Pro Bowl team. After the end of the season, however, the SNFL's new salary cap, traded him to the Minnesota Vikings.

In his first season with the Vikings, Warren passed for 4,264 yards, led the Vikings into the playoffs, and was chosen to his seventh straight Pro Bowl. In 1995 he had his second straight 4,000-yard season, appeared in his eighth consecutive Pro Bowl, and set a number of Viking franchise records, including touchdown passes in one season. Warren continued with the Vikings until 1997, when he moved to the Seattle Seahawks. In 1997 and

Warren Moon of the Kansas City Chiefs playing in his next-to-last game in October, 2000.

AP/Wide World Photos

1921

States, however, he showed beyond a doubt that he was one of the most talented players of his generation, in the process helping to eliminate a long-standing prejudice against African American quarterbacks. By the year 2000, it was clear from the number of African American quarterbacks in the NFL that Warren's work had indeed cleared the way for others to follow him.

Joe Horrigan

Additional Sources:

Gutman, Bill. *Great Quarterbacks of the NFL*. New York: Pocket, 1993.

Lieber, Jill. "NFL Plus/Inside the NFC Central." *Sports Illustrated* 81, no. 24 (December 12, 1994): 104-108.

Weisman, Larry. "Careers Come to Pass Moon on Culpepper: 'A Good Kid.'" *USA Today*, August 1, 2000, p. 12C.

ARCHIE MOORE
Archibald Lee Wright

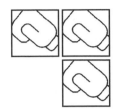

Sport: Boxing

Born: December 13, 1913 (or 1916)
   Benoit, Mississippi
Died: December 9, 1998
   San Diego, California

Early Life

Archibald Lee Wright was born on December 13, in either 1913 or 1916, depending upon whether one believes the testimony of his mother or of Archie himself. Archie was born into a poor family who made their home in Benoit, Mississippi. His father made a little money working on a local farm, but, throughout Archie's early childhood, the family struggled to make ends meet.

When Archie was still very young, his parents separated and, along with his older sister, he moved to St. Louis, Missouri, where he was raised by his aunt, from whom he acquired the surname Moore. Unfortunately, while attending Lincoln

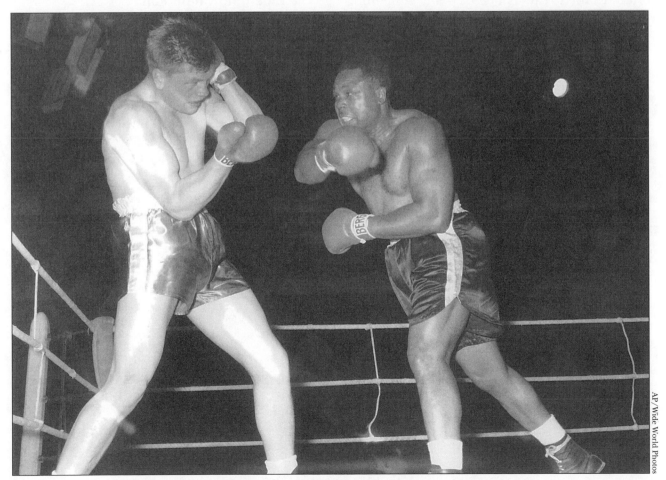

Archie Moore (right) won this 1957 bout against Belgian Alain Cherville.

High School in St. Louis, young Archie soon became involved in petty crime. He eventually ended up in reform school.

The Road to Excellence

Archie's early experiences with authority changed his entire outlook on life. After spending nearly two years at reform school, he returned to the outside world utterly determined to make something of himself. Unfortunately, during the Great Depression of the early 1930's, jobs were extremely scarce. As a result, Archie decided to join the Civilian Conservation Corps (CCC).

Archie was an eager seventeen-year-old, and he worked hard on numerous CCC projects. All his hard physical labor paid off, and Archie became supremely fit and strong. It was while working with the CCC that Archie first became involved with boxing. He had a few amateur contests, all of which he won. Archie saw that boxing offered him a real chance of doing something positive with his life. Consequently, he put all his energy into becoming a prizefighter.

Following a successful amateur career, Archie had his first professional bout in 1935, an impressive two-round victory over "Piano Man" Jones. Initially fighting as a middleweight, Archie rapidly discovered that his natural fighting weight was as a light heavyweight. Archie developed his professional boxing skills in fights in the St. Louis

area, where he was extremely successful, winning all but four of his forty-eight contests up to 1938.

In 1938, Archie moved to the West Coast in order to further his career. As he became more well known, Archie was nicknamed the "Old Mongoose," as a result of his canny defensive style and explosive punching power. Despite continued success in the ring, Archie was persistently pre\vented from getting a shot at the world light-heavyweight title. He was even forced to go to Australia to fight when he was refused important bouts in the United States.

Archie often became disillusioned with his managers, who consistently failed to arrange title fights for him. As a result, he frequently changed managers. This lack of continuity among his entourage was another reason why, although he was the number-one contender throughout the 1940's, Archie had to wait until 1952 for a shot at the world light-heavyweight crown.

The Emerging Champion

On December 17, 1952, in St. Louis, Archie fought for the world title against the champion, Joey Maxim. Even this long-overdue contest only came about because Archie agreed to receive a paltry $800 for the fight, with Maxim securing $100,000. Despite his advancing years, Archie outpointed Maxim to fulfill his dream. At last, and at the age of thirty-nine, Archie was light-heavyweight champion of the world.

RECOGNIZED WORLD LIGHT HEAVYWEIGHT CHAMPIONSHIPS

Date	Location	Loser	Result
Dec. 17, 1952	St. Louis, Mo.	Joey Maxim	15th-round win by decision
June 24, 1953	Ogden, Utah	Joey Maxim	15th-round win by decision
Jan. 27, 1954	Miami, Fla.	Joey Maxim	15th-round win by decision
Aug. 11, 1954	New York City, N.Y.	Harold Johnson	14th-round technical knockout
June 22, 1955	New York City, N.Y.	Carl (Bobo) Olson	3d-round knockout
June 5, 1956	London, England	Yolande Pompey	10th-round technical knockout
Sept. 20, 1957	Los Angeles, Calif.	Tony Anthony	7th-round technical knockout
Dec. 10, 1958	Montreal, Canada	Yvon Durelle	11th-round knockout
Aug. 12, 1959	Montreal, Canada	Yvon Durelle	3d-round knockout
June 10, 1961	New York City, N.Y.	Giulio Rinaldi	15th-round win by decision

RECOGNIZED WORLD HEAVYWEIGHT CHAMPIONSHIPS

Date	Location	Loser	Result
Sept. 21, 1955	New York City, N.Y.	Archie Moore (Rocky Marciano, winner)	9th-round knockout
Nov. 30, 1956	Chicago, Ill.	Archie Moore (Floyd Patterson, winner)	5th-round knockout

Although Archie was a popular champion, few expected him to retain his title for any length of time. Most people believed the Old Mongoose was simply too old. Archie, however, was not going to give up the title easily, after it had taken him nearly seventeen years to win it. Archie's extended boxing apprenticeship had developed him into a skillful strategist, which, in conjunction with his devastating punching power, enabled him to dominate his weight division for more than ten years.

Archie's first two defenses of the world title were against Joey Maxim, the former champion. Both bouts ended in points victories for Archie. Between 1954 and 1961, Archie went undefeated in eight title defenses and won numerous nontitle bouts. Indeed, Archie so dominated the light-heavyweight division that he, unsuccessfully and perhaps misguidedly, challenged for the heavyweight title, first against Rocky Marciano in 1955, then against Floyd Patterson in 1956.

One of Archie's most memorable fights was his titanic struggle against the Canadian Yvon Durelle in December, 1958. Archie was floored three times in the fourth round, and both fighters hit the canvas four times before Archie finally knocked out Durelle in the eleventh round. The rematch, eight months later, proved an anticlimax, with Archie winning easily in three rounds.

Continuing the Story

Archie's last title defense came in June, 1961, when he defeated the Italian Giulio Rinaldi. Archie never lost the light-heavyweight title in the ring. It was only inactivity that cost him his crown, when in February, 1962, the New York state and European boxing commissions stripped him of the title. At that point in time, he was the oldest world boxing champion of all time.

Archie retired after a third-round knockout over a wrestler, Mike DiBiase, in March, 1963. Having already starred in the film *The Adventures of Huckleberry Finn* in 1960, Archie continued to

---

STATISTICS

Bouts, 215
Knockouts, 129
Bouts won by decision, 54
Knockouts by opponents, 7
Bouts lost by decision, 13
Bouts lost by fouls, 2
Draws, 9
No contests, 1

RECORDS

Scored 129 knockouts as a professional, 145 overall—both current world records
At 48 years 51 days of age, the oldest professional boxer ever to hold any world title

HONORS AND AWARDS

1958	Neil Trophy
1966	Inducted into *Ring* magazine Boxing Hall of Fame
1987	Rocky Marciano Memorial Award
1990	Inducted into International Boxing Hall of Fame

---

do more film and television work. He also worked with youth and amateur boxers and trained and advised George Foreman during his career. The Old Mongoose must have been especially helpful during Foreman's comeback, for more than any other boxer, Archie Moore was adept at using an old head to defeat a younger opponent.

Summary

Archie Moore went astray early in his life but had the strength of character to bounce back. He discovered his talent for boxing and became determined to use his physical skills and mental ability to the utmost in order to make himself the best boxer he could possibly be. Despite numerous setbacks in his career, Archie eventually triumphed and became one of the greatest champions that professional boxing has ever seen.

David L. Andrews

Additional Sources:

Douroux, Marilyn G. *Archie Moore—the Ole Mongoose: The Authorized Biography of Archie Moore, Undefeated Light Heavyweight Champion of the World.* Boston: Branden, 1991.

Moore, Archie. *The Archie Moore Story.* London: Nicholas Kaye, 1960.

Moore, Archie, and Leonard B. Pearl. *Any Boy Can: The Archie Moore Story.* Englewood Cliffs, N.J.: Prentice-Hall, 1971.

BOBBY MOORE

Sport: Soccer

Born: April 12, 1941
Barking, London, England

Early Life

Robert Frederick Moore was born on April 12, 1941, in Barking, London, England, within a stone's throw of Dagenham, the hometown of his future manager, Alf Ramsey. Bobby had a very happy childhood. Robert and Doris Moore never had a lot of money, but they made sure that they gave their only child every support and encouragement.

From an early age, Bobby dreamed of playing soccer for England. When Bobby played for Barking Primary School, no one could have imagined that the dreams of the little blond boy would one day come true.

The Road to Excellence

Although Bobby was a good schoolboy soccer player, he was by no means exceptional. Consequently, it was something of a surprise that West Ham United, the local professional team, offered him a chance to play for their schoolboy team.

As a schoolboy, Bobby showed more promise at cricket than at soccer. He even captained the South of England Schools' cricket team. It was still soccer, however, that captured Bobby's imagination. He was determined to make the grade.

At West Ham, Bobby's keen positional play impressed his coaches. He was not the quickest or most mobile of players, but his ability to read the game enabled him to avoid potentially dangerous situations that might have exposed his limitations.

Bobby played as a central defender for West Ham's reserve teams, and his intelligent play helped him progress toward a spot on the first team. He was even selected to play for the England Youth team. In June, 1958, Bobby signed as

Bobby Moore is carried by his teammates after winning the FIFA World Cup in 1966.

a professional. Three months later, at the age of seventeen, he made his professional debut for West Ham in a game against Manchester United.

The 1960-1961 season saw Bobby establish

himself on the West Ham first team. Through sheer hard work, he had become a superb tackler. His tackling skill allowed him to steal the ball from opponents and then use the ball constructively in attack. By the time of his twenty-first birthday, Bobby was already one of the most accomplished defenders in the English game.

The Emerging Champion

Bobby's stylish and creative defensive play guaranteed his selection for England's national team. He won his first cap (an appearance on the national team) in May, 1962. International soccer posed no problems for Bobby, and he immediately starred in the England defense.

His rapid rise to the top was completed in May, 1963. An injury to the England captain, Jimmy Armfield, meant that at the tender age of twenty-two Bobby captained his country in a full international match against Czechoslovakia.

Bobby also found success at the club level. He was the captain of victorious West Ham teams in the 1964 Football Association and 1965 European Cup Winners' Cup finals. Both these games were played at Wembley Stadium, the home of the England international team. It was also at Wembley that Bobby was to experience the greatest triumph of his career.

In 1964, national team manager Alf Ramsey chose Bobby to lead England in the 1966 World Cup tournament, which was to be held in England. Although Bobby was quiet and reclusive in his private life, on the soccer field he was a dominating character. He constantly made himself available to receive the ball, and he acted with a calm authority at all times. These qualities made him a natural leader.

England's blond captain guided the team to the World Cup Final against West Germany. Perhaps Bobby's most valuable contribution during the tournament was the quick free kick he took to set up Geoff Hurst's equalizing goal. This intelligent piece of play paved the way for England's 4-2 victory over the West Germans.

On July 30, 1966, Bobby climbed the stairs to the Wembley Royal Box and joyfully accepted the World Cup Winners' Trophy from Queen Elizabeth II. Later he was voted Player of the Tournament by the sportswriters at the World Cup. England and Bobby were on top of the world.

Continuing the Story

In 1967, Bobby received the Order of the British Empire in recognition of his invaluable contribution to England's World Cup victory; he was still only twenty-five. The England captain was at his peak between 1966 and 1970, and he continued to star for both England and West Ham.

The 1970 World Cup finals, played in Mexico, provided Bobby with a further opportunity to display his immense talents. In a qualifying round game against Brazil, he played one of his best-ever games. That performance prompted the Brazilian star Pelé to describe Bobby as the finest defender in the world.

Ultimately, the Mexico tournament proved to be a disappointment for the England team and for Bobby. The team lost a heartbreaking quarterfinal game against an avenging West German team, and Bobby's participation was clouded by personal problems even before the tournament began.

Bobby was accused, wrongly, of stealing a bracelet from a shop in Colombia. The affair was blown up into an international incident. Throughout the affair, to his credit, Bobby conducted himself with the same calm integrity that he showed on the playing field.

After the 1970 World Cup, Bobby entered the twilight of his career. He played for England for the last time in 1973. That game against Italy was Bobby's 108th international appearance, at the time a world record.

In March, 1974, Bobby finally left West Ham and dropped down to the weaker Second Division to join Fulham. There he joined forces with

---

HONORS AND AWARDS

1964	English Football Association Cup champion English Footballer of the Year
1965	European Cup Winners' Cup champion
1966	World Cup champion World Cup Player of the Tournament British Broadcasting Corporation Sports Personality of the Year
1967	Order of the British Empire

MILESTONES

108 international appearances for England

his old England colleague Alan Mullery. These two seasoned professionals led Fulham to a miraculous appearance in the 1975 Football Association Cup Final. Unfortunately, the dream ended at Wembley as Fulham was beaten by, of all teams, West Ham.

Bobby retired in 1976 and had brief spells as the manager of non-league Oxford City and the professional club Southend United. Perhaps because of his reserved personality, Bobby did not relish the challenge of soccer management. After leaving soccer, Bobby wrote for national newspapers and helped to run a chain of pubs.

Summary

Bobby Moore became a great player because he was very dedicated and determined to get to the top. From an early age he identified his strengths and weaknesses and worked to perfect his game accordingly. As a youngster, Bobby had always dreamed of playing for England. In the end his career surpassed even his wildest dreams.

David L. Andrews

Additional Sources:

Henshaw, Richard. *The Encyclopedia of World Soccer.* Washington, D.C.: New Republic Books, 1979.

Hollander, Zander. *The American Encyclopedia of Soccer.* New York: Everett House, 1980.

Moore, Bobby. *My Soccer Story.* London: St. Paul, 1967.

Powell, Jeff. *Bobby Moore: The Authorized Biography.* London: Everest, 1976.

LENNY MOORE

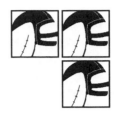

Sport: Football

Born: November 25, 1933
　　　Reading, Pennsylvania

Early Life

Leonard Edward Moore was born in Reading, Pennsylvania, on November 25, 1933. Reading is a small industrial and railroad city in the middle of Pennsylvania. Lenny was one of eight children in a hardworking family. Lenny's father was a laborer, and his mother was a cleaning lady.

The Road to Excellence

Lenny began his sports career at Reading High School, where his football coach was Andy Stopper, a man who would become his lifelong friend. Lenny excelled in football, basketball, and track and field because of his outstanding speed.

He played halfback and scored a record 22 touchdowns to lead the football team to a 9-1 record, the best record in the seventy-five-year history of the school. He played forward on the basketball team, which won the district championship. In the spring, Lenny ran the 100-yard dash, long-jumped, high-jumped, and was a member of the sprint relay teams.

Because of his speed and running ability, Lenny had offers of scholarships from twenty colleges. He chose Pennsylvania State University because it had an excellent football program and was near his home. Lenny played on the freshman team in 1953 because freshmen were not allowed to play on the varsity in the early 1950's. He moved up to varsity in 1954.

In his first season on the varsity,

Lenny was an immediate success, starting at offensive and defensive halfback, because players played both ways then. He led the team in rushing with 601 yards and scored 7 touchdowns.

During his junior season, Lenny was even better, leading Penn State to a 7-2 season. He was the first player in Penn State history to gain more

1929

than 1,000 yards in one season (1,082) and averaged 8 yards per carry. During Lenny's senior season, he was less successful but continued to lead the team in rushing. He received his college degree in the spring of 1956.

The Baltimore Colts decided to take a chance on this thin, 6-foot 1-inch, 190-pound young man because they needed a running back with speed who could also come out of the backfield and catch passes. He was their top draft choice in 1956.

Lenny proved to be an excellent choice, particularly when he teamed with free agent rookie quarterback Johnny Unitas. Lenny gained 649 yards rushing for a league-leading average of 7.5 yards per carry. He was named Rookie of the Year for the 1956 season.

The Colts dynasty began that season. Two years later, the Colts again won it all with players like Gene Marchetti, Gene "Big Daddy" Lipscomb, Alan Ameche, Raymond Berry, Unitas, and Lenny Moore. They won the league championship with a 9-3 record and faced the New York Giants in the 1958 championship game.

Many professional football experts consider that game to be the greatest in football history. Lenny began the game with a 60-yard pass reception, which led to the Colts' first touchdown. At the end of regulation, the game was tied 17-17 and went into sudden death.

The Giants received the kickoff but could not move the ball and punted to the Colts. The Colts then drove 80 yards for the winning touchdown and the National Football League (NFL) Championship.

The Colts won again in 1959. During those seasons, Lenny was used primarily as a pass receiver. He had outstanding years and made the All-Pro team in 1958, 1959, 1960, and 1961.

The Emerging Champion

Just as Lenny became an established professional star, disaster hit in the form of illness and injury. He missed the first two games of the 1963 season because he had to have an emergency appendix operation. Later in the season, a head injury caused him to miss five games. Altogether, he played in only seven games, gained 136 yards rushing, and caught 21 passes. Many experts believed his career was over.

In 1964, however, Lenny had his greatest season as a professional. He started the season as a second-team halfback, but when he was sent into the second game of the season against the powerful Green Bay Packers, he immediately caught a 58-yard touchdown bomb from Unitas. Later, he scored a 4-yard touchdown run to lead the Colts to a 21-20 victory over the heavily favored Packers.

The Colts offense came together behind Unitas and Lenny, and the team won 11 of their next 12 games. Lenny, who was used primarily as a running back, led the team with 584 yards rush-

STATISTICS

| Season | GP | Rushing | | | | Receiving | | | |
		Car.	Yds.	Avg.	TD	Rec.	Yds.	Avg.	TD
1956	12	86	649	**7.5**	8	11	102	9.3	1
1957	12	98	488	**5.0**	3	40	637	17.2	7
1958	12	82	598	**7.3**	7	50	938	18.8	7
1959	12	92	422	4.6	2	47	846	18.0	6
1960	12	91	374	4.1	4	45	936	20.8	9
1961	13	92	648	**7.0**	7	49	728	14.9	8
1962	10	106	470	4.4	2	18	215	11.9	2
1963	7	27	136	5.0	2	21	288	13.7	2
1964	14	157	584	3.7	**16**	21	472	22.5	3
1965	12	133	464	3.5	5	27	414	15.3	3
1966	13	63	209	3.3	3	21	260	12.4	0
1967	14	42	132	3.1	4	13	153	11.8	0
Totals	143	1,069	5,174	4.8	63	363	5,989	16.6	48

Notes: Boldface indicates statistical leader. GP = games played; Car. = carries; Yds. = yards; Avg. = average yards per carry or average yards per reception; TD = touchdowns; Rec. = receptions

HONORS AND AWARDS

1955	College All-American
1956	United Press International NFL Rookie of the Year
1957-61, 1964	*Sporting News* NFL Western Conference All-Star Team
1957, 1959-62, 1964-65	NFL Pro Bowl Team
1958-61, 1964	NFL All-Pro Team
1963	NFL All-Pro Team of the 1950's
1964	NFL Player of the Year Associated Press NFL Comeback Player of the Year Thorpe Trophy
1975	Inducted into Pro Football Hall of Fame Uniform number 24 retired by Indianapolis Colts

ing. More important, he scored a league-leading 16 touchdowns rushing and led the league in total touchdowns with 20 and in scoring with 120 points.

The Colts went on to a 12-2 season and the Western Conference Championship. Unfortunately, they lost the championship game to the Cleveland Browns 27-0.

Lenny was named as the Associated Press Comeback Player of the Year and as the league Player of the Year. He was also named to the All-Pro team and was selected to play in the Pro Bowl.

The 1964 season was a satisfying one for Lenny. He had overcome injury and illness to rise to the top of professional football and lead his team to the division championship.

Continuing the Story

Lenny played three more seasons with the Colts before he retired following the 1967 sea-son. His thirteen-year career was outstanding, both as a runner and as a pass receiver. He ran for 5,174 yards and caught 363 passes for 6,039 yards. Lenny scored a total of 113 touchdowns.

During his career, many honors came to Lenny. He was selected All-Pro five times and picked seven times for the Pro Bowl. His greatest honor came in 1975, when he was inducted into the Pro Football Hall of Fame. He was presented for induction by his old high school coach, Andy Stopper.

After his playing days were over, Lenny became one of the first African American announcers for CBS sports. He later was director of promotions for the Baltimore Colts until they moved to Indianapolis.

Lenny would go on to work in Juvenile Services for the State of Maryland. He and his wife, Edith, have nine children.

Summary

Lenny Moore came from a hardworking but poor family in Reading, Pennsylvania, to become a college and professional football star. He combined speed with good hand and running ability as few players had before. He became the model for professional football running backs of today.

C. Robert Barnett

Additional Sources:

Attner, Paul. "NFL: Football's One Hundred Greatest Players—Better than All the Rest." *The Sporting News* 223 (November 8, 1999): 58-59, 62.

Barber, Phil. "NFL: Football's One Hundred Greatest Players—The Hit Men." *The Sporting News* 223 (November 1, 1999): 12-16.

Pro Football Hall of Fame. http://www.pro footballhof.com.

PABLO MORALES

Sport: Swimming

Born: December 5, 1964
Chicago, Illinois

Early Life

The Cuban American Pablo Morales, Jr., was born on December 5, 1964, in Chicago, Illinois. Both his mother, Bianca, and father, Pablo Morales, Sr., emigrated to Chicago from their native Cuba in 1956. His father was a first-rate mechanic with Cadillac, but his first job in Chicago, when he spoke little English, was unloading railroad cars for sixty cents an hour.

In 1967, the Morales family moved to Santa Clara, California, home of the famed Santa Clara Swim Club, which had turned out more Olympic swimming champions than any other club. Pablo's mother wanted her children to take up swimming because she had nearly drowned in a miscalculated swim off Havana, in which she had overestimated her swimming stamina and ability. She had decided that this was not going to happen to her children. "My kids were in the pool before they were walking," she said. Pablo himself had early ambitions to be a success in sport.

Yet Santa Clara Swim Club coach George Haines remembers watching him through a fence when Haines went to the playground to watch his son Kyle. Kyle ran back and forth and young Pablo ran after him. He was quite knock-kneed, and Haines was sure he would never make it as any kind of an athlete.

The Road to Excellence

Entering the Santa Clara Swim Club under Haines and advancing there with Mitch Ivey, Pablo rapidly proved to be a fine swimmer and an athlete. In the national age-group rankings for the 100-meter butterfly, Pablo ranked number one at ten-and-under, eleven and twelve, thirteen and fourteen, and again at fifteen, sixteen, and seventeen. He grew to a lanky 6 feet 2 inches and

165 pounds. Pablo graduated from Ballarmine College Prep School in 1983. During his years there, Pablo swam in the Junior Olympic Nationals, placing first in the 100- and 200-meter butterfly and also placing in the 100- and 200-meter freestyle events. He went to the Soviet Union with the junior team in 1982 and again won two firsts in the butterfly. In 1983, he set a high school record for the fastest 100-meter butterfly ever

swum by a high school boy. The record he broke had belonged to Mark Spitz.

In his first year competing as a senior swimmer, he swam in United States Swimming's winter short-course Nationals, to finish a close second to Matt Gribble in the 100-meter butterfly and fifth in the 200. At the long-course outdoor event, he was again second to Gribble but worked his way up to second in the 200 and fourth in both the 400-meter individual medley races. He repeated his second-place 100 at the Pan-American Games and managed a first in the 200-meter butterfly in the Pan-Pacifics, a meet of teams from countries rimming the Pacific Ocean. In 1983, Pablo enrolled at Stanford, where he became the world's best butterflyer under his Stanford coach, Skip Kenney.

The Emerging Champion

Pablo's participation in the team sport water polo kept him interested when he might have succumbed to the monotony of training. Water polo is the swimmer's contact game, and it is very big in California high schools and colleges. Pablo was a regular each fall on the Stanford water polo team, which won the nationals in three of his four years on the team.

From the Pan-Pacifics through the Los Angeles 1984 Olympics and on to the Olympic trials for Seoul, South Korea, in 1988, Pablo was a brilliant, world-class swimmer who specialized in the 100-meter butterfly and the 400-meter medley relay (in which he swam the butterfly leg). On occasion, he was a big winner or high finisher in the finals of the individual medleys and the 200-meter butterfly. Pablo was principally a great sprinter and especially a short-course indoor sprinter in 25-yard pools, where his height, fast turns, and long push-offs on the turn walls gave him the edge. Pablo invariably led his races into the last lap, and only then did competitors such as Matt Gribble and Craig Beardsley

of the United States and Michael Gross of West Germany ever catch him.

Gribble was Pablo's greatest competition in the butterfly hundreds, often edging him out until the 1984 Olympic trials. Beardsley often beat him in the 200 until the Olympic trials, which were the biggest of Pablo's victories in both butterfly events. He also finished second in the 200-meter individual medley, beating such former world record holders as Jesse Vassallo and Bill Barrett. In the 1984 Olympics in Los Angeles, Pablo finished second and fourth to Michael Gross in the two butterfly distances, and second and fourth to Canadian world record holder Alex Baumann in the 200- and the 400-meter individual medleys. Pablo won his gold medal swimming the 100-meter butterfly leg on the 4×100 medley relay team. The other three Americans on the relay were Rick Carey, backstroke, Steve Lundquist, breaststroke, and Matt Biondi, freestyle. After the Olympics, Pablo was named American Swimmer of the Year.

Pablo always did well in the National Collegiate Athletic Association (NCAA) Championships in his four years at Stanford. He compiled

MAJOR CHAMPIONSHIPS

Year	Competition	Event	Place	Time
1983	Pan-American Games	100-meter butterfly	2d	54.62
		200-meter butterfly	6th	2:01.88
1984	Olympic Games	100-meter butterfly	Silver	53.23
		200-meter butterfly	4th	—
		200-meter individual medley	Silver	2:03.05
		4×100-meter medley relay	Gold	4:08.34
	NCAA Championships	100-yard butterfly	1st	47.02
		200-yard butterfly	1st	1:44.33
1985	NCAA Championships	100-yard butterfly	1st	46.52
		200-yard butterfly	1st	1:42.85
		200-yard individual medley	1st	1:46.08
		400-yard medley relay	1st	3:10.92
1986	World Championships	100-meter butterfly	1st	53.54
		200-meter individual medley	5th	2:03.88
		4×100-meter medley relay	1st	3:41.25
1986	NCAA Championships	100-yard butterfly	1st	46.37
		200-yard butterfly	1st	1:43.05
		200-yard individual medley	1st	1:45.43
		400-yard medley relay	1st	3:12.47
1987	NCAA Championships	100-yard butterfly	1st	46.47
		200-yard butterfly	1st	1:42.60
		200-yard individual medley	1st	1:45.42
		400-yard medley relay	1st	3:12.05

an impressive record, winning the 100-yard butterfly four times, the 200-yard butterfly four times, and the 200-yard individual medley three times. His eleven individual championship wins made him the most dominating influence in NCAA swimming history. He also swam on three winning Stanford medley relay teams. Pablo was a team leader and served as captain during his senior year.

Continuing the Story

For Pablo's swimming and academic accomplishments, he has won numerous awards, including the San Francisco Bay Area Sports Hall of Fame Athlete of the Year in 1984 and the prestigious Al Masters Award during his last two years at Stanford for the athlete attaining the highest standards of athletic performance, leadership, and academic performance. He was a two-time

Academic All-American and followed his graduation from Stanford in 1987 by enrolling in the Cornell Law School. Pablo's swimming career came to an end when he failed to make a second Olympic team in 1988. He was disappointed but felt it was time to change careers and work harder on his law studies. Pablo believes that every swim champion should defend and ultimately lose his athletic crowns in the water. He has no regrets because his brilliant swimming career ended with a loss. Ten years later, he was inducted into the International Swimming Hall of Fame.

Summary

Pablo Morales, one of Stanford's best scholar-athletes, went on to excel in the field of law. When one career ends at age twenty, it is a difficult adjustment to start another. Pablo is a wonderful example of this adjustment from being the best in the world to beginning anew in another field.

Buck Dawson

RECORDS

Set American records in the 100-yard and 200-yard butterfly, the 200-meter butterfly, and the 200-meter individual medley

World record in the 100-meter butterfly set at the Olympic trials (1984)

HONORS AND AWARDS

1984	Olympia Award
	Swimming World magazine Swimmer of the Year
	Athlete of the Year, Bay Area Sports Hall of Fame
1987	Sterling Award as the Outstanding Senior at Stanford University
1998	Inducted into International Swimming Hall of Fame

Additional Sources:

Levinson, David, and Karen Christenson, eds. *Encyclopedia of World Sport: From Ancient Times to Present.* Santa Barbara, Calif.: ABC-CLIO, 1996.

Mallon, Bill, and Ian Buchanan. *Quest for Gold: The Encyclopedia of American Olympians.* New York: Leisure Press, 1984.

Montville, Leigh. "Bravo, Pablo." *Sports Illustrated* 77, no. 5 (1992).

Wallechinsky, David. *The Complete Book of the Olympics.* Boston: Little, Brown and Company, 1991.

NOUREDDINE MORCELI

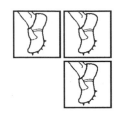

Sport: Track and field (long-distance runs)

Born: February 20, 1970
Tenes, Algeria

Early Life

Noureddine Morceli was born on February 20, 1970, one of nine children, six boys and three girls. His father worked in a building materials factory, and his mother was kept busy tending to the children. They were observant Muslims who practiced their religion seriously.

The other thing taken seriously in the household was running. At seven, Noureddine watched his older brother Abderrahmane place fourth in the 1,500 meters in the 1977 World Cup match in Dusseldorf, Germany. Noureddine grew up knowing that he wanted to run and believing that if he trained hard enough he could win any race. By the time he was eleven he had decided that he wanted to be world champion, and by twelve he had already run his first race. He ran a four-mile cross-country race on a beach, coming in fourth. Although he did not come in first, he knew that long-distance running would be his specialty. By the time he was fourteen, he could run for five hours.

The Road to Excellence

He took every race seriously. When, at sixteen, he had a bad race and placed sixth in the Algerian high school cross-country championships, he rededicated himself to his sport. He trained three times a day, until two weeks later he raced again and came in first. Again, he announced his intention of becoming the world champion. At seventeen, he nearly attained this goal when he placed second, behind Kenya's Kirochi, in the World Junior 1,500 meters.

Algerian Noureddine Morceli won the gold in the 1,500-meter run at the 1996 Olympics.

1935

After high school, Noureddine realized that he would need a better track if he were to achieve his goals. Speaking only limited English, with Arabic and French as his first two languages, he called coach Ted Banks at Riverside Community College in California. After giving Banks his athletic resume over the phone, he was invited to attend school in Riverside. He trained there for two years before leaving in 1990, when his community college track eligibility expired. By that time, however, at the age of twenty, he was ranked first in the world in the 1,500 meters. He was the youngest person to achieve that distinction.

His brother Abderrahmane took over as his coach and continued the rigorous training. In 1991 Noureddine won every race he entered. Early in the year in Seville, Spain, he won the indoor 1,500 meters, setting a world record. Nine days later he won the Indoor World Championships in the 1,500 meters. Six months later, on September 2, 1991, in Tokyo, Japan, he set a blistering pace in the 1,500 meters to win the Outdoor World Championships. That year established Noureddine as the man to beat.

He now set his sights on the Olympics. He entered the stadium in Barcelona, Spain, as the champion, having remained undefeated in both 1991 and 1992. Unfortunately, however, the gold eluded him. He struggled to keep his pace in a race filled with pushing and elbow throwing. The Kenyans boxed Noureddine in, making it impossible for him to run the race he had planned. He lost the race to Spanish runner Fermin Cacho and finished a disappointing seventh.

Despite the disappointment, Noureddine refused to let the loss truly defeat him. He returned to the rigors of training, hoping he would have his chance at Olympic gold again in four years.

The Emerging Champion

During the years between Olympics, Noureddine continued racing, winning, and setting

MAJOR CHAMPIONSHIPS			
Year	Competition	Place	Time
1,500 METERS			
1988	2d IAAF World Junior Championships	2d	3:46.93
1991	World Championships	1st	3:32.84
1992	Olympic Games	7th	3:41.70
1993	9th IAAF/Mobil Grand Prix Final	1st	3:31.60
	World Championships	1st	3:34.24
1994	7th IAAF World Cup in Athletics	1st	3:34.70
	10th IAAF/Mobil Grand Prix Final	1st	3:40.89
1995	IAAF/Mobil Grand Prix Final	1st	3:28.37
	World Championships	1st	3:33.73
1996	IAAF/MOBIL Grand Prix Final	2d	3:39.69
	Olympic Games	Gold	3:35.78
1997	World Championships	4th	3:37.37
CROSS COUNTRY			
1988	16th IAAF World Cross Country Championships	9th	24:45
1989	17th IAAF World Cross Country Championships	26th	27:05

world records. In 1995 he won his third consecutive world championship title in the 1,500 meters. He also established world records in the mile and the 3,000 meters. He said he hoped to own all the records, from 800 meters to the 10,000.

In the 1996 Olympic Games in Atlanta, he entered the stadium filled with confidence. Considered the greatest middle-distance runner at that time, he expected the others to be chasing him. During the race, however, Noureddine once again experienced difficulty. With only 400 meters left in the 1,500 meter race, Moroccan runner El Guerrouj surged forward to challenge Noureddine for the lead. Suddenly El Guerrouj's feet became tangled with Noureddine's and the Moroccan fell. Although Noureddine suffered a deep spike wound in his Achilles tendon, he continued running, pouring on speed and winning the race in three minutes, 35.78 seconds. Not only did he win the gold, but he achieved his fifty-third consecutive victory at 1,500 meters or the mile.

Continuing the Story

After the Olympics, Noureddine decided to take a much-needed break. In the interim, El Guerrouj filled the vacuum, winning the races that Noureddine had not entered and breaking Noureddine's records. In 1997, only days before Noureddine was to defend his title at the World Championships, one of his brothers died. He was not in peak psychological condition and, coming in fourth, suffered a stinging loss to his rival El Guerrouj.

His records continued to be toppled by El Guerrouj. Noureddine ended the 1998 season with only ten wins, but still he continued racing, refusing to retire. The next year, 1999, was another disappointing season, marked by a car crash in which Noureddine's car skidded off a road in Algeria and flipped over three times. He suffered bruises and cuts that required stitches. He was forced to discontinue his training and was unable to compete for over a month.

Not officially retired, he talked about racing in either the 1,500 or the 5,000 meters in the 2000 Olympic Games in Sydney. He no longer had the stamina, however, to beat the younger runners looking to establish their own world records. While contemplating whether to retire, he continued training in the mountains in both Algeria and the United States and spent more time with his wife, Swiss runner Patricia Bieri.

Summary

Noureddine Morceli dedicated himself to running while only a child, stating that he wanted to be the world champion. He never lost sight of that dream, pursuing it over many years and many miles. He endured a grueling training schedule in order to make the dream a reality. When he could not find proper facilities in Algeria, he left his home and came to the United States to find a suitable track. He established himself as the champion in the 1,500 meters and won race after race. In the Olympics, though, he struggled. He lost the 1992 competition but came back in 1996. During that race, although challenged and competing with an injury, he at last achieved his goal.

Deborah Service

Additional Sources:

Baxter, Kevin. "Not Running for Office as Olympics Approach." *Los Angeles Times*, May 17, 1992, p. 3.

Dupont, Kevin Paul. "Morceli Runs Down a Dream." *Boston Globe*, August 4, 1996, p. C7.

Post, Marty. "Prince of Times." *Runner's World* 28, no. 12 (December, 1993): 54.

"A Scream and a Prayer." *Sports Illustrated* 77 no. 5 (August 3, 1992): 46.

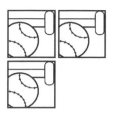

JOE MORGAN

Sport: Baseball

Born: September 19, 1943
Bonham, Texas

Early Life

Joe Leonard Morgan was born in Bonham, Texas, a small community north of Dallas, on September 19, 1943. Most of Joe's childhood, which he describes as an ordinary one, was spent in Oakland, California, where the Morgans moved in 1950.

His father, Leonard, always encouraged Joe to play ball and to develop his abilities to the fullest extent. The Morgans lived only a short walk from the old Oakland stadium. Joe and his father of-

Joe Morgan in 1975.

ten attended four or five games a week when the minor league Oakland Oaks were at home.

The Road to Excellence

Joe, who is 5 feet 7 inches in height and usually played in the big leagues at a weight of about 160 pounds, was always somewhat small for his age but remained confident of success. In sandlot games, he was often the first player chosen.

Joe also played on organized teams in Little League and in the Young American League, and in the Connie Mack, Babe Ruth, and American Legion leagues. He played shortstop for his Castlemont High School team, but his favorite big leaguers were both second basemen—Jackie Robinson and, especially, Nellie Fox, a small man who made good in a big way with the Chicago White Sox during the 1950's.

Joe attended junior college for one year in Oakland. There he attracted the attention of big-league scouts, who saw beyond his small size to appreciate his talent, his aggressive play, and his self-confidence. Joe shared his mother's respect for education and would eventually return to college to complete his degree after he retired. The chance to sign a contract with Houston in the National League in November, 1962, was too much for Joe to pass up.

In only two years, Joe climbed through the minor leagues. The first year was divided between Houston farm teams in Modesto, California, and Durham, North Carolina. After an outstanding

STATISTICS

Season	GP	AB	Hits	2B	3B	HR	Runs	RBI	BA	SA
1963	8	25	6	0	1	0	5	3	.240	.320
1964	10	37	7	0	0	0	4	0	.189	.189
1965	157	601	163	22	12	14	100	40	.271	.418
1966	122	425	121	14	8	5	60	42	.285	.391
1967	133	494	136	27	11	6	73	42	.275	.411
1968	10	20	5	0	1	0	6	0	.250	.350
1969	147	535	126	18	5	15	94	43	.236	.372
1970	144	548	147	28	9	8	102	52	.268	.396
1971	160	583	149	27	**11**	13	87	56	.256	.407
1972	149	552	161	23	4	16	**122**	73	.292	.435
1973	157	576	167	35	2	26	116	82	.290	.493
1974	149	512	150	31	3	22	107	67	.293	.494
1975	146	498	163	27	6	17	107	94	.327	.508
1976	141	472	151	30	5	27	113	111	.320	**.576**
1977	153	521	150	21	6	22	113	78	.288	.478
1978	132	441	104	27	0	13	68	75	.236	.385
1979	127	436	109	26	1	9	70	32	.250	.376
1980	141	461	112	17	5	11	66	49	.243	.373
1981	90	308	74	16	1	8	47	31	.240	.377
1982	134	463	134	19	4	14	68	61	.289	.438
1983	123	404	93	20	1	16	72	59	.230	.403
1984	116	365	89	21	0	6	50	43	.244	.351
Totals	2,649	9,277	2,517	449	96	268	1,650	1,133	.271	.427

Notes: Boldface indicates statistical leader. GP = games played; AB = at bats; 2B = doubles; 3B = triples; HR = home runs; RBI = runs batted in; BA = batting average; SA = slugging average

year at San Antonio in the Class AA Texas League, Joe became a big leaguer in 1965.

The Emerging Champion

One of the big influences in Joe's success as Houston's new second baseman was his hero, Nellie Fox, who was finishing his own career in Houston and who unselfishly helped his replacement. Joe believes that the best tip he got was to keep a positive attitude. For example, a player in a batting slump could still contribute to his team with heads-up play in the field.

A left-handed batter, Joe had a good eye and was patient at the plate. Between his hits and walks, he was often on base more than 250 times a season. He stole many bases and was a team leader in runs scored. At second, Joe had good range and became a master at making the double play.

Soon after Joe became a major leaguer, he married his high school sweetheart, Gloria Stewart. They had two daughters, Lisa and Angela.

After the 1971 season, Joe was traded to the Cincinnati Reds. Cincinnati already had the nucleus of a fine team, but Joe would improve the Reds at second base and also add speed on the base paths, something the team had lacked.

Joe soon won over Cincinnati fans with his competitiveness and enthusiasm and with his success at bat, in the field, and on the bases. In Joe's first season in Cincinnati, the Reds went to the World Series. Cincinnati won the World Series in both 1975 and 1976, and Joe's contribution to the Reds' success was recognized when he was voted the National League most valuable player in both seasons.

Continuing the Story

While with the Astros, Joe had had two knee injuries, including one that had cost him almost an entire season. He also missed quite a few games one year while he was on Army Reserve duty. Usually, however, Joe missed few games. After 1977, Joe's performance began to decline, his batting slumped, and injuries became more frequent.

Joe returned to the Astros as a free agent in 1980. He then moved on to the San Francisco Giants for two years and to the Philadelphia Phillies in 1983. Although Joe was no longer at his peak,

1939

all three teams benefited from his leadership and still sound play. Joe concluded his career with the Oakland Athletics.

In retirement, Joe would remain in the Oakland area, where he had several business investments. He also would announce baseball on television, becoming one of the best analysts of the game. Joe was inducted into the National Baseball Hall of Fame in 1990.

Some experts rank Joe as one of the two or three top second basemen of all time. During his first six years with the Reds, Joe's performance might well have surpassed that of any other second baseman in major league history. No one who has ever played this position did as many things as well as Joe was able to do at his peak.

Besides being a five-time Gold Glove winner, he hit for average, hit with power, and ran the bases exceptionally well. He also provided leadership and an example for teammates with his aggressive and intelligent play. Joe always seemed to know how he could contribute to his team—when to hit behind the runner, when to steal a base, where to position himself in the field, when to try for a sacrifice fly. The book Joe wrote for young ballplayers in 1976, *Baseball My Way*, made clear his approach. In the years after his playing days, Joe proved his abilities as a commentator by becoming a respected member of ESPN's broadcast team during the regular season. He has also appeared on NBC during the coverage of postseason play.

Summary

Joe Morgan played twenty full seasons in the big leagues. His greatest years were in Cincinnati, where he gained recognition as baseball's most complete player. Joe was deservedly proud of this.

Lloyd J. Graybar

Additional Sources:

Cohen, Joel H. *Joe Morgan, Great Little Big Man.* New York: Putnam, 1978.

Herskowitz, Mickey. "Despite His Small Stature, Joe Morgan Was a Big Success." *Baseball Digest* 59, no. 7 (2000).

Morgan, Joe. *Baseball My Way.* New York: Atheneum, 1976.

_____. *Joe Morgan: A Life in Baseball.* New York: W. W. Norton, 1993.

MAJOR LEAGUE RECORDS
Most home runs by a second baseman, 266

HONORS AND AWARDS	
1966, 1970, 1972-79	National League All-Star Team
1972	All-Star Game most valuable player
1973-77	National League Gold Glove Award
1975-76	National League most valuable player *Sporting News* Major League Player of the Year Seagram's Seven Crowns of Sports Award
1990	Inducted into National Baseball Hall of Fame Uniform number 8 retired by Cincinnati Reds

BOBBY JOE MORROW

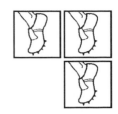

Sport: Track and field (sprints)

Born: October 15, 1935
Harlingen, Texas

Early Life

Bobby Joe Morrow was born on October 15, 1935, in Harlingen, Texas, a town situated at the southern tip of the state in the lower Rio Grande Valley, not far from the Mexican border. Bobby, however, was raised in nearby San Benito, Texas, on a cotton and carrot farm operated by his parents, Mr. and Mrs. Bob Floyd Morrow.

It was at San Benito High School where Bobby's athletic career began. There he played football and basketball and ran track. Track, though, was the sport in which he truly excelled. On the dirt track carved around the football field, Bobby ran the 100- and 220-yard dashes, occasionally the open 440, and legs on the 440 and mile relay teams.

During his high school career, Bobby won the Texas Schoolboy 100-yard dash championships in his junior and senior years and the 220-yard dash championship as a senior.

The Road to Excellence

Bobby credited his success in the sprints to Jake Watson, his high school track coach. Coach Watson's experiences as a sprinter in college, his knowledge about proper sprinting techniques, and his complete dedication to the sport of track and field helped Bobby develop sound running fundamentals and an intense desire to be the best. Coach Watson encouraged Bobby to continue running track in college, hinting of his excellent chances of representing the United States in the 1956 Summer Olympic Games to be held in Melbourne, Australia, in two years.

Every major college in Texas offered Bobby a track scholarship. After graduation, Bobby married his high school sweetheart, Jo Ann, and both decided to attend Abilene Christian College (ACC), a small liberal arts institution supported by members of the Church of Christ and located in Abilene, Texas. Their decision was twofold. ACC offered the type of religious education that Bobby desired, and the college had an excellent track program.

Bobby's addition to the ACC track team made a good track team even better. He was undefeated in the 100-yard dash his freshman year, and his time of 9.4 seconds was .1 of a second off the existing world record.

Bobby's sophomore track season, the Olympic year, was also successful. His record was 35-1,

his only loss being to Dave Sime of Duke University in the 100-yard dash. Sime's narrow win over the Texan motivated Bobby to work harder at practice each day. His hard work was rewarded when he defeated Sime by two yards in the 100-yard dash at a track meet in Bakersfield, California, two weeks before the Olympic trials that would determine who would make the United States Olympic team.

The Emerging Champion

Track coaches and athletes as well as sports journalists and fans began to sing the praises of Bobby Morrow. One such example was *Sports Illustrated,* a leading sports periodical, which put Bobby on its front cover. The magazine claimed that on any given day, at any distance up to 220 yards, Bobby was the equal of any sprinter in the world; it also predicted that, before the Olympics were over, Bobby would be ranked as the best. Oliver Jackson, ACC track coach, agreed that Bobby was the best sprinter in the world. Coach Jackson said he had never known anyone who wanted to win as much as Bobby did.

Bobby did win in the Olympic trials. He equaled the world record in the 100 meters as well as the American record in the 200 meters. To many people, Bobby seemed sure to become the first double sprint winner at the Olympic Games since Jesse Owens in 1936.

After the Olympic trials, however, Bobby experienced difficult times. Illness caused him to lose twenty pounds and prevented him from training

properly. His sprinting ability was now in question, and a medal in the Olympics was no longer considered a sure thing. Bobby's confidence was very low. He refused to participate in some pre-Olympic races in Australia because he could not stand to lose.

Continuing the Story

During the Olympics, Bobby did not lose. His renewed desire, dedication, and concentration contributed to a gold medal victory in the 100-meter dash. He added a second gold medal two days later and set a new Olympic record in the 200-meter dash. Later, Bobby added a third gold medal when he anchored the 400-meter relay and became the first man since Jesse Owens to win three gold medals.

Three Olympic gold medals did not end Bobby's track career. He returned to ACC to continue his education and that spring tied the world record in the 100-yard dash. Bobby was rewarded for his track accomplishments during the 1957 season by receiving the James E. Sullivan Memorial Award as the outstanding amateur athlete in the United States.

There were still some track goals that Bobby wanted to achieve. No one had ever accomplished a repeat performance by winning second gold medals in both sprint events in the Olympics. Bobby, now twenty-three and graduated from ACC, accepted the challenge. The commitment to the goal included total abstinence from tobacco and alcohol, a strict diet, at least ten hours of sleep each night, and regular weight training to improve his strength and endurance.

His enthusiasm and his hopes, however, soon turned to disappointment. Bobby's times in the 100 meters were not fast enough, and he realized that the 200-meter race was his best chance to make the 1960 Olympic team. He made the finals of the 200 in the Olympic trials but finished a distant fourth and did not make the team. This was his last race, and Bobby retired from track competition.

STATISTICS

Year	Competition	Event	Place	Time
1955	National AAU Outdoor Championships	100 meters	1st	9.5
1956	Olympic Games	100 meters	Gold	10.5
		200 meters	Gold	20.6 OR
		4×100-meter relay	Gold	39.5 WR, OR
	NCAA Outdoor Championships	100 yards	1st	10.4
		220 yards	1st	20.6
1956	National AAU Outdoor Championships	100 meters	1st	10.3
1957	NCAA Outdoor Championships	100 yards	1st	9.4
		220 yards	1st	21.0
1958	National AAU Outdoor Championships	100 meters	1st	9.4
		200 meters	1st	20.9

Notes: OR = Olympic Record; WR = World Record

Summary

Bobby Joe Morrow was more than a great sprinter and a three-gold-medal Olympic champion. Bobby was known for his sportsmanship, sterling Christian character, and deep sense of fair play. His great track ability and genuine humility continually won the respect of those with whom he associated—his teammates, track officials, opponents, and the people who cared to watch, his fans. Bobby was elected to the National Track and Field Hall of Fame in 1975.

William G. Durick

Additional Sources:

Bateman, Hal. *United States Track and Field Olympians, 1896-1980.* Indianapolis, Ind.: The Athletics Congress of the United States, 1984.

Hickok, Ralph. *A Who's Who of Sports Champions.* Boston: Houghton Mifflin, 1995.

Wallechinsky, David. *The Complete Book of the Olympics.* Boston: Little, Brown and Company, 1991.

Watman, Mel. *Encyclopedia of Track and Field Athletics.* New York: St. Martin's Press, 1981.

WILLIE MOSCONI

Sport: Billiards

Born: June 27, 1913
Philadelphia, Pennsylvania
Died: September 16, 1993
Haddon Heights, New Jersey

Early Life

Willie Mosconi was born in Philadelphia on June 27, 1913. He learned to play billiards in his father's pool hall. However, his father, Joseph William Mosconi, wanted him to join the Dancing Mosconis on the vaudeville entertainment circuit. To discourage him from playing billiards, Willie's father locked up the cues. Undaunted, Willie improvised by using a broomstick to shoot potatoes into the pockets. He honed his billiard skills while taking dance lessons in a school owned by an uncle.

By the age of six, the pocket-billiards prodigy was playing exhibition matches in New York City and Philadelphia for money. He never took lessons to learn how to play billiards. Instead, he mastered billiards by watching other people play the game. The hustlers who came to Philadelphia sought Willie out just so they could brag they had beaten the child star, but, by Willie's account, the hustlers often left town broke. When Willie was six, he scored a victory in which he sank 40 consecutive balls. However, he became bored with billiards and retired at age seven.

The Road to Excellence

Willie believed most of the great billiards players—including himself—were born with the talent. They were also showmen who knew how to please spectators. From the time he was a teenager, billiards provided him with his livelihood. He never thought of the game as a pastime or played merely for the fun of it. He only played for the money, which he used to feed his family.

In 1933, at the age of twenty, Willie won a sectional tournament, finished third in the National Championships, and earned a place, but no title, in the World Championships. Despite the fact he finished fifth, Brunswick Corporation, a manufacturer of billiards equipment, hired him to demonstrate its products. While traveling the country giving exhibitions on behalf of Brunswick, he perfected his famous trick shots.

Willie Mosconi lines up a shot at the New York Coliseum.

1944

RECORDS AND MILESTONES

Year	Record	Location, Venue
1950	Best grand average: 18.34 balls per inning	Chicago, World Tournament
1954	High run: 526 balls	Springfield, Ill., exhibition game
1956	Best game: run of 150 in one inning	Kinston, N.C., game vs. Jimmy Moore

After several unsuccessful attempts at the world championships title, Willie sought employment outside the world of professional billiards. When no job offer materialized in 1941, he returned to Philadelphia and competitive billiards.

The Emerging Champion

Willie won his first world championship in a marathon tournament of 224 games that lasted from November 26, 1940, to May 2, 1941. Between 1942 and 1953, Willie held the world title ten out of twelve possible times.

On many occasions, Willie said the best advice about billiards that anyone ever gave him was to hate the person he was playing. What Willie hated most was not the player, but rather the possibility of his own defeat. The killer instinct, the desire to beat an opponent by a score of 125-0, was critical to his success. Pocket billiards, he said, is a game of concentration played shot by shot. It is all about the control of the cue stick, the cue ball, the balls, the rails, and the pocket. A champion knows where all the balls will go from the first shot.

Willie rarely ever practiced more than an hour or two at a time. Billiards, he said, could only be mastered in competition against better players. The best lesson every player must learn is not to miss, because then he or she does not have to worry about anything else. Willie once beat thirteen-time world champion Ralph Greenleaf in a 1948 match that lasted only seventeen minutes because he did not want to miss a play at the Strand Theater in Times Square in New York City.

Continuing the Story

By 1950, Willie was a national celebrity. His rapid-fire play and trademark sports jacket and slacks only enhanced his image. His stardom won him a new role in the world of billiards. He was a technical adviser on the set of *The Hustler* (1961), which starred his friend Jackie Gleason

as a character named Minnesota Fats. Willie again served as a technical adviser for the sequel, *The Color of Money* (1986). Looking back on his career as a professional billiards player, Willie often said there was nothing he could not do with a billiard ball. He told journalists he retired after winning his fifteenth world championship because he got bored beating the same players year in and year out.

On December 27, 1956, Willie suffered a stroke at the billiards room he owned in Philadelphia. Sixteen months later, he was back playing billiards, however. His family said his recovery was so rapid because he was a relentless competitor who could not tolerate the idea of losing. After retiring from competition at age forty-three, Willie frequently played in exhibitions. In 1978, he played and defeated Minnesota Fats in a series of lucrative televised matches. Willie died of a heart attack on September 16, 1993, in his home in Haddon Heights, New Jersey.

Summary

Willie Mosconi ranks as one of the greatest pocket billiards players in the history of the sport. He won a record 77 percent of his tournament competitions, compared with a 71 percent record for billiards champion Ralph Greenleaf. Willie won the world championship in straight pool fifteen times between 1941 and 1957. He ran 526 consecutive balls without a miss in a straight-pool exhibition in 1954, calling the ball and pocket before every shot. His other heralded records included his best game ever, in which he sank 150 balls in a row in one inning (a perfect game) in 1956.

Willie was a tough competitor in tournament-length contests of 125 or 150 points and a veritable conqueror in longer challenge matches. He won twelve of his thirteen challenge matches by a combined score of 42,625 to 28,108, finishing, on average, more than 1,000 points ahead of his opponents. For him, billiards was an honorable and reputable profession, not a game for hustlers and suckers. Both in legend and fact, he ranks as a true gentleman of the sport.

Fred Buchstein

1945

Additional Sources:

Mosconi, Willie. *Willie Mosconi's Winning Pocket Billiards: For Beginners and Advanced Players with a Section on Trick Shots.* New York: Crown, 1995.

Mosconi, Willie, and Stanley Cohen. *Willie's Game: An Autobiography.* New York: Macmillan, 1993.

Shamos, Michael Ian. *The Illustrated Encyclopedia of Billiards.* New York: Lyons & Burford, 1993.

Stein, Victor. *The Billiard Encyclopedia: An Illustrated History of the Sport.* Minneapolis, Minn.: Blue Book, 1996.

ANNEMARIE MOSER-PROELL

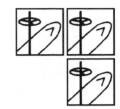

Sport: Skiing

Born: March 27, 1953
Kleinarl, near Salzburg, Austria

Early Life

Annemarie Proell was born on March 27, 1953, in Kleinarl, near Salzburg, in Austria. She was the sixth of eight children of a couple who farmed in the mountains of Austria.

Her parents were poor, but they were enthusiastic skiers and encouraged Annemarie to ski at an early age. When she was four years old, her father whittled her first pair of skis.

Skiing is popular in Austria, and children who excel in sports are often trained by professional coaches. The Proell family could not afford to send Annemarie to a coach, so she developed her own style of skiing. She was exceptionally strong, and her daredevil attitude made her well-suited for downhill racing.

Like many children who become successful, elite athletes, Annemarie loved her sport. Often she would skip breakfast to make a few runs before school began. Often she gave more attention to her skiing than her studies and "played hooky" to ski in the mountains.

The Road to Excellence

Annemarie's love of the outdoors and skiing coupled with her aggressive personality contributed to her early success in the sport. Her family

Annemarie Moser-Proell competes in the slalom during the 1971 World Cup in St. Gervais, France.

1947

had supported her early interest in skiing, and eventually she began to train with Karl Kahr, her first coach.

In 1969, at the age of fifteen, she tried out for the Austrian national ski team. The young blonde with freckles became the youngest member of the team. She weighed only 110 pounds and was 5 feet 6 inches tall; she was too slight for the sport. She soon began a training program

MAJOR CHAMPIONSHIPS

Year	Competition	Event	Place
1969	World Cup	Overall	17th
1970	World Championships	Giant slalom	14th
		Slalom	21st
		Downhill	3d
	World Cup	Overall	7th
		Giant slalom	3d
1971	World Cup	Overall	1st
		Giant slalom	1st
		Slalom	3d
		Downhill	1st
1972	Olympic Games	Giant slalom	Silver
		Slalom	5th
		Downhill	Silver
	World Cup	Overall	1st
		Giant slalom	1st
		Downhill	1st
1973	World Cup	Overall	1st
		Giant slalom	2d
		Downhill	1st
1974	World Championships	Giant slalom	4th
		Downhill	1st
	World Cup	Overall	1st
		Downhill	1st
1975	World Cup	Overall	1st
		Giant slalom	1st
		Downhill	1st
1977	World Cup	Overall	2d
		Giant slalom	3d
		Slalom	11th
		Downhill	2d
1978	World Championships	Giant slalom	3d
		Slalom	19th
		Downhill	1st
	World Cup	Overall	2d
		Giant slalom	5th
		Slalom	8th
		Downhill	1st
1979	World Cup	Overall	1st
		Giant slalom	12th
		Slalom	2d
		Downhill	1st
1980	Olympic Games	Giant slalom	6th
		Downhill	Gold

that enabled her to gain weight and the necessary strength needed for downhill racing, which requires both strength and endurance.

Her training program and additional size soon brought Annemarie success. By the time she was seventeen, she had become a successful performer with a nontraditional, flamboyant style. She excelled in all three ski-racing events—the downhill, the giant slalom, and the slalom—but her best event was the slalom.

With two years of intensive training, Annemarie was prepared for her first successful World Cup championship. In March, 1971, she won the championship with a victory in the giant slalom in Abetone, Italy. She ended the 1970-1971 season with a record total of 195 points.

Her World Cup victory helped reestablish Austria as a dominant power in downhill racing. Yet the success became difficult for the young champion, and the period following her World Cup victory was a difficult one for Annemarie. Often the intense and long periods of competition and the constant travel and absence of family and friends are difficult for young athletes. Annemarie missed her family and friends and the simple life of her hometown.

The difficulties of her lifestyle as an international sports champion affected Annemarie very much. Her relationship with the press became strained, she was often considered a difficult person with whom to work, and she was also rude to the press. These pressures did not affect Annemarie's performance, however; she continued to be successful on the international skiing circuit.

The Emerging Champion

In spite of the pressures of her life as a world champion, Annemarie continued to improve as a skier. In March of 1972, she claimed her second consecutive world championship title by winning the women's giant slalom at Heavenly Valley, California.

Later that year, Annemarie made her first appearance in the Winter Olympics in Sapporo, Japan. The Olympics proved to be a disappointment for both Annemarie and the Austrian team. One of her fellow skiers, Karl Schranz, was not permitted to participate on the Austrian team because he had received money for wearing a sponsor's shirt, thus jeopardizing his amateur

HONORS, AWARDS, AND RECORDS

1973	First skier to win all three World Cup Alpine events
1975, 1978-79	World Cup Competitor of the Year
1978	*Ski Racing* magazine Competitor of the Year

status. The internal problems on the team troubled Annemarie and were distracting to her and her teammates. She did not win the anticipated gold medal but won instead silver medals in the downhill and the giant slalom.

Annemarie once again survived the disappointments of her intense and competitive life as an international sports champion. She emerged in the 1972-1973 season in fine form. She became known as the "Flying Fraulein." Her nontraditional style was often considered awkward—feet well apart, arms locked to the thighs, crouched in an awkward squat—which often offended the purists. She became known for her quick start, and her risky style was considered intimidating to her opponents. Unlike her competitors, who stood upright from time to time in a race, Annemarie remained crouched throughout the entire run—an effort requiring great strength.

After her disappointing second-place finishes in the Olympics, Annemarie surprised the ski world when she won all eight downhill races in the 1973 World Cup competition. With these victories, she became the first skier, man or woman, to score a sweep in the three Alpine events. She also captured three giant slalom races and won her third consecutive World Cup Championship in 1973.

The year ended as it had begun for Annemarie, with another record-breaking feat. In late December, she broke Jean-Claude Killy's amateur record of eighteen World Cup victories and set a new record of twenty-eight. At the age of nineteen, she had won more races than any other skier.

Continuing the Story

In 1973, Annemarie married Herbert Moser, a soccer player who worked for the ski company that sponsored her travels. She took Herbert's name and thereafter was known as Annemarie Moser-Proell.

Annemarie's dominance of downhill racing continued the next year. She won 11 of 12 downhill races and placed fifth in the slalom and seventh in the giant slalom. She won her fourth consecutive World Cup championship by a margin of more than 100 points.

The next year brought a mixture of joy and sadness for Annemarie. On February 23, she won the giant slalom at Naeba, Japan, and won her fifth consecutive World Cup title. On March 20, she lost to Lise-Marie Morerod in a slalom race in Ortisei, Italy. After her defeat, she announced her retirement. Her decision to retire was caused by the disappointment of her loss and because she wanted to spend more time with her family. Also, she had become disappointed with the Austrian team.

For one year, Annemarie did not compete. She remained at home with her family. After that year, she missed competitive skiing and returned to the slopes for the 1976-1977 season.

Returning to World Cup competition in 1977, Annemarie continued to dominate the downhill events. She finished first in the downhill at the World Championships and the World Cup in 1978, she won the downhill and the overall titles at the 1979 World Cup, and she won the gold in the downhill at the 1980 Olympics in Lake Placid.

Summary

Annemarie Moser-Proell dominated women's skiing during the 1970's and she is widely considered the greatest woman alpine skier of all time. During her twelve-year career, she won six World Cup titles and posted sixty-two wins overall, the most of any female alpine skier. Her independent and aggressive personality contributed to her nontraditional and challenging style of racing. She endured the rigors of many years of intense international competition to become known as the "Queen of the Mountain" for many years.

Susan J. Bandy

Additional Sources:

Levinson, David, and Karen Christenson, eds. *Encyclopedia of World Sport: From Ancient to Present.* Santa Barbara, Calif.: ABC-CLIO, 1996.

Schapp, Dick. *An Illustrated History of the Olympics.* New York: Alfred A. Knopf, 1975.

Wallechinsky, David. *The Complete Book of the Olympics.* Boston: Little, Brown and Company, 1991.

EDWIN MOSES

Sport: Track and field (hurdles)

Born: August 31, 1955
Dayton, Ohio

Early Life

Edwin Corley Moses was born on August 31, 1955, in Dayton, Ohio. He was the second of three sons. Both of Edwin's parents were educators, so Edwin grew up in an environment of learning.

Edwin's father, Irving Sr., was an elementary school principal, and his mother, Gladys, was a curriculum supervisor. His parents had also been athletes in college, so the Moses boys grew up with an appreciation for both academics and athletics.

In addition to building science projects and reading books, Edwin played various sports. The combination of sports participation and a keen intellect helped Edwin to develop the athleticism that would make him one of the most dominant athletes in modern sports history.

The Road to Excellence

Edwin revealed no sign of incredible athletic ability as a youngster, however. Although he was an All-Star baseball catcher and a football defensive back at Fairview High School, his coaches discouraged him from considering a sports career, claiming he did not have the size or aptitude for those sports. Besides, everyone knew Edwin was more interested in track, the sport he fell in love with while watching the Dayton Relays as a third-grader.

Edwin Moses won the 400-meter hurdles in the 1984 Olympic trials. He later won the Olympic gold.

Edwin, however, was more serious about his schoolwork than his track. He won an academic scholarship to Morehouse College in Atlanta, Georgia, where he majored in physics and engi-

STATISTICS

Year	Competition	Event	Place	Time
1976	Olympic Games	400-meter hurdles	Gold	47.64 WR
1977	World Cup	400-meter hurdles	1st	47.58
	U.S. Nationals	400-meter hurdles	1st	47.45
1979	World Cup	400-meter hurdles	1st	47.53
	U.S. Nationals	400-meter hurdles	1st	47.89
1981	U.S. Nationals	400-meter hurdles	1st	47.59
1983	World Championships	400-meter hurdles	1st	47.50
	U.S. Nationals	400-meter hurdles	1st	47.84
1984	Olympic Games	400-meter hurdles	Gold	47.75
1986	Goodwill Games	400-meter hurdles	1st	
1987	World Championships	400-meter hurdles	1st	47.46
1988	Olympic Games	400-meter hurdles	Bronze	47.56

Note: WR = World Record

neering. In his senior year, Edwin finally began to realize his ability in track.

At the Florida Relays in Gainesville in March, 1976, Edwin ran the 400-meter intermediate hurdles in 50.1 seconds. His performance was so impressive that the Olympic coach, Leroy Walker, predicted that Edwin would win the gold medal at the 1976 Olympiad in Montreal, Canada. The games were just five months away.

Edwin continued to improve. Using his knowledge of physics, and with a tremendous desire to excel, Edwin began to revolutionize the event. He trained himself to maintain thirteen paces between hurdles, two less than the world's best racers. His 9-foot, 9-inch stride and his great endurance allowed him to "float" over the ten hurdles while recording blazing speeds. He set an American record of 48.30 seconds at the 1976 Olympic trials.

In a few months, Edwin had risen to the level of a top, world-class competitor. Little did anyone know he would remain at that level for nearly fifteen years.

The Emerging Champion

On July 25, 1976, in Montreal, Canada, Edwin Moses won the Olympic gold medal. Not only did he win, but he also set the world record at 47.64 seconds, a feat he would better three times. Edwin was less well known for his succession of world records, however, than he was for what is known simply as "The Streak."

Edwin's unbelievable streak of 122 consecutive victories began on September 2, 1977, and lasted for nine years, nine months, and nine days. During that time, his dominance in the intermediate hurdles made him one of the world's most famous and respected athletes. As an example of his fame, a crowd of five thousand fans once gathered simply to watch him practice.

Even after his streak-ending defeat by Danny Harris on June 4, 1987, Edwin continued to race, winning a bronze medal at the 1988 Olympiad in Seoul, South Korea. His list of accomplishments is more than impressive; it may never be matched.

He made four Olympic teams (1976, 1980, 1984, and 1988) and won three Olympic medals, two golds and a bronze. (The United States team did not compete in the 1980 games in Moscow.) He is a two-time world champion and winner of countless other titles. Many experts predict that the 47.02 world record he set in West Germany on his birthday in 1983 may not be broken until well into the twenty-first century.

Only a few individuals have run the 400-meter hurdles in less than 48 seconds; Edwin accom-

RECORDS

World record in 400-meter hurdles in 1977 (47.45)

World record in 400-meter hurdles in 1980 (47.13)

World record in 400-meter hurdles in 1983 (47.02)

Had an unbeaten string in the 400-meter hurdles that exceeded 122 races, stretching from mid-1977 through mid-1987

Ranked number 1 in the world 9 times, and number 2 twice

HONORS AND AWARDS

1976-77, 1980	DiBeneditto Award
1977	World Trophy
	Dieges Award
1980	Track and Field News World Athlete of the Year
1981	Jesse Owens Award
	Track Athlete of the Decade
1983	Sullivan Award
1984	Sports Illustrated Sportsman of the Year
1985	Inducted into U.S. Olympic Hall of Fame
1994	Inducted into National Track and Field Hall of Fame

plished that twenty-seven times. No other track athlete can claim that type of dominance.

Edwin's persistent work ethic, along with his constant desire to improve, caused him to be ranked number one in the world nine times. Using advanced training techniques that involved computer analysis and his knowledge of physics, Edwin spent long hours on the track perfecting his skills. Quite often his wife, Myrella, would be holding the stopwatch and lending moral support.

Continuing the Story

For all the support Edwin has received, he has also helped others in many ways. He is a powerful spokesperson against drug abuse and a strong proponent of athletes' rights. He served as a member of the Athlete's Advisory Council of the United States Olympic Committee (USOC). He was also the chairperson of the USOC Substance Abuse Committee and of the Athletic Congress's Year-Round Drug-Testing Committee.

In 1988, Edwin became interested in bobsledding and joined his fellow track Olympian, Willie Gault, in a bobsled team tryout. Edwin's speed and strength, as well as his competitive spirit, helped him to excel in both the two-person and the four-person bobsled events.

Teaming with experienced bobsled driver Brian Shimer, Edwin sped to a World Cup medal, a rare achievement in United States bobsledding. Edwin tried out for the U.S. Winter Olympics bobsled team, but he failed to qualify.

Following his retirement from competition, Edwin remained active. He became a licensed scuba diver as well as a private pilot. He also returned to school to work toward a masters degree in business administration at Pepperdine University.

Summary

Edwin Moses was one of the world's most dominant track athletes. "The Streak" may never be equaled, and his world record seems safe from serious challenge. By making four Olympic teams, Edwin established himself as one of the all-time greatest Olympians.

Edwin is revered for more than just his hurdling career. His courageous work against drug abuse has made him one of the most respected figures in sports. Although his attempt to race bobsleds speaks well for his versatility, it also illustrates another undeniable fact: Edwin Moses is clearly one of the greatest competitors of recent times.

William B. Roy

Additional Sources:

Bateman, Hal. *United States Track and Field Olympians, 1896-1980.* Indianapolis, Ind.: The Athletics Congress of the United States, 1984.

Hickok, Ralph. *A Who's Who of Sports Champions.* Boston: Houghton Mifflin, 1995.

The Lincoln Library of Sports Champions. 16 vols. Columbus, Ohio: Frontier Press, 1993.

Wallechinsky, David. *The Complete Book of the Olympics.* Boston: Little, Brown and Company, 1991.

Watman, Mel. *Encyclopedia of Track and Field Athletics.* New York: St. Martin's Press, 1981.

RANDY MOSS

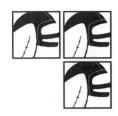

Sport: Football

Born: February 13, 1977
Rand, West Virginia

Early Life

Randy Moss was raised by a single mother in Rand, West Virginia, a predominantly African American community. At an early age Randy showed athletic prowess. At Dupont High School in Belle, West Virginia, he played both football and basketball. One of his basketball teammates was Jason Williams, who went on to play basketball for the NBA's Sacramento Kings.

On two separate occasions the West Virginia Sportswriters' Association named Randy "Mr. West Virginia" for his outstanding basketball performance. However, Randy decided to pursue a career in football. He enrolled at Florida State University but left that school before the end of his freshman year, enrolling at Marshall University in Huntington, West Virginia, in 1996.

The Road to Excellence

At Marshall, Randy, who was a wide receiver, led the football team to two winning seasons and to a 1997 victory in the Motor City Bowl. He caught 174 passes for 3,529 yards and scored 54 touchdowns. In 1997 he finished fourth in the balloting for the Heisman Trophy and won the Biletnikoff Award as the best college receiver in the nation.

In January, 1998, Randy announced that he would leave Marshall to pursue a career in professional football. A West Virginia hero, particularly to Marshall University fans, Randy sent an open letter to Marshall supporters, telling of his decision to leave the university without a degree and indicating that his future plans included obtaining a college diploma.

Minnesota Viking Randy Moss in August, 2000.

Randy was picked by the Minnesota Vikings in the first round of the National Football League (NFL) draft in 1998. Many observers felt that Randy, who was the twenty-first player picked,

1953

STATISTICS

Season	GP	Rec.	Yds.	Avg.	TD
1998	16	69	1,313	19.0	17
1999	16	80	1,413	17.7	11
2000	16	77	1,437	18.7	15
Totals	**48**	**226**	**4,163**	**18.4**	**43**

Notes: GP = games played; Rec. = receptions; Yds. = yards; Avg. = average yards per reception; TD = touchdowns

might have been chosen earlier in the draft if it had not been for his reputation as a trouble-maker. He had had several brushes with the law, including a domestic-violence charge for beating the mother of his child. In July, 1998, Randy signed a $4.5 million four-year contract as a wide receiver with the Vikings and reported to training camp.

The Emerging Champion

Randy quickly distinguished himself in his career with the Vikings, although off the field there was some criticism of his haughty attitude toward the media. Randy, who, at the time of signing, stood 6 feet 3½ inches and weighed 210 pounds, was prized by the Vikings for his speed and agility. These qualities immediately turned him into a star. In 1998 the Associated Press, *College and Pro Football Weekly,* and *Football Weekly* named him Offensive Rookie of the Year. *Sports Illustrated* named him Rookie of the Year, as did *The Sporting News* and *The Football News.*

In that same year the Professional Football Writers of American named Randy NFC Rookie of the Year. He was named All-Rookie by four magazines and All-Pro by the Associated Press and five magazines. He earned the NFL Best at Each Position award for wide receivers, was named to the All-Madden team, and was selected for *Pro Football Weekly*'s All-NFC and All-NFL teams. In November, 1998, he was named NFL Offensive Rookie of the Month, and several times during his first season he was honored as NFC Player of the Week.

In his 1998 debut season Randy set records and broke records nonstop. He set a new NFL record for touchdown receptions by a rookie, with 17. He was the only rookie to be selected for

the 1999 Pro Bowl, in which he was a starter, and the first Viking rookie ever to score 2 touchdowns in an initial NFL game. He was one of only four NFL players ever to score in their first games, the others being Chuck Foreman in 1973, Sammy White in 1976, and James Brim in 1987.

Randy tied Cris Carter's Viking record for most consecutive games with touchdown catches in a season (7) and set a team record for most games with a touchdown pass in a season (11), breaking Carter's previous record of 10. Randy broke the team record for touchdowns of 40-plus yards with 10, breaking Gene Washington's record of 5.

Although his second season was somewhat less spectacular, in the 2000 Pro Bowl Randy had 9 catches and 212 yards, both of which were Pro Bowl records, and he was named the game's most valuable player. During his third season, in 2000, he caught 77 passes and scored 15 touchdowns and ended the year still regarded as one of the league's brightest stars.

Continuing the Story

In 1999 Randy announced that he would like to play not only professional football but also professional basketball, reminding the media that he had been an outstanding high school basketball player in West Virginia. The Minnesota Timberwolves confirmed that Randy and his agent had contacted that team about his playing for them in his off-season from football. Vikings management indicated that it had no problem with Randy pursuing a career in basketball so long as he met his contractual obligations to the Vikings. Randy, however, decided that a professional basketball career should wait until he built up his athletic prowess further.

After going to work for the Vikings, Randy was sometimes labeled haughty and uncooperative. In 1999 he received much criticism for failing to show up to sign autographs for a group of youngsters in Deerfield Beach, Florida. Randy maintained that he had done nothing wrong and that the entire matter was a result of miscommunication. A few weeks later he redeemed himself somewhat by showing up in Charleston, West Virginia, and standing for hours so that five hundred youngsters there could meet him and get his autograph.

Summary

From an early age Randy Moss was identified as a natural athlete who possessed speed and agility. Unfortunately, Randy developed a reputation not only as a quick, natural athlete but also as a troublemaker. At the start of the twenty-first century there was some question as to whether Randy would be able to translate his physical ability into successful careers in both professional football and basketball.

Annita Marie Ward

Additional Sources:

Holler, John. *Minnesota Vikings: Fact and Trivia.* South Bend, Ind.: E. B. Houchin, 1998.

Nelson, Julie. *Minnesota Vikings: NFL Today.* Mankato, Minn.: Smart Apple Media, 2000.

Stewart, Mark. *Randy Moss: First in Flight.* Breckenridge, Colo.: Twenty-first Century Books, 2000.

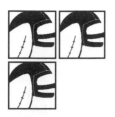

MARION MOTLEY

Sport: Football

Born: June 5, 1920
  Leesburg, Georgia
Died: June 27, 1999
  Cleveland, Ohio

Early Life

Marion Motley was born on June 5, 1920, in Leesburg, Georgia. When Marion was three years old, his family moved to Canton, Ohio, where his father worked as a laborer in a local foundry. One of four children of Blanch and Shakeful Motley, Marion grew up only a few miles from the present site of the Pro Football Hall of Fame.

Marion's first exposure to organized sport came as a member of his grade school's basketball team. It was, however, in pickup games played in vacant lots and playgrounds in his poor and predominantly African American neighborhood that Marion learned to play baseball and football.

The Road to Excellence

While a student at Canton's McKinley High School, Marion began to truly develop as an athlete. Although he played baseball, basketball, and football, it was at football that he excelled. By his senior year, Marion was considered one of the finest running backs in the state. His Bulldogs teams lost only three games during his three varsity seasons. These were all to Massillon High School, which was coached by Paul Brown, who would later play an important role in Marion's life.

After graduating from high school, Marion enrolled at South Carolina State University, but in 1940 he decided to rejoin his high school coach, Jimmy Aiken, who was then head football coach at the University of Nevada. At Nevada, Marion set several small-college records and earned honorable mention All-American ranking. This was something of a rarity for a small-college player in those days.

After suffering a knee injury during his senior year, Marion returned to Canton and went to work in a steel mill. Then, on Christmas Day, 1944, he enlisted in the Navy. Marion was stationed at Great Lakes Naval Base, Illinois, and became a member of the Great Lakes Navy football team that in 1945 defeated a heavily favored Notre Dame team 39-7. The Great Lakes team was coached by former Masillon High School coach Paul Brown.

Marion Motley in 1948.

1956

STATISTICS

Season	GP	Car.	Rushing Yds.	Avg.	TD	Rec.	Receiving Yds.	Avg.	TD
1946	13	73	601	8.2	5	10	188	18.8	1
1947	14	146	889	6.1	8	7	73	10.4	1
1948	14	157	**964**	6.1	5	13	192	14.8	2
1949	12	113	570	5.0	8	15	191	12.7	0
1950	12	140	**810**	5.8	3	11	151	13.7	1
1951	11	61	273	4.5	1	10	52	5.2	0
1952	12	104	444	4.3	1	13	213	16.4	2
1953	12	32	161	5.0	0	6	47	7.8	0
1955	7	2	8	4.0	0	0	0	0.0	0
AAFC Totals	53	489	3,024	6.2	26	45	644	14.3	4
NFL Totals	54	339	1,696	5.0	5	40	463	11.6	3

Notes: Boldface indicates statistical leader. GP = games played; Car. = carries; Yds. = yards; Avg. = average yards per carry *or* average yards per reception; TD = touchdowns; Rec. = receptions

The Emerging Champion

Upon discharge from the Navy, Marion again returned to Canton. Meanwhile, Paul Brown was hired as the first-ever coach of the Cleveland Browns of the All-America Football Conference (AAFC). Hoping for an opportunity to play professional football, Marion wrote to his Navy coach and asked for a tryout. Although he was first told that the team had enough running backs, Marion was later invited to the Browns' training camp. As it turned out, the Browns were actually more interested in Marion as a roommate for an African American player named Bill Willis than as a running back.

During the early years of professional football, there were very few African American players. In fact, for thirteen years, beginning in 1933, there were no African American players in professional football. Then, in 1946, the Los Angeles Rams signed two African American players, and a few weeks later, the Browns signed Willis. Their desire for another African American player to room with Willis gave Marion the opportunity he needed.

Although he began practicing with the second team, within days Marion worked his way into the Browns' starting lineup. During that first season, things were rough for Marion. Players often made insulting racial remarks and some deliberately attempted to cause him injury.

Finally, in 1947, in a game in Buffalo against the Bills, an official named Tommy Hughitt penalized a player for unsportsmanlike conduct after he deliberately stepped on Marion's hands after a play had ended. Hughitt informed the player that such behavior would no longer be tolerated. Marion contends that, thanks to Hughitt's stand, there were few such racially motivated incidents after that day.

Although many baseball fans recognize Jackie Robinson as the man who broke baseball's "color barrier," most do not realize the tremendous contributions made by Marion Motley to professional football.

Continuing the Story

Just as his role as an African American pioneer was overshadowed by Jackie Robinson, Marion's professional football career was somewhat overshadowed by his teammate, quarterback Otto Graham. It was the accurate passing of Otto that was the most popular element of the Cleveland Browns' very successful first decade (1946-1956). It was together, however, that the two popularized the draw and trap plays for which the Browns were famous. Together, the two stars also established the fullback as an effective pass receiver.

When Otto had trouble finding an open receiver, he knew his fullback, Marion, would be nearby to catch a short pass and turn it into a big gain. With his speed and size, Marion would run straight ahead and, if necessary, over opponents who stood in his way.

The draw play, which called for Otto to fake

1957

the pass, then hand off to Marion, became one of the Browns' most successful plays. According to Coach Brown, it was discovered by accident. Once, when Otto got a fierce pass rush from the defense, he in desperation handed the ball to Marion. In their haste to get to the quarterback, the defense ran right past Marion, who then swept through them for a big gain. In a short time, the draw play became Marion's most dangerous weapon.

How to stop Marion was always a concern for opposing defenses. If an opponent decided to drop back to stop the pass, Marion would take advantage and run up the middle. If they decided to stay up close and try to stop Marion from running the draw play, Otto would simply throw the ball over them.

Summary

As effective as Marion Motley was as a runner, he did not carry the ball with the frequency that the average running back does today. There really is no way to tell how many yards he might have gained if he carried the ball as often.

There is little doubt, however, that his hard-charging style, combined with his pass-catching ability, revolutionized the fullback position. Also, and perhaps more important, his role as an African American pioneer forever changed professional football for the better.

Joseph Horrigan

HONORS, AWARDS, AND RECORDS	
1946-48	All-AAFC Team
1950	NFL All-Pro Team
	Sporting News NFL All-Star Team
	NFL record for the highest single-game average in yards per carry (17.1)
1951	NFL Pro Bowl Team
1963	NFL All-Pro Team of the 1940's
1968	Inducted into Pro Football Hall of Fame

Additional Sources:

Hickok, Ralph. *A Who's Who of Sports Champions.* Boston: Houghton Mifflin, 1995.

LaBlanc, Michael L., and Mary K. Ruby, eds. *Professional Sports Team Histories: Football.* Detroit: Gale, 1994.

Porter, David L., ed. *African American Sports Greats: A Biographical Dictionary.* Westport, Conn.: Greenwood Press, 1995.

_____. *Biographical Dictionary of American Sports: Football.* Westport, Conn.: Greenwood Press, 1987.

ALONZO MOURNING

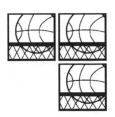

Sport: Basketball

Born: February 8, 1970
Chesapeake, Virginia

Early Life

Alonzo Mourning, Jr., was born to Alonzo, Sr., and Julia Mourning on February 8, 1970, in

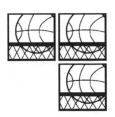

The 1999 Defensive Player of the Year, Alonzo Mourning, plays against Canada in a 2000 exhibition game.

Chesapeake, Virginia. In 1982, the Mournings separated and divorced. The couple had been arguing constantly, and, to avoid taking sides, the twelve-year-old moved in with a family friend, Fanny Threet, who inspired his career and repaired the once-frayed relationship with his father. The retired schoolteacher and her husband, Robert, made a home for Alonzo until he left for Georgetown University in Washington, D.C. Alonzo began to get into trouble, so the Threets, his teachers, and friends urged the gangly teen to play basketball.

The Road to Excellence

Alonzo played for Indian River Junior High School, but the nearly 6-foot 4-inch boy was more likely to trip over his feet than score. In the end, hard practice paid off. Eventually Alonzo "could erase a shot faster than chalk from a blackboard." The seventh grader's popularity spread as quickly as the nickname "Zo," by which he is still known.

Bill Lassiter, the Indian River team's coach, acknowledged Alonzo's skills but knew they needed refinement. At sixteen, Alonzo was invited to Pittsburgh's prestigious Five Star Basketball Camp. During the following year, as a junior, Alonzo led a state championship team, with a per-game average of 21.8 points, 11 rebounds, and 9.6 blocked shots. He attracted college recruiters and, with Lassiter's help, chopped a long list to five schools, finally choosing Georgetown.

The university's coach, John Thompson, invited Alonzo to try out for the 1988 U.S. Olympic basketball team.

The only high-schooler in the crowd, Alonzo was the second-to-last player cut, but he honed his skills in contests against more seasoned veterans. One of the highlights occurred in an exhibition game when he scored against lifelong idol Patrick Ewing.

The Emerging Champion

In 1989 the Georgetown freshman blocked 169 shots to set a national record. From the beginning reporters tagged him as NBA material, but the judgment proved premature. Alonzo's second year was embroiled in controversy. The fun-loving teen was tied to—and later testified against—Rayful Edmond III, a Washington, D.C., cocaine dealer. Later that year, Alonzo was accused of making a racist remark to the University of Connecticut's Israeli forward Nadav Henefeld. In the end, those involved agreed the comment was not anti-Semitic. An injured foot sidelined Alonzo for nine games during his junior year. Some sportswriters began to question the player's promise, but not the NBA.

Many professional teams hoped the aggressive Alonzo might drop out of college and enter the NBA draft. Alonzo knew he was not ready. He wanted to mature as a player and finish his sociology degree. Those goals changed his behavior. During the summer before his senior year, Alonzo worked out with fellow Georgetown alumni Patrick Ewing and Dikembe Mutombo. Sometimes he worked so hard that Thompson had to chase him out of the weight room. A new Alonzo was visible in the senior year.

In addition to the completion of a 1992 sociology degree, the Georgetown center averaged 21.3 points and 10.7 rebounds per game. He blocked 118 shots. Alonzo was the first college player named Big East Conference Player, Defensive Player, and Tournament Player in the same year. He was also named the Big East Tournament's most valuable player.

Continuing the Story

The Charlotte Hornets picked Alonzo up in the 1992 draft. In only forty-nine games in that first 1993 season, he set a shot-blocking record and a single-season high with 634 free-throw attempts. He made the NBA All-Rookie First Team and racked up the top rookie scoring average for the Hornets. Also, he shared credit for leading the team to its first playoff series.

He had a series of injuries during the next season but drew honors outside the NBA. Alonzo joined the Olympic Dream Team II and won a gold medal at the World Basketball Championships in Canada. Those wins were omens for his third NBA season. The Hornets smashed the fifty-win barrier for the first time. Alonzo was one of four NBA players who led the team in scoring, rebounding, blocked shots, and field goals. At the end of the 1994-1995 season, he was traded to the Miami Heat, where the center signed a contract for about $13 million per year through 2003 and became the franchise player, meaning the team would be built around him.

Alonzo suffered an injury during his first season with the Heat but still started seventy games.

STATISTICS

Season	GP	FGA	FGM	FG%	FTA	FTM	FT%	Reb.	Ast.	TP	PPG
1992-93	78	1,119	572	.511	634	495	.781	805	76	1,639	21.0
1993-94	60	845	427	.505	568	433	.762	610	86	1,287	21.5
1994-95	77	1,101	571	.519	644	490	.761	761	111	1,643	21.3
1995-96	70	1,076	563	.523	712	488	.685	727	159	1,623	23.2
1996-97	66	885	473	.534	565	363	.642	656	104	1,310	19.8
1997-98	58	732	403	.551	465	309	.665	558	52	1,115	19.2
1998-99	46	634	324	.511	423	276	.652	507	74	924	20.1
1999-00	79	1,184	652	.551	582	414	.711	753	123	1,718	21.7
2000-01	13	141	73	.518	55	31	.564	101	12	177	13.6
Totals	547	7,717	4,058	.526	4,648	3,299	.710	5,478	797	11,436	20.9

Notes: GP = games played; FGA = field goals attempted; FGM = field goals made; FG% = field goal percentage; FTA = free throws attempted; FTM = free throws made; FT% = free throw percentage; Reb. = rebounds; Ast. = assists; TP = total points; PPG = points per game

During the second season, he led the team to a record sixty-one wins, the Atlantic Division title, and the Eastern Conference finals. In 1996-1997 he led the Heat in rebounds (9.9), blocked shots (2.86), and field goal percentage (.534) and was the number-two scorer, averaging 19.8 points per game.

During the 1997-1998 season, he again led in scoring (19.2), field goals (.551), and blocked shots (2.24). On April 1, 1999, Alonzo blocked his 611th shot to become the Heat's high scorer. That was just part of an outstanding season. Alonzo was named to the 1998-1999 NBA First Team and led the Heat in scoring (20.1) and field goals (.511). He led the team and the NBA in rebounds (11), blocked shots, (3.91) and double-doubles (29), which earned him a spot on the NBA All-Defensive First Team and the Defensive Player of the Year award. After another failed trip to the 1999-2000 playoffs, he was named Defensive Player of the Year again.

After winning a gold medal with the U.S. men's team at the Sydney Olympics, Alonzo was diagnosed as having a life-threatening kidney disease. It appeared that he not only would miss the entire 2000-2001 season, but that his career might be over. To everyone's surprise, however, he returned in time to play the last thirteen games of the season and three playoff games before Miami was eliminated.

Summary

Alonzo Mourning's life had a rough start, but his journey proves that bad situations can be turned great through sports. The once-gangly teen worked hard to mold himself into an international champion. He left Georgetown University with a degree and top Big East honors, and he became an Olympic gold medalist. He led the Charlotte Hornets to more wins than ever before. After he moved to Miami in 1996, he gained a wide range of NBA honors, including two Defensive Player of the Year awards.

Vincent F. A. Golphin

Additional Sources:

Fortunato, Frank. *Sports Great Alonzo Mourning.* Springfield, N.J.: Enslow, 1997.

Gutman, Bill. *Alonzo Mourning: Center of Attention.* Brookfield, Conn.: Millbrook Press, 1997.

Rosenthal, Bert. *Alonzo Mourning.* Philadelphia: Chelsea House, 1998.

Swann, Phillip. "Alonzo Mourning, Saved by the Game." *Boys' Life,* January, 1989, 26.

CARLOS MOYA

Sport: Tennis

Born: August 27, 1976
Palma de Majorca, Spain

Early Life

Carlos Moya was born on August 27, 1976. He was the third and youngest child of Andreu Moya and Pilar Llompart. His parents, who owned a hotel, often played tennis, and he grew up with a racket in his hands. By the time he was six years old, Jofre Porta began coaching him. He also played soccer and basketball, which contributed

Spaniard Carlos Moya was a finalist at the 1998 ATP Tour World Championship.

to developing his athletic abilities and conditioning.

The Road to Excellence

As a boy, Carlos won a number of local and regional tournaments. By the time he was twelve, he began to show exceptional promise as a tennis player. When he was a teenager, he was coached by Alberto Tous, a former tennis professional from Majorca. Carlos won many junior tournaments in the Balearic Islands off the coast of Spain, where Majorca is located, and he also reached the semifinals of the Junior Spanish Championships.

Carlos and his coach knew that to achieve major success as a tennis player, he would need more intensive training and rigorous competition. At age seventeen, he moved to Barcelona to train at the Saint Cugat High Performance Center, where he began working with Juan Bautista Avendano, as well as other coaches. He was also able to raise the level of his game through competition with highly ranked Spanish players who trained at the center in Barcelona.

In 1994 Carlos started to play professional tennis on the Association of Tennis Professionals (ATP) tour. He began by entering Challenger tournaments on the satellite circuit, primarily in Spain. Victories in several of these tournaments brought his ranking to number 346. He continued this path in 1995. By the end of that year, he had won his first regular ATP tournament in Buenos Aires, Argentina, and his ranking had climbed to 63, a jump of 283 points.

During 1996 Carlos became a respected player on the ATP international circuit, maintaining his ranking in the top thirty. He entered the four Grand Slam tournaments for the first time, losing in the first round at the Australian Open and at Wimbledon and in the second round at the French Open and the U.S. Open. However, he reached the semifinals or finals of several other tournaments, and he won the Spanish Championships and the Croatia Open. In addition, he joined an elite group of Spanish players in Davis Cup competition. The experience that he gained, along with his hard work and talent, made him poised to become one of the best players on the men's professional tennis tour.

The Emerging Champion

All the potential and early success came together for Carlos in 1997, when he emerged as a top contender for major professional tennis championships. At the Australian Open, where he had lost in the first round in the previous year, he was a surprising finalist. En route to the final, he defeated several top players, including Boris Becker of Germany and Michael Chang of the United States. Although he lost in the final to number-one-ranked Pete Sampras, Carlos's strong showing at this Grand Slam tournament demonstrated that he had become a major force in professional tennis. He did not do as well in the other Grand Slam events that year, but he won several professional tournaments and ended the year ranked seventh in the world.

His best Grand Slam season came in 1998 with his most important professional victory, at the French Open. The red clay courts of the Roland Garros Tennis Center, where this Grand Slam tournament is played, are a favorite surface for Spanish players. Indeed, Carlos had to defeat several highly ranked clay-court players, including Chilean Marcelo Rios and his countrymen and friends Felix Mantilla in the semifinals and Alex Corretja in the finals. He won three other tournaments, reached the semifinal of the U.S.

Open, and was a finalist at the ATP Tour World Championship in Hanover, Germany, where the tables were turned when he lost to Corretja. He ended the year ranked fifth in the world, and by the early part of 1999 his continuing high level of performance lifted him to the number-one ranking on the ATP tour.

Continuing the Story

Carlos's position as the number-one male professional tennis player was a short one, lasting only a few weeks, because he had no victories in several of the major tournaments in the spring of 1999. More important, he suffered a stress fracture of his vertebrae, which caused him to miss about eight months for recuperation through the later part of 1999 and into the 2000 season. Additional injuries to his toe and finger frustrated his efforts at a comeback. However, he expressed optimism that he could regain the form that brought him success as a top-ten player and French Open champion.

Summary

Spain has produced a high number of excellent professional tennis players, but most of them have specialized in clay-court tennis, which emphasizes ground strokes, fitness, patience, and endurance. Carlos Moya has these characteristics as a tennis player, but he has developed a more versatile, all-court game, and he is equally comfortable playing at the net. The flair of his game and his versatility have made him more than just a clay-court player. His demonstrated ability to win on a variety of surfaces has brought him a Grand Slam championship and, for a short period, the number-one ranking in men's professional tennis. He has achieved a high level of performance in his sport, and he is poised to continue to improve his record in tennis.

Karen Gould

Additional Sources:
Bodo, Peter. "Spanish Fly." *Tennis* 34, no. 7 (November, 1998): 18-22.
Clarey, C. "Fiesta at the French." *Tennis* 34, no. 4 (August, 1998): 82-84.
Malinowski, M. "The World According to Carlos Moya." *Tennis* 35, no. 8 (October, 1999): 16.

MAJOR CHAMPIONSHIPS

1998	French Open

SHIRLEY MULDOWNEY

Sport: Auto racing

Born: June 19, 1940
Schenectady, New York

Early Life

Shirley Roque Muldowney was born on June 19, 1940, in Schenectady, New York. Her mother, Mae Roque, was a laundress, and her father, Belgium Benedict "Tex" Roque, was a professional prizefighter. Tex taught petite Shirley how to defend herself against bullies at her tough neighborhood school; he also used to take her on his lap to "steer" as he sped along country roads.

In 1956, Shirley met Jack Muldowney, the best hot-rodder in town. At sixteen, with her new driver's permit, she began to drive Jack's Mercury—at 120 miles per hour one night—and then quit school to marry him. (To keep a promise to her father, she got her diploma eight years later.) Jack built Shirley's first fast car, a 1940 Ford Coupe with a Cadillac engine, and got her interested in drag racing.

The Road to Excellence

One year after their marriage, Shirley and Jack had a son, John. Shirley kept driving and Jack worked on her cars. Her reputation as a hot-rodder grew, as well as her fascination with speed. In the late 1950's, stock car drivers were covering the quarter-mile track—1,320 feet—in as little as 7 seconds.

During the 1960's, Shirley raced stock cars, developing her driving technique and reaction time. She also fought authorities from the National Hot Rod Association (NHRA) because they did not want to give women professional status. Shirley and other women persisted until they got the right to apply for NHRA approval.

In 1971, Shirley won her first major race and finished the season ranked in the top five. Touring constantly was difficult, however. Whereas Shirley wanted to race full-time, Jack

wished for a quieter life at home working at his gas station. They divorced in 1972.

That was when Conrad "Connie" Kalitta, a top drag racer, became Shirley's crew chief and agent. He promoted Shirley as "Cha Cha" Muldowney and booked her in drag strips all over the country. Her driving impressed the crowds. Even after suffering two serious track fires in 1972 and 1973, Shirley went on. She decided to enter Top Fuel drag racing.

The Emerging Champion

Shirley was proud to have three drag racing greats sign her application for a Top Fuel license

National Hot Rod Association

in 1974: Don Garlits, Tommy Ivo, and Connie Kalitta. Connie remained her crew chief and Rahn Tobler became her mechanic. Shirley's main interest was speed. Top Fuel cars, named after a potent blend of nitromethane and methanol, could cover the quarter mile in 6 seconds or less.

Shirley's dragster, which looked like a 25-foot hot pink arrow on wheels, shot her into stardom. She was the first woman to qualify for a national Top Fuel event and win the final round. In 1976, she became the first woman to win an NHRA title. Also, she was the first woman to run the quarter mile in less than 6 seconds, win a Winston World Championship (1977), and earn a place on the Auto Racing All-American team. In 1977, after twenty-one years of driving, she was named the NHRA World Champion in Top Fuel.

Even so, some racers doubted her skill, claiming that her low weight (108 pounds) gave her an advantage. Others, however, recognized her strengths: her ability to focus on the job at hand, her quickness, and her studious approach to driving. Most important, she was cool under stress.

Shirley had to fight for her future, however. In 1977, when her long partnership with Kalitta ended, the racing world did not think she could keep winning and gave him credit for her success. Worse, she could not get a sponsor, even though Connie had called her "the best pure driver" he had ever seen. Her agent said it was because she was a woman. Shirley agreed. She had always had to fight for acceptance in the male-dominated world of racing.

Shirley had to enter many more races to support herself and her young pit crew, which now included her son. At the 1980 opening race, their dedication paid off: Shirley and her team won their first big victory without Kalitta and set a 255-miles-per-hour record. That year, Shirley clocked 5.705 seconds at the Gatornationals and won

eleven national events. She had more runs over 250 miles per hour and under 6 seconds than any other driver. Her 1980 world title silenced her critics. She became the first person ever to win the NHRA Top Fuel World Championship more than once. In 1982, she won it again and, to the delight of her fans, beat Kalitta to win the United

NHRA TOP FUEL VICTORIES	
1976-77, 1980	Spring Nationals
1977	Summer Nationals Grand Nationals
1977, 1980, 1982	Top Fuel World Championship Winston World Finals
1980	Fall Nationals
1980, 1982-83	Winter Nationals
1981	Southern Nationals
1981-82	Gatornationals
1982	North Star Nationals U.S. Nationals

RECORDS

First driver to win three NHRA Top Fuel World Championships

Only woman driver to win the U.S. Nationals (1982)

First woman driver to win an NHRA title event (1976)

Twice set record for the fastest speed in drag racing history, the second time at 312.5 miles per hour (1998)

First woman to be licensed to drive as a Top Fuel drag racer by the NHRA (1973)

HONORS AND AWARDS

1975-77, 1980, 1982	American Auto Racing Writers and Broadcasters Association Auto Racing All-American Team
1976-77	*Drag News* Top Fuel Driver of the Year
1977	U.S. House of Representatives Outstanding Achievement Award
1979	Charter Member, NHRA 250-Mile-an-Hour Club
1981-82	*Car Craft* magazine All-Star Team, Top Fuel Driver
1982	Jerry Titus Memorial Award
1985	*Car Craft* magazine Ollie Award
1986	American Auto Racing Writers and Broadcasters Association Comeback Driver of the Year
1989	Charter Member, Cragar Four-Second Club
1990	Inducted into Motorsports Hall of Fame of America
1997	U.S. Sports Academy's Top 25 Pro Female Athletes, 1972-97

1965

States Nationals at Indianapolis. She was the best in the sport.

Continuing the Story

Shirley's life was chronicled in the 1983 Hollywood film *Heart Like a Wheel*. The forty-four-year-old racer was at the height of success when her career took a violent turn. In June, 1984, a front-tire blowout threw her pink dragster into a destructive 600-foot-rollover near the end of a drag strip outside Montreal. Her legs, pelvis, and right hand were shattered. Her left knee was bent backward, and her right thumb and left foot were almost severed. It took eighteen months of operations, therapy, misery, and determination before she could walk again.

With her left ankle permanently fused and one leg shorter than the other, a triumphant Shirley Muldowney returned to racing in January, 1986, at the Firebird International Raceway in Phoenix, Arizona. Her new dragster was decorated with the name of her new sponsor, and it had new tubeless front tires Goodyear had developed to protect drivers from accidents like hers. There was nothing new, however, about Shirley's skill as a racer: Her first run was just .03 seconds slower than her all-time best. She had returned to racing, she said, because driving dragsters was what she did best.

In 1990, Shirley left the NHRA to compete in match racing in the United States and overseas. During the early 1990's, she set twelve track records for speed throughout the United States. She returned to NHRA competition in 1995, and in 1996 she won three national events back to back and finished second in top fuel points.

Shirley continued her record-breaking career in 1998 when her 4.69 second run at 312.5 miles per hour during a qualifying round at the Northern Nationals was the quickest and fastest ever recorded in the history of NHRA competition. In 2000, Shirley improved her best career speed to 319.22, a track record at the nationals in Cordova, Illinois.

Summary

Shirley Muldowney's comeback from a near-fatal crash in 1984 demonstrated her superb skill, stamina, and mental toughness. Her passion for racing has inspired fans and fellow drivers alike, and her belief that she can go faster than anyone else makes her not only a champion driver but also a true racer.

JoAnn Balingit

Additional Sources:

Cockerham, Paul W. *Drag Racing*. Philadelphia, Pa.: Chelsea House, 1997.

Jackson, Bob. *Inside the World of Drag Racing*. Osceola, Wis.: Motorbooks International, 1987.

Radlauer, Ed. *Drag Racing: Then and Now*. Chicago: Children's Press, 1983.

GERD MÜLLER

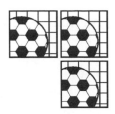

Sport: Soccer

Born: November 11, 1945
　　　　Zinzen, Bavaria, Germany

Early Life

Gerdhardt Müller was born in the small village of Zinzen, in Bavaria, Germany, on November 11, 1945. World War II had ended only three months earlier, and Europe was at peace for the first time in six years. Still, times were difficult for Germany, which had to rebuild itself after the ravages of war. Gerd's early life reflected the harshness of the times. His father died when Gerd was a young boy, and he had to leave school at the age of fifteen. He became an apprentice weaver.

Gerd was born with soccer "in his blood," but as soon as he was old enough to kick a ball in earnest, he discovered that Zinzen possessed no properly marked soccer fields. For years, he and his schoolfriends would improvise with hats and coats for goalposts and anything they could find for a soccer ball.

Gerd Müller takes a shot on goal in 1967.

1967

The Road to Excellence

Even though Gerd had no proper playing facilities, his talent shone through. When he was seventeen, he arranged to have a trial with TSV Nördlingen, the soccer club nearest to his home. Traveling the seven miles home by bus after the trial, he felt triumphant. The Nördlingen coaching staff had been impressed by his skills and had offered him a contract.

Gerd's first match for Nördlingen was the first time he had played on a properly marked-out field. He had to wear borrowed soccer shoes, because he possessed none of his own, but that did not put him off his game, and he scored 2 goals. Over the next two seasons, he scored a total of 46 goals for Nördlingen. Many clubs became interested in signing him, but some decided that Gerd lacked the speed and all-around mobility to be effective in challenging the best defenses. Gerd was small for a striker (he stood only 5 feet 8 inches tall), and at the time, he was also overweight. His teammates at Nördlingen nicknamed him "Dicker" (Fatty).

Wilhelm Neudecker, the president of the Bayern Munich soccer club, was impressed by Gerd's goal-scoring abilities, however. In 1964, he persuaded the Bayern coach, Tchik Cajkovski, to sign him, even though Cajkovski was not enthusiastic. Cajkovski regarded Gerd as "a bear amongst racehorses." Gerd was soon to prove him wrong, scoring 2 goals in his debut for Bayern's senior team and a total of 35 goals in his first season. His performance helped Bayern win promotion to West Germany's highest league, the Bundesliga.

The Emerging Champion

In 1966-1967, Gerd shared top scoring honors in the Bundesliga, with 28 goals. He also won a West German Cup Winners' Medal and made his first appearance for West Germany's national team. Gerd was well on the way to becoming one of the most lethal strikers in the history of the game. He had lost weight and sharpened his reflexes. He excelled in the penalty area and was adept at turning half-chances into goals. He seemed to be able to score goals with either foot and from almost impossible angles. After receiving the ball, he could pivot and turn in a moment, in either direction, leaving opposing defenders beaten. His skills were the result of endless practice. In training sessions, Gerd would arrive an hour earlier and leave an hour later than the other players in order to perfect his goal-scoring skills.

Gerd's years of playing produced a steady stream of successes. In 1967, he won another West German Cup Winners' Medal and a European Cup Winners' Medal. In the semifinal of the latter competition, he scored 4 goals against the Belgian team Standard Liege. He also scored 4 goals for West Germany in a 6-0 win against Albania. By 1969, Gerd was playing regularly for his country. In the same year, Bayern Munich won the Bundesliga title for the first time in their history. The team's success was due in large measure to Gerd's goal-scoring exploits. He was the league's top scorer with 30 goals and gained the nickname "Der Bomber."

In the World Cup finals in Mexico in 1970, Gerd was the tournament's leading scorer, with 10 goals. These included the winning goal against England in the quarterfinal and two goals against Italy in the semifinal, which West Germany lost by 4-3. Then at the top of his profession, Gerd was voted European Player of the Year.

Continuing the Story

In 1972, Gerd scored twice for West Germany in that team's 3-0 European Championship final victory over the Soviet Union. It was the prelude to three years of amazing success for Der Bomber. From 1972 to 1974, Bayern Munich won the Bundesliga championship each year, and Gerd was the leading goal scorer in the Bundesliga in each of those years, with 40, 36, and 30 goals.

One of Gerd's greatest triumphs came in the World Cup final in West Germany in 1974. He achieved every player's dream by scoring the winning goal against Holland. It was a typical Müller effort. Just before halftime, Gerd collected a pass from his teammate Rainer Bonhof inside the penalty area. The pass had arrived behind Gerd, but he controlled the ball, turned quickly, and shot past the Dutch goalkeeper, Jan Jongbloed, almost in one movement.

For the last five years of his career with Bayern Munich, Gerd was involved in a dispute with West

HONORS, AWARDS, AND RECORDS

1966-67, 1971	West German Cup champion
1967	European Cup champion
1967, 1969	West German Player of the Year
1969, 1972-74	West German League champion
1970	European Player of the Year (Ballon d'Or)
	World Cup high scorer (10 goals)
1972	European Championship champion
1974	World Cup champion
1974-76	European Cup champion
	World Cup all-time high scorer (14 goals)

MILESTONES

63 international appearances for West Germany
68 international goals

Germany's soccer administrators and did not play for his country again. His international record, however, speaks for itself: He scored 68 goals in 63 matches for West Germany, a feat that few players from any country can match. He also scored 365 goals in 427 Bundesliga games, and more than 600 goals in all competitions.

In 1979, Gerd moved to the United States, where he played for the Fort Lauderdale Strikers in the North American Soccer League. He left Florida in 1981 and retired to Munich. He would continue to watch his old team play, as well as to contribute a soccer column to a European newspaper.

Summary

Gerd Müller was the most successful striker in West German soccer history and one of the deadliest goal-scorers ever. He seemed to possess a "sixth sense" for positioning, particularly in the penalty area, and whenever he had the ball, there was danger for the opposing defense. Gerd played a large part in making West Germany the outstanding national team in the world in the early and mid-1970's.

Bryan Aubrey

Additional Sources:

Henshaw, Richard. *The Encyclopedia of World Soccer.* Washington, D.C.: New Republic Books, 1979.

Hollander, Zander. *The American Encyclopedia of Soccer.* New York: Everett House, 1980.

CHRIS MULLIN

Sport: Basketball

Born: July 30, 1963
Brooklyn, New York

Early Life

Christopher Paul Mullin was born on July 30, 1963, in the borough of Brooklyn in New York City to Rod Mullin, a customs inspector, and Eileen Mullin, a homemaker. He was the third of five children. At a young age, Chris was taught by his father to value hard work; his father also taught him that involvement in team sports helped a person to learn how to cooperate with others toward a common goal. Although his parents did not push Chris, he grew up with a strong desire to achieve.

While in grammar school, Chris began spending long hours at night shooting baskets. When he was ten, Chris won the Elks National Free Throw Contest by making 23 of 25 shots. He enjoyed playing basketball so much that at the age of twelve, he stopped participating in swimming and baseball. In high school, he became one of the best players in the city. He first attended Power Memorial High School, but he then transferred to Xaverian, where he helped his team to win the New York state championship.

The Road to Excellence

Although recruiters from across the country were interested in Chris, he decided to stay close to home and attend St. John's University, which was merely a commuter train ride away in the borough of Queens. Moreover, the St. John's basketball coach, Lou Carneseca, had a national reputation. Carneseca had seen Chris play when Chris was still in grammar school, and he told the boy even then that he wanted to coach him.

Chris had become an excellent basketball player by constant practicing. He was a smart player and a great shooter. Chris felt at home playing for St. John's. His girlfriend, Liz Con-

Courtesy of Golden State Warriors

nolly, kept the statistics for the basketball team. During his four years at St. John's, Chris earned a reputation as a team player who had extraordinary court vision. If he did not have a clear shot, Chris could find someone who did.

A solid performer during his freshman and sophomore years, Chris raised his level of play remarkably during his junior year. He shot better than 57 percent from the field, averaged 22.9 points per game, and was named to several All-American teams. He was also named to play for the United States in the 1984 Summer Olympics. At the Games in Los Angeles, Chris averaged 12 points per game and helped the U.S. team to win the gold medal. During his last year at St. John's, Chris averaged 19.8 points per game and helped

1970

his team reach the Final Four of the National Collegiate Athletic Association (NCAA) championship tournament. He was named to every All-America team as a senior.

The Emerging Champion

In the 1985 National Basketball Association (NBA) draft, Chris was chosen in the first round by the Golden State Warriors with the seventh pick overall. Although he was eager to play professionally, moving to the Oakland, California, area was a tough adjustment for him and his family. He was not sure that he really wanted to move that far away from home, but this was his chance to play in the NBA, and he resolved to make the most of his opportunity.

At 6 feet 7 inches tall, Chris was capable of playing both the guard and the small forward positions. He was not a great leaper, nor did he possess great speed, but he made up for these deficiencies by having keen court awareness and a wonderful shooting touch from anywhere on the court. When Chris joined the Warriors, however, he was shocked to find that the team did not function as a cohesive unit. Chris was used to hard work and constant practice, but the other members of the team did not appreciate his work ethic. Eventually, Chris became discouraged and began to lose interest in training.

Chris averaged 14.0 points per game in his first year with Golden State and 15.1 in his second, good totals for a young player. Soon, however, he began drinking heavily to make up for his disappointment with his life away from his home and friends. Critics were beginning to believe that Chris was merely another college star who could not make the transition into the NBA. Luckily for Chris, Don Nelson became the new Warrior's coach before the 1987-1988 season. Nelson was a former player who as a coach had earned a reputation for expecting a total commitment to the team from his players.

Nelson was the first person to confront Chris about his drinking problem. The coach demanded that Chris get help, telling him that otherwise he was through as a player. It took some time for Chris to accept that he was an alcoholic and that he needed to seek treatment, but in December of 1987, he checked himself into Centinela Hospital in Los Angeles. His parents were with him. Because his father was a recovering alcoholic, Chris knew that he could count on his father's support. Chris was in a rehabilitation program for a month. He was told that he could never drink alcohol again. Chris decided to enter into an intense fitness program to help in his recovery and to get himself ready to play basketball again.

STATISTICS

Season	GP	FGM	FG%	FTM	FT%	Reb.	Ast.	TP	PPG
1985-86	55	287	.463	189	.896	115	105	768	14.0
1986-87	82	477	.514	269	.825	181	261	1,242	15.1
1987-88	60	470	.508	239	.885	205	290	1,213	20.2
1988-89	82	830	.509	493	.892	483	415	2,176	26.5
1989-90	78	682	.536	505	.889	463	319	1,956	25.1
1990-91	82	777	.536	513	.884	443	329	2,107	25.7
1991-92	81	830	.524	350	.833	450	286	2,074	25.6
1992-93	46	474	.510	183	.810	232	166	1,191	25.9
1993-94	62	410	.472	165	.753	345	315	1,040	16.8
1994-95	25	170	.489	94	.879	115	125	476	19.0
1995-96	55	269	.499	137	.856	159	194	734	13.3
1996-97	79	438	.553	184	.864	317	322	1,143	14.5
1997-98	82	333	.481	154	**.939**	249	186	927	11.3
1998-99	50	177	.477	80	.870	160	81	507	10.1
1999-00	47	80	.428	37	.902	76	37	242	5.1
2000-01	20	36	.340	24	.857	41	19	115	5.8
Totals	986	6,740	.509	3,616	.865	4,034	3,450	17,911	18.2

Notes: Boldface indicates statistical leader. GP = games played; FGM = field goals made; FG% = field goal percentage; FTM = free throws made; FT% = free throw percentage; Reb. = rebounds; Ast. = assists; TP = total points; PPG = points per game

Continuing the Story

Chris came back to the Warriors in the best shape of his life. Before he started the fitness program, Chris had weighed 245 pounds. With the help of the Warriors' conditioning coach, Mark Grabow, Chris trimmed his weight to 210 pounds. Chris worked to keep himself sober and to keep himself physically fit for NBA basketball, and by the 1988-1989 season, he had raised his average to 26.5 points per game.

Chris, though, became more than merely a player who could score. He became a team leader who made his teammates better players. In 1992, his multiple skills were recognized when he was selected to be a member of the United States "Dream Team," which would compete at the Barcelona Summer Olympics. The Dream Team included such players as Michael Jordan and Magic Johnson, and they won the gold medal as expected.

On July 23, 1990, Chris's father died of lung cancer, but Chris remained determined to make his father proud. An injury kept him out of parts of the 1992-1993 and 1993-1994 seasons, but he worked hard to return to action. Knee and ankle injuries produced another disappointing season for Chris in 1994-1995, as he missed fifty-seven of the first fifty-nine games with the Warriors. After starting the first nineteen games in the 1995-1996 season, Chris was moved to a reserve role and averaged only 13.3 points per game, the lowest figure of his career to that point.

For the first time in five seasons, Chris was finally injury free for the 1996-1997 campaign. He played in seventy-nine games and averaged 14.5 points per game. On August 12, 1997, he was traded to the Indiana Pacers. Chris left the Warriors as the all-time franchise leader in games played and in steals, fourth in total points and assists, and fifth in blocked shots. With the Pacers, Chris led the NBA in free-throw percentage (.939) for the 1997-1998 season. He led the Pacers in three-point percentage in 1998-1999 and ranked second in the NBA. After another injury in the 1999-2000 season, Chris returned to

HONORS AND AWARDS	
1984-85	College All-American
1984, 1992	Gold Medal, Olympic basketball
1985	United Press International College Player of the Year U.S. Basketball Writers Association College Player of the Year Wooden Award
1989, 1991	All-NBA Second Team
1989-93	NBA All-Star Team
1990	All-NBA Third Team
1992	All-NBA First Team

the Pacers lineup in time to help them into the NBA finals against the Lakers. The Lakers prevailed, four games to two.

As of 2001, Chris had appeared in over seventy NBA playoff games, averaging 13.8 points, 3.3 rebounds, and 2.1 assists per contest. He had been selected as an NBA All-Star on five occasions. Known for his quick hands, crisp passing, and accurate shooting, Chris was one of only thirty-one players in NBA history to register over 15,000 points, 3,000 rebounds, and 3,000 assists. Chris married his college girlfriend, Liz Connolly, in the fall of 1991. They had three sons, Sean, Christopher, and Liam.

Summary

Chris Mullin overcame major obstacles to become an NBA star. Through hard work and the love and support of those close to him, Chris reinvented himself and, in the process, became one of basketball's all-time greats.

Jeffry Jensen

Additional Sources:

Bjarkman, Peter C. *The Biographical History of Basketball.* Chicago, Ill.: Masters Press, 1998.

Morgan, Terri. *Chris Mullin: Sure Shot.* Minneapolis, Minn.: Lerner Publishing, 1994.

Mullin, Chris, with Brian Coleman. *The Young Basketball Player.* New York: DK, 1995.

TORI MURDEN

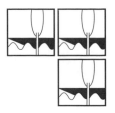

Sport: Rowing

Born: March 6, 1963
Brooksville, Florida

Early Life

Victoria E. "Tori" Murden was the youngest of three children born to educator Albert Murden and his wife, Martha. Tori earned a bachelor's degree in psychology from Smith College in 1985. She was captain of Smith's varsity basketball team as well as an outstanding scholar. By the time she was nineteen she was rowing competitively. After graduating from Smith, she earned a master of divinity degree from Harvard University in 1989 and a law degree from the University of Louisville in 1995. Her jobs have included running homeless shelters, working as a chaplain in an inner-city general hospital, and directing programs to rehabilitate depressed neighborhoods.

The Road to Excellence

In 1988, while a student at Harvard, Tori took off three months between semesters to join the nine-member International South Pole Expedition, which skied 750 miles across Antarctica to the geographic South Pole. Tori was one of two women who were the first to travel to the South Pole by an overland route. This expedition was also noteworthy in that it was the first one in which an American reached the South Pole via an overland route.

Tori achieved another first when she became the first woman to climb Mount Lewis Nunatuk in Antarctica. Other mountains she has climbed include Mount Silverthrone in Alaska and Mount Kenya in East Africa. She also participated in numerous ice climbing and kayaking expeditions.

In 1991, Tori devoted herself to training for a spot on the 1992 Olympic rowing team, which would compete in the Summer Games in Barcelona. Her specialty was the single scull racing boat. While driving to one of the trials, she was injured in a car accident. When Tori learned another rower, Michelle Knox, who was almost certain to make the team, needed a replacement boat, she loaned Michelle her equipment.

Rower Tori Murden in June, 1998, before her first attempt to row across the Atlantic.

1973

In 1996 Tori first thought of rowing across the ocean when she learned of the Port St. Charles Atlantic Rowing Race. She and a teammate joined thirty-two other teams seeking to row three thousand miles across the Atlantic. The adventure offered her the opportunity to test her courage and her belief in her own abilities and limitations. Tori and a high school friend, Louise Graff, were the sole American entrants and the only all-female team. They were forced to drop out of the race twice—after Tori became ill with food poisoning and then when the team's electrical equipment failed.

The Emerging Champion

After she returned to Louisville to live, Kenneth Crutchlow, founder of the Ocean Rowing Society, contacted Tori to determine her interest in attempting another Atlantic crossing in a rowboat. He had met her during the Atlantic race and was impressed by her fortitude and resolve in the face of obstacles. Crutchlow told her that Sector Sport Watches would sponsor the attempt to cross the Atlantic from west to east. At the time, only five rowers—all men—had completed the west-to-east journey. At first, Tori thought rough seas and contrary winds would make such a crossing impossible.

Persuaded she could successfully complete the journey, however, she set out on June 14, 1998, from Nags Head, North Carolina, heading to the coast of France. The 3,600-mile journey was expected to last more than one hundred days and carry her to Brest, France. Only eight days into the trip, the boat capsized, and she lost her communications equipment. Hurricanes Bonnie and Danielle battered her boat. Short of her goal by 950 miles, Tori activated her distress beacon and was rescued.

While not the record she hoped to set, Tori spent eighty-five consecutive days alone at sea—more than any other rower. She also set the record for the most continuous miles rowing by an American, man or woman. In the next-closest time, set in 1997, Peggy Bouchet of France had spent eighty days alone at sea when she attempted an east-to-west crossing of the Atlantic Ocean. Bouchet was rescued 120 miles east of Guadeloupe, her destination.

Continuing the Story

Tori's rowboat, the *American Pearl*, was designed to turn upright by itself. She and friends built the original craft from a kit during the summer of 1997. The 23-foot-long by 6-foot-wide boat was made of plywood and fiberglass. It was originally designed to carry a crew of two on a relatively calm east-to-west route between the Canary Islands and Barbados.

In 1999, she decided to make a second attempt to row across the Atlantic, this time east to west. This route is five hundred miles shorter, is warmer, and usually experiences fewer storms. On September 13, 1999, Tori set off in her 23-foot boat from the largest of the Canary Islands, Tenerife, which is just off the west coast of Africa. Her destination was Guadeloupe in the West Indies, and her goal was to become the first woman and the first American to row across the Atlantic Ocean.

The journey was grueling, requiring that Tori row twelve to fourteen hours a day. She finished the 3,333-mile journey in eighty-one days, seven hours, and forty-six minutes. She postponed her landing in the port city of Pointe-à-Pitre on the French Island of Guadeloupe by one day (December 2, 1999) in order to allow her backers, friends, and supporters to witness her arrival.

Summary

Tori Murden's feat—becoming the first woman and the first American to row solo across the Atlantic Ocean—is made even more incredible in that the death rate for people trying to cross an ocean in a rowboat is approximately one in nine. In addition to her Atlantic crossing and her world record for the longest time at sea by a

---

RECORDS AND MILESTONES

1988	First woman to climb Mount Lewis Nunatuk in the Antarctic
1989	First woman and first American to ski to the geographic South Pole
1998	Rowed 3,043 miles in 85 days, setting world record for most days at sea by a woman and most miles rowed solo continuously by an American
1999	First woman and first American to row across the Atlantic Ocean, solo and unsupported

woman solo rower, she was the first woman to reach the summit of Mount Lewis Nunatuk in the Antarctic and the first American to ski to the geographic South Pole. Tori said ocean rowing taught her that no one reaches his or her goal all at once. She wants to be remembered as a woman who tried to do something extraordinary and, after a few tries, succeeded.

Fred Buchstein

Additional Sources:

Barnette, Martha. "The Unsinkable Tori Murden." *Women's Sports and Fitness* 3 (June, 2000): 108.

Benham, Barbara. "The Far Shore." *Working Woman* 25 (August, 2000): 32-34.

Dodd, Christopher. *The Story of World Rowing.* London: Stanley Paul, 1992.

Moss, Deborah. "Victory at Sea." *Sports Illustrated* 91 (December 13, 1999): 98.

DALE MURPHY

Sport: Baseball

Born: March 12, 1956
Portland, Oregon

Early Life

Dale Bryan Murphy was born March 12, 1956, in Portland, Oregon. Dale comes from an athletic family. His great-grandfather was a semi-professional catcher and performed in rodeos in Nebraska. Ledger Bryan, his grandfather, was a center fielder as a young man in Oklahoma.

When Dale was in the fifth grade, his family moved to the San Francisco area. His father, who worked for Westinghouse, took him to major league baseball games in Oakland and San Francisco. Dale got to see his idol, Willie Mays, play for the Giants.

Atlanta Brave Dale Murphy in 1989.

AP/Wide World Photos

The Road to Excellence

After two years in California, the Murphys returned to Portland, where Dale played baseball and basketball at Woodrow Wilson High School. Jack Dunn, his baseball coach, was the first to recognize that his young catcher had major league potential. Dale was offered a baseball scholarship to Arizona State University but turned it down after he was selected first in the 1974 draft of amateur players by the Atlanta Braves.

Dale hit well in the minor leagues but displayed a wild arm from behind the plate. After fifty-eight games as a catcher with the Braves, he was converted to first base by manager Bobby Cox in 1978. After Dale found his new position almost equally difficult, the Braves became concerned about finding a spot where the 6-foot 4-inch, 210-pounder would do the least damage.

The Emerging Champion

Cox switched Dale to center field in 1980, and Dale quickly proved to be a natural outfielder, possessing the speed to run down balls other outfielders would not even come close to and a strong, accurate arm. Few base runners attempted to go for an extra base when Dale was in his prime. Despite being switched from one outfield post to another, depending upon the needs of his team, Dale received Gold Glove awards for his fielding skills for five consecutive seasons.

He gradually improved as a power hitter, having his best years from 1982 to 1985, when he led the National League in home runs, runs batted in, and slugging percentage twice each and in runs and walks once. He was named most valuable player in both 1982 (when the Braves finished first in the National League West for only the second time) and 1983.

Along with Mike Schmidt, Dale was the most feared power hitter in the National League during the 1980's. He even hit home runs in Hous-

STATISTICS

Season	GP	AB	Hits	2B	3B	HR	Runs	RBI	BA	SA
1976	19	65	17	6	0	0	3	9	.262	.354
1977	18	76	24	8	1	2	5	14	.316	.526
1978	151	530	120	14	3	23	66	79	.226	.394
1979	104	384	106	7	2	21	53	57	.276	.469
1980	156	569	160	27	2	33	98	89	.281	.510
1981	104	369	91	12	1	13	43	50	.247	.390
1982	162	598	168	23	2	36	113	**109**	.281	.507
1983	162	589	178	24	4	36	131	**121**	.302	**.540**
1984	162	607	176	32	8	**36**	94	100	.290	**.547**
1985	162	616	185	32	2	**37**	**118**	111	.300	.539
1986	160	614	163	29	7	29	89	83	.265	.477
1987	159	566	167	27	1	44	115	105	.295	.580
1988	156	592	134	35	4	24	77	77	.226	.421
1989	154	574	131	16	0	20	60	84	.228	.361
1990	154	563	138	23	1	24	60	83	.245	.417
1991	153	544	137	33	1	18	66	81	.252	.415
1992	18	62	10	1	0	2	5	7	.161	.274
1993	26	42	6	1	0	0	1	7	.143	.167
Totals	2,180	7,960	2,111	350	39	398	1,197	1,266	.265	.469

Notes: Boldface indicates statistical leader. GP = games played; AB = at bats; 2B = doubles; 3B = triples; HR = home runs; RBI = runs batted in; BA = batting average; SA = slugging average

ton's Astrodome, the most difficult of all major league stadiums for power hitters. He slugged 6 homers there in 1984, not only the most by a visiting player but more than all but one of the Astros. Dale combined speed with power, becoming, in 1983, only the sixth player to have more than 30 home runs and 30 stolen bases in the same season.

Most power hitters strike out frequently, and Dale would do so more often than most, almost once a game over his career thus far. He would be an awesome slugger in one game and flail away like an amateur the next. He led the league in strikeouts three times.

One of the most durable players in major league history, Dale played 740 consecutive games between 1981 and 1986, the twelfth longest such streak. The streak appeared over in its 676th game when Dale cut his hand after running into an outfield wall and received nine stitches, but he returned in the next game as a pinch hitter and hit a home run.

Dale was one of the most popular players of the 1980's, being voted to the National League All-Star team by the fans from 1982 through 1987 and receiving the most votes in 1985. He hoped to end his career with the Braves, but for a variety of reasons, including his salary and the team's commitment to younger players, he was traded to the Philadelphia Phillies during the 1990 season.

The following year, Dale hit 18 home runs with 81 runs batted in, but he was forced to miss most of 1992 because of injuries. He signed with the expansion Colorado Rockies in 1993 but decided to retire early in the season. The Atlanta Braves honored Dale, who holds thirteen franchise records, by retiring his number during the 1994 season.

Continuing the Story

Dale has received as much attention for his character and his off-the-field activities as for his accomplishments in baseball. Raised a Presbyterian, he was introduced to Mormonism in 1975 by teammate Barrl Bonnell, who baptized him following the season. He has been strongly active in the Mormon church ever since, teaching Bible classes to teenagers and donating 10 percent of his salary to the church. Unlike some contemporary athletes, however, Dale has not been a proselytizer for his religion who imposes his views on his teammates.

He met his wife, Nancy, while attending Brigham Young University after the 1978 season, and they were married in October, 1979. They wanted a large family and have six sons, Chad, Travis, Shawn, Tyson, Taylor, and Jacob. The Murphys' seemingly ideal family life has been tested by two miscarriages and by the health problems of Travis, born with Rubinstein-Taybi Syndrome, a rare disease that retards mental and physical development.

Dale is famous for being unable to refuse a request for his time, speaking to countless groups, devoting time to numerous charitable organizations, visiting people, especially children, in hospitals, giving endless autographs, and having his picture taken with strangers. He has said that because of his upbringing—his mother was a volunteer teacher of handicapped children—he cannot say no. For his off-the-field contributions to society, Dale won the Lou Gehrig Award in 1985

and was named, along with seven other similarly unselfish athletes, as a co-recipient of the *Sports Illustrated* Sportsman of the Year award in 1987.

Summary

Dale Murphy has been called the most admirable baseball superstar. His boyish awkwardness has earned him comparisons with everyone from Jimmy Stewart to John-Boy Walton. He blushes at cursing and catches fly balls with both hands in an era of showboating fielders. He rarely loses his temper, an unusual attribute for a free-swinging slugger. Perhaps the best example of his character and his commitment to excellence is his attending the winter instructional league after the 1982 season to work on his hitting. Such dedication paid off, with some observers considering him the National League's most improved player in 1983, even though he had been most valuable player the year before.

Michael Adams

HONORS AND AWARDS	
1980, 1982-87	National League All-Star Team
1982-83	National League most valuable player
1982-86	National League Gold Glove Award
1985	Lou Gehrig Award
1987	*Sports Illustrated* Co-Sportsman of the Year
1994	Uniform number 3 retired by Atlanta Braves

Additional Sources:

Kirkjian, Tim. "Graceful Exit." *Sports Illustrated* 78, no. 22 (1993).

Murphy, Dale, with Brad Rock and Lee Warnick. *Murph.* Salt Lake City, Utah: Bookcraft, 1986.

O'Keefe, John. "Dale Murphy, Braves' Double MVP." *Sports Illustrated* 91, no. 15 (1999).

EDDIE MURRAY

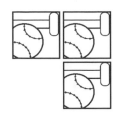

Sport: Baseball

Born: February 24, 1956
Los Angeles, California

Early Life

Eddie Clarence Murray was born on February 24, 1956, in Los Angeles, California, to Charles Murray, an hourly worker, and Carrie Murray. He was the eighth of twelve children. Eddie learned to play baseball at an early age by playing with his brothers and sisters in their own yard. Baseballs, though, were scarce in Eddie's impoverished neighborhood; sometimes he would get a chance to hit tennis balls, but often he had to make do with bottle caps or the plastic lids found on cans. When he was old enough, Eddie participated in Little League, Babe Ruth, and Connie Mack League baseball. He attended Locke High School in Los Angeles, where he played first base and pitched for the school team. Future major league players Ozzie Smith and Darrell Jackson also played with Eddie at Locke.

The Road to Excellence

On June 5, 1973, the Baltimore Orioles of the American League (AL) selected Eddie in the third round of the amateur draft. The Orioles signed him to a contract for a $25,000 bonus. Eddie would spend the next four years in the minor leagues. In 1973, he played in the Appalachian League at Bluefield, West Virginia. In fifty games with Bluefield, Eddie hit .287 with 11

home runs, and he was named Appalachian League Player of the Year.

Eddie was sent to Miami of the Florida State League for the 1974 season. Playing first base, he led the league in putouts with 1,114 and assists with 51; he also led all Florida State League first basemen with 113 double plays. In addition, he batted a respectable .289 and led the league in doubles with 29. Before the 1974 season ended,

Eddie Murray entered the tenth-place spot on the all-time hit list during this game in August, 1997.

AP/Wide World Photos

1979

STATISTICS

Season	GP	AB	Hits	2B	3B	HR	Runs	RBI	BA	SA
1977	160	611	173	29	2	27	81	88	.283	.470
1978	161	610	174	32	3	27	85	95	.285	.480
1979	159	606	179	30	2	25	90	99	.295	.475
1980	158	621	186	36	2	32	100	116	.300	.519
1981	99	378	111	21	2	22	57	78	.294	.534
1982	151	550	174	30	1	32	87	110	.316	.549
1983	156	582	178	30	3	33	115	111	.306	.538
1984	162	588	180	26	3	29	97	110	.306	.509
1985	156	583	173	37	1	31	111	124	.297	.523
1986	137	495	151	25	1	17	61	84	.305	.463
1987	160	618	171	28	3	30	89	91	.277	.477
1988	161	603	171	27	2	28	75	84	.284	.474
1989	160	594	147	29	1	20	66	88	.247	.401
1990	155	558	184	22	3	26	96	95	.330	.520
1991	153	576	150	23	1	19	69	96	.260	.403
1992	156	551	144	37	2	16	64	93	.261	.423
1993	154	610	174	28	1	27	77	100	.285	.467
1994	108	433	110	21	1	17	57	76	.254	.425
1995	113	436	141	21	0	21	68	82	.323	.516
1996	152	566	147	21	1	22	69	79	.260	.417
1997	55	167	37	7	0	3	13	15	.222	.317
Totals	3,026	11,336	3,255	560	35	504	1,627	1,914	.287	.470

Notes: GP = games played; AB = at bats; 2B = doubles; 3B = triples; HR = home runs; RBI = runs batted in; BA = batting average; SA = slugging average

Eddie was transferred to Asheville, North Carolina, to play for the team there, which was part of the Southern League. He remained in Asheville for the 1975 season. There, the coaching staff decided to make him a switch-hitter, so Eddie, a natural right-handed hitter, was taught to bat from the left side. On his first time batting left-handed, he hit a solid double. For the season, Eddie hit 17 home runs and batted .264. He remained in the Southern League for the start of the 1976 season, batting .298 and slugging 12 home runs before earning promotion to Rochester of the International League, the Orioles' top minor-league affiliate.

Rochester was Eddie's last minor-league stop. In fifty-four games with Rochester, Eddie hit .274 with 11 home runs and 40 runs batted in (RBIs). Baltimore's management believed that Eddie was more than ready to make the move to the major leagues, and he joined the Orioles for the 1977 season.

The Emerging Champion

In his first year with the Orioles, Eddie was used mainly as a designated hitter, although he did play part-time at first base and in the outfield.

He had an impressive first season with the Orioles, batting .283 with 27 home runs and 88 RBIs in 160 games, and he was named AL Rookie of the Year by the Baseball Writers Association of America. Baltimore's veteran first baseman Lee May helped Eddie to improve both his fielding and hitting skills. Standing 6 feet 2 inches and weighing 190 pounds, Eddie was built to be a home-run hitter; he could also hit for average. In 1978, Eddie became the Orioles' regular first baseman. Never one to seek out publicity, he quietly established himself as a remarkable athlete by his performances on the baseball diamond.

Eddie made steady improvement in fielding first base. In 1978, he led AL first basemen with 1,504 putouts, and in 1982 he won the first of three consecutive Gold Glove Awards. While his fielding became nothing short of topnotch, Eddie proved even more impressive at the plate. During his years with the Orioles, he was consistently among the league's leading home-run hitters and RBI men. In 1979 and 1983, he helped the Orioles to reach the World Series; although Baltimore lost the 1979 series to Pittsburgh, in 1983 Eddie and his teammates beat Philadelphia to become world champions.

1980

Eddie remained with the Orioles through the 1988 season. In his twelve years with the team, he slugged 333 home runs and batted .295, totals that established him as the best switch-hitter since Mickey Mantle.

Continuing the Story

After the 1988 season, Eddie was traded to the Los Angeles Dodgers of the National League (NL). In his first season with the Dodgers, his batting average tumbled to .247, but he managed to lead NL first basemen with a .996 fielding percentage. Eddie shook off his hitting slump the next year, batting a career-high .330. Although he had reached his mid-thirties, he remained a skilled first baseman and a crafty hitter.

After the 1991 season, Eddie signed as a free agent with the New York Mets. Never one who felt the need to talk to reporters, he had earned a reputation as a moody player, especially in the major media cities of Los Angeles and New York. Eddie believed that his performance on the field would do his talking for him. In 1992, he batted .261, but he drove in 93 runs. At thirty-seven, Eddie found himself to be a veteran fighting for respect, but he refused to believe that he was merely a once-great player whose best years were behind him. In 1993, he showed that he was still capable of being a force in baseball, batting .285 with 27 home runs and 100 RBIs. Eddie had proved himself to be one of the best ever to play the game, but there was still some baseball left in him. In 1994, he took the field as a Cleveland Indian; in his first game with Cleveland, he broke the all-time major league record for games played at first base.

The following year, Eddie batted .323 with 21 homers. He collected his three thousandth hit on June 30 at Minnesota and appeared in his third World Series, a losing effort against the Braves.

Eddie returned to Baltimore in 1996 in a trade for pitcher Kent Mercker. On September 6, he hammered his five hundredth career home run into the right-field bleachers at Camden Yards. He reinvigorated the struggling Orioles club, helping them to secure a wild card spot in the playoffs. Eddie and the Orioles upset Cleveland but eventually fell to the soon-to-be world champions, the Yankees.

Baltimore honored their former superstar by retiring Eddie's number, 33, in a formal ceremony on May 31, 1996. Eddie played briefly for the Angels and Dodgers in 1997 but announced his retirement prior to the 1998 season.

Summary

Eddie Murray's ability to hit for both power and average made him one of the most feared switch-hitters in baseball history. He supplemented his offensive skills with defensive excellence and steady play to become one of the top players of his generation.

Jeffry Jensen

Additional Sources:

Kuenster, John. "Eddie Murray Quietly Polishes His Hall of Fame Credentials." *Baseball Digest* 54, no. 8 (1995).

Singer, Tom. "Murray's Numbers Speak Louder than Words." *Sport* 86, no. 8 (1995).

HONORS AND AWARDS	
1977	American League Rookie of the Year
1978,1981-86	American League All-Star Team
1982-84	American League Gold Glove Award
1991	National League All-Star Team
1996	Uniform number 33 retired by Baltimore Orioles

TY MURRAY

Sport: Rodeo

Born: October 11, 1969
    Phoenix, Arizona

Early Life

Ty Murray was born outside Phoenix, Arizona, the youngest of Butch and Joy Murray's three children and their only son. Butch Murray trained horses and broke colts for a living, and Joy Murray won bull-riding trophies in her youth. Ty and his sisters learned to rope and ride as naturally as they learned to walk and talk. Ty's first shoes were cowboy boots, and by the time he was three he was riding calves unaided.

Ty's early passion for riding and his prodigious striving for excellence marked him as special from early childhood. In third grade, Ty was assigned to write a response to the question, "If you could accomplish anything in the world, what would it be?" Ty's response was specific and lofty: He wrote that he wanted to top the record of Jim Mahan, who won the Professional Rodeo Cowboy Association's All-Around Championship title six times. At that time, in the mid-1970's, no one thought that Mahan's record could ever be broken.

The Road to Excellence

Ty never wanted to be anything but a cowboy; virtually every activity he engaged in, and every decision he made, was bent toward that goal. To improve his balance, he walked along the tops of fences. He taught himself to ride a unicycle and, when that became easy, rode it while carrying weights in each hand. He saved money he earned doing chores and bought a bucking machine, which he rode until his thighs bled. At night, according to his mother, he slept in the "spurring position" used in bronc riding: toes out, heels in.

Ty began riding small bulls when he was nine years old. The second bull he ever rode threw and stepped

Prorodeo Hall of Fame and Museum of the American Cowboy, Colorado Springs, Colorado

on him, breaking his jaw. When Ty was thirteen, rodeo immortal Jim Mahan saw him ride at the Little Britches national finals in Colorado. The boy, Mahan remarked, was riding better at thirteen than Mahan had as a world champion. Already the style that would distinguish Ty was evident: clean, smooth, precise and, in Mahan's words, "almost Zen-like."

In high school, Ty continued to compete in rodeo and to hone his skills. He joined his school's gymnastics team expressly because he thought it would improve his coordination and balance. Although only in his late teens, he was already pushing the envelope of athleticism in his sport and honing what many consider the most disciplined physical machine in rodeo. In 1987, he won the National High School All-Around Cowboy title, competing in saddle bronc, bareback, and bull riding.

After completing high school, Ty moved to Texas and enrolled at Odessa College, a two-year school, small but with a premier rodeo program and conveniently located on the Professional Rodeo Cowboy Association (PRCA) circuit. In 1989, he claimed the National Intercollegiate Rodeo Association's all-around title and also competed in his first PRCA national finals, where he won his first professional All-Around Cowboy title, making him, at twenty, the youngest All-Around Cowboy winner in PRCA history.

The Emerging Champion

Ty returned to the PRCA finals for the next five years (1990-1994), and each year he walked away with the All-Around Cowboy championship title. This consistency is remarkable enough in itself, but even more so when one considers that Ty competed always in the most grueling "roughstock" events—bareback, saddle bronc, and bull riding. The physical toll these events exact, and their sky-high injury rates, tend to weed out all but the toughest competitors. Ty's ability to withstand and excel in these events is testimony to his discipline and toughness. "Timed events," calf roping, team roping, and steer wrestling, while requiring terrific skill and speed, are less physically arduous. Ty's choice of events amounted to a particularly grueling triathlon.

When Ty began riding professionally, he partnered, or shared driving and traveling expenses,

MAJOR CHAMPIONSHIPS AND HONORS		
1988	PRCA Resistol Overall and Bareback Rookie of the Year	
1989-1994, 1998	PRCA World All-Around Cowboy Champion	
1993, 1998	PRCA World Bull Riding Champion	

with veteran cowboy and longtime family friend Cody Lambert. Lambert had known Ty since his babyhood and mentored him in his riding, and he was known as one of the sharpest minds and most solid business heads in the sport. Eight years older than Ty, he undertook to teach him the ropes.

Lambert's intimate inside knowledge of stock contractors and events allowed him to know which rodeos were worth entering, based not only on the prize money but also on the quality of the stock. A good rider has a better chance to make money if the stock is tough. With Lambert's help, Ty not only won and continued winning, but also prospered financially. Ty's talent and grit probably predestined a rise to the top of his profession. There is no question, however, that Cody Lambert's presence in Ty's life—as friend and adviser—sped his ascent.

Continuing the Story

Despite his extraordinary athleticism, Ty has not been exempt from injuries. He has been sidelined repeatedly for damage to his knees and shoulders. What sets him apart is his ability to rebound after each setback, with skills and riding confidence seemingly unfazed by enforced layoffs. In 2000, Ty shifted his attentions from the PRCA, which had already yielded him seven All-Around Cowboy championships and numerous other honors, and focused more on his bull riding and on the highly lucrative Professional Bull Riders World Championship. This move allowed him not only to focus his energies but also to spend less time on the road.

Summary

Ty Murray is a rarity: a child prodigy who fulfilled the promise of his youth. From early childhood he was consumed by a love of rodeo and a driving ambition to break records and set new ones. He progressed steadily from youth rodeos to high school and college events, on to the professional circuit, gathering virtually every honor the sport has to bestow. By virtue of his innate talent, rigorous self-discipline, and steady determination, he has become one of the greatest athletes rodeo has ever seen.

Christel Reges

Additional Sources:

Coplon, Jeff. *Gold Buckle: The Magnificent Obsession of Rodeo Bull Riders*. San Francisco: HarperCollinsWest, 1995.

Hollandsworth, Skip. "Sweetheart of the Rodeo." *Texas Monthly*, May, 1999, 118.

Professional Bull Riders Online. http://www.PBRNOW.com.

STAN MUSIAL

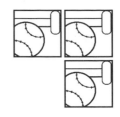

Sport: Baseball

Born: November 21, 1920
Donora, Pennsylvania

Early Life

In Donora, Pennsylvania, where Stanley Frank Musial was born on November 21, 1920, a young man from a working-class background could look forward to employment in the western Pennsylvania coal mines or in a steel mill. Lukasz Musial, a Polish immigrant, wanted something better for his children. When the Depression of the 1930's hit Donora, hc became even more determined to see his fifth child and first son, Stanley, attend college. Stan was thinking more about sports. He especially relished any opportunity to visit Forbes Field in Pittsburgh to see the Pirates play.

The Road to Excellence

At Donora High School, Stan starred in both basketball and baseball. The former sport offered the promise of a college scholarship, but Stan had set his heart on being a left-handed pitcher.

In 1937, still short of his seventeenth birthday, Stan was offered a professional baseball contract. Lukasz knew that only a small percentage of players in baseball's far-flung minor league system ever made it to the major leagues and that minor league salaries were pitifully small. When he rejected the offer, Stan cried, and Mrs. Musial talked Lukasz into giving their son a chance to pursue his dream.

At Williamson, Virginia, in 1938,

Stan won only six games, but he posted a 9-2 record the next year, and in 1940, at Daytona Beach, Florida, his strong hitting led to service in center field on days when he was not pitching. One day while diving for a fly ball, however, he fell heavily on his left shoulder. His pitching ca-

1985

reer, he soon learned, was over at age nineteen.

Prospects looked dim for Stan, already married and his wife expecting a baby, but his manager, Dick Kerr, and his wife took the young Musials into their home. Stan named their son Richard after their kind host.

In 1941, Stan attended a St. Louis Cardinals' tryout camp at Columbus, Georgia. His throwing arm was now very weak, but he could hit and run well, so the Cardinals assigned him to Springfield, Missouri, at Class C, one notch above the level at which he had labored in his first three seasons. He hit so well that he was promoted twice that year, the second time to the parent Cardinals.

In one season, he had progressed from a lame-armed outfielder in the low minors to a team that was battling the Brooklyn Dodgers for the National League pennant.

The Emerging Champion

The Cardinals lost the 1941 pennant, but Stan batted a spectacular .426 in a dozen games. The next year, however, manager Billy Southworth had second thoughts about Stan, who batted poorly early in the season, while his throwing arm remained woefully weak for an outfielder. Southworth stayed with him, though, and Stan improved steadily both afield and at bat.

In 1943, Stan enjoyed a remarkable year, winning the batting championship with a .357 average and leading the league in hits, doubles, and triples. From his unusual crouch, back turned almost squarely to the pitcher, he uncoiled like a cobra and sprayed hits in all directions. At the age of twenty-two, he won the National League most valuable player award.

The Cardinals, having lost fewer of their stars to military service than other teams, dominated National League teams during World War II. Stan batted .347 in 1944 as the Cardinals won their third straight pennant. In three full seasons, Stan had won the respect of National League base runners with his accurate throwing arm and had proven himself a contact hitter with better than average power.

In 1945, Stan served in the Navy. When he returned to St. Louis in 1946, some observers wondered whether he would keep up the pace against the league's best pitchers, many of whom

STATISTICS

Season	GP	AB	Hits	2B	3B	HR	Runs	RBI	BA	SA
1941	12	47	20	4	0	1	8	7	.426	.574
1942	140	467	147	32	10	10	87	72	.315	.490
1943	157	617	**220**	**48**	**20**	13	108	81	**.357**	**.562**
1944	146	568	**197**	51	14	12	112	94	.347	**.549**
1946	156	624	**228**	50	20	16	**124**	103	**.365**	**.587**
1947	149	587	183	30	13	19	113	95	.312	.504
1948	155	611	**230**	**46**	**18**	39	**135**	**131**	**.376**	**.702**
1949	157	612	**207**	41	13	36	128	123	.338	.624
1950	146	555	192	41	7	28	105	109	**.346**	**.596**
1951	152	578	205	30	12	32	**124**	108	**.355**	.614
1952	154	578	**194**	42	6	21	**105**	91	**.336**	**.538**
1953	157	593	200	53	9	30	127	113	.337	.609
1954	153	591	195	41	9	35	**120**	126	.330	.607
1955	154	562	179	30	5	33	97	108	.319	.566
1956	156	594	184	33	6	27	87	**109**	.310	.522
1957	134	502	176	38	3	29	82	102	**.351**	.612
1958	135	472	159	35	2	17	64	62	.337	.528
1959	115	341	87	13	2	14	37	44	.255	.428
1960	116	331	91	17	1	17	49	63	.275	.486
1961	123	372	107	22	4	15	46	70	.288	.489
1962	135	433	143	18	1	19	57	82	.330	.508
1963	124	337	86	10	2	12	34	58	.255	.404
Totals	3,026	10,972	3,630	725	177	475	1,949	1,951	.331	.559

Notes: Boldface indicates statistical leader. GP = games played; AB = at bats; 2B = doubles; 3B = triples; HR = home runs; RBI = runs batted in; BA = batting average; SA = slugging average

had been in the military since 1941. After all, he had been batting chiefly against pitchers classified as unfit for military duty, pitchers who, in 1946, would drift back to the minor leagues or out of baseball completely.

Continuing the Story

The postwar Musial—"Stan the Man," as admiring fans in Brooklyn's Ebbets Field dubbed him—proved to be even better. In 1946, he led the league again with a .365 average. For the fourth time in his first four full seasons, the Cardinals won the National League pennant.

Increasingly now he played first base, although he was often pressed into service in left, center, or right field. In his greatest year, 1948, he led the league in all important batting categories except home runs and missed tying Johnny Mize and Ralph Kiner for the lead in homers by one home run. He batted .376, the highest National League average since 1935. Forty-two years later, no subsequent National League had equaled that average for a single season.

For more than a decade after the war, Stan dominated batting statistics as few other ever have. He added six batting titles to his 1943 championship and virtually rewrote the National League record book. On his greatest single day, May 2, 1954, he became the first major leaguer to hit 5 home runs in a doubleheader.

Until 1959, Stan the Man knew little adversity on the diamond. That year, at age thirty-eight, he struggled to a .255 finish, his first sub-.300 season, and his mobility around first base, now his usual position, declined also. When he began the 1960 season even more slowly, manager Solly Hemus benched him for the first time since his rookie year. For several years he scarcely played at all, and fans wondered whether Stan was finished.

In late June, Hemus responded to a barrage of criticism by sending Stan back to left field. By September, he had raised his batting-average

MAJOR LEAGUE RECORDS
Five home runs in a doubleheader (1954)
Eight seasons as doubles leader
Five seasons as triples leader

NATIONAL LEAGUE RECORDS
Seventeen seasons hitting .300 or better (record shared)
Three seasons leading outfielders in fielding percentage (record shared)

HONORS AND AWARDS	
1943-44, 1946-63	National League All-Star Team
1943-44, 1946, 1948-54, 1957-58	*Sporting News* Major League All-Star Team
1943, 1946, 1948	National League most valuable player
1943, 1948, 1951, 1957	*Sporting News* Outstanding National League Player
1946, 1951	*Sporting News* Major League Player of the Year
1956	*Sporting News* Player of the Decade
1957	*Sports Illustrated* Sportsman of the Year
1969	Inducted into National Baseball Hall of Fame Uniform number 6 retired by St. Louis Cardinals

and runs-batted-in totals above his 1959 figures. He topped his 1960 totals in 1961, and, in a final burst of glory, batted .330 with 82 runs batted in in 1962 at the age of forty-one.

After the 1963 season, when he dropped back to .255, he retired. He had set many career records, some of which were later broken by Hank Aaron and one of which (most hits in the National League) was later broken by Pete Rose. A number of his records still stand. In 1969, he was voted into the National Baseball Hall of Fame.

Stan served one year as the Cardinals' general manager; in that year, 1967, St. Louis reigned as world champions. He continued as senior Cardinal vice president. President Lyndon Johnson named Stan director of the National Council on Physical Fitness, and he has remained active in a number of business enterprises.

Summary

Quiet and gentlemanly on and off the field, Stan Musial avoided the controversies that have often swirled around star players. Notoriously easy to sign, he was vastly underpaid for much of his career. To him, putting on a baseball uniform seemed a sufficient thrill. No one who ever saw

1987

the Cardinals' number 6 uncoil at the plate is likely to forget him.

Robert P. Ellis

Additional Sources:

Broeg, Bob. *Stan Musial: The Man's Own Story.* New York: Doubleday, 1964.

Goodman, Irv. *Stan Musial: The Man.* New York: Bartholomew House, 1961.

Lansche, Jerry. *Stan the Man Musial: Born to Be a Ballplayer.* Dallas: Taylor, 1994.

Musial, Stan, and Bob Broeg. *The Man, Stan: Musial, Then and Now.* St. Louis: Bethany Press, 1977.

_____. *Stan Musial: "The Man's" Own Story.* Garden City, N.Y.: Doubleday, 1964.

Robinson, Ray. *Stan Musial: Baseball's Durable Man.* G. P. Putnam's Sons, 1963.

MARIA MUTOLA

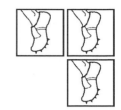

Sport: Track and field (middle-distance runs)

Born: October 27, 1972
Maputo, Mozambique

Early Life

Maria Mutola was born in Maputo, Mozambique, on October 27, 1972. Her father, Joao, worked as a railroad clerk, and her mother, Catarina, had a garden and sold her vegetables at a city market.

There was no way that anyone in that city would dream that Maria would be a track star. From the time she was young, Maria would play soccer with boys. She showed enough athletic ability to earn a spot on a boy's soccer club and was very competitive; she once scored the winning goal in a league championship game. This led the losing team to protest that girls should not be allowed to play soccer, especially with

Maria Mutola celebrates after winning the 800 meters at the 2000 Olympics.

1989

boys. Maria's team was forced to give up the winning title for this reason. Jose Craveirinha, Mozambique's most celebrated poet and a sporting philanthropist, read about Maria's story and suggested she try running.

The Road to Excellence

Maria was bitter about being kicked off the soccer team she loved. In order to see what the future held, however, it was the best thing that could have happened to her. Maria trained and practiced running under the leadership of Craveirinha's son, Stleo, a track and field coach.

Maria represented Mozambique for the first time in world-event running in the 800 meters at the 1988 Olympics at Seoul after very little training and at the age of fifteen. She went from being a soccer star and occasional runner in Mozambique to moving to Eugene, Oregon, to attend high school under an Olympic Solidarity Committee scholarship. She blossomed there, improving and mastering her running skills.

The Emerging Champion

In Eugene, Maria's talents put her in the running with the world's best, but her inexperience caused problems, particularly in the 1991 World Championships, where she finished fourth. After

that, she became the dominant 800-meter runner in the world and occasionally ran the 1,500 meters.

Maria was the first person from Mozambique to win a gold medal in an international athletics competition. After that feat in 1993, she remained one of the top 800-meter runners on the international circuit. Maria said her secret to focused running was the Christian background she received from her father. Before he died, he taught her the importance of faith in God, and with that, Maria believed she could do anything, including win Olympic medals.

Maria shot to prominence when she ran in the 800-meter and 1500-meter races in the Barcelona Olympics in 1992, where she placed fifth in the 800 meters and ninth in the 1,500. After the 800-meter run at the 1992 Barcelona Olympics, Maria began a three-year streak during which she won every 800-meter race she entered, including the 1993 world championship.

Continuing the Story

Her streak of forty-two consecutive 800-meter victories ended when Maria was disqualified in the semifinals of the 1995 World Championships for stepping out of her lane. That began a series of disappointments at major events. In 1996 at the Atlanta Olympics, Maria, who was the gold-medal favorite in the 800 meters, settled for the bronze behind Svetlana Masterkova of Russia and Ana Fidelia Quirot of Cuba.

However, Maria earned three victories on the international scene in 1998. In December, 1999, she ran a seasonal best, scoring 1:58.16 to win the women's 800-meter race in Malmo, Sweden. At the 1999 World Championships, she took the silver, crossing just .04 seconds behind Ludmila Formavona of the Czech Republic.

At the 2000 Olympic Games in Sydney, Maria took the gold medal for the 800-meter event, finishing in 1:56.15. This was her first Olympic gold.

Maria became interested in encouraging young people to practice not only track but also other sporting disciplines, especially people in her country who had many obstacles to athletic success. Among other things, she has donated funds to resurface a track and to develop a training program in Mozambique. She has also given funds to American programs that benefit the homeless and people with AIDS.

MAJOR CHAMPIONSHIPS				
Year	Competition	Event	Place	Time
1988	Olympic Games	800 meters	7th	2:04.36
1991	World Championships	800 meters	4th	1:57.63
1992	Olympic Games	800 meters	5th	1:57.49
	World Cup	800 meters	1st	2:00.47
	Olympic Games	1,500 meters	9th	4:02.60
1993	World Championships	800 meters	1st	1:55.43
	IAAF/Mobil Grand Prix Final	800 meters	1st	1:57.35
1994	World Cup	800 meters	1st	1:58.27
1995	IAAF/Mobil Grand Prix Final	800 meters	1st	1:55.72
1996	Olympic Games	800 meters	Bronze	1:58.71
1997	13th IAAF Grand Prix Final	800 meters	2d	1:56.93
	World Championships	800 meters	3d	1:57.59
1998	World Cup	800 meters	1st	1:59.88
1999	World Championships	800 meters	2d	1:56.72
2000	Olympic Games	800 meters	Gold	1:56.15
2001	World Championships	800 meters	1st	1:57.17

1990

Summary

Maria Mutola has been called one of the twenty best women distance runners of all time. She had more than fifty wins in the 800 meters from 1992 to 1996. Maria is the most famous athlete in her homeland, and she has given hope to the people of Mozambique, who had never claimed an Olympic medal winner before her.

Alex Mwakikoti

Additional Sources:

Cooper, Pam. "Mile Markers." *Runner's World* 35 (November, 2000): 17.

Layden, Tim. "Stepping Out." *Sport Illustrated* 93 (July 3, 2000): 76-77.

Patrick, Dick. "Mozambique Runner Beats Odds Going Abroad." *USA Today,* July 29, 1996, p. E4-E20.

DIKEMBE MUTOMBO

Sport: Basketball

Born: June 25, 1966
Kinshasa, Democratic Republic of
Congo

Early Life

Dikembe Mutombo, whose full name is Dikembe Mutombo Mpolondo Mukamba Jean Jacques Wamutombo, was born and raised in

AP/Wide World Photos

Center for the Atlanta Hawks, Dikembe Mutombo plays in November, 2000.

Kinshasa, the capital city of the Democratic Republic of Congo. He was the seventh of ten children born to Mukamba Mutombo, a Sorbonne-educated teacher and superintendent of schools in Kinshasa, and Biamba Mutombo, a housewife and Sunday school teacher.

Dikembe's first sport was soccer, and, with his height and impressive armspan, he was a talented goalkeeper. He did not begin playing basketball until his senior year in high school. Education was always of primary importance for the young Dikembe, and while his height and amazing potential were attracting international attention in basketball circles, it was a victory in an international science contest that won him an academic scholarship to Georgetown University, where he planned to study medicine.

The Road to Excellence

Georgetown Hoyas coach John Thompson had already heard about the impressive young Congolese man. Thompson was responsible for developing future National Basketball Association (NBA) superstars Alonzo Mourning and Patrick Ewing, and he looked forward to helping Dikembe realize his basketball potential. Ineligible to play his first year—he was unable to take the National Collegiate Athletic Association (NCAA)-required standard aptitude test (SAT), which was offered only in English—he took intensive English classes and began taking courses toward his pre-med degree. Eventually, he changed his course of study, and he finally graduated with a double degree in diplomacy and linguistics. Dikembe learned a wide variety of languages: English, French, Spanish, and Portuguese, and a number of African languages, including Tshiluba, Lingala, Kikongo, and Swahili.

1992

He was awarded an athletic scholarship after his first year at Georgetown. Once he was eligible to play in the NCAA, Dikembe took off quickly under John Thompson's tutelage, playing alongside Alonzo Mourning his first two years. The timing he had learned as a goalkeeper served him well, and he was an instant success as a shot blocker, setting a Big East Conference record in his first year as a player with 12 blocks in a single game. In his junior year, he shared the Big East Defensive Player of the Year award with teammate Mourning.

Dikembe had an opportunity to shine in his final year for the Georgetown Hoyas: He led the team in scoring, with an average of 15.2 points per game, 12.2 rebounds per game (a statistic that ranked him sixth in the nation), and 4.72 blocked shots a game (ranking fourth in the nation). He also led the team that year in field goal percentage, with an average of .586. He left Georgetown as the Hoyas' all-time leader in field goal percentage at .644 and the second-leading shot blocker (behind Patrick Ewing), with 354. Only one place remained for Dikembe to test his skill: the NBA. He was drafted as the fourth pick overall by the Denver Nuggets in 1991.

Continuing the Story

Dikembe quickly established himself as a force in the NBA. In his first year, he led the Nuggets in blocked shots (2.96 per game), rebounds (12.3 per game), and field goal percentage (.493). He was the only rookie to play in the 1992 All-Star game. In his next season, he improved his shot blocking and rebounding, averaging 3.5 blocked shots and 13 rebounds per game. He was ranked third in the NBA in both of these categories.

The next season, 1993-1994, would provide more success for Dikembe. In an amazing first-round playoff upset against the top-seeded Seattle Supersonics, he blocked 31 shots, setting a new NBA record for most blocks in a 5-game series. Although the Nuggets lost the conference semifinals to the Utah Jazz, Dikembe blocked 38 shots, setting another NBA record, this time for the most blocks in a 7-game series. He also led the league in blocks, with 4.1 blocks per game.

In the 1994-1995 season, Dikembe again led the league in blocked shots, with 3.91 per game, and won that year's NBA Defensive Player of the Year award. He led the league again in blocks in the 1995-1996 season with 4.49 blocked shots per

MILESTONES	
1994	Set an NBA Playoffs record with 31 blocked shots in a five-game series
1996	Tied a Nuggets franchise record with 31 rebounds
1997-1998	Led the NBA in total blocked shots for the 5th consecutive season, including a Nuggets' franchise record 336 in 1993-1994
1998	Blocked 2,000th career shot

STATISTICS

Season	GP	FGA	FGM	FG%	FTA	FTM	FT%	Reb.	Ast.	TP	PPG
1991-92	71	869	428	.493	500	321	.642	870	156	1,177	16.6
1992-93	82	781	398	.510	492	335	.681	1,070	147	1,131	13.8
1993-94	82	642	365	.569	439	256	.583	971	127	986	12.0
1994-95	82	628	349	.556	379	248	.654	1,029	113	946	11.5
1995-96	74	569	284	.499	354	246	.695	871	108	814	11.0
1996-97	80	721	380	.527	434	306	.705	929	110	1,066	13.3
1997-98	82	743	399	.537	452	303	.670	932	82	1,101	13.4
1998-99	50	338	173	.512	285	195	.684	610	57	541	10.8
1999-00	82	573	322	.562	421	298	.708	**1,157**	105	942	11.5
2000-01	75	556	269	.484	291	211	.725	**1,015**	76	749	10.0
Totals	760	6,420	3,367	.524	4,047	2,719	.672	9,454	1,081	9,453	12.4

Notes: Boldface indicates statistical leader. GP = games played; FGA = field goals attempted; FGM = field goals made; FG% = field goal percentage; FTA = free throws attempted; FTM = free throws made; FT% = free throw percentage; Reb. = rebounds; Ast. = assists; TP = total points; PPG = points per game

HONORS AND AWARDS

1994-1995, 1996-1998, 2000-2001	NBA Defensive Player of the Year
1994-1995, 1998-1999	NBA All-Defensive Second Team
1992, 1995-2000	NBA All-Star
1996	NBA Player of the Week ending December 1
1996-1998	NBA All-Defensive First Team
1997	NBA Player of the Week ending November 9
1997-1998	All-NBA Third Team NBA All-Interview Second Team
1998-1999	IBM Award
2000	NBA Player of the Week ending January 30

game, becoming the first player to lead the league in blocks for three consecutive seasons. After that year, Dikembe signed as a free agent with the Atlanta Hawks. He left the Denver Nuggets as their all-time leader in blocked shots with 1,486.

He was second in the NBA during the 1996-1997 season in both shot blocking and rebounding, and he won the NBA's Defensive Player of the Year award for the second time. He had another excellent year with the Hawks, earning yet another Defensive Player of the Year award for the 1997-1998 season. In 1999, Dikembe won the NBA's IBM award, earned by a computer-generated measure of a player's statistical contributions to his team.

Dikembe's best season came in 2000-2001. After an outstanding performance in the All-Star Game, he was acquired by the Philadelphia 76ers, whose coach, Larry Brown, had coached him in the All-Star Game. Dikembe led the league in rebounds and was again named Defensive Player of the Year. Dikembe then helped lead Philadelphia to the NBA Finals. The Sixers lost to the Lakers, but Dikembe surprised everyone with his strong offensive play. After the season ended, he signed a long-term contract with his new team.

Dikembe has been an impressive force off the basketball court as well. Aside from his own daughter, Carrie, Dikembe and his wife, Rose, have adopted four of his nieces and nephews. He founded the Dikembe Mutombo Foundation to aid poor and disadvantaged people in his country; in addition, he has donated $3 million for construction of a three-hundred-bed general hospital in Kinshasa. He sponsored the Zairean womens' basketball team when they competed in the 1996 Olympic Games in Atlanta. As a result of his work in the Democratic Republic of Congo and in the United States, Dikembe was awarded a President's Service Award, the highest honor for volunteer service, in 2000.

Summary

By the start of the twenty-first century, Dikembe Mutombo had been a six-time All-Star, had earned three rebounding titles and three Defensive Player of the Year awards, and had led the NBA five times in shot blocking. He had led his teams in rebounding every year he played. While he is most feared as a defender and a shot blocker, he had averaged over 12 points a game for his career and had one of the highest field-goal percentages in the league. Although he came to basketball late in his life, he certainly made a name for himself in the NBA.

Alexander Jordan

Additional Sources:

Brooks, Philip. *Dikembe Mutombo: Mount Mutombo.* Danbury, Conn.: Children's Press, 1996.

Stewart, Mark. *Dikembe Mutombo.* Danbury, Conn.: Children's Press, 1997.

Torres, John Albert. *Sports Great Dikembe Mutombo.* Berkeley Heights, N.J.: Enslow, 2000.

JOHN NABER

Sport: Swimming

Born: January 20, 1956
Evanston, Illinois

Early Life

John Phillips Naber was born January 20, 1956, in Evanston, Illinois, to Fred and Joan (Haskell) Naber. When John was four, his father, a management consultant, moved the family to Italy and later England. Because he was a tall, rather gangly youth whose bones grew far faster than his muscles, and because he lived in Europe, the young John did not play such typical American sports as football, baseball, and basketball. He did enjoy swimming, but in spite of a trip to visit the site of the ancient Olympic Games in Greece, he did not envision himself becoming an Olympic champion or the world's greatest backstroker.

When John and his family returned to the United States when he was thirteen, he brought home with him his love of swimming. Years later, John looked back and concluded that he had always enjoyed swimming because "I was really racing the stopwatch." Throughout his illustrious career, his continuing goal was to do a personal best by the end of each season, and he did, even the year after he won four gold medals and a silver at the Montreal Olympics, 1976.

The Road to Excellence

John did his first competitive swimming for Woodside High School, located just off Stanford University's campus in Woodside, California. After both his freshman and sophomore years, he won most improved athlete awards,

which, he would later say, proved how bad he had to have been when he started. By the end of his junior year, his coaches fully expected the sixteen-year-old John to qualify for the 1972 United States Olympic team. Just four months before the trials, however, he cracked his collarbone and spent the next two months with his arm in a sling. In spite of his inability to train, he missed making the Olympic team in the 100-meter backstroke by only .6 second. Naturally, to come so close was

disappointing, but for the first time, John Naber realized that he could become a world-class swimmer and, perhaps, even an Olympic champion. He would never again lose a backstroke race to an American swimmer.

The Emerging Champion

In the fall of 1973, John enrolled at the University of Southern California (USC). As an eighteen-year-old freshman, he won the first three of his ten individual National Collegiate Athletic Association (NCAA) titles. In addition to his favorite 100- and 200-yard backstroke events, he twice won NCAA titles in the 500-meter freestyle. While at USC, he also swam on five NCAA winning relay teams. During his four years, USC won four consecutive national team titles, and in each John Naber earned more points than any other swimmer. In the summer and winter National Amateur Athletic Union (AAU) meets, he also won eighteen individual and seven relay titles between 1973 and 1977.

In 1974, John won his first great international victory. Swimming against the East Germans in a dual meet held outside San Francisco, John swam against Roland Matthes, the 100- and 200-meter backstroke champion in the 1968 and 1972 Olympics, who had been undefeated for seven years. John defeated him in both races, but Matthes, who was swimming with an injured leg, retained his world records in both events. The stage was thus set for their confrontation at the 1976 Olympic Games in Montreal.

Continuing the Story

As early as 1972, John Naber predicted that it would take new world records of 55.5 seconds in the 100-meter backstroke and 2 minutes flat in the 200 meters to defeat Roland Matthes at the 1976 Olympic Games in Montreal. To provide himself with even more of a challenge, John also decided to try and make the United States team in the 200-meter freestyle and the two relays. At the trials, John earned his first world record in the 200-meter backstroke. After also qualifying in the 100-meter backstroke and the 200-meter freestyle, he was more than ready for his Olympic challenge.

On the second day of the competition at Montreal, John defeated Matthes in the 100-meter backstroke, swimming the event, as he had long planned, in the world-record time of 55.49. Forty-five minutes later, he broke another world record, this time in the 200-meter freestyle, but teammate Bruce Furniss edged him out for first place by .21 second. John went on to win gold medals in the 200-meter backstroke, the 4×200-meter freestyle relay, and the 4×100-meter medley relay. In the space of seven days, John Naber won four gold medals and a silver, breaking the existing world record in each event.

John majored in psychology and public relations at USC. Since his retirement from competitive swimming in 1977, he has

STATISTICS				
Year	Competition	Event	Place	Time
1973	World Championships	200-meter backstroke	3d	2:06.61
1974	NCAA Championships	500-yard freestyle	1st	4:26.855
		100-yard backstroke	1st	50.516
		200-yard backstroke	1st	1:48.951
1975	NCAA Championships	500-yard freestyle	1st	4:20.450
		100-yard backstroke	1st	49.947
		200-yard backstroke	1st	1:46.827
		400-yard medley relay	1st	3:19.221
1976	Olympic Games	200-meter freestyle	Silver	1:50.50
		100-meter backstroke	Gold	55.49 WR, OR
		200-meter backstroke	Gold	1:59.19 WR, OR
		4×200-meter freestyle relay	Gold	7:23.2 WR, OR
		4×100-meter medley relay	Gold	3:42.22 WR, OR
	NCAA Championships	500-yard freestyle	2d	4:19.71
		100-yard backstroke	1st	49.93
		200-yard backstroke	1st	1:46.95
		400-yard freestyle relay	1st	2:57.54
		800-yard freestyle relay	1st	6:33.13
		400-yard medley relay	1st	3:20.02
1977	Pan-American Games	500-meter freestyle	1st	—
		100-meter backstroke	1st	—
		200-meter backstroke	1st	—
	NCAA Championships	500-yard freestyle	2d	4:19.07
		100-yard backstroke	1st	49.36
		200-yard backstroke	1st	1:46.09
		800-yard freestyle relay	1st	6:28.01

Notes: OR = Olympic Record; WR = World Record

done swimming commentary for ESPN and NBC, given motivational speeches, and worked as a market consultant for various manufacturing firms. Intelligent, self-confident, and friendly, John Naber modestly concludes, "I'm just an ordinary guy who's accomplished some extraordinary things."

Summary

At 6 feet 6 inches and 195 pounds, John Naber had the ideal swimmer's body, but he also had the perfect attitude to be a great athlete. Always focused, he never seemed nervous; in fact, he often took a nap before a big race. Yet he was a fierce competitor whose world records in the 100- and 200-meter backstroke lasted until 1983. John was inducted into the International Swimming Hall of Fame in 1982 and the U.S. Olympic Hall of Fame in 1984.

Lewis H. Carlson

Additional Sources:

Besford, Pat. *Encyclopedia of Swimming*. New York: St. Martin's Press, 1976.

Hickok, Ralph. *A Who's Who of Sports Champions*. Boston: Houghton Mifflin, 1995.

Naber, John. "Building Character." *Swimming World and Junior Swimmer* 39, no. 6 (1998).

Schapp, Dick. *An Illustrated History of the Olympics*. New York: Alfred A. Knopf, 1975.

Wallechinsky, David. *The Complete Book of the Olympics*. Boston: Little, Brown and Company, 1991.

RECORDS
Won 25 National AAU titles (18 individuals, 7 relays)
Won a record 10 NCAA individual titles during his swimming career

HONORS AND AWARDS	
1975	Robert J. H. Kiphuth Award, Short Course
1976	Robert J. H. Kiphuth Award, Outdoor Long Course
	Robert J. H. Kiphuth Award, Indoor Long Course
	Southern California Athlete of the Year
	Lawrence J. Johnson Award
	AAU Swimming Award
	World Male Swimmer of the Year
1977	Outstanding California Athlete in the Pac-Eight Conference
	Sullivan Award
	Trophy of the International Committee for Fair Play (the first time an American is honored)
1982	Inducted into International Swimming Hall of Fame
1984	Inducted into U.S. Olympic Hall of Fame

NEDO NADI

Sport: Fencing

Born: June 9, 1894
  Leghorn, Italy
Died: January 29, 1940
  Rome, Italy

Early Life

Nedo Nadi was born on June 9, 1894, in Leghorn, Italy. He was born into a family of fencers. His father, Giuseppe, conducted a fencing school in Leghorn. From the time they were young children, Nedo and his younger brother, Aldo, worked out in their father's school and watched

Italian fencer Nedo Nadi in 1930.

some of the best fencers in Europe at work. It was valuable experience, for watching an opponent's footwork and movements, which is absolutely essential for a good swordsman, became second nature. Nedo's father would have limited his son to the foil, for he considered both the épée and the sabre to be inferior weapons. It was hard going against his father's wishes, but Nedo was determined to become proficient in all three weapons and secretly got instruction and practice in the other two weapons while training with his father in the use of the foil. What made Nedo a champion in the real sense of the word is that eventually he became master of all three weapons.

The Road to Excellence

Nedo started training at the age of seven and, by the age of thirteen, he was already a skillful fencer. In 1908, at the age of thirteen, he won the silver trophy in three-weapon work at the jubilee celebration for Emperor Francis Joseph I in Vienna, Austria. The victory was significant, for at the time, Vienna was the capital of the Austro-Hungarian Empire and the Hungarians especially were considered to be among the best swordsmen in Europe.

The Emerging Champion

Nedo became a world-class champion in 1912 at the Stockholm Olympics. His training in sabre was so thorough that he placed fifth, with seven wins. His use of the foil, however, was spectacular. He placed first, winning, at the age of eighteen, his first gold medal.

Nedo's fencing career was interrupted by World War I. He joined the Italian army and served with distinction in the cavalry, being decorated three times for bravery. Every free moment he could find, he practiced fencing, so by the time the war ended in 1918, he was again ready for wins at the Olympic contests, the goal of every good fencer.

There were no 1916 Olympics because of the war. The 1920 Olympics were held in Antwerp, Belgium, and it was here that Nedo made fencing and Olympic history, setting a record that would not be matched until fifty-four years later. He won gold medals in both the foil and the sabre individual contests. Nedo was captain of the Italian foil, épée, and sabre teams, and all three teams won gold medals in the team contests. That meant that Nedo set an Olympic record of winning five gold medals at one Games. Many considered him to be the greatest fencer of all time.

Continuing the Story

After the Antwerp Olympics, Nedo returned to Italy as a champion. Like his father, he decided to become a professional fencer and a coach. At the same time, he also became a journalist, writing a sports column for Italian newspapers to promote the sport of fencing. He married Roma Ferralasco, who also fenced.

In 1921, Nedo and his wife went to Buenos Aires, Argentina, where Nedo coached fencing and continued to write. In 1923, the couple returned to Italy, and Nedo continued to demonstrate his skill as a fencer on European tours. In 1925, he placed first in the International Tournament in Nice. The same year, with much publicity, he defeated French foil champion René Haussy.

In 1930, Nedo and his wife came to the United States, where Nedo demonstrated his skills as a fencer at exhibitions at the Plaza Hotel and the New York Athletic Club. Nedo fenced against Clovis Deladrier, the coach of the United States Naval Academy, and George Santelli, who had coached the United States Olympic team five times. Nedo defeated them both. Through these contests, Nedo helped to raise interest in fencing in the United States, which had not been known for producing good fencers. Nedo's good looks matched his skill as a swordsman, and he attracted large crowds whenever he performed.

Nedo returned to Italy and became president of the Italian Fencing Federation. In 1933, his

MAJOR CHAMPIONSHIPS			
Year	Competition	Event	Place
1906	Emperor Francis-Joseph Silver Cup Winner	—	—
1912	Olympic Games	Individual foil	Gold
1920	Olympic Games	Individual foil	Gold
		Individual sabre	Gold
		Team épée	Gold
		Team foil	Gold
		Team sabre	Gold
1924	World Fencing Championship	—	1st

best-known book, *With and Without the Mask,* was published in Milan. He continued teaching and coaching and accompanied Italian fencing teams around the world.

Then, in the late 1930's, tragedy struck. Nedo came down with a mysterious disease that no doctor could cure. The illness robbed him of all his strength. In January of 1940, at the age of forty-five, this great fencer died, leaving a record in fencing yet to be equaled.

Summary

Nedo Nadi's greatness as a fencer must be considered from three points of view: First, because of hard work and determination, he became a skillful fencer at a very early age; second, he became a master of all three weapons used in fencing; and third, through widely publicized demonstrations and matches, and because of his skills as a journalist and author, he helped to increase interest in the elegant, highly skilled sport of fencing.

Nis Petersen

HONORS AND AWARDS	
1930	World Champion of the Sword
	President of the Italian Fencing Federation

Additional Sources:

Evangelista, Nick. *The Encyclopedia of the Sword.* Westport, Conn.: Greenwood Press, 1995.
Nadi, Aldo. *The Living Sword: A Fencer's Autobiography.* Bangor, Maine: Laureate Press, 1996.

1999

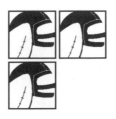

BRONKO NAGURSKI

Sport: Football

Born: November 3, 1908
Rainy River, Ontario, Canada
Died: January 7, 1990
International Falls, Minnesota

Early Life

Bronislaw (Bronko) Nagurski was born on November 3, 1908, in the village of Rainy River, Ontario, Canada. His parents were originally from the Ukraine in the Soviet Union. When Bronko was four years old, his parents moved from Rainy River to International Falls, Minnesota. There they established a small but successful grocery store and raised two sons and two daughters.

Bronko was known as a very hardworking boy. He built up his legs by running to and from school every day. In high school, Bronko played center on the International Falls High School basketball team and was on the track team in the shot put, discus, high jump, and relays. In football, Bronko played end, tackle, and guard; but the team did not win a game for two whole seasons.

When the principal at International Falls High School canceled a trip to a basketball tournament to punish two of his teammates, Bronko enrolled for his senior year at Bemidji High School. He had been a noteworthy player for International Falls, and the Bemidji coach was happy to have Bronko. The state high school association, however, ruled that Bronko could not play football at Bemidji because he lived outside the school district.

The Road to Excellence

Bronko graduated from Bemidji High School in 1926. He had always been big and strong for his age, and he loved football. He also wanted to go to college. Legend has it that the football coach from the University of Minnesota, Clar-

ence Spears, recruited Bronko after driving by a farm and seeing him plow a field without a horse. Actually, Bronko enrolled in Minnesota, unheralded and unrecruited, in 1926.

Freshmen were not eligible to play, so in 1927, Bronko showed what he could do. Playing on offense and defense, Bronko teamed with All-American Herb Joesting and Harold Hanson to achieve a 6-0-2 record for Minnesota. One of those tie games was at Notre Dame. It was the first

Bronko Nagurski in 1943.

AP/Wide World Photos

STATISTICS

| Season | GP | Rushing | | | | Receiving | | | |
		Car.	Yds.	Avg.	TD	Rec.	Yds.	Avg.	TD
1932	—	111	496	4.5	4	6	67	11.2	0
1933	—	128	533	4.2	1	1	23	23.0	0
1934	—	123	586	4.8	0	3	32	10.7	0
1935	—	50	170	3.4	1	0	0	0	0
1936	—	122	529	4.3	3	1	12	12.0	0
1937	—	73	343	4.7	1	0	0	0	0
1943	8	16	84	5.3	1	0	0	0	0
Totals	—	623	2,741	4.4	11	11	134	12.2	0

Notes: Statistics were not officially recorded in professional football until 1932. Some statistics are therefore unavailable. GP = games played; Car. = carries; Yds. = yards; Avg. = average yards per carry or average yards per reception; TD = touchdowns; Rec. = receptions

time in twenty years that the Fighting Irish had not defeated their opponent at home. The hero of the game was Bronko when he blocked a punt to set up the touchdown that tied the game. In Bronko's three years at Minnesota, the Gophers had an 18-4-2 record. The four losses came by a total of 5 points. Coach Spears said that Bronko was the most versatile player of all time and that he could be All-American at any of the eleven positions.

The Emerging Champion

In 1929, Bronko Nagurski was the first player named All-American at two positions: tackle and fullback. He is still considered the measuring stick for fullbacks even though, when asked in later years, he said he would probably be a linebacker in today's football.

Bronko was a punishing runner with the football, seeming to block for himself as he ran. Would-be tacklers seemed to bounce off of him. He never tried to sidestep them; he preferred to lower his head and shoulders at the last instant and bowl over his opponent. Yet, he was a gentle man off the field. He was kind and rarely argued. He had a high-pitched voice that made people feel relaxed after the initial shock of being close to such a big and strong man.

In 1930, this kind but tough man was given the chance to play for the Chicago Bears, at that time a very strong team. Bronko teamed up in the backfield with the immortal Red Grange, who later said that Bronko was the best player he had ever seen.

Continuing the Story

Bronko played nine seasons for the Bears. During that time, the Bears' record was 79-20-12. In 1932, they won the National Football League championship on a jump pass from Bronko to Red Grange. They played in the 1934 and 1937 championship games, only to lose to the Giants and the Redskins.

Bronko's professional playing career symbolized power and force. At 6 feet 2 inches and 235 pounds, he was a large athlete for his era. His championship ring was the largest ever made, at size 19½, until Chicago Bear William Perry's was made. He played both offense and defense with reckless abandon. Opponents would avoid him on the field because they knew he was powerful and strong.

His quarterback, Sid Luckman, said that Bronko was an exceptional person, not just the greatest athlete ever. Bronko was a humble champion.

There was not much money to be made in professional football in those days, so in the off-season, Bronko became a professional wrestler. He continued to wrestle professionally until 1960, long after he had retired from football for good, after a one-season comeback with the Bears during World War II to help them win a championship. He was inducted as a charter member into the Pro Football Hall of Fame in 1963.

Bronko went back to International Falls with his wife, Eileen, to raise four sons and two daughters. There he owned and managed a gas station until he retired in 1968. He suffered from arthri-

HONORS AND AWARDS

1929	College All-American
1951	Inducted into College Football Hall of Fame
1963	NFL All-Pro Team of the 1930's
	Inducted into Pro Football Hall of Fame
	Uniform number 3 retired by Chicago Bears

tis because of all of the pounding his body took, but he remained an active outdoorsman. He died in International Falls in 1990 at the age of eighty-one.

Summary

Bronko Nagurski remains a legend in football. When a modern ball carrier runs over tacklers, often the player is compared to Bronko. Yet,

Bronko was a peaceful man who later in life enjoyed the quiet of the forest and lakes of northern Minnesota. He did not play football for attention or to be a hero; he played because he loved the game. He played every game at full speed. He was a hero and a legend.

Kevin R. Lasley

Additional Sources:

Collins, David R. *Football Running Backs: Three Ground Gainers.* Champaign, Ill.: Garrard, 1976.

Olderman, Murray. *The Running Back.* Englewood Cliffs, N.J.: Prentice Hall, 1969.

Sugar, Burt R. *The One Hundred Greatest Athletes of All Time.* New York: Citadel Press, 1995.

Veccione, Joseph J., ed. *The New York Times Book of Sports Legends.* New York: Times Books, 1991.

AKINORI NAKAYAMA

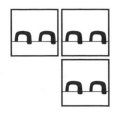

Sport: Gymnastics

Born: March 1, 1943
Nagoya, Japan

Japan's Akinori Nakayama receives the bronze medal in the men's combined gymnastics exercises at the 1968 Summer Olympic Games.

Early Life

Akinori Nakayama was born on March 1, 1943, in Nagoya, Japan. As a child, Akinori, destined to be a member of one of the greatest gymnastic dynasties of all times, was unaware that one of his gymnastic "fathers" was a Japanese American named Frank Endo.

Following World War II, Endo was assigned by the United States Army to serve as a translator in Japan (1947-1950). Having been an avid gymnast in high school, he sought a place to practice during off-duty hours. He subsequently met Takashi Kondo, who was Japan's representative to the International Gymnastics Federation. Kondo had been a member of Japan's 1932 and 1936 Olympic teams. Through Endo, Japan was able to catch up with the world of gymnastics in the postwar period. Akinori, too, would play an important role as a member of the world-famous Japanese men's gymnastic team.

In Japan, it is common for athletes to remain in a single sport for an entire career. During Akinori's time, in contrast, American boys and girls were encouraged to participate in a variety of sports. During his second year in junior high school, Akinori observed a gymnastic exhibition featuring the great Masao Takemoto, a two-time world champion in floor exercises. Later, Takemoto coached the Japanese men's team. Akinori knew immediately that gymnastics would be his sport. He was relatively small and deceptively frail, but soon he was able to make the most difficult elements look easy, thus proving that his appearance was misleading. Akinori's very relaxed yet precise style stayed with him throughout his career.

The Road to Excellence

Although it is difficult to trace his early competitive history, it is known that Akinori was an excellent gymnast during his years in high school. In junior high school, he had mastered the three events prescribed for boys. These were floor exercise, vaulting, and the parallel bars. Akinori would eventually win international gold medals in two of these events, though he had difficulty with the pommel horse.

Akinori particularly liked the horizontal bars, but he was continually frustrated by his inability to conquer the pommel horse as he would have liked. His training emphasized discipline, with absolutely no element being incorporated into his competitive routines until he had mastered it. He was also very careful about learning compulsory exercises and spent a great deal of time working on the international requirements. Such prescribed exercises once were required to be performed by all international gymnasts.

At age twenty-three, Akinori competed and won a place on Japan's national team. The National Gymnastic College in Osaka typically had four hundred struggling gymnasts trying out for this team, of whom only six or seven were selected. So it was that Akinori in his early twenties made the national team despite his comparatively lower scores on the horse.

Akinori was in great company as a member of the national team in 1966. His coach, Takashi Ono, was a veteran of five previous world and Olympic competitions. Coach Ono had been rated second in the world from 1956 to 1960 and was a member of Japan's 1960 World Championship team in Dortmund, Germany, which was the first of ten consecutive world and Olympic Championships won by the Japanese. Young Akinori

contributed immensely to the success of this team, which ruled men's gymnastics worldwide for twenty years.

The Emerging Champion

Akinori learned world-class gymnastics from his teammates Sawao Kato, Yukio Endo, and Eizo Kenmotsu, all of whom had been or were the world's best during his years on the national team in the 1960's and early 1970's. Every world-class gymnast will recall the influence of famous champions even though they never had met. Nakayama was surrounded with such talent every day.

In his first international meet, the World Championships at Dortmund, Germany, Akinori won two gold medals (floor exercise and horizontal bar) and placed third for the bronze medal in the prestigious all-around. His prime trait of making the difficult seem almost effortless impressed the international judges, and he immediately became the talk of the gymnastic world. Akinori's placid face and faint, "Mona Lisa-like" smile, a Nakayama trademark, were observed frequently in international gymnastics competitions through the early 1970's.

Akinori's continuing dilemma, the mastery of the pommel horse, was the root cause of his being denied first place in the all-around in international competitions. In one of these meets, he scored an 8.30 on the horse, very poor by international standards. This problem was not exclusively his own. The horse is the most difficult event for an all-around performer. To become a world or Olympic all-around champion one must master the pommels. Japanese men are also comparatively small in stature, which is generally advantageous in men's gymnastics. On the other hand, pommel horse specialists typically have been tall and lean. For example, at Akinori's first international meet, a Yugoslav named Miro Cerar won the gold on the horse. He had an ideal pommel horse body. Sadly, Akinori never won an international medal in this event, though he won at least one medal in every

MAJOR CHAMPIONSHIPS

Year	Competition	Event	Place	Event	Place
1966	World Championships	All-Around	3d	Rings	2d
		Floor exercise	1st	Vault	3d
		Horizontal bar	1st	Team	1st
1968	All-Japan	All-Around	1st		
	Olympic Games	All-Around	Bronze	Parallel bars	Gold
		Floor exercise	Silver	Rings	Gold
		Horizontal bar	Silver	Team	Gold
1970	World Championships	All-Around	3d	Parallel bars	1st
		Floor exercise	1st	Rings	1st
		Horizontal bar	2d	Team	1st
1972	Olympic Games	All-Around	Bronze	Rings	Gold
		Floor exercise	Silver	Team	Gold

other gymnastic discipline during his six years in world competition.

Continuing the Story

Akinori retired from active competition after the World Games in Varna, Bulgaria, in 1972. He had first entered international competition as a member of a gold medal team, and during his active years, Japan was always the top team in the world. He was third best in the world during his six years as a world-class gymnast and no doubt would have been first if he had been able to master the pommel horse. That was his greatest disappointment. As a coach, Akinori would emphasize this event with his teams at Chuyko University.

For a period of twenty years, from 1960 to 1980, the Japanese men's team dominated international gymnastics. Between 1970 and 1974, this legendary team actually swept the all-around event, winning all the gold and bronze medals and, with a single exception, the silvers as well. Akinori Nakayama was an important contributor to his team during this era of domination, winning eight gold, five silver, and five bronze medals. Four times he won the bronze medal for the all-around, and he might have won the gold or silver medals were it not for his teammates, who were equally talented but somewhat superior to Akinori on the pommel horse.

Summary

Akinori Nakayama will be remembered for his precision rather than his introduction of spectacular new tricks. His brilliant career with the foremost gymnastic team of the twentieth century is a model for those who aspire to be the best.

A. Bruce Frederick

MILESTONES

Helms International Award for Outstanding Athletic Performance

---

Additional Source:

"Akinori Nakayama." Yahoo! Sport: Olympic Games 2000. http://uk.sports.yahoo.com/ oly/oldgames/bio/9708.html. November 14, 2000.

JOE NAMATH

Sport: Football

Born: May 31, 1943
Beaver Falls, Pennsylvania

Early Life

Joseph William Namath was born on May 31, 1943, in Beaver Falls, Pennsylvania, a steel-mill town twenty-eight miles from Pittsburgh. Joe's father, who was a Hungarian immigrant, supported his family by working in the mill.

The neighborhood in which he grew up, called the Lower End, was predominantly African American. Consequently, many of Joe's childhood friends were African Americans. Joe's parents accepted his friends on equal terms and taught Joe to accept people on their own merits. Joe continued to be open and friendly to everyone, even after he became a celebrity.

The Road to Excellence

Because there were no organized activities for children in the Lower End, Joe and his friends entertained themselves by forming gangs and staging rock fights. When they entered junior high school, they exchanged rocks for balls. The same group of boys played basketball and football together in high school. Joe enjoyed playing basketball, but he excelled as a quarterback in high school, completing 84 out of 120 passes during his senior year. Joe acknowledged that this tremendous accomplishment would not have been possible without the efforts of his teammates, eleven of whom won scholarships.

Joe wanted to enter the University of Maryland but was unable to pass the College Board Ex-amination, even on his second try. Instead of becoming frustrated, Joe accepted Coach Bear Bryant's invitation to play for the Crimson Tide at the University of Alabama.

Winning a scholarship to the University of Alabama in 1961 presented him with obstacles that he had not even considered. Knowing Joe's reputation as a high school football star, his fellow players teased him unmercifully. Joe was also teased during his first semester because he defended African Americans during his informal debates with his teammates. Consequently, the normally outgoing Joe made friends very slowly.

Joe's independent ways and defiant manner also created some problems for him at the University of Alabama. He caused a small scandal as a nineteen-year-old sophomore when he was caught betting illegally at Miami's Tropical Park.

New York Jets quarterback Joe Namath in 1970.

STATISTICS

Season	GP	PA	PC	Pct.	Yds.	Avg.	TD	Int.
1965	13	340	164	.482	2,220	6.5	18	15
1966	14	471	232	.493	**3,379**	7.1	19	27
1967	14	491	258	.525	**4,007**	8.1	26	28
1968	14	380	187	.492	3,145	8.2	15	17
1969	14	361	185	.512	2,734	7.5	19	17
1970	5	179	90	.503	1,259	7.0	5	12
1971	4	59	28	.475	537	9.1	5	6
1972	13	324	162	.500	**2,816**	8.6	19	21
1973	6	133	68	.511	966	7.2	5	6
1974	14	361	191	.529	2,616	7.2	20	22
1975	14	326	157	.482	2,286	7.0	15	28
1976	11	230	114	.496	1,090	4.7	4	16
1977	4	107	50	.467	606	5.6	3	5
Totals	140	3,762	1,886	.501	27,661	7.4	173	220

Notes: Boldface indicates statistical leader. GP = games played; PA = passes attempted; PC = passes completed; Pct. = percent completed; Yds. = yards; Avg. = average yards per attempt; TD = touchdowns; Int. = interceptions

He was also suspended from the team briefly for breaking curfew. Afterward, Joe admitted that he had done a foolish thing and that Coach Bryant had done the right thing by punishing him.

The Emerging Champion

Although Joe had difficulty adjusting to college life, he had no trouble making the transition from high school to college football. In his sophomore year, Joe led a senior team to a 10-1 season. Newspapers across the nation heralded Joe's feats with headlines such as "Namath Bows, Wows, Tide Romps!" As a result of the publicity, Namath was harassed again, this time by the opposing team. He was angered and even motivated by the abuse, but he was never intimidated.

Joe's senior year with the Crimson Tide was his most triumphant and most arduous. In an early October game against North Carolina State, Joe's knee collapsed after he made a sudden stop. His knee collapsed again two weeks later in Florida and in late-December practice for the Orange Bowl. Incredibly, Joe played brilliantly, leading his team to a national championship in 1964, despite the fact that his knee was taped and heavily padded.

After the Orange Bowl, Joe became the first big-money free agent. The sports world was stunned by the $400,000 salary that the New York Jets paid him. That was considered a ridiculous sum at the time, but the owner was sure that "Broadway Joe" would bring victory and glamour to his team.

Before Joe began his professional career, he had to fly to New York in January, 1965, for surgery to his knee. After a piece of shredded cartilage was removed and a ligament was shortened, Joe had to undergo a grueling period of rehabilitation, bending his knee four hundred times a day. The press dubbed him, "The man with the $400,000 knee." By July, Joe's hard work had paid off, and he was ready to practice with the team.

Initially, Joe had as much trouble fitting in with the Jets as he had had being accepted by the Crimson Tide. The veteran players resented the fact that he was being paid more than they could ever hope to make in a lifetime of professional football. Joe's ability, hard work, and courage in the face of three knee operations eventually won him the team's respect.

From the beginning, Joe made it clear that his primary goal was "to become known as a good quarterback, not a rich one." In his first home game of 1966, Joe passed for 5 touchdowns. In 1967, he set a professional record by passing for 4,007 yards. Joe reached full maturity as a quarterback in the fall of 1968, when he led the Jets to the Eastern Division title. Just prior to Super Bowl III, Joe surprised the sports world by guaranteeing a Jet victory. Even though the Baltimore Colts were favored to win, Joe directed the near-perfect 16-7 upset that turned the football world upside down.

Continuing the Story

Following the Super Bowl, Joe became the biggest celebrity to hit New York since Babe Ruth. He captured the imagination of fans everywhere with his rugged good looks and his determination to do things his way. He courted scandal with his swinging bachelor lifestyle. He grew his hair long when other players did not, wore white shoes, put on panty hose for a commercial, and grew a Fu Manchu mustache, which he shaved off on television for money. He was a perfect hero for the nonconformist 1960's.

The 1969 season was extremely difficult for Joe and the championship Jets. In June, football commissioner Pete Rozelle asked Joe to sell his interest in an East Side Manhattan Bar, Bachelor's III, because it was frequented by professional gamblers. Joe denied that he had done anything wrong and resigned from the Jets on principle. His love of football prevailed, however, and two months later, he sold his interest in the bar and returned to the Jets. The team won the Eastern Division title but injuries prevented them from returning to the Super Bowl.

Joe's remaining years with the Jets were marked by pain and frustration. In 1970, he broke a bone in his passing hand and missed most of the season. He was sidelined again in 1971 when he tore some ligaments in his left knee. With the aid of metal braces on his knees, Joe continued to play with the Jets until 1975, but his passes were being intercepted with increasing frequency.

After being released by the Jets, Joe determined to prove that he was still the best quarterback in football. The Los Angeles Rams signed him on as a second-string quarterback in 1977 in the hopes that he would spur his team on to a Super Bowl victory. Joe tried to rebuild his tired body by swimming 1,600 yards a day, but with a knee that was practically immobile after five operations, Joe's valiant comeback was doomed.

Joe retired from football in 1978 and began a second career as a performer. In the early 1980's he sang and danced in nightclubs and in musicals such as *Damn Yankees* and *Li'l Abner.* The films that he made in the 1970's and 1980's, like *C.C. and Company* (1970) and *Chattanooga Choo Choo* (1984), prove that he was not afraid to make mistakes.

Because he still wanted to be part of football, he went into broadcasting in 1985. After a disastrous stint as color commentator on *Monday Night Football*, he almost gave up. He set his mind on improving, though, and was much more successful as color commentator for NBC in the late 1980's.

As part of his transition from glamorous young football player to conservative, middle-aged broadcaster, Joe shed his flamboyant image. He also stopped drinking in 1987.

In 1991 Joe had knee replacement surgery so he could walk with stability and without the pain that he had had since the middle of college. Joe became a spokesperson for the Classic Sports Network, which replayed vintage sporting events and shows on television. He also took a position with CBS Sportsline, a national on-line service in Fort Lauderdale. Joe and his wife, Tatiana, had two daughters, Jessica and Olivia, and settled in Tequesta, Florida.

Summary

Joe Namath will be remembered as one of the first professional athletes to achieve fame and fortune before he was a grown man. When he played up to his full potential, he was probably the best quarterback in the history of football. He awed his rivals with the strength and accuracy

---

HONORS AND AWARDS

1965	United Press International AFL Rookie of the Year *Sporting News* AFL Rookie of the year Bell Trophy
1966, 1968	AFL All-Star Game Co-Player of the Game
1966, 1968-70	AFL All-Star Team
1973	NFL Pro Bowl Team
1968	United Press International AFL Player of the Year *Sporting News* AFL Player of the Year Hickok Belt
1969	NFL Super Bowl most valuable player All-Time AFL Team
1972	All-NFL Team
1985	Inducted into Pro Football Hall of Fame Uniform number 12 retired by New York Jets

of his arm and his unusually fast drop-back into the pocket. He earned the respect of his fellow players and his fans through his ability to take punishment and bounce back from his injuries. Although his conduct off the field was criticized, Joe remained a person who knew what he wanted and cared little about what others expected him to be.

Alan Brown

Additional Sources:

Albrecht, Val K. *Larger than Life: Joe Namath*. Milwaukee, Wis.: Raintree Editions, 1976.

Chadwick, Bruce. *Joe Namath*. New York: Chelsea House, 1995.

Jackson, Robert B. *Joe Namath, Superstar*. New York: H. Z. Walck, 1974.

Sanford, William R., and Carl R. Green. *Joe Namath*. New York: Crestwood House, 1993.

MARTINA NAVRATILOVA

Sport: Tennis

Born: October 18, 1956
Prague, Czechoslovakia (now Czech Republic)

Early Life

Martina Navratilova's birthday is variously given as October 10, 1956, October 18, 1956, and October 18, 1957, possibly the result of the lack of cooperation between the Soviet Bloc nations and the rest of the world. She was born in Prague, Czechoslovakia. Her parents divorced shortly after her birth, and her father killed himself soon afterward. Her mother remarried, and Martina's stepfather and mother both encouraged her participation in sports in general and in tennis in particular.

When Martina was an infant, the family lived in the Krknose Mountains, and she learned to ski nearly as soon as she could walk. When Martina was five, the family moved to Revnice, a suburb of Prague, and she began to accompany her parents while they played in amateur tennis tournaments. Mirek Navratil, her stepfather, cut down an old racket for Martina to use, and, recognizing her natural ability, began to teach her the game.

The Road to Excellence

Eager to follow her idols, Margaret Court and Billie Jean King, Martina entered her first tennis tournament at age eight. Though officials protested that she was too small, she reached the semifinals. At age fourteen, Martina won her first national

title. She concentrated on sports, playing hockey and soccer and swimming and skiing to strengthen her body. By age sixteen, she had won three national women's tennis championships, as well as the national junior title, and became

Martina Navratilova at the 2000 French Open.

MAJOR CHAMPIONSHIP VICTORIES AND FINALS

1974, 1985	French Open mixed doubles (with Ivan Molina; with Heinz Gunthardt)
1975	French Open finalist
1975, 1982, 1984-85, 1987-88, 1986	French Open doubles (with Chris Evert; with Anne Smith; with Pam Shriver; with Andrea Temesvari)
1976, 1979, 1981-84, 1986	Wimbledon doubles (with Evert; with Billie Jean King; with Shriver)
1977, 1985	Wimbledon doubles finalist (with Betty Stove; with Shriver)
1977, 1978, 1980, 1983-84, 1986-87, 1989, 1990	U.S. Open doubles (with Stove; with King; with Shriver; with Hanna Mandlikova; with Gigi Fernandez)
1978-79, 1982-87, 1990	Wimbledon
1979	U.S. Open doubles finalist (with King)
1980, 1982-85, 1987-89	Australian doubles (with Betty Nagelsen; with Shriver)
1981, 1983, 1985	Australian Open
1981, 1985, 1989, 1991	U.S. Open finalist
1982, 1984	French Open
1983-84, 1986-87	U.S. Open
1985, 1987	U.S. Open mixed doubles (with Gunthardt; with Emilio Sanchez)
1985, 1993, 1995	Wimbledon mixed doubles (with Paul McNamee; with Mark Woodforde; with Jonathan Stark)
1988	Wimbledon finalist

OTHER NOTABLE VICTORIES

1975, 1987	Italian Open doubles (with Evert; with Gabriela Sabatini)
1975, 1981, 1986	U.S. Indoor Championship
1975	On winning Czechoslovakian Federation Cup team
1977, 1979, 1981, 1983-86	Virginia Slims Championship
1979, 1981-82	Avon Championship
1980, 1981-82	Avon Championship doubles (with King; with Shriver)
1981, 1984-85	U.S. Indoor Championship doubles (with Shriver)
1981, 1982, 1985	Canadian Open doubles (with Shriver; with Candy Reynolds; with Fernandez)
1982-83	Canadian Open
1982, 1986	On winning U.S. Federation Cup team
1983	On winning U.S. Wightman Cup team

the nation's top-ranked female tennis player. A left-handed player, Martina excelled nearly equally at singles and doubles play.

Martina was fascinated by the possibility of traveling to wonderful places and was thrilled when the Czechoslovakian Tennis Federation allowed her to play an eight-week tour sponsored by the United States Lawn Tennis Association (USLTA) in 1973. She did not win any titles during that tournament, but she went to the finals in the Italian Open and won the Junior Girls Championship at Wimbledon.

The next year Martina played in both the Italian and German opens, then returned to the United States for the Virginia Slims circuit. Her performance against the tough competition earned her the title of Rolex Rookie of the Year from *Tennis* magazine. Still, she was not happy with her game and resolved to work on her weaknesses. She returned home to Revnice and concentrated on strengthening both her body and her game.

The Emerging Champion

Her determination to win paid off, as she soon began to defeat opponents such as Margaret Court in the Australian Open, though she lost to Evonne Goolagong. A month later she beat Chris Evert, and then beat her again, and in Boston in March beat Evonne Goolagong. By the end of the year she had won several more titles and led the Czechoslovakian team to its first victory in the women's international cup match since 1963.

Martina's career entered a new phase in 1975. Her growing reputation resulted in frequent invitations to play in tournaments around the world, and especially in the United States. After an increasingly heated battle with the Czechoslovakian authorities over her freedom to play when and where she wanted, Martina defected to the United States during the U.S. Open. Having had to choose between her native country and the freedom to exercise her desire to play tennis led to difficulties for Martina. She reveled in her new-found and unaccustomed freedom, losing concentration on her game. Soon she was back on track, however, and became the first woman player to top $100,000 for the year after winning the Virginia Slims circuit in 1977.

Martina continued to rack up win after win. She came close to winning the Grand Slam twice, holding three major championship titles in 1983—Wimbledon, the U.S. Open, and the Australian Open—and three in 1984—Wimbledon, the French and U.S. opens. In 1986, a bittersweet triumph for Martina came at the battle for the Federation Cup, which was played in Prague. Now an American citizen, Martina won the hearts of the fans but not of the Czechoslovakian authorities. Annoyed and insulted by her growing popularity, the Czechoslovakian officials finally refused to allow the announcer to use Martina's name.

Continuing the Story

Martina's success had been nothing short of phenomenal. Her record of wins places her among the top four female tennis players, and she ranks among the top money-earners in the sports world. Her fierce determination to let nothing stand in her way—whether it be the repressive Czech government, her own weakness, or her opponent on the opposite side of the net—has made Martina a tough competitor to beat.

Her aggressive style extends to other aspects of her life, as well as her tennis game. She scoffed at the tendency of American women to compromise athletic conditioning and muscle tone for rounded, feminine bodies. Her attitude led to a frank admission of her bisexuality, but Martina refused to allow scandal to interfere with winning at tennis.

She also changed the shape of sports in other ways. While she was not the first to seek improvement for her mind and spirit, as well as her body, she was such a prominent success that others began to follow her path. Many younger athletes have benefited from her willingness to break

conventions. She describes her choices in her autobiography, *Martina* (1985).

Martina does have one soft spot, though—she established the Martina Foundation in 1983 to benefit underprivileged children worldwide. She also admits she misses her family and worried when she defected that the Communists would retaliate against them.

Though she was defeated at Wimbledon in 1988, Martina refused to give up, and she came back to win her ninth Wimbledon title in 1990. She continued to play, joining other top female athletes who refused to retire until their late thirties or forties.

After retiring from competitive tennis in 1995, Martina served as a tennis commentator for Home Box Office (HBO) from 1995 to 1999. In 2000, she was inducted into the International Tennis Hall of Fame. Martina also began playing doubles and mixed doubles on the women's tour again in 2000. With Mariaan de Swardt, she reached the quarterfinals in doubles at the 2000 Wimbledon.

Summary

Martina Navratilova was a major force in women's tennis, defecting from her native Czechoslovakia to pursue her goal. She won all the major titles in the United States, Europe, and Australia, and equaled or surpassed records set by previous tennis greats.

Mary Johnson

MILESTONES

Ranked number one in the world (1979, 1982-87)
Czechoslovakian Federation Cup team (1975)
U.S. Federation Cup team (1982-86)
U.S. Wightman Cup team (1983)
Grand Slam doubles (1984), 54 Grand Slam titles

HONORS AND AWARDS

1974	Rolex Rookie of the Year
1975	*Tennis* magazine Most Improved Player
1979, 1982-86	International Tennis Federation Player of the Year
1982-84	Women's Sports Foundation Professional Sportswoman of the Year
1983, 1986	Associated Press Female Athlete of the Year
1984	Inducted into Sudafed International Women's Sports Hall of Fame
2000	Inducted into International Tennis Hall of Fame

Additional Sources:

Blue, Adrianne. *Martina: The Lives and Times of Martina Navratilova.* Secaucus, N.J.: Carol, 1995.

Navratilova, Martina, with George Vecsey. *Martina.* New York: Knopf, 1985.

Schwabacher, Martin. "Martina Navratilova." In *Superstars of Women's Tennis.* Philadelphia: Chelsea House, 1997.

Zwerman, Gilda. *Martina Navratilova.* New York: Chelsea House, 1995.

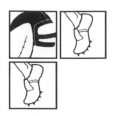

RENALDO NEHEMIAH

Sport: Track and field (hurdles) and Football

Born: March 24, 1959
   Newark, New Jersey

Early Life

Renaldo (Skeets) Nehemiah was born on March 24, 1959, in Newark, New Jersey. His father, Earl Nehemiah, was a sports enthusiast who encouraged his sons to participate in all types of athletics.

Renaldo grew up playing several sports but loved track more than any other. As a child, he would hurdle over his bedroom headboard, watching his technique in the mirror. By the time he was in high school, huge crowds would watch his fluid form as he skimmed effortlessly over high hurdles on the track.

With unbelievable speed and grace, Renaldo was clearly the best athlete at Scotch Plains High School. He was quarterback of the football team as well as the star track athlete. Local sports fans expected great things from Renaldo, and he delivered. By the time he was twenty, he had established himself as the greatest 110-meter high hurdler in the world.

Renaldo Nehemiah in a 1991 meet.

The Road to Excellence

Renaldo began hurdling seriously in the ninth grade, on a dare from a friend. Renaldo's efforts were more than a passing fancy, though, as he perfected his skills to become the country's premier track athlete. As a junior, he won the New Jersey 120-yard high hurdle championship, setting a record of 13.6 seconds.

Renaldo was even more impressive as a senior. He won the Eastern States high school championship, setting a national high school record of 12.9 seconds. He attracted worldwide attention, and many experts thought that Renaldo would become even better in the coming years.

Frank Costello, the track coach at the University of Maryland, was one who believed that Renaldo could be the world's greatest hurdler. He was right. As a University of Maryland student, and with Costello as coach, Renaldo became the number-one-ranked hurdler in the world from 1978 to 1981.

During that four-year period, Renaldo set thirteen world records, including seven indoor records in 1979. He won national championships in 1978, 1979, and 1980. Also in 1979, he won the National Collegiate Athletic Association (NCAA), Amateur Athletic Union (AAU), Pan-American Games, and World Cup championships. In April of that year, he set the outdoor 110-meter high hurdle record at 13.16 seconds. By the year's end, he would lower the record to 13.00 seconds, running the four fastest times in history in the process.

Hurdlers had been trying for generations to break the 13-second barrier. After a tremendous year in 1979, Renaldo seemed poised to glide through the barrier at the 1980 Moscow Olympic Games.

TRACK STATISTICS

Year	Competition	Event	Place	Time
1978	NCAA Championships	55-meter high hurdles	1st	7.16
1979	NCAA Championships	55-meter high hurdles	1st	6.90
	USA/Mobil Indoor Championships	60-yard high hurdles	1st	6.94
	Pan-American Games	110-meter high hurdles	1st	13.20 PAR
	World Cup	110-meter high hurdles	1st	13.39
1980	TAC Championships	110-meter high hurdles	1st	13.49

Note: PAR = Pan-American Games Record

The Emerging Champion

Unfortunately, the boycott of the Moscow Olympics prevented Renaldo from gaining Olympic glory, but it did not keep him from attaining another world record. In Zurich, Switzerland, on August 19, 1981, Renaldo Nehemiah excited the world with a flawless race that set the new standard at 12.93 seconds, a record that would endure for eight years.

The boycott left Renaldo with a decision about his career. Although he could have raced until the 1984 Olympiad, he decided instead to continue with sports in an entirely different field—professional football. Since Renaldo had won four Superstars championships—a multisport event that pits athletes from several different disciplines against each other—many football players encouraged him to consider playing pro football. Renaldo's speed, agility, and competitive spirit caused several pro football coaches to consider his potential as a wide receiver.

Although some experts doubted that the 6-foot 1-inch, 170-pound speedster would be able to make the transition to the hard-hitting world of pro football, Renaldo was eager to give it a try. In 1982, the San Francisco 49ers signed Renaldo to a four-year contract.

Renaldo soon dispelled the doubts about his toughness or willingness to play. He made several

FOOTBALL STATISTICS

Season	GP	Rec.	Yds.	Avg.	TD
1982	8	8	161	20.1	1
1983	16	17	236	13.9	1
1984	16	18	357	19.8	2
Totals	40	43	754	17.5	4

Notes: GP = games played; Rec. = receptions; Yds. = yards; Avg. = average yards per reception; TD = touchdowns

exciting catches and runs that confirmed his talent as well as his heart. Unfortunately, a string of injuries and lack of experience kept him from rising to the level of stardom he had achieved in track.

In his four years of football, he caught 43 passes for 754 yards and 4 touchdowns. In 1984, the 49ers won Super Bowl XIX, so Renaldo became a world champion in two sports, a rare and exciting accomplishment. When his contract expired, Renaldo wanted to continue his sports career, but not in football.

Continuing the Story

The exit from football led directly to a return to the track. With his amateur track status restored, the great high hurdler resolved to return to his championship form. He began his comeback with a victory in Viareggio, Italy, in August, 1986, running in 13.48 seconds. He continued to race well, eventually qualifying for the 1988 Olympic trials. Although he failed to make the team, he did not quit racing.

In spite of several setbacks involving injuries, the persistent competitor improved steadily, with his eye on the 1992 Olympiad. By 1991, he was the nation's fourth-best hurdler and the sixth-best in the world. His best time in 1991 was 13.22, a time competitive in any race.

Once considered a "boy-wonder," an athlete with skills far advanced for his age, Renaldo had become a senior competitor in a young man's sport. Nor was age his only obstacle; Renaldo's hiatus from track to pursue a demanding professional football career made his comeback even more unlikely.

Renaldo officially retired from competition in 1994, having been unable to make the U.S. Olympic team in 1988 and 1992. In 1997 he was elected to the National Track and Field Hall of Fame. After his retirement Renaldo made a name for himself in the business world as the director for track and field at Octagon, a sports marketing firm, representing all of the company's track and field clients, including two of the top hurdlers in the world, Allen Johnson and Mark Crear.

RECORDS
World indoor record in 50-meter high hurdles in 1979 (6.36)
World indoor record in 60-yard high hurdles in 1979 (6.89)
Two world records in 110-meter hurdles in 1979 (13.16; 13.00)
World indoor record in 50-yard hurdles in 1981 (5.96)
World outdoor record in 110-meter hurdles in 1981 (12.93)
American indoor record in 55-meter high hurdles in 1979 (6.89)
American indoor record in 60-yard hurdles in 1982 (6.82)

HONORS AND AWARDS	
1979	*Track and Field News* Indoor Athlete of the Year
	World Trophy
	DiBeneditto Award
1997	Inducted into National Track and Field Hall of Fame

Summary

Renaldo Nehemiah's astounding sports career is one that most athletes could only dream about. His phenomenal years as a hurdler left a trail of records that stood for more than a decade. Although he never had the opportunity to run for an Olympic gold medal, he was unanimously considered the world's best high hurdler in the late 1970's.

While Renaldo's professional football career was not as magnificent as his track career, he made a significant contribution to the world-champion San Francisco 49ers. In an inspirational comeback, Renaldo began a second career in track, re-establishing himself as one of the world's elite hurdlers.

William B. Roy

Additional Sources:

Bateman, Hal. *United States Track and Field Olympians, 1896-1980*. Indianapolis, Ind.: The Athletics Congress of the United States, 1984.

Hickok, Ralph. *A Who's Who of Sports Champions*. Boston: Houghton Mifflin, 1995.

Wallechinsky, David. *The Complete Book of the Olympics*. Boston: Little, Brown and Company, 1991.

Watman, Mel. *Encyclopedia of Track and Field Athletics*. New York: St. Martin's Press, 1981.

BYRON NELSON

Sport: Golf

Born: February 4, 1912
Fort Worth, Texas

Early Life

The top golfer of the late 1930's and 1940's was born on February 4, 1912, in Fort Worth, Texas, to John Byron and Madge Marie Nelson. John Byron Nelson, Jr.'s father was a grain merchant in Fort Worth, Texas, where Byron was born and subsequently grew up. The family lived in a home near the Glen Garden Club of Fort Worth, so when Byron was in his early teens, he began caddying after school at the club's golf course. It was not long before he learned the game, and from then on, he practiced whenever possible. When he was fourteen years old, he and his friend, Ben Hogan, tied for the caddy championship. Two years later, Byron went on to win his first event, the Glen Garden Club's junior title.

At sixteen, Byron left the Fort Worth public schools to work as a file clerk for a bankers' magazine and for the Fort Worth and Denver Railroad. In his free time, he always headed for the fairways.

The Road to Excellence

Byron's first important success as a golfer came in 1930, at age eighteen. He captured the Southwest Amateur crown, a triumph that hinted at what lay ahead for the young Texas golfer.

Two years later, in 1932, he turned professional. Unfortunately, his early efforts at tournament golf were not very successful. Those were the years of the Depression, so in his first year he won only $12.50. He did, however, tie for third in the Texarkana Open. For five rather lean years, Byron persisted. As the professional at the Texarkana Country Club in 1933, he earned a monthly salary of $60. He married Louise Shofner in June of the following year. To supplement his small income, he also taught golf at the Ridgewood, New Jersey, and Reading, Pennsylvania, country clubs. By the 1935 season, his income had jumped to $2,708, as he managed to win the New Jersey Open. That win enabled him to continue to play golf for a living.

Courtesy of Amateur Athletic Foundation of Los Angeles

While teaching golf, Byron also worked on a problem he had with his own swing. He discovered that his swing had a troublesome hook and figured out how to cure it. As a result, his performance improved, and he became a strong contender in tournament play from then on.

The Emerging Champion

Finally, in 1937, the years of perseverance paid off for Byron Nelson. He won his first major tournament, The Masters, where he exhibited exceptional putting skills, sinking a 30-footer on the tenth hole. At last his career was launched.

Only two years later, in 1939, he experienced his peak season. He won not only the United States Open but also the Western Open and the North and South Open. That same year, he earned the Vardon Trophy for the low-scoring average, and came in second in the Professional Golfers' Association (PGA) Championship.

By the time World War II called a halt to tournament golf in the United States, Byron held an exceptional record of wins and had established himself as a top-ranking American golfer. Byron's war-year wins on the fairways often have been downplayed because so many excellent contenders were off fighting instead of teeing off with him. Yet Byron, who was exempt from military service because of a blood-clotting condition, had proved himself as a consistent winner long before Pearl Harbor.

Byron spent the war years playing in golf exhibitions for the Red Cross or the United Service Organizations. In 1944, he won seven of twenty-two events, compiled a scoring average of 69.67, and earned a record $37,900 in War Bonds. The Associated Press (AP) voted him Male Athlete of the Year. Over a period of eighteen months beginning the following year, he achieved his most memorable accomplishment. He won eighteen of thirty-five tournaments, eleven of them in a row. No golfer will probably ever match this record; indeed, since Byron, none has ever won more than five consecutive tournaments. That year, 1945, it was easy for sportswriters to decide on the AP Male Athlete of the Year—Byron Nelson.

Continuing the Story

After winning every title he could in the United States, Byron began to have severe problems with his back. Crawling out of bed each morning was agony. He would arrive at tournaments leaning on his wife, and later he began skipping some of them entirely. He was tired of having to shake hands and attend lunches and of being the center of too much attention. He began to think more and more about ranching.

Exhausted after fourteen years of constant all-out effort, Byron retired in 1946, a few weeks after his caddie accidentally kicked his ball and cost him the United States Open. For all his victories, he was not able to save anything from his professional career. He found more profitable work as a rancher-businessman, managing his eight-hundred-acre Hereford ranch near Roanoke, Texas. He became a golfing commentator on ABC television and was considered one of the best coaches in America.

Byron Nelson was one of the most influential figures in the evolution of the golf swing. He had a way of drawing back his club in a "one-piece" movement, with no single part of his body dominating the move. His swing included a full shoulder turn but a restricted hip turn, and an extra-

MAJOR CHAMPIONSHIP VICTORIES	
1937, 1942	The Masters
1939	U.S. Open
1940, 1945	PGA Championship

OTHER NOTABLE VICTORIES	
1937, 1939, 1947	Ryder Cup Team
1939	North and South Open Phoenix Open Western Open
1940	Texas Open
1941-42, 1944-45	All-American Open
1941, 1945	Greensboro Open
1945	Canadian Open
1945-46	Los Angeles Open
1948	Texas PGA Championship
1951	Bing Crosby Invitational
1955	French Open
1965	Ryder Cup nonplaying captain

straight left arm to keep the club face square and hit the ball with extra leg drive. His club then pulled into the ball on the downswing, rather than pushed into it. This kind of swing increased the chances of consistent hitting.

Summary

Byron Nelson's forte was his consistent, powerful playing ability, which often caused him to be described as a mechanical golfer. Although his career was brief, he won forty-nine PGA tournaments and every other golf title and award there was to win in the United States. He constantly set records. His 1945 straight-victory record may never be broken.

Nan White

Additional Sources:

Davis, Martin. *Byron Nelson: The Story of Golf's Finest Gentleman and the Greatest Winning Streak in History.* New York: Broadway Books, 1997.

Grimsley, Will. *Golf: Its History, People, and Events.* Englewood Cliffs, N.J.: Prentice-Hall, 1966.

Nelson, Byron. *Byron Nelson: The Little Black Book: The Personal Diary of Golf Legend Byron Nelson: 1935-1947.* Arlington, Tex.: Summit, 1995.

_____. *How I Played the Game.* Dallas: Taylor, 1993.

RECORDS AND MILESTONES
Won a record eighteen tournaments (including one unofficial) in a single season, including a record eleven consecutive victories (Mar. 8, 1945, through Aug. 4, 1945)
Runner-up in the 1946 U.S. Open, the 1941 and 1947 Masters, and the 1939, 1941, and 1944 PGA Championships

HONORS AND AWARDS	
1939	PGA Vardon Trophy
1944-45	Associated Press Male Athlete of the Year
1953	Inducted into PGA Hall of Fame
1974	Inducted into PGA/World Golf Hall of Fame
	GWAA Richardson Award
	USGA Bobby Jones Award

ALEXEI NEMOV

Sport: Gymnastics

Born: May 28, 1976
Barashavo, Togliatti, U.S.S.R. (now
Russia)

Early Life

Alexei Nemov was born on May 28, 1976, in Barashavo, Togliatti, Russia. He never knew his father. An only child, he lived with his single mother in this small town on the Volga River. Alexei began gymnastics when he was five, after

All-around gold medalist Alexei Nemov was the most decorated athlete of the 2000 Games.

his mother brought him to a local gym. In his first competition he finished sixth out of six competitors.

The Road to Excellence

After Alexei had trained under three different coaches, fifteen-time Olympic medalist Nikolai Andrianov, then the Soviet national junior coach, noticed him. When Alexei was fourteen, he made the national team and went to train at the famed Round Lake facility near Moscow. He later graduated from the Togliatti Children's Education Institute.

He made his debut in the World Championships in 1993, qualifying first on floor before falling to fifth place in the finals. In the Brisbane World Championships in 1994, he was first in his qualifying session before he slipped to twelfth place in the all-around.

His big breakthrough was at the 1994 Goodwill Games, where he won the all-around by a large margin as well as four event finals. He won his first gold medal in a World Championships competition on the vault in 1995 and defended that title a year later. In 1996 he also earned a silver on the pommel horse and took the bronze on the parallel bars.

The Emerging Champion

At the 1996 Atlanta Games, Alexei lost the Olympic all-around title to China's Li Xioashuang by 0.049 point. A step out of bounds on the floor exercise meant he had to settle for the silver. However, he was the most successful gymnast of the Games, with the highest medal count of any athlete in Atlanta: six. He won a gold medal with the Russian team, a gold on vault, a silver in the all-around, and bronzes on high bar, pommel horse, and floor. He competed with a shoulder injury that was to be operated on immediately after the Games.

MAJOR CHAMPIONSHIPS

Year	Competition	Event	Place	Event	Place
1994	Goodwill Games	Team	1st	All-Around	1st
1995	World Championships	Team	4th	Vault	1st
1996	Olympic Games	Team	Gold	All-Around	Silver
		Vault	Gold	Floor exercise	Bronze
		Horizontal bar	Bronze	Pommel horse	Bronze
1997	World Championships	Team	3d	All-Around	26th
		Floor exercise	1st		
2000	Olympic Games	Parallel bars	Bronze	Floor exercise	Silver
		Team	Bronze	High bar	Gold
		Pommel horse	Bronze	All-Around	Gold

At the 1997 Worlds, Alexei was still recovering from his shoulder surgery. He struggled to twenty-sixth in the all-around. His grip tore on the rings, causing him to stop his routine, and he fell on his dismount from the high bar. He was still able to claim a gold on the floor exercise, however. Alexei realized he needed to bring his start values up to a higher level in order to compete with the Chinese gymnasts. Their routines' start values were 9.9 or 10.0, while Alexei's were a few tenths of a point less. An athlete cannot earn a score higher than his or her start value, no matter how well the maneuver is accomplished.

At the 1999 World Championships Alexei competed with a back injury; he said his separated vertebrae made it painful to walk. He still helped the Russian team win the silver medal, and he placed sixth in the all-around. He won the individual gold medal on the floor exercise with a score of 9.878, claiming his fourth Worlds gold in that event. He also took the gold on pommel horse with a score of 9.775, his fifth Worlds gold on that apparatus.

Continuing the Story

Alexei shone at the 2000 Olympics in Sydney, Australia. His demeanor in Sydney changed: In the past, the boyish athlete, dubbed "Sexy Alexei," had often flirted with the crowd or shrugged after a fall, not appearing to care much about his results. At these Games, Alexei focused more on winning because he knew he had a real chance to be on top. He said that he was also motivated by the birth of his son Alexei, Jr., who was born to Alexei's wife, Galina, on September 2, after Alexei had left for Sydney.

In the team competition he helped the Russians to a bronze medal behind China and Ukraine. In the all-around competition, he led the field, but his nearest competitor, China's Yang Wei, was only 0.113 point behind Alexei. Alexei's last event in the all-around was the parallel bars, on which he had a new routine that had been developed only ten days before the finals and had not been properly practiced. He performed almost perfectly, earning a 9.775 and clinching the gold medal. After this routine he finally allowed himself to wave and smile at the fans.

Alexei went on to win four more medals at the Games, making him the most decorated athlete of the Sydney Olympics. He took a gold on the high bar, a silver on the floor, and bronzes on the pommel horse and parallel bars.

Summary

Alexei Nemov will go down in history as the Olympian who won the most medals in both the 1996 and the 2000 Games, with six each time. He successfully combined artistry and physical power to climb to the top of the gymnastics world. His boyish charm and good looks helped attract attention to the sport of men's gymnastics.

Lauren Mitchell

Additional Sources:

Crumlish, John. "No Rush for Nemov." *International Gymnast* 39 (October, 1997).

Hockstader, Lee. "'Sexy Alexei' Has a Shirt to Put on His Back, but Not Much More." *The Washington Post*, September 2, 1996.

"Latvian Takes Gold, Nemov Completes Medals Trifecta." Fox Sports Online. http://www.foxsports.com/wires/pages/34/spt145134.sml. September 24, 2000.

"A Star Is Reborn." *International Gymnast* 42 (November, 2000): 42-47.

ERNIE NEVERS

Sport: Football

Born: June 11, 1903
     Willow River, Minnesota
Died: May 3, 1976
     San Rafael, California

Early Life

Ernest Alonzo Nevers was born to Nova Scotians George and Mary Nevers on June 11, 1903, in Willow River, Minnesota. Ernie was the youngest of eight children who spent their childhood living in northeastern Minnesota inns where their parents were innkeepers.

When Ernie was old enough to attend high school, his family lived in Superior, Wisconsin. At the time, Ernie was overweight and clumsy. As a member of Central High School's football team, he was used as a tackling dummy. Day after day, his young teammates tackled him in a sawdust pile. He put up with it because he knew he could not run or dodge very well. Meanwhile, he learned to be tough and invincible—invaluable qualities in an era when football could best be described as trench warfare. Ernie was well prepared for it from the start. At the same time, he also proved to be an outstanding basketball player. Before long, Ernie's football status improved. When his family moved to Santa Rosa, California, he became a star player at his new high school.

The Road to Excellence

When Ernie graduated from high school, he enrolled at Stanford University and was soon earning letters in basketball, football, and baseball. In fact, he became Stanford's greatest athlete and wore uniform number 1 (which was retired forever when he graduated). In football, Ernie was a relentless, hard-driving fullback, who ran over his opponents. People described him as a fury in football shoes because he was such an untiring, tough machine of a player. He also excelled at blocking, tackling, passing, and punting. Off the field, he was an example to all players, as he always kept himself in prime condition and was obedient to his training.

AP/Wide World Photos

HONORS, AWARDS, AND RECORDS

1925	Citizens Savings College Football Player of the Year
	Rose Bowl Co-Player of the Game
	Consensus All-American
	World Trophy
	Citizens Savings Northern California Athlete of the Year
1929-31	NFL All-Pro Team
1929	NFL record for the most points in a game (40)
	NFL record for the most rushing touchdowns in a game (6)
1951	Inducted into College Football Hall of Fame
	Inducted into Stanford University Sports Hall of Fame
1962	*Sports Illustrated* Best All-Time College Football Player
1963	Inducted into Pro Football Hall of Fame
	NFL All-Pro Team of the 1920's
1970	Pro Football Hall of Fame All-Time NFL Team
1991	Inducted into Rose Bowl Hall of Fame
	Uniform number 1 retired by Stanford University Athletic Department

Ernie first earned national recognition in 1925, as a senior. That year, he had broken his left ankle and had been sidelined for most of the season. When he finally was able to play again, he broke his right ankle. His coach, Glenn "Pop" Warner, made him a special brace so he could play in the Rose Bowl game against Notre Dame.

Stanford lost that game to the legendary Four Horsemen of Notre Dame, but not because of Ernie Nevers. Ernie's indomitable performance that day will be remembered as one of the finest in Rose Bowl history. On two broken, heavily taped ankles and a leg bandaged so tightly that his circulation was almost cut off, Ernie was like a knight leading his men to battle. He carried the ball 34 times in the full 60 minutes he played. He gained a fantastic 114 yards. Single-handed (and almost single-legged), he nearly matched the total yardage production of all Four Horsemen combined. From then on, Ernie Nevers was known as the kind of player who would give one hundred percent of himself in every game. That year, he made consensus All-American.

The Emerging Champion

In 1926, after pitching baseball for the St. Louis Browns, Ernie was invited to play professional football for the Duluth Eskimos. Although his professional career was to be one of the shortest in National Football League (NFL) history, he gave everything he had and more. As a rookie,

he missed only 29 minutes of play in his first twenty-nine games. Most of those minutes he missed because of an attack of appendicitis. When he saw his team fall behind, he put himself back into the game against doctor's orders, made a touchdown pass, and won the game.

Ernie and his team (soon known as the Ernie Nevers Eskimos) took to the road and helped popularize professional football nationally. The "Iron Men from the North" played in rain and storm, covering seventeen thousand miles by train, with a team of only thirteen players. Ernie was the team's star and coach. Actually, he was described as a one-man team, for he often stole the show in rushing, passing, kicking, and vicious tackling and blocking. Wherever he and his team traveled, crowds gathered to greet them.

After the 1928 season, Ernie injured his back and was forced to stop playing football. In 1929, however, he signed on with the Chicago Cardinals as the first player-coach in big-league professional history. There, he demonstrated his full talent as a fullback. He possessed an exceptional ability to cut and run once he had torn through the line of scrimmage. With amazing speed, he would dodge his way through the broken field. Not surprisingly, he made All-Pro at fullback in 1929, 1930, and 1931.

On November 28, 1929, Ernie Nevers set a one-game scoring record that may never be surpassed. In a Thanksgiving Day challenge of the Cardinals against the Chicago Bears, the final figures of the game read: Cardinals 40, Bears 6. In a remarkable performance, Ernie Nevers summoned all his talents to make 6 touchdowns and kick 4 extra points; he personally scored every one of those 40 winning points. That day, he earned his place in history as a "one-man team."

Continuing the Story

The following year, Ernie was seriously injured when a Green Bay lineman caused his wrist to snap. Although he usually made a comeback when battered and hurt, this time it was impossible. He retired in 1932 and was elected to the Pro Football Hall of Fame in 1963.

Ernie stayed involved with football, however. He worked as backfield coach for Stanford University and later at the University of Iowa. He coached the Cardinals again in 1939, but unsuccessfully.

Then, during World War II, Ernie served in the South Pacific as a captain in the United States Marine Corps. During that time, his wife, Mary Elizabeth Heagerty, whom he had married in 1926, died of pneumonia. After the war, Ernie settled in Tiburon, California, near San Francisco, where he married Margery Luxem in 1947. There he worked in public relations for a wholesale liquor company. Ernie died at home in California on May 3, 1976.

The Golden Boy from California, who was America's ideal of a sports hero, not only was handsome, courageous, and talented, but also, unlike most heroes, never let fame turn his head. As a star, he remained modest and uncontroversial. People everywhere liked him and his youthful spirit.

Summary

Ernie Nevers proved himself to be one of America's most versatile and talented football players, often single-handedly winning games as if he were indeed a "one-man team." He was a great fullback and a coach's dream come true. Even when injured, he could always be relied on to give a full 60 minutes of himself in every game he played. Ernie set a record for scoring the most points ever made by an NFL back in one game.

Nicholas White

Additional Sources:

Porter, David L., ed. *Biographical Dictionary of American Sports: Football.* Westport, Conn.: Greenwood Press, 1987.

Scott, Jim. *Ernie Nevers: Football Hero.* Minneapolis, Minn.: T. S. Denison, 1969.

Sugar, Burt R. *The One Hundred Greatest Athletes of All Time.* New York: Citadel Press, 1995.

PAULA NEWBY-FRASER

Sport: Triathlon

Born: June 2, 1962
Salisbury, Southern Rhodesia (now
Harare, Zimbabwe)

Early Life

Paula Newby-Fraser was the second of two children born to South African nationals in Salisbury, Southern Rhodesia. When she was four, Brian and Betty Newby-Fraser moved the family to Durban, South Africa, because of political upheaval in Southern Rhodesia. There, Paula's father's industrial painting business was the country's second largest. Paula credits her mother, a sociologist, educator, and progressive liberal, with being a role model for her ability to extend herself beyond boundaries.

Although her parents were not athletic, Paula took ballet and swimming lessons, played field hockey, and practiced Spanish dance. In junior high school she began swimming competitively, and by high school she had achieved national ranking. From the age of eight to sixteen, swimming consumed ninety minutes of training before school and two hours after school each day.

Paula stopped swimming at age sixteen because she could achieve no more as an amateur (South Africa, due to its apartheid policy, was banned from the Olympics) and did not believe she could support herself as a professional swimmer. She attended the University of Natal for the next six years, completely abandoning exercise.

The Road to Excellence

While working full time, Paula began jogging to lose the excess weight she had gained in college. She soon added weightlifting and aerobics classes to her routine. Late in 1984 she heard about triathlons, so she and her boyfriend purchased bicycles and began riding daily. Only eight weeks later she entered her first triathlon. She not only won the women's division but also set a new course record. Three months later, she won a national-level Ironman triathlon (a 2.4-mile swim, followed by a 112-mile bike race, followed by a marathon run), which earned

Triathlete Paula Newby-Fraser's winning time in the 1994 Ironman competition set a women's world record.

2025

MAJOR CHAMPIONSHIPS

Year	Race
1986, 1988, 1989, 1991, 1992, 1993, 1994, 1996	Hawaii Ironman Triathlon (world championship)
1988, 1990, 1991, 1992	Ironman Japan
1989, 1990, 1991, 1992	Nice International Triathlon
1989	World Duathlon
1991, 1992	Escape from Alcatraz
1991	Powerman Duathlon
1992, 1994, 1995	Ironman Europe
1994, 1995, 1997	Ironman Lanzarote
1996	Ironman Canada
1996, 1997	Ironman Australia
2000	Ironman South Africa

her a free trip to the Hawaii Ironman world championship race.

Paula's training for the Hawaii Ironman was casual compared to that of professional triathletes. She ran 25 to 30 miles a week, swam 2 or 3 miles, and occasionally rode her bike. Amazingly, she finished third—a fact that is often mentioned as evidence of her natural ability and her strong training base from her early years. After leaving Hawaii she spent some time in the triathlete community of San Diego, California. Enchanted by the lifestyle, she moved, at the age of twenty-three, to California for good, settling in Encinitas.

The Emerging Champion

After her impressive finish in her first Hawaii Ironman world championship race, Paula continued to improve her frequency of competition and her race results. She finished second in the 1986 Hawaii Ironman, but the winner was later disqualified, leaving her in first place in the women's division with $17,000 in prize money. She asked Paul Huddle, a professional triathlete and trainer, to help her increase her running and biking mileage. The two also began a long-term personal relationship.

Paula's 1988 Hawaii Ironman win has been called the greatest performance in endurance sports

history. Her time in the women's division, 9:01.01, broke the women's course record by thirty-four minutes and was beaten by only ten men.

Continuing the Story

Paula's 1988 Hawaii win was the start of an impressive string of accomplishments. Her 1992 Hawaii Ironman win—besides being the first time a woman had completed the Ironman in under nine hours—was the first perfect race in triathlon history. She performed the fastest swim, bike, and run of the race in the women's division. Her winning time in the 1994 Ironman Europe competition, 8:50.24, set a women's world record for the event. She began to be called the "Iron Queen," winning an unequaled eighth Hawaii Ironman world championship in 1996. One honor in which she took great pleasure was the 1990 Professional Sportswoman of the Year award, given by the Women's Sports Foundation. This international award, she felt, garnered broader recognition for her sport.

After winning her eighth world championship, Paula continued racing and training, although not as frequently or as intensely. As of early 2000 she had won twenty-two Ironman competitions (more than twice as many as triathletes Mark Allen, Erin Baker, and Dave Scott), including the inaugural Ironman South Africa in 2000. Besides competitions, her activities have included writing her training guide, *Peak Fitness for Women* (1995); cofounding the MultiSport School of Champions, which offers training camps for tri-

HONORS AND AWARDS

1990	Women's Sports Foundation Professional Sportswoman of the Year
1990, 1996	*Triathlete Magazine* Triathlete of the Year
1996	Inducted into Ironman Hall of Fame
1996	*Inside Triathlon* Triathlete of the Year
1996	U.S. Sports Academy, CNN, and *USA Today* Top 5 Professional Women Athletes of the Last 25 Years

athletes; and providing race-day analysis over the Internet for the 1999 Hawaii Ironman.

Summary

Paula Newby-Fraser's impressive list of accomplishments qualifies her as the greatest triathlete in the sport's history. She has contributed more to the sport than setting records and winning world championships, however. She has been an articulate and dedicated spokesperson for her sport, particularly for female competitors. She has also been an innovator—the first to use the smaller, 24-inch-diameter bike tires and the first female to incorporate weightlifting into her training. Her training routine focused on speed and rest at a time when other triathletes practiced "mega-mileage." Other professional triathletes have commended her consistency in training and her mental toughness in a sport that is psychologically as well as physically demanding. Paula herself felt fortunate to be able to make a living at a sport she loves.

Glenn Ellen Starr Stilling

RECORDS AND MILESTONES

1992	Hawaii Ironman course women's record time: 8:55:28
1994	Ironman women's world record time: 8:50:24

Additional Sources:

Cook, Jeff. *The Triathletes: A Season in the Lives of Four Women in the Toughest Sport of All.* New York: St. Martin's Press, 1992.

McAlpine, Ken. "Ironwoman." *Sports Illustrated* 87, no. 14 (October 6, 1997): 127A.

"Paula Newby-Fraser." In *Great Women in Sports*, by Anne Janotte Johnson. Detroit, Mich.: Visible Ink Press, 1996.

Ridge, Julie. "Enduring Greatness." *Women's Sports and Fitness* 11, no. 5 (June, 1989): 24-26, 28-29.

JOHN NEWCOMBE

Sport: Tennis

Born: May 23, 1944
Sydney, Australia

Early Life

John David Newcombe was born May 23, 1944, in Sydney, Australia, the son of George and Lillian Newcombe. His father was a dentist. Like most outstanding athletes, John took to his sport early; he began to play tennis when he was only seven years old. He did not concentrate on tennis exclusively but also played cricket and football.

In 1993 John Newcombe captained the Australian Davis Cup team to victory.

Clive Brunskill/Allsport

When John was still a boy, he became excited when listening on the radio to a Davis Cup match that pitted Australians Ken Rosewall and Lew Hoad against Americans Tony Trabert and Vic Seixas. John decided that he would like to take up the game in a serious way. An experienced local coach, Vic Edwards, saw John's talent and guided his initial efforts at serious play. By age ten, John was winning championship tournaments for juniors.

The Road to Excellence

John's game developed very rapidly, and he won the Australian Junior Championship for the first of three consecutive times in 1961. In 1963, he played for Australia's Davis Cup team for the first time; however, he suffered a setback, losing all his matches. Though not without talent, John lacked sufficient seasoning to win consistently at the championship level.

John had the necessary determination to work on his game for several years, so that he could rise from the ranks of talented players to attain greatness. He developed an unusual combination of skills that enabled him to do this. He was a very strong and aggressive player. His game featured a powerful serve, followed by a rush to the net and the use of volleying to gain the point. He also had a lethal overhead smash.

Unlike most players whose game stressed power, though, John was also a keen strategist. He was capable of detecting the slightest weakness in an opponent, at which he would pound away relentlessly. Against an opponent whose game also stressed power, John would often vary from his usual pattern and surprise his foe with crosscourt shots characteristic of defensive players such as Ken Rosewall. John tended to start his match slowly and would gradually build up the pace of action. He was especially dangerous if an opponent took an early lead. His record of comebacks in five-set matches was the best of any player's in the 1960's and 1970's.

The Emerging Champion

Given John's ability and determination, it is not surprising that his march to the top proved successful. In 1965, he won the Wimbledon doubles title and in 1967 the Wimbledon singles. In the latter tournament, John faced Clark Graebner, an outstanding American amateur, in his most difficult match. One of the sets of this match lasted 110 minutes. John showed his superb conditioning and determination by winning that set 17-15, and, more important, the match. By comparison, John's victory in the final was achieved without difficulty.

Also in 1967, John faced Graebner in another vital match. This time the scene of their confrontation was Forest Hills, and the U.S. National Championship singles title was at stake. John won the first two sets, but Graebner bounced back to take a commanding lead in the third. John was not to be denied, and, showing his unparalleled ability to rally when behind, John closed out Graebner to take the match in straight sets.

John turned professional in 1968 and continued his outstanding record. For the next several years, he was the game's dominant player, and in his first year as a professional he won over $174,000. He won the Wimbledon title in both 1970 and 1971. In the latter event, Stan Smith, a serve-and-volley player of great power, ran up an early lead against John in the final. By now the reader will be able to guess the upshot without difficulty. John came from behind to defeat Smith and win the tournament.

MAJOR CHAMPIONSHIP VICTORIES AND FINALS	
1963, 1966	Australian Championship doubles finalist (with Ken Fletcher)
1964	French Championship doubles finalist (with Tony Roche)
1965-66, 1968-70, 1974	Wimbledon doubles (with Roche)
1965, 1967	Australian Championship doubles (with Roche)
1966	U.S. National Championship finalist
1967	French Championship doubles (with Roche) U.S. National Championship U.S. National Championship doubles (with Roche)
1967, 1970-71	Wimbledon
1969, 1973	French Open doubles (with Roche; with Tom Okker)
1971, 1973	U.S. Open doubles (with Roger Taylor; with Owen Davidson)
1971, 1973, 1976	Australian Open doubles (with Roche; with Mal Anderson)
1972	U.S. Open doubles finalist (with Davidson)
1973	U.S. Open
1973, 1975	Australian Open
1976	Australian Open finalist

OTHER NOTABLE VICTORIES	
1965	Italian Championship doubles (with Roche)
1968-70	Professional World Doubles Tournament (with Roche)
1968	German Open
1969	Italian Open Canadian Open doubles (with Ron Holmberg)
1970	First National Classic doubles (with Roche)
1971	Canadian Open Swiss Open
1971, 1973	Italian Open doubles (with Roche; with Okker)
1972	U.S. Pro Championship doubles (with Roche)
1974	Japan Open WCT Finals

Continuing the Story

John's toughest opponents in both his amateur and professional careers were his fellow Australians, including Rosewall and Rod Laver. John's doubles partner, Tony Roche, deprived him of a U.S. title, but John had the consolation of knowing that he and Roche were the best doubles team of the late 1960's and early 1970's. In spite of a few major losses, however, John clearly ranks as best in the world in the period 1968-1971.

His style of play exacted a heavy toll on his body, and John developed back problems in the early 1970's that drastically reduced his world ranking. John plunged from best in the world to "also-ran" status, following his elimination in the early rounds of several tournaments.

Despite his impaired physical condition, John retained his iron determination. He once more resolved to overcome his problems and regain top ranking. John's efforts met with success in the 1973 U.S. Open. He faced Jan Kodes, the Wimbledon champion, in the final. Kodes at first baffled John by his scrambling recoveries of John's powerhouse shots, and he raced ahead in the match. John's power eventually wore Kodes down, however, and he could offer no defense to John's steady stream of service aces. John was once more U.S. champion.

In 1974, John defeated the young sensation Björn Borg in the finals of World Championship Tennis (WCT). After this victory, John's injuries proved too much for him, and he was compelled to retire from active play. He became a successful businessman, specializing in selling tennis programs to hotels. He owns a large number of tennis camps and resorts. John also has been honored to serve as Australia's Davis Cup captain.

Summary

John Newcombe at first seems cut from the same mold as most post-World War II players.

Strong and talented, John took up the game early and had the advantage of excellent coaching. His game emphasized the serve and volley. Unlike most players of this stripe, however, John was also a skilled strategist. In his ability to come back from a seemingly lost position, he was without equal. John dominated the game in the late 1960's and early 1970's, until injuries forced his retirement.

Bill Delaney

MILESTONES
Australian Davis Cup team (1963-76)
Served as president of the Association of Tennis Professionals

HONORS AND AWARDS	
1967, 1970-71, 1973, 1975	Ranked number 1 in the world
1978	"Broadcaster of the Year" JAKS Award
1986	Inducted into International Tennis Hall of Fame

Additional Sources:

Collins, Bud. "John Newcombe." In *Bud Collins' Tennis Encyclopedia*, edited by Bud Collins and Zander Hollander. 3d ed. Detroit: Visible Ink Press, 1997.

"John Newcombe." In *International Who's Who in Tennis*, edited by Jane Cooke. Dallas, Tex.: World Championship Tennis, 1983.

Newcombe, John. *Bedside Tennis*. New York: St. Martin's Press, 1983.

JACK NICKLAUS

Sport: Golf

Born: January 21, 1940
Columbus, Ohio

Early Life

Jack William Nicklaus was born January 21, 1940, in Columbus, Ohio. Jack was the first of two children born to Louis Charles and Nellie Helen (Schoener) Nicklaus. His father was the owner of a chain of drug stores, a successful pharmacist in Columbus, and a former president of the Ohio Pharmacy Board.

Jack attended Upper Arlington, Ohio, public schools and Ohio State University, which has granted him an honorary doctorate. Jack was an all-around athlete, enjoying participation in a variety of sports. Jack played golf, baseball, football, and basketball in high school, although golf was to become his primary activity.

Jack was introduced to golf at the age of ten by his father, who was playing golf on the order of a physician to aid in the strengthening of a leg which had suffered injury. Jack's first nine holes resulted in a score of 51, and a golfing legend was begun.

The Road to Excellence

As a junior member of the Scioto Country Club in Columbus, Jack enrolled in a golf class taught by the club professional, Jack Grout. Grout encouraged young golfers to hit the ball as far as they could and to worry about control later.

At the age of thirteen, Jack shot a round of 69 on the 7,095-yard course at Scioto. As a thirteen-year-old, Jack won the Ohio State Junior championship for players aged thirteen to fifteen. He also won the Columbus Junior Match-Play Championship and competed into the fourth round of

the United State Golf Association (USGA) Juniors tournament, all at the age of thirteen.

Jack spent four years at Upper Arlington High School in Columbus and built up an impressive list of accomplishments. At the age of fourteen, Jack was the Scioto Junior Club Champion, the Columbus Junior Match Play Champion, Columbus Junior Stroke Play Champion, and a medalist in his Tri-State (Ohio, Indiana, and Kentucky) High School Championship.

2031

MAJOR CHAMPIONSHIP VICTORIES

1959, 1961	U.S. Amateur
1962, 1967, 1972, 1980	U.S. Open
1963, 1965-66, 1972, 1975, 1986	The Masters
1963, 1971, 1973, 1975, 1980	PGA Championship
1966, 1970, 1978	British Open
1991, 1993	U.S. Senior Open

OTHER NOTABLE VICTORIES

1959, 1961	Walker Cup Team
1961	NCAA Championship
1963-64, 1966, 1971, 1973	World Cup Team member
1963-64, 1971, 1973, 1977	Tournament of Champions
1964	Phoenix Open
1964, 1968, 1971, 1975-76, 1978	Australian Open
1965	Memphis Open
1967, 1972	Westchester Classic
1967, 1972-73	Bing Crosby National
1967-68	Western Open
1968	American Golf Classic
1969	Andy Williams-San Diego Open
1969, 1971, 1973, 1975, 1977, 1981	Ryder Cup Team
1970-71	Byron Nelson Classic
1972, 1975	Doral-Eastern Open
1974, 1976, 1978	Tournament Players Championship
1975	Heritage Classic
1977-78	Jackie Gleason-Inverrary Classic
1982	Colonial National
1983, 1987	Ryder Cup Team captain
1990	Mazda Senior Tournament Players Championship
1990, 1995-96	Tradition at Desert Mountain, senior
1991	PGA Seniors Championship

The following year, Jack qualified for the United States Amateur Championship for the first time and again won the Junior Match Play Championship and the Stroke Play Championship, along with the Columbus District Amateur Championship. Jack qualified for the United States Open for the first time in 1957, although he missed the cut by ten shots after the first two rounds.

Jack stated in his 1978 autobiography that his father initiated and supported his involvement in the game during these early years. His father's values, strong character, and perspective were noted as significant to Jack's successes in life on and off the golf course.

The Emerging Champion

Jack chose to attend Ohio State University, although he received many scholarship offers from other schools. As a college student, he won the United States Amateur Championship twice (1959 and 1961) and was the runner-up to Arnold Palmer by two strokes in the 1960 United States Open.

Leading a very active college life and playing many sports while still a full-time student tended to keep Jack's school efforts at a minimum. Although Ohio State presented him with an honorary doctorate, Jack stated that not completing his undergraduate degree remained a source of regret.

Following the 1961 United States Amateur win, Jack began to seriously consider turning professional. He was spending much of his time working on his golf game, and he was also working to support his new bride, Barbara (wed July 23, 1960), and his first of five children (Jack II, born September 23, 1961). Jack announced that he was turning professional on November 8, 1961.

What happened next was simply history in the making. Although he did not take the professional golf world by storm, Jack had a successful first year on the tour. In his first seventeen tournaments, he had eight top-ten finishes, with five of these being second or third place.

His next tournament was one of the four major tournaments on the Professional Golfers' Association (PGA) tour—the United States Open. Jack defeated Arnold Palmer in a playoff to win the first of his now record twenty major titles.

In all, in 1962, his first year as a professional, Jack played in twenty-six United States events. Along with his win at the United States Open, he won the Seattle Open, Portland Open, and the World Series of Golf. Understandably, Jack was then nominated the Rookie of the Year and a legend was in the making.

Continuing the Story

Through the 1990 season, Jack's first year of eligibility on the senior tour (although still a member of the PGA tour), Jack had won more than ninety tournaments worldwide.

Jack is second on the all-time tournament winners list, with seventy PGA tour victories. Along with this, Jack has been in second or tied for second fifty-six times and placed third or tied for third thirty-five times. He has the lowest career scoring average (approximately 70.5), and for a number of years led the PGA tour in career earnings.

Jack Nicklaus has won twenty "majors" and finished second nineteen times, which is easily a record to be contended with for decades ahead. On the Senior PGA tour in 1990, Nicklaus won two of his four tournament entries, along with a second- and third-place finish in the other two.

Jack won both the PGA Seniors Championship and the U.S. Senior Open in 1991, and he won a second U.S. Senior Open victory in 1993. Following consecutive victories at the Tradition in 1995-1996, he had no tournament wins in 1997. An injured hip in 1998 hampered his play, but despite this difficulty he finished sixth at the Masters. He ended a remarkable streak of 154 straight appearances in major PGA championships when he decided not to compete in the PGA Championship in 1998.

Jack continued to play tournaments in 1999 and 2000, though

he appeared in fewer events. His best finish was a tie for ninth at the 2000 Tradition. Jack increasingly turned his attention to golf course design through his company, Golden Bear International. *Golf World* named him the Golf Course Architect of the Year in 1993.

Summary

What makes the Jack Nicklaus story even more compelling is that, throughout his career, he has been a devoted family man. As the father of five children, he has consistently been an active parent. Rarely has Jack played more than twenty tournaments, even during his most active years, making his accomplishments that

---

RECORDS AND MILESTONES

Co-holder (with Arnold Palmer) of the PGA Tour record for most consecutive years with a victory (seventeen), winning at least once every year from 1962 to 1978

First to reach $2 million, in 1973; $3 million, in 1977; $4 million, in 1983; and $5 million, in 1988; in PGA Tour career earnings

Only golfer to win all five major titles twice, while setting a record total of twenty major tournament victories

Accumulated a total of seventy PGA Tour victories, and a total of 18 international titles

Oldest winner of the Masters, in 1986, at forty-six years of age

Youngest winner of the Masters, in 1963, at twenty-three years of age

Leading money winner of the PGA Tour (1964-65, 1967, 1971-73, 1975-76)

HONORS AND AWARDS

1962	PGA Rookie of the Year *Golf Digest* Rookie of the Year
1964-65, 1967, 1972-73, 1975	*Golf Digest* Byron Nelson Award for Tournament Victories
1967, 1972-73, 1975-76	PGA Player of the Year
1972, 1975-76	GWAA Player of the Year
1974	PGA/World Golf Hall of Fame
1975	USGA Bobby Jones Award
1975-77	Seagram's Seven Crowns of Sports Award
1978	*Sports Illustrated* Sportsman of the Year GWAA Richardson Award
1980	Named Athlete of the Decade (1970's)
1980	Comeback of the Year Award
1982	Card Walker Award for outstanding contributions to junior golf Herb Graffis Award
1988	Named Golfer of the Century
1993	*Golf World's* Golf Course Architect of the Year

much more significant. Fellow competitor Chi-Chi Rodriguez summed up his career with the statement: "Jack Nicklaus is a legend in his spare time."

Another Nicklaus trademark is his balance, not only between his golf career and family involvement, but also in his business life. His booming golf course architecture project became his main career pursuit toward the end of the 1980's and in the early 1990's. He seems to enter each aspect of his life with the same tenacity and vigor, resulting in high levels of success.

Jack is arguably the greatest golfer ever to play the game. His records and list of achievements, on and off the golf course, leave the generations ahead much to aspire to.

Hal J. Walker

Additional Sources:

Nicklaus, Jack, with Ken Bowden. *Golf My Way.* New York: Simon and Schuster, 1974.

_____. *My Most Memorable Shots in the Majors.* Trumbull, Conn.: Golf Digest/Tennis, 1988.

Sampson, Curt. *The Eternal Summer: Palmer, Nicklaus, and Hogan in 1960, Golf's Golden Year.* New York: Villard, 2000.

Shaw, Mark. *Nicklaus.* Dallas, Tex.: Taylor, 1997.

Wukovits, John F. *Jack Nicklaus.* Philadelphia, Pa.: Chelsea House, 1998.

GREAT ATHLETES

Sport Index

TRACK AND FIELD

TRIATHLON

TRIPLE JUMP

Country Index

This index lists athletes by the countries—including some dependencies—with which they are most closely associated by virtue of their citizenship, residence, or membership on national teams. Many names are listed under more than one country, but some athletes are not listed under the countries in which they were born because they have no other meaningful ties with those countries. The index is intended to serve only as a guide and not be a definitive list of nationalities or birthplaces.

XIX

Name Index